GEOGRAPHICAL INDICATIONS AT THE CROSSROADS OF TRADE, DEVELOPMENT, AND CULTURE

Historically, few topics have proven to be so controversial in international intellectual property as the protection of geographical indications (GIs). The adoption of TRIPS in 1994 did not resolve disagreements, and countries worldwide continue to quarrel today as to the nature, the scope, and the enforcement of GI protection nationally and internationally. Thus far, however, there is little literature addressing GI protection from the point of view of the Asia-Pacific region, even though countries in this region have actively discussed the topic and in several instances have promoted GIs as a mechanism to foster local development and safeguard local culture. This book, edited by renowned intellectual property scholars, fills the void in the current literature and offers a variety of contributions focusing on the framework and effects of GI protection in the Asia-Pacific region. The book is available Open Access at http://dx.doi.org/10.1017/9781316711002.

Irene Calboli is Lee Kong Chian Fellow, Visiting Professor, and Deputy Director of the Applied Research Centre for Intellectual Assets and the Law in Asia (ARCIALA), School of Law, Singapore Management University. She is also Professor of Law at Texas A&M University School of Law and Transatlantic Technology Law Forum Fellow at Stanford Law School. An elected member of the American Law Institute, she has written extensively on the topic of geographical indications (GIs) and has acted as Expert on GIs for the World Intellectual Property Organization and the European Union Intellectual Property Office.

Ng-Loy Wee Loon is Professor at the Faculty of Law of the National University of Singapore. Her publications include the textbook on the Law of Intellectual Property of Singapore (2nd ed. 2014). She was the Founding Deputy Director at the Intellectual Property Academy of Singapore, and is currently a member of the Singapore's Copyright Tribunal and of the Singapore Domain Name Dispute Resolution Policy Panel. She is also Senior Counsel (*honoris causa*) (an appointment made by Singapore's Court of Appeal and Attorney-General).

Geographical Indications at the Crossroads of Trade, Development, and Culture

FOCUS ON ASIA-PACIFIC

Edited by

IRENE CALBOLI

Singapore Management University and Texas A&M University

NG-LOY WEE LOON

National University of Singapore

CAMBRIDGE UNIVERSITY PRESS

CAMBRIDGE
UNIVERSITY PRESS

University Printing House, Cambridge CB2 8BS, United Kingdom

One Liberty Plaza, 20th Floor, New York, NY 10006, USA

477 Williamstown Road, Port Melbourne, VIC 3207, Australia

4843/24, 2nd Floor, Ansari Road, Daryaganj, Delhi – 110002, India

79 Anson Road, #06–04/06, Singapore 079906

Cambridge University Press is part of the University of Cambridge.

It furthers the University's mission by disseminating knowledge in the pursuit of education, learning, and research at the highest international levels of excellence.

www.cambridge.org
Information on this title: www.cambridge.org/9781107166332
DOI: 10.1017/9781316711002

© Irene Calboli and Ng-Loy Wee Loon 2017

This work is in copyright. It is subject to statutory exceptions and to the provisions of relevant licensing agreements; with the exception of the Creative Commons version the link for which is provided below, the reproduction of any part of this work may take place without the written permission of Cambridge University Press.

An online version of this work is published at http://dx.doi.org/10.1017/9781316711002 under a Creative Commons Open Access license CC-BY-NC-ND 4.0 which permits re-use, distribution and reproduction in any medium for non-commercial purposes providing appropriate credit to the original work is given. You may not distribute derivative works without permission. To view a copy of this license, visit https://creativecommons.org/licenses/by-nc-nd/4.0

All versions of this work may contain content reproduced under license from third parties. Permission to reproduce this third-party content must be obtained from these third-parties directly. When citing this work, please include a reference to the DOI 10.1017/9781316711002

First published 2017

Printed in the United States of America by Sheridan Books, Inc

A catalogue record for this publication is available from the British Library.

ISBN 978-1-107-16633-2 Hardback

Cambridge University Press has no responsibility for the persistence or accuracy of URLs for external or third-party internet websites referred to in this publication and does not guarantee that any content on such websites is, or will remain, accurate or appropriate.

Contents

List of Contributors   *page* viii
Editors' Preface   xv

    PART I FRAMING THE DEBATE: THE STILL-CONTESTED ROLE OF GEOGRAPHICAL INDICATIONS IN THE GLOBAL ECONOMY   1

1 Geographical Indications between Trade, Development, Culture, and Marketing: Framing a Fair(er) System of Protection in the Global Economy?
Irene Calboli   3

2 From Geography to History: Geographical Indications and the Reputational Link
Dev S. Gangjee   36

3 The Limited Promise of Geographical Indications for Farmers in Developing Countries
Justin Hughes   61

4 Rethinking the Work of Geographical Indications in Asia: Addressing Hidden Geographies of Gendered Labor
Rosemary J. Coombe and S. Ali Malik   87

5 A Look at the Geneva Act of the Lisbon Agreement: A Missed Opportunity?
Daniel Gervais   122

    PART II GEOGRAPHICAL INDICATIONS AT THE CROSSROADS OF INTERNATIONAL AND NATIONAL TRADE   145

6 Geographical Indications and Mega-Regional Trade Agreements and Negotiations
Susy Frankel   147

7   Geographical Indications as Property: European Union
    Association Agreements and Investor–State Provisions
    Anselm Kamperman Sanders   168

8   How Would Geographical Indications from Asia Fare in
    Europe?
    Christopher Heath   186

9   Looking Beyond the Known Story: How the Prehistory of
    Protection of Geographical Indications in the Americas
    Provides an Alternate Approach
    Christine Haight Farley   212

10 European Union-Singapore Free Trade Agreement: A New
    Chapter for Geographical Indications in Singapore
    Susanna H.S. Leong   235

    **PART III   THE PROMISE AND PROBLEMS OF GEOGRAPHICAL
    INDICATIONS FOR LOCAL AND RURAL DEVELOPMENT**   257

11 Sunshine in a Bottle? Geographical Indications, the
    Australian Wine Industry, and the Promise of Rural
    Development
    Peter Drahos   259

12 Legal Protection of Geographical Indications as a Means to
    Foster Social and Economic Development in Malaysia
    Tay Pek San   281

13 The Use of Geographical Indications in Vietnam:
    A Promising Tool for Socioeconomic Development?
    Barbara Pick, Delphine Marie-Vivien, and Dong Bui Kim   305

14 'Vanity GIs': India's Legislation on Geographical
    Indications and the Missing Regulatory Framework
    Yogesh Pai and Tania Singla   333

15 Protection of Geographical Indications in Taiwan: Turning
    a Legal Conundrum into a Policy Tool for Development
    Szu-Yuan Wang   359

16 A Unique Type of Cocktail: Protection of Geographical
    Indications in China
    Haiyan Zheng   380

| 17 | The Potentials, and Current Challenges, of Protecting Geographical Indications in Sri Lanka
Naazima Kamardeen | 409 |

PART IV THE SHIFTING RELATIONSHIP BETWEEN GEOGRAPHICAL INDICATIONS, TRADITIONAL KNOWLEDGE, AND CULTURAL HERITAGE 437

18	The Geographical Indication Act 2013: Protection of Traditional Knowledge in Bangladesh with Special Reference to *Jamdani* *Mahua Zahur*	439
19	From Chianti to Kimchi: Geographical Indications, Intangible Cultural Heritage, and Their Unsettled Relationship with Cultural Diversity *Tomer Broude*	461
20	Geographical Indications, Heritage, and Decentralization Policies: The Case of Indonesia *Christoph Antons*	485
21	When Geographical Indications Meet Intangible Cultural Heritage: The New Japanese Act on Geographical Indications *Steven Van Uytsel*	508

Index 530

Contributors

Christoph Antons is Professor of Law in the Newcastle Law School, University of Newcastle, Australia. He is an Affiliated Research Fellow at the Max Planck Institute for Innovation and Competition, Munich, and Senior Fellow, Center for Development Research, University of Bonn. He is Project Leader of the following Australian Research Council Discovery projects: "Intangible Cultural Heritage Across Borders: Laws, Structures and Strategies in China and its ASEAN Neighbours"; "Building an Intellectual Property System: The Indonesian Experience," and "Food Security and the Governance of Local Knowledge in Agriculture in India and Indonesia." Recent book publications include INTELLECTUAL PROPERTY AND FREE TRADE AGREEMENTS IN THE ASIA-PACIFIC REGION (2015, edited with Reto M. Hilty) and the ROUTLEDGE HANDBOOK OF ASIAN LAW (2017).

Tomer Broude is the Sylvan M. Cohen Chair and Academic Director of the Minerva Center for Human Rights at the Hebrew University of Jerusalem. His interests are in public international law and international economic law, particularly international trade and investment, human rights, dispute settlement, development, and cultural diversity.

Dong Bui Kim is Senior Researcher at CASRAD, the Center for Agrarian Systems Research and Development, under the Vietnamese Academy of Agricultural Science, Hanoi, Vietnam. He is an agronomist engineer and holds a master's in geography from Montpellier University, France. In the past decade, he has been conducting research and development projects on GIs for twenty agricultural products in Vietnam, focusing on defining the specification of the products and establishing producers associations. Mr. Dong was a national expert at the Vietnamese Office of Intellectual Property for Geographical

Indications in the context of the international trade agreement between the European Union and Vietnam.

Irene Calboli is Lee Kong Chian Fellow, Visiting Professor, and Deputy Director of the Applied Research Centre for Intellectual Assets and the Law in Asia, School of Law, Singapore Management University. She is also Professor of Law at Texas A&M University School of Law and Transatlantic Technology Law Forum Fellow at Stanford Law School. She is an elected member of the American Law Institute, an associate member of the Singapore Academy of Law, and is currently serving, inter alia, in the Board of the European Policy for Intellectual Property Law Association, and as the Chair-Elect of the Art Law Section of the Association of American Law Schools.

Rosemary J. Coombe is the Tier One Canada Research Chair in Law, Communication, and Culture at York University in Toronto, where she teaches in the Department of Anthropology, the York and Ryerson Joint Graduate Program in Communication and Culture, and the Graduate Program in Socio-legal Studies. She holds a joint doctorate in Law and Anthropology from Stanford University. She has been awarded visitorships at Harvard, MIT, Iowa, American, DePaul, the University of Chicago, and the University of California, and has held research fellowships at the University of Utrecht, the Stellenbosch Institute for Advanced Study, and the University of Gottingen. Her award-winning book THE CULTURAL LIFE OF INTELLECTUAL PROPERTIES (1998) was reprinted in 2008 by Duke University Press.

Peter Drahos is a professor in the Regulatory Institutions Network at the Australian National University. He holds a Chair in Intellectual Property at Queen Mary, University of London, and is a member of the Academy of Social Sciences in Australia. He holds degrees in law, politics, and philosophy and is admitted as a barrister and solicitor.

Christine Haight Farley is Professor of Law at American University Washington College of Law. She teaches and writes about intellectual property, trademark law, international and comparative trademark law, design protection, and art law. Professor Farley served as Associate Dean for Faculty and Academic Affairs from 2007 to 2011 and as Co-Director of the Program on Information Justice and Intellectual Property from 2005 to 2009. She has been a visiting professor at law schools in France, India, Italy and Puerto Rico and is a Fulbright Specialist for intellectual property law.

Susy Frankel is Professor of Law, Chair in Intellectual Property and International Trade, and Director of the New Zealand Centre of International Economic Law, at Victoria University of Wellington. She is the President of the International Association for the Advancement of Teaching and Research in Intellectual Property (ATRIP), 2015–2017. Since 2008 she has been Chair of the Copyright Tribunal (NZ). She is a member of the editorial boards of the *Journal of World Intellectual Property Law* and the *Queen Mary Journal of Intellectual Property*. She teaches copyright, trademarks, patents, international intellectual property and international trade law. Susy's scholarship focuses on international intellectual property and particularly treaty interpretation, and the protection of indigenous peoples' knowledge and innovation.

Dev S. Gangjee is Associate Professor in Intellectual Property within the Oxford Law Faculty as well as a Tutorial Fellow at St Hilda's College. He is presently Director of the Oxford Diploma in IP Law and Practice, an Academic Member of the Oxford IP Research Centre, and on the Editorial Board of the Modern Law Review. Dev has acted in an advisory capacity for national governments, law firms, international organizations, and the European Commission on IP issues. His research focuses on branding and trademarks, GIs, and copyright law. Additional research interests include the history and political economy of IP, collective and open innovation, and the interface between IP and theories of development.

Daniel Gervais is Professor of Law at Vanderbilt University Law School and Director of the Vanderbilt Intellectual Property Program. He is Editor-in-Chief of the *Journal of World Intellectual Property* and Editor of www.tripsagreement.net. Before joining academia, he was Legal Officer at the GATT (now WTO); Head of Section at WIPO; and Vice-President of Copyright Clearance Center, Inc. (CCC). In 2012, he was elected to the Academy of Europe. He is a member of the American Law Institute and, as of 2015, President Elect of the International Association for the Advancement of Teaching and Research in Intellectual Property (ATRIP).

Christopher Heath is currently a Member of the Boards of Appeal at the European Patent Office in Munich and co-editor of THE INTERNATIONAL REVIEW OF INTELLECTUAL PROPERTY AND COMPETITION LAW (IIC). He studied at the Universities of Konstanz, Edinburgh, and the London School of Economics. He lived and worked in Japan for three years, and between 1992 and 2005 headed the Asian Department of the Max Planck Institute for Patent, Copyright, and Competition Law in Munich (now Max Planck Institute for Innovation and Competition). Dr Heath wrote his PhD thesis on Japanese unfair competition prevention law.

Justin Hughes is the Hon. William Matthew Byrne Professor of Law at Loyola Law School in Los Angeles, where he teaches international trade and intellectual property courses. Prior to Loyola, he taught at Cardozo Law School. From 2009 until 2013, Professor Hughes also served in the Obama Administration as Senior Advisor to the Undersecretary of Commerce for Intellectual Property. In that capacity, he was US chief negotiator at the Diplomatic Conferences that completed the Beijing Treaty on Audiovisual Performances (2012) and the Marrakesh Treaty for the Blind (2013). Educated at Oberlin and Harvard, Professor Hughes has also done democracy development work in Albania, Bosnia, El Salvador, Haiti, and Mali.

Naazima Kamardeen is Senior Lecturer, Department of Commercial Law, Faculty of Law, University of Colombo, where she teaches Intellectual Property Law at both undergraduate and postgraduate levels. She is also an attorney-at-law of the Supreme Court of Sri Lanka. She serves in the National Level Committee, which is drafting the Plant Variety Protection Law of Sri Lanka. She holds a PhD in Intellectual Property Law, specializing in issues of bio-piracy, patent law, and TRIPS. She has published in several journals, and her article on Community Rights to Intellectual Property was published in the *Journal of World Intellectual Property* in 2015.

Anselm Kamperman Sanders is Professor of Intellectual Property Law, Director of the Advanced Masters Intellectual Property Law and Knowledge Management (IPKM LLM/MSc), and Academic Director of the Institute for Globalization and International Regulation (IGIR) at Maastricht University. He acts as Academic Co-director of the Annual Intellectual Property Law School and IP Seminar of the Institute for European Studies of Macau (IEEM), and is Adjunct Professor at Jinan University Law School, Guangzhou, China. Anselm holds a PhD from the Centre for Commercial Law Studies, Queen Mary, University of London. He is a member of the European Commission expert group on development and implications of patent law in the field of biotechnology and genetic engineering.

Susanna H.S. Leong is a Professor of Law at the NUS Business School, National University of Singapore. She has published in several international and local academic journals and is the author of the book INTELLECTUAL PROPERTY LAW OF SINGAPORE (2013). Susanna is the Vice-Dean (Graduate

Studies) at the NUS Business School. She is also a Senior Fellow at the Intellectual Property Academy of Singapore, a member of the World Intellectual Property Organization (WIPO) Arbitration and Mediation Centre's Domain Name Panel, a member of the Regional Centre for Arbitration, Kuala Lumpur (RCAKL) Panel, and a member of the Singapore Copyright Tribunal.

S. Ali Malik is a PhD candidate in Socio-legal Studies at York University. He earned his MA in International Human Rights Law from the American University in Cairo and participates in the Institute for Global Law and Policy at Harvard Law School. Drawing on a diverse range of theoretical and methodological influences in critical international legal theory, social theory, and anthropology, his doctoral research is in the intersections of global law, intellectual property, and international development.

Delphine Marie-Vivien is Researcher in Law at the Centre de Coopération Internationale en Recherche Agronomique pour le Développement (CIRAD) and, since 2012, she has been based in Vietnam. From 2005 to 2008 she was a visiting researcher at National Law School, Bangalore. She has written extensively on comparative aspects of GIs between EU and Asian countries, the issue of the public-private governance of GIs, the link to the origin for handicraft goods, the certification mechanism, and the use of GIs to protect biodiversity. Her current research focuses on comparing GIs with other food standards and safety regulations. Her recent publications include the book THE PROTECTION OF GEOGRAPHICAL INDICATIONS IN INDIA: A NEW PERSPECTIVE ON THE FRENCH AND EUROPEAN EXPERIENCE (2015).

Ng-Loy Wee Loon is Professor at the Faculty of Law, National University of Singapore. Among her academic publications is her text on LAW OF INTELLECTUAL PROPERTY OF SINGAPORE (2nd edn. 2014). Outside of the university, her involvement in the legal landscape of Singapore includes the following: member of the Board of Directors of the Intellectual Property Office of Singapore (2000–2001); member of the Board of Governors of the IP Academy (2007–2011); member of Singapore's Copyright Tribunal (since 2009); member of the Singapore Domain Name Dispute Resolution Policy Panel (since 2014); IP Adjudicator with the Intellectual Property Office of Singapore (2014–2015).

Yogesh Pai is Assistant Professor of Law at National Law University, Delhi. He teaches and writes in the area of intellectual property law and policy. He has previously worked with the South Centre in Geneva, Centad, New Delhi, and was Assistant Professor of Law at National Law University, Jodhpur. Yogesh serves as legal member in an ad hoc committee constituted by the Government of India to assess the granting of compulsory licenses for affordable healthcare in India. Previously, he was part of an ad hoc expert committee formed in order to examine the need for utility models in India.

Barbara Pick is a PhD candidate at the London School of Economics and Political Sciences and an associate research fellow at the Centre de Coopération Internationale en Recherche Agronomique pour le Développement (CIRAD). Her research focuses on the relationship between GIs and development. Previously she worked as a legal and policy consultant for the European Patent Office and the Food and Agriculture Organization of the United Nations (FAO) where she researched national and regional policies related to plant genetic resources, including intellectual property rights, farmers' rights, access and benefit-sharing mechanisms, and biosafety.

Tania Singla holds an LLB with honors from the National Law University Delhi, India, and is currently an LLM candidate at Europa Institut, Universität Des Saarlandes, Germany. She is also the recipient of the DAAD Angela Merkel Scholarship 2016. Her current research focuses on contemporary developments in intellectual property, and she has previously written and addressed topics such as GIs and patent laws as a student fellow at the Centre for Innovation, Intellectual Property and Competition (CIIPC), National Law University, Delhi, under the supervision of Professor Yogesh Pai.

Tay Pek San is Associate Professor at the Faculty of Law, University of Malaya, Kuala Lumpur. She is also the legal advisor to the University of Malaya's Centre of Innovation & Commercialization, a committee member of the Intellectual Property Chapter of the International Chamber of Commerce (Malaysia), and a committee member for the Evaluation of Intellectual Property of the University of Malaya. She is a coauthor of the book INTRODUCTION TO CYBERLAW IN MALAYSIA (2004), and the author of the books PROTECTION OF WELL-KNOWN TRADE MARKS IN MALAYSIA (2007) and INTELLECTUAL PROPERTY LAW IN MALAYSIA (2013).

Steven Van Uytsel is Associate Professor at Kyushu University in Japan and specializes in competition law and cultural heritage law. He has been acting as expert to the International Research Centre for Intangible Cultural Heritage in the Asia-Pacific Region, a UNESCO Category II Center. He is also a Senior Research Fellow at the EU Institute Japan-Kyushu.

Szu-Yuan Wang is Assistant Professor at Graduate Institute for Intellectual Property Rights, Shih Hsin University, Taiwan. He teaches Intellectual Property Law, Intellectual Property Law and Antitrust Law, and International Intellectual Property Law. He has broad research interests, ranging from intellectual property law, law and economics, cultural property law, traditional and indigenous knowledge protection, and legal history. He read his LLB degree at National Taiwan University. He studied Roman law and legal history at the University of Glasgow, where he was awarded LLM degree. He obtained his PhD degree at Newcastle University. His thesis examined the theoretical foundation of intellectual property and explored the possible location of GIs in the IP territory.

Mahua Zahur is Senior Lecturer in the Department of Law of East West University. Previously she was Lecturer in the School of Law, BRAC University, Bangladesh. She holds an LLB and LLM degrees from the University of Chittagong. Her areas of research focus on intellectual property laws. She has attended many national and international conferences and seminars in this area. She is currently enrolled as an advocate of the Dhaka Bar Association and is a partner in a law chamber in Dhaka.

Haiyan Zheng is currently Director of Trademark Examination Division One, Trademark Office, State Administration for Industry and Commerce (SAIC), PR China. She has been working for the Trademark Office since 1998, dealing with trademark substantive examination, general affairs, legal affairs, and issues related to GIs of origin consecutively.

Editors' Preface

Why a book on geographical indications (GIs) with a focus on the Asia-Pacific region? Our reason is simple enough. For several decades, GIs have not received mainstream attention by national policy-makers in Asia-Pacific. Consider that on the international stage, the Lisbon Agreement for the Protection of Appellations of Origin and their International Registration (Lisbon Agreement)[1] has been of interest, at least so far, only to one country in Asia, namely, North Korea. Of course, this does not mean that there is no legal protection for GIs in this region; after all, GI protection is mandated by the Agreement of Trade-Related Aspects of Intellectual Property (TRIPS).[2] However, our sense was that GI laws in this region were enacted, at least initially, by the policy-makers primarily as a matter of compliance with international obligations without fully understanding the implications of these laws.[3] This state of affairs, we felt, deserved further investigation and attention by academics – especially now that many countries in the region are showing a growing interest for GIs, and GIs have appeared on the agenda in the bilateral or pluri-lateral negotiations for international trade agreements (FTAs) between countries in the region and other countries, in particular the

---

[1] Lisbon Agreement for the Protection of Appellations of Origin and Their International Registration, October 31, 1958, *as revised*, July 14, 1967, 923 U.N.T.S. 205.
[2] Agreement on Trade-Related Aspects of Intellectual Property Rights arts. 22–24, April 15, 1994, Marrakesh Agreement Establishing the World Trade Organization, Annex 1C, 1869 U.N.T.S. 299.
[3] This is borne out by observations made by some of the authors in this volume. To cite a few, the chapter authored by Tay Pek San (Chapter 12) reporting on Malaysia's experience with GIs writes that when the country enacted its GI Act 2000, there was "relatively little understanding of the benefits and potential impact" of GI protection. A similar message came from Szu-Yuan Wang (Chapter 15) reporting on Taiwan, when he described the country's struggles to understand this "foreign" transplant when it was amending its laws to protect GIs upon accession to the WTO in 2002. As the readers may observe, several other chapters in the volume express similar considerations and concerns.

European Union (EU). For example, the EU has recently concluded FTAs with South Korea, Singapore, and Vietnam and is also negotiating, or discussing the possibility to negotiate, similar agreements with Malaysia, India, and other countries in Asia-Pacific. And then there were the negotiations for a multilateral agreement of the Pacific that led to the adoption of the Trans-Pacific Partnership (TPP) in 2015 (but whose fate is, at present time, uncertain due to the recent withdrawal of the United States therefrom). GIs were a sticky topic in the TPP, as negotiating parties were almost evenly divided between countries supporting strong protection, and others, such as the United States, Canada, Australia, and New Zealand, which were less enamored of GIs.

Unsurprisingly, the EU's narrative on GIs is that GIs can play an important role in trade, rural development, and the conservation of national cultural heritage – a position that has been enshrined in the EU law on GIs since the adoption of the very first GI Regulation in 1992.[4] Today, this narrative is gaining consensus in several countries in Asia-Pacific, particularly those that are rich in agricultural products and traditional handicrafts. However, this narrative needs further testing and exploration, as enthusiasm for GIs could not necessarily harvest the results that several countries in the region may hope for. To this end, we convened a meeting of a group of scholars and other experts in March 2015 at the Faculty of Law of the National University of Singapore (NUS) to discuss the changing landscape of GI protection in this region and, to a certain extent, worldwide. We believed that a comprehensive analysis of these questions would assist policy-makers and trade negotiators in this region to formulate appropriate responses during FTA negotiations, in the adoption of national laws on GI protection and, beyond that and regardless of FTA negotiations, to review how the potential in their country's GIs may be actualized with best practices, quality-control programs for GI products, and the like. At the meeting, several themes were addressed, and in particular the following questions. What should policy-makers and trade negotiators in Asia-Pacific make of the claims and the rebuffs of benefits from GI protection? Is it true that a GI protection regime will provide higher economic returns to farmers and other holders of traditional knowledge through price premiums and enhance rural development and/or preserve indigenous knowledge and culture? What level of legal protection of GIs, if not that set out in TRIPS, will

---

[4] See recital 6 of the Council Regulation (EEC) No. 2028/1992 on the Protection of Geographical Indications and Designations of Origins for Agricultural Products and Foodstuff (stating that GIs have "proved successful with producers, who have secured higher incomes").

Editors' Preface   xvii

produce these benefits? Where are the success stories? Can these success stories be replicated in other countries, especially the developing countries in the Asia-Pacific region?

Our harvest was bountiful. We heard from those who warned of overstatements of the benefits that stronger GI protection can produce[5] and who unveiled the hidden costs of romanticizing the GI debate,[6] while others were optimistic, sometimes cautiously,[7] sometimes more openly.[8] We learned of real-life success stories[9] and of failures[10] in various countries – and success stories and failures occurring within the same country.[11] Even more importantly, we learned about the various factors that contributed to the success or failure in the case studies presented. As expected, we saw national politics, and even geopolitics, at play when there are fights over GIs between the central government and the local government in a country,[12] or between neighboring countries.[13] Our playfield also went beyond Asia-Pacific, and scholars discussed recent development in international law, above all the recent controversial adoption of the Geneva Act of the Lisbon Agreement in

---

[5] See, e.g., Justin Hughes (Chapter 3) focusing on the promised economic benefits; and Tomer Broude (Chapter 19) focusing on the preservation of intangible cultural heritage and promotion of cultural diversity.

[6] See, Rosemary J. Coombe & S. Ali Malik (Chapter 4) highlighting the socioeconomic marginalization of the Nepali-speaking women workers in the Darjeeling tea plantations in India even as this GI gains renown around the world, allowing others to reap the economic benefits.

[7] See, e.g., Irene Calboli (Chapter 1) supporting the positive aspects of GI protection as long as producers disclose the actual origin of all products' raw materials; Peter Drahos (Chapter 11) highlighting the possible positive aspects of GI protection in Australia in the wine sector; Steven Van Uytsel (Chapter 21) in the context of preservation of intangible cultural heritage in Japan.

[8] See Dev Gangjee (Chapter 2), highlighting how the current definition of GIs reflects not only a geographical but also an historical linkage between products and places; Barbara Pick, Delphine Marie-Vivien, and Dong Bui Kim (Chapter 13) supporting the importance of GIs in Vietnam.

[9] See Peter Drahos (Chapter 11) on the case study of the *Granite Belt* GI for wine in Australia.

[10] See Yogesh Pai and Tania Singla (Chapter 14) on the case study of the *Banarasi* GI for silk sarees in India.

[11] See Barbara Pick, Delphine Marie-Vivien, and Dong Bui Kim (Chapter 13) on the case studies of the *Hạ Long* GI for fried calamari (success story) and the *Lạng Sơn* GI for star anise (not so successful) in Vietnam.

[12] See Christoph Antons (Chapter 20) on Indonesia where the central government and local government can fight for control over GIs linked to national cultural heritage and traditions.

[13] See Tay Pek San (Chapter 12) on the dispute between Malaysia and Indonesia over ownership of the term *batik*, a textile art involving the practice of dyeing cloth through wax-resistant methods; Muhua Zahur (Chapter 18) on the resentment in Bangladesh when location-based products of Bangladesh such as *Jamdani* fabric were registered in India by Indian parties; and Szu-Yuan Wang (Chapter 15) on the registration of certain Taiwanese tea production districts as trademarks in China.

May 2015.[14] In addition, we were given an assessment of how Asian GIs would fare in Europe,[15] and how GIs are protected in the United States.[16] We were alerted to interesting features in national GI protection systems in this part of the world.[17] We understood better what reputation-based GIs really mean and their implications for nonagricultural products and even services.[18] We were given insight into the potency of the Investor State Disputes Settlement (ISDS) provisions, if incorporated into FTAs, in how they can be triggered by GI owners.[19] We saw the challenges facing policymakers in navigating conflicting provisions on GIs in EU-dominated FTAs and the TPP,[20] even as we were surprised by an alternative (not so anti-GI) approach taken by the United States that seems to be known by just a few, but could become very relevant in the global GI debate going forward.[21] Last, but not least, we were given important insights on the potential, and again controversial, role of GIs beyond trade and development and from a culture-related perspective.

Today, the presentations and discussion in our meeting have been translated into this volume, which presents itself as the first comprehensive guide on GI protection in Asia-Pacific. The readers will greatly benefit from learning more about the topic from the various contributions, which illustrate the many complexities, and contradictions, that still characterize the GI debate in this region. In their chapters, contributors employ a variety of research methodologies – from doctrinal analysis, to both quantitative and qualitative

[14] World Intellectual Property Organization (WIPO), Geneva Act of the Lisbon Agreement on Appellations of Origin and Geographical Indications and Regulations Under the Geneva Act of the Lisbon Agreement on Appellations of Origin and Geographical Indications, WIPO Document LI/DC/19 (May 20, 2015). *See* Daniel Gervais (Chapter 5) offering a recount and critique of the diplomatic conference leading to the adoption of the Geneva Act.
[15] *See* Christopher Heath (Chapter 8) discussing the various GIs from Asia currently protected in the EU.
[16] *See* Christine Haight Farley (Chapter 9).
[17] *See, e.g.*, Susanna Leong (Chapter 10) on Singapore, where the *sui generis* GI Act, if the 2014 amendments thereto are brought into force, will protect registered and unregistered GIs, with registered GIs enjoying a higher level of protection; Haiyan Zheng (Chapter 16) on China where GIs can be protected not only under trademark law as well as not just one but two *sui generis* regimes which are administered by different governmental agencies; and Naazima Kamardeen (Chapter 17) on Sri Lanka, where all agricultural products, regardless of whether they are wines or spirits, enjoy the enhanced level of protection mandated in art. 23 of the TRIPS Agreement for wines and spirits.
[18] *See* Dev Gangjee (Chapter 2).   [19] *See* Anselm Kamperman Sanders (Chapter 7).
[20] *See* Susy Frankel (Chapter 6).
[21] *See* Christine Haight Farley (Chapter 9) discussing the General Inter-American Convention for Trade-mark and Commercial Protection, February 20, 1929, 46 Stat. 2907, 124 L.N.T.S. 357 (referred to as both the Inter-American Convention and the Pan American Convention).

empirical studies, to theories related to law and development, law and culture, and gender studies. This richness of methodologies provides the readers with an important variety of perspectives, and ultimately contributes to the conclusion that the appropriate role of GI protection is often defined on a case-by-case basis. This volume develops across four themes: the first group of contributions sets the stage for the discussion, recounting the still-contested framework of GI protection, the promises of GIs, and their potential pitfalls; the second group addresses the growing role of GIs as a trade issue, both at the international and national level, with specific attention to different systems of GI protection; the third group digs deeper into the actual value of GIs in many of the countries in Asia-Pacific, and presents results that are, intentionally, contradictory in part; the fourth and last group tackles GI protection from the lenses of the preservation of culture, a narrative that is gaining traction in many countries, and which is interconnected with the discussions for safeguarding intangible cultural heritage led by the United Nations Organization for Education, Science, and Culture (UNESCO).

Our hope is that this volume, now in print, will be useful to a large variety of stakeholders, including academics, policy-makers, trade negotiators, legal practitioners, and representatives of producer and consumer associations. We also hope that this volume will lead the way for more research in this area in Asia-Pacific, especially more case studies of the practical application of GI protection to local and regional products.

To all who participated in this project, we express our deep appreciation. First of all, we thank the contributors to this volume. It has been our privilege to work with such an outstanding group of scholars and experts. We are also indebted to five additional participants to the March 2015 meeting, who offered important insights to the discussion and the perspectives presented in this volume: Kiyoshi Adachi, Denis Croze, Keri Johnston, Ignacio de Medrano Caballero, and Daren Tang. Several students assisted us in editing and preparing the manuscript for the final stage of publication before delivering it to our publisher, Cambridge University Press (CUP). In this respect, we thank Kyle Carney, Tave Parker Doty, Ellen Flint, Evangeline Lim, Victor Looi Yi En, Caitlin P. Schneider, Cherilyn Wong, and Huiling Xie. We are additionally grateful to John Berger, and the editorial staff of CUP, for their strong support to this project. Very special thanks also go to Professor Andrew Harding and Regana Zara Mydin, respectively the Director and Assistant Manager at the Centre for Asian Legal Studies (CALS) at the Faculty of Law of NUS at the time of our meeting in March 2015. Without the financial and administrative support from CALS, this project would not have been possible. We also thank the Applied Research Centre for Intellectual Assets and the Law in Asia (ARCIALA) of the Singapore Management University School of Law for providing the funds to cover the index of the book. Finally, we want to toast to the deepening of our friendship with each other as we worked together in this very worthwhile project. This volume is dedicated to our contributors, students, and those with a special interest in GIs. We also remember our colleague Dwijen Rangnekar, who has left us too soon and could not be part of this volume, but whose contributions in this area will stay with us for many decades to come.

Irene CALBOLI
NG-LOY Wee Loon
Singapore, August 2016

PART I

FRAMING THE DEBATE

The Still-Contested Role of Geographical Indications in the Global Economy

1

Geographical Indications between Trade, Development, Culture, and Marketing: Framing a Fair(er) System of Protection in the Global Economy?

Irene Calboli[*]

1 INTRODUCTION

This chapter analyzes some of the topics on the current debate involving geographical indications (GIs) of origin that will be further elaborated by the contributors to this volume from a variety of perspectives and angles. As the title indicates, this volume focuses on GI protection "at the crossroads of trade, development, and culture," with a specific focus on the countries in the Asia-Pacific region. This choice is due primarily to the fact that the analysis of issues related to GI protection in this region is, to date, not as extensive as the analysis in other regions, particularly in the Western world. This volume intends to fill this gap and aims, in particular, at analyzing the potential benefits, but also related problems, of GI protection for local and national development in Asia-Pacific countries. Trade- and culture-related issues, primarily issues related to the conservation and promotion of local culture and cultural diversity, are also central to the contributions to this volume. As the opening contribution of this volume, this chapter then aims at setting the stage and framing the context for other authors by offering an overview of the status of the GI debate, as well as emphasizing some of the trends that have become salient features of this debate in Asia-Pacific, and worldwide. These trends are, in particular, the following: the globalization of the GI debate beyond Western countries and beyond a "wine and cheese" agenda, or trade war, between primarily Western

---

[*] Lee Kong Chian Fellow, Visiting Professor and Deputy Director, Applied Research Centre for Intellectual Assets and the Law in Asia, Singapore Management University School of Law; Professor of Law, Texas A&M University School of Law. This chapter builds on my previous publications in this area.

3

interests; the increased attention for the potential benefits of GI protection by developing countries and the often neglected attention to the potential problems associated with GI protection for local producers in these countries; and the increasing loosening of the definition of GIs as symbols of true geographical origin in favor of a definition granting exclusive rights based on the "historical reputation" of GIs.

Building on this premise, Section 2 starts by discussing how, after almost a century of limited attention at the international level, GIs have become one of the hottest topics in international intellectual property law today. Born out of the French tradition in the nineteenth century, and originally reserved to identify, and protect, the geographical origin of wines against counterfeits, GI protection was later accepted by other European countries and eventually by the European Union (EU). Then, from Europe, GIs become a global phenomenon and a topic of international controversy in the past two decades. In particular, GIs were one of the hot issues at the negotiating table that led to the creation of the World Trade Organization (WTO) in the late 1980s and early 1990s. Discussions over GIs continued to dominate part of the WTO Doha Development Agenda, even though WTO Members never reached any agreement on the issue.[1] Still, despite the lack of consensus at the international level, an increasing number of countries became interested in GIs in the following years. This interest reached beyond Western countries. In particular, countries in Asia, Africa, and South America have adopted, to date, national policies on GIs and taken part in the discussion of the WTO Doha Development Agenda. In the past decade, provisions related to GI protection have also become an important component of bilateral and plurilateral international trade agreements (FTAs) between countries from all continents.[2] To some extent, this is the result of the pressure exerted by the EU in its attempt to export a pro-GI protection agenda outside Europe. But many countries have become interested in GIs regardless of this pressure. In 2015, discussions over GI protection also led to the adoption of the Geneva Act of the Lisbon Agreement for the Protection of Appellations of Origin and their International Registration (Geneva Act) under the auspices of the World

---

[1] Agreement on Trade-Related Aspects of Intellectual Property Rights, April 15, 1994, Marrakesh Agreement Establishing the World Trade Organization, Annex 1C, 1869 U.N.T.S 299 [hereinafter TRIPS]; World Trade Organization, Ministerial Declaration of November 14, 2001, WTO Doc. WT/MIN(01)/DEC/1, 41 I.L.M. 746 (2002) [hereinafter Doha Declaration].

[2] See *infra* Section 2.

Intellectual Property Organization.[3] Even though the Geneva Act was, at large, the result of Western pro-GI diplomacy, it was supported by countries outside Europe.

Moving from the international to the national level, Section 3 first reports that several jurisdictions in Asia-Pacific have currently adopted national *sui generis* systems for GI protection. These national laws are largely modelled after the system currently adopted in the EU. Countries that have implemented *sui generis* systems include, to date, Japan, South Korea, Bangladesh, Sri Lanka, Australia, Cambodia, Malaysia, and Singapore.[4] Several countries in Asia-Pacific have also established, or are discussing the establishment of national GI registries to register both national and foreign GIs.[5] Countries that already operate national GI registries in Asia-Pacific include Cambodia, India, Indonesia, Malaysia, Thailand, Vietnam, and other countries.[6] Several of the contributors to this volume explain in detail the laws, including the national reforms, which have been adopted in these countries. Building on these descriptions, Section 3 focuses on the potential benefits of GIs for socioeconomic development as well as for safeguarding national cultural heritage in Asia-Pacific, and in general.[7] However, Section 3 highlights that GIs do not per se constitute a magic recipe, and that the long-term success of GI products depends largely on local producers controlling and maintaining the quality of the products, and developing savvy marketing plans. This point is reiterated by many of the contributors to this volume, and is probably the most important observation directed to GI producers, local and regional communities.

---

[3] World Intellectual Property Organization (WIPO), Geneva Act of the Lisbon Agreement on Appellations of Origin and Geographical Indications and Regulations under the Geneva Act of the Lisbon Agreement on Appellations of Origin and Geographical Indications, WIPO Doc. LI/DC/19 (May 20, 2015) [hereinafter, Geneva Act]. For the original version of the Lisbon Agreement, *see* Lisbon Agreement for the Protection of Appellations of Origin and their International Registration, art. 2(1), October 31, 1958, *as revised* July 14, 2967, 923 U.N.T.S. 205 [hereinafter 1958 Lisbon Agreement].

[4] *See infra* Section 3.   [5] *Id.*

[6] Even though GI registries are not necessary to implement *sui generis* GI protection, these registries are seen today as formal tools to catalog existing GIs and promote awareness among producers and consumers. This point is elaborated, in particular, in the chapter authored by Naazima Kamardeen on Sri Lanka, in this volume.

[7] Irene Calboli, *Of Markets, Culture, and* Terroir: *The Unique Economic and Culture-Related Benefits of Geographical Indications of Origin*, in INTERNATIONAL INTELLECTUAL PROPERTY: A HANDBOOK OF CONTEMPORARY RESEARCH (Daniel J. Gervais ed., 2015) [hereinafter Calboli, *The Benefits of GIs*]; Tomer Broude, *Taking "Trade and Culture" Seriously: Geographical Indications and Cultural Protection in WTO Law*, 26 U. PA. J. INT'L. ECON. L. 623, 656–57, 674–79 (2005).

Section 4 tackles one of the most problematic aspects of the GI debate, namely the progressive loosening of the territorial linkage between GI products and GI regions in the definition of "geographical indications." This section supports the point that, although this territorial linkage has never been an absolute linkage since the first appearance of national laws regulating the use of geographical names, the current trend seems to privilege a considerably looser definition of GIs with respect to the actual geographical origin of the products, their ingredients, and manufacturing process. Hence, the traditional basis for granting exclusive rights on GIs is precisely the territorial linkage between the GI products and the regions – the deep connection between the products and the land, the *terroir* as it is defined in the French tradition.[8] In particular, Section 4 specifically recounts that, in 1958, the text of the Lisbon Agreement[9] defined "appellations of origin" as signs identifying products "exclusively or essentially" originating from a certain geographical region. This definition was weakened with the adoption of the Agreement on Trade-Related Aspects of Intellectual Property Rights (TRIPS) in 1994, which defines GIs as "indications which identify a good as originating in the territory ... where a given quality, reputation or other characteristic of the good is essentially [no longer exclusively] attributable to its geographical origin."[10] The TRIPS definition finds its origin in the language of the EU Regulations on GIs that were adopted in 1992.[11] In 2015, the trend of loosening the territorial linkage between the products' name and their actual origin was confirmed in the revision of the Lisbon Agreement finalized in Geneva (Geneva Act of the Lisbon Agreement), as the Geneva Act adopted a definition of GIs (in addition to "appellations of origin") that is identical to the definition in TRIPS.[12]

Naturally, granting exclusive rights to the name of products' locations facilitates the marketing of the products with famous geographical names in the global market – i.e., Champagne sparkling wine, Parmigiano Reggiano hard table cheese, Darjeeling tea, Kintamani coffee, or Kampot pepper. Yet, should this exclusivity be justified when the products do not entirely originate from the regions? Section 5 builds upon Section 4, and argues that when GIs do not identify products that are entirely local, GIs no longer fulfill the function for which they are legally protected – offering accurate information about products' geographical origin to consumers and incentivizing local development. Instead, GIs become marketing tools to sell GI products with

---

[8] Irene Calboli, *In Territorio Veritas: Bringing Geographical Coherence in the Definition of Geographical Indications of Origin under TRIPS*, 6(1) WIPO J. 57 (2014) [hereinafter Calboli, *In Territorio Veritas*].
[9] 1958 Lisbon Agreement, *supra* note 3, art. 2(1). [10] TRIPS, *supra* note 1, art. 22(1).
[11] *See infra* Section 4. [12] Geneva Act, *supra* note 3, art. 2(1)(i).

a competitive advantage – the GI name – on the international market. In this respect, GIs become tools that capitalize on the association between the names and the geographical locations even when this association is based simply on an historical reputation rather than on the accurate geographical origin of the products. To remedy this potential distortion, or misuse of GIs, Section 5 repeats a point that I made in my previous scholarships. In particular, this Section argues that GI protection should be limited only to the products that are entirely made in the GI-denominated regions.[13] Certainly, (re)creating the normative framework to implement such stricter interpretation of GIs in practice is a highly complex task that may require amending the current definition of GIs in TRIPS – which today protects products' "reputation" as much as the products' actual "geographical origin." Still, while recognizing the challenges of amending the definition in TRIPS, this section also proposes a more workable alternative, which could restore "geographical accuracy" under the current international framework for GI protection. In particular, this section suggests that GI producers disclose directly in the GI specification, as well as on the packaging and the advertising materials related to the products, the origin of all the ingredients, raw materials, and manufacturing steps of the products that do not originate from the GI-denominated regions. To this extent, this section turns to the language of Article 22(2) of TRIPS, which already prohibits the use of GIs to mislead consumers as to the origin of the products, and this provision should also apply to GI producers.[14] To date, this provision has been interpreted primarily as prohibiting competitors from using GI names misleadingly. Yet, the provision could (and should) apply also to GI producers and be interpreted as requiring that GI producers disclose the actual geographical origin of the entirety of the ingredients and manufacturing steps of products. This section concludes that this interpretation of Article 22(2) would benefit not only consumers but also the producers of raw materials and product ingredients, whose localities would be directly recognized in the global marketplace and production chain.[15] This

---

[13] *See* Calboli, *In Territorio Veritas*, *supra* note 8, at 63–66.
[14] TRIPS, *supra* note 1, art. 22(2).
[15] This conclusion is the result of an insightful conversation with Ms. Natalie Corthésy, Ph.D. candidate at Queen Mary University in London and lecturer at the University of West Indies at Mona, in December 2015. Ms. Corthésy's research focuses on the intellectual property protection of countries' names. She already supported and suggested a similar conclusion. Our conversation focused, in particular, on Jamaica, and the rights of Jamaican producers in being recognized for their agricultural products in the international market. I am grateful to Ms. Corthésy for highlighting the problems that developing countries' farmers face and the lack of academic discussion on this issue so far.

observation is of considerable relevance for developing countries, including in Asia-Pacific, as many products from these countries, including many GI products, are raw materials and agricultural products. These products are often sold to and used by foreign producers for their finished products, and rarely acknowledged in the packaging or advertising of the finished products.

2 THE GLOBAL, AND FRAGMENTED, DISCUSSION ON GEOGRAPHICAL INDICATIONS: FROM FRANCE TO EUROPE, TO THE WORLD

The discussion over GIs generally brings about images of European wines, beers, and cheeses, and with it the decade-long controversy over the names of these products between Europeans and New World producers, primarily producers of European immigrant origins. As other scholars and I have recounted in detail before, this controversy sees, on the one side, the struggle of the Europeans to prevent the New World from copying the geographical names of EU products[16] – primarily wines and cheeses – based on the argument that the New World free rides on these names and generally produces subpar replicas compared to the original products. In the New World, this argument is met, on the other side, with fierce resistance and the counter-argument that European producers are trying to monopolize names that have been used as generic terms for decades, if not centuries, in the New World by immigrants coming from Europe.[17] These two images certainly embody sharply different points of view over the GI debate. Yet, they also shed an important light over the historical origin of the GI controversy – one that is tackled, from different angles, by the contributions in this volume: namely, these images show how discussions about GIs, and the resulting controversy, were born and have long been dominated by Western interests, literally by

---

[16] *See, e.g.*, the contributions in DEV GANGJEE, RESEARCH HANDBOOK IN INTELLECTUAL PROPERTY AND GEOGRAPHICAL INDICATIONS (2016); *see also* the special issue of the *International Review of Intellectual Property and Competition Law*, 46(7) INT'L REV. INTELL. PROP. & COMPETITION L. (2015).

[17] This position is well summarized in the steady opposition to GIs by the representatives of the Consortium for Common Food Names in the United States. *See, e.g., Threats to Common Food Names More Widespread in EU Trade Deals and Other Geographical Indications Policies*, CONSORTIUM FOR COMMON FOOD NAMES (March 19, 2015), www .commonfoodnames.com/threats-to-common-food-names-more-widespread-in-eu-trade-deals -and-other-geographical-indications-policies/ (stating the actions taken in several countries to protect common food names such as "parmesan," "feta," and "bologna") [hereinafter CONSORTIUM FOR COMMON FOOD NAMES].

a "wine and cheese war" between the Old and New Worlds.[18] Western interests were clearly at the basis, and at the negotiating table, when the GI provisions in TRIPS were discussed and finalized in the early 1990s, even as the EU was the main proponent of GI protection and New World Western countries were the main opponents. Hence, despite the lack of overall agreement on the issue, both worlds agree on enhanced protection for wines and spirits[19] – since both (Western) worlds had, and have, important interests in wines and spirits, as the main producers and exporters of these products.[20] To the contrary, both worlds could not find a common solution with respect to the protection of the names for cheeses primarily due to the resistance of national dairy industries. Several decades after the conclusion of TRIPS, the "cheese war" between Old and New Worlds still rages on.

In the past decades, however, discussions about GIs have expanded beyond the West and reached the attention of other continents and developing countries. Notably, many countries in Asia, Africa, Central America, and South America have expressed interest in GI protection and, as a result, have implemented or are considering implementing specific provisions to protect GIs, including registration-based *sui generis* systems.[21] In this respect, it should be noted that several famous GI-denominated products come today from non-Western countries – Darjeeling tea, Ceylon tea, Kampot pepper, Kobe beef, and Blue Mountain coffee are just a few examples of famous non-Western GI products. Contributors to this volume address in detail several of the national initiatives to protect GIs, particularly with respect to the Asia-Pacific region, and elaborate on the legislative history, and where possible the practical application, of these laws. Additional evidence of the increasing interests by non-Western countries in the GI debate is shown by the fact that discussions over GI protection are no longer just about "wine and cheese" or agricultural and food-related products – the latter also part of the GI agenda of Western countries.

---

[18] To date, the "wine" part of this war has been largely resolved with ad hoc wine agreements between Western countries. See Agreement Between the European Community and the United States of America on Trade in Wine, E.C.-U.S., March 10, 2006, 2006 O.J. (L 87) 2 (EC), http://ttb.gov/agreements/us-eu-wine-agreement.pdf. The EU has concluded similar "Wine Agreements," inter alia, with Canada, Australia, and New Zealand. See Irene Calboli, *Time to Say Local Cheese and Smile at Geographical Indications? International Trade and Local Development in the United States*, 53 HOUS. L. REV. 373, 396–97 (2015) [hereinafter Calboli, *Say Local Cheese*].

[19] TRIPS, *supra* note 1, art. 23.   [20] Calboli, *Say Local Cheese*, *supra* note 18, at 384.

[21] An updated list of national laws on GIs can be found in the database of WIPO. See WIPO Lex, www.wipo.int/wipolex/en/ (last visited August 22, 2016).

Instead, discussions on GI protection now encompass proposals for expanding protection beyond agricultural products, foodstuffs, wines, and spirits in those countries that still limit protection to these products.[22] Several countries in Asia-Pacific, for example, have long offered protection as GIs to handicrafts and artisanal products beyond agricultural products and food stuff, and have promoted the expansion of protectable subject matter to encompass these products internationally.[23] Along the same lines, many non-Western pro-GI countries are promoting, along with Western pro-GI countries such as the EU, the adoption of the higher level of protection currently provided by TRIPS to wines and spirits for all GIs, again because this protection may better suit their national interests in international trade by offering the possibility to protect the names of their products also in the foreign countries where the products are exported and sold to.[24]

Still, even though discussions about GIs – more precisely discussions for and against GI protection – have certainly gone global today, it is important to remember that the modern system of GI protection originates from Europe and, more specifically, from the French laws protecting appellations of origin in the early twentieth century.[25] Remembering this fact is relevant both to better understand the development of the international movements supporting GI protection and to identify solutions to limiting a possibly excessive expansion of GI protection beyond the economic and normative reasons that were originally at the basis of this protection.

In particular, the origin of GI protection can be traced back to the attempts to prevent fraud in the marketplace for wines in France following the dramatic destruction of French vineyards by a pandemic of phylloxera in the late 1800s. Due to the pest, the production of French wine considerably diminished,[26] and this led to widespread counterfeits and adulterated products.[27] To counter this, France enacted a wine labeling law in 1905 prohibiting the misuse of wine names.[28] This law was revised in

---

[22] See discussion *infra* Section 3.
[23] See, e.g., Delphine Marie-Vivien, *A Comparative Analysis of GIs for Handicrafts: The Link to Origin in Culture as Well as Nature?* in RESEARCH HANDBOOK IN INTELLECTUAL PROPERTY AND GEOGRAPHICAL INDICATIONS 292 (Dev Gangjee ed., 2016).
[24] *Id.*
[25] For one of the most detailed reconstructions of the history and development of GI protection, *see* Dev Gangjee, RELOCATING THE LAW OF GEOGRAPHICAL INDICATIONS 93–96 (2012) [hereinafter Gangjee, RELOCATING GIs].
[26] *Id.* at 93–94.   [27] *Id.* at 94–95.
[28] Loi du 1er Août 1905 sur les Fraudes et Falsifications en Matière des Produits ou de Services, JOURNAL OFFICIEL DE LA RÉPUBLIQUE FRANÇAISE [J.O.] [OFFICIAL GAZETTE OF FRANCE], August 5, 1905, p. 4813.

1919,[29] and later in 1935.[30] Still, the adoption of the French laws in the early twentieth century was prompted primarily by the necessity to prevent unfair competition in the marketplace by unrelated parties using geographical names inaccurately while also securing the accuracy of the information about products' geographical origin for consumers.

To justify the protection of geographical names, however, the French laws enshrined into the normative framework of protection the notion that location, and more precisely the *terroir* – a deep connection between the products and the land, as mentioned in the Introduction – where the vine was grown and the wines were made, was a "key ingredient in differentiating between wines by indicating a distinct origin."[31] This notion represented a considerable step forward in explicitly protecting "geographical origin" from the previously existing laws on unfair competition and, above all, the protection granted to "indications of origin" in the 1883 Paris Convention for the Protection of Industrial Property.[32] Since then, the notion of *terroir* has been at the heart of the policy justifications for protecting GIs, including the basis of the argument that GIs are incentive for local and rural development due to the fact that they promote local products. To be precise, the 1891 Madrid Agreement for the Repression of False and Deceptive Indications of Source on Goods (the Madrid Agreement),[33] which predated the French Law of 1905 by a few years, already included a similar notion – the protection of "*regional* appellations concerning the source of the products of the vine."[34] Yet, French negotiators certainly influenced the language of the agreement. In 1958, the notion of *terroir* was then confirmed in the Lisbon Agreement, whose imprint from the French laws also cannot be overstated. Certainly the most comprehensive system of protection for appellations of origin adopted at the international level, the Lisbon Agreement also included

---

[29] Loi du 6 Mai 1919 Relative à la Protection des Appelations d'Origine, JOURNAL OFFICIEL DE LA RÉPUBLIQUE FRANÇAISE [J.O.] [OFFICIAL GAZETTE OF FRANCE], May 8, 1919, p. 4726.
[30] Décret-loi du 30 Juillet 1935 Relatif à la Défense du Marché du Vins et au Régime Economique de l'alcool, JOURNAL OFFICIEL DE LA RÉPUBLIQUE FRANÇAISE [J.O.] [OFFICIAL GAZETTE OF FRANCE], July 31, 1935, p. 8314 (creating a system based on controlled appellations of origin).
[31] GANGJEE, RELOCATING GIs, *supra* note 25, at 83.
[32] Paris Convention for the Protection of Industrial Property, March 20, 1883, *as revised* July 14, 1967, 21 U.S.T. 1583, 828 U.N.T.S. 305, arts. 10(1) and 10bis [hereinafter Paris Convention], forbidding "false, fictitious, or deceptive trade names," and the use of any misleading indications (but not specifically geographical indications).
[33] Madrid Agreement for the Repression of False and Deceptive Indications of Source on Goods, April 14, 1891, 828 U.N.T.S. 163 [hereinafter Madrid Agreement].
[34] Madrid Agreement, *supra* note 33, art. 2.

a system of international registration. However, both the Lisbon Agreement and the Madrid Agreement had few signatories and the majority were countries from Europe.[35] In May 2015, a revised text of the Lisbon Agreement was adopted after a Diplomatic Conference held in Geneva. Supporters of the Geneva Act of the Lisbon Agreement hoped that the new agreement may facilitate a membership increase.[36] To date, for example, several countries in Asia-Pacific are evaluating the feasibility of joining the revised Lisbon Agreement and the international registration system. Still, the Geneva Act was adopted amidst many controversies and it may not achieve the success hoped for by its proponents.

Ultimately it was only in 1994, with the adoption of TRIPS, that GIs really entered the international stage on a full scale since all WTO Members had to include a minimum-level GI protection in their national laws as part of the obligations established by TRIPS.[37] The same obligation applied to the countries that joined the WTO after 1994, many of which were countries from the Asia-Pacific region.[38] Still, non-Western countries were, at large, not active parts in negotiating these provisions, even though several of these countries participated in subsequent negotiations related to the advancement of TRIPS' built-in GI agenda.[39] In particular, TRIPS established a double system of protection: a "floor level" of protection for all GIs against misleading and unfair competition-based uses of GIs;[40] and an enhanced level of protection for GIs identifying wines and spirits against usurpation of the GI names, including when "the true origin of the goods is indicated or the [GI] is used in translation or accompanied by expression such as 'kind', 'type', 'style', 'imitation', or the like."[41] TRIPS also established several

---

[35] As of March 2017, only twenty-eight States are contracting parties to the 1958 Lisbon Agreement, and twenty-seven States are signatories of the 1967 Stockholm Revisions. *See Contracting Parties, Madrid Agreement*, WORLD INTELL. PROP. ORG., www.wipo.int/treaties/en/ShowResults.jsp?lang=en&treaty_id=3. Only thirty-six States are contracting parties of the Madrid Agreement. *See Contracting Parties, Lisbon Agreement* and *Contracting Parties, Stockholm Act*, WORLD INTELL. PROP. ORG., www.wipo.int/treaties/en/registration/lisbon/.

[36] As of March 2017, only fifteen States have signed the Geneva Act. *See Contracting Parties, Geneva Act*, WORLD INTELL. PROP. ORG., www.wipo.int/treaties/en/registration/lisbon/.

[37] TRIPS, *supra* note 1, arts. 22–24.

[38] For the alphabetical list of the countries that are members of the WTO, which also indicates the date in which the countries joined the WTO, *see Members and Observers*, WORLD TRADE ORG., www.wto.org/english/thewto_e/whatis_e/tif_e/org6_e.htm.

[39] For a background to the current debate at the WTO, and the respective proposal by various groups of countries, see TRIPS: Geographical Indications, Background and the Current Situation, WORLD TRADE ORG., www.wto.org/english/tratop_e/trips_e/gi_background_e.htm#wines_spirits.

[40] TRIPS, *supra* note 1, art. 22(2). [41] *Id.* art. 23.

limitations to GI protection as a result of the requests of anti-GI advocates. These include provisions on generic terms and the possibility of "grandfathering" existing rights for trademarks that were in use or had been registered in good faith before the date of the implementation of TRIPS in the WTO Member States where the mark was registered, or before the GI was protected in its country of origin.[42]

Nevertheless, the GI provisions in TRIPS did not fully satisfy the requests of the pro-GI countries, which managed to include into TRIPS the commitment to continue the negotiation – in the form of a built-in agenda mandating further negotiations on GIs.[43] In particular, TRIPS binds WTO Members to hold future negotiations in order to (a) discuss the creation of a multilateral system of notification and registration of GIs (similar to the one already in force under the Lisbon Agreement) for wines and spirits[44] and (b) "to enter into negotiations aimed at increasing the protection of individual geographical indications [to the level of GIs for wines and spirits]."[45] Because of the delay in pursuing these negotiations – due again to the opposition of anti-GI countries – GI protection was also included in the agenda for discussion in the Doha "Development" Round of WTO negotiations in 2001.[46] The Doha version of the WTO GI agenda included again the creation of a multilateral register, no longer just for wines and spirits, but for all GIs, and the possibility of extending the higher level of protection provided to wines and spirits to all GIs.[47] However, no agreement on any of these issues could be reached when WTO Members met in 2003 in Cancun, Mexico.[48] As a result, multilateral negotiations on GIs have been stalled ever since, and more than a decade after the meeting

---

[42] TRIPS, *supra* note 1, art. 24(4)–(5). The multinational controversies over several names such as Feta, Fontina, Asiago, and Parmesan as well as the litigation for the rights to the GI (or mark) "Budweiser" across several countries are some of the most famous examples of potential national divergences, and in turn (legal) conflict, regarding the relationship between GIs and, respectively, generic names and registered marks. See CONSORTIUM FOR COMMON FOOD NAMES, *supra* note 17; Christopher Heath, *The Budweiser Cases: A Brewing Conflict*, in LANDMARK INTELLECTUAL PROPERTY CASES AND THEIR LEGACY 181 (Christopher Heath & Anselm Kamperman Sanders eds., 2011).
[43] TRIPS, *supra* note 1, arts. 23(4), 24(1).   [44] *Id.* art. 23(4).   [45] *Id.* art. 24(1).
[46] See Doha Declaration, *supra* note 1. For a detailed analysis of the Doha Declaration, *see* TRIPs: Issues, Geographical Indications, WORLD TRADE ORG., http://wto.org/english/tratop_e/trips_e/gi_e.htm (last visited August 22, 2016).
[47] See Doha Declaration, *supra* note 1, 18.
[48] For more details about the WTO negotiations in Cancun, *see* TRIPS: Geographical Indications, Background and the Current Situation, WORLD TRADE ORG., www.wto.org/english/tratop_e/trips_e/gi_background_e.htm (last visited August 22, 2016).

in Cancun and two decades since the adoption of TRIPS, there is no sign that WTO countries may restart negotiations on the TRIPS' built-in GI agenda any time soon.[49]

Because of this impasse, discussions about GIs have continued primarily as part of FTA negotiations in recent years. Several of these FTAs, and the resulting "FTA maze," are addressed at length in this volume, from the perspectives of both pro-GI and GI-skeptic countries. In a nutshell, pro-GI countries, led by the EU, seem to have been particularly successful in advancing their GI protection agenda as part of the FTA strategy. For example, the EU has negotiated the protection of a long list of EU GIs, including the "claw back" of several terms that are protected as GIs in the EU and were considered generic terms in the jurisdictions of several negotiating parties, in the EU–Canada Comprehensive Trade Agreement,[50] and in the FTAs concluded with Korea, Vietnam, and several South American countries.[51] To date, EU negotiators are continuing to press the EU GI agenda in trade talks with, inter alia, India, Japan, Malaysia, Australia, New Zealand, and the United States.[52] The EU is also discussing the extension of its previous stand-alone agreement on GIs with China, through which both the EU and China had registered ten GIs from the other parties in their national, or regional for the EU, jurisdictions.[53] Considering the importance of China, and Asia, as the export destination for EU products, these results are certainly good news for the EU. To counter the EU strategy, GI-skeptic countries have also engaged in trade negotiations, including GI provisions. This has been the case primarily with the Trans-Pacific Partnership (TPP), which was

---

[49] *See* WORLD TRADE ORGANIZATION, *Article 27.3b, Traditional Knowledge, Biodiversity*, WTO Doc. TN/C/W/61 (April 21, 2011), www.wto.org/english/tratop_e/trips_e/art27_3b_e.htm.

> *Status of Play* – Delegations continued to voice the divergent views that have characterized this debate, with no convergence evident on the specific question of extension of Article 23 coverage: some Members continued to argue for extension of Article 23 protection to all products; others maintained that this was undesirable and created unreasonable burdens.

Id. at 4.

[50] *See* Comprehensive Trade and Economic Agreement, Can.-EU, Consolidated CETA Text, ch. 22, art. 7, Intellectual Property, September 26, 2014, http://trade.ec.europa.eu/doclib/docs/2014/september/tradoc_152806.pdf [hereinafter CETA, Intellectual Property Chapter]. *See* Calboli, *Say Local Cheese*, *supra* note 18, at 408–18 (discussing the EU's strategy as part of CETA and suggesting a compromising solution for the TTIP negotiations).

[51] For details on the FTAs concluded by the EU and other countries, or currently under negotiation, *see European Commission's Trade Policy Portal*, EUR. COMM'N, http://ec.europa.eu/trade/policy/accessing-markets/intellectual-property/geographical-indications/ (last visited August 22, 2016).

[52] *Id.*

[53] *See Geographical Indications (GI)*, EU-CHINA TRADE PROJECT (II), www.euctp.org/index.php/en/agriculture-food-safety/geographical-indications-gi.html (last visited August 22, 2016).

finalized in 2015, and includes provisions related to "generic terms" and registered marks that may be protected as GIs in other countries.[54] Still, because of the diverging interests of various TPP members, the final draft of the TPP leaves signatories free to negotiate different provisions in other FTAs, subject only to minimum requirements[55] – again a partial victory for pro-GI advocates. Moreover, the United States officially withdrew from the TPP in January 2017, and the agreement may never be ratified by the remaining parties.[56]

3 THE POTENTIAL BENEFITS, PROMISES, AND PROBLEMS OF GEOGRAPHICAL INDICATIONS FOR ECONOMIC AND SOCIAL DEVELOPMENT

As indicated in Section 2, besides being one of the most relevant topics of discussion in international trade today, the benefits derived by adopting a national system of GI protection have been discussed also at the national level in a growing number of countries. In particular, GI-related legislations have recently been adopted or updated in several countries, including in Asia-Pacific, as detailed by the chapters in this volume. Notably, new or updated laws have been recently adopted, inter alia, in Japan,[57] Bangladesh,[58] Singapore,[59] Indonesia,[60] and Cambodia.[61] In other countries, such as Sri

---

[54] See Trans-Pacific Partnership Agreement, ch. 18, arts. 18.30–36 Intellectual Property, October 5, 2015, https://ustr.gov/sites/default/files/TPP-Final-Text-Intellectual-Property.pdf [hereinafter TPP]. When the TPP was finalized, the TPP members were Australia, Brunei Darussalam, Canada, Chile, Japan, Malaysia, Mexico, New Zealand, Peru, Singapore, the United States, and Vietnam. But the United States withdrew from the TPP in early 2017. See infra n.56.

[55] Id. art. 18.36. Several TPP members – Vietnam, Malaysia, and Singapore – have concluded, or are discussing, FTAs with the EU.

[56] See Office of the United States Trade Representative (USTR), *The United States Officially Withdraws from the Transpacific-Partnership*, https://ustr.gov/about-us/policy-offices/press-office/press-releases/2017/january/US-Withdraws-From-TPP. (last visited 1 February 2017).

[57] *Tokutei Norin Suisan Butsu to no Meisho no Hogo ni Kansuru Horitsu* [Act for the Protection of the Names of Designated Agricultural, Forestry and Fishery Products and Foodstuffs], June 25, 2014, *available at*, www.maff.go.jp/j/shokusan/gi_act/outline/pdf/do c4.pdf. (last visited August 22, 2016).

[58] The Geographical Indication (Registration and Protection) Act of 2013 (Bangl.).

[59] Geographical Indications Act, No. 19 of 2014 (Sing.), not yet in force. When this Act enters into force, it will replace the Geographical Indications Act (Cap 117B, 1999 rev edn.) (Sing.).

[60] See Law No. 20 of October 27, 2016, concerning Trade Marks and Geographical Indications amending Law No. 15of 2001 concerning Trade Marks (Indonesia).

[61] The Law on Geographical Indications of Goods ("GI Law") of Cambodia entered into force on January 20, 2014. *See Protected Geographical Indications in Cambodia*, AGENCE FRANCAISE DE DEVELOPPEMENT, www.afd.fr/webdav/shared/PORTAILS/PAYS/CAMBODGE_2/PDF/Brochure%20GI%20-%20Cambodia%20-%20EN.pdf (last visited August 22, 2016).

Lanka,[62] Australia,[63] and New Zealand,[64] among others, legislative reforms about the current status of GI protection are pending or being discussed. In this respect, it is important to note that these reforms are also taking place in countries that have traditionally been skeptical of GI protection, such as Australia, which is currently debating a possible extension of GI protection for wines to other agricultural products.[65] A similar discussion may soon start in New Zealand, a country that is currently considering a bill to implement more detailed requirements and clarification for the current level of GI protection to wines. As mentioned earlier, the growing participation of Asia and non-Western countries in discussions on GIs also brought more attention to the request of expanding GI protection to nonagricultural products, namely handicrafts and artisanal goods, such as wood-carved and pottery products, textiles, and so forth. Developing countries are large producers of these products and seek their protection not only at the national level but also internationally. For example, pressure from developing countries (in exchange of protection for EU GIs in their jurisdictions) is certainly part of the reasons why the EU is now considering expanding GI protection beyond agriculture-based products,[66] and the proposal for a new Regulation in this respect has already received the unanimous approval of the EU Parliament.[67]

---

[62] Intellectual Property Act, No. 36 of 2003, § 160 (Sri Lanka); Consumer Affairs Authority Act, No.9 of 2003, § 30 (Sri Lanka).

[63] Wine Australia Corporation Act of 1980; Australian Grape and Wine Authority Act of 2013.

[64] Fair Trading Act of 1986 (N. Z.).

[65] *See* WILLIAM VAN CAENEGEM, JEN A. CLEARY & PETER DRAHOS, PROVENANCE OF AUSTRALIAN FOOD PRODUCTS: IS THERE A PLACE FOR GEOGRAPHICAL INDICATIONS? (2015), *available at* https://rirdc.infoservices.com.au/items/15-060; William Van Caenegem, Jen A. Cleary, & Peter Drahos, *Pride and Profit: Geographical Indications as Regional Development Tools in Australia*, 16 J. ECON. & SOC. POL'Y (2014), *available at* http://epubs.scu.edu.au/jesp/vol16/iss1/5/.

[66] In 2015, the European Commission published a report evaluating the opportunity to extend GI protection for nonagricultural products. *See Results of the Public Consultation and Public Conference on Making the Most Out of Europe's Traditional Know-How: A Possible Extension of Geographical Indication Protection of the European Union to Non-Agricultural Products*, at 36–37, COM (2014) 469 final (January 20, 2015), http://ec.europa.eu/docsroom/documents/10565/attachments/1/translations/en/renditions/pdf. This report followed a study commissioned by the EU Commission. *See* Insight Consulting et al., *Study on Geographical Indications Protection for Non-Agricultural Products in the Internal Market* (2013), http://ec.europa.eu/internal_market/indprop/docs/geo-indications/130322_geo-indications-non-agri-study_en.pdf.

[67] On September 22, 2015, the European Parliament considered the protection of nonagricultural GIs and called "on the Commission to propose without delay a legislative proposal with the aim of establishing a single European system of protection of geographical indications for non-agricultural products." Comm. on Legal Affairs, *Report on the*

Certainly, the rise in attention to GIs is again, at least with respect to some countries, the direct effect of FTA negotiations, particularly with the EU. This is the case, for example, of Singapore, a country with no national GIs, which has updated the existing law and adopted a registration-based system of GI protection as part of the obligations undertaken under the EU-Singapore FTA.[68] Other countries, however, already had comprehensive national GI regulations well before negotiating FTAs – this is the case of Vietnam, for instance, a country with a long-standing tradition of GI protection before the EU-Vietnam FTA.[69] Still, several of the countries, in Asia-Pacific (and elsewhere), that decided to implement a *sui generis* system of protection, including a registration system, may have done this under the indirect influence from the EU, because of previous colonial ties, or in order to imitate the EU system as a proven successful system in this area when they had to implement the minimum standards of protection mandated under TRIPS. This may be the case of countries such as Bangladesh, Cambodia, China, India, Indonesia, and Thailand among others. All these countries have a registration-based system for GI protection today. In certain instances, several countries in Asia-Pacific seem also to have been influenced by successful experiences of neighboring countries in this respect. For example, it cannot be excluded that, once India implemented a system of GI protection, this triggered discussions about adopting a similar protection in neighboring countries.[70] Presently, several of the member countries of the Association of South-East Asian Nations (ASEAN) are also stepping up their GI protection based both on a variety of FTA negotiations in the region and the example of successful GI experiences, such as those in Thailand and Vietnam.

In general, this renewed attention to GIs is driven primarily by the belief (or the hope) that GI protection can, or at least may, benefit the national

---

Possible Extension of Geographical Indication Protection of the European Union to Non-Agricultural Products, EU Doc. A8-0259/2015, at 6/26, ¶ 3 (2015), www.europarl.europa.eu/sides/getDoc.do?pubRef=-//EP//NONSGML+REPORT+A8-2015–0259+0+DOC+PDF+V0//EN.

[68] *See* Geographical Indications Act, No. 19 of 2014 (Sing.). *See* also EU-Singapore Free Trade Agreement, EU-Sing., September 20, 2013, http://ec.europa.eu/trade/policy/countries-and-regions/countries/singapore/.

[69] Civil Code of Vietnam (1995), art. 786 (Vietnam). In 2015, the EU and Vietnam concluded the EU-Vietnam FTA. *See EU-Vietnam Free Trade Agreement: Agreed Text as of January 2016*, EUR. COMM'N, February 1, 2016, http://trade.ec.europa.eu/doclib/press/index.cfm?id=1437.

[70] This is the case of Sri Lanka and Bangladesh, for example, following the adoption of GI protection in India. *See* the chapters by Naazima Kamardeen and Mahua Zauhr in this volume.

economies of the countries adopting these laws. Several of the contributions to this volume discuss the potential benefits, but also the possible pitfalls, of GI protection in several countries in Asia-Pacific.

In particular, as I have recounted before, one of the staple arguments in support of GI protection – in Europe, Asia, and worldwide – is precisely the proposition that granting exclusive rights on geographical names associated to products coming from certain regions would translate into incentivizing and promoting local and rural development in those regions.[71] This argument rests on the consideration that groups of regional producers would be motivated to start investing, or continue to invest, in the production of certain types of products that traditionally originate from a given region, if they can secure exclusive rights on the geographical names of that region. This is because, in the view of the producers, obtaining exclusive rights on the GIs would guarantee the ability to capture the full profit for the quality and characteristics of the products, including the added value that the GIs could give to the products – e.g., the fact that consumers locally, nationally, or internationally may be willing to pay a premium price for sparkling wine from Champagne, tea from Darjeeling, and pepper from Kampot.

Hence, in order to secure these exclusive rights, collectivities of regional producers should work together to identify a common process that defines the uniqueness of the GI products, and submit the products' specification with the application to register the GI. Producers should also identify quality control bodies, both internal and external, to certify the conforming of the products to the specification.[72] Once the GI is registered, the collectivity of producers (which generally also remain competitors in the intra GI market) is bound by

---

[71] See Calboli, *The Benefits of GIs*, *supra* note 7, at 447–52 (summarizing the economic arguments in favor of GI protection); *see also* GANGJEE, RELOCATING GIs, *supra* note 25, at 183 (noting that GIs are protected due to the possibility to "generate improved incomes and tangible benefits for groups of rural or marginalized groups"). *See also, e.g.,* Sarah Bowen, *Embedding Local Places in Global Spaces: Geographical Indications as a Territorial Development Strategy*, 75 RURAL SOC. 209 (2010); GIOVANNI BELLETTI & ANDREA MARESCOTTI, GI SOCIAL AND ECONOMIC ISSUES 15 (2006), *available at* www.origin-food.org/2005/upload/SIN%20-%20WP2%20FinalReport%20DEF.pdf.

[72] This is a very important step in the process of GI registration, which traditionally sees the involvement of the state, as a certifying public authority, and the selection of private, yet independent, bodies for quality control. For example, the quality control body for the GI Parmigiano Reggiano is the Organismo di Controllo Qualità Produzioni Regolamentate. *See* ORGANISMO DI CONTROLLO QUALITÀ PRODUZIONI REGOLAMENTATE [Organism for Quality Control of Regulated Productions], www.ocqpr.it/ (last visited August 22, 2016). The quality control body for the GI Prosciutto di Parma is Istituto Parma Qualità. *See* ISTITUTO PARMA QUALITÀ [Institute Parma Quality], www.parmaqualita.it/ (last visited August 22, 2016).

the specification, and this guarantees the consistency of the quality and characteristics that consumers expect to find in all GI-denominated products.[73]

In other words, GIs facilitate not only local development by tying producers to the land, but also producers' cooperation to maintain the quality of the products for the collectivity. Overall, the impact of GI protection on development continues to strengthen when GI-denominated products become established in the marketplace, as GIs incentivize the producers to continue to invest in the quality of the products.[74] Moreover, since the land is the essential wealth, the heart, upon which the fortune of the GI producers is constructed, GIs also function as incentives for producers to adopt long-term strategies for safeguarding and enhancing the well-being of the land. In particular, GI producers are aware that the long-term health of the land and the resources of the region are crucial for the long-term success of GI products and generally work together to maintain the well-beingness of the region. Besides benefitting GI producers, this can have positive spillover on the region landscapes and in turn several other industries built around the GI products – for example, a variety of service providers, the tourism industry, including eco-tourism, and regional retailer of GI products and the producers of products that can accompany the sale of GI products.

Moreover, whereas GIs permit producers to capture the added value of GI products, GIs also operate as "badges of accountability" for those producers who decide to produce subpar products or simply not respect the requirements listed in the GI specification. In particular, under the current normative framework of GI protection, these producers will be forbidden from using the GI unless they return to producing following the mandated standards. In light of this possibility, the importance of quality control on GI products cannot be overstated. In this respect, several countries in Asia-Pacific have recently implemented or have revamped the systems of quality control

---

[73] For example, all European GIs for agricultural products and food stuff are registered in the online database "DOOR." *See* DOOR, *Denomination Information*, EUR. COMM'N, http://ec.europa.eu/agriculture/quality/door/list.html (last visited August 22, 2016). Moreover, the websites of many registered PDOs and PGIs indicate the specifications and quality control related to the products.

[74] *See* GANGJEE, RELOCATING GIS, *supra* note 25, at 266 ("Since consumers are willing to pay more for such goods, this encourages farmers to invest in making the transition from producing un-differentiated bulk commodities, towards producing higher quality niche products"). *See also* Michelle Agdomar, *Removing the Greek from Feta and Adding Korbel to Champagne: The Paradox of Geographical Indications in International Law*, 18 FORDHAM INTELL. PROP. MEDI & ENT. L.J. 541, 586–87 (2008) (noting that granting property rights through geographical indications allows producers to control the quality of their goods in order to build consumer confidence).

of GI-denominated products in order to effectively ensure that the products comply with the product specifications.[75]

The second argument in support of GI protection is that GIs provide consumers with relevant information about the GI products.[76] In particular, from a public policy standpoint, GIs offer to consumers, including retailers purchasing GI-denominated products for resale, information that can reduce the information asymmetries that consumers usually face compared to producers at the time of purchase. In other words, GIs offer additional information about the quality and characteristics of the products, and this offers consumers the possibility to make a better-informed decision about their purchase.[77] GIs can also offer relevant information about the safety and the health of the products because they offer information about the origin and the practices that go into making the products.[78] Similarly, GIs can provide information about the impact of the manufacturing and other practices used to produce the GI-denominated products on the environment, and even labor practices, including overall human rights. Again, this set of information could assist consumers in identifying potentially healthier foods for their individual needs, or artifacts made with traditional or environmentally friendly manufacturing techniques for those countries that provide GI protection beyond food-related products. As mentioned earlier, GIs can even reduce possible "contagion effects" due to negative incidents in a given geographical market for a certain type of product.[79] This was the case, for example, with respect to the scandal of the contaminated "mozzarella di bufala campana," a GI-denominated product from Italy.[80] In this case, consumers could use the information provided by the GI to know that they should avoid the products

---

[75] See, e.g., Trong Binh Vu & Duc Huan Dao, *Geographical Indication and Appellation of Origin in Vietnam: Reality, Policy, and Perspective*, INSTITUTE OF POLICY AND STRATEGY FOR AGRICULTURE AND RURAL DEVELOPMENT – MISPA PROJECT (2006), *available at* www.fao.org/fileadmin/templates/olq/documents/documents/GI%20and%20AO%20in%20Vietnam.pdf [hereinafter, Binh & Huan, *GI and Appellation of Origin*]; *see also* Chuthaporn Ngokkuken & Ulrike Grote, *Challenges and Opportunities for Protecting Geographical Indications in Thailand*, 19 ASIA-PAC. DEV. J. 93 (2012).

[76] See Calboli, *The Benefits of GIs*, *supra* note 7, at 435; GANGJEE, RELOCATING GIs, *supra* note 25, at 183 (GIs are protected because they "must *actually* provide useful information to consumers in an established market").

[77] Agdomar, *supra* note 74, at 586–87 (noting that GIs constitute methods of improving asymmetrical information as they signal quality and expertise and enable consumers to distinguish between premium-quality products and low-end products).

[78] Id. at 587–88.   [79] See Calboli, *The Benefits of GIs*, *supra* note 7, at 447–52.

[80] See Michael McCarthy & John Phillips, *Italy's Toxic Waste Crisis, the Mafia – and the Scandal of Europe's Mozzarella*, THE INDEPENDENT (March 22, 2008), www.independent.co.uk/news/world/europe/italys-toxic-waste-crisis-the-mafia-ndash-and-the-scandal-of-europes-mozzarella-799289.html.

originating in the affected region, while they could safely continue to purchase the generic product "mozzarella di bufala" from other regions.

In addition to the arguments that GI promotes economic development and reduces information asymmetries from consumers, another argument has been brought forward in recent years to justify GI protection. This argument is directly addressed by several contributions in this volume and centers on the proposition that GIs can protect the cultural identity of local and regional communities, which in turn may contribute to promoting cultural diversity.[81] The growing importance of GIs under the lenses of culture-related concerns finds additional support in two separate conventions that have been recently adopted under the patronage of the United Nation Educational, Scientific and Cultural Organization (UNESCO): the 2003 Convention for the Safeguarding of the Intangible Cultural Heritage[82] and the 2005 Convention on the Protection and Promotion of the Diversity of Cultural Expressions.[83] Under the UNESCO framework, GIs seem well suited for the protection of culture-based interests because GI products frequently relate to local and traditional knowledge of the region where the products are made.[84] Thus, granting exclusive rights to GIs could serve to promote the continuation of traditional manufacturing techniques, which could otherwise succumb to the competition of mass production techniques. Moreover, GIs directly contribute to reinforcing local identities by again promoting the making and selling of local products. As others and I have suggested, this may promote greater product diversity in an economy where products would be otherwise increasingly similar due to the globalization of trade and the de-localization of product manufacturing.[85]

---

[81] In this respect, see Calboli, *The Benefits of GIs*, supra note 7, at 439; see also, e.g., Toshiyuki Kono, *Geographical Indication and Intangible Cultural Heritage*, in LE INDICAZIONI DI QUALITÀ DEGLI ALIMENTI 289 (Benedetta Ubertazzi & Esther Muñiz Espada eds., 2009); Tomer Broude, *A Diet Too Far? Intangible Cultural Heritage, Cultural Diversity, and Culinary Practices*, in DIVERSITY IN INTELLECTUAL PROPERTY: IDENTITIES, INTERESTS, AND INTERSECTIONS 472 (Irene Calboli & Srividhya Ragavan eds., 2015).

[82] Convention for the Safeguarding of the Intangible Cultural Heritage, October 17, 2003, in force April 20, 2006, 2368 U.N.T.S. 1, available at http://unesdoc.unesco.org/images/0013/00 1325/132540e.pdf.

[83] Convention on the Protection and Promotion of the Diversity of Cultural Expressions, October 20, 2005, 2440 U.N.T.S. 346 available at http://en.unesco.org/creativity/sites/creativ ity/files/passeport-convention2005-web2.pdf.

[84] See, e.g., Teshager W. Dagne, *Harnessing the Development Potential of Geographical Indications for Traditional Knowledge-based Agricultural Products*, 5 J. INTELL. PROP. L & PRAC. 441, 447 (2010).

[85] See Calboli, *The Benefits of GIs*, supra note 7, at 439; Dev Gangjee, *Geographical Indications and Cultural Heritage*, 4 WIPO J. 92, 99 (2012).

Hence, as Justin Hughes pointedly observes in this volume, for all their potential benefits for local development and culture, GIs are not a magic recipe for success for local producers. Instead, several of the GIs that have been registered in the EU, and elsewhere, to date, have not brought to their producers more than some modest returns and, at times, the same returns as non-GI products. This has been proven true, in particular, with respect to raw materials and non-processed agricultural products.[86] As a result, this partially questions the value of GIs for these products. In turn, this raises question about the value of GI protection for developing countries, as many of the GIs registered and protected in these countries are for raw materials and non-processed agricultural products. Moreover, developing countries often lack the infrastructure to enact strict quality control programs, and appropriate marketing of the products. Similarly, foreign enterprises are often deeply involved in the management of GIs in developing countries, which may lead to their business interests prevailing over long-term local (and thus national) development.[87] This could become problematic for local communities, particularly when foreign businesses push for excessive production and fast-paced growth of the products' quantities.[88] More generally, the success of any GI products can become a double-edged sword and lead to inconsiderate exploitation of the land and natural resources without proper management of the GIs and a long-term strategic plan for the growth and development of the products. In turn, this could directly and negatively affect the local environment, and overall the sustainability of the production of the GI products themselves. A telling example in Asia-Pacific is the case of "Phu Quoc," which was registered as a GI for fish sauces in Vietnam in 2001. After obtaining the GI registration, national (and foreign) producers overproduced without implementing a rigorous system of quality control for the products for several years. This led to unwelcome results for the local environment, and the simultaneous rise of counterfeits.[89] Only recently, a control body for the Phu Quoc products was established and the body has stepped up in controlling the quality and authenticity of the products.

---

[86] ARETÉ, STUDY ON ASSESSING THE ADDED VALUE OF PDO/PGI (2013), http://ec.europa.eu/agriculture/external-studies/2013/added-value-pdo-pgi/exec-sum_en.pdf.

[87] See Bowen, *supra* note 71.

[88] See, e.g. Jennifer Barnette, *Geographic Indications as a Tool to Promote Sustainability? Café de Colombia and Tequila Compared*, 39 ECOLOGY L. Q. 102 (2012).

[89] For a detailed discussion on the "Phu Quoc" registration process, see Binh & Huan, *GI and Appellation of Origin*, *supra* note 75.

4 TERROIR WITH LESS TERROIR? THE RISE OF "REPUTATION-BASED" GEOGRAPHICAL INDICATIONS, THE LOOSENING TERRITORIAL LINKAGE, AND RISKS THEREOF

This section argues that GI protection becomes more questionable when the products do not entirely originate from the GI regions and GI producers use a partially de-localized production model for their products. Unfortunately, despite the claims of "geographical purity" supported by pro-GI advocates, this partially delocalized model of production for GI products seems today to be more the norm than the exception, with the blessing of international law and most national laws on GIs. Hence, when GIs do not identify fully locally made products, GI protection can easily transform in subsidies and thus confirm the concerns that are often expressed by GI skeptics. In essence, as I argued in my previous scholarship, granting exclusive rights when GIs do not identify fully locally made products risks to transform GIs into a marketing tool rather than signs of the accurate geographical origin of the products at issue.[90] This, in my opinion, seems to run against the very rationale for protecting GIs in the first place – the linkage between the products and the land, in other words the commonly celebrated unique relationship between the products and the *terroir*.

Certainly, it should be noted that the relationship between the *terroir* and the products originating from the land has been partially romanticized. In particular, this relationship was never absolute and overly strict, despite the (often conveniently painted) arguments of GI supporters. This was already the case with respect to the first laws on GIs – or, more precisely, their predecessors "indications" and "appellations" of origin – in the legal landscape. Yet, as mentioned in Section 2, starting with the French laws of the early 1900s, and a few years prior with the Madrid Agreement, it is accurate to say that the broad justification for protecting indications of geographical origin was enshrined in the notion that these indications deserved separate protection from other distinctive signs – primarily trademarks – because of the special relationship between the location from which the products originate and the overall characteristics of the products. In 1958, the definition of "appellations of origin" in the Lisbon Agreement codified this notion in Article 2(1), which reads that "appellations of origin" are the "geographical name[s] of a country, region, or locality, which serve to designate a product originating therein, the quality and characteristics of which are due *exclusively or essentially* to the geographical environment, including natural and human

---

[90] Calboli, *In Territorio Veritas*, supra note 8, at 62–63.

factors."[91] Article 2(2) of the Lisbon Agreement further clarified that "[t]he country of origin is the country whose name, or the country in which is situated the region or locality whose name, constitutes the appellation of origin which has given the product its *reputation*."[92]

Certainly, despite its strong emphasis on the "geographical environment," the very language of the Lisbon Agreement already reflected some flexibility in the definition of "appellations of origin." Notably, Article 2(1) does not impose an "exclusive" connection between the products and the land, but just an "exclusive or essential" connection. Moreover, the definition in Article 2(1) adds "human factors" to "natural factors" with reference to the "exclusive or essential" elements of the products' quality or characteristics. As supported by prominent scholars, reference to human factors may be seen as evidence to support a system of GI protection focused on localities as the place not only where products are grown but also where the products are made, possible with ingredients and raw materials partially originating from outside the region. Last, but not least, the Lisbon Agreement also refers to the notion of product "reputation," a concept later found in TRIPS, even though the combined reading of Article 2(1) and 2(2) indicates that the use of the wording "reputation" in Lisbon is a narrow one, meaning primarily that protectable appellations of origin are the names of those geographical locations that have given reputation to a certain product coming from those locations. As explained in the remainder of this section, the concept of "reputation" has later emerged as an (almost) independent justification for protecting GIs today – a tendency that Dev Gangjee explores in this volume based on both a "geography" and "history" approach.

Still, the major loosening of the definition of GIs away from a strict interpretation of the notion of "geographical origin" was the direct result of the adoption of TRIPS in 1994. Notably, Article 22(1) of TRIPS blends the concept of *terroir* – in its romantic interpretation as absolute relationship between the products and the land – with a much wider concept of "reputation" compared to the concept in the Lisbon Agreement. In particular, Article 22(1) of TRIPS defines GIs as "indications which identify a good as originating in the territory ... or a region or locality in that territory, where a given quality, reputation or other characteristic of the good is *essentially* attributable to its geographical origin."[93] In other words, the provision in

---

[91] 1958 Lisbon Agreement, *supra* note 3, art. 2(1) (emphasis added).   [92] *Id.* art. 2(2).
[93] TRIPS, *supra* note 1, art. 22(1). The definition in TRIPS was certainly influenced by WIPO's definition of GIs as "sign[s] used on goods that have a specific geographical origin and possess qualities, reputation or characteristics that are essentially attributable to that origin." World Intellectual Property Organization (WIPO), *What is a Geographical Indication?* www.wipo .int/geo_indications/en/ (last visited August 22, 2016).

TRIPS makes of the linkage between products and the land just an "essential" and no longer an "exclusive or essential" element for GI protection. This loosening of "geographical accuracy" in the TRIPS' definition of GIs is exacerbated by the fact that TRIPS includes the notion of "reputation" front and center in the definition of GIs, treating "reputation" as an equally significant element for GI protection as the other characteristics and qualities of the GI-denominated products. In other words, following TRIPS, producers in a given region are able to claim exclusive rights on the geographical names of the region with respect to their products even though the products may be manufactured with ingredients entirely originating from outside the region, simply because the name of the region has, historically, been linked with the products and has given to the products their reputation (most likely because the products were first made, or became famous when they were made, in the region).

As I mentioned in the Introduction, it is a known fact that the language of Article 22(1) of TRIPS was heavily influenced by the language of the existing EU Regulations at the time of the TRIPS negotiations, and that the EU strongly supported this language. Notably, Council Regulation (EEC) No. 2081/92 of July 14, 1992, on the protection of GIs and designations of origin for agricultural products and foodstuffs[94] protected two different types of GIs: "geographical indications" (PGIs), which were defined as "the name[s] of a region, a specific place or, in exceptional cases, a country, used to describe an agricultural product or a foodstuff" that are "originating in that region, specific place or country" and "which possess a specific quality, *reputation* or other characteristics attributable to that geographical origin *and the production and/or processing and/or preparation of which take place in the defined geographical area*";[95] and "designations of origin" (PDOs), which were defined as "the name[s] of a region ... used to describe an agricultural product or a foodstuff" that are "originating in that region, specific place or country" and "the quality or characteristics of which are *essentially or exclusively* due to a particular geographical environment with its inherent natural and human factors, and the production, processing and preparation of which take place in the defined geographical area."[96] For the latter type of GIs, the PDOs, a stronger link with the territory was required under EU law, but that was not the case for PGIs. Moreover, Regulation No. 20181/92 provided that "certain geographical

---

[94] Council Regulation 2081/92 of July 14, 1992 on the Protection of Geographical Indications and Designations of Origin for Agricultural Products and Foodstuffs, 1992 O.J. (L 208) 1, [hereinafter Regulation 2081/92].
[95] Id. art. 2(2)(b).   [96] Id. art. 2(2)(a).

designations shall be treated as designations of origin where the raw materials of the products concerned *come from a geographical area larger than or different from the processing area.*"[97] Regulation 2081/92 was later amended and replaced, but today's Council Regulation (EC) No. 1151/2012 (Agricultural Products and Foodstuff Regulation)[98] and Council Regulation (EC) No. 479/2008 (Wine Regulation)[99] repeat almost verbatim the same definitions for PGIs and PDOs. Council Regulation (EC) No. 119/2008 (Spirits Regulation) only refers to "geographical indications" for spirits.[100] Despite their differences in the requirements to qualify as PGIs or PDOs, both types of GIs enjoy the same level of (enhanced) protection in the EU.

Besides the influence of the EU Regulations on the definition in TRIPS, in May 2015, a provision blending Article 22(1) of TRIPS and the EU definitions was introduced into the Geneva Act of the Lisbon Agreement,[101] which amends the definition in Article 2(1) of the Lisbon Agreement. In particular, similar to EU law, the Geneva Act definition now includes two types of GIs, namely "geographical denominations" and "geographical indications." More specifically, Article 2(1) of the Geneva Act defines (i) geographical "denominations" as signs which "designate a good as originating in that geographical area, where the quality or characteristics of the good are due exclusively or essentially to the geographical environment, including natural and human factors, *and which has given the good its reputation*";[102] and (ii) geographical "indications" as signs which "consist of or contain the name of a geographical area, or another indication known as referring to such area, which identifies a good as originating in that geographical area, where a given quality, *reputation* or other characteristic of the good is *essentially* attributable to its geographical origin."[103] In this respect, Article 2(1)(i) of the Geneva Act

[97] *Id.* art. 2(4). The provision put the following conditions: "provided that: the production area of the raw materials is limited; special conditions for the production of the raw materials exist, and there are inspection arrangements to ensure that those conditions are adhered to."
[98] Regulation 1151/2012 of the European Parliament and of the Council of November 21, 2012, on Quality Schemes for Agricultural Products and Foodstuff, 2012 O.J. (L 343) 1, art. 5(1)–(3).
[99] Council Regulation 479/2008 of April 29, 2008, on the Common Organization of the Market in Wine, Amending Regulations 1493/1999, 1782/2003, 1290/2005, 3/2008 and Repealing Regulations (EEC) No 2392/86 and 1493/1999, 2008 O.J. (L 148) 1, art. 34(1)(a)–(b). In addition, art. 31(1)(c) includes in the definition of "designation" certain "traditional used names" provided that "(a) designate a wine; (b) refer to a geographical name; (c) meet the requirements referred to in paragraph 1(a)(i) to (iv) [of Article 34(1)(a)]; (d) undergo the [relevant] procedure conferring protection on designations of origin and geographical indications."
[100] Regulation 110/2008, of the European Parliament and of the Council of January 15, 2008, on the Definition, Description, Presentation, Labeling and the Protection of Geographical Indications of Spirits Drinks and Repealing Council Regulation (EEC) 1576/89, 2008 O.J. (L 39) 16, art. 15.
[101] Geneva Act, *supra* note 3, art. 2.   [102] *Id.* art. 2(1)(i).   [103] *Id.* art. 2(1)(ii).

merges the language of Article 2(1) and 2(2) of the Lisbon Agreement, adding to the definition of "geographical denomination" (previously "appellations of origin") the wording *"which has given the product its reputation."*[104] Article 2(1)(ii) repeats the TRIPS and EU definition for "geographical indications," and refers to "reputation" as an element sufficient, per se, for granting exclusive rights on GIs.[105] Article 2(2) of the Geneva Act then enlarges the scope of the definition even more in Article 2(1) by defining "geographical area" as potentially also "the *entire territory* of the Contracting Party of Origin [thus a whole country] or a region, locality or place in the Contracting Party of Origin."[106] This area can now consist also "of a trans-border geographical area, or a part thereof."[107]

In summary, the review of the development of the current definition of GIs directly reflects a far less stringent relationship between GI products and the *terroir* than the one that is often purported in the GI debate. This review shows, in particular, a progressive loosening of this linkage, at least in terms of the dependence of the products from the physical and natural resources of the GI regions. It also shows the rising importance of the human factors, traditionally a partially less relevant element in the GI debate compared to the physical and natural resources, as a qualifying element per se for claiming exclusive rights on geographical names. More problematically, it empowers national authorities to grant GI rights based simply on the reputational link between products and geographical names. Not surprisingly, the loosening of the strictness of this territorial linkage matches changes in international trade, including trade facilitations and a larger access to raw materials from foreign markets at reduced, or no longer existent, tariff barriers. Under the current system, GI producers could have the best of both worlds – claiming exclusive rights on famous locations that grant a competitive advantage to their products against competitors on the one side, and the possibility of accessing cheaper raw materials in foreign markets, if not cheaper human factor, at least in part, for processed GI products, including handcrafts and artisanal goods. Hence, this system no longer accurately identifies the geographical origin of the GI products nor fulfills the functions that are at the core of GI protection:

---

[104] *Id.* art. 2(1)(i).   [105] *Id.* art. 2(1)(ii).
[106] *Id.* art. 2(2).
[107] Geneva Act, *supra* note 3, art. 2(2). This option could resolve several ongoing disputes between neighboring countries over the origin of certain products, such as Basmati rice or Emmentaler cheese. See Basmati, Registration No. 4076214 (India); Emmentaler Tradition Switzerland, Registration No. 583659 (S.Z.); Allgäuer Emmentaler, Dossier No. DE/PDO/ 0017/0459 (Germany); Emmental de Savoie, Dossier No. FR/PGI/ 0017/0179 (France).

incentivizing local and rural development, and offering accurate information to consumers.

As I mentioned before, the protection of GIs – well-known GIs in particular – certainly offers an important legal alternative in a world in which agricultural subsidies, and other trade subsidies, are increasingly scrutinized as barriers to international trade. In this respect, GIs permit producers to continue to secure some "monopoly rent" against competing products in the international market.[108] Not surprisingly, the loosening of the definitions of GIs has been supported precisely by those nations and stakeholders representing GI-intensive countries and industries, such as the EU. Yet, this begs the following question: is this "modern" system of GI protection compatible with the historical objectives of this protection? Moreover, under the current system, the blame and shame for any problems related to products not fully originating from GI-denominated regions may be erroneously passed on to other GI producers, including those who entirely produce their products in the GI-denominated area. Ultimately, as I elaborate in the following section, this modern system of protection could be made compatible with the traditional objectives of GI protection, should GI producers clearly disclose the actual geographical origin of the raw materials, product ingredients, and manufacturing steps that do not originate from the GI region. This is of particular importance to, and thus should interest, developing countries in Asia-Pacific and elsewhere, as these countries are strong producers, and exporters, of (mostly agricultural) raw materials and non-processed products, which are, or could be, used by other countries' producers.

5 FULL DISCLOSURE REQUIRED: THE CASE FOR A SYSTEM OF PROTECTION BASED ON A MORE FLEXIBLE, BUT STILL ACCURATE, NOTION OF "GEOGRAPHICAL ORIGIN"

Based on the considerations in Section 4, it is not an exaggeration to state that the system of GI protection that is currently being embraced by TRIPS and other relevant international agreements and national legislations directly favors a flexible notation of "geographical origin," which does not necessarily include the origin of all the ingredients and steps of manufacturing that are used and needed for the production of the GI products. In this respect, criticisms by GI skeptics exposing the inconsistency between this reality and the arguments put forward by GI supporters that GI deserves special

---

[108] See Justin Hughes, *Champagne, Feta, and Bourbon: The Spirited Debate About Geographical Indications*, 58 HASTINGS L.J. 299, 345 (2006).

protection because of the linkage between the products and the *terroir* are thus well taken. Still, these criticisms should not let us lose sight of the actual and potential benefits that a system of GI protection which is focused on accurate information, can otherwise bring to both consumers and local development. Moreover, we should not forget that the criticisms expressed against GI protection often derive from supporters of an anti-GI agenda, an agenda that frequently aims to protect the national interests of businesses that use (misusing them in the view of this author) foreign GIs to identify their generic national products – frequently adding to the packaging of these products additional misleading elements, such as flags, national symbols, and color schemes reminiscent of the foreign countries from where the GIs originate and that are famous for their GI products.

Ultimately, as the contributions to this volume illustrate from a variety of different angles, as much as GI protection favors a certain set of interests – those of localities with strong agricultural or artisanal traditions and the businesses in these localities that grow or manufacture products related to these traditions – the lack of appropriate GI protection favors another set of interests – those of businesses producing similar products to be sold under names that are similar to the existing geographical names even though the products do not share any geographical link with those locations. Disputes over terms like Budweiser, Champagne, or Parma between business interests in different countries are illustrious examples of these conflicting interests.[109] Accordingly, the arguments put forward by GI skeptics should also be carefully vetted as these arguments may also not offer optimal solutions for consumers and (national and/or local) economic development. For example, in some instances, the use of GI names in unrelated contexts in different countries does indeed derive from decades of usage by immigrant communities, or is due to the fact that the GI terms have indeed become generic terms in those countries. In this case, specific exceptions should be, and generally have been, carved out with legal solutions. Hence, these cases are less frequent than GI skeptics tend to purport. In contrast, in several cases, the inappropriate use of GIs by third parties in foreign countries seems to be done with the specific intent to exploit the association generated by these terms with certain (famous) foreign geographical places in order to create a sense of déjà vu and reassurance in consumers, especially in other jurisdictions where these "GI look-alike" products compete with authentic GI products. This is certainly the case with respect to the names of many cheeses available in the market in New World countries today.

---

[109] See Calboli, *In Territorio Veritas*, supra note 8, at 66.

Still, despite these flaws in the arguments of GI skeptics, a more rigorous interpretation of the notion of "geographical origin," one that better complies with the normative objectives that have been traditionally invoked to justify GI protection, is nevertheless needed to restore legitimacy in the arguments supported by GI advocates in favor of GI protection, especially when these arguments are used to request that other countries agree to adopt additional protection beyond the level currently provided for in TRIPS. As I mentioned earlier and have also argued in my previous scholarship,[110] in the absence of a considerable "refocus" toward greater geographical accuracy (i.e., toward a system in which GIs effectively convey accurate information about products' geographical origin), GI protection may become nothing more than a monopoly (and more problematically one not limited in time) on geographical names for possibly no other sound reasons than the historical reputation of a certain location. In this case, however, GI protection no longer brings about the benefits that communities had hoped for in terms of local development – as part of the products would be made outside the regions. Likewise, the use of GIs may result in increasing, rather than decreasing, the information asymmetries between producers and consumers as to the actual origin and quality of the products at issue. In other words, from badges of geographical origin and associated characteristics, GIs may become just badges of misleading information to induce consumers to believe that products originate from a region, even though, in practice, the ingredients may originate, at least in part, elsewhere, or simply badges of a reputation that is associated to a location only based on past traditions which no longer exist.

In a previous article, in 2014,[111] I argued in support of the adoption of a narrower and more geographically coherent definition of GIs to resolve the risks of geographical inaccuracy, or inconsistency, which may plague the current system of GI protection. This narrower approach, I argued, could be based on limiting the granting of GI protection only to those products that are actually grown in the GI regions, or effectively originate from these regions with respect to the entirety of the ingredients and manufacturing steps necessary to manufacture the finished products. To reach this result, I suggested that one option could be to delete the wording "reputation" from Article 22(1) of TRIPS, and with it the possibility to grant exclusive rights on GIs just based on the "reputation" of the GI products without any additional link to the actual quality and characteristics of these products. Likewise, I suggested the removal

---

[110] *Id.* at 63–66.   [111] *Id.*

of the word "essentially" from the definition of GIs in Article 22(1), so that GIs would be defined as "indications which identify a good as originating in the territory of a Member, or a region or locality in that territory, where a given quality, or other characteristic of the good, is attributable to its geographical origin."[112] Alternatively, I suggested the introduction into TRIPS' definition in Article 22(1) the wording "essentially or exclusively" as in the 1958 version of the Lisbon Agreement.[113] In my opinion, this language would better reflect a very high level of geographical connection between the products and the GI-denominated areas. Today, in light of the 2015 Geneva Act of the Lisbon Agreement, this proposal should include amending the new definition in the Geneva Act discussed in Section 4, as this definition has been modeled after TRIPS.

However, as I already acknowledged in 2014, amending TRIPS is likely to be an impossible task today, due to the current gridlocking of trade negotiations within the WTO and the collapse of the Doha multilateral agenda.[114] Moreover, many countries have implemented a definition of GIs similar to TRIPS, thus any amendment of TRIPS should be followed by the amendments of these national laws. This would certainly result in an equally complex, if not again an impossible, task to achieve in practice.

Still, a perhaps less radical but effective proposal for a refocus of the current system of GI protection toward a system based on a stricter territorial linkage and more transparent disclosure of the geographical origin of the products may nonetheless be possible under the current framework. In particular, after further thinking and discussing this issue, I have reached the conclusion that the key for such a solution lies in interpreting the definition of Article 22(1) in light of the provision in Article 22(2) of TRIPS, which forbids any misleading use of a GI and states that "interested parties" are entitled to oppose "(a) the use of any means in the designation or presentation of a good that indicates or suggests that the good in question originates in a geographical area other than the true place of origin *in a manner which misleads the public as to the geographical origin of the goods.*"[115] As noted in Section 2, this provision provides the minimum protection for all GIs against misleading uses. Yet, nothing in the language of the provision seems to indicate that only GI producers can invoke Article 22(2) to oppose the misleading use of GIs by third parties. Instead, the provision clearly applies to *all* misleading use of a GI. This may include all the cases in which GI producers use a GI to identify products that do not fully originate from the region, should the public believe

[112] Id. [113] Id. [114] Id. [115] TRIPS, *supra* note 1, art. 22(2).

that the products entirely originate from the region. In other words, this may include the cases in which GI producers turn to ingredients or raw materials, or partially prepare the products with labor from outside the region, and do not disclose these facts to consumers who purchase the products believing that they originate in their entirety from the region.

Thus, based on the assumption that Article 22(2) of TRIPS could be invoked also to prohibit the misleading use of GIs by GI producers, a solution that could potentially address the geographical inaccuracy, or inconsistency, and the (at least partial) lack of transparency of the current system could be the following: GI producers could be required to clearly disclose the actual geographical origin of any raw materials, ingredients, and manufacturing steps of the products that do not originate from the GI region at the point of sale and on the packaging of their products.

In particular, Article 22(2) of TRIPS could be interpreted as providing that, should producers not disclose this information to consumers in a transparent and explicit manner, GI producers may then be held accountable for using GIs "in a manner which misleads the public as to the geographical origin of the goods" and thus denied the right to use the said GIs. To the contrary, when producers disclose the actual origin of any raw materials, ingredients, and manufacturing steps of the products that do not originate from the GI region, they would be seen as complying both with Articles 22(1) and 22(2) of TRIPS, or more precisely their equivalent provisions in the national jurisdictions where the GIs are registered and/or protected. In practice, information about the quality and actual origin of the ingredients and raw materials used for the products may already be listed in the product specification, even though it is unclear if national laws require such disclosure as a requirement for registering GIs.[116] Moreover, consumers rarely consult product specifications, if they are aware of the existence of these specifications at all. Instead, consumers generally rely on the information that they can find directly on the product packaging and

---

[116] For example, the specification of the PDO "Prosciutto di Parma" permits that the pigs used for the final products, the Parma ham, originate from outside the Parma region, precisely from eleven different regions of Italy. Notably, "[t]he raw material comes from a geographical area that is larger than the production area, and which includes the administrative districts of the following Italian Regions: Emilia-Romagna, Veneto, Lombardy, Piedmont, Molise, Umbria, Tuscany, Marche, Abruzzo and Lazio (Italy)." *See* Specification and Dossier Pursuant to Article 4 of Council Regulation 2081/92 of July 14, 1992, on the Protection of Geographical Indications and designations of Origin for Agricultural Products and Foodstuffs, 1992 O.J. (L 208) 6, www.prosciuttodiparma.com/pdf/en_UK/disciplinare.28.11.2013.en.pdf.

advertising.[117] Accordingly, by requiring producers to fully disclose the geographical origin of raw materials, ingredients, and manufacturing steps on the packaging on the products and related product advertising consumers would be made aware of the actual origin of all these various components. This not only would allow consumers to make better informed purchasing decisions; it would also incentivize GI producers to select materials, ingredients, and human factors of a quality on par with the reputation of the products, lest consumers may no longer purchase the GI products.

Equally relevant, this obligation could benefit the producers in the localities from which the raw material ingredients originate, or the workers that provide some of the manufacturing steps of the products. Today, these producers and workers disappear in the production chain of the GI products, and their work is not at all recognized even though their role in the final quality, and the overall success of the products, cannot be overstated – simply put, there would not be Swiss chocolate without cocoa beans from cocoa plantations that are certainly not located in Switzerland.[118] This observation is of particular importance for countries that are primarily producers and exporters of agricultural products, and in particular for developing countries, including developing countries in Asia-Pacific – many of which have registered GIs for agricultural products.[119] As noted also in a 2013 study, raw materials command a much lower premium price than finished products in general,[120] and in countries whose GIs are primarily agricultural and raw-materials-based, GI

---

[117] See, e.g., Annette Kur, *Quibbling Siblings: Comments to Dev Gangjee's Presentation*, 82 CHI.-KENT. L. REV. 1317, 1320–321 (2007) (noting "[a]s most of us are laymen in the field, we have to trust the competent authorities to do their job correctly" and that "the informing effects that protected GIs have on consumers resulting from the fact that the products bear, in addition to the GI itself, the indications 'PDO' ..., 'PGI' ..., or their equivalents in other languages-appear modest at best").

[118] Ammini Ramachandran, *Indian Cocoa Grown for Swiss Chocolate*, ZESTER DAILY (June 21, 2012), http://zesterdaily.com/agriculture/indian-cocoa-grown-for-swiss-chocolate/ (stating that Swiss Chocolat Noir is made from cocoa from Kerala, India). Kaspar Meuli, *Facing Cocoa Shortage, Swiss Chocolate Makers Aim to Boost African Production*, WORLDCRUNCH (January 2, 2012), http://www.worldcrunch.com/business-finance/facing-cocoa-shortage-swiss-chocolate-makers-aim-to-boost-african-production (stating that "[m]ore than half of the cacao beans transformed into chocolate in Switzerland come from [Ghana]").

[119] An analysis of the GIs that are registered in ASEAN indicates that a large part of these GIs comprises of agricultural products, such as pineapples, rice, sugar coffee, tea, etc. *See* ASEAN GI DATABASE, www.asean-gidatabase.org (last visited August 22, 2016).

[120] ARETÉ, *supra* note 86, at 6 (this study was commissioned by the EU Commission and proves, with data, that "[a]s for agricultural raw materials, price premiums for raw materials for GI production were very limited or absent in the majority of cases. Significant price premiums for GI production over standard production were observed in less than one third of the cases").

producers do not seem to receive a fair share from the current GI system compared to the producers of fully developed GI products. Instead, processed products, like wine and cheese, tend to enjoy higher premium prices over competing products, even when they are made, in part, with foreign ingredients – again the case of Swiss chocolate is on point.[121] In this respect, a more transparent system of GI protection requiring full disclosure would both be compatible with the current language of TRIPS and make a stronger case in support of GI protection everywhere.

6 CONCLUSION

This chapter highlighted how the debate over GI protection remains controversial under multiple fronts. Notably, as the title of this volume summarizes, GIs are today at a crossroads between trade, development, and culture-related interests. In particular, this chapter illustrated how the GI debate, and related controversy, continues to dominate international trade negotiations – at this time no longer (or not only) under the umbrella of the WTO, but primarily as a topic addressed in bilateral and multilateral FTAs. Moreover, attention to GIs is no longer just a "European thing," even though the EU has largely built its trade negotiations' agenda over obtaining protection, or enhancing the existing protection, for its GIs. Instead, many countries outside the EU, including in Asia-Pacific, have turned their attention to GIs and implemented national systems of GI protection driven by the beliefs (and hopes) that this could promote local development as well as assist marketing their products in the global market. Hence, this chapter has also highlighted that GIs do not represent, per se, a magic tool for local development. Thus, a wise development strategy should always include strict quality control protocols, long-term plans to maintain product quality, and thoughtful marketing strategies.

While highlighting the economic benefits of GI protection, this chapter also emphasized that GIs should not become pure marketing tools for GI producers. In this respect, it argued that the current definition of GIs has drifted toward a looser linkage between GIs and their historical justification: the territorial linkage between the products and the regions. Notably, GI protection today extends to products that only "essentially" originate from GI-denominated regions, which permit producers to partially (or mostly) outsource the raw materials, ingredients, or manufacturing steps of GI products, and still enjoy exclusive rights on the GI names. This chapter criticized this

---

[121] See *supra* note 118.

development as not being in line with the normative justifications for GI protection and possibly a violation of Article 22(2) of TRIPS. Instead, this chapter supported a narrower definition of GIs to reflect a closer linkage with the *terroir*, with this link implemented in the form of a requirement that GI producers disclose the actual origin of all the raw materials, ingredients, and manufacturing steps of the GI products to consumers at the point of sale, and on the product packaging and advertising. This requirement is compatible, and perhaps even mandated, under a sensible interpretation of Article 22(2) of TRIPS, and would benefit a more transparent system of GI protection, both to the advantage of producers – GI producers and the producers of the foreign materials, ingredients, and labor of GI products – and consumers.

2

From Geography to History: Geographical Indications and the Reputational Link

Dev S. Gangjee[*]

1 INTRODUCTION

For much of its history, the notion of a distinctive link between regional products and their places of origin has been articulated in the language of *terroir*. This polysemous term acts as a cipher for the influence of geographical origin on the end product's quality.[1] As one leading scholar of the concept describes it: 'Historically, *terroir* refers to an area or terrain, usually rather small, whose soil and micro-climate impart distinctive qualities to food products. The word is particularly closely associated with the production of wine.'[2] This type of causal relationship – where the physical geography factors within a region leave their distinctive traces upon the end product – is reflected in the definition of a geographical indication (GI) found in Article 22.1 of the Agreement on Trade-Related Aspects of Intellectual Property Rights (TRIPS).[3]

According to Article 22.1, a GI is a sign that identifies 'a good as originating in the territory of a [WTO] Member, or a region or locality in that territory, where a given *quality*, reputation *or other characteristic* of the good is

---

[*] Associate Professor, Faculty of Law, University of Oxford. The author is grateful to the editors of this volume and the contributors for their comments on the initial draft of this chapter.
[1] See Daniel W. Gade, *Tradition, Territory, and Terroir in French Viniculture: Cassis, France, and Appellation Contrôlée*, 94(4) ANNALS ASS'N AM. GEOGRAPHERS 848 (2004); Cornelis Van Leeuwen & Gerard Seguin, *The Concept of Terroir in Viticulture*, 17 J. WINE RES. 1 (2006); Marion Demossier, *Beyond Terroir: Territorial Construction, Hegemonic Discourses, and French Wine Culture*, 17 J. ROYAL ANTHROPOLOGICAL INST. 685 (2011).
[2] Elizabeth Barham, *'Translating Terroir' Revisited: The Global Challenge of French AOC Labeling*, in RESEARCH HANDBOOK ON INTELLECTUAL PROPERTY AND GEOGRAPHICAL INDICATIONS 57 (Dev Gangjee ed., 2016).
[3] Agreement on Trade-Related Aspects of Intellectual Property Rights, 15 April 1994, Marrakesh Agreement Establishing the World Trade Organization, Annex 1C, LEGAL INSTRUMENTS – RESULTS OF THE URUGUAY ROUNDS vol. 31, 33 I.L.M. 1125, 1197 (1994) [hereinafter TRIPS].

essentially attributable to its geographical origin' (emphasis added). However, this chapter will focus on the relatively ignored option bracketed between qualities and characteristics – reputation. Ironically, reputation is the least talked about form of linkage between product and place. The analysis which follows considers the question of when a product's reputation can be said to be essentially attributable to its geographical origin.

This is a question worth investigating because it relates to the very foundation of GI protection. The basis for treating GIs as a distinct intellectual property (IP) regime rests on the notion of a verifiable link between a product and its place of origin.[4] In the words of the World Intellectual Property Organization (WIPO):

> It is important for the justification of the elements of the definition to be made in the most objective manner possible with a view to giving the link a precise and specific form, since this constitutes the basis for the protection of a [GI]. The grant of an exclusive right to a denomination is made only insofar as this right is justified by objective elements and forms of proof. These elements and proof help to make the subject matter for which protection is sought and the reason for such protection understandable, while using, for example, specifications containing these elements in methodological and concrete terms.[5]

The necessity for a causal and objectively verifiable link was also endorsed by the Institut National de l'Origine et de la Qualité (INAO), which has regulated GIs in France since its inception in 1935.[6] When registering a protected designation of origin (PDO) or protected geographic indication (PGI), a demonstration of the causal interaction between the specificities or characteristics of the area and the characteristics of the product is expected to be provided.[7]

Yet despite the justificatory significance of the link, scholars working in this field have noticed a countervailing trend – a general loosening of the link

---

[4] For the origins of this link and its justificatory functions in GI regimes, see DEV GANGJEE, RELOCATING THE LAW OF GEOGRAPHICAL INDICATIONS (2012) [hereinafter GANGJEE, RELOCATING GIs].

[5] WIPO, *Geographical Indications*, at 32, WIPO Doc. SCT/10/4 (23 March 2003).

[6] On the institutional mission of the Institut National de l'Origine et de la Qualité (INAO), see Delphine Marie-Vivien, Laurence Bérard, Jean-Pierre Boutonnet & François Casabianca, *Are French Geographical Indications Losing Their Soul? Analyzing Recent Developments in the Governance of the Link to the Origin in France*, WORLD DEVELOPMENT (forthcoming 2016).

[7] INAO, GUIDE DU DEMANDEUR D'UNE APPELLATION D'ORIGINE PROTÉGÉE (AOP) OU D'UNE INDICATION GÉOGRAPHIQUE PROTÉGÉE (IGP) À L'EXCEPTION DES VINS ET DES BOISSONS SPIRITUEUSES (April 2015) 23 (' *La démonstration d'une interaction causale entre les spécificités de l'aire et les spécificités du produit est attendue*') (April 2015).

requirement accompanied by less demanding scrutiny. Driven by the desire to reach strategic multilateral compromises and develop an international consensus in favour of GI protection, proponents of GIs have been relaxing definitional criteria and overlooking enduring ambiguity for decades. In recent work, Irene Calboli has argued for a return to a more rigorous GI definition, which does not stray too far from *terroir*.[8] The PGI[9] is cast as the culprit for the lowering of standards, with its permissive approach to a reputational link and its relatively undemanding requirement that only one stage of the product's life cycle (its production, *or* processing, *or* preparation) take place within the defined region of origin.

In recent work, I have explored the flexibilities and blind spots contained within the European Union's (EU) GI registration system for agricultural products and foodstuffs, including the limitations of a public certification process when verifying the link between product and place. Within this two-stage process, both the national registrar and the European Commission ultimately work with, and are constrained by, the product specification that is submitted.[10] A registrar can be provided with a PGI specification that is entirely silent on certain aspects of production, that permits the sourcing of raw materials for a PGI from outside the specified region or that describes the reputation link by merely referring to a few historical sources. Despite this being a unitary EU-wide system operating according to harmonised standards, there is very limited guidance provided by the Commission in terms of the criteria to be satisfied.[11]

Delphine Marie-Vivien is also interested in the apparent attenuation of the link requirement for PGIs, but she explores the potential to accommodate

---

[8] Irene Calboli, *In Territorio Veritas: Bringing Geographical Coherence in the Definition of Geographical Indications of Origin under TRIPS*, 6(1) WIPO J. 57 (2014); Irene Calboli, *Geographical Indications of Origin at the Crossroads of Local Development, Consumer Protection and Marketing Strategies*, 46 IIC 760 (2015); Irene Calboli, *Of Markets, Culture and Terroir: The Unique Economic and Culture-Related Benefits of Geographical Indications of Origin*, in INTERNATIONAL INTELLECTUAL PROPERTY LAW: A HANDBOOK OF CONTEMPORARY RESEARCH 433 (Daniel Gervais ed., 2015).

[9] See *infra* Section 3.

[10] Dev Gangjee, *Proving Provenance? Geographical Indications Certification and Its Ambiguities*, WORLD DEVELOPMENT (forthcoming 2017).

[11] In the European Union (EU), a modest seven-page guide for GI applicants exists. *See* European Commission, *Guide to Applicants: How to Complete the Single Document*, http://ec.europa.eu/agriculture/quality/schemes/guides/guide-for-applicants_en.pdf (last visited 23 April 2016). In contrast, the guidelines for registry examiners for the unitary Community Trade Mark (the EU Trade Mark from 2016) run into thousands of pages. *See* European Union Intellectual Property Office, *Trademark Guidelines*, https://oami.europa.eu/ohimportal/en/trade-mark-guidelines (last visited 23 March 2016).

human factors within this less deterministic (in a physical geography sense) form of link. The PGI model has the flexibility to incorporate traditional crafts and textiles within the present EU approach towards GI protection. Therefore, for Marie-Vivien, reputation is the potential vector for admitting such products into the EU's conceptual framework of GIs.[12] Crafts, textiles and non-agricultural GIs in general are of interest not just for the EU but for countries in Asia and Africa as well. Thus, reputation as a form of linkage between product and place is presently both a cause for concern – because its loose application undermines the justifications for GI protection – and a potentially flexible option to incorporate non-agricultural products, which demonstrate an appropriate historic connection with a place. Both its peril and potential make this an opportune moment to study the question taken up by this chapter.

Section 2 will identify five reasons why we need to think about the content of the reputation link more closely. While reputation is increasingly being relied upon in GI legislation as well as registration systems, there is a curious absence of criteria that would help to establish this type of link. Section 3 will establish that assistance cannot be found in the drafting history of TRIPS or other contemporaneous legal instruments. It will review the circumstances under which the reputation link was introduced and show that it is normatively hollow. This history suggests that it was incorporated into the draft text of TRIPS as an acceptable compromise, not only between New World opponents and Old World proponents at the General Agreement on Tariffs and Trade (GATT) negotiations leading up to TRIPS, but also as a viable solution for members of the European Community (EC), who were divided over which types of GIs ought to be recognised within Europe. Indeed, reputation was rather hastily incorporated within a framework otherwise premised upon *terroir*. Therefore, if we are to make meaningful sense of a reputation, which is essentially attributable to origin, then this type of link should be informed by the overall purpose and objectives of *sui generis* GI protection. The potential components of the reputation link are unpacked in Section 4, which will also relate these criteria back to the foundations for GI protection. Section 5 concludes.

---

[12] Delphine Marie-Vivien, *The Protection of Geographical Indications for Handicrafts: How to Apply the Concepts of Natural and Human Factors to All Products*, 4 WIPO J. 191 (2013); Delphine Marie-Vivien, *A Comparative Analysis of GIs for Handicrafts: The Link to Origin in Culture as Well as Nature?* in Research Handbook on Intellectual Property and Geographical Indications 292 (Dev Gangjee ed., 2016).

2 WHY WE NEED TO TALK ABOUT REPUTATION

There are at least five compelling reasons why we should think more carefully about reputation as the basis for the link between product and place. First, the GI definition in Article 22.1 of TRIPS is by now well established as the international reference point. This is evident in national or multilateral definitions that map on to Article 22.1.[13] Reputation is therefore an independent and sufficient basis for satisfying the definition of a GI. However, it is a form of linkage that will inevitably be subjected to testing. The ongoing TRIPS negotiations regarding the establishment of a multilateral register for wine and spirit GIs have witnessed deliberations on whether registration notifications should include 'details of the quality, reputation or other characteristics of the wine or spirit essentially attributable to its geographical origin'.[14] The requirement for such details at the time of international registration is also reflected in the 'work-in-progress' composite text of the multilateral register.[15] A notification could include a declaration of conformity with the definition of a GI in Article 22.1 of TRIPS. Not satisfying Article 22.1 could potentially be a basis for refusing protection within the territory of a participating member.[16] Yet, the reputation link in Article 22.1 remains poorly understood.

Second, the TRIPS definition of GIs has recently been accommodated within Article 2(1)(ii) of the Geneva Act of the Lisbon Agreement 2015.[17] The Lisbon system has established an international registration system for qualifying geographical designations, which are recognised at the national level. Scrutinising international registrations for compliance with the

---

[13] A review by the WTO of the existing legislation in 2003 confirmed that the notion of GI, as defined by TRIPS, formed the basis for several national definitions. See WTO, Review under Article 24.2 of the Application of the Provisions of the Section of the TRIPS Agreement on Geographical Indications, at 42, WTO Doc. IP/C/W/253/Rev.1 (24 November 2003) ('many but not all of the definitions include reputation as a specific characteristic related to the geographical origin of a product that might justify protection of the [Indication of Geographical Origin] designating that product').

[14] World Trade Organization (WTO), Chairman's Report, TRIPS Council Special Session: Multilateral System of Notification and Registration of Geographical Indications for Wines and Spirits, WTO Doc. TN/IP/18, at 15 (9 June 2008).

[15] See WTO, Chairman's Report, Multilateral System of Notification and Registration of Geographical Indications for Wines and Spirits: Report to the Trade Negotiations Committee, WTO Doc. TN/IP/21, at B.2 (21 April 2011).

[16] Id. at E.2.

[17] WIPO, Geneva Act of the Lisbon Agreement on Appellations of Origin and Geographical Indications and Regulations under the Geneva Act of the Lisbon Agreement on Appellations of Origin and Geographical Indications, WIPO Doc. LI/DC/19 (20 May 2015) [hereafter Geneva Act].

definition of a GI is once again a concern here, but a more immediate one. Where the 'reputation ... of the good is essentially attributable to its geographical origin', it will now qualify for international registration. The Geneva Act provides for both the initial refusal of the effects of international registration by a Contracting Party (Article 15) and the possibility of subsequent invalidation (Article 19). Both refusal and invalidation proceedings require the grounds to be stated.[18] During the deliberations leading up to the adoption of the Geneva Act, 'grounds based on failure to meet the definition of an appellation of origin or a geographical indication' were specifically envisioned as a reason for invalidation.[19] Similarly, a refusal to recognise a GI can be based on any ground, including failure to satisfy the definitional provisions.[20] Thus, a more developed sense of when a reputation is 'essentially attributable' to the product's geographical origin is a necessary prelude to any such challenges.

If the first two reasons relate to multilateral obligations and international norms, the next three draw upon developments within the EU context, but the insights are more broadly applicable. The third reason is conveyed most conveniently by statistics. As of 29 February 2016, the Database of Origin and Registration (DOOR) indicated that PGI registrations were maintaining their lead over PDO registrations in the EU[21] – there were 671 registered PGIs and 604 registered PDOs.[22] One principal difference between the two types of GI is that for a PGI to be registered a product's 'given quality, reputation or other characteristic is essentially attributable to its geographical origin', whereas for a PDO, the product's 'quality or characteristics are essentially or exclusively due to a particular geographical environment with its inherent natural and human factors'.[23] It is evident that the reputational basis for registration, with its attendant flexibility, is proving to be popular.

---

[18] See respectively Geneva Act, *supra* note 17, at art. 15(1)(b); Regulations under the Geneva Act, *supra* note 17, at 9(2)(iii), 10(1)(ii); Regulations under the Geneva Act, *supra* note 17, at 13(1)(v).

[19] WIPO, *Notes on the Basic Proposal for the New Act of the Lisbon Agreement on Appellations of Origin and Geographical Indications*, at 19.01, WIPO Doc. LI/DC/5 (22 December 2014).

[20] *Id.* at 15.03.

[21] The definition and difference between protected denominations of origin (PDOs) and protected geographical indications (PGIs) are elaborated upon in Part III.

[22] See European Commission, *Agriculture and Rural Development*, http://ec.europa.eu/agriculture/quality/door/list.html (last visited 21 April 2016).

[23] See Council Regulation 1151/2012, art. 5, 2012 O.J. (L323/1).

Fourth, recent pronouncements from the Court of Justice of the European Union (CJEU)[24] have confirmed that the EU's harmonised regime for GI protection, set out in Regulation 1151/2012 and its predecessors, is exhaustive and pre-empts national GI registration systems *to the extent that they regulate the same subject matter.*[25] Therefore, where a regional product's reputation is causally attributable to its geographical origin, it can no longer be protected by national protection systems, such as passing off or unfair competition law, which have historically protected GIs.[26] As a recent dispute concerning *Greek Yoghurt* highlights, such a geographical designation has to be registered at the EU level, failing which it is apparently left vulnerable, without any legal protection at the national level.[27] The objective is to channel all suitably qualified subject matter into the unitary EU regime in order to achieve complete harmonisation. However, the CJEU case law suggests that simple geographical designations can continue to be protected at the national level, for instance, under unfair competition law. The court has recently summarised the position as follows:

> [It] is apparent from the case-law that whilst the aim of Regulation No 2081/92 [which previously regulated GIs for agricultural products and foodstuffs] is to provide a uniform and exhaustive system of protection ... that exclusivity does not preclude, however, the application of rules governing the protection of geographical designations which fall outside its scope ... It is apparent [both from the preamble to the Regulation and the PGI definition] that the rules on protection laid down by that provision cover only designations relating to products for which there is a specific link between their characteristics and their geographical origin.[28]

---

[24] Formerly the European Court of Justice (ECJ).
[25] This was emphatically confirmed by the CJEU Grand Chamber. *See* Case C-478/07 Budějovický Budvar National Corporation v. Rudolf Ammersin GmbH (C-478/07) [2009] E.C.R. I-7721; 2009 E.T.M.R. 65, at 106–29 (*Budweiser II*).
[26] WIPO, *Document SCT/6/3 Rev. on Geographical Indications: Historical Background, Nature of Rights, Existing Systems for Protection and Obtaining Protection in Other Countries,* at 16, WIPO Doc. SCT/8/4 (2 April 2002).
[27] This was argued before the UK Court of Appeals. *See* Fage UK Ltd. v. Chobani UK Ltd. [2014] EWCA (Civ) 5. The issue was whether 'Greek Yoghurt' could potentially be registered as a GI at the EU level as a PGI. If it could, in principle, then there would be no other form of protection available at the national level. The tort of passing off had already been established at trial and the appellant, Chobani, attempted to escape its consequences by arguing, ultimately unsuccessfully, that Greek Yoghurt had a PGI-type reputation and would qualify in principle under the harmonized EU regime, so passing off protection was pre-empted at the national level. The author must declare that he acted as a consultant for the respondent, Fage, in this matter.
[28] Case C-35/13, Kraft Foods Italia v. Associazione fra produttori per la tutela del 'Salame Felino' and Others, 2014 [Unreported] at 28–29.

Consequently, it seems that the CJEU endorses a distinction between a PGI-type reputation that is objectively or causally attributable to origin and a non-PGI type reputation, where a product may be subjectively or 'romantically' connected to its region of origin in the eyes of consumers but for which there is no objective basis. The latter may still be protected under national unfair competition law, provided it does not unjustifiably impede the free movement of goods within the internal market. In the United Kingdom (UK), this distinction was at issue in *Greek Yoghurt*, where subjective reputation was described in the following manner:

> It is impossible to do much more than speculate as to why that substantial proportion of the relevant public think that [thick and creamy] Greek yoghurt is special. Some may ... make a romantic association between Greek yoghurt and a Greek holiday. Some may think that Greeks use manufacturing methods that give it its special thick and creamy texture. Few would probably know how or why.[29]

Ultimately, what mattered for the requirements of the tort of passing off was that a subjectively held and commercially valuable reputation contingent upon Greek origin existed which could be protected against misrepresentation. We therefore need clearly identified and workable criteria in order to distinguish between these two types of reputation associated with geographical origin, because only subjective reputation will continue to be protected at the national level within the EU.

The fifth reason for seeking greater clarity is that the European Commission is proposing to extend the EU's GI regime to non-agricultural products and handicrafts. Its interest was signalled in a Green Paper in 2014,[30] which drew upon a prior study exploring the potential to register crafts and textile products from across the EU.[31] The Commission's proposal recognises that non-agricultural products may also possess a link to a region, which can either be a *terroir* or reputation-based link:

> This link to a geographical location can also apply to non-agricultural products. In some cases, such as marble and stone, the strength of the link

---

[29] Fage UK Ltd. v. Chobani UK Ltd. [2013] EWHC (Ch) 630 [115]. The issue of whether passing off was pre-empted was only raised on appeal, see [2014] EWCA Civ 5.

[30] *Commission Green Paper Making the Most Out of Europe's Traditional Know-How: A Possible Extension of Geographical Indication Protection of the European Union to Non-Agricultural Products*, COM (2014) 469 final (15 July 2014) [hereinafter *Green Paper*].

[31] *See* INSIGHT CONSULTING ET AL., STUDY ON GEOGRAPHICAL INDICATION PROTECTION FOR NON-AGRICULTURAL PRODUCTS IN THE INTERNAL MARKET FINAL REPORT (2013), http://ec.europa.eu/internal_market/indprop/docs/geo-indications/130322_geo-indications-non-agri-study_en.pdf.

is comparable to that for agricultural products ... In principle, the stronger the link, the more credible and authentic a product will be in the eyes of the consumer. However, certain GIs may be based entirely on human rather than natural inputs, or on reputation.[32]

Reputation attributable to geographical origin could be used as a criterion in addition to, or as an alternative to, a particular quality or inherent characteristic of the product. This would allow GI protection to be extended only to products that have already developed a recognised reputation among consumers.[33]

If reputation is to be put to work in this context, then we need to better understand how it can be anchored in or 'essentially attributable' to the place of origin.

3 REPUTATION: A COMPROMISE OR COMPROMISED?

Historical research confirms that we are unlikely to find the answers we seek within the text or *travaux* of TRIPS. This section documents (a) how reputation was included within the TRIPS definition as a compromise; and (b) how it was an incompletely conceived compromise, because reputation was hastily amalgamated within a paradigm otherwise dominated by a *terroir*-based approach to GI protection. This compromise unfolded in two broad stages. To fully account for the presence of the reputation link in TRIPS, we have to first acknowledge a prior reconciliation within Europe as part of the historical backdrop to the EU's own harmonised GI regime for agricultural products and foodstuffs.

3.1 Two Paradigms of Geographical Indication Protection

Wine is the archetypal GI product. Since the latter part of the nineteenth century, successive legislative experiments directed at regulating wine appellations in France showcase the extent to which *terroir*-thinking gradually characterised the nature of the link between product and place.[34] The transition from the *appellation d'origine* (AO) to the *appellation d'origine contrôlée* (AOC) reveals that a naturally deterministic understanding of *terroir*, which was reliant on physical geography factors such as soil, sunlight,

---

[32] Green Paper, supra note 30, at 16–17.   [33] Id. at 18.
[34] This transition is comprehensively documented in Chapter 3 of GANGJEE, RELOCATING GIs, supra note 4; See also Alessandro Stanziani, French Collective Wine Branding in the Nineteenth–Twentieth Centuries, in RESEARCH HANDBOOK ON INTELLECTUAL PROPERTY AND GEOGRAPHICAL INDICATIONS 13 (Dev Gangjee ed., 2016).

orientation and elevation, gave way to a more holistic understanding which also included production techniques and human influences.[35] The *terroir* approach was adopted by Southern European countries with a wine-growing tradition, including Italy, Spain and Portugal. Within this paradigm, *reputation was an additional factor* to be considered cumulatively, after an objectively verifiable causal connection was established between a product's qualities and its region of origin.

The paradigm is perhaps best exemplified by Article 2 of the Lisbon Agreement of 1958.[36] Article 2(1) requires that the 'quality or characteristics of [the product] are due exclusively or essentially to the geographical environment', while Article 2(2) additionally stipulates that when identifying the country of origin we have to look for the country containing the place 'which has given the product its reputation'. This is made explicit in Lisbon's Geneva Act of 2015, where Article 2(1)(i) defines an appellation of origin as 'any denomination ... consisting of or containing the name of a geographical area, or another denomination known as referring to such area, which serves to designate a good as originating in that geographical area, where the quality or characteristics of the good are due exclusively or essentially to the geographical environment, including natural and human factors, *and which has given the good its reputation*' (emphasis added).

By contrast, in other European jurisdictions, GIs were protected under unfair competition law.[37] Historically, unfair competition has been used in different senses. It is variously an umbrella term for a cluster of tortious actions (or their equivalents in *delict*), an individual tort by itself or the basis for a specific statutory regime. What unites the different approaches is their emphasis on misconduct. All of these iterations seek to regulate the activities of traders in the marketplace and enable courts to cry foul when business practices overstep their limits. For example, while it may be permissible for a trader to claim her goods are better than those of a rival, or even to claim that those of her rival are objectively inferior, it will not be permissible to lie to customers about the source or quality of her goods, or unjustifiably

---

[35] For the origins and competing accounts of *terroir*, see Laurence Bérard, Terroir *and the Sense of Place*, in RESEARCH HANDBOOK ON INTELLECTUAL PROPERTY AND GEOGRAPHICAL INDICATIONS 72 (Dev Gangjee ed., 2016).

[36] Lisbon Agreement for the Protection of Appellations of Origin and their International Registration, 31 October 1958, *as revised* 14 July 1967, 923 U.N.T.S. 205. For a comparison between TRIPS and Lisbon definitions, including the approach to reputation, *see* Daniel Gervais, *The Lisbon Agreement's Misunderstood Potential*, 1 WIPO J. 87 (2009).

[37] *See* HERMAN COHEN JEHORAM, PROTECTION OF GEOGRAPHIC DENOMINATIONS OF GOODS AND SERVICES (1980); WIPO, *supra* note 26, at 11–17.

disparage the products of her rival.[38] Consequently, WIPO identifies 'at least one objective that is common to all different approaches, and that is to provide those in trade with an effective remedy against unlawful and dishonest business practices of their competitors'.[39] Germany and the UK are two prominent jurisdictions that favoured such an approach to GI protection.[40]

As opposed to the information being specified *ex ante*, in a *cahier des charges* or product specification required by registration-based systems under the *terroir* paradigm, the unfair competition approach adopted a different methodology for identifying a regional product, determining its region of production and legally recognizing those entitled to use the geographical name on their products. These answers would only crystallise within the context of an individual dispute, on a case-by-case basis. Furthermore, recognition and protection were dependent upon the communicative content of the sign. The designation would inevitably be protected against deceptive uses or misrepresentations and, depending on the national regime in question, potentially against misappropriating or free-riding uses as well. Protection in turn was contingent upon consumer perception. From the consumers' perspective (and that of the trade), did a geographical designation used on certain products have a reputation in the market? Would the relevant public expect the product to come from a specific region? Would they expect it to be made in accordance with certain techniques and processes (for example, a minimum ageing requirement for whisky) even if they were unclear on the precise details? If so, consumer expectations would be protected together with the reputation of the product.

It is crucial to point out that within the unfair competition paradigm the paramount consideration is whether a valuable reputation exists in the marketplace for a regional product. Its existence could be established through direct and indirect evidence such as sales figures, mentions in the media or consumer surveys. That reputation *did not have to be essentially or causally attributable to geographical origin* in the manner that the *terroir* approach requires.[41] Reputed geographical designations were treated in the same way as

[38] WIPO INTERNATIONAL BUREAU, PROTECTION AGAINST UNFAIR COMPETITION: ANALYSIS OF THE PRESENT WORLD SITUATION 48, 54–60 (1994).
[39] WIPO, *supra* note 26, at 12.
[40] *See* GANGJEE, RELOCATING GIs, *supra* note 4, at 115–124; Dev Gangjee, *Spanish Champagne: An Unfair Competition Approach to GI Protection*, in INTELLECTUAL PROPERTY AT THE EDGE 105 (Rochelle Cooper Dreyfuss & Jane C. Ginsburg eds., 2014).
[41] *See* Friedrich-Karl Beier & Roland Knaak, *The Protection of Direct and Indirect Geographical Indications of Source in Germany and the European Community*, 25 INT'L REV. INTELL. PROP. & COMPETITION L. 1, 2 (1994).

trade names or unregistered (trade) marks, which also had reputations worth protecting. Given this detachment from any *terroir*, i.e. causal connection requirement, an unfair competition approach to GIs can range beyond agricultural products to accommodate reputed manufactured as well as artisanal products, such as Solingen steel, Brussels lace and Swiss clocks. It can also scale up to protect national-level reputations for products such as Jamaican rum, which would otherwise be impermissible under a *terroir* approach where homogenous geographical features need to be identifiable within a region.

3.2 Accommodating Reputation within a Terroir Paradigm: The EU Compromise

The extent to which the *terroir* and unfair competition approaches to GI protection were equally legitimate was directly tested before the CJEU in the decades preceding the adoption of a harmonised EU-wide system of protection. Throughout the 1970s and 1980s, only the former was recognised as a legitimate category. During this period, the case law was characterised by suspicion towards national labelling regimes that protected simple or quality-neutral GIs of source, which could potentially have operated as disguised restrictions on the free movement of goods within the common market.[42] The French AO concept, with its purportedly objective link between origin and quality, provided an acceptable basis for prohibiting the use of appellations by those outside the designated regions. It would take several years before the Court acknowledged the protection of a valuable reputation, alongside the prevention of unfair competition, as an alternative basis for restricting the use of geographical designations. Two prominent decisions of the CJEU bracket this transition.

In the *Sekt/Weinbrand* decision,[43] the validity of German legislation, which restricted the use of certain wine designations, was challenged. It reserved the designations 'Sekt' and 'Weinbrand' to domestic products and the appellation 'Praedikatssekt' to wines produced in Germany from a fixed minimum proportion of German grapes. The German law further prescribed that imported sparkling wine and wine brandy not in compliance with these conditions had

---

[42] Geographical designations indicating national territories, but without any objectively verifiable link associated with the territory, could be disguised campaigns to appeal to patriotic buying. For a convenient summary of the free movements backdrop, *see* VADIM MANTROV, EU LAW ON INDICATIONS OF GEOGRAPHICAL ORIGIN: THEORY AND PRACTICE 113–118 (2014).

[43] Case C-12/74, Commission v. Germany, 1975 E.C.R 181.

to use different terminology ('Schaumwein' and 'Branntwein aus Wein').[44] The European Commission queried the German legislation's compatibility with the former Article 28 (now Article 34 of the Treaty on the Functioning of the European Union (TFEU)) on the basis that by claiming generic terms as indirect geographical designations, it favoured domestic production and operated as a measure equivalent to a quantitative restriction on imports. Germany responded that while it might be a restriction, it was justified on the basis of protecting consumers and legitimate producers against unfair competition. Therefore, it was a permissible exception to Article 28 contained in Article 30 (now Article 36 TFEU). In dismissing the German argument, the CJEU made the following observation:

> These [wine] appellations only fulfil their specific purpose [i.e. to safeguard producers against unfair competition and prevent consumers being misled] if the product which they describe does in fact possess qualities and characteristics which are due to the fact that it originated in a specific geographical area.
>
> As regards indications of origin in particular, *the geographical area of origin* of a product *must confer on it a specific quality and specific characteristics* of such a nature as to *distinguish it from all other products* (emphasis added).[45]

Since this qualitative link was not invoked, restrictions on these terms were found to be unjustified. It should be noted that the outcome of the decision was not considered objectionable. Such expressions were arguably generic at the time, so in trying to artificially impose a specific geographical limitation, the contested legislation was vulnerable on this ground alone. However, the reasoning that was applied proved divisive.

The controversy stemmed from the implication that reputation-based geographical designations did not fall within the limited exceptions to the free movement of goods principle. As the AO appeared to be the only legitimate category of GI worthy of being exempted from a free movements challenge, the decision provoked forceful critiques.[46] A measure of their potency is the

---

[44] As required by WEINGESETZ 1971 [LAW ON VINE PRODUCTS] Bundesgesetzblatt I [BGBL] No. 63/1971 and WEINGESETZ 1971 [SPARKLING WINES AND SPIRITS OBTAINED BY DISTILLING WINE] Bundesgesetzblatt I [BGBL] No. 64/1971.

[45] Case C-12/74, Commission v. Germany, 1975 E.C.R. 181, at 7.

[46] *See, e.g.*, Derrick Wyatt, *Free Movement of Goods and Indications of Origin*, 38 MOD. L. REV. 679 (1975); Friedrich-Karl Beier, *The Need for Protection of Indications of Source and Appellations of Origin in the Common Market: The Sekt/Weinbrand Decision of the ECJ*, 16 INDUS. PROP. 152 (1977).

outcome in the CJEU's subsequent *Exportur* decision.[47] Here, the issue was whether the Spanish geographical designations 'Touron Alicante' and 'Touron Jijona' could be used on nougat confectionery produced in France. These were protected designations under a Franco-Spanish Treaty,[48] notwithstanding the absence of an objective or *terroir*-based link. The Court held that despite this, such designations 'may nevertheless enjoy a high reputation amongst consumers and constitute for producers established in the places to which they refer an essential means of attracting custom. They are therefore entitled to protection.'[49] Celebrating this vindication of the reputational basis for GI protection, Professor Beier argued that any harmonised EU regime which represented the AO ideal alone would have been a 'monstrosity'.[50]

With this eventual judicial recognition of both the *terroir* and reputation approaches, there is ample evidence that the EU's harmonised regime for agricultural products and foodstuffs, introduced by Regulation 2081/92,[51] institutionalised this compromise. It fused these two distinct approaches together within a common framework premised upon registration-based legal recognition. The Regulation begins with the concession that 'existing practices make it appropriate to define two different types of geographical description, namely protected geographical indications and protected designations of origin'.[52] The solution was therefore to create two 'doorways' into the GI registration system in Article 2. PDOs could be applied to products of which 'the *quality or characteristics* ... are *essentially or exclusively due* to a particular geographical environment with its inherent natural and human factors' (emphasis added). In contrast, PGIs envisioned a looser form of link and were available for products 'which [possess] a specific *quality, reputation or other characteristics attributable to* that geographical origin and the *production and/or processing and/or preparation* of which take place in the defined geographical area' (emphasis added). However, both

---

[47] Case C-3/91, Exportur SA v. LOR SA and Confiserie du Tech SA, 1992 E.C.R. I-5529.

[48] *See* Convention between the French Republic and the Spanish State on the Protection of Designations of Origin, Indications of Provenance, and Names of Certain Products, 27 June 1973, Journal Officiel de la République Française [J.O.], 18 April 1973, p. 4011.

[49] Case C-3/91, Exportur SA v. LOR SA and Confiserie du Tech SA, 1992 E.C.R. I-5529, at 28.

[50] Friedrich-Karl Beier, *Case Comment: Court of Justice – Case No. C-3/91 'Turron'*, 25 Int'l Rev. Intell. Prop. & Competition L. 73, 81 (1994).

[51] Council Regulation 2081/92 of 14 July 1992, Protection of Geographical Indications and Designations of Origin for Agricultural Products and Foodstuffs, 1992 O.J. (L 208/1).

[52] *Id.* at 10.

types of GIs would be granted equal protection. This 'two doorways' compromise has been maintained in the successors to Regulation 2081/92, namely Regulation 510/2006 and Regulation 1151/2012.[53]

The existence of two different types of GIs attests to the underlying fissures and factionalism in the lead up to the original Regulation. Writing at the time of its enactment, one commentator noted that on '14 July 1992, contrary to common belief and indeed much to general amazement, the EC Regulations on the "protection of designations of geographical origin" ... were passed by the European Council despite the number of disputed issues which remained unresolved until the last moment'.[54] The initial French memorandum submitted in 1988 was restricted to designations of origin, along the lines of the AO, which was subsequently supported by Italy and Spain.[55] However, the draft text of the Commission's proposed Regulation contained references to both PGIs and PDOs.[56] The influence of the AO model remains visible in the Opinion of the Economic and Social Committee, which reveals glimpses of *terroir*-thinking at crucial junctures. Thus, while acknowledging the importance of protecting a product's reputation, the Committee noted that the 'special characteristics of the food involved derive from their origin, soil conditions, geographical and climatic environment, the varieties and species used, and the way they are prepared or produced. It is these factors which give the product its name and reputation in the marketplace.'[57]

During this phase, the drafting process involved negotiations between two competing Northern and Southern groups. Marina Kolia observed that when the proposals reached the European Parliament in September of 1991, GI

---

[53] See respectively Council Regulation No 510/2006 of 20 March 2006, Protection of Geographical Indications and Designations of Origin for Agricultural Products and Foodstuffs, 2006 O.J. (L 93/12) art. 2; Council Regulation No 1151/2012 of 21 November 2012, Quality Schemes for Agricultural Products and Foodstuffs, 2012 O.J. (L 343/1).

[54] Marina Kolia, *Monopolizing Names of Foodstuffs: The New Legislation*, 4 EUR. INTELL. PROP. REV. 333, 333 (1992).

[55] Francois Vital, *Protection of Geographical Indications: The Approach of the European Union*, in SYMPOSIUM ON THE INTERNATIONAL PROTECTION OF GEOGRAPHICAL INDICATIONS (1999). For an excellent general background, see Onno Brouwer, *Community Protection of Geographical Indications and Specific Character as a Means of Enhancing Foodstuff Quality*, 28 COMMON MKT. L. REV. 615 (1991).

[56] See Council Proposal on the Protection of Geographical Indications and Designations of Origin for Agricultural Products and Foodstuffs, at 90 SEC (1991) 2415 final (21 January 1991), and as amended by COM (1992) 32 final (18 March 1992).

[57] See Opinion of the Socio Economic Committee on the 'Proposal for a Council Regulation (EEC) on the Protection of Geographical Indications and Designations of Origin for Agricultural Products and Foodstuffs', 1991 O.J. (C 269/62) 1.2.

protection was again restricted to PDOs and 'the applicants were required to produce convincing evidence that the product's characteristics were essentially due to the geographical origin'.[58] The European Parliament did not accept the proposal in this form and the draft Regulation returned to the Commission, where it was further debated. At this stage, Germany began 'to promote the idea of a very broad category under which all geographical names would be mutually recognised'.[59] When faced with the option of a single broad definition, which would have diluted the cachet of the AO concept, negotiators revived the PGI as an alternative option. Eventually, an acceptable compromise was arrived at in the form of two distinct pathways into registration and the crisis was averted.

3.3 The EU Compromise as the Multilateral Template

There is a convincing documentary trail which reveals that the internal compromise between the German (unfair competition prevention by emphasising reputation) and French (*terroir* logic premised on a qualitative link) approaches went on to inform the EC's position in multilateral negotiations. The EC's recognition of a reputation-based link was visible in its proposal during – the ultimately unsuccessful – WIPO negotiations for the revision of the Paris Convention[60] in 1990. The issue under discussion was whether there was an alternative to the existing categories of a simple, quality-neutral indication of source (IS) (e.g., Made in China) and the more demanding AO (e.g., Bordeaux).

> [The EC Representative suggested that] in order for a geographical indication to be 'protectable', some kind of link must exist between the geographical area to which the indication refers and the goods which originate from that area. [The EC further suggested that] protectable geographical indications should be those which 'designate a product as originating from a country, region, or locality where a given quality, reputation or other characteristic of the product is attributable to its geographical origin, including natural and human factors'. It was explained that this 'quality link' was broader than the

---

[58] Marina Kolia, *Monopolising Names: EEC Proposals on the Protection of Trade Descriptions of Foodstuffs*, 14 EUR. INTELL. PROP. REV. 233, 235 (1992).

[59] *Id.* at 235–36.

[60] Paris Convention for the Protection of Industrial Property, *opened for signature* 20 March 1883, 21 U.S.T. 1583, 828 UNTS 305 (revised at Brussels on 14 December 1900, at Washington on 2 June 1911, at The Hague on 6 November 1925, at London on 2 June 1934, at Lisbon on 31 October 1958, and at Stockholm on 14 July 1967, and as amended on 28 September 1979).

restrictive definition of 'appellation of origin' under the Lisbon Agreement ... [According to the EC proposal] the link need not consist of a given quality but may consist of a given 'reputation or other characteristic' and such characteristic need not be 'exclusively or essentially' attributable to its geographical origin.[61]

Two important ingredients of the TRIPS definition – the stand-alone reputation option to establish the link and the relative loosening of this link – were introduced at this stage.[62] The EC was also very clearly drafting its own harmonised GI regime in accordance with its position during the Uruguay Round negotiations. The Commission's draft for Regulation 2081 specifically notes:

[The draft Regulation] also broadly reflects the position which the Community has defended in the international negotiations on intellectual property in GATT.
  In the Uruguay Round negotiating group on intellectual property, the Community proposed a definition of, and appropriate protection for, geographical indications, including designations of origin, which the Commission has taken into account.[63]

During the Uruguay Round negotiations, it is widely acknowledged that the EC was the driving force behind the TRIPS GI provisions.[64] As for the drafting of Article 22.1, a helpful resource was the Secretariat's synoptic table of proposals accumulated by early 1990.[65] The EC's proposed definition closely resembled the final TRIPS version with its reputation link option, save for the addition of 'geographical origin, including natural and human factors'. The core of this definition remained stable until the final TRIPS text was adopted, presumably because it was acceptable to those countries which protected GIs either under unfair competition or trademark law.[66]

---

[61] WIPO Secretariat, *Report Adopted by the Committee of Experts*, WIPO Doc. GEO/CE/I/3, at 49 (1 June 1990).
[62] For the drafting history of the TRIPS GI provisions, *see* GANGJEE, RELOCATING GIs, *supra* note 4, at 191–236.
[63] Proposal for a Council Regulation, *supra* note 56, at 9–10.
[64] Most recently acknowledged by the negotiators themselves; *see* JAYASHREE WATAL & ANTONY TAUBMAN, THE MAKING OF THE TRIPS AGREEMENT: PERSONAL INSIGHTS FROM THE URUGUAY ROUND NEGOTIATIONS 28, 98, 116, 147, 178, 194, 197 (2015).
[65] *See* Group of Negotiations of Goods (GATT), *Synoptic Tables Setting Out Existing International Standards and Proposed Standards and Principles*, GATT Doc. MTN.GNG/NG11/W/32/Rev.2, at 68–69 (2 February 1990) (The only other proposed definition is a much broader Swiss one, similar to the simple indication of source).
[66] The differences between the trademark approach and the appellation approach have been explored in Daniel Gervais, *A Cognac after Spanish Champagne? Geographical Indications as*

Countries that were opposed to *sui generis* GI protection, including the US and Australia, found the relatively broad definition with its acknowledgement of reputation acceptable. This definition established common ground by including certification and collective marks within the GI definition. After all, these were established categories of marks and potential vectors for the protection of a collectively sustained reputation.

Therefore, while the TRIPS definition was ultimately acceptable as a bridge to span the – primarily trans-Atlantic – divide over GIs, the origins of this European proposal can be traced to an internecine dispute between European neighbours. However, the compromise superficially glosses over a fundamental distinction: the unfair competition or trademark approach was amenable to protecting a regional product's reputation *without any necessity for a causal link requirement*. The very existence and commercial value of the reputation was a sufficient basis for protection. This proves to be an awkward fit within a GI definition, which originated in a *terroir* paradigm and saw reputation, as an additional factor, dependent upon the existence of a causal connection between a product's desirable qualities or characteristics and its geographical origin.

Once this history is retrieved, there are clear traces that the two paradigms of *terroir* and unfair competition have been inelegantly fused together within TRIPS. Clashing styles of conceptual architecture remain obvious. For a start, there is the central puzzle of having to prove that a product's commercially valuable reputation is also essentially attributable to geographical origin in a causally verifiable manner. Section 4 considers how we might best make sense of this. Furthermore, how are we to define the boundaries of the region of origin for a product which has a reputation-based link? A study by WIPO observed that the standard criterion for delimiting a region of origin includes natural features (rivers, contour lines); geographical characteristics (soil drainage, climate, elevation); human influences (choice of plant variety, method of production); historical associations; and economic considerations (equivalence of yield).[67] Several of these criteria are more relevant for a *terroir* link and will be inapplicable for reputation-based products.

Moreover, TRIPS suggests that the name of an entire country could qualify as a GI. While this is acceptable under a reputation-based approach, it is unlikely under a *terroir* one, which requires a geographical region to be both

---

Certification Marks, in INTELLECTUAL PROPERTY AT THE EDGE 105 (Rochelle Cooper Dreyfuss & Jane C. Ginsburg eds., 2014).
[67] WIPO Secretariat, *The Definition of Geographical Indications*, WIPO Doc. SCT/9/4 at 20 (1 October 2002).

relatively homogenous and distinctive in order to influence the product.[68] Finally, while TRIPS applies to goods, it does not prohibit GIs being recognised for services. Switzerland, Estonia, Uruguay, Peru, Korea and Morocco are some countries that recognise GIs for services in the hospitality, banking, financial, or health and traditional healing sectors.[69] While a well-regarded local service may give rise to a valuable reputation – perhaps solely based on human factors with their attendant mobility – and qualify for protection under the unfair competition paradigm, how is this essentially attributable to geographical origin? These are just some of the unresolved questions that have arisen from the fusion of two previously distinct paradigms.

4 FROM GEOGRAPHY TO HISTORY: AN 'ESSENTIALLY ATTRIBUTABLE' REPUTATION

Now for the difficult question: what kind of reputation ought to be 'essentially attributable' to geographical origin? Without clear guidance, there is a very real risk that the established unfair competition or trademark approach to measuring reputation will be inappropriately transplanted into the *sui generis* GI context. For these regimes, establishing a sign's reputation is relevant primarily in two situations:

(a) Does the trademark applicant's or unfair competition claimant's sign qualify for protection? Here, a sign may initially be a descriptive or otherwise unsuitable term (e.g., STAPLES for office supplies),[70] but over time and through marketing efforts, the relevant public can be taught that the sign indicates a specific commercial source. The success of this process of education is measured via the doctrines of acquired distinctiveness or secondary meaning.[71]

(b) What is the scope of protection available? Reputed or famous trademarks are granted a broader penumbra of protection both under the likelihood of confusion test (which prevents use of the trademark on dissimilar goods or services, or even in the absence of registration) and via causes of action

---

[68] GANGJEE, RELOCATING GIs, *supra* note 4, at 218–20.
[69] Irina Kireeva & Bernard O'Connor, *Geographical Indications and the TRIPS Agreement: What Protection Is Provided to Geographical Indications in WTO Members?* 13 J. WORLD INTELL. PROP. 275, 282 (2010).
[70] *See* STAPLES, http://www.staples.co.uk (last visited 22 April 2016).
[71] For US recognition, *see* 15 U.S.C. § 1052(f); for EU recognition, *see* Council Directive 2008/95/EC, art. 3(3) 2008 O.J. (L299/25) (A trademark which is non-distinctive to begin with can be registered 'if, before the date of application for registration and following the use which has been made of it, it has acquired a distinctive character').

collectively referred to as 'dilution' which all rely on a non-confusing but otherwise wrongful association being made between the claimant and defendant's signs.[72]

These approaches seek to determine (a) what percentage of the relevant public are familiar with the sign; and (b) for certain types of claims such as tarnishment, what do the public think about the sign to begin with? Therefore, reputation has a quantitative as well as a qualitative dimension, but it is concerned with contemporary consumer perception. This is reflected in the direct, as well as circumstantial, categories of evidence that are admissible to establish its existence. Therefore, in both the EU and the US, courts will consider factors such as the market share of the product sold under the sign; the intensity, geographical extent and duration of use; the investment in advertising and promotion; the extent of consumer recognition via survey evidence; trade recognition; and unprompted media coverage.[73] However, the trademark and unfair competition approaches focus on *whether the reputation exists* at the relevant time and *not how it came about*, let alone why it *arose in a particular place*.

So when is a reputation 'essentially attributable' to its geographical origin? The answer to this is a work in progress, but presently cumulative evidence relating to three aspects is required:[74]

(a) contemporary reputation;
(b) historic reputation; and
(c) the history of the product, including the specific production techniques which gave rise to the distinctive product within that region.

The three aspects are interrelated and overlap with each other. Therefore, contemporary reputation can be gauged by resorting to familiar categories of evidence (consumer surveys, sales figures, trade opinion, etc.) that are similar to the trademark or unfair competition approach. However, there is an important difference. The purpose here seems to be to measure continuity, or

---

[72] *See generally* FREDERICK W. MOSTERT, FAMOUS AND WELL-KNOWN MARKS: AN INTERNATIONAL ANALYSIS (2nd edn., 2004).
[73] The US factors, which vary across circuits, are conveniently summarized in BARTON BEEBE, TRADEMARK LAW: AN OPEN-SOURCE CASEBOOK Part I, 41–54 (2nd edn., 2015). For the EU, *see* Cases C-108/97 & 109/97, Windsurfing Chiemsee v. Boots, 1999 E.C.R. I-2779, at 49–51 (acquired distinctiveness); Case C-375/97, General Motors v. Yplon, 1999 E.C.R. I-5421, at 27 (establishing reputation for dilution protection).
[74] INAO Guide, *supra* note 7; European Commission, *supra* note 11, at 6–7; World Intellectual Property Organization (WIPO), Geographical Indications, WIPO Doc. SCT/10/4, at 23–26 (25 March 2003).

ongoing vitality, as opposed to the extent of the product's fame or renown. Thus, it should be proved that the designation continues to function as a GI for consumers in at least the country of origin. In turn, continuity suggests that the present reputation rests on the product's historic reputation. One of the central tasks here is to identify the characteristic features which set this product apart – characteristics which have made it distinctive when compared with similar cheeses or textiles or crafts. These characteristic features have sustained the product's historic reputation over time. The purpose of the historical analysis is therefore to establish a basis for the product's reputation – which is attributable to its distinctive features. Finally, regarding the product's history, the aim is to identify a causal connection between the product's distinctive or characteristic features, which have sustained the historic as well as contemporary reputation, and the natural and/or human factors within the geographical region of origin.

For reputation-based GIs, this often involves the identification of specific production techniques (human factors) and an explanation for why they historically developed within that region, in response to environmental, socio-economic or cultural conditions specific to a place. The reputation link can be restated as follows: *(a) contemporary reputation builds upon (b) historic reputation, which accreted over time around the specific or distinctive features of the product, and (c) these features of the product in turn were causally attributable to natural/human factors specific – but not necessarily unique – to the region of origin.*

This is the 'turn to history' alluded to in this chapter's title. The historical evidence required by stages (b) and (c) is directed towards identifying the 'first uses of the name, accompanied as far as possible by the first descriptions of the product'.[75] The historical evidence should link the name of the product to a specific geographical region through the context surrounding the uses of the name. It should also identify the distinctive features of the product, which give the product a stable core of identity over time, and this provides the foundation for developing a reputation. Bérard and Marchenay identify some of the sources that can substantiate this.[76] While documentary sources are helpful, a local product may have only been known in the region of origin or have been produced primarily for domestic consumption, thereby leaving few textual traces. Oral history can therefore fill in the gaps or even provide much of the basic data.

---

[75] *Id.* at 23.
[76] Laurence Bérard & Philippe Marchenay, From Localized Products to Geographical Indications: Awareness and Action 23–25 (2008).

The oral history of a product can be compiled through multiple interviews across the product's supply chain and with members of the local community. In terms of documentary sources, of

> particular interest are various works by an increasing number of learned societies [in the 19th and 20th centuries] that relied on the testimony of local experts. Other sources of information range from administrative and technical reports to agricultural journals, treaties and statistics. Food and gastronomic history can also help to shed light on these products ... [Sources] range from administrative documents (surveys, censuses, statistics, decrees, legal cases, regional commodity prices), travel logs and food guides to directories of regional specialities and motoring and touring guides [as well as] local archives.[77]

These sources should be cross-referenced with local-level economic data relating to production where possible. There is of course a difference between a rigorous historical approach, which adopts valid historiographical and methodological techniques, and an instrumental account, which selectively dips into historical materials to tell a partial story or which embraces mythological origins.[78]

This approach to 'essentially attributable' reputation is evident for PGIs in the EU, as some recent registrations have illustrated. Take the example of the 'Polvorones de Estepa', a soft and crumbly Spanish Christmas confection (shortbread) made from flour, sugar, milk and nuts from the city of Estepa in Andalucia.[79] Its product specification states that the 'link between "Polvorones de Estepa" and the geographical area is based on the product's reputation. That reputation is over a century old. In that time, the confections have been made to the same recipe.'[80] Historical materials are used to establish that (i) an identifiable or stable product recipe has existed for some time; (ii) the product has enjoyed a reputation for some centuries; and (iii) confectioners were

---

[77] Id. at 24–25.
[78] The conflict between instrumental accounts drawing selectively on historical materials or taking them out of context (i.e. advocacy) and the more objective approach of professional historians is familiar to legal historians. See e.g., Mathew J. Festa, Applying a Usable Past: The Use of History in Law, 38 SETON HALL L. REV. 479 (2008); Jonathan Rose, Studying the Past: The Nature and Development of Legal History as an Academic Discipline, 31 J. LEGAL HIST. 101 (2010).
[79] Dossier No. ES/PGI/0005/01218. The description is available at http://ec.europa.eu/agriculture/quality/door/list.html (last visited 2 April 2016).
[80] See European Commission, Publication of An Amendment Application Pursuant to Article 50(2)(a) of Regulation (EU) No 1151/2012 of the European Parliament and of the Council on Quality Schemes for Agricultural Products and Foodstuffs ('Polvorones de Estepa') 2015 O.J. (C 338/10), at 5 (13 October 2015).

employed in that region to meet the demand from Seville and Madrid (making this a socio-economic origin story).[81] Documentary sources draw on the archives of a convent, which includes old recipes; the contributions of an individual confectioner (e.g. a method of baking and a process of refining and toasting the flour) who provided what would become the modern template; evidence of product sales dating back to 1959; and more recent (1980s and 1990s) references from the press, especially around the time of Christmas, as well as the product's inclusion within inventories of traditional foods.[82]

Another product that illustrates the historical approach to reputation is 'Carnikavas nēģi' for fresh or cooked Latvian river lampreys.[83] The specification states that the 'link between the product and the geographical area is based on the reputation of "Carnikavas nēģi" and the skills of the local fishermen and fish processors who preserve ancient traditions and methods'. Since fishing was a major source of income for the region, special techniques were developed to discover optimum fishing spots based on knowledge of the habits of the fish, influence of weather conditions and the need to adapt to the river changing its course. Ensuring that fishing practices favour sustainable fish stocks is also recorded in the specification. The specification very clearly claims that the product's reputation, which can be traced back to the seventeenth century, is attributed to the human skills – relating to both fishing and processing – which have been passed down through the generations: 'The taste characteristics of "Carnikavas nēģi" are connected with the skills of the residents of Carnikava in catching and preparing them; these skills have been preserved since the 17th century and are based on manual work and experience.'[84]

Therefore, this more overtly historical approach to the product emphasises the human contribution. Bérard and Marchenay underscore this by saying that

> historical rooting entails an identification of the skills and practices that have been developed and transmitted by successive generations. Historical depth must be linked to the collective know-how that has been passed down to the present generation, while bearing in mind that the transmission of know-how does not rule out evolution. Otherwise, history threatens to serve as a means of justifying would-be heritage products on the basis of a place's reputation – not on the specific qualities of the product concerned.[85]

[81] Id. [82] Id. [83] Dossier No. LV/PGI/0005/01153.
[84] Publication of an application pursuant to Article 50(2)(a) of Regulation (EU) No 1151/2012 of the European Parliament and of the Council on Quality Schemes for Agricultural Products and Foodstuffs ('Carnikavas nēģi') [2014] O.J. C 336, p, 27 (26 September 2014) at 5.1–5.3.
[85] Bérard & Marchenay, supra note 76, at 21–22.

Bringing human skills into the frame – via the link requirement, where the natural and human factors in a region have a causal influence on the distinctive features of the product – implies that we should be concerned with 'living history'. Mere long-standing production in a region is not sufficient; it is the human skills and techniques which give the product its distinctive features over time, and there is often a place-based explanation for how and why these skills and techniques arose and have adapted. Consequently, the human contribution has a normative dimension. Such products deserve protection because of the collective, inter-generational transmission of *savoir faire*, or potentially because local products help to actively make the place itself.[86]

5 CONCLUSION

For a legal regime initially founded upon a causation narrative drawn from physical geography, the turn to history is admittedly difficult but also contains intriguing possibilities. The purpose of this chapter was to set out a more GI-specific approach to reputation, by asking when it ought to be essentially attributable to the place of origin. This historical turn is worth engaging with because in the absence of a more appropriate reputational link between product and place, *sui generis* GI protection becomes unjustifiable. If contemporary commercial reputation becomes the benchmark, the boundary with trademark or unfair competition law breaks down and the justification for GIs, as a separate regime based on the causal connection between product and place, collapses.

Two concluding case studies illustrate the danger of adopting a simplified notion of reputation. In 2006, JAM NAGAR[87] was applied for as a GI for petrol, fuel, liquefied petroleum gas and diesel-related goods before the Indian GI registry. The applicant, Reliance, had established what it claims is the world's largest fuel refinery complex at Jamnagar in Gujarat, in western India.[88] The refinery complex had won awards and the applicant alluded to the superior (technological) quality of its refinery processes, which it claimed

---

[86] Bérard, *supra* note 35, at 86–87 ('People construct their spatial spheres of action by setting boundaries, by occupation and by transformation, designating and distinguishing a given place ... Localised agri-food production is a part of that process, helping to foster a sense of place through a wealth of specialised products that engage with local society in all sorts of ways and on all sorts of production levels').

[87] GOVERNMENT OF INDIA, GEOGRAPHICAL INDICATIONS JOURNAL VOL. 12, Application Nos. 38, 39, 41 & 42 (1 January 2006) (the author must disclose that he filed an opposition to the application, which was eventually withdrawn).

[88] *See* Reliance Industries Limited, *Petroleum Refining & Marketing*, www.ril.com/OurBusinesses/PetroleumRefiningAndMarketing.aspx (last visited 23 April 2016).

had earned the refinery complex a positive contemporary reputation. However, nowhere did it explain why a sign designating a relatively new and highly industrial complex could satisfy the 'essentially attributable' requirement on the basis of quality, characteristics or reputation. This seems to be a clear case of contemporary commercial reputation being a sufficient basis for GI registration.

The second case study relates to an ongoing dispute at the time of writing, concerning the PGI 'Piadina Romagnola', a flat bread made in the area around the Italian Adriatic coast of the Romagna Riviera.[89] The dispute is complicated and involved a challenge both to the definition of the geographical region by a producer excluded from it and by small-scale 'kiosk' producers of piadene sold in side-street outlets.[90] In an appeal to the CJEU seeking to cancel the PGI, it was noted that 'these organisations disputed the fact that, for the purposes of the envisaged PGI, industrially-produced piadine were being treated as equivalent to piadine produced on a small-scale basis and sold in street-side outlets'.[91] Despite these objections, the Italian authorities registered the application, which allowed the industrially produced flat bread to use the PGI, thus ignoring the history in the product specification which records that small-scale, artisanal production is what gave rise to the reputation in the first place.[92] The historic basis for reputation should inform the definition of acceptable production techniques, whereas in this case the reputation is instead viewed as an autonomous, commercially valuable intangible. Such a reputation can certainly be protected as certification marks or against unfair commercial practices, but not as a GI insofar as a meaningful link to the region of origin is required. The proposal considered in this chapter is suggested as one plausible method of satisfying that link to origin for products with a reputation.

---

[89] Dossier No. IT/PGI/0005/01067. I am grateful to Andrea Zappalaglio for bringing this controversy to my attention.

[90] For an overview, see LINDA BRUGIONI, *The Strange Case of the Protection of Piadina Romagnola PGI*, in BIRD & BIRD FOOD LAW DIGEST (3rd edn., 2015), www.twobirds.com /en/news/articles/2015/global/food-law-digest--3rd-edition--2015/food-law-digest-3rd-edition -2015.

[91] As noted in an appeal to the CJEU seeking to cancel the PGI, see Case T-43/15 R, CRM Srl v. Comm'n, 2015 Order of the President of the General Court, at 5.

[92] As the specification records: 'The consolidation over the centuries of this tradition and the specific production techniques were the basis for the birth, in the 1970s, of the small-scale commercial production of "Piadina Romagnola"/"Piada Romagnola" at small outlets (kiosks) for immediate serving. The widespread and visible presence in Romagna of kiosks producing and selling "piadine" for immediate consumption is a characteristic feature of the territory, well-known to locals and tourists alike.'

3

The Limited Promise of Geographical Indications for Farmers in Developing Countries

Justin Hughes[*]

1 INTRODUCTION

Among the various fields of intellectual property, geographical indications (GIs) law is arguably the smallest in terms of economic importance and the most complex in terms of principles and justification. To get a sense of the relative importance of GIs, in 2012–2013, India had over 43,000 patent applications, over 8,000 design registration applications, over 194,000 applications for trademark registration, but only 24 applications for protection of GIs.[1]

While GI law is rooted in the idea of *terroir* (a concept we consider below), discussions about GI protection can bring in strands of trademark law, unfair competition, agriculture policies, rural development, environmental protection, and – more distantly – protection of traditional cultural expression and traditional knowledge. These connections can easily lead to simplistic and sometimes false narratives about the potential benefits from different sorts of legal protection of GIs. This chapter describes some of the forces benefiting and burdening effective GI labeling with today's consumers.

Because those consumers *do* show an interest in geographic origins, despite the occasional hype, GIs can be – in many circumstances – a useful tool in raising rural incomes in developing countries. Because GI-based marketing

---

[*] Honorable William M. Byrne Professor of Law, Loyola Law School, Los Angeles. Copyright © 2016 by the author. Permission is hereby granted for noncommercial reproduction of this chapter in whole or in part for educational or research purposes, including the making of multiple copies for classroom use, subject only to the condition that the name of the author, a complete citation, and this copyright notice and grant of permission be included in the copies.

[1] The actual numbers are 43,674 (patents), 8,337 (designs), and 194,216 (trademarks). UNITED NATIONS ECONOMIC COMMISSION FOR AFRICA, INNOVATION, COMPETITION, AND REGIONAL INTEGRATION: ASSESSING REGIONAL INTEGRATION IN AFRICA VII, Table 6.4 at 110 (2016) [hereinafter UNECA, INNOVATION, COMPETITION, AND REGIONAL INTEGRATION]. Information obtained by the report authors from Office of Controller General of Patents, Designs and Trademarks of India, 2012–13.

can help developing farmers, *properly calibrated* legal protection of GIs should be part of a "development agenda" for jurisdictions with significant rural economies. In that spirit, this chapter lays out some of the factors determining whether and how GI marketing (and GI legal protection) can help any particular rural region. With those issues in mind, we will consider a few specific examples.

2 GEOGRAPHICAL INDICATIONS AND *TERROIR*

"Geographical indications" is an umbrella term for the various legal mechanisms used to protect geographical designators that tell consumers both the geographic origin of a product *and* something about the product's quality and characteristics. The legal standards of protection vary as does the moniker used to designate the protected name ("appellations of origin," "protected geographical indication," "protected designation of origin," "collective mark,"[2] etc.). Whatever the name used, true appellation laws – and now geographical indications laws – have been traditionally justified by the idea of *terroir*: that a particular land is a key input for a particular product. The *terroir* idea is that the product's qualities "come with the territory" and that there is, as I have described elsewhere, an "essential land/product qualities nexus."[3]

For example, the French government's Institut national de l'origine et de la qualité (formerly the Institut national des appellations d'origine) explains an appellation d'origine contrôlée (AOC) this way:

> [It] guarantees a close link between the product and the terroir, which is a clearly defined geographical area with its own geological, agronomical, climatic, etc. characteristics, as well as particular disciplines self-imposed by the people in order to get the best out of the land. This notion of terroir encapsulates both natural and human factors, and means that the resulting product may not be reproduced outside its territory.[4]

In the context of wine (but in concepts that apply broadly), terroir can be understood as "the environmental conditions, especially soil and climate, in

---

[2] Justin Hughes, *Champagne, Feta, and Bourbon: the Spirited Debate about Geographical Indications*, 58 HASTINGS L. J. 299, 301 (2006). A term used not just in jurisdictions that protect GIs through trademark law regimes but also in some scholarly commentary. *See, e.g.* Alessandro Stanziani, *Wine Reputation and Quality Controls: The Origin of the AOCs in 19th Century France*, 18 EUROPEAN J OF L. & ECON. 149 (2004).

[3] Hughes, *supra* note 2, at 301.

[4] Institute National de Appellations d'Origine, *History and Genesis of the AOC* www.inao.gouv .fr/public/textesPages/History_and_concepts350.php?mnu=350 (last visited May 4, 2016).

which grapes are grown and that give a wine its unique flavor and aroma."[5] As one Australian wine critic has written: "terroir ... translates roughly as 'the vine's environment[,]' but has connotations that extend right into the glass: in other words, if a wine tastes of somewhere, if the flavours distinctly make you think of a particular place on the surface of this globe, then that wine is expressing its terroir."[6]

The *terroir* theory in this classic form has always been somewhat "cultural" and largely ignored in many quarters of the agricultural sciences. In his seminal 1947 *The Soil and Health*, Sir Albert Howard – one of the fathers of modern organic farming – does not mention any such concepts.[7] In 302 pages detailing how to produce better crops of coffee, tea, cotton, cocoa, wheat, tomatoes, and various fruit, Howard's concern is the general *quality* of soil and maintaining soil fertility through natural means, but he never takes up the question of whether enduring variations in soils and climate would produce enduring variations in foodstuffs.[8] It simply wasn't an issue for the science-minded but contrarian Howard.

More and more, we understand that the most factually sound *"terroir"* is microclimatic, i.e., that each field (or small cultivated block) is its own *terroir* based on particular soil composition, relationship to sunshine, wind, rainfall, and drainage. In other words, *single appellations are rarely consistent in key geology, flora, and climate*. In fact, the larger the appellation, the more the variation. Geological studies have shown between ten and sixty soil types for the AOC *Alsace grand cru*.[9] Discussing "Bordeaux" as an appellation, Thierry Desseauve has noted that it "represents all forms of *terroir*, all kinds of microclimates, all situations, and finally all kinds of wines and prices."[10]

---

[5] www.dictionary.com/browse/terroir (last visited May 4, 2016). The Oxford dictionaries offer as definitions of *terroir* both "The complete natural environment in which a particular wine is produced, including factors such as the soil, topography, and climate" and "The characteristic taste and flavor imparted to a wine by the environment in which it is produced." www.oxforddictionaries.com/us/definition/american_english/terroir (last visited May 4, 2016).

[6] Max Allen, Sniff Swirl & Slurp: How to Get More Pleasure Out of Every Glass of Wine 24 (2002).

[7] Sir Albert Howard, The Soil and Health (Devin-Adair, 1947). The book was republished by the University of Kentucky Press in 2006.

[8] The closest thing to a discussion of *terroir* comes from a correspondent, Friend Sykes, in one of the appendices to The Soil and health in which Sykes proposes that "the best thoroughbreds are all bred on land with high lime content – either limestone or chalk." *Id.* at 292.

[9] B. Burtschy, *Dix terroirs, quatre cépages, cinquante grand crus. L'équation enfin résolue*, Revue du Vin de France, March 2000, at 54.

[10] Yves Rousset-Rouard & Thierry Desseauve, La France face aux vins du Nouveau Monde 120–21 (2002).

Similarly, the United States' designated "American Viticultural Areas" (AVAs) are probably just "too big ... to have real viticultural meaning."[11] But this is genuinely a problem for appellations of *all* sizes. One French wine guide notes that *within* the *Le Minervois* AOC (a small region) there are four regions that are differentiated from each other by their *terroir* and climate.[12] Many northern California vintners have studied soil and slope characteristics to the point of dividing individual *vineyards* into "flavor blocks," i.e., miniature *terroirs* that are viticulted differently.[13] Even in the case of salmon, writer Rowan Jacobsen observes that each particular stream may be its own *terroir*,[14] undermining any *terroir* meaning to "Alaskan" or "Norwegian" salmon.

But if this is the reality of *terroir*, appellations like "Bordeaux," "Napa Valley," or "Burgundy" make little sense from a *terroir* perspective. Nationwide appellations like "Feta" or "Irish whiskey" make no sense at all. Large (but not too large) geographic areas like "Idaho potatoes," "Parma ham," and "Melton Mowbray Pork Pies" may make sense from the perspective of consistent cultural traditions, but the problem is that those traditions are *transportable* – a contentious point underlying the Europe/New World feud over GIs.

Not surprisingly, over time, there has been a loosening of the connection between *terroir* and GI law. The 1958 Lisbon Agreement requires that a product's "quality and characteristics" be "due exclusively or essentially to the geographical environment" while recognizing that "human factors" could contribute to this equation.[15] In contrast, the definition of "geographical indications" in the TRIPS Agreement requires that the "given quality,

---

[11] Rod Smith, *Savoring Sonoma/The Wines*, L.A. TIMES, June 1, 2005, at F5 ("The Sonoma Coast AVA was created primarily as a marketing tool for large wineries and is too big (nearly half of the county) to have real viticultural meaning.").

[12] JACQUELINE GARDAN, LIVRE DE CAVE: PRÉCIS A L'USAGE DE L'AMATEUR ÉCLAIRÉ 77 (Porphyre ed., 1991) ("Quatre regions se différencient par leur terroir et leur climat.").

[13] W.H. Terry Wright, *Diverse Geology/Soils Impact Wine Quality, Practical Winery & Vineyard*, September/October 2001, at Vol. XXIII, No. 2, www.sonomagrapevine.org/pages/growerstool box/gtgeology_soils.html (noting this about Benziger Family Winery and describing "a rich smorgasbord of rock types and a complicated geological history" producing a "high diversity of soil types, each a niche with its own conditions of texture, structure, and nutrients" in Sonoma County). *See also World-Class Vineyard Uses GIS to Fine-Tune All Its Operations*, ArcNews, Fall 2013 (describing operations at Scheid Vineyards in Monetrey; here "GIS" means "geographical information systems") available at www.esri.com/esri-news/arcnews/fal l13articles/world-class-vineyard-uses-gis-to-finetune-all-its-operations.

[14] As in Rowan Jacobsen's view "that every stream's salmon are genetically distinct, having conformed to their terroir." ROWAN JACOBSEN, AMERICAN TERROIR 172 (2010).

[15] Lisbon Agreement for the Protection of Appellations of Origin and their International Registration, art. 2(1), October 31, 1958, 923 U.N.T.S. 189 (English text of Stockholm revision

reputation, or other characteristic of the good is essentially attributable to its geographical origin."[16] The 2015 Geneva Act revising the Lisbon Agreement offers two different definitions of a protectable GI: one mimics the TRIPS "geographical indication" definition while the other recites the 1958 Lisbon formulation *but adds* "and which has given the good its reputation."[17]

No one knows whether there is any difference between product qualities being "essentially" or "exclusively" due to the land, so it is unclear what the loss of "exclusively" means. What is clear is that the addition of "reputation" to the legal definitions could, broadly read, obviate any land/qualities connection of the sort that has been fundamental to the notion of appellations.[18] As Irene Calboli writes, this "allows GI producers to partially 'de-territorialize' the production of GI-denominated products" and "this partial 'delocalization' runs against the very rationale for GI protection – the linkage between the products and the *terroir*."[19] And this is exactly the case with some GIs, such as the United Kingdom's "Melton Mowbray Pork Pies" and India's "Feni" liquor.

3 GEOGRAPHICAL INDICATIONS PROTECTION – MAGIC-LIKE CLAIMS, UNPROVEN RESULTS

If the justification for legal protection of GIs has shifted in recent years, the strength of the European Union's advocacy for GIs – mainly on behalf of France and Mediterranean Member States – has not. Here is an example of the European Commission's claims about GIs in a more somber moment:

---

begins at 215), available at www.wipo.int/wipolex/en/details.jsp?id=12586 (revised at Stockholm on July 14, 1967, and as amended on September 28, 1979) [hereinafter 1958 Lisbon Agreement].

[16] Agreement on Trade-Related Aspects of Intellectual Property Rights, art. 22(1), April 15, 1994, Marrakesh Agreement Establishing the World Trade Organization, Annex 1C, The Legal Texts: The Results of the Uruguay Round of Multilateral Trade Negotiations 320 (1999), 1869 U.N.T.S. 299, 33 I.L.M. 1125, 1197 [hereinafter TRIPS].

[17] Geneva Act of the Lisbon Agreement on Appellations of Origin and Geographical Indications and Regulations under the Geneva Act of the Lisbon Agreement on Appellations of Origin and Geographical Indications, WIPO Document LI/DC/19 (May 20, 2015) [hereinafter Geneva Act], www.wipo.int/meetings/en/details.jsp?meeting_id=35202.

[18] Bernard O'Connor, *The Legal Protection of Geographical Indications*, 2004 INTELL. PROP. Q. 1, 52 ("This definition expands the concept of appellation of origin contained in Art. 2 of the Lisbon Agreement to protect goods which merely derive a reputation from their place of origin without possessing a given quality or other characteristics which are due to that place."); Hughes, *supra* note 2, at 315–16 (same).

[19] Irene Calboli, *Time to Say Local Cheese and Smile as Geographical Indications of Origin? International Trade and Local Development in the United States*, 53 HOUS. L. REV. 373, 387 (2015).

> The protection of geographical indications matters economically and culturally. They can create value for local communities through products that are deeply rooted in tradition, culture and geography. They support rural development and promote new job opportunities in production, processing and other related services.[20]

This statement is unimpeachable: GIs do "matter," "can" do the things claimed, and appear to "support" rural development.

But at other times the Commission takes a more rhetorical tack. For example, a 2012 study commissioned by the European Union found that for 2,768 GI products from 27 EU countries in 2010 "[t]he average price premium for GI products was found to be 2.23, which means that GI products were sold 2.23 times as high as the same quantity of non-GI products, *which shows that using GIs can achieve a higher market price*."[21]

Of course, the evidence does not "show" that. Even if all the data are correct, what we have is a *correlation* (not *causation*) between GI protection and higher prices for GI products as compared to non-GI products in the same categories. Perhaps products bearing GIs command a price premium because they simply are, on the whole, *better* – with or without the GI labeling; or perhaps the products bearing GIs command a price premium because they are simply more famous, with or without the GI labeling; or perhaps they are better advertised. Ironically, the higher average price may even be because of non-EU demand for the GI-labeled products in jurisdictions that do not provide the heightened level of legal protection that the European Union claims is necessary (i.e., demand in the United States, Japan, China, etc.).

A more extreme claim is found in the 2009 "Teruel Declaration" of OriGin, an NGO dedicated to promoting GIs:

> By providing jobs for millions of individuals around the world, helping preserve the environment and ensuring that the globalization of markets does not encroach on the diversity, quality and tradition of origin products, Geographical Indications (GIs) play a vital role in our economies and societies. Producers, both from developing and developed countries,

---

[20] http://ec.europa.eu/trade/policy/accessing-markets/intellectual-property/geographical-indications/.

[21] Catherine Saez, *GIs The "Darling" of Europe, But Protection a Challenge for All, Producers Say*, IP WATCH, May 28, 2013 (describing report of Michael Erhart, head of agricultural product quality policy at the European Commission, emphasis added), available at www.ip-watch.org/2013/05/28/gis-the-darling-of-europe-but-protection-a-challenge-for-all-producers-say/.

increasingly rely on GIs for the sustainable development of their communities.[22]

This passage is well beyond the usual overstatements from trade associations or nonprofits. Instead of focusing on increased price premiums (even without a causal analysis), OriGin makes a blanket statement that GIs "provid[e] jobs for millions of individuals" – as if the underlying products themselves would not sell *at all* without the GI protection. Unfortunately, some otherwise intelligent people buy into this kind of rhetoric. In a 2005 paper presented at a World Intellectual Property Organization (WIPO) meeting, a Kenyan government official reasoned that "GI protection would transform African farmers from raw material producers to exporters of differentiated products easily identifiable in the global marketplace"[23] and argued that GI protection against usurpation or dilution would "benefit" dozens of local Kenyan products – even though these products are *generally unknown* in developed economies.[24]

3.1 No Across-the-Board Effects

But thoughtful people concerned about rural development know that strong legal protection of GIs is not such magic. Laws *by themselves* do not create commercial or reputational value: EU-level GI protection globally would not suddenly make "Asembo mangoes" or "Muruanga bananas" into premium-price products. As Carlos Correa has said, "geographical indications, like trademark, may in some cases play a decisive role in generating a premium over and above the price of equivalent goods, while in other cases their contribution cannot be distinguished from that attributable to the product itself."[25] Bald claims about the economic value of GIs ignore the fact, as Carlos Correa has wisely observed, that "the final price of the product that incorporates an intellectual property component is a poor indicator of the

---

[22] Organization for an International Geographical Indications Network, TERUEL DECLARATION (Teruel, June 26, 2009) at 1.

[23] James Otieno-Odek, *The Way Ahead – What Future for Geographical Indications?* WIPO – ITALIAN GOVERNMENT, WORLDWIDE SYMPOSIUM ON GEOGRAPHICAL INDICATIONS, Parma, Italy, June 27–29, 2005, at 5.

[24] While Otieno-Odek mentioned some products that might have reputations in OECD countries (like Mt. Kenya coffee), his list included "Kisii tea, Kericho tea, kangeta, miraa, meru potato, kikuyu grass, Mombasa mango, Machakos mango, Asembo mango, Muranga bananas and Kisii bananas" as well as "Molo lamb, Kitengela ostrich meat, Omena fish and Mursik milk," *Id.* at 3.

[25] Carlos Correa, *Protection of Geographical Indications in Caricom Countries* (September 2002) at 18, available at http://ctrc.sice.oas.org/geograph/crnm/Geographical.pdf.

value of the intellectual property itself"[26] and that "[s]eeking to quantify the current and, particularly, the potential, value generated by the use of a geographical indication is an extremely difficult task."[27]

In the words of a 2008 study commissioned by the European Commission to study the effect of "protected designation of origin" (PDO) and "protected geographical indication" (PGI) status:

> A key limitation of the evaluation of the scheme is that, at the present time, data on the administrative implementation of the PDO and PGI scheme and on the PDO/PGI products are scant as, typically, Member States do not monitor the administrative and statistical aspects of the scheme such as the value or volume of production, sales, and prices of PDO and PGI products.[28]

As that 2008 study further explained, although there are case studies claiming positive relationships between PDO/PGI status and improved prices, "[t]he limited number of case studies does not allow one to draw firm conclusions for the overall population of PDOs and PGIs."[29]

There are a number of good reasons why it is extremely difficult to figure out what impact GI legal protection has on the price of GI-labeled products, let alone whether *different levels of legal protection* might have different impacts on those prices:

[1] For some products, it is difficult if not impossible to disentangle premiums produced by trademark-protected *brands* and any premium produced by the GI. Scotch whisky would be a prime example.

[2] For some products, the price premium apparently *preceded* the formal GI status. For example, this is clear from the *application* for PGI status made by the Melton Mowbray Pork Pie Association:

> Melton Mowbray Pork Pies are clearly distinct from other pork pies in their packaging, design and marketing at point of sale. They carry a price premium compared to other pork pies on the market place of 10–15 percent because they have a specific reputation that sets them apart as different and worth paying for.[30]

---

[26] *Id.* at 19.   [27] *Id.* at 18.
[28] London Economics, *Executive Summary, Evaluation of the CAP Policy on Protected Designations of Origin (PDO) and Protected Geographical Indications (PGI)* 3 (November 2008) [hereinafter 2008 London Economists Study].
[29] *Id.* at 6.
[30] EC No: UK/PGI/005/0335/13.02.2004, Official Journal of the European Union, April 4, 2008, section 4.6 at C 85/20, available at http://eur-lex.europa.eu/LexUriServ/LexUriServ.do?uri= OJ:C:2008:085:0017:0020:EN:PDF.

[3] Studies and reports showing that *local* citizens place a premium on *local* GIs simply do not help us understand the mechanisms by which we could induce developed world consumers to pay more for products from *distant* developing locales.

[4] Even where a protected GI appears to command a price premium, the GI labeling and marketing often imposes higher production costs so the *net* price premium is unknown. In its 2008 review of eighteen case studies of EU-protected GIs, a consulting firm hired by the European Commission found that "[i]n 14 out of 18 cases, the price of a PDO/PGI product is higher than the price of the comparator product" but that "[i]n 10 cases, the costs of producing a PDO/PGI is higher than the cost of producing its comparator."[31]

One serious attempt to measure the effect of a legally protected GI is Dwijen Rangnekar's study of "Darjeeling" tea in the WTO's 2004 World Trade Report.[32] "Darjeeling" received GI protection as a certification mark in a number of jurisdictions in the 1980s – the United Kingdom, the United States, Canada, Japan, Egypt, and a number of European countries;[33] it has also been protected as a certification mark in India for decades.[34] Rangnekar and his colleagues found that (at least this level of) legal protection of the *Darjeeling* GI has had no noticeable effect on price over a twenty-year period. According to the report, "[t]he results obtained suggest that GI protection has increased the price of Darjeeling tea in total by less than 1 per cent in real terms over the 1986–2002 period. This result is suggestive of only a very modest price premium effect of GI protection."[35] Of course Darjeeling is a very famous kind of tea, suggesting dimmer outcomes for less known GIs.

3.2 Why People Believe in Geographical Indications Magic

If the evidence is so mixed, what is the attractive power of stronger GI protection? How does the GI rhetoric take hold with people who do not come from privileged and famous agricultural locales like Champagne, Napa, or Parma? Developing countries are surely not looking to guarantee that they will pay *more* to producers of Champagne, Bourbon, Roquefort, and Feta.

---

[31] 2008 London Economists Study, *supra* note 28, at 9.
[32] Dwijen Rangnekar, *The International Protection of Geographical Indications: The Asian Experience*, paper presented at UNCTAD/ICTSC Regional Dialogue on IPRs, Innovation, and Sustainable Development, Hong Kong, November 8–10, 2004.
[33] *Id.* at 28.   [34] *Id.* at 8–9.   [35] 2008 London Economists Study, *supra* note 28, at 9.

The answer is pretty straightforward: there is something quite appealing about a law that will protect the name and integrity of one's local products and supposedly propel those products into international recognition. Most people have some points of pride for their geographic homes and that local pride is often centered on food. The European Commission's message is simple: *your home probably has a unique and special local product and it would command respect and price premiums globally if only it had stronger legal protection.*

That is an understandably seductive message, whether for people in Bergamo, Italy, who take "pleasure in consuming local products" and "regularly choose their own lard, salami and cheeses over other, even more prestigious, varieties"[36] or, half way around the world, for coffee farmers in the Highlands of Papua New Guinea who "think they are constantly being underpaid for their coffee, because it is better than all other coffee"[37] (even though Papua New Guineans generally *do not drink coffee*[38]). In this sense, strong GI protection becomes a matter of "respect" for their local products.[39]

4 THE GOOD AND BAD OF GEOGRAPHIC ORIGINS MARKETING

We should also recognize that GI-based marketing must respond to changing consumer tastes and concerns, only some of which benefit GIs.

4.1 *The Appeal of Geographic Origin Marketing*

A GI label can be, for a wide range of consumers, *at least* an indicator of the geographic origin of the product. In other words, geographic origin information may be important to the consumer for reasons completely separate from quality or characteristics (the *terroir*); in that context the GI label will serve a market and marketing function broader than the function attributed to it by GI theory. For example, interest in geographic origin of foodstuffs may be rooted in any of the following:

---

[36] Jillian R. Cavanaugh, *Making Salami, Producing Bergamo: The Transformation of Value*, 72:2 ETHNOS: JOURNAL OF ANTHROPOLOGY 155 (2007).
[37] PAIGE WEST, FROM MODERN PRODUCTION TO IMAGINED PRIMITIVE: THE SOCIAL WORLD OF COFFEE FROM PAPUA NEW GUINEA 148 (2012).
[38] Most Papua New Guineans are Seventh Day Adventists who do not drink coffee.
[39] *See generally* Daniel Gervais, *Traditional Innovation and the Ongoing Debate on the Protection of Geographical Indications*, in INDIGENOUS PEOPLES' INNOVATION 121 (Peter Drahos & Susy Frankel eds., 2012) (suggesting that developing countries may be attracted to GI protection of indigenous products because of GI's potential ability to promote respect).

- a desire to lessen transportation effects on the planet, e.g., a Californian consumer might prefer Guatemalan or Costa Rican coffee over Ethiopian coffee;
- a desire to support countries with better human rights, worker rights, or democracy records, e.g., a preference for Costa Rican over Guatemalan coffee;
- a desire to support fellow countrymen, whether patriotic or nationalistic, e.g., a preference for Hawaiian Kona coffee over Sulawesi or Jamaican Blue Mountain coffee;
- a simple desire for a more specific, nonindustrial (or less industrial) narrative.

It is not hard to see strands of evidence supporting these different consumer interests – and how this connects or does not connect with protection of GIs.

Consider the first of these: the trend toward "localization." As Daniel Gervais notes, some consumers' insistence on geographic origin labeling "partly stems from a desire to buy more locally produced products and to reduce the carbon footprint of their consumption patterns."[40] We see this trend not only in the rise of farmers' markets and farm-to-table restaurants but in industrial producers informing customers of local sourcing – as when McDonald's in Switzerland assures its customers that they work with Swiss agricultural partners.[41]

This trend toward geographic identification can rely on – and strengthen – GI-based marketing, but it does not require full-fledged GI laws.[42] More importantly, to the degree consumers show preferences for local production, this does not bode well for *developing* country farmers using GIs to extract economic rents from *developed* country consumers. On the other hand, as a growing middle and upper middle class emerges in cities like Mumbai, Chengdu, Johannesburg, Kuala Lumpur, and Sao Paulo, this trend might

---

[40] Daniel Gervais, *Irreconcilable Differences? The Geneva Act of the Lisbon Agreement and the Common Law*, 53 HOUS. L. REV. 339, 346 (2015).

[41] Brochure, McDonald's: Une excellente qualité, garantie par des partenaires suisses et européens (undated, but from 2009 to 2013) (on file with the author). Actually, the brochure is obliquely worded, naming many Swiss food sector partners but not directly saying what comes from Swiss agricultural production.

[42] David A. Wirth, *Geographical Indications, Food Safety, and Sustainability Challenges and Opportunities*, paper presented at 145th EAAE Seminar "Intellectual Property Rights for Geographical Indications: What is at Stake in the TTIP?", April 14–15, 2015, Parma, Italy ("Some consumers also seem to be particularly interested in purchasing locally-produced food, lending greater importance to non-GI indications of the locality of origin") (on file with the author).

produce parallel "local" substitution – if, for example, Mumbai residents increasingly prefer Goan Feni over "western" liquors.

4.2 Geographical Indications Marketing Amid an Abundance of Labels

In a broader perspective, today the geographic source information that is provided by GI labeling competes with a growing array of labels conveying information about (a) the product, and (b) what in international trade is called "process and production methods." The former include "organic," "non-GMO," and "gluten-free"; the latter include "shade-grown," "sustainable," and "fair trade."

We do not have any meaningful empirical evidence on how consumers – consumers in different places and different socioeconomic groups – respond relative to these different labels. There is no question that consumers are paying and expect to pay price premiums for products that are guaranteed to have many of these characteristics. But we do not know if consumers will pay *more* for geographic origin labeling than for organic, more for GI certified labeling than fair trade certified labeling, etc. For example, imagine a study that showed us the different price points that Australian or Japanese, Singaporean or American consumers would pay for the following different labeling/certifications:

> "Organic French Roast coffee"
> "Papua New Guinea coffee"
> "Organic Papua New Guinea coffee"
> "Fair trade certified Dark Roast coffee"
> "Fair trade certified Papua New Guinea coffee"

That kind of empirical evidence would more meaningfully guide policy makers for at least three reasons: first, whether for Papua New Guinea coffee growers or Colorado iced tea bottlers, *each* of these certification processes costs time, effort, and money;[43] second, some retail outlets are available or foreclosed based on different labeling and rural practices;[44] and, third, there is

---

[43] Annie Gasparro and Leslie Josephs, *The Gatekeeper to Organic Heaven*, WALL STREET JOURNAL, May 7, 2015, at B1 (describing how one small vegan cheese producer spent $3,000 getting certified organic and a bottled ice tea producer saying "grueling certification processes are worth the money to get its iced tea on Whole Foods shelves").

[44] *Id.* (for example, Whole Foods – one of the United States' premier retailers to high-income food consumers – is much more likely to carry products with fair trade or organic labeling).

good reason to think that consumers are or at some point *will* start suffering "label fatigue."[45]

While not the subject of this chapter, there is also a real danger that GI labeling will be misunderstood by consumers as signifying some guarantee of organic, natural, non-GMO, or fair trade production.[46] That connection is implied by comments about GIs enhancing "sustainability," but sustainability of rural *economies* and "sustainable" farming are quite different. For example, according to one French consumer group study, French wine producers only use 3.7 percent of France's farmland but account for 20 percent of that country's pesticide use.[47] Indeed, *organic* winemakers in Burgundy have been fined and threatened with prosecution for *refusing* to use pesticides.[48] The confusion of GI labeling with production guarantees ("organic") could accrue to benefit developing countries' farmers, but price premiums through consumer confusion is surely not an acceptable policy objective.

5 A COMPLEX DECISION, HOPEFULLY FOR FARMERS

All of this produces a complex picture for policy makers who would help farmers in developing countries. One must assess the relative costs and benefits of different production and labeling practices that "de-commodify"

---

[45] Ulrike Grote, *Environmental Labeling, Protected Geographical Indications, and the Interests of Developing Countries*, 10 ESTREY CENTRE J. INT'L L. & TRADE POL. 94, 96 (2009) ("A proliferation and multiplication process for labels in different markets is on-going, and it has resulted in decreased transparency and labeling fatigue from the perspective of consumers"). Or as anthropologist Paige West asks us about origin and fair trade labeling, "[w]hat happens when people get tired of hearing about people from the global South?" WEST, *supra* note 37, at 255.

[46] Gervais, *Irreconcilable Differences*, *supra* note 40, at 345 (noting that GI labeling "ties into – or may be confused with – 'fair trade' labels and certification processes concerning the sourcing of an increasingly wide range of products, many of which come from the developing world"); see DANIEL JAFFEE, BREWING JUSTICE: FAIR TRADE COFFEE, SUSTAINABILITY, AND SURVIVAL 92 (2014) (noting that in rural Oaxaca coffee "producers understandably conflate the tangible requirements of organic production with the less familiar concept of fair trade").

[47] Elaine Sciolino, *In France, Pesticides Get in Way of Natural Wines*, N.Y. TIMES, March 2, 2015, available at www.nytimes.com/2015/03/04/dining/in-france-pesticides-get-in-way-of-natural-wines.html?_r=0; *Lab Tests on French Wines Find Pesticide Residue in Every Bottle*, FOOD SAFETY NEWS, September 30, 2013 (reporting that even organic wine contained pesticide residues); see also UFC-Que Choisir, *Vins: La peste soit des pesticides*, September 24, 2013, available at www.quechoisir.org/alimentation/production-agricole/cultures/enquete-vins-la-peste-soit-des-pesticides.

[48] *Pesticides in French Wine*, N.Y. TIMES, March 2, 2015, available at www.nytimes.com/2014/01/03/opinion/pesticides-in-french-wine.html?_r=0.

local production. And that assessment has to be in the context of *what is possible in that locale.*

In the case of GIs – whether a *sui generis* system or a certification marks approach – one will need to define the geographic area for eligible production. This process can easily become highly politicized. Ironically, drawing the geographic boundaries should be easier when the GI seems to have little prospective reputational value. The next element is defining the production standards: ingredients, from where raw ingredients can be sourced, recipes, aging and fermentation practices, permissible technologies for distillation and/or storage, etc. As Dwijen Rangnekar notes:

> A GI requires documentation of the production rules, thus the need for the relevant group of producers in the region and across the supply chain to arrive at some consensus. All this raises questions of participation, debate, disagreement, cooperation and all the messiness of politics and economics of who is involved, who is excluded, and who is leading the process of rule-making.[49]

In the case of certification marks, a private leadership group can pretty much establish their own production standards; in the case of *sui generis* GI law, the producers will have to work with government agencies in what will be extended, detailed public–private sector collaboration.

Central government involvement also raises two other very important issues: capacity and extraction of economic rents. Simply put, the central government may try to extract economic rents by controlling when the GI designation can be used and by whom. There is always a danger that the GI will be used to strengthen a government's role in the market – and that may or may not help rural citizens. The capacity issue is also a serious one. For example, economist Tyler Cowen has observed that "[m]ost African nations simply cannot afford the requirements for safety, labeling, and control that European-style regulation imposes on them."[50]

Fair trade and organic production and certification practices also impose a substantial burden in terms of training, labor, and community disciplines.[51] It

---

[49] Dwijen Rangnekar, *Geographical Indications and Localisation: A Case Study of Feni* (UK Economic and Social Research Council, 2009), version available at http://papers.ssrn.com/sol3/papers.cfm?abstract_id=1564624##.

[50] TYLER COWEN, AN ECONOMIST GETS LUNCH 163 (2012).

[51] *Coffee: A Major PNG Export*, BUSINESS ADVANTAGE PNG, September 1, 2012 (noting that in Papua New Guinea "the requirements of organic certification can often be beyond the capacity of smallholders") at www.businessadvantagepng.com/coffee-a-major-png-export/. *See generally* JAFFEE, *supra* note 46 (detailing difficulties coffee growers in rural Oaxaca, Mexico face in meeting and maintaining both fair trade and organic standards).

may be that there is a broader international community of NGOs that can bring "off-the-shelf" organic, fair trade, and environmentally friendly production systems to rural communities, bypassing central governments. But there are also substantial efforts from the NGO community to help those who would pursue GI labeling.

Farmers, activists, and policy makers should also consider carefully the price differentials that different labeling produces. Discussions of organic, fair trade, and GI labeling are replete with claims about the higher prices that de-commodification brings, but we must focus on (a) whether farmers, rural workers, and rural communities are actually receiving the economic premiums, and (b) if and when higher production costs wipe out the value of those premiums.

With these issues in mind, let's briefly consider three parables of de-commodification of developing country foodstuffs – Ethiopian coffee, Goan "Feni" liquor, and Papua New Guinea coffee.

5.1 Ethiopian Coffee and the Problem of Quality Control

Humanity's consumption of coffee began in Ethiopia; the modern, high-end global coffee market is closely identified with Starbucks. So the feud that erupted in 2006 between Ethiopia and Starbucks over Ethiopian coffee names had all the makings of a good news story.

In the past few decades, Ethiopia has taken varied approaches to coffee production, but despite these shifts there seems to be agreement that "[t]he coffee value chain in Ethiopia involves a large number of intermediaries and is largely state-controlled."[52] Beginning in March 2005 – during a period of relative liberalization – the Ethiopian government sought US trademark registration for three geographic names used for Ethiopian coffees: HARRAR, YIRGACHEFFE, and SIDAMO. The Ethiopians sought to register the names as *regular* trademarks. The United States Patent and Trademark Office (USPTO) quickly granted the registration application for YIRGACHEFFE.[53] But the HARRAR and SIDAMO applications were held up.[54]

---

[52] Till Stellmacher, *Prospects and Challenges of Forest Coffee Certification in Ethiopia: The Need to Effectively Link Economic Benefits and Biodiversity Conservation*, 2008 paper at 4, available at http://userpage.fu-berlin.de/~ffu/akumwelt/bc2008/papers/bc2008_9_Stellmacher.pdf.
[53] USPTO Registration number 3126053. The application for YIRGACHEFFE was filed on March 17, 2005; published for opposition on April 11, 2006, and granted on August 8, 2006.
[54] *Making the Origin Count – Two Coffees: Ethiopia and the Starbucks Story*, 5 WIPO MAGAZINE, October 2007 at 2, 3 (reporting that USPTO initially denied the HARRAR application in October 2005 and the SIDAMO application in August 2006).

Starbucks had already applied for a trademark that *included* "Sidamo"; its application was for SHIRKINA SUN-DRIED SIDAMO.[55] More broadly, Starbucks publicly argued that it was a bad idea to grant regular trademarks to these Ethiopian place names, arguing that they are "geographically descriptive terms" and urging "a geographic certification program" to ensure that the names were used to "represent quality products that come from a specific region."[56] For their part, the Ethiopians recognized that seeking trademarks for the names was a "new approach," but said it was justified by the situation of small coffee farmers and traders in the country.[57]

After receiving a blitz of bad publicity – much of it fomented by Oxfam – Starbucks softened its position, and in November 2006, Starbucks and Ethiopia reached an entente.[58] Eventually, SIDAMO and HARRAR obtained USPTO trademark registration.[59] Starbucks made some sort of promise to help promote the Ethiopian coffees, and Ethiopia gave Starbucks royalty-free licenses to use the three trademarks in conjunction

---

[55] USPTO Serial number 78431410. The application was for SHIRKINA SUN-DRIED SIDAMO; filed on June 8, 2004; published for opposition in December 27, 2005; and abandoned on July 8, 2006. "Shirkina" is an Amharic word for partnership. See www.starbucksstore.com/products/shprodde.asp?SKU=439270. The press sometimes misunderstood this. See, e.g., ETHIOPIAN COFFEE: Every bean counts, BRANDS STRATEGY, September 14, 2007, at 48 (describing Starbuck's application correctly, but stating that if Starbucks had received the trademark, Ethiopian farmers "could have lost the right to name their own product").

[56] Starbucks Press Release, *Starbucks Sets the Record Straight on Press Coverage Regarding Starbucks, the Ethiopian Government, and Oxfam*, October 26, 2006, available at www.starbucks.com/aboutus/pressdesc.asp?id=714.

[57] *Starbucks and EIPO Reach Agreement*, TEA AND COFFEE TRADE JOURNAL, June 1, 2007 at 62 (Ethiopian government offices "[w]e realize our approach to trademarking and licensing these coffees brands that originate in and represent the best of Ethiopia's coffee heritage is a new approach").

[58] After a meeting between Starbucks CEO and the Ethiopian Prime Minister, the former announced that "Starbucks and the Ethiopian government agreed that they will work together toward a solution for the protection and use of Intellectual Property Rights of Ethiopian coffee names." Press Release, *Starbucks and the Ethiopian Government Agree to Work Together Toward a Solution that Supports the Ethiopian Coffee Farmers*, November 29, 2006, available at www.starbucks.com/aboutus/pressdesc.asp?id=729. Starbucks subsequently sponsored Ethiopia as the first "African Portrait Country" at the annual meeting of the Specialty Coffee Association of America in 2008. *Country Takes Center Stage at US Specialty Coffee Conference*, THE DAILY MONITOR (ETHIOPIA), April 30, 2008.

[59] SIDAMO – USPTO registration number 3381739; application dated March 17, 2005; published for opposition on November 27, 2007; and registered on February 12, 2008. HARRAR – USPTO registration number 3457979; application dated March 17, 2005; published for opposition on April 15, 2008; and registered on July 1, 2008.

with its sales of Ethiopian coffees – the same as Ethiopia had done for other coffee retailers.[60]

There are different ways to interpret the Ethiopia/Starbucks dispute. In the dominant public interpretation, Starbucks was already using these geographic names in conjunction with Ethiopian coffees (as the result of buying bona fide Ethiopian beans at auction), and Starbucks did not want to start paying additional trademark-licensing fees to the Ethiopian government. In this narrative – according to Oxfam – Starbucks was trying to avoid paying $US 88–90 million a year to Ethiopia.[61] It is anyone's guess how Oxfam got these numbers, and clearly those numbers were false in the sense that Ethiopia soon granted Starbucks royalty-free licenses for the trademarks.

The idea that Starbucks was not paying enough for the geographically labeled product certainly feeds into the GI advocates' narrative, fueling further misunderstandings. For example, in 2009, a University of Hannover professor characterized the dispute as one in which "[t]he Ethiopian government wants to protect coffee originating in those specific regions by using GIs as opposed to labeling as proposed by Starbucks."[62] Of course, that is just the *opposite* of what happened: Starbucks had proposed the traditional GI mechanism in the United States (certification marks) and Ethiopia has insisted on regular trademarks (i.e., just "labeling").

As both sides tried to provide popular explanations of their positions, the story did not become much clearer. In a YouTube video, counsel for Ethiopia argued that "[a] certification mark provides much weaker control in the holder of the certification mark."[63] Given that certification marks get the same level of protection under US trademark law (Lanham sections 32 and 43), what was Ethiopia's lawyer trying to say in asserting that a certification mark gives less "*control?*" The point he may have been trying to make is that once a coffee roaster/retailer purchases coffee beans genuinely produced in the applicable region (and pursuant to any quality controls the certification mark requires), the coffee roaster/retailer would be free to use the appropriate mark

---

[60] See, e.g., ETHIOPIAN COFFEE: Every Bean Counts, BRANDS STRATEGY, September 14, 2007 at 48; Ethiopia: Starbucks to Sign Licence Agreement with EIPO, 34 COFFEE & COCOA INTERNATIONAL 4 (June/July 2007); see Janet Adamy, Starbucks, Ethiopia Agree on Licensing, WALL ST. J., June 21, 2007, at B6.

[61] Ethiopia is Now Trademarking its Specialty Coffees, THE FOOD INSTITUTE REPORT, November 19, 2007 at 5 (Oxfam America reporting that trademarks would bring Ethiopia an additional $US 88 million).

[62] U. Grote, Environmental Labeling, Protected Geographical Indications and the Interests of Developing Countries, 10 ESTEY CENTRE JOURNAL OF INTERNATIONAL LAW AND TRADE POLICY, volume 1, 94, 95 (2009).

[63] Robert Winter, Arnold & Porter, January 29, 2007: www.youtube.com/watch?v=2DiWK81j7fg.

(HARRAR, SIDAMO, or YIRGACHEFFE). He may have also meant that certification marks would give the Ethiopian government less leverage over its own farmers – again, as long as the farmer meets the certification mark standards, the farmer cannot be denied the right to sell his coffee as HARRAR, SIDAMO, or YIRGACHEFFE. In contrast, with regular trademarks the Ethiopian government is not required to be even-handed either with Starbucks or its farmers; that really does give it more "control," particularly if the country's farmers are increasingly selling directly to coffee roasters/retailers.

But is that the sort of control we want to give an undemocratic, non-transparent central government over its farmers? One trade industry report ominously characterized the Ethiopian government's efforts this way: "[w]hile certification marks are commonly used as a means of identifying products associated with a particular geographic region, *the Ethiopian government elected to assert traditional trademark rights to identify itself as the ultimate source of the country's specialty coffees.*"[64] In other words, Oxfam's intervention was clearly helpful to the central government in Addis Ababa but not to the provincial farmers. The effort to obtain regular trademarks may manifest the central government's fear that, over time, they will not be able to stop direct sales between farmers and foreign buyers – and, therefore, will be cut out of the usual middleman rents that African governments have extracted.[65]

In another interpretative variation, does the quest for regular trademarks manifest an admission by the Addis Ababa government that practically speaking *it cannot police even minimal certification standards*? This was the suggestion made implicitly by Ron Layton, the head of "Light Years," an NGO trying to help African countries capitalize on their intellectual property:

> So what's wrong with the regional [certification] model? Layton argues that certification – while it works well for a smaller country like Jamaica – would be too difficult to implement in Ethiopia. There are literally millions of Ethiopians moving coffee beans to only a handful of distributors like Starbucks.[66]

---

[64] ETHIOPIAN COFFEE; *Trademark versus geographical certification*, BRAND STRATEGY, September 14, 2007 at 49 (emphasis added).

[65] *See generally*, Justin Hughes, *Coffee and Chocolate – Can We Help Developing Country Farmers through Geographical Indications?* September 29, 2010 (describing how African governments and capital elites have historically extracted economic rents from rural cocoa and coffee producing areas), available at http://papers.ssrn.com/sol3/papers.cfm?abstract_id=1684370&rec=1&srcabs=1671676&alg=5&pos=4 (last visited May 4, 2016).

[66] Joshua Gallu, *Starbucks, Ethiopia, and the Coffee Branding Wars*, DER SPEIGEL Online (English), November 16, 2006, available at www.spiegel.de/international/0,1518,448191,00.html. One Ethiopian official has said the same thing: "[o]ur coffee is grown on four million very

The Limited Promise of GIs for Farmers

A 2007 report on Ethiopia's efforts similarly commented that "geographic certification" is valuable, but "it can be a costly mark to maintain" and that "[a]s the majority of Ethiopian farmers still live in extremely basic conditions, it is not a cost they can afford to absorb."[67] And Ethiopian officials have been very blunt in their claim that the Harrar, Sidamo, and Yirgacheffe names "refer[red] not to geographical locations, but to distinctive coffee types"[68] and that "[t]he coffee varieties *were not strictly regional* ... so wine-style designations would have made no sense."[69] A benign interpretation of all these statements is that officials in Addis Ababa realize that they cannot establish an effective, dependable system for geographical certification, let alone additional quality controls that EU officials associate with true GIs.

Finally, the denouement of this story also warrants our attention. Did the increased control of the three important Ethiopian geographic coffee labels in the world's biggest coffee-consuming market help? My own site visits to Starbucks in different cities and review of Starbucks coffee guides show a general *absence* of Ethiopian coffees in Starbucks stores *for years* following the dispute. For example, a 2010 brochure for Starbucks in China shows eighteen different coffee offerings; of these, seven are single-source country or region coffees, none of which are Ethiopian GIs.[70]

Indeed, in September 2013, Starbucks introduced into its US stores "a new single-origin coffee from the birthplace of coffee, Ethiopia."[71] The coffee is called "Ethiopia" and the words "Sidamo," "Harrar," and "Yirgacheffe" do not appear *anywhere* in the packaging or promotional materials.[72] This "Ethiopia"

---

small plots of land. Setting up a certification system would have been impracticable and too expensive. Trademarking was more appropriate to our needs. It was a more direct route offering more control." *Making the Origin Count – Two Coffees: Colombia – 50 Years of Evolving Strategies*, 5 WIPO MAGAZINE, October 2007 at 3.

[67] ETHIOPIAN COFFEE: *Every bean counts*, BRANDS STRATEGY, September 14, 2007 at 48. See also *Direct from the Source, Coffee in Ethiopia*, THE ECONOMIST (U.S. edition), April 19, 2008 (head of EIPO says that there was neither time nor money for Ethiopia "to pursue a complicated certification process").

[68] *Making the Origin Count – Two Coffees*, *supra* note 66, at 3.

[69] See *Direct from the Source, Coffee in Ethiopia*, *supra* note 67 (quoting Getachew Mengistie, head of EIPO).

[70] Starbucks, *Discover the Finest Coffee in the World* (2010) (on file with the author). The regional coffees offered in the brochure are Columbia Nariño Supremo, Guatemala Antigua, Sulawesi, Sumatra, Sumatra Decaf, Kenya, and Rwanda.

[71] Starbucks press release, September 23, 2013, available at https://news.starbucks.com/news/starbucks-honors-the-birthplace-of-coffee-with-ethiopia [hereinafter Starbucks Ethiopia Press Release].

[72] Another page for the Ethiopia coffee says: "On the ancient slopes flanking Africa's Great Rift Valley, coffee trees first emerged from the rich, volcanic soil." But no mention of the three regions. http://store.starbucks.com/ethiopia-whole-bean-011028995.html (last visited May 4,

coffee "joins Starbucks selection of 20 core and 10 traditional and seasonal whole bean coffees offered at Starbucks retail stores nationwide";[73] it is also one of twelve single-origin coffees offered by Starbucks online.[74] As for Ethiopia's protected marks, Starbucks appears to offer online only "Starbucks® Ethiopia Yirgacheffe® Espresso Verismo® Pods" in their coffee pod section.[75] The internal search engine on the Starbucks site also brings up "Starbucks Reserve Sun-Dried Ethiopia Sidamo" and "Starbucks Reserve Sun-Dried Ethiopia Harrar," but neither of these can be found on the "reserve coffees" page as of May 4, 2016.[76]

From Oxfam's perspective, this might indicate bad faith on the part of Starbucks, but it might also be simply supply and quality issues;[77] or Starbucks' need to rotate among different single-origin coffees; or Starbucks' concern that "Sidamo" and "Harrar" coffees simply cannot be guaranteed to come from those places. Whatever the explanation, the Ethiopia coffee names saga is a sobering story on quality control and geographic guarantees, government relations to farmers, and the fact that promotion of developing country GIs will often rest with the goodwill of corporations in the developed world.

5.2 *Some Observations on Goa's Cashew Apple Feni*

In 2009, Dwijen Rangnekar published an extremely thorough and detailed case study of the development of GI status for "Feni" liquor from Goa, India.[78] Rangnekar's research is a case study on the successful establishment of a

---

2016). Starbucks also offers an "Ethiopia Gemadro" single-origin estate coffee. http://store.starbucks.com/ethiopia-gemadro-single-origin-estate-011040514.html (last visited May 4, 2016).
[73] Starbucks Ethiopia Press Release, *supra* note 71.
[74] See http://store.starbucks.com/coffee/whole-bean-and-ground/ (last visited May 4, 2016).
[75] See http://store.starbucks.com/starbucks-ethiopia-yirgacheffe-espresso-verismo-pods-011030279.html?&srule=Featured&start=0&sz=12&cgid=starbucks-verismo-pods (last visited May 4, 2016).
[76] COWEN, *supra* note 50, at 163.
[77] Germany and Saudi Arabia each import far more Ethiopian coffee than the United States, the latter for obvious geographic reasons. *See Ethiopian Coffee Consumers Vote for Quality amid Rising Prices*, ETHIOPIAN NEWS, May 9, 2011 (showing the US as the third-largest market for Ethiopian coffee in 2009/10), www.ethiopian-news.com/ethiopian-coffee-consumers-vote-quality-rising-prices/; USDA Global Agricultural Information Network Annual Ethiopia Coffee Report, GAIN Report No.: ET-1302, May 14, 2013 (showing the US as the fifth-largest market for Ethiopian coffee in 2011/12 after Germany, Saudi Arabia, France, and Belgium).
[78] Dwijen Rangnekar, *Geographical Indications and Localisation: A Case Study of Feni* (UK Economic and Social Research Council, 2009), version available at http://papers.ssrn.com/sol3/papers.cfm?abstract_id=1564624## [hereinafter Rangnekar, *Case Study of Feni*].

protected GI: any local leader or NGO working on agricultural development and considering tools for de-commodifying farmers' production would profit from reading his report.

"Feni" is the name of a liquor that has been produced for centuries in Goa state in India. There are two principal types of Feni: coconut Feni, which was probably first, and Feni made from cashew apples, a tree that was imported in the sixteenth century from Brazil when Goa was under Portuguese rule.[79] Cashew apple Feni is typically made from fruits that have been allowed to fall to the ground before they are collected.[80] The apples are crushed, traditionally by foot but then by "stone-mortar crusher[s] using draught animals" and now mechanical crushers.[81] The juice is fermented for two to four days and then distilled in pot-stills that are of local design.[82] Historically, Feni was a triple-distilled liquor, but Rangnekar reports that there is now "a certain consensus towards a double-distilled Feni."[83]

It is not clear how the effort at GI registration got started, but a group of Feni producers organized as the "Feni Association" and worked extensively with the Goa Chamber of Commerce and the Goa Government Department of Science and Technology in drafting an application for protected GI status under India's 1999 GI law. The application was submitted to the central Indian government in December 2007 and ultimately approved in February 2009.[84] This private-local government group rose to the bureaucratic challenge, "demonstrat[ing] a substantial effort in assembling the information for a GI application, coordinating the various interests and groups concerned with Feni, then responding to the examination process of the GI registry."[85]

Preparing that application required agreeing upon specifications. Rangnekar reports that research was undertaken by "an informal committee involving journalists and archivists, agronomists and scientists, and bottlers and distillers."[86] Armed with those results, "distillers, bottlers and retailers

---

[79] Id. at 24.
[80] Id. ("The apples are generally left to fall to the ground before being collected, as this is an indication that the kernel/nut is mature ... The cultural wisdom against plucking apples from the tree is that the unripe apple will give the Feni a bitter taste.")
[81] Id. at 25.
[82] Id. at 26–27 (detailing evolution of different pot-still designs and construction).
[83] Id. at 28.   [84] All these facts are recounted at id. at 30.   [85] Id. at 6.
[86] Id. at 7 ("An informal committee involving journalists and archivists, agronomists and scientists, and bottlers and distillers, was assembled. Details of the distilling process were scripted, its history was researched and collected, and chemical analysis was conducted and documented.").

need[ed] to agree to some minimum standards related to Feni while not excluding or marginalising the rich diversity and tradition of Feni-distilling."[87]

The Feni narrative demonstrates many of the basic issues in establishing a protected GI to benefit rural farmers, workers, and families. For example, although the process for preparing the GI application was elaborate and *apparently* inclusive, at the end of the day most Feni *distillers* did not know about the application (as compared to most Feni *bottlers*, who consolidate supply from individual distillers).[88] The decision to use the name "Feni" but exclude coconut Feni from the GI definition means, as Rangnekar says, a "loss of history and practice [that] is not entirely easy."[89] It also likely means consumer confusion going forward.[90]

Aspects of the Feni GI definition exclude a substantial number of distillers[91] while the permissible sourcing of cashew apples from *anywhere*[92] may, over the long term, work to the benefit of Goan distillers and bottlers, but to the detriment of Goan farm labor. On the other hand, Feni distribution channels suggest that the benefits of the GI might accrue disproportionately to *bottlers* who can send Feni beyond Goa's borders instead of individual *distillers* who tend to supply bars, tavernas, and restaurants.[93] Indeed, this is implicit in the idea of Feni being "launched as a global liquor" like tequila.[94] The different interests and involvement of Feni

---

[87] *Id.* at 8.

[88] *Id.* at 35 ("most distillers were not involved in the GI debate in Goa. For that matter, a mere 2% confirmed knowledge about the GI application in comparison to over 80% of bottlers").

[89] *Id.* at 31.

[90] For example, one website currently describes coconut Feni in detail and says "Feni has got the status of Geographical Indication (GI)." In smaller print, the webpage mentions that the GI registration is only for cashew apple Feni and since that is the only time cashew apple Feni is mentioned, a reader might easily think all GI Feni is coconut. See *Goan Fenny/Feni*, Indian Mirror, www.indianmirror.com/culture/indian-specialties/Goanfeni.html (last visited May 12, 2016).

[91] For example, in his fieldwork Rangnekar concludes that "the most popular level" of alcoholic content for Feni "lies outside the GI specifications." Rangnekar, *Case Study of Feni*, supra note 78, at 49.

[92] *Id.* at 42 (noting that the "lack of clarity on the geographic origin of cashew apples" shows the "tacit acceptance of the practice of cashew apples being transported from beyond Goa's borders" and that this practice might already be necessary to meet local demand). See also *id.* at 9.

[93] *Id.* at 37. As a 2012 report says, "[a]round three-fourths of the distillers sell their produce to bars directly." Raunaq Sahu, *The Goan Feni Industry: Challenges*, The Centre for Civil Society, CCS Working Paper No. 261 at 4 (2012) available at http://ccs.in/internship_papers/2012/261_feni-industry_raunaq-sahu.pdf [Sahu's report appears to have been written under an internship program, i.e., the author may be a student].

[94] Rangnekar, *Case Study of Feni*, supra note 78, at 40. The Goa activists pursuing the GI protection referred to Tequila as "an example to emulate." Id. at 42.

distillers and Feni bottlers also reflect educational and socioeconomic differences: less than 8 percent of distillers completed their high school education but over 85 percent of bottlers did.[95]

Finally – as I have emphasized earlier in this chapter – the mere creation of the GI protection does not establish *demand* for the product: Rangnekar concludes that the export market is currently limited to "Goa's diaspora" and the reputation of Feni – promulgated in tourist books on Goa – as a local "fire water" means that "the tourist will be an unreliable and unlikely ambassador for a future export market."[96] This is a real challenge because Feni production had already been in decline prior to the GI registration – despite otherwise growing alcohol consumption in India.

The question is whether GI status can *help* reverse that decline over time. As one Indian observer asked in 2012, "[w]hy hasn't the Goan feni industry been able to grow, despite it being granted the GI status?"[97] As of 2013, Feni distiller Gurudatta Bhakta concluded, "[t]he GI has not helped much in the promotion of cashew feni."[98] One major reason appears to be other Indian regulations hampering Feni sales *in India* outside Goa state.[99] But the broader reason is that GI status itself only helps when there is a commitment to building the product's reputation through improvement of product quality, consistent production (both of which may undermine traditional practices and biodiversity), and promotion. As one person central to the Goan Feni industry said, "It is now up to us as to how we take this forward."[100]

---

[95] Sahu, *supra* note 93, at 5.   [96] Rangnekar, *Case Study of Feni*, *supra* note 78, at 50.

[97] Sahu, *supra* note 93, at 1. Chandu Gopalakrishnan, *Hic! Feni Fights to Regain Turf in Goa*, Economic Times of India, July 1, 2010 ("But even after obtaining the GI status, production of feni continues to decline, putting in danger the already-meagre export prospects") available at http://articles.economictimes.indiatimes.com/2010–07-01/news/28392598_1_feni-gurudatta-bhakta-cashew-apple. But in fairness that comment is made only one year after GI status.

[98] As quoted in Joseph Zuzarte, *The Rise of Cashew Feni*, Streets, March 14, 2013, available at http://goastreets.com/the-heady-rise-of-cashew-feni/.

[99] Sahu, *supra* note 93, at 5. Joseph Zuzarte, *GI-certified Cashew Feni Still "Legal" only in Goa*, The Times of India, April 4, 2013 (reporting that because of Feni's "country liquor" classification "[f]our years after it received a geographical indication (GI) certificate cashew Feni can still not be sold legally in other parts of the country") available at http://timesofindia.indiatimes.com/city/goa/GI-certified-cashew-feni-still-legal-only-in-Goa/articleshow/19369766.cms. The Goan government was seeking such a reclassification as of 2016.

[100] Zuzarte, *The Rise of Cashew Feni*, *supra* note 98 quoting Mac Vaz, a marketer of Feni. Vaz spoke of the need for "the industry [to] gain[s] the consumers' trust and for this we also need to protect ourselves from those few within the industry who consistently weaken and tamper with the quality of the beverage for fast and greater money."

5.3 Some Observations on Papua New Guinea Coffee

In her 2012 book, *From Modern Production to Imagined Primitive: The Social World of Coffee from Papua New Guinea*, anthropologist Paige West has provided us with a rich account of the socioeconomics of coffee in one of Asia's least developed regions.[101] In many ways, coffee production in the Highlands of Papua New Guinea is the opposite of Feni production in Goa. The Feni GI story happens in a comparatively rich and sophisticated polity (Goa state) in a mega-state with a sophisticated and robust legal system (India); as emblematic as Feni might be of Goa, the alcohol's production is not a dominant element of the local economy.

In contrast, coffee production in Papua New Guinea occurs in a country with a very small population and lacking a legal and policy infrastructure on par with that of the Indian subcontinent. More importantly, unlike Feni, coffee production *is the* economy for the Highlands of Papua New Guinea. While extractive industries are important to Papua New Guinea exports, "coffee is the only [Papua New Guinea] export commodity owned and operated by the local people,"[102] and coffee production is the most significant source of income for most people in the Highlands of Papua New Guinea.[103] According to West, "[b]etween 86 and 89 percent of coffee grown in PNG is 'smallholder' coffee, grown by landowners who live in relatively rural settings with small family-owned and family-operated coffee gardens."[104]

Not surprisingly, there have been efforts to de-commodify Papua New Guinea coffee along many of the marketing metrics identified above. Single-origin Papua New Guinea coffee is definitely present in the United States market: as of 2016, Peet's Coffee sells "New Guinea Highlands" coffee; the Coffee Bean and Tea Leaf chain offers both "organic Papua New Guinea" and "Papua New Guinea Sigri Estate" coffees; and Amazon carries Papua New Guinea coffees from at least half a dozen smaller roasters with many of these labeled as organic, fair trade, or "direct trade."[105] It would be much more

---

[101] WEST, *supra* note 37, at 148. [102] *Id.* at 10.
[103] *Id.* at 110–11. See also, *Coffee: A Major PNG Export*, *supra* note 51 ("[i]t is estimated that 2.5 million Papua New Guineans rely on coffee as their main source of income").
[104] WEST, *supra* note 37, at 7.
[105] In a May 15, 2016, survey of the Amazon website, companies marketing Papua New Guinea coffees included Camano Island Coffee Roasters, Clipper, CoffeeAM, Coffee Bean Direct, Heirloom Coffee LLC, Lavanta Coffee Roasters, and RhoadsRoast Coffees. The Camano Island, Clipper, and Heirloom companies offered organic Papua New Guinea coffees; Clipper and Lavanta offered fair trade or "direct trade" products. Another website, pngcoffee.com, offers "exclusive, rare organic coffees from Papua New Guinea." www.pngcoffee.com/about.html (last visited May 4, 2016).

difficult to determine what amounts, if any, of organic or fair trade Papua New Guinea coffees are going into blends like Starbucks "Estima" fair trade or "Yukon" organic coffees.

From her anthropologist's perspective, West sees these different labeling schemes as all aimed at giving Papua New Guinea coffee "a set of meanings that distinguish it from other coffees"[106] because "[c]onsumers are willing to pay more for coffee that has a particular story or a particular history."[107] West is direct in her conclusion about how both fair trade and geographic origin marketing work: "[w]ith certified and single-origin coffees the images used to sell the products are also manipulated to make consumers feel as if they are also making other people's lives better through the act of buying."[108]

Again, the situation with Papua New Guinea coffee reinforces some basic truths about the potential for GIs as against the spectrum of claims made by GI advocates. First, West concludes that while *most* Papua New Guinea coffee production comes from small individual farms, *better*-quality coffee comes from the larger, more industrial, less "traditional" sources of production.[109] In other words, whatever demand exists for Papua New Guinea coffee is *not* a function of small-batch, artisanal production. Second, any level of legal protection of the GI does not matter if the GI has no reputation with consumers – and it may be that Papua New Guinea is simply not that well known.[110] Third, even among those who know Papua New Guinea coffee, unless the coffee has a reputation for distinctiveness or excellence[111] the GI

---

[106] WEST, *supra* note 37, at 13.   [107] *Id.* at 17.   [108] *Id.* at 25.
[109] *Id.* at 142 ("Without the blending that coffee buyers and factories undertake, the coffee grown in villages would have no value on the market. According to factory owners in Goroka, village-processed coffee is too wet, and much of it has been stored improperly at airstrips waiting for planes, causing it to develop a musty smell and taste. The factories ... mix the musty coffee with properly processed green bean from well-run plantations so that it can be sold."). *Id.* at 168–69 (details on factory-processed Papua New Guinea coffee being superior to what is partially processed by villagers). *See also* Wikipedia, *Coffee Production in Papua New Guinea* ("the coffee grown by the small farmers, which is organically grown, on occasions, do not match with the quality of the estate grown coffee"), available at https://en.wikipedia.org/wiki/Coffee_production_in_Papua_New_Guinea (last visited May 4, 2016).
[110] WEST, *supra* note 37, at 230 (describing interviews of 100 Columbia University students born between 1983 and 1989 of which 48 percent "had no idea that Papua New Guinea produced coffee at all").
[111] Coffee connoisseurs are often critical or unenthusiastic about Papua New Guinea coffees. *See, e.g.*, "Papua New Guinea," Sweet Maria's Coffee Library (offering many criticisms and that generally "[t]he main problems in PNG come with poor coffee processing and poor dry-milling"), available at http://legacy.sweetmarias.com/library/content/papua-new-guinea-1 (last visited May 4, 2016).

may not carry a significant price premium – in which case emphasis on marketing through organic and fair trade channels *may* produce better results.[112] Not surprisingly, in 250-plus pages describing Papua New Guinea Highlands coffee production, West devotes almost no words to origin certification for Papua New Guinea coffee; at the local level, enhanced legal protection of Papua New Guinea as a GI is simply not seen as a priority to increase economic rents for Papua New Guinea coffee farmers.

6 CONCLUSION

GIs are a policy tool that can, *in some circumstances*, improve conditions in rural areas through price premiums paid for GI-labeled products. But the most important word in that sentence is "can," not "will" or "do." Instead of the simplistic promotion one hears from GI advocates, the United Nations Economic Commission for Africa's 2016 study on IP policy struck the right tone:

> Geographical indication protection may be extended under collective trademarks, through a special geographical indication regime, or through disciplines on unfair competition. For some local agricultural products that have niche markets and high-value customers, geographical indication protection may add value and generate economic benefits in certain regions. However, increased geographical indication protection does not itself guarantee better market access unless quality is assured by, for example, producers' complying with importing countries' sanitary, phytosanitary and other quality regulations. Moreover, extended geographical indication protection could restrict local production of products that infringe foreign geographical indications. Therefore, a full cost-benefit analysis must inform the design of the national geographical indication regime.[113]

That conclusion for African countries applies with equal force to the rural areas of Asia, Oceania, and the Americas. Those seeking to help de-commodify foodstuffs produced in developing countries must carefully examine each situation, including looking at the comparative costs and benefits that might accrue from fair trade, organic, or other labeling schemes. In short, the promise of geographical indications may be real – but it is a limited promise, not a money-back guarantee.

---

[112] *Coffee: A Major PNG Export*, *supra* note 51 ("Organic certification is considered the quickest and easiest way of adding value to [Papua New Guinea] coffee ... This certification, plus the sale of coffee under the internationally recognised Fairtrade brand, has the potential to enable growers to achieve higher incomes.").
[113] UNECA, INNOVATION, COMPETITION, AND REGIONAL INTEGRATION, *supra* note 1, at 68.

4

Rethinking the Work of Geographical Indications in Asia: Addressing Hidden Geographies of Gendered Labor

Rosemary J. Coombe[*] and S. Ali Malik[**]

1 INTRODUCTION: HOPES FOR GEOGRAPHICAL INDICATIONS AND ACKNOWLEDGING THEIR LIMITS

Geographical indications (GIs)[1] are widely perceived to provide prospects for new forms of rural development, community autonomy, preservation of cultural traditions, and even the conservation of biological diversity when

---

[*] Rosemary J. Coombe is the Tier One Canada Research Chair in Law, Communication and Culture at York University. She gratefully acknowledges the research and editorial assistance of Laura Fox and Jackie Ewald.
[**] S. Ali Malik is a PhD candidate in the Sociolegal Studies Program at York University.
[1] The 1994 Trade-Related Aspects of Intellectual Property Agreement (TRIPS Agreement) established GIs as a distinctive category of intellectual property. Indications of source, appellations of origin, denominations of origin, and collective trademarks and certification marks are herein collectively denoted as marks indicating conditions of origin (MICOs) to reflect this broader field of legal vehicles. In some common-law jurisdictions, recognition is possible without registration if the MICO is an indication of source for consumers. Some countries in the Global South employ the term GI as a generic name for a new form of protection established by new legislation to comply with the TRIPS Agreement. Because the TRIPS Agreement leaves discretion with member countries regarding the means and forms of such protections, countries may name their protections GIs, but utilize governance frameworks historically applied to denominations of origin or collective trademarks, for example. See Article 22(1), Agreement on Trade-Related Aspects of Intellectual Property Rights, April 15, 1994, Marrakesh Agreement Establishing the World Trade Organization, Annex 1C, LEGAL INSTRUMENTS -RESULTS OF THE URUGUAY ROUND, vol. 31, 33 I.L.M. 1125 (1994) [hereinafter TRIPS Agreement]. They may also fuse elements from diverse legal vehicles and add new ones. See DANIELE GIOVANNUCCI ET AL., GUIDE TO GEOGRAPHICAL INDICATIONS: LINKING PRODUCTS AND THEIR ORIGINS 8 (2009), *available at* www.intracen.org/Guide-to-Geographical-Indications-Linking-Products-and-their-Origins/. Many countries have entrenched contemporary GIs as forms of state property when historically they would have been held by collective stakeholders such as producer associations that upheld quality controls and were responsive to local conditions. Moreover, some states in Asia have allowed traders to use them as if they were producers, which may alienate their governance from those who create the goods that bear them. *See*

the production of goods encourages the stewardship rather than the depletion of the natural resources from which they are made.[2] They may also provide an effective means to protect traditional environmental knowledge (TEK) and traditional cultural expressions (TCEs),[3] enable the sustainable use of genetic resources, contribute to maintaining agricultural landscapes, and utilize TEK that might otherwise be lost.[4] Consequently, the European Union has promoted their extension across the Global South as a rural development strategy that, not incidentally, supports European interests in global trade.[5] Asian countries have seen in GIs a means to protect artisanal knowledge,[6] viewing human factors such as producer know-how, skills, and practices as linked to a particular territory and its means of production. The broader group of legal vehicles we refer to as marks indicating conditions of origin (MICOs) are attractive to development practitioners who hope to prevent social inequalities by creating community controls over economic activities that tie rural areas

---

N. S. Gopalakrishnan, Prabba S. Nair, & Arayind K. Babu, *Exploring the Relationship between Geographical Indications and Traditional Knowledge: An Analysis of the Legal Tools for the Protection of GIs in Asia* (Geneva: International Centre for Trade and Sustainable Development, Working Paper, 2007).

[2] *See, e.g.,* PHILIPPE CULLET, INTELLECTUAL PROPERTY PROTECTION AND SUSTAINABLE DEVELOPMENT (2005).

[3] For traditional knowledge (TK), *see,* Teshager W. Dagne, *Harnessing the Development Potential of Geographical Indications for Traditional Knowledge-based Agricultural Products,* 53 J. OF INTELL. PROP. L. & POL'Y 441 (2010); Shivani Singhal, *Geographical Indications and Traditional Knowledge,* 3 J. OF INTELL. PROP. L. & POL'Y 732 at 738 (2008); David Downes, *How Intellectual Property Could Be a Tool to Protect Traditional Knowledge,* 25 COLUM. J. ENVTL. L. 253 at 281 (2000); and sources cited in Nicole Aylwin & Rosemary J. Coombe, *Marks Indicating Conditions of Origin in Rights-Based Sustainable Development,* 47 U.C. DAVIS L. REV. 753, at 773–74 (2014). For traditional cultural expressions (TCEs), *see,* MICHAEL BLAKENEY ET AL., EXTENDING THE PROTECTION OF GEOGRAPHICAL INDICATIONS: CASE STUDIES OF AGRICULTURAL PRODUCTS IN AFRICA 120–34 (Michael Blakeney et al. eds., 2013); DAPHNE ZOGRAFOS, INTELLECTUAL PROPERTY AND TRADITIONAL CULTURAL EXPRESSIONS 176–77 (2010).

[4] JORGE LARSON GUERRA, RELEVANCE OF GEOGRAPHICAL INDICATIONS AND DESIGNATIONS OF ORIGIN FOR THE SUSTAINABLE USE OF GENETIC RESOURCES (2007), *available at* http://underutilized-species.org/Documents/PUBLICATIONS/gi_larson_lr.pdf. *See also,* JORGE LARSON GUERRA, GEOGRAPHICAL INDICATIONS, IN-SITU CONSERVATION AND TRADITIONAL KNOWLEDGE (2010) ICTSD Policy Brief No. 3, *available at* http://ictsd.org/i/publications/100736/.

[5] Rosemary J. Coombe, Sarah Ives, & Daniel Huizenga, *Geographical Indications: The Promise, Perils and Politics of Protecting Place-Based Products, in* THE SAGE HANDBOOK OF INTELLECTUAL PROPERTY, 207, 210 (Mathew David & Debra Halbert eds., 2014); Cerkia Bramley & Estelle Biénabe, *Why the Need to Consider GIs in the South?, in* DEVELOPING GEOGRAPHICAL INDICATIONS IN THE SOUTH 1–14 (Cerkia Bramley, Estelle Biénabe, & Johann Kirsten eds., 2013).

[6] Delphine Marie-Vivien, *The Protection of Geographical Indications for Handicrafts: How to Apply the Concepts of Natural and Human Factors to All Products,* 4 WIPO J. 191 (2012).

into larger markets and forge collective rights indivisible from locality.[7] For rural economies, GIs are extolled as providing "a physical and conceptual structure for affirming and valuing the unique socio-cultural and agro-ecological characteristics of a particular place"[8] which may have spillover effects that contribute to regional branding and foster tourism.

Nonetheless, there is considerable evidence that poorly designed GI systems negatively transform the conditions of production they are celebrated as sustaining.[9] Such systems have a tendency to conflate nature and culture and to uniquely depoliticize relations of production in their regions of application. The discourse advocating their adoption and celebrating their use relies on a "social imaginary" of place-based products that projects a harmonious community, represented "holistically, possessing singular traditions and rooted in a particular place characterized by a naturally bounded and distinctive ecosystem."[10] This social imaginary binds traditions to territory through an Orientalist lens in which peoples collectively share narratively romanticized bonds to a natural environment shaped by their labors into an authenticated place. The use of GIs tends to imbue products with distinct attributes that simply reflect local biodiversity and cultural distinction, both presumed to be isomorphic with a community. Thus a stable, unified, and harmonious place is ideally imagined, represented, and, ultimately perhaps, even experienced. In neoliberal terms, this is a "win-win" scenario where tradition, culture, and knowledge are simply integrated into global markets and legally protected in a global trading system. This social imaginary presumes a unified community that will receive uniform benefits from its use, a scenario which usually has little factual basis, as we have explored elsewhere.[11]

Diverse stakeholders in supply chains are assumed to all share similar interests in developing a region's reputation through the marking of distinctive goods. Nonetheless, GI premiums are rarely shared equitably, particularly in

---

[7] Aylwin & Coombe, *supra* note 3, at 777. [8] GIOVANNUCCI ET AL., *supra* note 1, at 8.

[9] Sarah Bowen & Ana Valenzuela Zapata, *Geographical Indications, Terroir, and Socioeconomic and Ecological Sustainability: The Case of Tequila*, 25 J. RURAL STUD. 108 (2009); Tomer Broude, *Taking "Trade and Culture" Seriously: Geographical Indications and Cultural Protection in WTO LAW*, 26 UNIV. OF PENN. J. OF INTL. ECON. LAW 623 (2005); ANITA SAY CHAN, NETWORKING THE PERIPHERIES: TECHNOLOGICAL FUTURES AND THE MYTH OF DIGITAL UNIVERSALISM 23–52 (2014).

[10] Rosemary J. Coombe, Sarah Ives, & Daniel Huizenga, *The Social Imaginary of Geographical Indicators in Contested Environments: The Politicized Heritage and the Racialized Landscapes of South African Rooibos Tea*, in THE SAGE HANDBOOK OF INTELLECTUAL PROPERTY 224, 225 (Mathew David & Deborah Halbert eds., 2014).

[11] *Id.*; Rosemary J. Coombe & Nicole Aylwin, *Bordering Diversity and Desire: Using Intellectual Property to Mark Place-based Products*, 43 ENV'T & PLAN. A: SOC'Y & SPACE 2027 (2011).

the Asian context, where traders are treated as if they are producers and constitute the most powerful actors in the value chain.[12] As Basole's fieldwork in the Banaras textile industry revealed, artisans see very little of the GI premium and the system does little to assist those facing destitution.[13] It is interpreted in a way that imposes outside notions of authenticity, prevents the community from innovating, and is biased toward distributing value toward merchants and traders.[14] GIs imposed from the top-down tend to favor more powerful actors. Benefits rarely trickle down to small producers or individual artisans; traders and master weavers with bargaining power in the supply chain are often the primary beneficiaries of increased revenues in a cottage industry in which it is very difficult for traditionally non-weaving castes to find any access. Consumers often have little or no idea of who the producer is, and producers have scant information about how their products are marketed.[15]

Such limitations of GIs in practice are not unique to the South Asian context. State-driven GI strategies that focus primarily upon increased productivity and export earnings tend to further deprive small producers and privilege industrial elites wherever they are introduced.[16] Even in the European context, experts caution against the general promotion of GIs and urge attention to their governance when assessing their capacities to propel equitable rural development.[17] The oldest appellations of origin were developed to protect aristocratic traditions and continue to reflect class-based privilege, concentrate control over governance in small elites, restrict the upward mobility of smallholders, discourage the formation of or supplant cooperatives, and entrench poor agricultural working conditions.[18] Many MICO regimes have reduced rather than increased local biological and cultural

---

[12] Gopalakrishnan, Nair & Babu, *supra* note 1.
[13] Amit Basole & Deepankar Basu, *Relations of Production and Modes of Surplus Extraction in India, Part-II Informal Industry*, 46 ECON. & POL. WKLY. 63 (2011).
[14] Amit Basole, *Authenticity, Innovation, and the Geographical Indication in an Artisanal Industry: The Case of the Banarasi Sari*, 18 J. WORLD INTELL. PROP. 127 (2015).
[15] Soumya Vinayan, *Intellectual Property Rights and the Handloom Sector: Challenges in Implementation of Geographical Indications Act*, 17 J. INTELL. PROP. RTS. 55 (2012).
[16] Coombe, Ives, & Huizenga, *supra* note 5, at 217.
[17] Elizabeth Barham, *Translating Terroir: The Global Challenge of French AOC Labelling*, 19 J. RURAL STUD. 127 (2003).
[18] *See* Daniel W. Gade, *Tradition, Territory, and Terroir in French Viniculture: Cassis, France, and Appellation Contrôlée*, 94 ANNALS ASS'N AM. GEOGRAPHERS 848 (2004); Warren Moran, *Rural Space as Intellectual Property*, 12 POL. GEOGRAPHY 263 (1993); Warren Moran, *The Wine Appellation as Territory in France and California*, 83 ANNALS ASS'N AM. GEOGRAPHERS 694 (1999).

diversity.[19] Moreover, the dominant social imaginary offered by proponents for GIs tends to be localized in activities of marketing, which do not merely misrepresent social realities but shape them, naturalizing hierarchical labor relations[20] and influencing the ways stakeholders come to understand their relationships to these products.[21] Although marketing strategies are ideally formulated with the input of various stakeholders in the supply chain, the most well-connected corporate producer bodies and owners of large agricultural holdings have the greatest influence, shaping these narratives in ways that reinforce their privileges. Rather than merely promoting unique differences that pre-exist them, "GIs are being cultivated to promote products, processes and methods traditional to places, and traditions are being cultivated to support these marketing vehicles."[22]

Given the diversity of current GI regimes, few generalizations about their promise or performance as a global category seem warranted without greater empirical study of the actual conditions governing their use. Local regulatory mechanisms need to be analyzed within a broader scope of inquiry that is attentive to local conditions of class, ethnicity, and gender. Most academic scholarship ignores the social relations between workers, landowners, producers, and the degree to which MICO institutions represent their respective interests. Few scholars studying GIs consider political movements for decolonization or postcolonial forms of emancipation. In the South and Southeast Asian context, we should consider the propensity of GI governance to challenge or to further entrench patterns of plantation agriculture, peasant dispossession, and the legacies of exploitative labor relations. In this chapter we show how current uses of MICOs encourage tendencies toward socio-economic marginalization, reinforce local divisions of labor, and obscure colonial patterns of landholding. If the World Intellectual Property Organization's development agenda is to have any meaning, we need to focus on MICOs as forms of local governance, and ask to what extent they might govern differently – to challenge rather than reinforce entrenched social hierarchies,[23] contribute to rights-based development,[24] or achieve social justice objectives.[25]

---

[19] See Aylwin & Coombe, *supra* note 3 (for these reasons the authors argue that rights-based sustainable development principles should guide the creation and governance of new MICOs).
[20] SARAH BESKY, THE DARJEELING DISTINCTION: LABOR AND JUSTICE ON FAIR-TRADE PLANTATIONS IN INDIA (2014).
[21] Paola Filippucci, *A French Place without a Cheese: Problems with Heritage and Identity in Northeastern France*, 44 FOCAAL-EUROPEAN J. ANTHROPOLOGY 72 (2004).
[22] Coombe, Ives, & Huizenga, *supra* note 5, at 214.
[23] Debarati Sen, *Fair Trade vs. Swaccha Vyāpār: Women's Activism and Transnational Justice Regimes in Darjeeling, India*, 40 FEMINIST STUD. 444 (2014).
[24] Aylwin & Coombe, *supra* note 3. [25] Coombe, Ives, & Huizenga, *supra* note 10.

We will first describe some of the ideological tendencies in MICO rationales and consider how a famous GI, Darjeeling Tea, is used to protect goods considered traditional to a region in India. We then provide some insight into contemporary Southeast Asian political ecology to show why MICOs and their governance should be considered matters of pressing global concern. Finally, we explore emerging politics, practices, and policies in value chain governance that might ground Asian MICOs in alternative norms to meet the needs of wider constituencies while advancing environmental as well as social justice objectives.

2 EXISTING LANDSCAPES OF GEOGRAPHICAL INDICATIONS: DARJEELING TEA

The Darjeeling Tea GI is widely celebrated as having extended IP-based justice to the Global South;[26] it was the first of India's now over 230 registered GIs.[27] There is no doubt that it has been a marketing success in raising export earnings. The Tea Board of India controls this GI as a form of national IP, designating select plantations as natural garden homes for a unique tea, based in a *terroir* constituted primarily, we would suggest, through tropes of enchantment. Anthropologist Sarah Besky collected hundreds of Tea Board papers like this one:

> What is it that makes the world's tea aficionados rush to Darjeeling during spring-time to "book" the first flush teas? The answer? ... Darjeeling Tea just happens ... To science, Darjeeling Tea is a strange phenomenon. To the faithful, it is a rare blessing. Thankfully, the Darjeeling Tea Estates have always lived by their faith-by humbly accepting this unique gift of nature and doing everything to retain its natural eloquence. So, Darjeeling tea, hand-plucked by local women with magician's fingers, withered, rolled and fermented in orthodox fashion, with the sole intention of bringing out the best in them.[28]

It is easy to dismiss such romanticism as mere advertising, but Besky draws our attention to the labor conditions that support it. So-called "Indian" Darjeeling

---

[26] Pradyot Ranjan Jena et al., *Geographical Indication Protection and Rural Livelihoods: Insights from India and Thailand*, 29 ASIAN-PAC. ECON. LITERATURE 174 (2015); Pradyot Ranjan Jena & Ulrike Grote, *Changing Institutions to Protect Regional Heritage: A Case for Geographical Indications in the Indian Agrifood Sector*, 28 DEV. POL'Y REV. 217 (2010).

[27] GI Registry Government of India, *State Wise Registration Details of G.I. Applications* (15 September 2003), http://ipindia.nic.in/girindia/treasures_protected/registered_GI_18November2015.pdf. For an up-to-date list of Indian GIs, see Intellectual Property India, *Geographical Indications Registry*, http://ipindia.nic.in/girindia/ (last visited 8 March 2016).

[28] BESKY, *supra* note 20, at 89.

Tea is picked nearly entirely by Nepali-speaking women, descendants of the indentured women from Nepal who brought this tea and their knowledge of its cultivation to a region that was incorporated into India in 1947. In the GI campaign, gendered, arduous, and exploitative industrial plantation toil (still locally disparaged as "coolie" labor) is erased, replaced by the craftwork of angelic guardians whose TEK is deployed in their gentle care of tea gardens – where they are naturally placed and affectively bound. To cite another Tea Board advertisement, "Perhaps it is the warmth of their touch which gives the brew such sweetness."[29]

This advertising imagery has a real impact on people's lives and livelihoods. Besky reminds us that Darjeeling Tea is understood as national cultural patrimony, intangible cultural heritage, and the basis for a new industry – tea tourism – in which women are disciplined to "perform" the smiling docility of the GI's social imaginary. These women make $1 a day, work sixty-hour weeks, and are tied to plantations by debt; they inherit rather than choose their jobs and are reliant upon plantation owners for housing, healthcare, schools, and access to subsistence plots on environmentally degraded lands. In neocolonial, patriarchal labor conditions, such widespread gendered representations warrant serious consideration. Do they improve or undermine workers' capacities to critique conditions of production or to articulate ways to transcend them? To the extent that such branding supports a new industry whose profitability is dependent upon meeting tourists' expectations, to what extent will the capacities of women to transform their less than idyllic working conditions be enhanced?

The GI region comprises eighty-seven plantations, populated by semi-bonded labor; many were revived by the GI. It is not co-extensive with the Darjeeling district of West Bengal, where the same tea is cultivated by Adivasis (tribal or indigenous peoples), who are wholly excluded from this new market. The indication also excludes Nepal's own smallholder co-operatives – viewed as imitators from whom Darjeeling needs to be protected.[30] Much of this tea is certified as fair trade, a practice that reproduces a patronizing narrative in which a Northern, modern, urban consumer savior provides an empowering lifeline for a Southern, traditional, impoverished, rural peasant.[31] Historically, fair trade certification disregarded disparities in gender, was not sympathetic to unions, and seemed to prefer peasant producers lacking any organization

---

[29] *Id.* at 98.
[30] Ironically, it is rumored that at least some of the "green leaf" that went into the processed tea was cheaper tea smuggled in from Adivasi co-operatives in Nepal. *See Id.* at 103.
[31] Lindsay Naylor, *"Some Are More Fair Than Others": Fair Trade Certification, Development, and North–South Subjects*, 31 AGRIC. & HUM. VALUES 273, 277–78 (2014).

other than co-operatives.[32] Instead of bringing Western consumers closer to workers in a relation of greater justice, the administration of the Darjeeling mark creates greater distance between the female tea pluckers and consumers – some of whom are tourists dressing up as smiling tea-pickers to mimic the Tea Board advertisements (!). The workers have new jobs to add to their toil – posing for pictures and singing for visitors – captive creatures in a practice they describe as "turning the plantation into a zoo."[33]

In neighboring smallholder plots, anthropologist Debarati Sen reports, Nepali tea pluckers also feel objectified:

> You know that smiling woman on that tea package is not us. It's nice to know people around the world care about us so much, but why now? Where were these people when we had no roads, when no one gave us loans, when we ate only stale rice? What can they do for us if they do not care about what we women want?[34]

These farmers criticize the nature of fair trade justice and empowerment because of its lack of support for their own efforts to improve their communities, contest local patriarchies, resist the domination of local middlemen, and engage in entrepreneurial activities to meet their family needs with dignity.

Historically, because these women were squatters on abandoned plantations, whose rights to the lands they worked were unrecognized, they could not access the state-subsidized, high-yielding Green Revolution technologies targeted for plantations. In short, they learned to cultivate illegal tea with manure and homemade compost, a tradition of knowledge born of poverty and necessity. When, in the 1990s, organic tea was newly valued in global markets, plantations were forced to give up chemical fertilizers; their productivity declined 30 per cent. To augment supplies, plantation managers made agreements with these illegal producers who were assisted by NGOs to register themselves and market their tea as "co-operatively produced" rather than become wholly subsumed under the plantation labels.

Although nearly all of this tea is farmed by women, the advent of global consumer interest prompted underemployed local men to seize these new opportunities, quickly assuming management of the co-operatives as middlemen with the new international agencies. Controlling the new profits, they invested these in ways that did not support or provide benefits to the women whose labors had sustained the organic production from which the community was now benefitting. Women's efforts to diversify the local economy received no

---

[32] Eileen Davenport & Will Low, *The Labour behind the (Fair Trade) Label*, 8 CRITICAL PERSP. ON INT'L BUS. 329 (2012).
[33] BESKY, *supra* note 20, at 111.   [34] Sen, *supra* note 23, at 444.

assistance and their organic quality-control work attracts no compensation. The men do not use any part of the fair trade premium to support female entrepreneurial activities; indeed, women are sexually shamed for engaging in such immodest work. Nevertheless, they still consider themselves far better off than the female plantation workers whose celebrated labor supports the GI.

Certification bodies, then, need to attend to the local dynamics that affect exclusion and marginalization. Fair trade certification still has a long way to go in making all stages in value chains transparent; labor relations are notoriously difficult to discern and improve.[35] A heated global debate has emerged in which Fair Trade USA (which wants to expand fair trade's certification to more plantations) has splintered off from the Fair Trade Labelling Organizations International (FLO). The move has been criticized by the group Equal Exchange as a dilution of the fair trade ethos because it enables large corporations such as Nestlé and Starbucks to represent more of their products as ethically produced.[36] The distinction between smallholders and plantations, however, is only one way of addressing the "proper laboring subject of fair trade."[37] Fair trade was originally an agricultural justice movement forged through "bottom-up partnerships between Latin American [smallholder] coffee producers and Northern activists."[38] In the Indian tea industry, however, it was implemented in a largely top-down fashion.[39] Fair trade in Asia is not linked to political struggles amongst plantation workers, and neglects the colonial legacies of a feudal order in which large holdings with absentee owners produced largely non-indigenous crops for colonial elites with the inadequately compensated labor of racialized and socially marginalized peoples.[40]

If inclusion of plantation-based goods in fair trade incorporates these goods into a market, it does little to provide any form of political recognition for plantation laborers. It appears to exclude them into the "global community of solidarity and interdependence" between producers and consumers that the fair trade movement propounds as an alternative to global capitalism.[41]

---

[35] Daniel Berliner et al., *Governing Global Supply Chains: What We Know (and Don't) about Improving Labor Rights and Working Conditions*, 11 ANN. REV. L. & SOC'Y 193 (2015).

[36] Sarah Besky, *Agricultural Justice, Abnormal Justice? An Analysis of Fair Trade's Plantation Problem*, 47 ANTIPODE 114 (2015). Darjeeling Tea plantations were amongst the first in the world to be fair trade certified, whereas "Equal Exchange sells Darjeeling tea grown only on cooperatives" arguing that it better achieves justice for workers.

[37] *Id.* at 1142.   [38] *Id.*   [39] *Id.*

[40] Phyllis Robinson, *Transforming the Tea Industry: From Plantations to a Small-Farmer Model*, SMALL FARMERS BIG CHANGE (17 February 2010), http://smallfarmersbigchange.coop/2010/02/17/transforming-the-tea-industry-from-plantations-to-a-small-farmer-model-2/.

[41] *Id.* at 1144 (citing JOHN BOWES, THE FAIR TRADE REVOLUTION (London: Pluto Press, 2011); APRIL LINTON, FAIR TRADE FROM THE GROUND UP: NEW MARKETS FOR SOCIAL JUSTICE

Plantation workers are denied representation and voice in the framing of transnational justice by Fair Trade USA, which insists upon describing industrial agricultural enterprises as "farms" to avoid issues of land tenure and labor organization.[42] Equal Exchange ignores the historical forces which have divided peoples into those who have the opportunity as landholders to cultivate crops and co-operativize, and those whose political marginalization was more deeply entrenched by colonial rule, while ignoring gender and ethnicity:

> [I]n Darjeeling[,] Nepali tea pluckers, like ethnically-marked plantation and large farm workers in other parts of the world, are multiply oppressed. As plantation workers, many lack full access to participation in a global economic order. As Nepalis within India, all struggle for recognition as well as full domestic political representation.[43]

Both co-operative and plantation workers are linked as much by their shared struggle for representation within the Indian state as by their experience of economic hardship.[44] Fair trade certification evades these political struggles and thereby "ignores – and by extension reinforces – the deep-seated ethnic marginalization that has sustained the Darjeeling tea industry for nearly 180 years."[45] Such selective political attention, however, is not necessary to certification systems; alternative forms of transnational solidarity are possible. In order to address other forms of oppression based on cultural, linguistic, ethnic, and gender identity, however, GIs must attend to the ways in which people make their own claims and give voice to their needs. As we shall explore, this concern with representation and voice is precisely the way in which new MICOs are evolving. In the meantime, hundreds of thousands of people across Asia are being pushed into plantation agriculture under conditions that promise to exacerbate climate change, rural insecurity, and human rights abuses.

3 THE CRISIS OF BIOCULTURAL DIVERSITY IN SOUTHEAST ASIAN POLITICAL ECOLOGY

A great tract of Earth is on fire. It looks as you might imagine hell to be. The air has turned ochre: visibility in some cities has been reduced to 30 metres. Children are being prepared for evacuation in warships; already some have choked to death. Species

---

(Seattle: University of Washington Press, 2012); SARAH LYON & MARK MOBERG, FAIR TRADE AND SOCIAL JUSTICE: GLOBAL ETHNOGRAPHIES (New York: NYU Press, 2010)).

[42] Equal Exchange similarly downplays workers in the factories that process tea, even as it champions small farmers and co-operatives.
[43] Besky, *supra* note 36 at 1152.   [44] Id.   [45] Id. at 1151.

are going up in smoke at an untold rate. It is almost certainly the greatest environmental disaster of the 21st century ... Fire is raging across the 5,000km length of Indonesia ... currently producing more carbon dioxide than the US economy. And in three weeks the fires have released more CO_2 than the annual emissions of Germany ... Orangutans, clouded leopards ... the Sumatran tiger ... are among the threatened species being driven from much of their range ... After the last great conflagration, in 1997, there was a missing cohort in Indonesia of 15,000 children under the age of three, attributed to air pollution. This, it seems, is worse ... It's not just the trees that are burning. It is the land itself. Much of the forest sits on great domes of peat ... the fires ... smoulder for weeks, sometimes months, releasing clouds of methane, carbon monoxide, ozone and exotic gases such as ammonium cyanide.[46]

3.1 Deforestation, Plantation Agriculture, and the Decline of Swidden Cultivation

Palm oil may be the largest cause of deforestation, land-grabbing, and labor exploitation in the world. It permeates our food chain; it is in almost half of all supermarket products.[47] Indigenous peoples and communities inhabit the frontlines of palm oil expansion; they face loss of lands, threats to security, and marginal economic benefits from a new monoculture plantation economy, powered by global corporate demand for the most widely consumed vegetable oil on the planet.[48] For years, the palm oil sector has manifested incontrovertible evidence of the widespread loss of forests, burning of peatlands, stealing of community lands, and the use of child and slave labor.

The expansion of palm oil plantations in Indonesia is part of a massive increase in commercial agriculture across upland Southeast Asia. Swidden agriculture, also known as shifting cultivation,[49] is the traditional land use system in this region; until recently it was the most extensive

---

[46] George Monbiot, *Indonesia is Burning. So Why Is the World Looking Away?* THE GUARDIAN (30 October 2015), www.theguardian.com/commentisfree/2015/oct/30/indonesia-fires-disaster-21st-century-world-media.

[47] Rainforest Action Network, *Testing Commitments to Cut Conflict Palm Oil. 2015: The Year to Drive Change – Progress Report* https://d3n8a8pro7vhmx.cloudfront.net/rainforestactionnetwork/pages/5884/attachments/original/1435772500/RAN_TESTING_COMMITMENTS_2015_FINAL.pdf?1435772500 (last visited 9 March 2016).

[48] Id.

[49] Alan D. Ziegler et al., *Recognizing Contemporary Roles of Swidden Agriculture in Transforming Landscape of Southeast Asia*, 25 CONSERVATION BIOLOGY 846 at 846 (2010) (citing Ole Mertz et al., *Swidden Change in Southeast Asia: Understanding Causes and Consequences*, 37 HUM. ECOLOGY 259 (2009)).

landscape in Southeast Asia.[50] Rapid transitions in land use in the humid tropical uplands of Southeast Asia are replacing swidden agriculture and displacing its traditional practitioners.[51] Hundreds of forest species, managed by communities dependent upon them for subsistence/sustenance and marketable products, may also be at risk.

Governments denounce swiddening, associating it with deforestation, inefficient carbon sequestration, and degradation of soil and water resources.[52] However, these rotational crop systems "include a wide range of land use and management practices that affect carbon cycling differently,"[53] providing various kinds of regrowth,[54] with fallows offsetting planting-phase CO_2 emissions.[55] Governments have never, however, measured impacts across the landscapes people cultivate over time.[56] Swiddening is difficult to measure because it is represented by a large number of distinct landscape features, which may be in transition and mistaken for other land uses, with swidden fallows considered to be "wasteland/abandoned/unused" or

---

[50] Committee on Sustainable Agriculture and the Environment in the Humid Tropics, NATIONAL RESEARCH COUNCIL (U.S.) (eds.), SUSTAINABLE AGRICULTURE AND THE ENVIRONMENT IN THE HUMID TROPICS (Washington: National Academy Press, 1993). DOI: 10.17226/1985; Dietrich Schmidt-Vogt et al., *An Assessment of Trends in the Extent of Swidden in Southeast Asia*, 37 HUM. ECOLOGY 269 (2009).

[51] Janice Alcorn & Antoinette G. Royo, *Best REDD Scenario: Reducing Climate Change in Alliance with Swidden Communities and Indigenous Peoples in Southeast Asia*, in SHIFTING CULTIVATION AND ENVIRONMENTAL CHANGE: INDIGENOUS PEOPLE, AGRICULTURE AND FOREST CONSERVATION 289–306 (Malcolm F. Cains ed., 2015).

[52] Jefferson Fox et al., *Policies, Political Economy and Swidden in Southeast Asia*, 37 HUM. ECOLOGY 305 (2009), available at http://link.springer.com/article/10.1007%2Fs10745-009-9240-7. See also, Mertz, supra note 49.

[53] Jefferson Fox, J. C. Castella, & A.D. Ziegler, *Swidden, Rubber and Carbon: Can REDD+ Work for People and the Environment in Montane Mainland Southeast Asia?* (CCAFS Working Paper No. 9, 2011), available at www.ccafs.cgiar.org.

[54] Biomass and carbon stocks in swidden systems change dramatically between the planting and mature fallow phases, with forms of regrowth ranging from grasslands to mature secondary forests. Gabriela Vargas-Cetina, supra note 19 (citing Bruun et al., supra note 52; Kanok Rerkasem et al., *Consequences of Swidden Transitions for Crop and Fallow Biodiversity in Southeast Asia*, 37 HUM. ECOLOGY 347 (2009).

[55] Scientists have shown that CO_2 originally resulting from the burning phase is or may be offset by carbon sequestered during the fallow phases and that longer fallows may be optimal. T. B. Bruun et al., *Environmental Consequences of the Demise of Shifting Cultivation in Southeast Asia*, 37 HUM. ECOLOGY 347 (2009).

[56] Mertz supra note 49. H. J. GEIST & E. F. LAMBIN, WHAT DRIVES TROPICAL DEFORESTATION? A META-ANALYSIS OF PROXIMATE AND UNDERLYING CAUSES OF DEFORESTATION BASED ON SUBNATIONAL CASE STUDY EVIDENCE (LUCC International Project Office, 2001); Tuisem Shimrah, K. S. Rao, & K. G. Saxena, *The Shifting Agricultural System (Jhum) and Strategies for Sustainable Agroecosystems in Northeast India*, 39 AGROECOLOGY & SUSTAINABLE FOOD SYSTEMS 1154 (2015).

"residual/miscellaneous,"[57] rather than recognized as part of an agricultural system. Climate change mitigation policy has made research into these systems imperative because they are rapidly disappearing in mountain regions of Asia as farmers are pushed by national policies and pulled by market forces toward high-value commercial crops, especially rubber and oil palm.[58]

Long before swiddens were denigrated as environmentally destructive,[59] they were discouraged and their cultivators often criminalized throughout South and Southeast Asia.[60] Most colonial and postcolonial states engaged in coercive efforts to eradicate swiddening as economically inefficient and socially uncivilized. If scientific research no longer supports these prejudices,[61] swiddening's historical practitioners continue to bear stigma.

[57] Christine Padoch et al., *The Demise of Swidden in Southeast Asia? Local Realities and Regional Ambiguities*, 107 DANISH J. OF GEOGRAPHY 29, 32 (2007).
[58] Fox, Castella, & Ziegler, *supra* note 53.
[59] Wolfram Dressler & Juan Puhlin, *The Shifting Ground of Swidden Agriculture on Palawan Island, the Philippines*, 27 AGRIC. & HUM. VALUES 445 (2010).
[60] Bram Büscher & Wolfram Dressler, *Commodity Conservation: The Restructuring of Community Conservation in South Africa and the Philippines*, 43 GEOFORUM 367 (2012); Fox et al., *supra* note 52; Jonathan C. Newby et al., *Smallholder Teak and Agrarian Change in Northern Laos*, 11 SMALL SCALE FORESTRY 27 (2011); Peter Vandergeest & Nancy Peluso, *Political Ecologies of War and Forests: Counterinsurgencies and the Making of National Natures*, 101 ANNALS ASS'N AM. GEOGRAPHERS 587 (2011); in Cambodia, the dominant development paradigm stressed principles of civilization and modernity in which upland peoples were at best bearers of culture that was nostalgically reified, or at worst, primitive relics of another era in need of assimilation. See Neal B. Keating, *Kuy Alterities: The Struggle to Conceptualise and Claim Indigenous Land Rights in Neoliberal Cambodia*, 54 ASIA PAC. VIEWPOINT 309 (2013); Jonathan Padwe, *Highlands of History: Indigenous Identity and its Antecedents in Cambodia*, 54 ASIA PAC. VIEWPOINT 282 (2013); in Vietnam, swidden agriculture was the feature that the central government used to identify ethnic minorities as being "at the starting point of the evolutionary ladder." Rob A. Cramb et al., *Swidden Transformations and Rural Livelihoods in Southeast Asia*, 37 HUM. ECOLOGY 323, 339 (2009) (citing T. D. NGUYEN, CULTURE, SOCIETY AND PEOPLE IN THE CENTRAL HIGHLANDS (Ho Chi Minh City: Social Science Press, 2005). See generally, Asian Indigenous Peoples Pact, *REDD+ Implementation in Asia and the Concerns of Indigenous Peoples* (Chiang Mai, Thailand, International Working Group for Indigenous Affairs, 2011), AIPP, www.iwgia.org /iwgia_files_publications_files/0654_REDD_Plus_Implementation_in_Asia_and_the_Conc erns_of_Indigenous_Peoples.pdf (last visited 9 March 2016). State foresters and resource managers continued to entertain colonial ideologies that considered swiddening to involve unplanned indiscriminate slashing and burning, misunderstanding its systemic nature and integration with local culture and social structure. See MALCOLM F. CAIRNS, VOICES FROM THE FOREST: INTEGRATING INDIGENOUS KNOWLEDGE INTO SUSTAINABLE UPLAND FARMING (2007).
[61] Asia Indigenous People Pact & International Working Group for Indigenous Affairs, *Shifting Cultivation, Livelihood and Food Security: New and Old Challenges for Indigenous Peoples in Asia*, AIPP & IWGIA, www.iwgia.org/iwgia_files_publications_files/0694_AIPPShifting_cult ivation_livelihoodfood_security.pdf (last visited 9 March 2016); Alcorn & Royo *supra* note 51; Dietrich Schmidt-Vogt, *Second Thoughts on Secondary Forests: Can Swidden Cultivation be*

Widely vilified, considered primitive and obstacles to progress, they have faced policies of harassment, eviction, and sedentarization throughout Southeast Asia.[62] In the Philippines, for example, the Spanish used the Regalian Doctrine to categorize and divide the nation into two social groups: Christians who, being closer to God, were the productive social class that occupied lowlands with title; and a tribal pagan minority who, by avoiding proselytization, were considered primitive uplanders occupying public domain without title.[63]

There continue to be clear political and strategic advantages for states in differentiating between agricultural and forest lands; rights of tenure were attached to the former while the latter was claimed as state domain. By misrecognizing fallows and secondary forests of swidden agriculture as forest terrain, not only could these be described as environmentally degraded, but they could also be seized by states and opened up to migrant farmers for permanent agriculture, while swiddeners were criminalized for further cultivating them.[64] Across Asia swiddeners lost lands to illegal logging, livestock grazing, long-term cultivation of annual crops, greenhouse horticulture, coercive development projects, and, most recently, monoculture tree plantations.[65] Their antagonists insist upon the greater productivity and environmental sustainability of these new practices despite considerable evidence to the contrary.[66]

Swiddeners in the Philippines were the first to align with NGOs and join global social movements pressing for land and livelihood rights as indigenous peoples with cultural identities tied to these agroforestry systems.[67] Regional groups now press for such recognition.[68] The Asian Indigenous Peoples' Pact

---

Compatible with Conservation?, in SHIFTING CULTIVATION AND ENVIRONMENTAL CHANGE: INDIGENOUS PEOPLE, AGRICULTURE AND FOREST CONSERVATION 388–40 (Malcolm F. Cains ed., 2015); Herwasono Soedjito, *Shifting Cultivators, Curators of Forests and Conservators of Biodiversity: The Dayak of East Kalimantan, Indonesia*, in SHIFTING CULTIVATION AND ENVIRONMENTAL CHANGE: INDIGENOUS PEOPLE, AGRICULTURE AND FOREST CONSERVATION 420–48 (Malcolm F. Cains ed., 2015).

[62] Fox et al., *supra* note 52. [63] *Id.* at 445–48.
[64] Carol Colfer, Janice Alcorn, & Diane Russell, *Swidden and Fallows*, in SHIFTING CULTIVATION AND ENVIRONMENTAL CHANGE: INDIGENOUS PEOPLE, AGRICULTURE AND FOREST CONSERVATION 62, 63–64 (Malcolm F. Cains ed., 2015).
[65] Schmidt-Vogt et al., *supra* note 50; Alcorn & Royo *supra* note 51; MARCUS COLCHESTER, PALM OIL AND INDIGENOUS PEOPLE IN SOUTHEAST ASIA (2011); Fox et al., *supra* note 52.
[66] Alan D. Ziegler et al., *Environmental Consequences of the Demise in Swidden Agriculture in Southeast Asia: Hydrology and Geomorphology*, 37 HUM. ECOLOGY 361 (2009).
[67] Alcorn & Royo, *supra* note 51, at 292.
[68] See longer discussion in Rosemary J. Coombe, S. Ali Malik, & Marc Griebel, *Culturalized Properties in Neoliberal Futures: Frontiers of Dispossession and Indigenous Assertion*, in

(AIPP) estimates that close to two-thirds of the world's 370 million indigenous peoples are in Asia, and that between 14 and 34 million of these groups practice shifting cultivation in Southeast Asia.[69] Increasingly, they work with international environmental organizations to document the TK of swiddeners and the ecosystem services (ecoservices) they deliver. Swiddening is practiced largely by ethnic minorities, historically disparaged as hill tribes; it has been suggested that "the notion of indigeneity took shape as a counter-discourse intended to refute the claim that shifting cultivators were forest destroyers."[70] Regional indigenous organizations are now supported by transnational environmental and food security organizations alarmed by the environmental and social consequences of intensified agriculture.[71] They argue that shifting cultivation is important to local food security and nutrition, closely tied to ritual cycles, and constitutive of local cultural identities; in 2014, the United Nations Food and Agriculture Organization (FAO) Assistant Director General and Regional Representative for Asia and the Pacific asserted that swidden agriculture was the cultural heritage of indigenous communities.[72] Although many shifting cultivators may choose to transition to intensive agricultural production, others want to maintain swiddens, not only for the security they provide against landlessness,[73] but because their decline undermines collective decision-making, customary land claims, and community governance.[74]

Many indigenous farmers willingly adopt new forms of agriculture, but others have little choice; although earlier shifts to smallholder commercial agriculture appear to have been voluntary, the recent rise of commercial estates (particularly in Malaysia, Indonesia, and the Philippines) has led to a widespread, rapid, and often brutal demise of this agroforestry system[75] with

---

INTELLECTUAL PROPERTY, CULTURAL PROPERTY, AND INTANGIBLE CULTURAL HERITAGE (Christoph Antons & William Logan eds., 2017).

[69] AIPP & IWGIA, *supra* note 61, at 2.

[70] DEREK HALL, PHILIP HIRSCH, & TANIA MURRAY LI, POWERS OF EXCLUSION: LAND DILEMMAS IN SOUTHEAST ASIA 172 (2011).

[71] In 2014, for example, under the sponsorship of the FAO, the Norwegian Rainforest Foundation, and the Danish Ministry of Foreign Affairs, the AIPP gathered representatives from Southeast Asia to address the value of swidden systems.

[72] CHRISTIAN ERNI (ED.), SHIFTING CULTIVATION, LIVELIHOOD AND FOOD SECURITY: NEW AND OLD CHALLENGES FOR INDIGENOUS PEOPLES IN ASIA (2015), *available at* www.fao.org/3/a-i4580e.pdf.

[73] Cramb et al., *supra* note 60, at 332.   [74] *Id.*

[75] *Id.* at 328. *See* ZAHARI ZEN, COLIN BARLOW, & RIA GONDOWARSITO, OIL PALM IN INDONESIAN SOCIO-ECONOMIC IMPROVEMENT: A REVIEW OF OPTIONS (Canberra: Department of Economics, Research School of Pacific and Asian Studies, Australian National University Working Paper 11/2005, 2005), *available at* http://rspas.anu.edu.au/economics/publish/papers/wp2005/wp-econ-2005-11.pdf; John F. McCarthy & Rob A. Cramb, *Policy Narratives, Landholder Engagement, and Oil Palm Expansion on the Malaysian and*

significant local and global environmental consequences. Policies promoting industrialized agriculture and timber farming in Asia are responsible for accelerating rates of deforestation[76] and raising greenhouse gas emissions[77] by reducing total carbon stocks.[78] Increases in agricultural productivity have generated high rates of erosion and enhanced probability of landslides, sedimentation in rivers, declines in water quality, and stream desiccation caused by irrigation. When monoculture plantations are planted with non-native species at relatively high latitudes and elevations, water shortages occur.[79] In Asia, the multiple-use forest reserves where swidden communities reside are more effective at fire prevention than other so-called protected areas, suggesting that swidden demise and regional conflagration are integrally related.[80]

3.2 Undermining Indigenous Livelihood Security and Ecosystem Services

Numerous studies show swiddening to be a rational, economical, and environmental choice for resource-poor farmers, providing ecoservices in hydrology, biodiversity, and carbon storage that may help to mitigate climate change.[81] Swiddening requires relatively large forested landscapes and affords

Indonesian Frontiers, 175 THE GEOGRAPHICAL J. 112 (2009); Colfer, Alcorn, & Russell, *supra* note 64; Yurdi L. Yasmi, Lisa Kelley, & Thomas Enters, *Forest Conflict in Asia and the Role of Collective Action in its Management* CAPRi, Working Paper No. 102, 2010); MARCUS COLCHESTER & SOPHIE CHAO, CONFLICT OR CONSENT? THE OIL PALM SECTOR AT A CROSSROADS (2013), *available at* www.forestpeoples.org/topics/palm-oil-rspo/publication/2013/conflict-or-consent-oil-palm-sector-crossroads.

[76] Jonah Busch et al., *Structuring Economic Incentives to Reduce Emissions from Deforestation within Indonesia*, 109 PROC. NAT'L ACAD. SCI. 1062, 1063 (2012).

[77] Alessandro Baccini et al., *Estimated Carbon Dioxide Emissions from Tropical Deforestation Improved by Carbon-Density Maps*, 2 NATURE CLIMATE CHANGE 185 (2012).

[78] Studies have shown aboveground carbon declining more than 90 per cent when swidden systems with long fallow periods are replaced by rotational systems with short fallow periods or by continuous cycles of annual crops, and reductions of soil organic carbon from 10 percent to 40 percent resulting from the conversion to continuous annual agriculture with the largest declines associated with plantations. See Bruun et al., *supra* note 55, at 379.

[79] Roy C. Sidle et al., *Erosion Processes in Steep Terrain – Truths, Myths and Uncertainties Related to Forest Management in Southeast Asia* (2006) 224 FOREST ECOLOGY & MGMT. 199; Alan D. Ziegler et al., *supra* note 69; Maite Guardiola-Claramonte et al., *Local Hydrologic Effects of Introducing Non-native Vegetation in a Tropical Catchment*, 1 ECOHYDROLOGY 13 (2008); Maite Guardiola-Claramonte et al., *Modeling Basin-Scale Hydrologic Effects of Rubber (Hevea brasiliensis) in a Tropical Catchment*, 3 ECOHYDROLOGY 306 (2010); Jane Qui, *Where the Rubber Meets the Garden*, 457 NATURE 246 (2009).

[80] Andrew Nelson & Kenneth M. Chomitz, *Effectiveness of Strict vs. Multiple Use Protected Areas in Reducing Tropical Forest Fires: A Global Analysis Using Matching Methods*, PLoS ONE (16 August 2011), http://journals.plos.org/plosone/article?id=10.1371/journal.pone.0022722.

[81] Bruun et al., *supra* note 55; Cramb et al., *supra* note 60.

lower short-term economic return, but provides benefits that permanent agriculture does not. Biodiversity benefits under swidden are greater than monoculture plantations or other agroforestry options;[82] not only maintaining, but increasing biodiversity in some regions, as secondary succession[83] in swidden fallows provides diverse habitats and preserves genetic resources.[84] Shifting cultivation also maintains a diversity of human food sources[85] and plant species, with a variety of local uses,[86] as evidence throughout the region indicates.[87] Even farmers who undertake commercial farming are reluctant to abandon swiddens because they function as important social safety nets against market fluctuations, climate shifts, forest fires, encroachments from migrants, and logging.[88] Few swidden households in the region have the asset base that the new agriculture demands or access to the land, credit, and networks needed for maintaining intensified production.[89] Although commercial agriculture raises the income of former swidden farmers, their vulnerability increases with specialization, leaving them indebted and pushing them into wage labor. Some peoples continue to uphold swidden practices because they consider it part of their cultural identity;[90] others find new markets for swidden crops. Nearly all hold significant agricultural TEK, the loss of which

---

[82] Soil fertility, plant biomass, and species richness of plants may decline over time in swidden systems, but maintenance of lengthy fallow and short cropping periods both slow this decline and regenerate secondary forests. See Fox et al., *supra* note 52, at 323 (internal citations omitted).

[83] Secondary succession occurs after an ecosystem has been disturbed and plant species succeed one another. Soedjito, *supra* note 61, at 421, 423.

[84] The diversity of fallows provides microenvironments that enable a greater variety of plant and animal species than a more uniform forest or a farming environment could afford. It has been estimated that demographic density would have to be multiplied at least five times before showing any significant modification to the value of biodiversity or of ecosystem functions in some swidden regions. See Laurent Chazee, *Valuation and Management of Forest Ecosystem Services: A Skill Well Exercised by the Forest People of Upper Nam Theun, Lao P.D.R in* SHIFTING CULTIVATION AND ENVIRONMENTAL CHANGE: INDIGENOUS PEOPLE, AGRICULTURE AND FOREST CONSERVATION 559–76 (Malcolm F. Cains ed., 2015).

[85] Christine Padoch & Miguel Pinedo-Vasquez, *Saving Slash and Burn to Save Biodiversity*, 42 BIOTROPICA 550 (2010).

[86] Schmidt-Vogt, *supra* note 61. These include food, medicine, textile fibres, biofuel, handicrafts, and construction.

[87] Rerkasem et al., *supra* note 54; Shimrah, Rao, & Saxena, *supra* note 56; Janet Sturgeon, *Transformation of a Landscape: Shifting Cultivation, Biodiversity and Tea in* SHIFTING CULTIVATION AND ENVIRONMENTAL CHANGE: INDIGENOUS PEOPLE, AGRICULTURE AND FOREST CONSERVATION 850–60 (Malcolm F. Cains ed., 2015).

[88] Cramb et al., *supra* note 60, at 337–38; Colfer, Alcorn, & Russell, *supra* note 64, at 71; Malcolm Cairns & Harold Brookfield, *Composite Farming Systems in an Era of Change: Nagaland, Northeast India*, 52 ASIA PAC. VIEWPOINT 56 (2011).

[89] See Dressler & Puhlin, *supra* note 59, at 454.   [90] *Id.* at 456.

the global community sought to avoid when the Convention on Biodiversity (CBD) recognized the significance of local communities' knowledge, innovation, and practices in preserving biodiversity and maintaining genetic resources.

The landscape and species diversity that swiddening maintains contrasts starkly with the changes in land use being encouraged by or pressed upon peoples across Southeast Asia; plantation agriculture, particularly, results in deteriorated soil quality.[91] Nearly all alternative land-use scenarios proposed in the region produce more decreased stocks of soil organic carbon and fewer ecoservices than provided by swiddens.[92] Nonetheless, "global forest governance initiatives and national governments continue to press for the replacement of swidden with other land uses, such as monocrops considered to be better for carbon and livelihood outcomes."[93] Scientific debates are ongoing, but bring little relief or political leverage to peoples dispossessed from these traditional agroforestry systems. Many commentators propose territorial solutions based on park protection that recognize synergistic linkages between biological and cultural diversity, which became apparent when the criminalization of indigenous agriculture in many areas simultaneously facilitated both detribalization and the erosion of culturally rooted resource management practices.[94] Nonetheless, new models are emerging for recognizing

---

[91] Bruun et al., *supra* note 55, at 381–83.

[92] Maintaining swidden systems with long fallows provides greater benefits in terms of providing carbon absorption, hydrological properties, reducing soil erosion, enhancing floral diversity, and supporting soil nutrient cycling than monocropping, annual crop rotations, or protected forests. See Wolfram Dressler et al., *Examining How Long Fallow Swidden Systems Impact upon Livelihood and Ecosystem Services Outcomes Compared with Alternative Land-Uses in the Uplands of Southeast Asia*, 7 J. DEV. EFFECTIVENESS 1 (2015); Ole Mertz et al., *The Last Swiddens of Sarawak, Malaysia*, 41 HUM. ECOLOGY 109 (2013); Christine Padoch & Terry C. H. Sunderland, *Managing Landscapes for Greater Food Security and Improved Livelihoods*, 64 UNASYLVA 3 (2013); Cornelia Hett et al., *A Landscape Mosaics Approach for Characterizing Swidden Systems from a REDD+ Perspective*, 32 APPLIED GEOGRAPHY 608 (2012).

[93] Given the range of ecosystem services that swiddeners perform, consideration was given to compensating communities in REDD+ climate negotiations; new ways of valuing swiddens are considered imperative. The concept of ecosystem services is a neoliberal market-based vehicle in which external beneficiaries of environmental services would remunerate local communities who manage ecosystems so as to deliver those services. It is largely rejected by activists and scholars who believe that payments meant for communities are likely to be expropriated if they are administered by Asian states and such a scheme is likely to be used as an opportunity for states to craft new pretexts for enabling corporate landgrabbing. See Delphine Marie-Vivien et al., *Trademarks, Geographical Indications and Environmental Labelling to Promote Biodiversity: The Case of Agroforestry Coffee in India*, 32 DEV. POL'Y REV. 379 (2014).

[94] Malcolm F. Cairns, *Ancestral Domain and National Park Protection: A Logical Union? A Case Study of the Mt. Kitangland Range National Park, Bukidnon, Philippines*, in SHIFTING

biocultural heritage as an aspect of what are increasingly known as biocultural rights.[95]

3.3 Women's TEK in Swidden Agriculture

The contribution of Asian women in ensuring household economy and nutritional security through their management of natural resources has only recently become the subject of scholarly research.[96] Elderly women hold encyclopedic TEK derived from years of informal experimentation with biodiversity.[97] In many mountainous ecosystems, women's lifelong need for location-specific knowledge makes them "the backbone of food, medicinal, and nutritional security."[98] Theoretically, men and women have equal needs and opportunities to conserve biocultural diversity for sustaining livelihoods in the face of socio-economic, agricultural, and climate change,[99] but women face greater challenges to maintain livelihoods in shifting mountain ecosystems.[100] Policy makers and planners in Southeast Asia seldom consider

---

CULTIVATION AND ENVIRONMENTAL CHANGE: INDIGENOUS PEOPLE, AGRICULTURE AND FOREST CONSERVATION 598–99 (Malcolm F. Cains ed., 2015).

[95] SANJAY KABIR BAVIKATTE, STEWARDING THE EARTH: RETHINKING PROPERTY AND THE EMERGENCE OF BIOCULTURAL RIGHTS (2014).

[96] Fikram Berkes & Nancy J. Turner, *Knowledge, Learning and the Evolution of Conservation Practice for Social–Ecological System Resilience*, 34 HUM. ECOLOGY 479 (2006); Ranjay K. Singh, Jules N. Pretty, & Sarah Pilgrim, *Traditional Knowledge and Biocultural Diversity: Learning from Tribal Communities for Sustainable Development in Northeast India*, 53 J. ENV'T & PLAN. MGMT. 511 (2010); Carol J. Pierce Colfer et al., *Gender Analysis: Shifting Cultivation and Indigenous People*, in SHIFTING CULTIVATION AND ENVIRONMENTAL CHANGE: INDIGENOUS PEOPLE, AGRICULTURE AND FOREST CONSERVATION 920–57 (Malcolm F. Cains ed., 2015).

[97] Honey Bee, *A Union for a Century* CENTENARIAN (July 2012), www.sristi.org/hbnew/files/ce netenarian/khapriben-chotiyabhai-rathwa-english.pdf. Honey Bee, *The Age of Motorcycles, Medicines, and Electricity*, CENTENARIAN (July 2012), www.sristi.org/hbnew/files/cenetenar ian/khapriben-chotiyabhai-rathwa-english.pdf.

[98] Ranjay K. Singh, Orik Rallen, & Egul Padung, *Elderly Adi Women of Arunachal Pradesh: Living Encyclopedia and Cultural Refugia in Biodiversity Conservation of the Eastern Himalaya, India*, 52 ENVTL. MGMT 712, 713 (2013) (citing Tara Devi Dhakal & Brigitte Leduc, *Women's Role in Biodiversity Management in the Himalayas*, in GENDER PERSPECTIVES IN MOUNTAIN DEVELOPMENT: NEW CHALLENGES AND INNOVATIVE APPROACHES 16–17 (2013).

[99] Michael Kollmair, *Challenges and Opportunities for Women in the Changing Himalayas*, in GENDER PERSPECTIVES IN MOUNTAIN DEVELOPMENT: NEW CHALLENGES AND INNOVATIVE APPROACHES 2–4 (2010).

[100] MANOHARA KHADKA & RITU VERMA, GENDER AND BIODIVERSITY MANAGEMENT IN THE GREATER HIMALAYAS TOWARDS EQUITABLE MOUNTAIN DEVELOPMENT (2012), *available at* www.cbd.int/undb/countries/np/undb-np-icimod-gender.pdf.

women's knowledge and experience in devising policies for biodiversity conservation at the ecosystem level.[101]

Women play key roles in rice cultivation, seed selection, conservation of vegetable crops, and the use and storage of produce; they are responsible for agricultural innovations dependent upon systematic observation, careful experimentation, and adaptation. Historically they had considerable autonomy and greater sexual freedom, characteristics "interpreted as indications of depravity by dominant groups," which reinforced notions that swiddeners were "primitive" – the ultimate "others" whose agricultural practices were irrational and in need of reform.[102] Negative attitudes toward women's agricultural work contributed to the generalized regional disapproval of swidden systems. In rice-growing swidden regions of Borneo, Sarawak, Java, Kalimantan, Laos, Thailand, and Nepal, women were active cultivators who led the harvesting rituals. They appear to have dominated the collection and trade of non-timber forest products in the fallows from which they have been dispossessed.

Moving into monocropping deprives women of access to resources necessary for maintaining an adequate living, forcing them to travel further and work much harder to provide food and fuel for their families and livestock. The TEK of shifting cultivation in South and Southeast Asia is increasingly held by women resisting industrial agriculture or maintaining swiddening instead of, or alongside, commercial crop activity. Often, only elderly women are left to safeguard and transmit swidden-related rituals and practices,[103] which are likely to disappear if their values are no longer appreciated. Asian indigenous peoples' organizations concerned about the decline of swidden cultivation emphasize the key role of women's TEK and the need to encourage its transmission.[104] In addition to better support for the production and marketing of non-forest timber products, they seek to have barter systems[105] and seed exchanges recognized as vital to biocultural conservation. They hope to develop value chains in "the promotion of a sustainable creative economy" involving "the marketing of indigenous handicrafts, designs, and other creative products as means of livelihood and promotion of indigenous cultures."[106] Novel usages of intellectual property seem inevitable in these emerging conditions, and new forms of MICOs could serve these purposes.

---

[101] Singh, Rallen, & Padung, *supra* note 98, at 714.   [102] *Id.*   [103] Chazee, *supra* note 84.
[104] Erni, *supra* note 72; AIPP & IWGIA, *supra* note 61.
[105] Ranjay K. Singh, *Barter System, Biodiversity and Livelihoods of Tribal Communities: Cultural Diversity and Conservation in Eastern Himalaya, Arunachal Pradesh*, 98 CURRENT SCI. 1280 (2010).
[106] AIPP & IWGIA, *supra* note 61, at 11.

Much of the most extensive knowledge of women's TK comes from the seven sister states of Northeast India.[107] Home to more than 166 distinct tribes, the region features a multiplicity of forest-dependent cultural communities that practice traditional swidden agriculture and govern resources through indigenous institutions.[108] It thus has a rich heritage of culturally embedded TK, which protects biodiversity and local ecosystems.[109] Tribal women in the region are major stakeholders and custodians of knowledge, conserving food and medicinal plants in both "jhum" lands (the regional name for swiddening) and home gardens.[110] As agricultural plant scientist Ranjay K. Singh laments, "despite the rich knowledge of women, and their role in conserving biocultural diversity as experimenters, conservators and stabilisers of foods, medicines and other indigenous resources, their contribution is rarely recognised at the policy level."[111] Although there are numerous TK protection initiatives in India, no area of national government has shown significant interest in assessing the erosion of tribal TK and its implications for biodiversity and the continuing resilience of indigenous livelihoods in the region.[112]

The state of Arunachal Pradesh is considered one of the biodiverse areas of the country. It is home to 26 tribes and 110 ethnic groups, who largely reside in

---

[107] Assam, Arunachal Pradesh, Nagaland, Tripura, Mizoram, Meghalaya, and Manipur – which border Bhutan, China, Myanmar, and Bangladesh – constitute one of the most bioculturally diverse regions of India. See Jimmy Y. Yumnam, *Rich Biodiversity of Northeast India Needs Conservation*, 95 CURRENT SCI. 297 (2008); Ranjay K. Singh & R. C. Srivastava, *Biocultural Knowledge and Adi Community: Conservation and Sustainability in the Biodiversity Hotspot of Arunachal Pradesh*, 96 CURRENT SCI. 883 (2009).

[108] Yumnam, *supra* note 107; Department of Planning, Arunachal Pradesh Human Development Report (ADHDR) (2005), *available at* http://planningcommission.nic.in/plans/stateplan/index.php?state=b_sdrbody.htm.

[109] P. S. RAMAKRISHNAN, A. K. DAS, & K. G. SAXENA, CONSERVING BIODIVERSITY FOR SUSTAINABLE DEVELOPMENT 246 (1996); P. S. RAMAKRISHNAN ET AL., TRADITIONAL ECOLOGICAL KNOWLEDGE AND MANAGING BIOSPHERE RESERVES IN SOUTH AND CENTRAL ASIA (2002); Anaminka Singh, Ranjay K. Singh, & A. K. Sureja, *Cultural Significance and Diversities of Ethnic Foods of Northeast India*, 6 INDIAN J. TRADITIONAL KNOWLEDGE 79 (2007).

[110] Ranjay K. Singh, *Conserving Diversity and Culture: Pem Dolma*, 15 HONEY BEE 12–13 (2004); Sunita Mishra, Ranjay K. Singh, & Anamika Singh, *Dynamics of Adi Women's Traditional Foods in Varying Socio-Ecological Systems of Arunachal Pradesh: A Source of Learning and Inspiration*, in THE NEW CULTURES OF FOOD: MARKETING OPPORTUNITIES FROM ETHNIC, RELIGIOUS AND CULTURAL DIVERSITY 203–22 (Adam Lindgreen & Martin K. Hingley eds., 2009).

[111] Ranjay K. Singh et al., *Traditional Knowledge and Biocultural Diversity: Learning from Tribal Communities for Sustainable Development in Northeast India*, 53 J. ENVIRON. PLAN. & MGMT 511, 512–13 (2010).

[112] Ranjay K. Singh & R. C. Srivastava, *Biological Geographical Indicators of Traditional Knowledge Based Products and Green Technology from Arunachal Pradesh: An Initiative for Safeguarding IPR of Communities*, 9 INDIAN J. TRADITIONAL KNOWLEDGE 689 (2010).

forest areas on which they are dependent for socio-cultural, food, and livelihood requirements.[113] Most tribal groups have maintained distinctive indigenous landraces for subsistence and ritual purposes.[114] Although such groups do not yet face absorption into commercial or plantation agriculture, increasing population levels, rapid urbanization, greater incorporation into market economies, transitions to individual land ownership, and the breakdown of extended families are threatening women's TEK, while modern educational systems tend to make children less interested in maintaining the communal ways of life that rely upon it. Top-down development projects encouraging commercial cultivation of oranges, pineapples, and ginger (as well as the recent introduction of exotic crops) have reduced numbers of indigenous crop species and wild-growing plants in jhum lands.[115]

In 2003, the Arunachal government reviewed its developmental policies and formulated state policies indicating an interest in promoting TK-related biodiversity and protecting the IP of knowledge holders.[116] Singh and his collaborators used participatory research methodologies to identify Adi and Monpa community knowledge holders, document their TK, and design biocultural conservation activities, including community knowledge gardens, the promotion of TK-based microenterprise, and contests to enhance appreciation for TK in the area.[117] These village-based participatory TK workshops were amongst the first in India, and recorded practices relating to food, medicine, agriculture, animal husbandry, handicrafts, cosmetics, and biodiversity conservation. Biodiversity contests in local schools tested children's TK and generated new enthusiasm. Recipe contests validated elderly women's knowledge of nutritional health[118] while revitalizing customary lateral and vertical networks of knowledge sharing (these traditionally enabled cross-cultural transfers and refinements of knowledge on ethnomedicine and facilitated the flow of genetic resources from one biome to another).[119] Indigenous

---

[113] Id.
[114] Singh, Pretty, & Pilgrim *supra* note 96; Ranjay K. Singh, *Community Based Forest Resources Management through Socio-Cultural Institutions: Dynamics of Biodiversity Conservation and Subsistence Living of Adi Tribe under Subtropical Ecosystem in Eastern Himalayas*, CANADIAN SOCIETY OF ECOLOGICAL ECONOMICS (2007) (paper presented at the International Conference "Sustaining Communities and Development in the Face of Environmental Challenges").
[115] See RAMAKRISHNAN ET AL., *supra* note 109.   [116] APHDR, *supra* note 108.
[117] Singh, Pretty, & Pilgrim, *supra* note 96, at 527–28.
[118] Ranjay K. Singh & Anamika Singh, *Biodiversity and Recipe Contests: Innovative Socioecological Approaches to Capture Ecological Knowledge and Conserve Biodiversity in Arunachala Pradesh*, 12 INDIAN J. TRADITIONAL KNOWLEDGE 240 (2003).
[119] Singh, Rallen, & Padung, *supra* note 98, at 729.

women were trained to understand Free, Prior and Informed Consent (FPIC) principles, and how to manage and update TK databases, microenterprises, and screen practices for their market potential. These activities have enhanced valuation of biocultural resources and appear to have revitalized interest in using and developing ethnomedicines and domesticating food plant species, resulting in a heightened sense that the area's plants, animals, and related cultural practices were part of a tribal collective biocultural heritage rather than individual properties.[120] Significantly, "biological geographical indicators" were proposed as a MICO to designate new TK-based goods and technologies.[121] MICOs might be used to duplicate these efforts in other regions in Asia to support women in maintaining swiddens.

3.4 Gendered Labor in Emerging Plantation Economies

Shifts from swiddening to commercial agriculture weaken biodiversity and women's TEK while introducing practices of land and resource dispossession, creating communal insecurity and conditions of precarity ripe for the abuse of women and children. The consequences of oil palm plantations for women have only recently become the subject of critical attention and there is a paucity of empirical research in the field.[122] One significant exception is a study by anthropologist Tania Li commissioned to address the gendered impacts of Indonesian oil palm expansion under both smallholding and plantation models.[123] Most of Indonesia's oil palm is on the island of Sumatra, but Kalimantan was the main region of expansion from 2005 to

---

[120] Singh, Pretty, & Pilgrim, *supra* note 96, at 518–28.
[121] Singh & Srivastava, *supra* note 112, at 691.
[122] One study explored the social impact on a Dayak village in West Kalimantan, finding that women lost lands for subsistence farming, lost rubber income, were denied status as landholders, and were particularly vulnerable as plantation workers. *See* Julia & Ben White, *Gendered Experiences of Dispossession: Oil Palm Expansion in a Dayak Hibun Community in West Kalimantan*, 39 J. PEASANT STUD. 995 (2012). The NGO Down to Earth considered the introduction of oil palm in Papua, finding that women lost access to forest lands and resources, received only precarious plantation work, had difficulty feeding their families, and faced greater domestic violence. *See* Yuliana Langowuyo, *Women and Oil Palm in an Investment Region*, DOWN TO EARTH (October 2014), www.downtoearth-indonesia.org/story/women-and-oil-palm-investment-region. Women workers are more often treated as casual labor and exposed to serious health hazards because oil palm plantations in Indonesia tend to use hazardous pesticides banned elsewhere.
[123] Tania Murray Li, *Social Impacts of Oil Palm in Indonesia: A Gendered Perspective from West Kalimantan*, OCCASIONAL PAPER 124. CENTER FOR INTERNATIONAL FORESTRY RESEARCH (2014), *available at* www.cifor.org/publications/pdf_files/OccPapers/OP-124.pdf. The report draws upon Li's student team's empirical research in one district of West Kalimantan from 2010 to 2012.

2013, adding 1.5 million ha of plantations and a much smaller area (228,000 ha) of smallholdings. Her study illustrates some striking historical tendencies of the impacts of palm oil industries upon women in swidden regions.

Historically, the Indonesian state designated huge areas of territory as "concession lands" which were thereby available for oil palm development. Such territory appears to have deemed public domain under state forestry law, where the customary land rights of swiddeners were unrecognized.[124] Although little oil palm is planted on what the state considers to be primary forest land[125] (a category which may reflect only the longer length of swidden fields lying fallow in an area), much of it is planted on lands from which customary landholders are now excluded. They can neither farm independently nor access what were until recently considered common resources necessary for rural security of livelihood. The state, which has not historically recognized these lands, issues plantation licenses that require companies "to negotiate with communities and individuals for release of their customary rights," so that "customary rights are only recognized provisionally and contingently, just enough to facilitate their release to corporations."[126] People cede these lands in return for small payments or vague promises of inclusion in future smallholder schemes; many, it appears, do not understand these "releases" as permanent alienations. Oil plantations are sites of the most violent of Indonesian land conflicts, which are likely to escalate as former landholders become squeezed between plantations, unable to make a living on smallholdings or bestow lands to their children.[127] Unless they become employees of plantations, former landholders are likely to become unemployed or casual laborers paid below provincial minimums.[128]

---

[124] Douglas Sheil et al., *The Impacts and Opportunities of Oil Palm in Southeast Asia: What Do We Know and What Do We Need to Know?* (2009), available at www.cifor.org/library/2792/the-impacts-and-opportunities-of-oil-palm-in-southeast-asia-what-do-we-know-and-what-do-we-need-to-know/.

[125] Krystof Obidzinski et al., *Environmental and Social Impacts of Oil Palm Plantations and Their Implications for Biofuel Production in Indonesia*, 17 ECOLOGY & SOC'Y 1 (2012).

[126] Li, *supra* note 123, at 4.

[127] John F. McCarthy, *Where is Justice? Resource Entitlements, Agrarian Transformation and Regional Autonomy in Jambi, Sumatra*, in COMMUNITY, ENVIRONMENT AND LOCAL GOVERNANCE IN INDONESIA: LOCATING THE COMMONWEAL 169–98 (Carol Warren and John F. McCarthy eds., 2009); Tania Murray Li, *Centering Labour in the Land Grab Debate*, 38 J. OF PEASANT STUD. 281 (2011); Lesley Potter, *New Transmigration "Paradigm" in Indonesia: Examples from Kalimantan*, 53 ASIA PAC. VIEWPOINT 272 (2012).

[128] Obidzinski et al., *supra* note 125; Hariati Sinaga, *Employment and Income of Workers on Indonesian Oil Palm Plantations: Food Crisis at the Micro Level*, 1 FUTURE OF FOOD: J. ON FOOD, AGRIC. & SOC'Y 64 (2013).

Smallholder schemes in which holders might independently farm lands to which they would eventually receive title were historically introduced alongside state and corporate plantations that absorbed the labor of swiddeners and transmigrants. By the late 1990s, companies were reluctant to engage in further smallholder regimes, and since 2004 the law has required that only 20 per cent of lands need to be developed in partnerships with smallholders.[129] Partnerships only pay the smallholder a monthly dividend for oil palm cultivation and such payments are much lower than the yields from independent planting.[130] Independent smallholders plant oil palm on lands held individually, collectively, purchased from others, or claimed by the state as forest land (which was generally acquired by refusing rights to indigenous farmers). Since 2000 there has been a large increase in smallholders' cultivation of palm, solely or in combination with other crops, given increasing prices. Farmers may be successful where they have access to roads, mills, credit, and plants, but the threshold for entry remains too high for most former swiddeners. Successful oil palm smallholders (often government employees) tend to acquire more lands from surrounding swiddeners, which increases rural income inequalities.[131]

Historically, government allocations under transmigration and smallholder schemes recruited married householders, but registered lands only in the names of the husband, thereby stripping women of their joint rights under customary law. Recently, plantations have ceased to approach conjugal units as recruits, instead hiring a small core workforce of single young men, while recruiting women as temporary employees. Women's land rights are no longer secure in cases of divorce; men can sell or mortgage lands without their wives' consent, and take monthly payments directly. To the extent that smallholders have any voice in livelihood conditions, it is through plantation-based

---

[129] Companies resist even this requirement and in some areas refuse any role for smallholders. Historical discussions of the reluctance of both state and corporate plantations to work with smallholders are discussed in McCarthy & Cramb, *supra* note 75; Piers Gillespie, *How does Legislation Affect Oil Palm Smallholders in the Sanggau District of Kalimantan, Indonesia?* 14 AUSTRALASIAN J. NAT. RESOURCES L. & POL'Y 1 (2011); John F. McCarthy, Piers Gillespie, & Zahari Zen, *Swimming Upstream: Local Indonesian Production Networks in "Globalized" Palm Oil Production*, 40 WORLD DEV. 555 (2011); Colchester & Chao, *supra* note 76; MARCUS COLCHESTER, NORMAN JIWAN, & EMILOLA KLEDEN, INDEPENDENT REVIEW OF THE SOCIAL IMPACTS OF GOLDEN AGRI RESOURCES' FOREST CONSERVATION POLICY IN KAPUAS HULU DISTRICT (2014), *available at* www.forestpeoples.org/topics/palm-oil-rspo/publication/2014/independent-review-social-impacts-golden-agri-resources-forest.

[130] McCarthy, Gillespie, & Zen, *supra* note 129, at 555; Colchester & Chao, *supra* note 76.

[131] John F. McCarthy, *Surfing and Crashing in the Indonesian Oil Palm Boom*, JAKARTA POST (March 28, 2008), www.thejakartapost.com/news/2008/03/27/surfing-and-crashing-indonesian-oil-palm-boom.html.

co-operatives; however imperfect such institutions,[132] their exclusion of women denies them any voice in plantation life.[133]

In regions where swiddens are most intact, women want to add palm oil cultivation to their other crops to avoid releasing lands to outsiders and to retain them for future generations. Lack of roads, capital, and planting material, however, ensures that smallholding is primarily for local elites. The more lands are dominated by smallholder monocropping, the more limited other farmers' crop choices become and the more nutrition declines. Landlessness is worst for those closest to the plantation core that have lost access to most if not all subsistence resources, often transmigrants who relinquished customary lands in the areas from which they came to take advantage of plantation employment. Women, who must anchor households and support children when men migrate, face the direst situations, often becoming the casual day laborers of plantation economies who face the greatest health risks.

The historical trajectory toward impoverishment that Li describes for one area in West Kalimantan is cause for alarm and will potentially recur on other land frontiers in Indonesia. Two possible futures for oil palm development remain: the continued expansion of government-supported monocropped corporate plantations and the promotion of independent oil palm smallholdings as part of mixed agroforestry systems, supported by many UN organizations, social movements, and NGOs. Only independent oil palm smallholdings are likely to achieve environmental and social justice certification, particularly given ongoing conflicts over corporate enclosures. Just 10 per cent of palm oil in Indonesia can be certified by the Roundtable on Sustainable Palm Oil (RSPO),[134] which sets very minimal conditions. Smallholders will require greater organization and the capacity to develop local institutions, but only they will be able to meet "standards for sustainable, equitable, and socially responsible oil palm development."[135] The rights and livelihoods of both women and children are at stake. With reports of forced and child labor on plantations increasing in Indonesia, Malaysia, and Papua

---

[132] The limitations of co-operatives in Indonesia are discussed in David Henley, *Custom and Koperasi: The Cooperative Ideal in Indonesia*, in THE REVIVAL OF TRADITION IN INDONESIAN POLITICS: THE DEPLOYMENT OF ADAT FROM COLONIALISM TO INDIGENISM 87–112 (Jamie S. Davidson & David Henley eds., 2007).

[133] Mia Siscawati & Ava Mahaningtyas, *Gender Justice: Forest Tenure and Forest Governance in Indonesia*, in THE CHALLENGES OF SECURING WOMEN'S TENURE AND LEADERSHIP FOR FOREST MANAGEMENT: THE ASIAN EXPERIENCE (2012), *available at* www.rightsandresources.org/documents/files/doc_5224.pdf

[134] Li, *supra* note 123, at 39.   [135] *Id.* at 40.

New Guinea,[136] new means of certifying conditions of oil palm production that do protect biocultural diversity and women's access to livelihood resources are essential.

4 FUTURE LANDSCAPES FOR MICOS

The term "conflict palm oil" brings consumers' attention to their own complicity in Asian conflicts, because palm oil is ubiquitous in manufactured household food products such as cookies, instant noodles, and potato chips. There are no consumer markets in the world in which everyday goods do not contain this oil.[137] The conditions of palm oil plantation have attracted international attention; activists pressure the largest purchasers in the global food industry to adopt more responsible practices. As a consequence:

> [I]n the last two years, more than twenty of the world's largest consumer brands and palm oil traders have announced new palm oil procurement commitments, which are intended to eliminate sourcing from growers associated with on-going deforestation, climate pollution, and human rights abuses ... Working with allies from around the world, Rainforest Action Network (RAN) is exposing the supply chains that link Conflict Palm Oil to the foods Americans are sold, focusing on a group of large corporate palm oil end-users we call the Snack Food 20.[138]

The Snack Food 20 could fundamentally transform palm oil production by supply-chain mapping and monitoring, developing procurement policies for the protection of rainforests and peatlands, respecting the rights of communities to give or withhold FPIC to land development, insisting that plantation lands be acquired only from those who hold title, respecting workers' rights, eliminating child labor, banning burning and reducing greenhouse emissions, including smallholders in supply chains, and practicing equitable benefit sharing.[139] Given the growing conflicts between companies and communities and the increasingly dire ecological crisis fuelled by palm oil intensification, third-party verification of compliance is urgently needed.

Many companies surpassed the inadequate standards of the RSPO, committing to ambitious deadlines for cutting suppliers trafficking conflict palm oil by the end of 2015 (which were largely unrealized). When Kit Kat bars were

---

[136] Palm oil has been listed on the US Department of Labor's *List of Goods Produced by Child Labor or Forced Labor* since 2010. See Monbiot, *supra* note 47.

[137] A partial list would include brands such as Campbell Soup, Dunkin' Donuts, Heinz, Hershey, General Mills, Kelloggs, Kraft, Krispy Kreme, Mars, and Smuckers.

[138] Rainforest Action Network, *supra* note 47, at 2.   [139] *Id.*

clearly linked to rainforest destruction in Indonesia in 2010, Nestlé began verifying that its sources were not associated with destruction of high conservation value and high-carbon stock forests. Far less has been done to protect labor rights. Unilever recognized that it had a palm oil problem after Dove personal care products were similarly exposed in 2008, but its 2013 commitment allegedly lacked "both clear requirements and a deadline for suppliers to end destruction of rainforests, peatlands and abuse of human and labour rights in all operations."[140] Some corporations have released stronger commitments since 2013, while others, such as Hormel Foods and Kraft Heinz Company, still inadequately pressure suppliers; PepsiCo could play a vital role in transforming the worst conditions in Indonesia and Malaysia.[141]

Ultimately, environmentalists want a moratorium on the clearance of forests and development of peatlands, halting further expansion until comprehensive assessments identify the conservation and climate change values of these regions. Others seek to ascertain whether indigenous peoples and local communities are fully consenting to palm oil development on their customary lands, and to ensure protection of their water sources, food systems, and livelihoods.[142] Certification regimes need to find means of identifying suppliers operating plantations on lands acquired through coercion. The transformation of global palm oil supply chains will be a massive undertaking, in which corporations must assume new forms of transnational governance. Through such chains, nearly all consumers are linked to Asian indigenous peoples and become complicit in their dispossession. Even if some of the proposed certifications are developed and implemented, new MICOs must be forged to meet environmental and human rights objectives.

Contemporary struggles around private standards and certifications for goods have become much more conscious of their capacity to represent interests, uphold power relations, provide representation, and engender voice.[143] Interest in the institutional dimensions of value chains has put new emphasis upon how local actors engage them and shape their structures, processes, values, and outcomes.[144] Increasingly, labor, food safety, and agricultural practice standards are converging, with workers and small producers recognized as active participants in tackling social and environmental

---

[140] Id. at 8. [141] Id. [142] Id.
[143] Valerie Nelson & Anne Tallontire, *Battlefields of Ideas: Changing Narratives and Power Dynamics in Private Standards in Global Agricultural Value Chains*, 31 AGRIC. & HUM. VALUES 481 (2014).
[144] Anne Tallontire et al., *Beyond the Vertical? Using Value Chains and Governance as a Framework to Analyse Private Standards Initiatives in Agri-food Chains*, 28 AGRIC. & HUM. VALUES 427 (2011).

problems. The United Nations Research Institute for Sustainable Development, for example, has focused on Social and Solidarity Economy approaches to production and exchange, which share explicit economic and social objectives:

> [T]hey reconnect economic activity with ethical values and social justice, aim to satisfy human needs, build resilience, expand human capabilities, empower women, foster workplace democracy, and/or promote ways of living, producing and governing that are more caring of both people and the environment.[145]

This new model addresses sustainability and labor issues at a landscape or industry level.[146] It develops and influences standards rooted in the capacity of workers and smallholders to articulate their own needs in a variety of forums, public and private, building multi-scalar alliances that create pressures for change, while engaging external actors as brokers and facilitators to help communities realize social and economic aspirations. Another key shift is the recognition that global value chains operate within territorial institutional dynamics. Creating change involves engaging key actors to work collaboratively across a sector on multiple issues, moving beyond farm-level interventions to landscape and industry-wide initiatives.[147]

> These systems support negotiations with companies, improving the bargaining power of specific communities and enabling grievances to be addressed. In some cases this has led to a redistribution of benefits towards local communities, requiring companies to obtain FPIC, or pay royalties for locally extracted resources. These systems can therefore provide recognition of stakeholders' rights, and a capacity to have their concerns heard. As in fair trade, enclaves of coproduction emerge where coordinated joint efforts between companies, NGOs and/or State actors come together – as developmental interventions – to generate relatively inclusive smallholder outcomes.[148]

Such private regulatory vehicles are likely to be ineffective in the absence of public regulatory standards, because they attempt to redistribute benefits in a way that conflicts with the local constellations of power and interest reflected

---

[145] Nelson & Tallontire, *supra* note 143, at 485–86 (citing, Geneva: United Nations Research Institute for Social Research, *Potential and Limits of Social and Solidarity Economy*, UNRISD, www.unrisd.org/80256B3C005BD6AB/search/513E84D6BA2D56EEC1257AF A00469157?OpenDocument (last visited 9 March 2016).
[146] *Id.* at 493.   [147] *Id.*
[148] Jeremy McCarthy, *Certifying in Contested Spaces: Private Regulation in Indonesian Forestry and Oil Palm*, 33 THIRD WORLD Q. 1871 (2010).

in public policies. Few would argue that forms of certification will substitute for recognition of indigenous title; critics suggest that certifying products emerging from regions characterized by land conflicts ratifies bad policies and weakens customary rights claims. Certification may redistribute benefits but doesn't provide public accountability; it may extend "the extraction of resources without conferring effective forms of redress or recognition on groups claiming resource rights."[149] In the absence of community rights, companies have enormous bargaining power and communities often settle for what they can get. Oil palm certification, for example, continues to be dominated by industry, does not apply throughout the whole value chain, and finds no demand in large consumer and manufacturing markets such as China and India. Such certifications do, however, publicize local conditions and provide opportunities for new forms of political pressure toward these ends.

Gender equity is increasingly considered in mapping value chains that follow plantation crops.[150] Proponents of certifications to enhance social justice insist that the entire value chain must be considered if equities are to be secured,[151] which must include employment conditions, too often overlooked in fair trade justifications and in MICOs more generally. Certifications must address conditions of both formal and informal employment as well as the impact of conditions of production upon women's reproductive work.[152] In regions where development has devolved to municipal authorities, old plantation industries such as tea (which have both a female labor force and a female consumer base) have been receptive to new certifications.[153]

It is unlikely that MICOs will develop in a fashion that is more equitable to small producers, more sensitive to gender relations, or more attuned to biocultural diversity without collective organization, greater differentiation amongst marked products, and considerable transnational support.[154] More relational forms of institutional support need to be developed in process-based approaches to GIs, to avoid them simply becoming forms of geographical branding.[155] Although it is often assumed that such supports must

---

[149] Id.
[150] Allison Loconto, *Can Certified-Tea Value Chains Deliver Gender Equality in Tanzania?* 21 FEMINIST ECO. 191 (2015). *See also*, the discussion of Just Change tea in Coombe & Aylwin, *supra* note 11, at 2032–36.
[151] Stephanie Barrientos, Catherine S. Dolan, & Anne Tallontire, *A Gendered Value Chain Approach to Codes of Conduct in African Horticulture*, 31 WORLD DEV. 1511 (2003).
[152] Lone Riisgaard et al., *Integrating Poverty and Environmental Concerns into Value-Chain Analysis: A Strategic Framework and Practical Guide*, 28 DEV. POL'Y REV. 195 (2010).
[153] Loconto, *supra* note 150, at 194–96.   [154] Id.
[155] Ricky Conneely & Marie Mahon, *Protected Geographical Indications: Institutional Roles in Food Systems Governance and Rural Development*, 60 GEOFORUM 14 (2015).

come from states, a number of initiatives indicate that transnational relationships between organized civil society groups may fulfill similar functions. Self-determined forms of certification link producers and consumers in transnational networks of solidarity. Many small-scale producer cooperatives have withdrawn from Fair Trade USA, for example, because producers get little input into standards of certification that don't consider the circumstances of their lives.[156] A new Small Producers' Symbol (Si´mbolo de los Pequen˜os Productores – SPP) certification system under the Latin American Fair Trade network began certifying groups in 2011, using standards for production created by small producers attempting to address their everyday socio-economic issues; "in assessing standards, the SPP attempts to create direct relations and dignified living through dialogue – articulated as an economy of trust."[157] Significantly, geographer Lindsay Naylor argues that this MICO "creates new ways of participating in economic activities and performing economic identities that are focused on place-based ways of living" and suggests a geographical basis for such indications.[158]

Initiatives to counter gender discrimination and to forge networks of female solidarity may be driven by producers and workers as well as by consumers.[159] Café Femenino, for example, is a Fair Trade coffee brand developed in the Andean foothills of Northern Peru, under which multiple capacity-building gender empowerment projects are clustered.[160] Members of a female-owned co-operative grow the coffee on lands owned by women, which supports community development initiatives in health, literacy, transportation, and youth employment. Use of the Café Femenino mark accrues an extra two cents a pound for the women and the same amount again for the community foundation.[161] Profits are also distributed to a women's shelter and crisis foundation, as well as women's hospitals and

---

[156] *See* Sarah Lyon, *Maya Coffee Farmers and Fair Trade: Assessing the Benefits and Limitations of Alternative Markets*, 29 CULTURE & AGRIC. 100 (2007); SARAH LYON, COFFEE AND COMMUNITY: MAYA FARMERS AND FAIR-TRADE MARKETS (2011); Marie-Christine Renard & Allison Loconto, *Competing Logics in the Further Standardization of Fair Trade: ISEAL and the Si´mbolo de Pequen˜os Productores*, 20 INT'L J. SOC'Y. AGRIC. & FOOD 51 (2013); Erin Smith & William Loker, *"We Know Our Worth": Lessons from a Fair Trade Coffee Cooperative in Honduras*, 71 HUM. ORG. 87 (2012).
[157] Naylor, *supra* note 31, at 280. [158] *Id.* at 281.
[159] *See* longer discussion in Coombe and Aylwin, *supra* note 11, at 2037.
[160] John-Justin McMurtry, *Ethical Value-Added: Fair Trade and the Case of Café Femenino*, 86 J. BUS. ETHICS 27 (2009).
[161] *Id.* at 38.

a breast cancer research foundation in Canadian consumer communities.[162] The ethical aspect of the added value that this MICO creates is deliberately extended through the entire supply chain. The economic benefits have encouraged families to put more land in women's names, securing greater economic independence and more equity in local gendered divisions of labor.

Another prospect is provided by alternative food networks, wherein civil society groups mobilize "to vindicate the cultural value of food in terms of taste, its conditions of production and its ecological and cultural dimensions as part of the landscape that supports the economy of the smallholder family."[163] They promote local vernacular economies and self-governance through voluntary certifications. Largely involving producers and consumers in close proximity, such initiatives centrally involve women as farmers, mothers, food providers, and monitors of family nutrition and health who are concerned with agrochemicals, genetic modification, and labor conditions to create relationships of trust between producers and consumers in processes of food governance that are more democratic than those provided by third-party certifications.[164] Alternative food networks often involve female smallholders engaged in multicropping and the preservation of native plant varieties and are dominated by women who understand the integral relationship between agriculture, territory, and food. They offer intriguing possibilities for translation and adaptation in Asian contexts.

There is also hope that "GI production systems based on well-managed extractive activities [can be used to] promote the conservation of natural vegetation and forested areas with benefits to ecosystem and landscape conservation,"[165] and biocultural diversity treated as "an asset that can be developed through GI differentiation."[166] For example, forest biologists, agricultural scientists, and ecologists argue that a landscape with a reputation as a well-managed sustainable environment rich in biodiversity is one that can support a GI for a production system that maintains biodiversity.[167] Such "green GIs" are most successful when they are initiated by local producers,

---

[162] Imperial Coffee and Services Inc., *Café Femenino Project Empowers Women*, IMPERIAL (2 September 2015), http://imperialcoffee.com/2015/09/02/cafe-femenino-project-empowers-women/.
[163] Ronald Nigh & Alma-Amalia González Cabañas, *Reflexive Consumer Markets as Opportunities for New Peasant Farmers in Mexico and France: Constructing Food Sovereignty Through Alternative Food Networks*, 39 AGROECOLOGY & SUSTAINABLE FOOD SYSTEMS. 317 (2015).
[164] *Id.* at 329–30.   [165] *Id.* at 8.   [166] *Id.*
[167] Marie-Vivien et al., *supra* note 93, at 380–85.

give biodiversity objectives primacy, and provide specifications for their use that prioritize local environmental practices.[168] Nonetheless, it is doubtful that benefits will be realized in countries where institutions for supply-chain governance are weak, trends toward agroindustrialization are already established, and there is little state support for local organizations or community governance.[169] Again, new forms of support and collaboration will be essential.

One final set of values that might inform new initiatives for developing MICOs emerges from the growing recognition of biocultural rights. Norms linking biodiversity maintenance and TEK protection have been evolving under the auspices of the CBD since 1992. In countries where the indigenous status of minority ethnic groups is precarious, unacknowledged, or refused, the relationship between "traditional" peoples, local communities, and natural environments is recognized through an acknowledged interrelationship between biological and cultural diversity. Biocultural diversity has emerged as a hybrid good to be pursued in support of the livelihood resources, identities, and political interests of local communities[170] alongside political principles of FPIC that fulfill state obligations to "take into consideration indigenous and local communities' customary laws, community protocols and procedures when accessing TK associated with genetic resources."[171]

Biocultural community protocols are legal vehicles that indigenous peoples use in environmental and biodiversity negotiations to regulate the interface between international legal instruments and the locally held collective heritage resources that internationally ground indigenous rights.[172] Many social movements and UN bodies embrace these principles, but the prospect of marking goods and services as indicating places of origin that comply with

---

[168] Claude Garcia et al., *Geographical Indications and Biodiversity in the Western Ghats, India: Can Labelling Benefit Producers and the Environment in a Mountain Agroforestry Landscape?*, 27 MOUNTAIN RES. & DEV. 206 (2007).

[169] LARSON, ICTSD Policy Brief No. 3, *supra* note 4.

[170] Reiner Buergin, *Contested Rights of Local Communities and Indigenous Peoples in the Context of the Biocultural Turn in Environmental and Development Discourses*, 49 MOD. ASIAN STUD. 2022 (2015).

[171] Krystyna Swiderska, *Protecting Traditional Knowledge: A Holistic Approach Based on Customary Laws and Bio-Cultural Heritage*, in CONSERVING AND VALUING ECOSYSTEM SERVICES AND BIODIVERSITY 331–44 (Karachepone N. Ninan ed., 2009).

[172] UNEP, BIOCULTURAL COMMUNITY PROTOCOLS: A COMMUNITY APPROACH TO ENSURING THE INTEGRITY OF ENVIRONMENTAL LAW AND POLICY (2009), available at www.unep.org/communityprotocolsPDF/communityprotocols.pdf; HOLLY SHRUMM AND HARRY JONAS (eds.), BIOCULTURAL COMMUNITY PROTOCOLS: A TOOLKIT FOR COMMUNITY FACILITATORS: INTEGRATED PARTICIPATORY AND LEGAL EMPOWERMENT TOOLS TO SUPPORT COMMUNITIES TO SECURE THEIR RIGHTS, RESPONSIBILITIES, TERRITORIES, AND AREAS (2012); Bavikatte, *supra* note 95, at 227–30.

these norms is only beginning to be explored. Means to verify compliance with the FPIC of indigenous peoples (which in many cases will be based on customary or "living law") and to certify and communicate such compliance are still being devised.[173] The International Institute for Environment and Development (IIED) Report considering "Intellectual Property Tools for Products Based on Biocultural Heritage" suggests that some types of GIs might be used by associations of small producers to recognize and support group rights; used appropriately and controlled by local communities, they can protect traditional methods, support sustainable development, and might be further developed to mark products "derived from the collective biocultural heritage of indigenous people."[174]

Alejandro Argumedo argues that MICOs, collectively owned and run in accordance with community self-determined rules which correspond with customary law principles, offer real economic and political benefits to indigenous communities. In countries with state-held GIs, collective trademarks are better vehicles for indigenous communities but a new regime of "biocultural heritage indications" that builds upon this legal vehicle might "open up the current IPR [Intellectual Property Rights] system to millions of poor rural communities."[175] As this chapter went to press, the IIED, the University of Leeds, and Asociacion ANDES (Peru) were widely consulting experts on the best means to develop a biocultural heritage (BCH) indication regime for marking products and services.[176]

---

[173] BRENDAN TOBIN, INDIGENOUS PEOPLES, CUSTOMARY LAW AND HUMAN RIGHTS: WHY LIVING LAW MATTERS 178 (2014).

[174] Graham Dutfield, Alejandro Argumedo, & Krystyna Swiderska, *Designing an Effective Biocultural Heritage Indication Labeling System* (2015), *available at* http://pubs.iied.org/14655IIED.

[175] ALEJANDRO ARGUMEDO, COLLECTIVE TRADEMARKS AND BIOCULTURAL HERITAGE. TOWARDS NEW INDICATIONS OF DISTINCTION FOR INDIGENOUS PEOPLES IN THE POTATO PARK, PERU 5 (2013). Argumedo is an agricultural development expert and Director of Association ANDES, an internationally linked indigenous NGO; he was instrumental in establishing an indigenous, community-run Potato Park in Pisaq, Peru. The Park has been informally using a collective trademark since 2005 and bases the rules governing its use on principles derived from an Andean cosmovision – the *ayllu*, a holistic territorial approach to life and development that informs all activities in which biocultural heritage goods and services are produced and marketed (10–11). The use of the collective mark helps to protect the communities from appropriation of genetic resources, and functions to communicate the collective nature of ayllu production processes and Quechua knowledge and innovation systems (14). It also helps to ensure cohesion between villages, increases people's pride in their local heritage, and encourages greater reflexivity about community values in development while educating others about indigenous community rights. The mark also independently generates revenue to the extent that tourists value it as authenticating the goods and souvenirs they take home.

[176] Dutfield, Argumedo, & Swiderska, *supra* note 174, at 3–5.

5 CONCLUSION

In this journey through tea plantations, oil palm frontiers, and tribal women's gardens, we have attempted to illustrate that GIs and other MICOs have largely worked in Asia to hide or obscure racialized conditions of gendered labor. They have done little to illuminate the hidden and unappreciated work of conservation and biocultural regeneration that women do across the region. Nonetheless, MICOs which can be held and governed locally according to living law and rights-based development criteria and certified for new markets have the potential to be shaped in ways that respect and value the work that women do in rural Asia while contributing to the maintenance of those biocultural heritage resources which have traditionally sustained rural communities. New values are emerging for managing supply chains that recognize the environmental and cultural labors of women in ways that support their livelihoods. The adoption and adaptation of such models in Asian contexts should be welcomed and encouraged.

5

A Look at the Geneva Act of the Lisbon Agreement: A Missed Opportunity?

Daniel Gervais[*]

1 INTRODUCTION

In May 2015, a number of World Intellectual Property Organization (WIPO) member states adopted a new Act of the Lisbon Agreement for the Protection of Appellations of Origin and their International Registration 1985 (Lisbon Agreement).[1] A question that surfaced both during the negotiations and since the signing ceremony is whether this new Act will be palatable to countries using a common-law trademark approach for the protection of geographical indications (GIs) instead of the mostly European approach of using a *sui generis* (non-trademark) system.[2] This question applies, for example, to several

---

[*] Professor of Law, Vanderbilt University Law School, and Director of the Vanderbilt Intellectual Property Program. A US-focused version of this chapter is published in the Houston Law Review. Daniel Gervais, *Irreconcilable Differences? The Geneva Act of the Lisbon Agreement and the Common Law*, 53 HOUSTON L. REV. 339 (2015).

[1] Lisbon Agreement for the Protection of Appellations of Origin and Their International Registration, October 31, 1958, *as revised*, July 14, 1967, 923 U.N.T.S. 205 [hereinafter Lisbon Agreement], www.wipo.int/treaties/en/text.jsp?file_id=285856/; World Intellectual Prop. Org. [WIPO], Geneva Act of the Lisbon Agreement on Appellations of Origin and Geographical Indications and Regulations under the Geneva Act of the Lisbon Agreement on Appellations of Origin and Geographical Indications, WIPO Document LI/DC/19 (May 20, 2015), [hereinafter Geneva Act], www.wipo.int/meetings/en/details.jsp?meeting_id=35202.

[2] For example, "Champagne" is a GI protected under a *sui generis* regime in France and the rest of Europe. In France, this protection reflects a recognized link between the land (and know-how concerning its use) and a product – a concept known as *terroir*. Terroir has received various forms of legal protection dating back to at least the fifteenth century. See PAUL S. KINDSTEDT, CHEESE AND CULTURE 214 (2012). CHAMPAGNE is now protected under the system of *Appellations d'Origine Contrôlée* (AOC). *Id.* at 308. More recent regulations are contained in the Code de la Propriété Intellectuelle [C. PROP. INTELL.] [INTELLECTUAL PROPERTY CODE] art. L 721–1 to -10 (Fr.), www.legifrance.gouv.fr/affichC ode.do?cidTexte=LEGITEXT000006069414; and the Law of the 30th of July 1935. Décret législatif du 30 juillet 1935 – Défense du Marché des Vins et Régime Économique de l'Alcool [Law of July 30, 1935, Defense of Wine Market and Economic Regime of Alcohol],

countries involved in the now likely defunct Trans-Pacific Partnership (TPP) Agreement but also in other regional trade arrangements including the draft Regional Comprehensive Economic Partnership (RCEP).[3]

GIs matter on several levels. They have deep roots in the *terroir*, a French word designed to encapsulate a blend of land, tradition, and human know-how.[4] In the Geneva Act context, this raises a question, namely whether this notion of *terroir* is commensurate with modern international trade rules, at least as trade is practiced outside of Europe (in say, RCEP countries).[5] *Terroir* matters to many producers and many countries, and not just in Europe. In parts of the "Old World," however, it is not an exaggeration to say that some countries link *terroir* to national identity.[6] Many so-called "New World" producers of wines, spirits, and agricultural products see things differently. While they also recognize the economic value of identifying the geographic origin for certain products – for example, in the United States (US), Florida orange juice, Idaho potatoes, Napa Valley wines, and Vidalia onions – they are concerned about possible restrictions on the use of terms they consider generic (meaning terms that, in their view, primarily describe a type of product, not its geographic origin).[7]

Several developing country producers have similar concerns about the protection of foreign terms—often belonging to producers in former colonial powers – that have become, or may become, generic in their country or region.

JOURNAL OFFICEL DE LA RÉPUBLIQUE FRANÇAISE [J.O.] [OFFICIAL GAZETTE OF FRANCE], July 31, 1935, p. 8314.

[3] *See* Trans-Pacific Partnership, October 5, 2015, https://ustr.gov/sites/default/files/TPP-Final-Text-Intellectual-Property.pdf. The twelve countries party to the TPP are Australia, Brunei Darussalam, Canada, Chile, Japan, Malaysia, Mexico, New Zealand, Peru, Singapore, the United States, and Vietnam. *See* Office of the US Trade Representative, *What is the TPP*, https://ustr.gov/tpp/ (last visited February 9, 2016). As to the Regional Comprehensive Economic Partnership (RCEP), it is a proposed trade agreement (FTA) between the member states of the Association of Southeast Asian Nations (ASEAN) (Brunei, Cambodia, Indonesia, Laos, Malaysia, Myanmar, the Philippines, Singapore, Thailand, Vietnam), on the one hand, and Australia, China, India, Japan, New Zealand and South Korea, on the other hand. The United States is not party to the RCEP discussions (as of February 2017).

[4] *See* Justin Hughes, *Champagne, Feta, and Bourbon: The Spirited Debate about Geographical Indications*, 58 HASTINGS L. J. 299, 300–02, 306–08, 352 (2006).

[5] *See supra* note 3.

[6] *See* KOLLEEN M. GUY, WHEN CHAMPAGNE BECAME FRENCH: WINE AND THE MAKING OF A NATIONAL IDENTITY 2 (2007) ("Much like the nation, champagne and its *terroir* are believed to possess eternal, natural qualities. The wine can be seen as an objective manifestation of the French 'soul,' the guardian of supreme spiritual values."); Emily C. Creditt, *Terroir vs. Trademarks: The Debate over Geographical Indications and Expansions to the TRIPS Agreement*, 11 VAND. J. ENT. & TECH. L. 425, 427 (2009).

[7] *See* J. THOMAS MCCARTHY, MCCARTHY ON TRADEMARKS AND UNFAIR COMPETITION §§ 19:92.50 (2nd edn. 1999).

Their situation is not uniform, however. Those who live in countries rich in traditional knowledge (many of which are developing countries), for instance, see the expansion of GI protection as a way to repair historical wrongs and, more broadly, as a way to de-Westernize intellectual property rules, which some consider systematically discriminatory because they favor Western methods of marketing and production and Western goods.[8] Several developing nations consider GIs as a way of protecting and globally marketing their rural and traditional products at a higher price, which they assert would lead to "development from within," that is, "an alternative development strategy that prioritizes local autonomy and broad, community-wide development goals."[9]

GIs affect prices, though not for every product and not in a uniform way. There are examples that illustrate the capture of additional rents due to the (consumers') perception of higher quality associated with certain geographical origins. For some products, this ties into – and may sometimes be confused with – "fair trade" labels and certification processes concerning the sourcing of an increasingly wide range of products, many of which come from the developing world (e.g., coffee, tea, cocoa, etc.).[10] Recent research also suggests that GI protection impacts food consumption patterns and can lead to shifts in agricultural models.[11]

GIs tend to focus production on a nation's comparative advantage in making a product whose origin infuses it with a higher market

---

[8] "Western" is used here not as a geographical reference but as a reference to the most industrialized nations. Peter Yu has suggested that the discriminatory use of GIs may lead developing countries to be more self-interested in higher levels of intellectual property protection. *See* Peter K. Yu, *TRIPS and Its Achilles' Heel*,' 18 J. INTELL. PROP. L. 479, 523–24 (2011).

[9] *See* Sarah Bowen, *Development from Within? The Potential for Geographical Indications in the Global South*, 13 J. WORLD INTELL. PROP. 231, 232 (2010) (noting that "diverse stakeholders" find GIs a useful tool for rural development). *See generally* Daniel Gervais, *Traditional Innovation and the Ongoing Debate on the Protection of Geographical Indications*, in INDIGENOUS PEOPLES' INNOVATION 121, 121–47 (Peter Drahos & Susy Frankel eds., 2012) (suggesting that developing countries may be attracted to GI protection of indigenous products because of GI's potential ability to promote respect, prevent misappropriation and misuse of traditional cultural expressions, empower communities, and encourage community innovation and creativity).

[10] For a review of fair trade labeling standards, see, for example, *Our Standards*, FAIRTRADE INT'L, www.fairtrade.net/our-standards.html (last visited February 8, 2016).

[11] *See* Elizabeth Barham, *Translating Terroir: The Global Challenge of French AOC Labeling*, 19 J. RURAL STUD. 127, 127 (2003) (arguing that expanded AOC systems create "new forms of local–global connections"). "As part of its initiative on 'Quality Linked to Geographical Origin,' the Food and Agriculture Organization (FAO) of the United Nations sponsored case studies on GIs and developing countries, culminating in regional seminars in Morocco and Chile in 2007 and a conference in Rome in 2008." Bowen, *supra* note 9, at 232.

value.[12] As such, GIs may have a deep environmental significance and form an increasingly relevant part of agricultural and food policy.[13] It is not surprising, therefore, that the debate surrounding the protection of GIs has captured the attention of a number of consumer groups, many of which insist on proper labeling of products, notably to indicate their origin. Their insistence stems not only from a desire to buy more locally produced products and to reduce the carbon footprint of their consumption patterns but also from the "quality assurance" factor[14] associated with a number of GIs.[15]

How does this translate into the Lisbon Agreement context? As of this writing (March 2017), no common-law jurisdiction is party to the Lisbon Agreement.[16] There are a number of reasons that explain this lack of enthusiasm. As this chapter elaborates in the following pages, many common-law jurisdictions use trademarks, collective marks, and certification marks to protect geographic symbols and names. This has a number of both normative and administrative implications, including use requirements, possible loss or diminution of right due to acquiescence and abandonment or genericness, and the payment of maintenance fees, to mention just the main effects. These characteristics define the gap that needs to be bridged between the Lisbon system and the common law. This chapter's purpose is to explore whether the Geneva Act succeeded in building this bridge.

---

[12] Cerkia Bramley, Estelle Biénabe, & Johann Kirsten, *The Economics of Geographical Indications: Towards a Conceptual Framework for Geographical Indication Research in Developing Countries*, in THE ECONOMICS OF INTELLECTUAL PROPERTY 109, 121 (2009), www.wipo.int/edocs/pubdocs/en/economics/1012/wipo_pub_1012.pdf.

[13] See William van Caenegem, *Registered GIs: Intellectual Property, Agricultural Policy and International Trade*, 26 EUR. INTELL. PROP. REV. 170, 172–73 (2004) (stating that the momentum behind the EU appeals for greater GI protection "comes from Mediterranean EU states, Italy, Portugal, Spain, and above all France, where traditional, specialised, small scale, non-commoditised agricultural practices remain relatively commonplace, with a fair degree of rural processing").

[14] See Alberto Francisco Ribeiro de Almeida, *Key Differences between Trade Marks and Geographical Indications*, 30 EUR. INTELL. PROP. REV. 406, 410 (2008) (listing positive public effects of GIs).

[15] See David Goodman, *Rural Europe Redux? Reflections on Alternative Agro-Food Networks and Paradigm Change*, 44 SOCIOLOGIA RURALIS 3, 9–10 (2004).

[16] As of October 2015, the list of parties to the Lisbon Agreement is as follows: Algeria, Bosnia and Herzegovina, Bulgaria, Burkina Faso, Congo, Costa Rica, Cuba, Czech Republic, Democratic People's Republic of Korea, France, Gabon, Georgia, Haiti, Hungary, Iran, Israel, Italy, Mexico, Montenegro, Nicaragua, Peru, Portugal, Republic of Moldova, Serbia, Slovakia, the former Yugoslav Republic of Macedonia, Togo, and Tunisia. See *Contracting Parties-Lisbon Agreement*, WORLD INTELL. PROP. ORG., www.wipo.int/treaties/en/ShowResults.jsp?lang=en&treaty_id=10 (last visited January 11, 2016).

To do so, the chapter proceeds as follows. The first part briefly describes the functioning of the Lisbon system, and the second part compares the Lisbon system with the common-law system of protection for geographic identifiers as marks.

2 GEOGRAPHICAL INDICATIONS UNDER THE LISBON AGREEMENT

2.1 *Terminological Issues*

Article 1 of the 1958 Lisbon Agreement requires member states to protect appellations of origin "as such."[17] The Geneva Act of the Lisbon Agreement on Appellation of Origin and Geographical Indications 2015 (Geneva Act)[18] is more flexible on this front. In addition to its reference to the 1958 notion of "appellations of origin," the Geneva Act also refers to "geographical indications," bringing it in line with the language used in the Agreement on Trade-Related Aspects of Intellectual Property Rights (TRIPS Agreement).[19]

The Geneva Act applies to

> any indication protected in the Contracting Party of Origin consisting of or containing the name of a geographical area, or another indication known as referring to such area, which identifies a good as originating in that geographical area, *where a given quality, reputation or other characteristic of the good is essentially attributable to its geographical origin.*[20]

The TRIPS Agreement defines geographical indications as

> indications which identify a good as originating in the territory of a Member, or a region or locality in that territory, *where a given quality, reputation or other characteristic of the good is essentially attributable to its geographical origin.*[21]

---

[17] Lisbon Agreement, *supra* note 1, art. 1(2); *see* Hughes, *supra* note 4, at 312–13, 312 n.79.
[18] Geneva Act, *supra* note 1, art. 2(1)(ii).
[19] Agreement on Trade-Related Aspects of Intellectual Property Rights, 1993, art 22.1, April 15, 1994, Marrakesh Agreement Establishing the World Trade Organization, Annex 1C, 1869 U.N.T.S. 299 [hereinafter TRIPS Agreement]. TRIPS uses and defines only the term geographical indications. It refers neither to Lisbon, nor to the notion of appellation of origin.
[20] Geneva Act, *supra* note 1, art 2(1)(ii) (emphasis added).
[21] TRIPS Agreement, *supra* note 19 art 22.1 (emphasis added). For a full analysis of the distinction between TRIPS and the original 1958 definitions, see Daniel J. Gervais, *Reinventing Lisbon: The Case for a Protocol to the Lisbon Agreement (Geographical Indications)*, 11 CHI. J. INT'L L. 67, 83–87 (2010).

Incorporating the language contained in the TRIPS Agreement, and thus common to all WTO members in the Geneva Act, is an improvement. While the Geneva Act obligates members to protect both registered appellations of origin and geographical indications on their territory, it also dropped the "as such" language and further provides that each "Contracting Party shall be free to choose the type of legislation under which it establishes the protection stipulated in this Act."[22] Dropping the "as such" language may have solved the terminological quandary that countries not using the notion of "appellation of origin" in their legal system may have had with the 1958 text.

2.2 Level of Protection Issues

The 1958 Lisbon Agreement obligates countries to provide protection of geographical indications against "any *usurpation* or imitation, even if the true origin of the product is indicated or if the appellation is used in translated form or accompanied by terms such as 'kind,' 'type,' 'make,' 'imitation,' or the like."[23] "Usurpation" is not a term commonly used in international intellectual property laws and treaties.[24] The *travaux*[25] define usurpation as the "illicit adoption" of an appellation and provide "counterfeiting" as a possible synonym.[26] The *travaux* also make clear that it is up to each country to decide the remedies that should be available.[27] It is difficult to reconcile this language with the TRIPS Agreement because that Agreement provides for two different levels of protection of geographical indications.

---

[22] Geneva Act, *supra* note 1, arts. 9, 10(1).
[23] Lisbon Agreement, *supra* note 1, art. 3 (emphasis added).
[24] The term is also used in the Bangui Agreement Relating to the Creation of an African Intellectual Property Organization, Constituting a Revision of the Agreement Relating to the Creation of an African and Malagasy Office of Industrial Property, art. 47, March 2, 1977, WORLD INTELL. PROP. ORG., www.wipo.int/wipolex/en/other_treaties/text.jsp?file_i d=181150#P3099_400022 (last visited November 20, 2015).
[25] *Travaux* are the "[m]aterials used in preparing the ultimate form of an agreement or statute, and esp. of an international treaty; the draft or legislative history of a treaty." *Travaux préparatoires*, BLACK'S LAW DICTIONARY (10th edn. 2014).
[26] Union Internationale pour la Protection de la Propriété Industrielle, Actes de la Conférence Réunie à Lisbonne du 6 au 31 Octobre 1958, at 815 (1963) [hereinafter *Actes*]. The *Actes* (including mostly the *travaux préparatoires*) of the Lisbon Conference were published in French only. Translations are the Author's own.
[27] *Id.* at 818; *see also* Lisbon Agreement, *supra* note 1 art. 8 (stating that a "competent Authority" of each member state or an "interested party" in each member state may take legal action under the agreement).

Under Article 22.2(a) of the TRIPS Agreement, which may apply to products of any kind (thus to agricultural and nonagricultural products), a potential right-holder must provide the means for interested parties to prevent the use of designations that might mislead the public, a level of protection that resembles trademark protection. A higher level of protection for *wines and spirits* was agreed upon in the TRIPS Agreement. Article 23 of the TRIPS Agreement prohibits use of a GI on wine or spirits originating outside the region specified by the GI.[28] The prohibition stands even if the true origin of the wine or spirits is indicated, a translation is used, or the indication is "accompanied by expressions such as 'kind,' 'type,' 'style,' 'imitation' or the like."[29] There is almost what looks like a presumption that the public might be misled – or that the competing use constitutes an act of unfair competition – when dealing with GIs on wines and spirits. This higher level of protection for wines and spirits is closer to the standard of the 1958 Lisbon Agreement, and probably even more so now because the Geneva Act replaced the right against "usurpation" with a three-legged right.

Article 11 of the Geneva Act provides a right that combines elements of Articles 16.3 (protection of well-known marks) and 22.2 (protection of geographical indications) of the TRIPS Agreement. Specifically, member countries must provide legal means to prevent any unauthorized use of the GI in three situations: (1) goods of the same kind as those to which the GI applies (including use in translated form or accompanied by terms such as "style," "kind," "type," "make," "imitation," "method," "as produced in," "like," "similar," or the like); (2) goods or services not of the same kind, if use would suggest a connection expanded to include, "where applicable," a right against uses liable "to impair or dilute in an unfair manner, or take unfair advantage of, that reputation" of the GI; and (3) "any other practice liable to mislead consumers as to the true origin, provenance or nature of the goods," including use amounting to imitation of the protected appellation or indication.[30]

This is a "TRIPS plus" outcome both because the higher level of protection in the TRIPS Agreement (without the need to show deception or confusion) is limited to wines and spirits[31] and because the TRIPS Agreement does not provide protection against "imitation." The Geneva Act is a de facto expansion by (and for) Lisbon members of GI protection to products other than wines and spirits – a measure sought by a number of WTO members, especially in the developing world. The Lisbon standard does not require confusion. This

---

[28] TRIPS Agreement, *supra* note 19, art. 23.1. [29] Id. [30] Geneva Act, *supra* note 1, art. 11.
[31] TRIPS Agreement, *supra* note 19, art. 23.

level of protection, unlike trademark law, requires no evaluation of the local consumer even (or especially) in a market where a GI protected under Lisbon may be neither known (by a significant proportion of the relevant public) nor used.

Finally, under the Lisbon system, one could argue that registration creates a worldwide public notice of the claim leading, normatively and/or doctrinally, to a presumption of confusion of sorts, requiring a ban on the use of the GI even with words such as "like" or "style." The TRIPS Agreement provision on a possible notification and registration system does not go that far in that it does not specify the legal effect of registration in the system, the establishment of which must still be negotiated.

2.3 Registration-Related Issues

The 1958 Lisbon Agreement established a multilateral registry for appellations of origin.[32] The Geneva Act made several improvements to the administrative operation of the register and generally modernized the system of registration of both geographical indications and appellations of origin. Without offering an exhaustive list of such improvements, the Geneva Act made the role of national offices much clearer. Applicants may be required to pay per-country fees and fees to use the protected indication, but not maintenance fees to the member country in which they seek protection.[33]

The Geneva Act also introduced a clearer system to refuse new GIs (and then withdraw refusals in whole or in part) and a new system allowing interested parties to "request the Competent Authority to notify a refusal in respect of the international registration."[34] In contrast, the text of the 1958 Lisbon Agreement did not mention grounds for refusal of a GI submitted by another Contracting Party and had no detailed provision on withdrawals.[35]

---

[32] Lisbon Agreement, *supra* note 1, art. 5.
[33] The issue of maintenance fees was the topic of heated debate during the conference. Maintenance fees had been mentioned in square brackets in early versions of the draft Geneva Act but did not make it into the final version. *Compare* Geneva Act, *supra* note 1, arts. 7–8, WIPO Document LI/DC/3 (November 14, 2014) (providing in Article 7 an "Alternate A" and an "Alternate B" for a "maintenance fee," and stating in Article 8 that nonpayment of a maintenance fee will result in the cancellation of a registration).
[34] *See* Geneva Act, *supra* note 1, arts. 15–16; *see also id.* rule 9 (explaining how Contracting Parties are to notify the International Bureau of the refusal); *id.* rule 10 (explaining what the International Bureau does not consider as a valid refusal); *id.* rule 11 (stating the procedure for withdrawal of refusal).
[35] *Compare* Geneva Act, *supra* note 1, rules 9–10 (specifying the required contents of a valid refusal), *with* Lisbon Agreement, *supra* note 1, art. 5 (requiring only that the basis of the refusal be included).

Under the 1958 Lisbon Agreement, a court or other competent authority in the country where protection is claimed could invalidate an appellation.[36] The Geneva Act more or less maintains this system but includes much clearer rules and a specific process.[37]

The topic of fees was a major issue during the Diplomatic Conference. Under the system based upon the 1958 Lisbon Agreement, applicants had to pay a *single fee once* to WIPO and their application would be deemed valid (subject to refusal by individual members) for essentially forever in all Lisbon member states where it was not initially refused or later invalidated.[38] This fee (which was 500 Swiss francs or approximately US $525, but doubled as of January 1, 2016) is paid to, and retained by, WIPO. There is no country designation and no "per-country" fee, unlike, say, the Madrid system for trademarks, the Hague system for designs, or the Patent Cooperation Treaty (PCT).[39] No renewal fee is ever required.[40] This is administratively different from the situation with several other IP rights, and also arguably incompatible with the current practice of common-law jurisdictions that protect GIs as trademarks. Trademarks can be considered abandoned and canceled for nonuse, and a registration, renewal, or maintenance fee is typically payable.[41] Under the Geneva Act, country designation was introduced and per-country fees are now possible for the initial registration and for use of the indication, but not maintenance fees.[42] This is likely to become a major bone

---

[36] *See* Lisbon Agreement, *supra* note 1, art. 5 (stating that once an appellation is registered with the International Bureau, an authority in any of the countries party to the Agreement may invalidate an appellation in their own country within one year of notice of the registration).

[37] *See* Geneva Act, *supra* note 1, arts. 15–16 (using similar wording as the Lisbon Agreement that an authority may invalidate an appellation registered with the International Bureau); *id.* rules 9–10 (detailing the requirements for a notification of refusing, including the process of how the International Bureau will handle irregular notifications of refusals that do not contain all the required information).

[38] Lisbon Agreement, *supra* note 1, arts. 5, 7.

[39] *Schedule of Fees*, WORLD INTELL. PROP. ORG., www.wipo.int/export/sites/www/hague/en/fees/pdf/sched.pdf (last visited February 8, 2016) (containing the fee schedule for the Hague System for Designs); *Individual Fees under the Madrid Protocol*, WORLD INTELL. PROP. ORG., www.wipo.int/madrid/en/madridgazette/remarks/ind_taxes.html (last visited February 8, 2016); *PCT Fee Tables*, WORLD INTELL. PROP. ORG., www.wipo.int/export/sites/www/pct/en/fees.pdf (last visited February 8, 2016); *Payment of Fees – Lisbon System*, WORLD INTELL. PROP. ORG., www.wipo.int/about-wipo/en/finance/lisbon.html (last visited February 8, 2016).

[40] The Lisbon Agreement specifically provides for the absence of renewal. Lisbon Agreement, *supra* note 1, art. 7.

[41] In the United States, since 1989, the renewal term has been ten years. *See* MCCARTHY, *supra* note 7, §§ 19:142, 19–422. Also, under US law, cancelation is possible after three years of nonuse. *See* 15 U.S.C. § 1127 (2012) ("Nonuse for 3 consecutive years shall be prima facie evidence of abandonment").

[42] *See supra* note 33.

of contention within WIPO member states, due to the disagreements over the protection of GIs and the limited membership to the Lisbon Agreement, and the Geneva Act, among WIPO members.

2.4 Genericness Issues

The 1958 Lisbon Agreement was fairly flexible in several respects but not on genericide. Genericide is the loss of an appellation when it becomes generic, and is thus unable to function as an indication of geographic origin in a given market.[43] The language of the 1958 Lisbon Agreement prevents invalidation for genericness in the country where protection is claimed, unless the appellation has become generic *in its country of origin*.[44] This is a rare mandatory application of *lex originis* in international intellectual property.[45] A country *joining* the Lisbon system has one year to determine whether it will refuse to protect any previously registered appellations.[46] For appellations registered *after* a country has joined, there is a twelve-month period to make such a decision. After that period has lapsed, however, it becomes much more complicated to refuse protection. An issue might surface in common-law jurisdictions here, especially if the owner of a Lisbon GI does nothing while the GI is used (with his knowledge but without his consent) either by a competitor or generically by several users.

It is a well-established principle of international intellectual property that the law of the country of protection (*lex loci protectionis*) would typically govern issues of genericide. Thus, a court or other competent authority determines the validity of a copyright, trademark, or patent in its own jurisdiction. The Paris Convention for the Protection of Industrial Property (Paris Convention)[47] makes it clear that this does not directly affect the same trademark or a patent on the same invention in other

---

[43] *See, e.g.*, Deborah J. Kemp & Lynn M. Forsythe, *Trademarks and Geographical Indications: A Case of California Champagne*, 10 CHAP. L. REV. 257, 266 (2006); *see also* Daniel J. Gervais, *The Lisbon Agreement's Misunderstood Potential*, 1 WORLD INTELL. PROP. ORG. J. 87, 96–97 (2010) (discussing how a country may refuse a registration if the name is generic in its country).

[44] Lisbon Agreement, *supra* note 1, art. 6.

[45] *Cf.* Graeme B. Dinwoodie, *Developing a Private International Intellectual Property Law: The Demise of Territoriality?* 51 WM. & MARY L. REV. 711, 731 (2009) (arguing that the United States applies *lex originis* in authorship copyright law by giving special weight to "the nationality of the authors and the place of first publication").

[46] Lisbon Agreement, *supra* note 1, art. 14.

[47] *See* Paris Convention for the Protection of Industrial Property, March 20, 1883, *as revised* July 14, 1967, 21 U.S.T. 1629, 828 U.N.T.S. 305 [hereinafter Paris Convention].

jurisdictions – a principle known as the independence of patents and trademarks.[48] In the case of infringement, the law of the country where protection is claimed (*lex loci delicti*) typically applies.[49] It would be strange indeed if a court could not find a patent or mark invalid unless it had been found invalid in the inventor's or trademark owner's country of origin. Yet that was, and still is, the system under the 1958 Lisbon Agreement.

Implementing this provision functionally requires a *sui generis* system because countries that protect GIs using trademarks assess genericness *in their territory* and not in the mark's country of origin. In previous scholarship, I have suggested that the Lisbon system should eliminate this obstacle to make it possible for countries protecting GIs under trademark systems to join. Unfortunately, the Geneva Act, while it uses language that differs from the 1958 Lisbon Agreement text, essentially maintains a version of the *lex originis* regime, especially in its Article 12, which reads: "Subject to the provisions of this Act, registered appellations of origin and registered geographical indications cannot be considered to have become generic in a Contracting Party."[50]

In sum, as already noted the Geneva Act, like the 1958 Lisbon Agreement, allows a Lisbon member to reject a GI within twelve months of registration if it is generic in their territory.[51] It will also allow its members to maintain coexistence of a GI and a trademark and protect prior trademark rights. However, if the GI gets protection under the Lisbon system and later becomes generic in a Lisbon Agreement member state, for example, because of inaction or even acquiescing by the holder of the GI, then it is far from clear under either the 1958 Lisbon Agreement or the Geneva Act how that Lisbon member could find this GI generic if the GI is not generic in its country of origin.[52] If that is so, then there is at least one irreconcilable difference between the Lisbon Agreement and the common law.

---

[48] Paris Convention, *supra* note 47, arts. 4*bis*, 6 (proclaiming the independence of patents and marks).

[49] See *id.* arts. 6*quinquies*(B), 10*ter*(2); Berne Convention for the Protection of Literary and Artistic Works art. 6*bis*, September 9, 1886, 1161 U.N.T.S. 3 (amended Sept. 28, 1979). see also Pamela E. Kraver & Robert E. Purcell, *Application of the Lanham Act to Extraterritorial Activities: Trend Toward Universality or Imperialism?* 77 J. Pat. & Trademark Off. Soc'y 115, 121–22 (1995) (discussing choice of law principles, including *lex loci delicti*).

[50] Geneva Act, *supra* note 1, arts. 8(1), 12.

[51] Lisbon Agreement, *supra* note 1, art. 5(3), (4); Geneva Act, *supra* note 1, art. 15(1).

[52] Lisbon Agreement, *supra* note 1, art. 6; Geneva Act, *supra* note 1, art. 12.

2.5 Conflicts with Prior Trademarks and Generic Terms

The 1958 Lisbon Agreement allows its members to adopt or continue to use one of three approaches in managing conflicts between trademarks and GIs (however those are protected under national law): (1) a "first in time, first in right" approach; (2) a "coexistence approach" (that is, a GI and trademark with similar legal effect); or (3) a "GI superiority approach," under which the GI wins the conflict, except perhaps where the previous trademark is considered well known.[53]

"First in time, first in right" usually is understood to mean first *in the territory of the jurisdiction concerned*.[54] One could see a degree of irony in the case of GIs because GIs very often have been in use for decades or more before the registration of a trademark that would defeat the use of such GIs in a country other than the country of origin.[55] Yet, as a matter of trademark law, the analysis focuses on the domestic market and is largely a question of the domestic consumer's perception – although this perception may include

---

[53] Lina Montén, *Geographical Indications of Origin: Should They Be Protected and Why? – An Analysis of the Issue from the US and EU Perspectives*, 22 Santa Clara Computer & High-Tech. L.J. 315, 328–30 (2006). For example, while the EU has a GI superiority approach in most cases, its regulations provide protection for prior, well-known marks. See Council Regulation No 510/2006 of March 20, 2006, on the Protection of Geographical Indications and Designations of Origin for Agricultural Products and Foodstuffs, art 3(4), 2006 O.J. (L 93) 12, 14–15 (EC). The European Union's Council Regulations provide that a "designation of origin or geographical indication shall not be registered where, in the light of a trademark's reputation and renown and the length of time it has been used, registration is liable to mislead the consumer as to the true identity of the product." In sum, EU law provides that prior well-known trademarks prevail over GIs and allows coexistence of prior trademarks not considered to be well-known. *Id.*

[54] *See* Frederick W. Mostert, Famous and Well-Known Marks: An International Analysis 2–34 (2nd edn. 2004) (arguing that the principle of "first in time, first in right" should be applied to resolve for GI–trademark conflicts); *see also* Dev Gangjee, *Quibbling Siblings: Conflicts Between Trademarks and Geographical Indications*, 82 Chi.-Kent L. Rev. 1253, 1262 (2007) ("Given the similarity of function and therefore presumed epistemological backcloth for both trademarks and GIs, the principle of 'first in time, first in right' has been suggested as a means of resolving such conflicts."). A number of trade agreements have enshrined this principle. *See, e.g.*, Free Trade Agreement, Austl.-U.S., art. 17.2(4), May 18, 2004, KAV 6422; *see also* Chase C. Rhee, Principles of International Trade (Import-Export): The First Step Toward Globalization 48 (5th edn. 2012) (regarding the US-Singapore Free Trade Agreement, which applies the principle of "first in time, first in right").

[55] *See Geographical Indication Protection in the United States*, US Patent and Trademark Office, www.uspto.gov/sites/default/files/web/offices/dcom/olia/globalip/pdf/gi_system.pdf (last visited February 8, 2016) ("The United States has provided protection to foreign and domestic GIs since at least 1946, decades prior to the implementation of the TRIPS Agreement (1995) when the term of art 'geographical indication' came into wide use."). I am grateful to Keri Johnston (of MARQUES) for this insight.

knowledge gained through advertising of a famous mark not in use or not yet widely used in the territory concerned.[56] The Geneva Act thus allows, but does not mandate, a country party to it to apply the "first in time, first in right" principle in resolving GI–trademark disputes.[57]

It is worth recalling the four main features that apply to WTO members under the TRIPS Agreement. First, a member of the World Trade Organization (WTO) must refuse or invalidate the registration of a trademark that contains or consists of a geographical indication if (1) the goods do not originate in the territory indicated; and (2) use of the indication in the trademark for such goods in the territory of the "member" concerned is *of such a nature as to mislead* the public as to the true place of origin.[58] Second, for GIs used in connection with wines and spirits, however, deception (misleading the public as to the true place of origin) does not need to be present.[59] Third, Article 24.5 of the TRIPS Agreement then allows a WTO member to protect those who were using or applied for registration of a trademark (or were "grandfathered") in the WTO member concerned either before the TRIPS Agreement became applicable in the WTO member concerned or before the indication in question was protected in its country of origin.[60] Fourth, Article 24.6 of the TRIPS Agreement provides that WTO members may decide not to protect a geographical indication used in connection with foreign goods or services[61] when the relevant indication "is identical with the term customary in common language as the common name for such goods or services in the territory of that Member."[62]

In *EC–Trademarks and Geographical Indications I*, a WTO dispute-settlement panel explained that the coexistence of a protected indication and a trademark can be considered, under certain circumstances a limited exception justifiable under Article 17 of the TRIPS

---

[56] This situation is reflected in TRIPS Article 16, which provides that in determining whether a trademark is well known for the purposes of applying Article 6*bis* of the Paris Convention (which only applies to identical or similar goods but which TRIPS extends to both dissimilar goods and services), WTO "Members shall take account of the knowledge of the trademark in the relevant sector of the public, including knowledge in the Member concerned which has been obtained as a result of the promotion of the trademark." TRIPS Agreement, *supra* note 19, art. 16; Paris Convention, *supra* note 47, art. 6*bis*.

[57] Geneva Act, *supra* note 1, art. 13(1).   [58] TRIPS Agreement, *supra* note 19, art. 22.3.

[59] *Id.* art. 23.2.

[60] *Id.* art. 24.5; *see also* World Intellectual Prop. Org. [WIPA], *Possible Solutions for Conflicts between Trademarks and Geographical Indications and for Conflicts between Homonymous Geographical Indications*, 11–12, WIPO Doc. SC/5/3 (June 8, 2000).

[61] TRIPS Agreement, *supra* note 11, art. 24.6.   [62] *Id.*

Agreement.[63] In other words, the coexistence of a protected indication and a nonfamous trademark is a permitted exception to *trademark rights*.[64] In sum, the TRIPS Agreement allows – but does not mandate – continued application of "first in time, first in right" by each WTO member.[65]

The Geneva Act is clearer on this point than the 1958 Lisbon Agreement in that it provides specific conflict rules, which mostly allow for prior trademark rights to be protected, and, like the text of the 1958 Lisbon Agreement, allows GIs to be rejected for genericness in a member country *at the time that country joins the system*. Because the genericide prohibition was maintained in the Geneva Act, it would make it difficult, however, to reconcile the new Act with "first in time, first in right" in the case of a GI that was used but becomes generic as a geographic term in a country, if the owner of the GI then tries to prevent its use, or the use of a similar term, by a third party as a trademark or even otherwise (e.g. a descriptive use). A country joining the Geneva Act may thus limit its option to use to its full extent the exception regime under the TRIPS Agreement as interpreted in the WTO dispute-settlement process.[66]

3 COMMON-LAW GEOGRAPHICAL INDICATIONS

3.1 *Geographical Indications and a Free Market Economy*

Attaching an intangible yet measurable (that is, a higher price due to the intellectual property rent) value to the identification of the geographic origin

---

[63] Panel Report, *European Communities – Protection of Trademarks and Geographical Indications for Agricultural Products and Foodstuffs: Complaint by the United States*, ¶ 7.688, WT/DS174/R (March 15, 2005); Panel Report, *European Communities – Protection of Trademarks and Geographical Indications for Agricultural Products and Foodstuffs: Complaint by Australia*, ¶ 7.644–7.686, WT/DS290/R (March 15, 2005).

[64] And thus allowed under Article 17 of TRIPS. See TRIPS Agreement, *supra* note 19, art. 17 ("Members may provide limited exceptions to the rights conferred by a trademark ..."). The report of the dispute-settlement panel mentioned in the previous note concluded, "with respect to the coexistence of GIs with prior trademarks, the Regulation is inconsistent with Article 16.1 of the TRIPS Agreement but, on the basis of the evidence presented to the Panel, this is justified by Article 17 of the TRIPS Agreement." *Complaint by Australia*, *supra* note 64, ¶ 7.686; *Complaint by the US*, *supra* note 64, ¶ 7.688. In countries that use certification marks and/or the torts of "unfair competition" and "passing off" in this context, such a conflict would be between two trademarks, not between a trademark and "something else," such as a GI.

[65] Essentially, under TRIPS Article 24.5, a prior trademark continues to be registrable and its owner may continue to use the mark. This must be interpreted together with Article 16.1.

[66] State practice subsequent to the adoption of a treaty is one of the relevant factors in that treaty's interpretation. Vienna Convention on the Law of Treaties art. 31(3)(b). May 23, 1969, 1155 U.N.T.S. 331 (entered into force January 27, 1980).

of a product seems to postulate the existence of a correlative, measurable difference in *actual quality*, that is, an objectively quantifiable difference between products of different origin but similar composition – say, a wine produced from Pinot Noir grapes in Napa Valley, New Zealand, or Bourgogne (Burgundy).[67] One could posit that this measurable difference – assuming that one *can* measure it – lies in natural factors such as soil and climate. This now brings us to the *terroir*. Indeed, a system of protection for denominations of geographic origin emphasizes the cluster of factors traditionally amalgamated under the term *terroir*: tradition, know-how, and a link between product and land.[68] *Terroir* is used as a marketing tool to extract additional rents.

A consumer who does not share the history and culture of the French, Italian, or Spanish *terroir* may not easily identify with the conventions and practices that were used to define the quality of a product (say, a red wine) at its point of origin. That same consumer *can* nonetheless attribute a higher value or quality to a product for a different set of reasons. Even if the higher price resulting from the linkage between a product and its origin is arguably or even demonstrably irrational – say, because no measurable objective quality differentiates the product and its non-GI equivalent – that is not a fatal argument against GI protection: trademarks also sometimes perform an "irrational" yet well-accepted function in guiding consumer behavior.[69] Put differently, and more concretely, using a consumer's belief that *brie* cheese will be not just different but *better* because it was produced in Meaux[70] (France), as opposed to in an unknown location in some industrial plant or even in a known cheese producing location (such as the US state

---

[67] *See* DAVID BIRD, UNDERSTANDING WINE TECHNOLOGY: THE SCIENCE OF WINE EXPLAINED 1–16 (2005).

[68] *See* Irene Calboli, *Of Markets, Culture and Terroir: The Unique Economic and Culture-Related Benefits of Geographical Indications of Origin*, in INTERNATIONAL INTELLECTUAL PROPERTY 433, 434 (Daniel J. Gervais ed., 2015) (describing *terroir* as a "deep traditional connection to the land – where the products are grown, processed, or manufactured").

[69] *See* McCarthy, *supra* note 7, § 2:38 (discussing the criticism that trademarks create irrational consumer preferences).

[70] "Meaux" is the name of a town near Paris, France. Brie de Meaux is a protected indication, but "Brie" is not. BRIE DE MEAUX is Lisbon entry no. 686 and was registered on October 5, 1983. *See (686) Brie de Meaux*, WORLD INTELL. PROP. ORG., www.wipo.int/ipdl/en/lisbon/key.jsp?KEY=686 (last visited February 9, 2016). Wisconsin also produces "brie" cheese. *See Brie*, WIS. CHEESE, www.eatwisconsincheese.com/wisconsin-cheese/article?cid=9 (last visited February 9, 2016) ("Wisconsin has become an important source of Brie for American consumers").

of Wisconsin), is not incompatible with the principles of a "free" market economy.[71]

3.2 Geographical Indications as Marks

Geographical indications, like trademarks, depend on reputation and associated goodwill.[72] To paraphrase Professor Dev Gangjee, they share the same epistemological backcloth.[73] Reputation is an element mentioned in both the Lisbon Agreement and the TRIPS Agreement.[74] "Normal" trademarks, collective marks, and certification marks can be used as symbols of or ways to suggest geographic origin.

A feature of common law–based trademark law is the so-called "first in time, first in right" approach, according to which the first user in a given territory will have senior rights. Using the US system as an exemplar of such an approach, a geographic designation of origin must not clash with a preexisting trademark if it is to be protected under a trademark system.[75] Similarly, a geographic term that is generic in the US cannot acquire trademark status.[76] A term that is merely descriptive can be protected as a mark once it acquires secondary meaning.[77]

In the case of a geographic *certification mark*, there is a *collective goodwill* linked to a region or locality. This notion of collective goodwill emerged in the United Kingdom in the so-called "Drinks" cases.[78] Collective goodwill is goodwill shared by a group of producers. Any producer part of the group may file a claim in civil courts to protect the goodwill – without having to show control over or agreement of the collective.

---

[71] Unless the perception is based on deceptive marketing practices, but that is typically handled under a different area of law.
[72] See McCarthy, *supra* note 7, § 2:38, at 2–76.   [73] See Gangjee, *supra* note 54, at 1262.
[74] Lisbon Agreement, *supra* note 1, art. 2(2); TRIPS Agreement, *supra* note 19, art. 22.1.
[75] See McCarthy, *supra* note 7, § 16:1.   [76] See *id.* § 14:18.
[77] See *id.* § 11:25. The rule is a bit more complicated, but the details are not necessary for our purposes.
[78] Bollinger v. Costa Brava Wine Co. Ltd. [1961] RPC 116 (Ch.) (Eng.); Vine Prods. Ltd. v. Mackenzie & Co Ltd. [1969] RPC 1 (Ch.) at 4 (Eng.) (citing Bollinger v. Costa Brava Wine Co. Ltd. [1960] RPC 16 (Ch.) (Eng.)). These cases have a progeny in the UK. John Walker & Sons Ltd. v. Henry Ost & Co Ltd. [1970] RPC 151 (Ch.) (Eng.); HP Bulmer Ltd. v. Bollinger S.A. [1978] RPC 79 (C.A.) (Eng.); Erven Warnink Besloten Vennootschap v. J Townend & Sons (Hull) Ltd. [1979] AC 731 (HL) (Eng.). The same happened in other common-law jurisdictions. Canada: Institut National des Appellations d'Origine des Vins et Eaux-de-Vie v. Andre Wines Ltd. (1990) 30 C.P.R. 3d 279 (Can. Ont. C.A.); Dairy Bureau of Canada v. Annable Foods Ltd. (1993) 46 C.P.R. 3d 289, 309 (Can. B.C. Sup. Ct.); New Zealand: Comite Interprofessionel du Vin de Champagne v. Wineworths Group, Ltd. [1991] 2 NZLR 432 (HC).

US courts have also recognized that goodwill can be shared but they have generally taken a less liberal approach on the right of action by individual users. They have given the holder of a certification mark more control over its use and enforcement. For example, in *State of Idaho Potato Comm'n v. G & T Terminal Packaging, Inc.*, the Ninth Circuit found that selling genuine Idaho potatoes using the name IDAHO constituted counterfeiting of the certification mark IDAHO for potatoes because the mark owner had not had the opportunity to exercise quality control.[79] The owner of the mark "acts as the representative of the mark users."[80] Hence, as a matter of trademark law, the owner of a certification mark – not the State – controls the certification standards. Examples of US geographic certification marks include FAMOUS IDAHO POTATOES, FAMOUS POTATOES GROWN IN IDAHO, GROWN IN IDAHO IDAHO POTATOES, and PREMIUM PACKED IDAHO POTATOES for (unsurprisingly) Idaho potatoes; PARMIGIANO-REGGIANO, ROQUEFORT, STILTON, and REAL CALIFORNIA for cheese; PARMA for ham; DARJEELING for tea; WASHINGTON for apples; and THE FLORIDA SUNSHINE TREE for citrus.[81]

Certification marks have also been used in a more typical "Lisbon" context: booze. The three US "Cognac" cases serve as milestones on the road to GI protection via trademark law. The first case dates back to 1944.[82] The case involved applications for the trademarks COLOGNAC and CALOGNAC for brandy. Oppositions to those applications were filed by a "genuine" (French) Cognac maker.[83] The oppositions were not made on the basis of preexisting registrations for other marks (such as COGNAC). Instead they were made under the terms of the statute in force at the time, which allowed certain parties (this would emerge in the case, as we shall see) to oppose the use of

---

[79] State of Idaho Potato Comm'n v. G & T Terminal Packaging, Inc., 425 F.3d 708, 721–22 (9th Cir. 2005).
[80] McCarthy, *supra* note 7, §19:92.50, at 19–305.
[81] FAMOUS IDAHO POTATOES FAMOUS POTATOES GROWN IN IDAHO, Registration No. 2,403,069; PARMIGIANO-REGGIANO, Registration No. 1,896,683; ROQUEFORT, Registration No. 571,798; STILTON, Registration No. 1,959,589; REAL CALIFORNIA CHEESE, Registration No. 1,285,675; PARMA HAM, Registration No. 2,014,628; DARJEELING, Registration No. 1,632,726; WASHINGTON, Registration No 1,528,514; THE FLORIDA SUNSHINE TREE, Registration No. 932,033. The vast majority of certification marks in the United States are not for geographic origin. This majority includes marks registered by unions and various standardization bodies, such as Underwriters' Laboratories. *See* JEFFREY BELSON, SPECIAL REPORT: CERTIFICATION MARKS 26–28 (2002).
[82] The date matters because, although the case is silent on that point, sympathy for France may have been a factor at that particular juncture in US history.
[83] Otard, Inc. v. Italian Swiss Colony, 141 F.2d 706 (C.C.P.A. 1944).

descriptors as marks if those descriptors would confuse or mislead the consumer. Reversing both the Examiner of Trade-Mark Interferences – who had not recognized the opposer's right to oppose the applications – and the Commissioner of Trademarks, the Court of Customs and Patent Appeals confirmed the opposer's standing and agreed with the opposer.[84] The Court stated the following in a passage that has the unmistakable aroma of an "Old World" GI perspective:

> Cognac is a name applied to a type of brandy distilled from wines made from grapes grown in a limited territorial region of France, often referred to as the Cognac district, the boundaries of which are defined by French law ... there is a certain quality in the soil of the region which gives to the grapes there grown a particular character or flavor, which enters into the brandy made from them, and that that quality of soil is not found elsewhere in France, nor, it is claimed, in any other part of the world. It is recognized as a superior brandy.[85]

The second case, four decades later, dealt with applications for two similar derivatives of Cognac, namely COLOGNAC and CALOGNAC.[86] The case evidently bears strong resemblance to the previous one, but here the opposer was not an individual producer of Cognac but rather an entity responsible under French law for defending the word Cognac.[87] Between the two cases, Congress had adopted the 1946 Trademark (Lanham) Act, which contained a specific provision for certification marks.[88] Indeed, one of the Board's first steps in this second case was to note that the statute defined certification marks and included marks used to denote a geographic origin.[89] The 1946 statute also contained the now familiar prohibition of the registration of a mark that, "when applied to the goods of the applicant, is primarily geographically descriptive or deceptively misdescriptive of them."[90] The Board's approach was consonant with trademark law principles, putting the focus squarely on consumer deception:

---

[84] *Id.* at 709–11. [85] *Id.* at 708.

[86] Bureau Nat'l Interprofessionnel du Cognac v. Int'l Better Drinks Corp., 6 U.S.P.Q.2d 1610, 1615 (T.T.A.B. 1988). The application was filed in 1984. *Id.* at 1610.

[87] *Id.* at 1610–11. [88] Trademark Act, 15 U.S.C. §§ 1052(d), (e), 1054 (1946).

[89] *Bureau Nat'l Interprofessionnel du Cognac*, 6 U.S.P.Q.2d at 1614. The terminology was new, but not the notion of a collectively owned mark. Section 62 of the Trade-Marks Act of 1905 referred to standardization marks. Trade Marks Act 1905, 9 Edw. 7 c. 15, § 62 (Eng.). The statute was amended in 1936 and again in 1938 to provide for registration of collective marks owned by foreign associations. *See* S. REP. NO. 1770 (1938). Some of these marks were used to denote a form of certification by the foreign association. *Id.*

[90] Trademark Act, *supra* note 88, § 1052(e)(2).

> [I]f a mark is the name of a place known generally to the public, purchasers who encounter goods bearing the mark would think that the goods originate in that place [i.e., purchasers would make a "goods-place association" ...], [if] the goods do not come from the named place, and the deception is material to the purchasing decision, the mark is deceptive under Section 2 (a); if the deception is not material to the purchasing decision, the mark is primarily geographically deceptively misdescriptive under Section 2(e)(2) of the Act.[91]

In the third and final case, decided a decade later, the opposer, the French Institut National des Appellations d'Origine, was also a "GI defending entity" responsible for defending several protected wine and spirit appellations of origin in France.[92] The Board applied Section 2(d) of the Lanham Act, which deals with the likelihood of confusion with a preexisting mark, and decided that the test was the same as for other marks:

> There is nothing in the language of Section 2(d) which mandates or warrants application of one level of likelihood of confusion analysis ... in cases where the plaintiff's mark is a trademark or service mark, but a different and more limited likelihood of confusion analysis in cases where the plaintiff's mark is a certification mark.[93]

In other words, a showing of deception was unnecessary. Certification marks should be treated for purposes of an infringement analysis in the same way as ordinary trademarks. While the opinion parallels the previous case, it is worth noting that the Board also recognized protection of the COGNAC mark under *labeling regulations*.[94]

Overall, the picture that emerges from the Cognac cases and others shows a willingness to recognize collective goodwill in the form of (common-law) certification marks.[95] The application of trademark law by US courts and other authorities suggests that common law can protect symbols of geographic origin

---

[91] *Bureau Nat'l Interprofessionnel du Cognac*, 6 U.S.P.Q.2d at 1615.
[92] Institut Nat'l des Appellations d'Origine v. Brown-Forman Corp., 47 U.S.P.Q.2d 1875, 1877 (T.T.A.B. 1998). Apparently, the applicant's concoction actually contained some French brandy. *Id.* at 1880.
[93] *Id.* at 1890.
[94] *Id.* at 1878, 1885–96. The regulation is 27 C.F.R. § 5.22(d)(2) (2014) (recognizing French governmental authority to designate and regulate Cognac grape brandy distilled in the Cognac region of France).
[95] This actually started with Pillsbury-Washburn Flour Mills Co v. Eagle, 86 F. 608 (7th Cir. 1898). For a fuller discussion of this topic (from which this part of the Article is derived), *see* Daniel Gervais, *A Cognac after Spanish Champagne? Geographical Indications as Certification Marks*, in INTELLECTUAL PROPERTY AT THE EDGE 130, 135–36 (Rochelle Cooper Dreyfuss & Jane C. Ginsburg eds., 2014).

used in trade beyond the US *sui generis* mechanism used for alcohol labels. Unfortunately, for the future of the Lisbon system, using trademark law to protect GIs implies the ability to remove a mark not used by its owner from the register. More generally, trademark law in common law jurisdictions implies (1) a requirement of use to register, (2) the payment of renewal or maintenance fees, and (3) a level of protection tied to the existence of a likelihood of confusion except for famous or well-known marks.[96] None of these are allowed, at least explicitly, under the Geneva Act even though they were raised on several occasions by delegations at the Diplomatic Conference. The Geneva Act does allow member countries to impose examination and use fees, however, as well as declarations of intention to use a GI.[97]

3.3 The Future of the Lisbon System

As of the date of the Diplomatic Conference that adopted the Geneva Act of the Lisbon Agreement in May 2015, the so-called Special Union (of Lisbon members) had twenty-eight member states.[98] Many of the members will likely join the Geneva Act, which is also open to intergovernmental organizations such as the European Union and Organisation Africaine de la Propriété Intellectuelle (OAPI).[99] Even if several OAPI members join Lisbon, how much they will use it (that is, how many GIs they will actually register) is unclear. Indeed, some OAPI members are already members of the "old" Agreement and have not used it much.[100] North African countries such as

---

[96] On the protection of well-known marks, the TRIPS Agreement requires WTO members to take account "of the knowledge of the trademark in the relevant sector of the public, including knowledge in the Member concerned which has been obtained as a result of the promotion of the trademark." TRIPS Agreement, *supra* note 19, art. 16.2.

[97] Geneva Act, *supra* note 1 art. 7(4); WIPO Document LI/DC/19, *supra* note 1, rule 5(4)(b).

[98] See *supra* notes 1, 16; see also World Intellectual Prop. Org. [WIPO], *Contracting Parties or Signatories of Treaties Administered by WIPO: Lisbon Agreement for the Protection of Appellations of Origin and Their International Registration*, www.wipo.int/export/sites/www/treaties/en/documents/pdf/lisbon.pdf (last visited November 20, 2015). The term "Special Union" (that is, the group of parties to the Lisbon Agreement) is used in the Lisbon Agreement (1958), *supra* note 1, art. 1, and in the Geneva Act, *supra* note 1, art. 21.

[99] Geneva Act, *supra* note 1, art. 22(2). The OAPI has seventeen members, most of which are French-speaking sub-Saharan African countries. *États Membres*, ORGANISATION AFRICAINE DE LA PROPRIÉTÉ INTELLECTUELLE, www.oapi.int/index.php/en/aipo/etats-membres (last visited February 9, 2016).

[100] The following countries are members of both agreements: Burkina Faso, Congo, Gabon, and Togo. See *Contracting Parties or Signatories of Treaties Administered by WIPO – Lisbon Agreement for the Protection of Appellations of Origin and Their International Registration*, *supra* note 98; *Etats Members*, *supra* note 99.

Morocco and Tunisia, together with Algeria, which is already party to the "old" (1958/1967) Act, may also join the Geneva Act membership. A few Latin American countries might do so as well, adding to the existing five members of the old Agreement (Costa Rica, Cuba, Mexico, Nicaragua, and Peru).[101] More importantly, European membership will likely broaden to include most or all EU members (including Germany, who is not currently a Lisbon member) and possibly Moldova and Russia, among others. This means a potential of approximately fifty to fifty-five member states. If the European Union were to join backed by all its member states, it would potentially have a majority vote in the Special Union (which it could exercise as a single vote on behalf of all twenty-eight EU members).[102]

The denouement of the Geneva Act story may be complicated, however. Despite the strength of the opposition manifested at the closing plenary by a number of common-law jurisdictions, the art of trade negotiations is such that anything is possible. Smaller common-law jurisdictions might find it harder to resist EU trade pressure to join Lisbon. Some of the nations that negotiated the moribund TPP recently introduced *sui generis* GI legislation that may make it easier for them to agree to join Lisbon, for example, as part of a trade deal with the European Union.[103] The list of bilateral EU trade agreements with a GI focus might soon include India.

Then, multinational companies, including those based in the common law world, that use terms they consider generic or descriptive on their products may find Lisbon members in the path of their trade transactions with other nations, including members of the Association of Southeast Asian Nations (ASEAN), where the cost of protecting foreign GIs (and implementation of the Geneva Act) could be low, and may bring substantial beneficiaries in trade dealings with the European Union.[104] Even so, a question that remains is what

---

[101] Haiti is also a member. *See Contracting Parties or Signatories of Treaties Administered by WIPO – Lisbon Agreement for the Protection of Appellations of Origin and Their International Registration, supra* note 98.

[102] *See* Lisbon Agreement, *supra* note 1 art. 22(b)(4)(ii) (allowing any Contracting Party that is an intergovernmental organization to vote in place of its members).

[103] *See, e.g.*, Geographical Indications of Goods (Registration and Protection) Act, 1999, No. 48 Acts of Parliament, 1999 (India); Geographical Indications Act, 2000 (Act 602) (Malay.); Geographical Indicators Regulation, 2007, Gov. Reg. No. 51 (2007) (Indon.).

[104] According to an April 2015 press release announcing the restart of EU-ASEAN trade talks, "[t]he EU is ASEAN's second-largest trading partner with total trade amounting to $248 billion in 2014 and was Southeast Asia's largest source of foreign direct investment in 2014 with $29.1 billion, or 21.3% of foreign inflows to the region." *See EU and ASEAN to Jumpstart Trade Agreement Talks* EURACTIV (April 27, 2015), www.euractiv.com/sections/trade-society/eu-and-asean-kick-start-free-trade-agreement-talks-314100 (last visited February 9, 2016).

the European Union will be prepared to concede to get ASEAN countries to adhere to the Geneva Act.

More importantly, normative countermeasures, such as definitions of prior rights or genericness standards incompatible with the Lisbon standard, may emerge. The TPP text was not easy to reconcile with Article 12 of the Geneva Act (providing for genericide only in the country of origin of the GI): it provides that a GI may become generic in each country that protects it, leading to its potential invalidation in such country.[105] The apparent TPP failure probably pushes this back to diplomatic *oubliettes*. More generally, adequate heed should be paid to the renewed emphasis on the role of certification marks to protect GIs which has surfaced in various fora.

4 CONCLUSION

The adoption of the Geneva Act of the Lisbon Agreement was a clear chance to update the Lisbon Agreement to reconcile the Lisbon system on two fronts: doctrinally, with the common law; and administratively, by allowing countries that protect GIs under trademark law (often as certification marks) to continue to do so as Lisbon members. That did not happen, however, at least not clearly. The absence of consensus – indeed, the deep divide – at the Diplomatic Conference and the stated[106] incompatibility of the Geneva Act with trademark-based GI systems are unlikely to prove productive in the short- to medium term for GI holders, authorized users

---

[105] The TPP text available as of November 2015 is not easy to reconcile with Article 12 of the Geneva Act on genericide only in the country of origin of the GI, in that it provides that a GI may become generic in each country that protects it, leading to its potential invalidation in such country. Article 18.32.(3) provides "No Party shall preclude the possibility that the protection or recognition of a geographical indication may be cancelled, or otherwise cease, on the basis that the protected or recognised term has ceased meeting the conditions upon which the protection or recognition was originally granted in that Party." Trans-Pacific Partnership, *supra* note 3, 18.32(3).

[106] Reference is made here to statements, notably by Australia, Japan, Korea, and the United States, during the closing plenary of the Diplomatic Conference that adopted the Geneva Act (May 20, 2015). The author attended the event and this is from personal knowledge as the Records of the conference had not yet been published as of this writing. However, archived webcasts of all official meetings are available. *Diplomatic Conference for the Adoption of a New Act of the Lisbon Agreement*, WORLD INTELL. PROP. ORG., www.wipo .int/webcasting/en/index.jsp (last visited November 20, 2015) (select "LI/DC: Diplomatic Conference for the Adoption of a New Act of the Lisbon Agreement for the Protection of Appellations Of" in the Videos on Demand Search Bar, scroll to and select "LI/DC – Tues 19 – English Afternoon Main Committee I"; the US delegation makes its proposal between 1:29:50 and 1:33:10).

of GIs, users of generic denominations, or consumers. The bridge between the Lisbon system and the common law has not been built by the Geneva Act. Some useful foundations were laid, but much remains to be done. The bridge, if it is ever built, will not be the result of a normative encounter. It will be made of trade bricks.

PART II

GEOGRAPHICAL INDICATIONS AT THE CROSSROADS OF INTERNATIONAL AND NATIONAL TRADE

6

Geographical Indications and Mega-Regional Trade Agreements and Negotiations

Susy Frankel[*]

1 INTRODUCTION: THE EXCESSES OF THE TRADE-RELATED APPROACH

In the presentation of this chapter in draft form, I asked the following question, 'how do you spot a dodgy international intellectual property claim?' One possible answer to that question is that those who own intellectual property (IP) rights in one jurisdiction, where those rights have developed from local or regional policies, want those locally grounded rights exported to other legal systems in order to protect IP-related products exported to those jurisdictions. That proposition alone cannot be the only way to spot a 'dodgy IP claim' because that is a description of many international IP negotiations where there are attempts to gain at least some international agreement on minimum standards of protection. The 'dodgy' aspect arises when incumbents want more protection (without convincing evidence that more protection is needed), and in seeking that greater protection, those incumbents suggest that newcomers will gain immeasurable bounty. This is exactly how the European Union presents its geographical indications (GIs) policy to its trading partners. The argument usually involves three steps. First, multiple GIs have worked in Europe. Second, there are one or two instances of GIs working for developing countries. The following statement from the European Commission illustrates these first two steps:

> The protection of geographical indications matters economically and culturally. They can create value for local communities. Over the years European countries have taken the lead in identifying and protecting their geographical indications. They support rural development and promote new job opportunities in production, processing and other related services.

---

[*] Professor of Law, Chair in Intellectual Property and International Trade, Faculty of Law, Victoria University of Wellington.

> For example: Cognac, Roquefort cheese, Sherry, Parmigiano Reggiano, Teruel and Parma hams, Tuscany olives, Budějovické pivo, and Budapesti téliszalámi.
>
> Geographical indications are becoming a useful intellectual property right for developing countries because of their potential to add value and promote rural socio-economic development. Most countries have a range of local products that correspond to the concept of geographical indications but only a few are already known or protected globally.
>
> For example: Basmati rice or Darjeeling tea through products that are deeply rooted in tradition, culture and geography.[1]

The third step proffered to complete this argument is that because GIs 'with commercial value are exposed to misuse and counterfeiting',[2] GI protection EU style should be the global legal norm in order to prevent this misuse and counterfeiting.

While there is plenty of truth in these statements – after all no one doubts the value of using the origin of a product to sell it when that origin has cachet – there is also a considerable weakness in the logic that purportedly links the three propositions. This weakness is because the success of GIs (as a legal model for exploiting the value in origin of goods) from one territory does not mean that success can be easily replicated in other territories. First, what makes GIs valuable, at least initially, is the place with which the GI-branded product is associated. Such associations (if they are genuine) are not identically replicable. More importantly, the success of GIs is dependent on multiple factors, including investment and infrastructure around the business, industry, place and communities concerned. The legal framework alone, for GIs, is unlikely to create development of the local industry without those other factors being present. Some chapters in this book suggest positive uses of GIs in Asia for those other than Darjeeling tea and Basmati rice,[3] but a remarkable amount of literature (including the above-quoted statement from the European Union) pinpoints these as examples of how developing countries could succeed in improving their agricultural economy with GIs. This sort of statement is often proffered without an appropriately corresponding analysis of the transferability of the GI mechanism to other communities and other products. In fact, as developing countries repeatedly have shown, the removal of agricultural subsidies in the developed world would make a real difference and enable developing countries to compete in world markets for agricultural

---

[1] *Geographical Indications*, EUROPEAN COMMISSION, http://ec.europa.eu/trade/policy/accessing-markets/intellectual-property/geographical-indications/ (last visited 21 March 2016).
[2] *Id.* [3] See, in particular, the chapters in Part III of this volume.

products. In a manner prescient of an EU-directed path with GIs, most developed countries have not removed agricultural subsidies (with the notable exception of New Zealand) and, in order for developing countries to compete with developed countries, large developing countries now also subsidise agriculture.[4] The losers are those countries that cannot afford subsides, particularly the small developing countries, which may agree to implement GI regimes when they are in trade negotiations. This is the kind of outcome that happens when the 'weak bargain with the strong'.[5]

Just as the GI policy of one country may not be a good fit for another country, evidence that GIs have been effective as a development tool in one community is not evidence that the same model of GIs will be effective in all communities.[6] As William van Caenegem, Peter Drahos and Jen Cleary have discussed, the success of GIs as a tool in certain parts of the Australian wine industry, for example, is attributable not only to GIs but to certain other factors which are not simply replicable by enacting GI laws.[7] Their research demonstrates that certain industries have benefited from investment accompanied by GIs in Australia.[8] This research reveals that a careful calculus is required. The authors suggest that if that benefit of GIs is to be replicated, then Australian autonomy over the design of any law to extend GI protection is crucial.

The international minimum standards for GIs should not be moulded on a legal regime that cannot accommodate appropriate differences between different countries and even different communities in those countries. The benefits of GIs to local communities are only possible with appropriate

---

[4] See, e.g., Jason Clay, *Are Agricultural Subsidies Causing More Harm Than Good?*, THE GUARDIAN (8 August 2013), www.theguardian.com/sustainable-business/agricultural-subsidies-reform-government-support (concluding 'global economic progress requires a recalibration of how we approach today's challenges. Agricultural subsidies can be a blunt instrument that can impede progress and slow economic growth if they're wielded without precision and a specific cut-off date. We'll only succeed in protecting our planet – and our food security – if we change how we think about subsidies and how we use them.').

[5] I borrow this phrase from Peter Drahos, *When the Weak Bargain with the Strong: Negotiations in the World Trade Organization*, 8 INT'L NEGOT. 79–109 (2003), http://papers.ssrn.com/sol3/papers.cfm?abstract_id=418480.

[6] For an expansion of this argument in relation to traditional knowledge, see Susy Frankel, *The Mismatch of Geographical Indications and Innovative Traditional Knowledge*, 29 PROMETHEUS 253 (2011), http://papers.ssrn.com/sol3/papers.cfm?abstract_id=1953033.

[7] William van Caenegem, Peter Drahos & Jen Cleary, *Provenance of Australian Food Products: Is There a Place for Geographical Indications?* RURAL INDUSTRIES RESEARCH AND DEVELOPMENT CORPORATION, AUSTRALIA GOVERNMENT (July 2015), https://rirdc.infoservices.com.au/items/15-060.

[8] *Id.* at 68–70. Interestingly, in relation to the wine industry, the authors note that it is difficult to gauge the benefit of GIs, but that they seem to be enhancing the industry. *Id.* at 22.

legal framing to meet and enhance local needs. GIs can be part of a package to enhance development, but a legal mechanism without associated investment cannot effectively function as a source of development. GIs being "part of a package" means exactly that rather than a top-down imposition through trade agreements of a framework and detailed laws designed for the economic conditions of others. Put differently, there is no 100 per cent right or wrong position on GIs even though the debate is polarized. The reality is that one size does not fit all, but several sizes may fit some or possibly even many.

Perhaps the most significant argument against the export of EU-style GI law to developing countries is that while such export has been going on for some time, there are relatively few success stories in developing countries. This would seem to be because a successful *sui generis* GI regime requires infrastructure and related investment in development, which may be missing. Just as pharmaceutical patents are predominantly a cost to those who do not produce pharmaceuticals, establishing a GI protection regime is largely a cost to those who lack the resources and infrastructure to exploit the origin of goods, in the form of an IP right, in the global economy. In such places, registered GIs will largely be foreign-owned.[9]

The approach of trying to force a one-size-fits-all model is certainly not the exclusive domain of the European Union in its trade agreements.[10] While the United States does not seek to export GI laws through its trade agreements, it does export its view of how trademark law should dominate and how GIs, if and where they exist, should not trump trademarks, but rather trademarks should prevail over GIs.[11] Much of the global GI debate is thus characterized by a trans-Atlantic debate and the dominant parties in that debate seek to

---

[9] Global trade rules about origin of goods have many detailed rules that are separate from Intellectual Property (IP) rules. As the World Trade Organization (WTO) explains, 'rules of origin are the criteria needed to determine the national source of a product. Their importance is derived from the fact that duties and restrictions in several cases depend upon the source of imports.' *Technical Information on Rules of Origin*, WTO, www.wto.org/english/tratop_e/roi_e/roi_info_e.htm (last visited 21 March 2016).

[10] *See generally* THE STRUCTURE OF INTELLECTUAL PROPERTY LAW: CAN ONE SIZE FIT ALL? (Annette Kur & Vytautas Mizara eds., 2001); GRAEME B. DINWOODIE & ROCHELLE C. DREYFUSS, A NEOFEDERALIST VISION OF TRIPS: THE RESILIENCE OF THE INTERNATIONAL INTELLECTUAL PROPERTY REGIME (2012); Daniel J. Gervais, INTELLECTUAL PROPERTY IP CALIBRATION, IN INTELLECTUAL PROPERTY, TRADE AND DEVELOPMENT 86–116 (Daniel J. Gervais ed., 2014).

[11] *See Geographical Indication Protection in the United States*, UNITED STATES PATENT AND TRADEMARK OFFICE (USPTO), www.uspto.gov/sites/default/files/web/offices/dcom/olia/globalip/pdf/gi_system.pdf (last visited 21 March 2016).

recruit support for their respective positions in countries around the world through bilateral and mega-regional trade agreements.

The Agreement on Trade-Related Aspects of Intellectual Property Rights (TRIPS Agreement) GI requirements are minimum standards.[12] In other words, members of the TRIPS Agreement can implement GI-style protection in a variety of ways. This flexibility around implementation is reinforced by the general provision in the TRIPS Agreement that allows for countries to implement the obligations in their own legal system in a manner they deem appropriate.[13] It is well documented that since the TRIPS Agreement came into force there has been a proliferation of free trade agreements (FTAs).[14] These FTAs were initially predominantly bilateral and now frequently involve multiple parties and so are plurilateral, such as the Trans-Pacific Partnership (TPP).[15] Plurilaterals are often mega-regional agreements. Even though negotiations such as the Trans-Atlantic Trade and Investment Partnership (TTIP) are between the European Union and the United States rather than multiple parties, because of the size of the economies of those two parties, such an agreement is mega-regional in terms of the volume of trade it could cover. Geopolitically, the mega-regionals seem to be in competition with each other. The TPP did not include the European Union or China, and the Association of South-East Asian Nations (ASEAN) plus six parties negotiation for the Regional Comprehensive Economic Partnership (RCEP) does not include the United States, for example.[16] While at the time of this writing, the TPP will likely not come into force because of the United States withdrawal from it, the TPP IP chapter is emerging in other trade negotiation forums as proposals for negotiation. The text of the TPP relevant to this chapter was introduced into the RCEP negotiations. There is much opposition to such proposals.[17]

---

[12] Agreement on Trade-Related Aspects of Intellectual Property Rights, Marrakesh Agreement Establishing the World Trade Organization, 15 April 1994, 1867 U.N.T.S. 154, Annex 1C [hereinafter TRIPS Agreement].

[13] TRIPS Agreement, art. 1.1.

[14] The World Trade Organization records that since its formation in 1995 over 400 regional trade agreements have been entered into and many are still being negotiated. Many but not all include IP chapters. See Regional Trade Agreements: Facts and Figures, WORLD TRADE ORGANIZATION, www.wto.org/english/tratop_e/region_e/regfac_e.htm (last visited 3 June 2016).

[15] Trans-Pacific Partnership, NEW ZEALAND FOREIGN AFFAIRS & TRADE, www.tpp.mfat.govt.nz/text (last visited 21 March 2016) [hereinafter TPP]. As of January 2017 it seems unlikely that the TPP will ever come into force ads the united States has withdrawn form it.

[16] For a general discussion, see David A. Gantz, The TPP and RCEP: Mega-Trade Agreements for the Pacific Rim, 33 ARIZ. J. INT'L & COMP. L. 57, 59, 63 (2016).

[17] See, for e.g., Intellectual Property Watch, Hundreds Of Civil Society Groups Urge RCEP Negotiators To Reject Imported TPP Clauses, 30 November 2016), www.ip-watch.org/2016/11/30/hundreds-civil-society-groups-urge-rcep-negotiators-reject-imported-tpp-clauses/.

Some bilateral FTAs designed and entered into by large economies, particularly the United States or the European Union (known as economic partnerships), articulate one of those major economies' stance on GIs. Both the United States and the European Union through these FTAs recruit as many countries as possible to one GI stance or another. The trans-Atlantic rivals are dealing with this policy and legal framework collision in the TTIP.[18] At the political level, the rhetoric captures the difficulty:[19]

> Wisconsin Republican Paul Ryan, chairman of the House Ways and Means Committee, which has jurisdiction over matter of trade policy, condemns European GIs as trade barriers and vows that 'for generations to come, we're going to keep making gouda in Wisconsin. And feta, and cheddar and everything else'.[20]
>
> At the same time, the EU Trade Commissioner Cecilia Malmström laments that Italian cheeses are being 'undermined by inferior domestic imitations' in the United States and vowed to solve the problem through TTIP by 'getting a strong agreement on geographical indications'.[21]

In Section 2, certain approaches to GI protection in mega-regionals and bilateral FTAs are discussed. Section 3 considers some of the incompatibilities between the EU-dominated and US-dominated approaches. Section 4 raises questions about countries that purport to trade in both regimes, which include Singapore, Korea, Australia and New Zealand. The chapter concludes that unless a compromise is worked out in ongoing trade agreements such as the TTIP and the RCEP (or the proposed Free Trade Area of the Asia-Pacific (FTAAP)),[22] the GI debate will worsen, and as it does, the casualties will be small and medium-developing countries and those whose trade agreements have obligated them to both regimes.

---

[18] K. William Watson, *Geographical Indications in TTIP: An Impossible Task*, CATO INSTITUTE (October 2015), www.cato.org/publications/cato-online-forum/geographical-indications-ttip-impossible-task.

[19] *Id.*

[20] *Id.* (citing Adam Behsudi, *US to Europe: Don't Move My Cheese*, POLITICO (June 20, 2015), www.politico.com/story/2015/07/us-to-europe-dont-move-my-cheese-120387).

[21] *Id.* (citing *EU Trade Commissioner Expects Italian Cheese Exporters to Benefit from Lower Tariffs, Strong GI Protections in TTIP*, CHEESE REPORTER (26 June 2015), http://npaper-wehaa.com/cheese-reporter/2015/06/s3/#?article=2545800).

[22] The Free Trade Area of the Asia-Pacific (FTAAP) is a proposal for a free trade agreement (FTA) of the Asia Pacific between the Asia Pacific Economic Cooperation (APEC) nations which is being designed to bridge the Trans-Pacific Partnership (TPP) and Regional Comprehensive Economic Partnership (RCEP).

2 MEGA-REGIONAL AGREEMENTS

The European Union is a large region. Its policy on GIs is summarized above.[23] In contrast, the TTP takes a trademark-centric approach. The TPP was signed on 4 February 2016,[24] and, as noted above, it is unlikely to come into force. It does, however, provide a detailed example of United States' GI trade policy and the text is not dead as it is being used in other trade negotiation forums, most notably RCEP. This part refers to the TPP text as it is public, and at the time of this writing the exact state of the RCEP negotiations in relation to the same text is not publicly known. The TPP required that the parties to it protect country names from misuse in a misleading manner.[25] In addition, the text defined a GI as

> an indication that identifies a good as originating in the territory of a Party, or a region or locality in that territory, where a given quality, reputation or other characteristic of the good is essentially attributable to its geographical origin.[26]

This definition is substantively identical to the definition in the TRIPS Agreement and thus immediately flags that the TPP would have gone no further than the TRIPS Agreement in the extent of its protection of GIs.[27] The TPP did, however, delineate a relationship between GIs and trademarks that the TRIPS Agreement does not. The part of the TPP dealing with GIs sets out what might broadly be described as the United States' preferred approach. In particular, GIs may be protected through trademarks, a *sui generis* system or other legal means.[28] Significantly, there was a requirement that 'each Party shall also provide that signs that may serve as geographical indications are capable of protection under its trademark system'.[29] This would have required parties to the TPP with *sui generis* GI regimes to ensure that the trademark regime provides the same protection. This was a significant gain for the United States, as under the TRIPS Agreement it is quite possible for parties to have a GI system that does not accommodate trademark registrations for protection within the same regime. The various EU GI systems[30] are a quintessential

---

[23] In addition, many members of the European Union (EU) are members of the Lisbon Agreement, *see* Daniel Gervais' chapter in this book.
[24] It will come into force when a sufficient amount of trade coverage is covered by the ratifying parties.
[25] TPP, art. 18.29.   [26] TPP, art. 18.1:1.   [27] TRIPS Agreement, art. 22.1.
[28] TPP, art. 18:30.   [29] TPP, art. 18.19.
[30] The EU has an extensive GI framework with multiple regimes, including protected designations of origin (PDOs). PDOs are applicable to agricultural products that are produced, processed and prepared in a particular geographical area using a recognized method or other sort of know-how; protected geographical indications (PGIs) that apply to agricultural

example of non-trademark-embracing GI systems. So while the TRIPS Agreement *allows* for the recognition of GIs in trademark regimes, the TPP *required* it.

The TPP also included several grounds for opposing the registration of GIs. These grounds included where the GI applied for causes confusion with a trademark which is the subject of an existing registration or even a pending application.[31] Significantly, GIs could be opposed when the GI is a 'term customary in common language as the common name for the relevant good', i.e., the name is generic.[32] The agreement included guidelines for determining what amounts to customary in the common language, in particular 'how consumers understand the term'.[33] Again, this approach was *required* under the TPP but is a permissible approach under the TRIPS Agreement.[34] The United States' potential gain in the TPP had the effect of standing in the way of the EU approach of clawing back generic names, because arguably any list of required names for clawback purposes in future agreements will be inconsistent with the TPP. Some parties to the TPP (and RCEP) have existing GI obligations with the European Union. There is potential for conflicting obligations among the various agreements and so these countries and others will have had to work out (and no doubt will also have to do so as disputes arise) which obligations apply. Australia has already agreed to some EU clawbacks.[35] Vietnam has agreed to recognize and protect certain EU GIs.[36] Singapore has agreed with the European Union to review whether the EU GI list should be registered in Singapore.[37] Further, as one commentator notes, 'by exporting

---

products that are linked to a geographical area; and traditional speciality guaranteed (TSG), which applies to products that have a particular traditional character related to either the product's composition or means of production. This summary shows the wide catchment of the European system. *See generally*, European Commission, *Agriculture and Rural Development Quality Policy*, http://ec.europa.eu/agriculture/quality/schemes/index_en.htm (last visited 1 June 2016).

[31] TPP, art. 18.32:1(a). [32] TPP, art. 18.32:1(c). [33] TPP, art. 18.32:2.
[34] The substantive obligations for protection of GIs in the TRIPS Agreement are found in arts. 22–23 and are not as specific as the TPP language, but broadly require laws to prevent users that mislead the public. *See* TRIPS Agreement, art. 22.2(a).
[35] EU-Australia Wine Agreement (entered into force on 31 August 2010, replacing the 1994 Agreement) (as a result of which Australian wine producers will not be able to continue the use of many names, including 'Champagne', 'Port', 'Sherry', 'Amontillado' and 'Claret').
[36] EU-Vietnam Free Trade Agreement, 20 January 2016, Chapter 12 Intellectual Property, art. 6.3.1. The reciprocal obligation on the EU is in art. 6.3.2, http://trade.ec.europa.eu/doclib/press/index.cfm?id=1437 (last visited 1 August 2016).
[37] EU-Singapore Free Trade Agreement, 29 June 2015, Chapter 11 Intellectual Property [hereinafter EU-Singapore FTA], art 11.17.3 and Annex 11-A, List of Names to be Applied for Protection as Geographical Indications in the Territory of Parties, http://trade.ec.europa.eu/doclib/press/index.cfm?id=961 (last visited 1 August 2016).

the principle of co-existence between geographical indications and trade marks the EU is chipping away at regulatory diversity in the area of geographical indications'.[38] That 'chipping away' will likely be harder, if not impossible, in some countries depending on what happens to the mega-regional trade agreements.

In order to have made the TPP compatible with other agreements, it attempted to set other trade agreements in a TPP-aligned framework. There was a general clause relevant to all of the TPP agreement and applicable to FTAs that bind at least two parties that provided that

> [i]f a Party considers that a provision of this Agreement is inconsistent with a provision of another agreement to which it and at least one other Party are party, on request, the relevant Parties to the other agreement shall consult with a view to reaching a mutually satisfactory solution.[39]

The above article did not, however, deal with the significant overlaps with agreements made with one TPP party and a non-member of the TPP, such as the European Union. However, as noted above, the TPP parties (and RCEP parties) included several parties who have either existing agreements with the European Union (such as Singapore and Australia) or negotiations with the European Union (such as Canada) that include provisions about GIs. For GIs, there was an explicit regime to deal with the overlap of agreements between TTP parties and non-parties. The result of this was a somewhat complex two-page clause which in essence seeks to make contradictory and opposing approaches to GIs functionally compatible.[40] The central rule was that

> [n]o Party shall be required to apply this Article to geographical indications that have been specifically identified in, and that are protected or recognised pursuant to, an international agreement involving a Party or a non-Party, provided that the agreement:
>
> (a) was concluded, or agreed in principle, prior to the date of conclusion, or agreement in principle, of this Agreement;
> (b) was ratified by a Party prior to the date of ratification of this Agreement by that Party; or
> (c) entered into force for a Party prior to the date of entry into force of this Agreement for that Party.[41]

The remaining parts of this article explained how information must be provided and how other parts, relating to opposition and

---

[38] BILLY A. MELO ARAUJO, THE EU DEEP TRADE AGENDA: LAW AND POLICY 157 (2016).
[39] TPP, art. 1.2:2.   [40] TPP, art. 18.36.   [41] TPP, art. 18.36:6.

administrative procedures, should apply even to prior protected GIs. Under the terms of the TPP, parties must have made available procedures to oppose and review GI registrations. It also required that analogous procedures were applicable to GIs that precede the TPP, even where that GI protection arises under other agreements.[42] The details of procedures required are somewhat complex.

The irony of this complexity is that the TPP was supposed to make trade easier. The practical results of the relationship between the above-described provisions (and an array of additional side-letters relating to GIs[43]) remain to be tested.

To illustrate some of the complexity, consider an agreement made between South Korea and Australia. Australia was part of the TPP and South Korea is not yet a party.[44] A side-letter to navigate the differences between Australia's and the European Union's approaches to GIs, when South Korea has agreements with both, provides that

> [f]inally, I confirm that Korea will allow third parties to oppose any proposal to designate any term as a GI, whether these proposals are made pursuant to the Korea-EU FTA, or to any other future agreements with other trading partners. In addition, before Korea identifies additional terms as GIs under the Korea-EU FTA, it will provide, by published administrative guidelines, that designations of asserted GIs may be opposed in Korea on the grounds that would include: (1) the term is generic in Korea; (2) the term is confusingly similar to a pre-existing trademark or geographical indication that was either previously applied for or registered or established through use; (3) the term is confusingly similar to a well-known trademark; and (4) the term does not meet the definition of a GI.[45]

As mentioned above, another mega-regional trade agreement of particular importance to the Asia Pacific region is RCEP.[46] The general negotiation principles of RCEP state that

---

[42] TPP, art. 18.36:1–5.
[43] The side-letters are negotiated alongside the agreement and often explain positions in relation to particular articles and in relation to the TPP between some, but not all, of the parties to the agreement.
[44] South Korea is one of several countries that have suggested interest in joining the TPP. South Korea has existing trade agreements with most TPP members.
[45] *Letter from Korean Ministry of Trade Industry and Energy to Department of Foreign Affairs and Trade, Australia*, DEPARTMENT OF FOREIGN AFFAIRS AND TRADE (24 March 2014), https://dfat.gov.au/trade/agreements/kafta/Documents/letter-on-geographical-indications-korea.pdf.
[46] The negotiating members of RCEP include Association of South-East Asian Nations members (Brunei, Myanmar, Cambodia, Indonesia, Laos, Malaysia, the Philippines, Singapore, Thailand and Vietnam) plus six other nations (New Zealand, Australia, China, South Korea, Japan and India). *See The Second Regional Comprehensive Economic Partnership (RCEP),*

> [t]he text on intellectual property in the RCEP will aim to reduce IP-related barriers to trade and investment by promoting economic integration and cooperation in the utilization, protection and enforcement of intellectual property rights.[47]

A purported working draft of the negotiations dated October 2014[48] proposes protection of trademarks that pre-date GIs[49] and more broadly provides that

> [e]ach Party recognises that geographical indications may be protected through various means, including through a trademark system, provided that all requirements under the TRIPS Agreement are fulfilled.[50]

As noted above, South Korea and Japan are reputed to have introduced equivalent proposals to those that are found in the TPP IP chapter as a possible model for negotiation in RCEP.[51]

It is important to include in this group of trade agreements that have been negotiated after the TRIPS Agreement, the mega-economy bilaterals, particularly as these are significant in the GI debate. As noted above, the negotiations between the European Union and the United States in the TTIP are significant. If those trading blocs can reach a workable compromise, then much of the rest of the world may also be able to do so.

The Canada-EU Trade Agreement (CETA) negotiation shows a kind of complicated compromise.[52] In CETA, GIs are defined as

> an indication which identifies an agricultural product or foodstuff as originating in the territory of a Party, or a region or locality in that territory, where a given quality, reputation or other characteristic of the product is essentially attributable to its geographical origin.[53]

ASSOCIATION OF SOUTHEAST ASIAN NATIONS, www.asean.org/the-second-regional-comprehensive-economic-partnership-rcep/ (last visited 3 June 2016).

[47] *Guiding Principles and Objectives for Negotiating the Regional Comprehensive Economic Partnership*, Ministry of Foreign Affairs and Trade, www.mfat.govt.nz/assets/_securedfiles/FTAs-in-negotiations/RCEP/Guiding-Principles-and-Objectives-for-Negotiating-the-Regional-Comprehensive-Economic-Partnership.pdf (last visited 21 March 2016).

[48] *Chapter on Intellectual Property Regional Comprehensive Economic Partnership (RCEP) Free Trade Agreement* (Working draft), KNOWLEDGE ECOLOGY INTERNATIONAL (KEI) (10 October 2014), http://keionline.org/sites/default/files/RCEP-TNC6-WGIP3-ASEAN-Draft%20oIP%20Text-10Oct2014.pdf.

[49] *Id.* 6. [50] *Id.* 7.

[51] *Leaked IP Chapter, Regional Comprehensive Economic Partnership (RCEP) FTA*, KEI (3 October 2014), www.keionline.org/node/2239.

[52] *EU-Canada Comprehensive Economic and Trade Agreement* (CETA), EUROPEAN COMMISSION, http://ec.europa.eu/trade/policy/in-focus/ceta/ (last visited 21 March 2016).

[53] *Id.* art. 7.

Notably, this definition explicitly excludes the application of GI rules to non-agricultural and foodstuff products, which the European Union extends some GIs to and proposes to extend GIs even further.[54]

The CETA text provides a general requirement for the protection of GIs that are listed in annexes to the agreement.[55] The protection must still be provided even where the true origin of the product is indicated or when the GI is used in translation or accompanied by expressions such as kind, type, style and the like.[56] The parties must also 'determine the practical conditions under which the homonymous indications ... will be differentiated from each other'.[57]

There are some detailed exceptions, including that Canada shall not be required to provide laws to prevent the use of some terms including asiago, feta, fontina, gorgonzola and Munster, when such terms are accompanied by expressions such as kind, type, style and imitation.[58] The combination of names and terms, e.g. 'feta style', must be both legible and visible.[59]

Overall CETA is a well-developed – even if complex – compromise between the extremities of the GI debate. At one extreme of the debate is insistence on the necessity of a *sui generis* GI system and at the other extreme the view that only trademarks are appropriate and necessary. There is some considerable detail required to reach CETA's compromise and these details accentuate some of the incompatibility of the approaches found in the other mega-regionals.

3 POLICY INCOMPATIBILITIES OF APPROACHES TO GEOGRAPHICAL INDICATIONS IN TRADE AGREEMENTS

This section does not discuss the various technical differences between GI and trademark systems, but rather focuses on some of the policy incompatibilities that have arisen and arguably are becoming entrenched in the mega-regional framework. As a starting point, the extension of local success to the global arena raises questions about the normative basis for so doing and the consistency between local policy and globalization of that policy.

---

[54] *Geographical Indications for Non-agricultural Products*, EUROPEAN COMMISSION, http://ec.europa.eu/growth/industry/intellectual-property/geographical-indications/non-agricultural-products/index_en.htm (last visited 21 March 2016).
[55] CETA, art. 20.19:2.   [56] CETA, art. 20.19:3.
[57] CETA, art. 20.20.1. A provision also provides for negotiation regarding homonymous GIs with third parties. CETA, art. 20.20:2.
[58] CETA, art. 20.21:1.   [59] Id.

The origins and justifications for GIs, which are linked to local conditions such as the *terroir*,[60] risk distortion when linked to other parts of the world through the global trading. The overall basis for the claim for greater global harmonization of GIs is to protect the products that are 'genuinely' GI-labelled, not just in the domestic market, but also in foreign markets. As noted above, it is in export markets (both existing and potential) that the European Union claims its GI products are unfairly imitated. Notably, however, there can be no claim over making equivalent products,[61] and the complaint is about applying the GI to them. While there are some notoriously bad products which draw on GI products and their names, there are plenty of high-quality products which compete with GI products, both nationally and internationally, but that have not used GIs to acquire a market share.[62] The GI approach assumes that such products may be better off with GIs, but that is not necessarily so.[63] Moreover, until appropriate analysis of local conditions, including investment and infrastructure, is in place, such claims are mere assertions calculated to push the GI export agenda rather than to encourage quality local-made food.

A localized reputation (even if extensive) is not, however, the same as a globalized reputation and so the need for export protection for many GI products is not necessarily obvious to the importing markets. The ubiquitous example of champagne is exactly on point. The value of the GI is intimately connected to the geographical region as both product and production factors are dependent on features of the Champagne region.[64] International protection, outside of the European Union, of champagne (and other GI products) occurs under various regimes. These include *sui generis* recognition of GIs on

---

[60] For an overview of *terroir* as part of the French appellation of origin system, see DEV GANJEE, RELOCATING THE LAW OF GEOGRAPHICAL INDICATIONS 83 (2012).

[61] GI advocates emphasize the difference between their products and others of like style (even when they are made in niche markets and with quality ingredients) because of the regional differences in *terroir* and ingredients emanating from the *terroir*. For example, no one can make the equivalent of Roquefort because they do not have the same caves and grapes; even the caves and grapes one metre outside of Champagne are allegedly different from those found within the region.

[62] Examples include New Zealand milk powder and even cheeses and wines, which while the products use geographical names they have not been marketed on a GI basis to date. Analogous examples exist all around the world.

[63] It is even less likely to be the case where the products have not yet developed to a level where they compete in export markets, such as many of the agricultural products of developing countries. Processed primary products are more relevant to the GI context.

[64] See the description of champagne characteristics in the passing-off cases Bollinger v. Costa Brava Wine Co Ltd [1960] RPC 16 and Wineworths Group Ltd v. Comite Interprofessionel du Vin de Champagne [1992] 2 NZLR 327 (CA).

similar grounds to the European Union, clawback provisions in trade agreements that have made 'ungeneric' the generic[65] and claims to distinctive reputation in the local market that can give rise to either a certification or collective trademark and in some jurisdictions grounds for action under a common-law doctrine such as passing off.[66] The latter two approaches can include geographical and place-based arguments as relevant to reputation and consumer perceptions; however, neither trademarks nor passing off necessarily depends on any direct connection to place for any protection.[67]

One might even argue that calibrations of local law, which are framed and developed to meet local needs (that is exactly what GIs represent), are the antithesis of the case for globalization. The framework of IP that utilizes minimum standards and domestic discretion, including modes of implementation, within the minimum standards framework creates the mechanism through which the global is reflected in the local and vice versa. The question, in relation to GIs (and all IP), is how prescriptive should the minimum standards be and thus how much autonomy is left to local discretion and how much is governed by international rules. The greater the level of prescription at the international level, the less room for national discretion and the more likely that the international obligation will be based on models designed for the conditions of some, but not all, economies. This is the top-down approach (edging towards a one-size-fits-all approach), which the trade agreements, discussed in Section 1 of this chapter, exemplify. The TRIPS Agreement, on the other hand, leaves much GI detail to national autonomy. However, neither the European Union nor the United States are prepared to stop at the TRIPS Agreement minimum standards level of protection, but rather seek to globalize their own agendas.

The fundamental objection to too much global harmonization or inflexible rules is the risk that GIs, rather than protecting genuine culturally anchored outputs, function as barriers to trade. As the development of globalized IP rules has shown, particularly in other areas such as patents, globalized rights

---

[65] See, for example, EU-Australia Wine Agreement, *supra* note 34.

[66] See Dev S. Gangjee, *Spanish Champagne: An Unfair Completion Approach to GI Protection*, in INTELLECTUAL PROPERTY AT THE EDGE: THE CONTESTED CONTOURS OF IP 105–29 (Rochelle Cooper Dreyfuss & Jane C. Ginsburg eds., 2014); Daniel Gervais, *A Cognac after Spanish Champagne? Geographical Indications as Certification Marks*, in INTELLECTUAL PROPERTY AT THE EDGE: THE CONTESTED CONTOURS OF IP 130–56 (Rochelle Cooper Dreyfuss & Jane C. Ginsburg eds., 2014).

[67] In Ervin Warnick v. Townend & Sons [1979] A.C. 73, the House of Lords recognized the plaintiffs' claim in passing off and dismissed the defendant's argument that the plaintiffs, makers of Advocaat, could not use passing off because unlike the Champagne makers they did not rely on a geographic area for their reputation.

tend to favour incumbents over new entrants. So how much protection is enough protection? Put differently, what protection of GIs globally is a legitimate use of IP as a non-tariff trade barrier and what level of GI protection exceeds that level?[68]

Internationally, IP is protected in different jurisdictions on the basis that the promise of exclusivity can provide an incentive for innovation and creativity. There is much commentary about the effectiveness and ineffectiveness of incentives and in which arenas they work and when they do not.[69] The argument that GIs can assist with rural development that is consistent with cultural and sustainable practices is a kind of incentive argument. The counterargument is that GIs can sometimes be used to disincentivize innovation because they require production processes to conform to rules that do not allow for innovative alterations.[70] Neither representation of GIs is true all of the time, but both are true sometimes.

In most areas of IP, both incentivizing and disincentivizing goes on. Balancing these tensions is core to how the IP regime (and some quasi-property IP rules) functions. It is known that exclusivity restricts third-party users and, thus, IP rights block immediate follow-on innovation, but temporal restrictions justify the imposition of exclusive rights.[71] Trademarks and GIs are different because they do not have temporal restrictions (unless fees are not paid) and so their overreach can cause disincentivizing effects with no possibility of change. In trademark law, this takes the form of trademarks substituting for copyright (and in some jurisdictions, design) after expiry of the

---

[68] Trade barriers are often divided into tariff and non-tariff barriers. All of IP is a non-tariff trade barrier. The TRIPS Agreement is a recognition of a globally agreed level of IP protection in a framework that has long characterized IP rights as an exception to the principles of the GATT Agreement, including free movement of goods, which provides in art. XX:

> subject to the requirement that such measures are not applied in a manner which would constitute a means of arbitrary or unjustifiable discrimination between countries where the same conditions prevail, or a disguised restriction on international trade, nothing in this Agreement shall be construed to prevent the adoption or enforcement by any contracting party of measures ... (d) *necessary* to secure compliance with laws or regulations *which are not inconsistent with the provisions of this Agreement*, including those relating to customs enforcement ... the protection of patents, trade marks and copyrights, and the prevention of deceptive practices.

Id.

[69] *See generally* William Fisher, *Theories of Intellectual Property, in* NEW ESSAYS IN THE LEGAL AND POLITICAL THEORY OF PROPERTY 168–99 (Stephen R. Munzer ed., 2001); ROBERT MERGES, JUSTIFYING INTELLECTUAL PROPERTY (2011).

[70] *See* Justin Hughes, *Champagne, Feta and Bourbon: The Spirited Debate about Geographical Indications*, 58 HASTINGS L. J. 299–386 (2006).

[71] In patents and copyright, the length of protection is severely contested precisely because of the limitations the rights place on follow-on creativity and innovation.

copyright.[72] With GIs, the danger is that the GI protects too much both in the jurisdiction of origin and in export markets. As far as export markets are concerned, the issue is whether GI protection in the export market really incentivizes local development that is consistent with cultural and sustainable practices. In the jurisdiction of origin, consider, for example, the quintessential example of a GI protecting a product created through local practice. If that protection is extended to protect the method of production, then, in fact, the GI is protecting know-how (as opposed to innovation). This know-how is an area that copyright and patent protection, in particular, are supposed to not cover.[73] Copyright protects original works. Patents are granted for processes and products, provided they are inventions that are new, involve inventive step and are useful.[74] There is a fine line between protecting these things and protecting know-how. The cumulative effect of both protecting the know-how of process and production methods through GIs, by extending the GI justification relating to the commodification of products, and requiring protection of GIs when they are used beyond their locality in export markets, means that GI protection is all encompassing. At that point, what is left? Where is the space for innovation in and around existing IP? Unless GIs are appropriately framed, they will become the latest mechanism for IP overreach.

The preference for property or property-style rules to govern IP is based on the proposition that property comes after (*ex post*) creation or innovation and so the potential grant of property rights incentivizes creativity and innovation. Put differently, IP rights are a goal to reach and a reward when that goal is reached.[75] Subsidies are thought to do the opposite because they are *ex ante* to creativity and innovation. This is why the World Trade Organization (WTO) system allows subsidies to be challenged where they amount to trade barriers. The details of impermissible subsidies, for WTO members, are found in the WTO Subsidies and Counterveiling Measures Agreement (SCM).[76] In that framework, the issues of particular interest to the relationship between IP and subsidies, is the rules around research subsidies. In the early stages of the SCM the rules allowed subsidies for research and development without questioning

---

[72] Irene Calboli, *Overlapping Rights: The Negative Effects of Trademarking Creative Works*, in THE EVOLUTION AND EQUILIBRIUM OF COPYRIGHT 52 (Susy Frankel & Daniel Gervais eds., 2014).

[73] One could argue about whether in fact this is the case. [74] TRIPS Agreement, art. 27.1.

[75] Some authors have explored other incentive models, particularly in patents such as prizes, *see* Joseph E. Stiglitz, *Prizes, Not Patents*, PROJECT SYNDICATE (6 March 2007), www.project-syndicate.org/commentary/prizes–not-patents; *see also* Daniel J. Hemel & Lisa L. Ouellette, *Beyond the Patents-Prizes Debate*, 92 TEX. L. REV. 303–82 (2013).

[76] *Agreement on Subsidies and Countervailing Measures*, WTO, www.wto.org/english/docs_e/legal_e/24-scm.pdf (last visited 21 March 2016).

them (these were known as green light subsidies). The SCM contained a provision that later moved these 'green light' subsidies to amber status. This made such subsidies actionable, rather than permissible simply because they were connected to research.[77] In other words, research subsidies could be challenged under the SCM rules.

When IP rights overprotect, they take on the economic characteristics of subsidies.[78] Too many incentives can lead to a lack of innovation. When it is 'raining carrots',[79] one hardly needs to pursue costly innovation if substantive reward can be obtained from the existing regime. Expanded GI protections in foreign markets for products that do not necessarily retain their initial reputation in those foreign markets are, therefore, arguably overprotected. If the rationale for GIs is protection of the local to generate rural development, then that rationale does not simply slip over into export markets. In the export market, the desirability of protecting the local may simply disappear if the local product cannot compete with exports. The local product may, however, be cheaper and as the GI product is a speciality good it is often higher priced. That price may be justified on the assumption, which is perpetuated by both producers and consumers, of better quality. Global GI rules do not require proof of quality and they should probably not be formulated to do so because the necessary administration and resources to retain such a system are very costly and totally impractical for many countries.

Irene Calboli argues that the connection between the GI and the *terroir* should be strictly enforced so as to maintain the proper scope of GI protection.[80] In many ways, this argument is attractive because it is an attempt to

---

[77] *See* SUSY FRANKEL, TEST TUBES FOR GLOBAL INTELLECTUAL PROPERTY ISSUES: SMALL MARKET ECONOMIES 68–91 (2015).

[78] *See id.* Also, see the discussion in the WTO Appellate Body's report about whether a patent is the equivalent of a subsidy. The issues arose in a complaint about the alleged subsidizing of the United States (US) aircraft industry. The facts are complex and involve much more than patents, but the patent-relevant point was whether the allocation of patent rights under contracts between government agencies and Boeing amounted to a subsidy. Based on the submission of the parties, the panel assumed, for the sake of argument, that the allocation of patent rights to government-financed research could constitute a subsidy. WTO Appellate Body Report, *United States – Measures Affecting Trade in Large Civil Aircraft (Second Complaint)*, WTO, WT/DS353/AB/R (12 March 2012), www.wto.org/english/tratop_e/dispu_e/353abr_e.pdf (last visited 21 March 2016).

[79] A carrot is often used as a colloquial term for an incentive. 'Raining carrots' means that there is an excess of incentives.

[80] Irene Calboli, *Geographical Indications of Origin at the Crossroads of Local Development, Consumer Protection and Marketing Strategies*, 46 INT'L REV. INTELL. PROP. & COMPETITION L. 760, 760–80 (2015).

decouple overprotection, for what she calls 'market-strategies', from deeply held place-based cultural claims. Further, there are numerous examples where local culture cannot sustain global markets and attempts to do so undermine local traditions and can create sustainability and development issues. These sorts of issues will vary from place to place, just as the effectiveness of GIs varies.

If Calboli's argument is correct, then it is also an important reason why GIs are not often a good fit for traditional knowledge, especially where the claimants of traditional knowledge have been dispossessed of their land at one time or another or permanently, which is often the case with indigenous peoples.

I have argued elsewhere that the GI framework is not a good framework for protecting many aspects of traditional knowledge.[81] The argument is multifaceted, but in essence rejects the similarities between GIs and claims to traditional knowledge (collective nature of ownership and possibility of indefinite protection) as for the most part superficial similarities. GIs enable the commodification of tradition, and claims for protection of traditional knowledge are often not about commodification.[82] In addition, the resources that are needed for the development of communities seeking traditional knowledge protection will not be achieved through having to pay for the costs of a GI framework and registration without investment in real development and infrastructure.[83]

That said, there is a similarity between what might be an appropriate GI framework of minimum standards and the appropriate framework for protecting traditional knowledge. If both frameworks are aligned with their normative underpinnings, which ought to be primarily about local communities, then any global minimum standards of protection should enable some considerable flexibility in implementation. This flexibility allows for appropriately calibrated domestic application based on local needs and rural development. Such drivers of GI policy are unlikely to be realized by detailed harmonized norms, but through a framework of minimum standards. The same case for a

---

[81] Frankel, *supra* note 6.   [82] *Id.*, at 14.
[83] As noted above, this has been the success for GIs for the Australian wine industry. The Australian Aborigine peoples cannot boast of such success, or at least not yet. Willian van Caenegem, Jen A. Cleary, & Peter Drahos, *Pride and Profit: Geographical Indications as Regional Development Tools in Australia*, 16 J. ECON. & SOC. POL'Y 3 (2014). In relation to regional development, the authors suggest that locally tailored GI policies should be considered if they can assist Aboriginal Communities, noting that Australians 'are also prepared to pay more for products emanating from specialist niche sectors, such as from Aboriginal country, culture and community'. *Id.*

pluralistic approach to traditional knowledge can be made. To be clear, however, the appropriate framework for traditional knowledge is not the GI commoditization framework, but the similarity may be that pluralistic approaches need to be incorporated into the respective legal frameworks if the systems remain true to their normative drivers.[84]

It is important to remember that GIs, as intangible IP rights, are separate legal entities from the goods to which they attach. Using IP analogies, extensive GI protection has a parallel to some aspects of well-known trademarks. Well-known trademarks receive significant worldwide protection.[85] Small- and medium-sized businesses cannot hope for this level of protection globally and often this means the businesses of small and medium countries cannot rival large economies on the international stage. Well-known GIs are not those of small- and medium-sized businesses either.

If the normative underpinning of GIs is the drive for local culture and sustainability, then that alone does not obviously require global rules. In fact, such aims may be more achievable without global rules. To the extent that minimum standards in GIs around the globe can be sufficiently broad to allow for local differences, such as the CETA compromise discussed above, the regime may work. The normative basis for harmonized rules is, however, somewhat hazy outside of the need to strike a trade deal. It may, therefore, be that not only are the multifaceted approaches to GIs well and truly here to stay; they may have to learn to function better together and support both legal and cultural diversity.

4 TRADING IN BOTH THE EU AND THE US GEOGRAPHICAL INDICATIONS REGIMES

As noted in Section 1 of this chapter, there are several countries with trade agreements, with both the European Union and the United States, that purport to operate (one might say with prodigious care) under both trade regimes and other countries that are poised to do so. Carefully calibrated local laws might be able to meet the demands of both frameworks, but as noted

---

[84] There also is a practical difference between GIs and traditional knowledge. There is an international standard for GIs, but there is no international protection for traditional knowledge. Thus, a very narrow aspect of traditional knowledge is protected through the GI system, which in essence favours the protection of Western versions of traditional knowledge.

[85] TRIPS Agreement, art. 15(2)–(3); Paris Convention for the Protection of Industrial Property, 20 March 1883 (as amended 28 September 1979), 21 U.S.T. 1583, 828 U.N.T.S. 305 (protecting well-known trademarks in Article 16*bis*).

above, such approaches are complex, expensive and require legal ingenuity and perhaps even fictions on some occasions.

Trade agreements are not only about GIs (or IP rights); they are also about goods and often include considerable negotiation, even if not resolution, about dairy products and the reduction of subsidies and market access. The European Union uses GIs to protect dairy products whereas the United States, Australia and New Zealand for the most part do not. That is not to suggest that other IP rights such as trademarks do not play an extensive role in the dairy sector. They most certainly do, and dairy products are one of the most contentious sectors in the international GI debate.

To illustrate further the problem of complex overlaps and potential incompatibilities of GI provisions in trade agreements, consider the following. New Zealand exports not only dairy products but also commodities used in dairy products such as milk. Imagine a product made in Australia and called 'parmesan' (and trademarked with other names) that includes New Zealand milk products. That product is made by an Australian company with New Zealand owners and is marketed under a label that alludes to Italian culture. It does not use the protected GI (or certification trademark in Australia and New Zealand) 'Parmigiano-Reggiano'. Instead, the packaging utilizes techniques to suggest 'Italian style', such as green and red colouring. Under Australia's and/or New Zealand's trade agreements with Singapore (and other countries) that product has market access to Singapore. Under some trade agreement rules, such a product uses what is described as a common name (which is not recognized as a GI) and the mere use of colour does not give rise to protectable rights. It is arguable that this use of 'geography' could raise a GI issue in countries that have GI regimes. For the avoidance of doubt, it is not clear that Singapore's GI regime will allow such concerns to be raised in a dispute, but it may. Another point of the example is to show that when Singapore (and other countries in analogous positions) agreed to create a *sui generis* GI regime with the European Union, it already had trade and market access obligations in relation to goods that it had to take into account and will have to continue to take into account when implementing and enforcing its GI regime.

In relation to GIs alone, the need to take into account existing trade agreements is evident in the text of the US-Singapore and EU-Singapore trade agreements.[86] The agreement with the United States embodies a

---

[86] At the time of writing, both Australia and New Zealand are negotiating trade agreements with the EU and are likely to enter into analogous complexities. The difference, however, is that unlike Singapore, these negotiations are post-TPP.

first-in-time-first-in-right principle.[87] The later EU-Singapore agreement provides, therefore, that a GI that conflicts with a prior existing trademark in Singapore is capable of being registered only with the existing consent of the trademark holder.[88] Whatever can be said about the ingenuity of Singaporeans to try to navigate the conflicting interests of its trading partners, such a complex regime requires extensive legal knowledge and resources, which will not be a solution available to many countries, and particularly developing countries.

This sort of balancing of interests is precisely why the CETA rules look as detailed as they do, but it is not at all clear that Singapore's rules or indeed those in CETA and potential regimes, like the text of the TPP, are compatible. At a high level, they may appear to be so, but that remains to be tested. It is difficult to see how countries that have signed up to several regimes can easily make their obligations compatible.

5 CONCLUSION

On a case-by-case basis, incompatibilities in GI frameworks may be ironed out if and when disputes are resolved. The tug of war between the European Union and the United States to control the international GI framework is, however, costing other trading nations too much in the negotiation and implementation process. The complex hybridized systems are imposed via top-down models rather than generated locally on a fit-for-purpose basis.

Incumbents of the GI system seek international harmonization rather than any flexible minimum standards that would allow various cultures to calibrate and adjust their laws according to local needs. At the same time, the major opponent of the GI system, the United States, seeks its version of trade-mark requirements as a way to 'correct' EU policy. Neither approach is satisfactory. In both scenarios, the only likely winners are those whose products are well known.

---

[87] United States-Singapore Free Trade Agreement, US-Sing., art. 16.2(2), January 1, 2004, https:// ustr.gov/sites/default/files/uploads/agreements/fta/singapore/asset_upload_file708_4036.pdf (last visited 1 June 2016).

[88] EU-Singapore FTA, *supra* note 36, art. 11.21(2) n.19.

7

Geographical Indications as Property: European Union Association Agreements and Investor–State Provisions

Anselm Kamperman Sanders[*]

1 INTRODUCTION

Under European Union (EU) law, geographical indications (GIs) are protected under three guises: the protected GIs (PGI), the protected designations of origin (PDOs), and the traditional specialities guaranteed (TSGs). For the EU, the protection of its GIs in and outside of Europe is a very relevant economic issue, as the value of GI products in 2010 was estimated at €54.3 billion, of which the sale of wines accounts for more than half.[1] It is no surprise that the EU is vigorously trying to obtain protection for its GIs in major trade partner nations. However, in the context of the World Trade Organization (WTO), New World nations, most notably the North Americas, Australia and New Zealand, have consistently rejected the notion of a multilateral register for GIs that is dominated by European claims. Thus, it comes as no surprise then that in the context of the WTO negotiation mandate contained in the Agreement on Trade-Related Aspects of Intellectual Property Rights (TRIPS)[2] under Article 23,[3] no significant progress has been made or can be expected in the near future.

---

[*] Professor of Intellectual Property Law, Director of the Advanced Masters Intellectual Property Law and Knowledge Management (IPKM LL.M/MSc), and Academic Director of the Institute for Globalization and International Regulation (IGIR), Maastricht University.

[1] See Final Report of And-International on the external study: 'Value of production of agricultural products and foodstuffs, wines, aromatised wines and spirits protected by a geographical indication (GI)' (October 2012), http://ec.europa.eu/agriculture/external-studies/value-gi_en.htm.

[2] See Agreement on Trade-Related Aspects of Intellectual Property Rights, 15 April, 1994, Marrakesh Agreement Establishing the World Trade Organization, Annex 1C, 1869 U.N.T.S. 299 [hereinafter TRIPS].

[3] See id. art. 23(4), which mandates that 'negotiations shall be undertaken in the Council for TRIPS concerning the establishment of a multilateral system of notification and registration of geographical indications'.

As a result of this stalemate at the multilateral level, the strategy of the EU has been to place the protection of GIs at the heart of its intellectual property (IP) chapters in bilateral trade and investment agreements (BTIAs). In particular, Article 3(1)(e) of the Treaty on the Functioning of the European Union (TFEU)[4] provides the EU with the exclusive competence to deal with common commercial policy.[5] According to Article 207(1) of the TFEU,[6] this includes commercial aspects of IP. Not surprisingly, the number of EU BTIAs is quickly growing and the EU-South Korea[7] and EU-Singapore[8] Free Trade Agreements (FTAs), the recent Canada-EU Trade Agreement (CETA)[9] and the EU-Vietnam Trade Agreement[10] all contain annexes listing the GIs that are to be protected in the partner countries as part of the trade deal.

The nature of BTIAs, however, is that these are mixed agreements dealing with issues of tariffs and trade, but also with investment protection and, increasingly, investor–state dispute settlement (ISDS). In the context of the ongoing negotiations ISDS has become a highly controversial issue, including in the negotiation surrounding the Transatlantic Trade and Investment Partnership Agreement (TTIP).[11] The controversy lies in the fact that the

---

[4] Consolidated Version of the Treaty on the Functioning of the European Union, 10 October 2012, 2012 O.J. (C 326) 1 [hereinafter TFEU].
[5] *See* id. Art. 3(1)(e). *See* Case 22/70, Comm'n v. Council, 1971 E.C.R. 263 [hereinafter ERTA]:

> Each time the Community ... adopts provisions laying down common rules ..., the Member States no longer have the right, acting individually or even collectively, to undertake obligations with third countries which affect those rules. ... When such common rules come into being, the Community alone is in a position to assume and carry out contractual obligations towards third countries affecting the whole sphere of application of the Community legal system. ... To the extent to which Community rules are promulgated for the attainment of the objectives of the Treaty, the Member States cannot, outside the framework of the Community institutions, assume obligations which might affect those rules or alter their scope.

[6] TFEU, art. 207(1).
[7] EU-South Korea Free Trade Agreement, EU-S. Kor., 16 September 2010, 54 O.J. (L 127) 1, 46–47, http://eur-lex.europa.eu/legal-content/en/ALL/?uri=OJ:L:2011:127:TOC.
[8] EU-Singapore Free Trade Agreement, EU-Sing., 20 September 2013, http://ec.europa.eu/trade/policy/countries-and-regions/countries/singapore/.
[9] Comprehensive Trade and Economic Agreement, Can.-EU, Consolidated CETA Text, ch. 22, Intellectual Property, 26 September 2014, http://trade.ec.europa.eu/doclib/docs/2014/september/tradoc_152806.pdf [hereinafter CETA].
[10] EU-Vietnam Free Trade Agreement, EU-Viet., 5 August 2015, http://trade.ec.europa.eu/doclib/docs/2015/august/tradoc_153674.pdf [hereinafter EU-Vietnam FTA].
[11] The Transatlantic Trade and Investment Partnership (TTIP) is currently still under negotiation. Further details can be seen at *In Focus: Transatlantic Trade and Investment Partnership (TTIP)*, Eur. Comm'n, http://ec.europa.eu/trade/policy/in-focus/ttip/ (last visited 2 June 2016).

policy freedom of a signatory state to an agreement containing ISDS may become limited on account of investor expectations that have to be honoured. The controversy is remarkable to the extent that ISDS has been a prominent feature in international trade and investment frameworks since the mid-1970s. In fact, the proliferation of ISDS in bilateral agreements is so widespread and affects so many trading nations globally[12] that it is almost surprising that relatively few cases have been brought so far claiming violations under these provisions. Also regional trade agreements like the North American FTA (NAFTA)[13] and the Trans-Pacific Partnership Agreement (TPP)[14] contain ISDS clauses.

However, the concept of ISDS is relatively new in the field of IP. This is due to the fact that IP only became a global trade issue relatively recently through the integration of IP standards and IP enforcement in the WTO framework. That said, IP is also peculiar in the sense that the valuation of IP as an object of property that can be viewed as an investment is also a relatively new concept. Even now, various approaches to valuation according to income-based, market-based and review of cost-based approaches, coupled with diverging reporting standards, yield different results.[15] Still, the number of ISDS complaints is rising and the first cases involving core issues of IP expropriation are currently pending.

Of all IP rights, the EU regime on the protection of GIs invites a substantial involvement of public authority in defining GI specifications, as well as the quality maintenance thereof. This means that any change in the specification may give rise to an investor–state dispute. This chapter charts the likelihood that GIs may become a bone of contention under constitutional expropriation protection laws, WTO disputes and ISDS, and concludes that given the nature of GI protection's inclusion of specifications, there is a higher state involvement, and accordingly, a higher likelihood that measures negatively affecting a GI proprietor's rights can be attributed to a state.

---

[12] A short internet search also reveals that ISDS is not exclusive to trade deals involving Western nations. Asian countries are equally parties to such agreements, also when it concerns their regional trade and investment partners.

[13] North American Free Trade Agreement, US-Can.-Mex., 17 December 1992, 32 I.L.M. 289 (1993) [hereinafter NAFTA].

[14] Trans-Pacific Partnership, ch. 18, Intellectual Property, 5 November 2015, https://medium.com/the-trans-pacific-partnership/intellectual-property-3479efdc7adf#.ux18hliwo [hereinafter TPP, Intellectual Property Chapter].

[15] See *Final Report from the Expert Group on Intellectual Property Valuation* (29 November 2013), https://ec.europa.eu/research/innovation-union/pdf/Expert_Group_Report_on_Intellectual_Property_Valuation_IP_web_2.pdf.

2 GEOGRAPHICAL INDICATIONS AND SPECIFICATIONS IN THE EUROPEAN UNION

The EU PGI, PDO and TSG schemes operate on the basis of registration in the Database of Origin and Registration (DOOR).[16] There are also product-specific regimes and databases, such as the E-BACCHUS[17] for wines and E-SPIRIT DRINKS[18] for spirits. EU law also protects GIs for aromatized wine products.[19] Generally, EU law applies to products originating from EU Member States and third countries that comply with EU rules. Alongside the existing public registries, there are several certification schemes for agricultural products and foodstuffs in the EU. These range from compliance obligations with compulsory production standards to additional voluntary requirements relating to environmental protection, animal welfare, organoleptic qualities, etc. Also, all kinds of 'fair trade' or 'slave free' epithets fall within these voluntary regimes. All these regimes should, however, be in compliance with the 'EU best practice guidelines for voluntary certification schemes for agricultural products and foodstuffs',[20] in order to be in compliance with EU law.

In 2005, the United States (the US) and Australia successfully challenged the legitimacy of EC Regulation 2081/92[21] on GIs for agricultural products and foodstuffs, which was the regulation in force at the time, before the WTO. The regulation contained a number of contentious provisions, namely on (1) the equivalence and reciprocity conditions in respect of GI protection; (2) procedures requiring non-EU nationals, or persons resident or established in non-EU countries, to file an application or objection in the European Communities through their own government, but not directly with EU Member States; and (3) a requirement on third-country governments to provide a declaration that structures were in place on their territory enabling the inspection of compliance with the specifications of the GI registration. On all three points, the WTO Panel[22] found violations of Article 3(1) of

---

[16] See DOOR, Eur. Comm'n, http://ec.europa.eu/agriculture/quality/door/list.html (last visited 5 June 2016).

[17] See E-Bacchus, Eur. Comm'n, http://ec.europa.eu/agriculture/markets/wine/e-bacchus/.

[18] See E-Spirit-Drinks, Eur. Comm'n, http://ec.europa.eu/agriculture/spirits/.

[19] Council regulation 1601/91 of 10 June 1991, laying down general rules on the definition, description and presentation of aromatized wines, aromatized wine-based drinks and aromatized wine-product cocktails, 1991 O.J. (L 149) 1.

[20] Commission Communication – EU best practice guidelines for voluntary certification schemes for agricultural products and foodstuffs, 2010 O.J. (C 341) 4, 5.

[21] Council Regulation 2081/92 of 14 July 1992, on the protection of GIs and designations of origin for agricultural products and foodstuffs, 1992 O.J. (L 208) 1–8.

[22] Complaint by the United States, *EC – Trademarks and Geographical Indications for Agricultural Products and Foodstuffs*, WTO Doc. WT/DS174/R (adopted 20 April 2005);

TRIPS[23] and Article III(4) of the General Agreement on Tariffs and Trade 1994 (GATT),[24] and that the GATT violations were not justified by Article XX(d) of GATT.[25] In the Australian Report, the WTO Panel further found that these inspection structures did not constitute a 'technical regulation' within the meaning of the Agreement on Technical Barriers to Trade (TBT).[26] As a result, the EU changed its regime in March 2006 to ensure compliance with the WTO regime, currently primarily through the Foodstuffs Regulation,[27] and corresponding provisions in the other Regulations.[28] The scope or protection extends to consumer deception;[29] commercial use in comparable products;[30] commercial use exploiting reputation;[31] and misuse, imitation or evocation[32] in relation to the registered GI. The enforcement of a GI is, however, a private law issue.

More interesting, for the purpose of this chapter, however, is the product specification – its establishment, inspection and enforcement – as this requires the involvement of public authority. The definition of the product according

---

Complaint by Australia, *EC – Protections of Trademarks and Geographical Indications for Agricultural Products and Foodstuffs*, WTO Doc. WT/DS290/R (adopted 20 April 2005); see also Lothar Ehring, *National Treatment Under the GATT 1994*, in THE PRINCIPLE OF NATIONAL TREATMENT IN INTERNATIONAL ECONOMIC LAW – TRADE, INVESTMENT AND INTELLECTUAL PROPERTY 34–54 (Anselm Kamperman Sanders ed., 2014) [hereinafter THE PRINCIPLE OF NATIONAL TREATMENT IN INTERNATIONAL ECONOMIC LAW]; Anselm Kamperman Sanders, *National Treatment Under the TRIPS Agreement*, in THE PRINCIPLE OF NATIONAL TREATMENT IN INTERNATIONAL ECONOMIC LAW, *supra*, at 286–99.

[23] See TRIPS, art. 3(1) (obligating National Treatment (NT) in respect of WTO Member States).
[24] See General Agreement on Tariffs and Trade, 15 April 1994, Marrakesh Agreement Establishing the World Trade Organization, Annex 1A, Legal Instruments – Results of the Uruguay Round, art. III(4), 1867 U.N.T.S. 187 (1994) [hereinafter GATT 1994].
[25] GATT 1994, art. XX(d) (providing that an exception can be made to measures falling foul of the mandated standards if they are 'necessary to secure compliance with laws or regulations').
[26] See Agreement on Technical Barriers to Trade, GATT Secretariat. *Uruguay Round of Multilateral Trade Negotiations: Legal Instruments Embodying the Results of the Uruguay Round of Multilateral Trade Negotiations done at Marrakesh on 15 April 1994* (2003), GATT Doc. MTN/FA II-A1A-6 (15 December 1993) [hereinafter TBT], www.wto.org/english/docs_e/legal_e/17-tbt.pdf.
[27] Regulation 1151/2012 concerning certain foodstuffs and certain non-food agricultural products (the 'Foodstuffs Regulation'), 2012 O.J. (L 343), 1–29.
[28] Regulation 1308/2013 concerning wines and sparkling wines, 2013 O.J. (L 347) 671–854; Regulation 110/2008 on the definition, description, presentation, labelling and the protection of geographical indications of spirit drinks, 2008 O.J. (L 39) 16–54; Council Regulation 1601/91 of 10 June 1991, laying down general rules on the definition, description and presentation of aromatized wines, aromatized wine-based drinks and aromatized wine-product cocktails, 1991 O.J. (L 149) 1–9.
[29] 2012 O.J. (L 343), art. 13(c)–(d).   [30] 2012 O.J. (L 343), art. 13(a).   [31] *Id.*
[32] *Id.* art. 13(b).

to precise specifications and its analysis by national authorities is a process integral to the registration of the GI at the EU level.

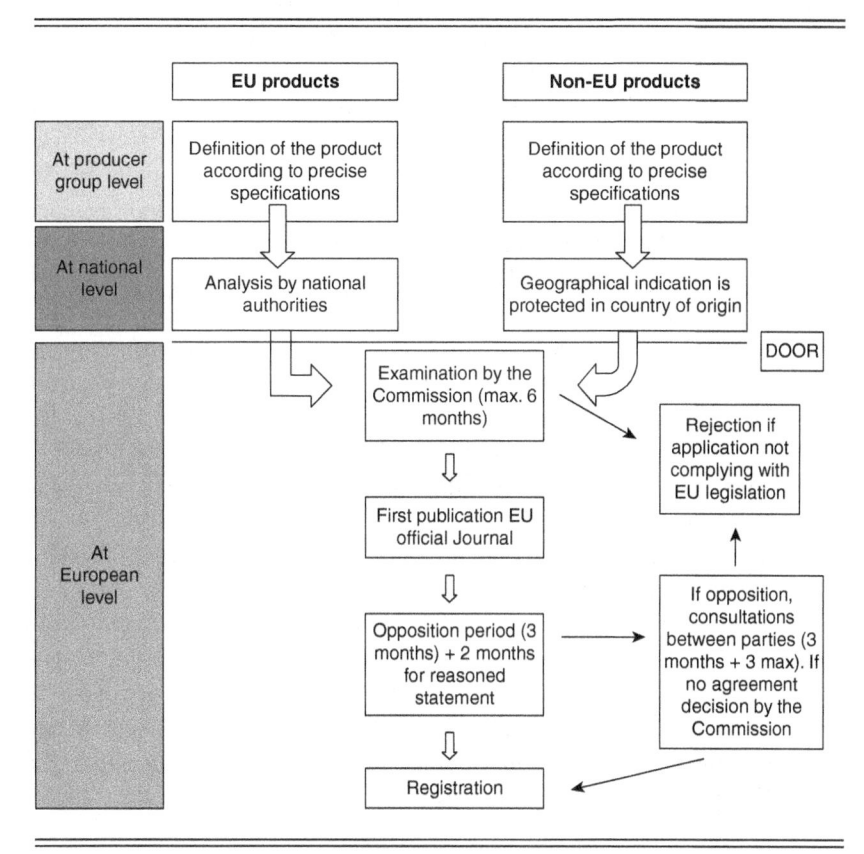

Figure 7.1 *Source:* European Commission, http://ec.europa.eu/agriculture/quality/schemes/index_en.htm

The definition of the product comprises the following elements: the product name, applicant details, product class, the name of the product, the description of the product, a definition of the geographical area, proof of the product's origin, a description of the method of production, the linkage between the product and the area, the nomination of an inspection body and labelling information.[33] For PDOs, all production steps must take place within the geographical area, whereas for PGIs at least one production step must take place within the geographical area. It is also at this point where

---

[33] *See Guide to Applicants,* EUR. COMM'N, http://ec.europa.eu/agriculture/quality/schemes/guides/guide-for-applicants_en.pdf (last visited 5 June 2016).

specific rules concerning slicing, grating, packaging and the like of the product to which the registered name refers may be stated and justified. Given the fact that these types of conditions on repackaging or slicing result in geographical restrictions having strong protectionist and anticompetitive effects, they are among the most controversial specifications.

In 1997, the Consorzio del Prosciutto di Parma,[34] the Italian trade association of 200 traditional producers of Parma Ham, sought injunctions against Asda Stores in the United Kingdom to restrain them from selling pre-sliced packets of prosciutto as 'Parma Ham', a protected PDO. The ham was sliced by a supplier of Asda outside the production region, and pre-packaged without supervision by the inspection body responsible for enforcing EU production regulations. The slicing of the ham itself cannot be problematic as such,[35] but the question is whether slicing the ham away from the consumer's eyes and offering them as a pre-packaged product not bearing the Consorzio's mark would be infringing upon the PDO. The Consorzio's argument was that the consumer could not verify the origin, and the quality of the ham could not be guaranteed. The Court of Justice of the European Union (CJEU[36]) held[37] that protection conferred by a PDO did not normally extend to operations such as grating, slicing and packaging the product. The CJEU, however, stated that those operations were prohibited to third parties outside the region of production only if they were expressly laid down in the specification, and if this condition was brought to the attention of economic operators by adequate publicity in Community legislation. The latter was not yet the case under the old regime.[38] Under Article 8.2[39] of Regulation 1151/2012, the product specification is now to be included in the single document that is contained in the DOOR register, and the Consorzio can now enforce its slicing and packaging rules.

The specification also contains the names of the inspection bodies responsible for enforcing EU production regulations.[40] In each Member State,

---

[34] See PROSCIUTTO DI PARMA, www.prosciuttodiparma.com/ (last visited 5 June 2016).
[35] One can follow the hilarious videos of the 'Prosciutto di Parma DOP slicing instruction' videos on YouTube. ProsciuttodiParmaDOP, *English Tutorial: Preparing and Slicing Parma Ham*, YOUTUBE (16 October 2012), www.youtube.com/watch?v=_qfVIzmqlGE.
[36] Formerly European Court of Justice (ECJ).
[37] Case C-108/01, Consorzio del Prosciutto di Parma en Salumificio S. Rita SpA v. Asda Stores Ltd and Hygrade Foods Ltd., 2003 E.C.R. I-5163.
[38] Regulation 2081/92 on the protection of geographical indications and designations of origin for agricultural products and foodstuffs, 1992 O.J. (L 208) 1–8.
[39] 2012 O.J. (L 343), art. 8(2).
[40] For a list of inspection bodies, see EUR. COMM'N, http://ec.europa.eu/agriculture/quality/schemes/compliance-authorities_en.pdf (last visited 5 June 2016).

public authorities or government agencies are entrusted with this task. When it comes to defining or redefining the specification, however, quite a lot of state involvement can be observed. A case on point is the enlargement in 2009, actively supported by the Italian government, of the area of production for 'Italian Prosecco'.[41] The production of this sparkling wine has been traditionally confined to the Veneto Region around Venice, but it was suddenly 'strategically' expanded to include the town of Prosecco, which is located in the Friuli-Venezia Giulia Region near Trieste and the Slovenian border. This is the place where the Prosecco grape variety is believed to have originated from. Yet, upon accession to the EU in 2013, Croatia found that its sweet Prošek dessert wine, which is different from Italian Prosecco in all aspects of methods of production and grapes used, could no longer coexist in the EU with Italian Prosecco.[42]

In short, GIs are peculiar in the sense that they constitute a type of IP right where a lot of state involvement can be observed, especially in the drafting, maintenance and alteration of the GI's specification. This may lead to the consortium of GI producers, or the (semi-)state authority itself to alter a GI specification after the GI has been registered. As a consequence, this may give rise to investor–state disputes by private parties that may consider themselves affected by these changes or the recognition of GIs in general (in that they may no longer be able to market their products under the same or similar names), since many of these measures leading to the definition of the GI's specification can be directly or indirectly attributed to the state.

3 GEOGRAPHICAL INDICATIONS AS PROPERTY

Like other IP rights, GIs are protected as proprietary interests. This becomes apparent from the WTO Panel report in *EC – Trademarks and Geographical Indications*,[43] but even more so in the context of the European Convention on Human Rights (ECHR).

In the case of *Anheuser-Busch v. Portugal*, the European Court of Human Rights (ECtHR) held that the protection provided for by Article 1 of the

---

[41] See *Prosecco Wine*, WINE-SEARCHER, www.wine-searcher.com/regions-prosecco (last visited 7 November 2013), for a brief summary; Filippo Mattia Ginanni, *The 2009 Prosecco DOC Reform*, WINE & SPIRIT EDUC. TR., www.wsetglobal.com/documents/julian_brind_scholarship_2015_prosecco_reform__filippo_ginanni.pdf.

[42] See Anselm Kamperman Sanders, *Geographical Indications of Origin: When GIs Become Commodities, All Gloves Come Off*, 46 IIC-INT'L REV. INTELL. PROP. & COMPETITION L. (IIC) 755–59 (2015).

[43] 1992 O.J. (L 208) 1–8.

Protocol No.1 to the ECHR,[44] which guarantees the right to property,[45] is applicable to IP as such.[46] This means that the owner of an intellectual 'possession' is protected in respect of (1) the peaceful enjoyment of property; (2) deprivation of possessions and the conditions thereto; and (3) the control of the use of property by the state in accordance with general interest. Inherent in the convention is the recognition that a fair balance needs to be struck between the demands of the general interests of society and the requirements of the protection of the individual's fundamental rights.[47]

Since 2000 the EU Charter on the Protection of Fundamental Human Rights[48] recognized similar principles that EU citizens can rely on. In *Scarlet Extended v. Sabam*,[49] the CJEU held:

> The protection of the right to intellectual property is indeed enshrined in Article 17(2) of the Charter of Fundamental Rights of the European Union

---

[44] See Monica Carss-Frisk, A Guide to the Implementation of Article 1 of the Protocol No. 1 to the European Convention on Human Rights, *in* HUMAN RIGHTS HANDBOOK (Eur. Council, Human Rights Handbooks No. 4, 2001), www.echr.coe.int/LibraryDocs/DG2/HRHAND/D G2-EN-HRHAND-04(2003).pdf.

[45] Convention for the Protection of Human Rights and Fundamental Freedoms Protocol 1 art. 1, 4 November 1950, 213 U.N.T.S. 222 (European Convention on Human Rights) [hereinafter ECHR]:

> Every natural or legal person is entitled to the peaceful enjoyment of his possessions. No one shall be deprived of his possessions except in the public interest and subject to the conditions provided for by law and by the general principles of international law.
> The preceding provisions shall not, however, in any way impair the right of a state to enforce such laws at it deems necessary to control the use of property in accordance with the general interest or to secure the payment of taxes or other contributions or penalties.

[46] Anheuser-Busch Inc. v. Portugal, App. No. 73049/01, 44 Eur. H.R. Rep. 42, para. 72 (2007) (stating that 'Article 1 of Protocol No. 1 is applicable to intellectual property as such', but in the case at hand decided that legitimate regulatory interests may justify interference with the right of property in line with the court's general approach to interference with the right to property). See also Anselm Kamperman Sanders, Professional Case Comment, *Case No. 73049/01 of the Grand Chamber of the ECHR, Anheuser-Bush Inc. v. Portugal*, 4 EUR. HUMAN RIGHTS CASES (EHRC) 433–37 (2007).

[47] See James v. the United Kingdom, 8 Eur. H.R. Rep. A98, para. 46 (1986).

[48] Charter of Fundamental Rights of the European Union art. 17, 18 December 2000, 2000 O.J. (C 364) 1, on the right to property provides:

> 1. Everyone has the right to own, use, dispose of and bequeath his or her lawfully acquired possessions. No one may be deprived of his or her possessions, except in the public interest and in the cases and under the conditions provided for by law, subject to fair compensation being paid in good time for their loss. The use of property may be regulated by law in so far as is necessary for the general interest.
> 2. Intellectual property shall be protected.

[49] Case C-70/10 Scarlet Extended v. Société Belge des auteurs, compositeurs et éditeurs SCRL (SABAM), 2011 E.C.R. I-11959.

('the Charter'). There is, however, nothing whatsoever in the wording of that provision or in the Court's case-law to suggest that that right is inviolable and must for that reason be absolutely protected ... The protection of the fundamental right to property, which includes the rights linked to intellectual property, must be balanced against the protection of other fundamental rights.

Opinions on how this balance should be struck, however, naturally differ, depending on one's perspective. In a European case, *British American Tobacco*,[50] involving challenges to restrictions on advertising, branding and trademark communication in relation to tobacco products, the CJEU held that restrictions on trademark use requiring labels to display health warnings by taking up 30 per cent of the front and 40 per cent of the back of a cigarette package[51] amount to a legitimate restriction that still allows for a normal use of the trademark. The tobacco companies had argued that there is a de facto expropriation of their property in the trademark. A similar argument was made in the well-publicized constitutional challenge case to the Australian Tobacco Plain Packaging Act 2011.[52] The High Court of Australia in *BAT v. Commonwealth of Australia*[53] held that there was no acquisition of property that would have required so-called 'just terms' protection under the Australian constitution. Yet it is the Australian Tobacco Plain Packaging Act 2011 that has also produced two WTO challenges to tobacco plain packaging, by Ukraine[54] and by a number of other states.[55] Although Ukraine suspended its proceedings on 28 May 2015, the litigation by Honduras, Cuba, Indonesia and the

[50] Case C-491/01, The Queen v. Secretary of State for Health, ex parte British American Tobacco (Investments) Ltd and Imperial Tobacco Ltd., 2002 E.C.R. I-11453.
[51] Current requirements are even more stringent under Directive 2014/40/EU, of the European Parliament and of the Council of 3 April 2014, on the approximation of the laws, regulations and administrative provisions of the Member States concerning the manufacture, presentation and sale of tobacco and related products and repealing Directive 2001/37/EC, 2014 O.J. (L 127) 1, with Arts. 8–10 amounting to a '75% rule' in terms of the package having to display health warnings.
[52] See Tobacco Plain Packaging Act 2011 (Austl.).
[53] British American Tobacco Australasia Limited and Ors v. Commonwealth of Australia, 2012 250 CLR 1.
[54] Complaint by Ukraine, *Australia – Certain Measures Concerning Trademarks, and Other Plain Packaging Requirements Applicable to Tobacco Products and Packaging*, WTO Doc. WT/DS343/1 (13 March 2012).
[55] Complaint by Honduras, *Australia – Certain Measures Concerning Trademarks, Geographical Indications and Other Plain Packaging Requirements Applicable to Tobacco Products and Packaging*, WTO Doc. WT/DS435/1 (4 April 2012 [hereinafter *Australia – Certain Measures Concerning Trademarks*); Complaint by Dominican Republic, *Australia – Certain Measures Concerning Trademarks*, WTO Doc. WT/DS441/1 (18 July 2012); Complaint by Cuba, *Australia – Certain Measures Concerning Trademarks*, WTO Doc. WT/DS458/1 (3 May

Dominican Republic remains unaffected. Plain packaging also sparked investor–state disputes.[56] These cases raise questions on the remaining policy freedom that nation states have in regulating the use or exercise of IP in light of societal interests, such as public health, in the context of multilateral and bilateral trade agreements, and investment protection agreements.

4 INVESTOR–STATE DISPUTE SETTLEMENT AND WTO LAW

Bilateral free trade and investment agreements may provide additional protection to investors in relation to their investments that are then considered to be 'possessions' in the state where such investments have been made. The question is then to what extent protection granted by means of bilateral agreements changes the legal relations between WTO Members. Although the annexes to EU BTIAs list GIs that are to be protected under the agreement,[57] it remains to be examined what their effect under the WTO Dispute Settlement Understanding (DSU) is.

The WTO Appellate Body, in *Mexico – Taxes on Soft Drinks*,[58] rejected the notion that parties can modify WTO obligations by means of an FTA, whereas the WTO Panel in *Peru – Additional Duty*[59] was not so categorically opposed. In the latter case, there are numerous references to Peru's freedom to maintain a price range system (PRS) under an FTA with complainant Guatemala. The WTO Panel, however, observed that the FTA in question was not yet in force, and that its provisions should therefore have limited legal effects on the dispute at hand. Peru's arguments in respect of the FTA were that, even assuming that Peru's PRS was WTO-inconsistent, Peru and Guatemala had modified between themselves the relevant WTO provisions to the extent that the FTA allowed Peru to maintain the PRS. Upon appeal, the Appellate Body stated:

> [W]e are of the view that the consideration of provisions of an FTA for the purpose of determining whether a Member has complied with its WTO obligations involves legal characterizations that fall within the scope of appellate review under Article 17.6 of the DSU.[60]

2013); and Complaint by Indonesia, *Australia – Certain Measures Concerning Trademarks*, WTO Doc. WT/DS467/1 (20 September 2013).

[56] See *infra* Section 5.   [57] See *supra* Section 1.
[58] Appellate Body Report, *Mexico – Tax Measures on Soft Drinks and Other Beverages*, WTO Doc. WT/DS308/AB/R, (adopted 6 March 2006).
[59] Panel Report, *Peru – Additional Duty on Imports of Certain Agricultural Products*, WTO Doc. WT/DS457/R (adopted 27 November 2014) [hereinafter Additional Duty Panel Report].
[60] Appellate Body Report, *Peru – Additional Duty on Imports of Certain Agricultural Products*, 5.86 WTO Doc. WT/DS457/AB/R (adopted 20 July 2015).

However, it also considered that WTO Members cannot modify WTO provisions such that these become WTO-inconsistent, even if these changes 'merely' operate bilaterally *inter partes* and not amongst all WTO Members. In particular, the Appellate Body held:

> We note, however, that Peru has not yet ratified the FTA. In this respect, it is not clear whether Peru can be considered as a 'party' to the FTA. Moreover, we express reservations as to whether the provisions of the FTA (in particular paragraph 9 of Annex 2.3), which could arguably be construed as to allow Peru to maintain the PRS in its bilateral relations with Guatemala, can be used under Article 31(3) of the Vienna Convention in establishing the common intention of WTO Members underlying the provisions of Article 4.2 of the Agreement on Agriculture and Article II:1(b) of the GATT 1994. In our view, such an approach would suggest that WTO provisions can be interpreted differently, depending on the Members to which they apply and on their rights and obligations under an FTA to which they are parties.[61]

In the case at hand, this means that Peru under the FTA is only allowed to maintain a WTO-consistent PRS, which should meet the requirements of Article XXIV[62] of the GATT 1994, which permits certain specific deviations from WTO rules. All such departures require that the level of duties and other regulations of commerce applicable in each of the FTA members to the trade of non-FTA members shall not be higher or more restrictive than those applicable prior to the formation of the FTA.[63]

In *Turkey – Textiles*,[64] the Appellate Body held that the justification for measures that are inconsistent with certain GATT 1994 provisions requires the party claiming the benefit of the defence provided for by Article XXIV GATT 1994 lies in closer integration between the economies of the countries party to such an agreement. It is clear that Peru's PRS measure cannot be interpreted as a measure fostering closer integration; rather, it results in the opposite. The GI 'claw-back' annexes to EU BTIAs can arguably be held to contain obligations that approximate the economies of the parties to the agreement, providing the holder of such a GI legal certainty not only as to the protection and enforcement of the GI but also as to the protection of an 'investment' in terms of production and marketing of a GI product.

---

[61] Additional Duty Panel Report, *supra* note 60, at ¶ 5.106.
[62] GATT 1994 art. XXIV(5) (providing that parties can form custom unions or free trade areas, subject to certain conditions being met).
[63] GATT 1994 art. XXIV(5)(a).
[64] Appellate Body Report, *Turkey – Restrictions on Imports of Textile and Clothing Products*, WTO Doc. WT/ DS34/AB/R (adopted 19 November 1999).

The WTO Dispute Settlement Body has meanwhile established dispute settlement panels in relation to Australia's tobacco plain packaging measure. GIs are part of the property package on which the claim is based. The five complainants are arguing that the measure is inconsistent with Australia's WTO obligations under TRIPS,[65] TBT[66] and the GATT 1994.[67] In respect of trademarks and GIs, the claim is that restrictions on their use amount to an expropriation of property. There is only one caveat that will be of relevance to a decision in these cases[68] in the context of TRIPS, and that is that in *EC – Geographical Indications*, the panel held:

> [T]he TRIPS Agreement does not generally provide for the grant of positive rights to exploit or use certain subject matter, but rather provides for the grant of negative rights to prevent certain acts. This fundamental feature of intellectual property protection inherently grants Members freedom to pursue legitimate public policy objectives since many measures to attain those public policy objectives lie outside the scope of intellectual property rights and do not require an exception under the TRIPS Agreement.[69]

5 INVESTOR–STATE DISPUTE SETTLEMENT AND GEOGRAPHICAL INDICATIONS

The ISDS case of *Philip Morris Asia v. Australia*[70] shows that investor–state disputes can be brought in support of, or as an alternative to, constitutional and WTO challenges. In this case, Philip Morris Asia challenged the tobacco plain packaging legislation under the 1993 Agreement between the Government of Australia and the Government of Hong Kong for the Promotion and Protection of Investments. The arbitration was conducted under the United Nations Commission on International Trade Law (UNCITRAL) Arbitration Rules 2010.[71] In a decision of 18 December 2015,

---

[65] TRIPS, *supra* note 2. [66] TBT, *supra* note 26. [67] GATT 1994 art. III(4).
[68] See *supra* notes 54 & 55. The Chair of the panel informed the Dispute Settlement Body on 10 October 2014 that the panel expects to issue its final report to the parties in the second half of 2016.
[69] See Panel Report, *EC – Trademarks and Geographical Indications*, 7.210, WTO Doc. WT/DS/174R (adopted 15 March 2005).
[70] Philip Morris Asia Limited (Hong Kong) v. The Commonwealth of Australia, Case No. 2012–12 (Perm. Ct. Arb. 22 June 2011), www.pcacases.com/web/view/5.
[71] *UNCITRAL Arbitration Rules*, U.N. COMM'N INT'L TRADE L., www.uncitral.org/uncitral/en/uncitral_texts/arbitration/2010Arbitration_rules.html (last visited 6 June 2016).

the Tribunal hearing the case ruled that it had no jurisdiction to hear Philip Morris Asia's claim.

However, it is important to realize that the proliferation of ISDS clauses in bilateral trade agreements is increasing. Investor–state dispute settlement revolves around the question of whether expropriation, directly or indirectly, has been conducted according to the principles of Fair and Equitable Treatment (FET). FET is determined through applying principles of (1) reasonableness, (2) consistency, (3) non-discrimination, (4) transparency and (5) due process. In this context, the legitimate expectations of an investor are taken into consideration in order to assess whether the state has expropriated in bad faith, through coercion, by means of threats or harassment. Due to the fact that there is no true harmonized multilateral dispute settlement system in relation to investment disputes, the interpretation and application of these principles are not uniform. Due to the confidential nature of arbitration, not all arbitration reports are public. The most concrete expressions of what legitimate investor expectations are can be found in statements made in published cases that seem to indicate that a balance must be struck.

For example, in *International Thunderbird v. Mexico*,[72] a NAFTA dispute conducted under UNCITRAL Arbitration Rules, the panel held:

> [A] situation where a Contracting Party's conduct creates reasonable and justifiable expectations on the part of an investor (or investment) to act in reliance on said conduct, such that a failure by the NAFTA Party to honour those expectations could cause the investor (or investment) to suffer damages.[73]

Conversely, in *Saluka v. Czech Republic*,[74] an investor–state dispute also conducted under UNCITRAL Arbitration Rules, the panel held:

> No investor may reasonably expect that the circumstances prevailing at the time the investment is made remain totally unchanged. In order to determine whether frustration of the foreign investor's expectations was justified and reasonable, the host State's legitimate right subsequently to regulate domestic matters in the public interest must be taken into consideration as well.[75]

---

[72] International Thunderbird Gaming Corporation v. The United Mexican States, NAFTA, Arbitral Award (26 January 2006), www.iisd.org/pdf/2006/itn_award.pdf.

[73] *Id.* at 49, para. 147.

[74] Saluka Investments BV (The Netherlands) v. Czech Republic, Partial Award, (Perm. Ct. Arb. 17 March 2006), http://archive.pca-cpa.org/SAL-CZ%20Partial%20Award%20170306ba57.pdf?fil_id=105.

[75] *Id.* at 66, para. 305.

There are few ISDS cases involving IP.[76] These are cases that have been argued under the rules of the International Centre for Settlement of Investment Disputes (ICSID), which is an independent branch of the World Bank.

First, there was a failed attempt at arguing a trademark infringement case under investor–state dispute settlement in *AHS v. Niger*.[77] In this case, although a concession to service Niger's national airport had been terminated, there was continued use of seized equipment and uniforms bearing the trademarks of the complainant. The panel held that it had no jurisdiction, as IP enforcement is a civil matter that cannot be raised in the context of the ISDS expropriation complaint.

Second, there is the ongoing case of *Philip Morris v. Uruguay*[78] that is argued under the Uruguay-Switzerland FTA,[79] and where the legitimacy of plain packaging tobacco products is challenged. In this case jurisdiction has been established and proceedings on the merits are to follow.

Third, there is a NAFTA[80] case argued under UNCITRAL Arbitration Rules. In *Eli Lilly v. Canada*,[81] pharmaceutical company Eli Lilly sought damages for $100 million CAD and challenged changes to the patentability requirements in respect of utility or industrial applicability, leading the Canadian patent office to invalidate two of Eli Lilly's patents for the Strattera attention-deficit disorder pill and the Zyprexa antipsychotic treatment. Eli Lilly argued that the interpretation of the term 'useful' in the Canadian Patent Act by the Canadian courts led to an unjustified expropriation and a violation of Canada's obligations under NAFTA on the basis that it is arbitrary and discriminatory. Canada conversely argued that Eli Lilly's claims were beyond the jurisdiction of the Tribunal. Ultimately, in March 2017, the Tribunal dismissed Eli Lilly's claims and confirmed that Canada was in compliance with its NAFTA obligations.[82]

---

[76] For a comprehensive overview, see H. Grosse Ruse-Khan, *Litigating Intellectual Property Rights in Investor-State Arbitration: From Plain Packaging to Patent Revocation* (Univ. Cambridge, Legal Studies Research Paper Series No. 52, 2014).

[77] AHS Niger and Menzies Middle East and Africa S.A. v. Republic of Niger, ICSID Case No. ARB/11/11 Award (15 July 2013), www.italaw.com/sites/default/files/case-documents/italaw3034.pdf.

[78] Philip Morris Brands Sàrl v. Oriental Republic of Uruguay, ICSID Case No. ARB/10/7, www.italaw.com/cases/460.

[79] Agreement Between the Swiss Confederation and the Oriental Republic of Uruguay on the Recipocal Promotion and Protection of Investments, 7 October 1988, 1976 U.N.T.S. 389.

[80] NAFTA, *supra* note 13.

[81] Eli Lilly and Co. v. The Government of Canada, ICSID Case No. UNCT/14/2 NAFTA (7 November 2012).

[82] Eli Lilly and Co. v. The Government of Canada, ICSID Case No. UNCT/14/2 Final Award (16 March 2017).

Cases involving IP can be and are clearly brought if measures negatively impacting upon the 'investment' can be attributed to a state that has submitted to ISDS. Issues such as IP enforcement or thresholds for patentability as such appear to be outside of the remit of ISDS, as these are civil or administrative matters where access to judicial review is usually provided. However, complaints over (arbitrary or discriminatory) denial of justice may not be. In the cases described above, one can argue that the general measures taken are neither of an arbitrary nor discriminatory nature. GI specifications, on the other hand, are discriminatory by nature since they are always specifically targeted, and this characteristic exceeds the already exclusionary nature of an IP right. This is because, as we have seen, the definition of the product comprises not only the product name and related labelling but also the description of the product, a definition of the geographical area, proof of the product's origin, a description of the method of production, the linkage between the product and the area, the nomination of an inspection body empowered to police the specification.

This means that there are a number of actions that may have an immediate impact, not only on the existence and exercise of a GI, but also on its value and costs. The example of the Italian Prosecco DOC reform[83] comes to mind, as an enlargement of the geographical area, but also a possible reduction thereof has immediate effects for producers within and outside of the area. Production methods may also be subject to changes. Changes to production requirements resulting from a raise in food safety standards may be legitimized within the context of the WTO Agreement on the Application of Sanitary and Phytosanitary Measures (SPS).[84] Many of the GI production requirements are, however, steeped in a tradition and culture that solicit the demand for a particular product. If one, for example, orders Limburg Grotto Cheese,[85] one expects the cheese to have been ripened through completely natural processes by exposure of the cheese to the atmosphere of a limestone cave that contains the *Brevibacterium Linens* that produces a cheese with a pungent odour. The cheeses ripen on oak wooden boards and need to be turned regularly. This is a delicate operation as the fungi growing on the cheeses are poisonous. The result of food safety standards (no oak, stainless steel racks, etc.) has been that the traditional production for the traditional connoisseur

---

[83] See *supra* note 41.
[84] See Agreement on the Application of Sanitary and Phytosanitary Measures, 15 April 1994, Marrakesh Agreement Establishing the World Trade Organization, Annex 1, 1867 U.N.T.S. 493.
[85] The 'Duchy of Limburg' was a state in the Holy Roman Empire (1065–1794) and a part of the German Confederation (1839–1867). Since 1839 'Limburg' is a province in Belgium, and a province in the Netherlands. Furthermore, it is the name of a town in Belgium, and in Germany it is used in respect of various cities, towns, a castle, abbey and airfield.

consumer has now moved literally and figuratively underground. As a result, only the more industrial producers remain around to sell a product that is compliant with legal standards. They are selling a product that may be safer (although this is often disputed) but is certainly far less traditional than the consumer is led to believe. Phasing-out rules concerning slicing, grating, packaging, etc. stem from a desire to free the market from anticompetitive restrictions, but arguably these could also be measures that have a negative impact on the investments made by producers benefitting from GI specifications containing such rules. These forms of proprietary protection of GIs via individual regulations are also open to non-European entities, as we have seen above. So, a US association that holds an EU GI, such as the Idaho Potato Commission,[86] could then also sue before the special ISDS courts envisaged under the TTIP[87] for a weakening or strengthening of protection standards in Europe. In most cases, after all, the measure can be attributed to the state, and despite attempts by EU Member States to deny private parties the right to invoke international treaties, the CJEU has affirmed the direct effect of international treaties that bind the EU.[88]

6 CONCLUSION

More than any other IP, a GI displays a very high level of state involvement in relation to specifications that do not directly concern the exercise of the IP right in terms of protection against consumer confusion and the like, but that very much influences the value of the GI for its owner. Definitions of territory, methods of production, sanitary and phytosanitary standards, and other more nefarious rules concerning slicing, grating, packaging, etc. can be changed at the behest of members of the consortium, but also of (semi-)state authorities or

---

[86] *See* IDAHO POTATO COMM'N, https://idahopotato.com (last visited 6 June 2016).
[87] EU-Vietnam FTA, *supra* note 10.
[88] Case C-104/81, Hauptzollamt Mainz v. C.A. Kupferberg, 1982 E.C.R. 3641. *See also* Case C-265/03, Igor Simutenkov v. Ministerio de Educación y Cultura and Real Federación Española de Fútbol (EU-Russia Partnership Agreement), 2005 E.C.R. I-2579 (precluding imposing limits in fielding individual sportsmen from non-EEA members). *But see* Case C-240/09, Lesoochranárske zoskupenie VLK v. Ministerstvo životného prostredia Slovenskej republiky (Aarhus Convention), 2011 E.C.R. I-1255 (holding that in the absence of EU rules governing the matter, it is for the domestic legal system of each Member State to lay down the detailed procedural rules governing actions for safeguarding rights which individuals derive from EU law); Joined Cases C-404 & C-4055/12P, Council v. Stichting Natuur en Milieu and Pesticide Action Network Europe (Aarhus Convention), 2015 EUR-Lex CELEX LEXIS 62012CJ0404 (13 January 2015) (holding that an NGO has no standing to invoke the Aarhus Convention in a challenge to the postponement of clean air requirements).

agencies. Insofar as these lead to a negative impact on members of the consortium, or third parties, there appears to be an increase in the options to challenge such measures under domestic constitutional and WTO rules, or bilateral and regional trade and investment agreements containing ISDS. These ISDS clauses are commonly included in recent US and EU trade and investment agreements, also those with Asian partners. To date, only a limited number of such cases that have been brought involve IP rights. The likelihood of success appears limited, but several key cases are still pending. In ISDS complaints over IP enforcement, tribunals seem hesitant to accept jurisdiction over these cases. In the plain packaging tobacco cases, the question will be the extent to which WTO Members have policy freedom in articulating exceptions to WTO obligations.

EU GI specifications are very targeted and individual in nature, so that any measure affecting them may be considered arbitrary or discriminatory much more easily as compared to general policy measures affecting the use, grant or scope of a trademark, design, copyright or patent right. Furthermore, many specifications are rooted in culture and custom rather than in science and utility, which raises the chances of a dispute over arbitrariness and discrimination in standards imposed when determining issues of culture and custom. Finally, measures affecting GI specifications are often attributable to a public authority or agency. This combination increases the likelihood of success of claims for protection of GIs as property and investments. If, for example, an EU company takes over (i.e., invests) a business located in Vietnam or Korea that is involved in the production of a GI product, and the Vietnamese or Korean authority redefines the geographical area in such a way that the EU company can no longer use that GI, this could give rise to an ISDS case. The same could be true for a US company making investments in Asian jurisdictions. This should be taken into consideration when drafting or changing GI product specifications.

8

How Would Geographical Indications from Asia Fare in Europe?

Christopher Heath[*]

1 INTRODUCTION AND STRUCTURE

Asian countries are discovering geographical indications (GIs).[1] There are two reasons for this. First, the recognition that GIs can serve as an advantageous identifier for the marketing of domestic products abroad. Second, a system for the protection of GIs has become an obligation under bilateral and multilateral agreements. The question of how GIs from Asia can be protected abroad thereby becomes of interest. This chapter analyses how Asian GIs would fare in Europe.[2] 'Would', because as of yet there is very little actual experience in this respect. Very few GIs from Asia have been registered in Europe, be it as GIs or trademarks, and even fewer have been litigated. The examples used in this chapter demonstrate how 'foreign' GIs can, did or did not find protection in Europe, either at the level of European Community law or the domestic laws of individual European Union (EU) Member States.

This chapter is divided into four sections. Section 2 gives a brief overview of the interplay between social, economic and legal considerations when approaching the topic of protecting domestic GIs abroad. Section 3 discusses the possibilities for Asian GIs to obtain protection in Europe, be it under the *sui generis* protection offered by EU law or on the basis of bilateral or international agreements. Section 4 discusses protection under EU trademark

---

[*] Member of the Board of Appeal, European Patent Office; former Head of the Asia Department, Max-Planck Institute for Innovation and Competition.

[1] Geographical indications (GIs) are understood here in a rather broad sense as any indication that, in the course of trade, may serve as a geographical identifier for goods or services.

[2] The reverse already exists. The European Union (EU) has commissioned a study as to how European GIs can be protected abroad: 'Geographical Indications and TRIPs: 10 Years Later... A Roadmap for EU GI Holders to Get Protection in Other WTO Members', available at http://trade.ec.europa.eu/doclib/docs/2007/june/tradoc_135088.pdf.

law in different contexts: protection against registration of geographical names by third parties, protection based on trademark registration, protection based on the registration of a collective mark and protection once a trademark has received well-known status. Section 5 discusses non-proprietary protection in the context of unfair competition prevention law, namely as a guarantee of the 'freedom to operate' and market access.

2 GEOGRAPHICAL INDICATIONS AT THE CROSSROADS OF CULTURE, LAW AND ECONOMY

Try to discuss GIs in a country with a strong heritage in food and beverages such as Italy, and tempers flare. Most consider it a huge injustice that Americans sell 'Parmesan' cheese that does not originate from Italy (and often tastes like grated wood), but would readily admit that neither 'Parmesan' nor 'Parmigiano' are protected indications in Italy itself (only Parmigiano Reggiano is). 'Tokaj' and 'Prosecco' are considered local indications by most Italians, yet few know or acknowledge that the fame of Tokaj is based on Hungarian Tokaj being sold to the Tsars of Russia, and even fewer know that 'Prosecco' is a place (let alone where it is on a map).[3] If they did, they would discover that this little village up the Karst region of Triest belonged to the Habsburg monarchy for almost 600 years, and the fame of the sparkling wine owes more to the Austrian Empire than to Italy. Particularly when it comes to national heritage and history, there is often a mismatch between local and global perception, and GIs are no exception. While for many, 'Pilsener' beer comes from Pilsen, 'Budweiser' beer from Budweis (Ceske Budejovice) and Bavarian beer from Bavaria, others take the view that 'Pilsen' is generic, 'Budweiser' comes from Anheuser Busch and Bavarian beer may come from Bavaria, or is generic, or may come from the Dutch brewery 'Bavaria'. The same issues are discussed in the Asia-Pacific region. Australians strongly feel that 'Ugg' boots are Australian; Indians insist that 'Basmati' rice must originate from India (or, maybe, from Pakistan); and Thais feel the same about 'Jasmine' rice, while for many European consumers, these indications sound just as generic as Afghan dogs, bone China or Singapore Sling. Things are not helped by the fact that well-reputed indications often face an erosion from piggybackers: 'Kobe beef' produced in the United States and Australia is an example.[4]

[3] John Brunton, *Lovely Bubbly: A Taste of Italy's Prosecco Region*, THE GUARDIAN (3 August 2010), www.theguardian.com/travel/2010/aug/03/prosecco-wine-tasting-tour-italy.
[4] See Larry Olmsted, 'Food's Biggest Scam: The Great Kobe Beef Lie', FORBES (12 April 2012), www.forbes.com/sites/larryolmsted/2012/04/12/foods-biggest-scam-the-great-kobe-beef-lie/#493 8377434d7. Olmsted covers the misuse of the term 'Kobe beef' in a four-part series of articles.

All this of course also has financial implications. Particularly, the European Union makes mantra-like claims about the financial benefits that GIs bring to producers (and paid for by consumers, of course).[5] Whether the figures are correct or inflated, it is certainly true that business identifiers through proper marketing can turn into extremely valuable brands and premium prices for products. 'Champagne' may be the most prominent example, but also the recognition of 'Café de Colombia', a relatively recent indication, should not be underestimated.[6]

The question is then how and to what extent the cultural and financial interests in GIs can be safeguarded and enforced by legal means. In this respect, one should distinguish three different levels of legal protection. First, the freedom to operate; second, non-proprietary protection of an indication based on the principles of unfair competition (that is, protection against misleading use); and, third, proprietary protection based on registration, against the use of the indication for either similar or, at the highest level of protection, dissimilar goods.

The freedom to operate is normally guaranteed where the marketing of goods under an indication does not infringe third-party rights and is not considered misleading. Third-party rights may become an issue either where the GI in question has been registered by someone else (rare but possible, e.g., where two countries use the same indication, such as Ginseng in North and South Korea) or, more common, where conflicting trademark rights exist. The latter has been a particularly contentious issue in trade negotiations (see Section 3). Although unlikely, it may be that in accordance with local consumer perception even a true GI is considered misleading, e.g., where two different locations sharing the same name produce similar goods. Wines from 'Cordoba' could originate in Argentina or Spain.

The freedom to operate guarantees market access but does not allow the exclusion of others. In case the indication is considered generic, proprietary

---

[5] See the *External Study on the Value of Production of Agricultural Products and Foodstuffs, Wines, Aromatised Wines and Spirits Protected by a GI*, EUR. COMM'N (October 2012), http://ec.europa.eu/agriculture/external-studies/value-gi_en.htm, which puts the figure of GI products sold in 2010 at 54.3 billion euros. The study also concludes that GI-indicated products are sold at 2.23 times the price of comparable products that do not bear a GI. Irene Calboli correctly points out that such mark-up can only be justified when these claims for premium products are reflected in distinct ingredients and methods of production. Often, this is not the case, although consumers are made to believe so. See Irene Calboli, *Geographical Indications of Origin at the Crossroads of Local Development, Consumer Protection and Marketing Strategies*, 46 INT'L REV. INTELL. PROP. & COMPETITION L. 760, 772 (2015).

[6] See 2007 O.J. (L240) 7; CAFÉ DE COLOMBIA, www.cafedecolombia.com (last visited 21 May 2016).

protection may not be available at all, nor would an action for misleading use succeed (e.g., 'Pilsener beer' would be considered generic in most countries). In order to avoid such genericide, significant efforts and investment are often necessary so as to prevent generic use. The example of 'Greek Yoghurt'[7] demonstrates that this is possible, and producers of Basmati rice, Jasmine rice or Kobe beef may well consider a proactive enforcement strategy in Europe. Different from the laws on trademarks and GIs, remedies under unfair competition law can only be obtained at a national level based on domestic consumer perception. Such course of action may be the only avenue where the indication in question cannot be protected in its home country (as was the case for Greek Yoghurt).

3 THE FRAMEWORK OF GEOGRAPHICAL INDICATIONS PROTECTION IN EUROPE

3.1 Regulations 2081/92 and 1151/2012

The first laws that allowed for European Community-wide protection of agricultural products were Regulations 2081/92 of 14 July 1992,[8] 2082/92[9] and 1848/93,[10] while Regulation 1234/2007[11] was limited to wines and spirits. No protection is available, to date, for non-agricultural and non-food items (carpets, porcelain, crystal, etc.). In particular, GIs are divided, under EU law, into protected designations of origin (PDOs), protected GIs (PGIs) and traditional specialties guaranteed (TSGs).[12] PDOs have the strongest geographical link, and, with (notable) exceptions, must meet three requirements. The product must originate from a certain place, must essentially derive its characteristics from the geographical environment or local human factors, and must be processed in the area itself.

---

[7] See infra Section 5.
[8] Council Regulation No. 2081/92 of 14 July 1992 on the protection of GIs and designations of origin for agricultural products and foodstuffs, 1992 O.J. (L 208) 1.
[9] Council Regulation No. 2082/92 of 14 July 1992 on certificates of specific character for agricultural products and foodstuffs, 1992 O.J. (L 208) 9.
[10] Commission Regulation No. 1848/93 of 9 July 1993 laying down detailed rules for the application of Council Regulation (EEC) No 2082/92 on certificates of specific character for agricultural products and foodstuffs, 1993 O.J. (L 168) 35.
[11] Council Regulation No. 1234/2007 of 22 October 2007 establishing a common organisation of agricultural markets and on specific provisions for certain agricultural products, 2007 O.J. (L 299) 1.
[12] See Quality Policy, EUROPEAN COMMISSION, http://ec.europa.eu/agriculture/quality/schemes/index_en.htm (last visited 4 May 2016) (explaining the three schemes for protecting the names and agricultural products and foodstuffs).

Initially, non-EU indications could only be registered upon reciprocity, that is, as long as the countries at issue permitted GI registration in their jurisdiction. However, the obligations under the Agreement on Trade-Related Aspects of Intellectual Property Rights (TRIPS)[13] by the World Trade Organization (WTO) required an amendment of the reciprocal arrangements envisaged under EU law, in that national treatment obligations under TRIPS did, amongst others, not permit a registration of non-EU indications only upon reciprocal possibilities of protection for EU indications abroad. The amendment followed a complaint by Australia and the United States to the WTO.[14] Following the WTO ruling on the case, the European Union amended the text of the Regulations and allowed foreigners to register their indications under conditions comparable to those of EU nationals.[15] The currently applicable Regulations 1151/2012[16] (agricultural products) and 1308/2013[17] (alcoholic beverages) no longer require reciprocity in order to register non-EU GIs.

In particular, the following GIs from Asia have already been registered, or have been applied for registration to the European Commission as of 1 April 2016:[18]

1. Mrech Kampot 'Poivre de Kampot' (Cambodia) (registration)[19]
2. Kafae Doi Tung / กาแฟดอยตุง (Thailand) (registration)[20]
3. Kafae Doi Chaang / กาแฟดอยช้าง (Thailand) (registration)[21]
4. ข้าว สังข์ หยด เมือง พัทลุง Khao Sangyod Muang Phatthalung (Thailand) (application)[22]

---

[13] See Agreement on Trade-Related Aspects of Intellectual Property Rights arts. 22–24, 15 April 1994, Marrakesh Agreement Establishing the World Trade Organization, Annex 1C, 1869 U.N.T.S. 299 [hereinafter TRIPS].

[14] Panel Report, European Communities – Protection of Trade Marks and Geographical Indications for Agricultural Products and Foodstuffs, WT/DS174/R (adopted 15 March 2005).

[15] See Council Regulation (EC) No. 510/2006 on the protection of GIs and designations of origin for agricultural products and foodstuffs, 2006 O.J. (L 93) 12.

[16] Regulation 1151/2012 of the European Parliament and of the Council of 21 November 2012 on quality schemes for agricultural products and foodstuffs, 2012 O.J. (L 343) 1.

[17] Regulation 1308/2013, of the European Parliament and of the Council of 17 December 2013 establishing a common organisation of the markets in agricultural products and repealing Council Regulations (EEC) No 922/72, (EEC) No 234/79, (EC) No 1037/2001 and (EC) No 1234/2007, 2013 O.J. (L 347) 671.

[18] DOOR, EUR. COMM'N, http://ec.europa.eu/agriculture/quality/door/list.html (last visited 21 May 2016).

[19] 2016 O.J. (L 41) 1.   [20] 2015 O.J. (L 185) 4.   [21] 2015 O.J. (L 185) 5.

[22] DOOR, Denomination Information, EUR. COMM'N, http://ec.europa.eu/agriculture/quality/door/appliedName.html?denominationId=8850 (last visited 21 May 2016).

5. ข้าวหอมมะลิทุ่งกุลาร้องไห้ Khao Hom Mali Thung Kula Rong-Hai (Thailand) (registration)[23]
6. 东山白卢笋 Dongshan Bai Lu Sun (China) (registration)[24]
7. 平谷大桃 Pinggu Da Tao (China) (registration)[25]
8. Phú Quốu (Vietnam) (registration)[26]
9. 盐城龙虾, Yancheng Long Xia (China) (registration)[27]
10. 镇江香醋 Zhenjiang Xiang Cu (China) (registration)[28]
11. 金乡大蒜 Jinxiang Da Suan (China) (registration)[29]
12. Darjeeling (India) (registration)[30]
13. 龙井茶, Longjing cha (China) (registration)[31]
14. 琯溪蜜柚 Guanxi Mi You (China) (registration)[32]
15. 陕西苹果 Shaanxi ping guo (China) (registration)[33]
16. 蠡县麻山药 Lixian Ma Shan Yao (China) (registration)[34]
17. Kangra Tea (India) (application)[35]
18. Kopi Arabika Gayo (Indonesia) (application)[36]

Still, compared to the number of registered EU GIs, the number of Asian applications or registrations is quite small.[37] This is not surprising given the fact that comparable systems of registration for GIs have been introduced in Asia quite recently[38] or have still not been adopted.

3.2 *Scope of Protection*

Article 13(1) of Regulation 1151/2012[39] prohibits any direct or indirect commercial use of a protected indication, any imitation or evocation, or any other practice that misleads the consumer. Particularly, the notion of 'evocation' is relatively broad and includes translations and alliterations.[40] This is of

[23] 2013 O.J. (L 41) 3. [24] 2012 O.J. (L 330) 12. [25] 2012 O.J. (L 310) 17.
[26] 2012 O.J. (L 277) 1. [27] 2012 O.J. (L 219) 3. [28] 2012 O.J. (L 153) 4.
[29] 2011 O.J. (L 285) 6. [30] 2011 O.J. (L 276) 5. [31] 2011 O.J. (L 122) 67. [32] *Id.* [33] *Id.*
[34] *Id.*
[35] DOOR, *Denomination Information*, Eur. Comm'n, http://ec.europa.eu/agriculture/quality/door/appliedName.html?denominationId=10144 (last visited 21 May 2016).
[36] *Id.*
[37] According to the Association of Southeast Asian Nations (ASEAN) GI Database that has been created by ECAP, the total number of registered GIs in ASEAN was 178, as on 20 March 2006. ASEAN GI Database, www.asean-gidatabase.org (last visited 21 May 2016).
[38] For Japan, see Sachiko Tanaka, *Analysis of a Newly Enacted Law in Japan on Geographical Indications*, 40 AIPPI Japan (International Edition) 71 (2015).
[39] Regulation 1151/2012 of the European Parliament and of the Council of 21 November 2012 on Quality Schemes for Agricultural Products and Foodstuffs, art. 13(1), 2012 O.J. (L343) 1.
[40] *See also* Case C-132/05, Comm'n v. Federal Republic of Germany (Parmesan), 2008 E.C.R. I-957. Note that the national courts determine 'evocation' based on the perception of domestic

particular importance where GIs are known in a number of linguistic varieties, depending on the transliteration or historical connotation. As noted below, the issue of transliteration has been expressly stipulated in the EU-South Korea Free Trade Agreement (FTA),[41] and is a sensible addition in all cases where the GIs originate from a country with a non-Latin alphabet.

Different from trademark law, also as noted below, there is no specific provision that would protect well-known or well-reputed indications against the use for dissimilar goods, although one could argue that the concept of 'evocation' under Article 13(1) of the Regulation is broad enough to prevent the use of non-similar goods.[42] One should be aware, though, that there is no case law on this point.

Conflicts between GIs and similar trademarks used on identical or similar products are resolved on the basis of priority of registration. Even where the trademark registration precedes the registration for a GI and there are no grounds for invalidating such marks, the GI may be registered and used so that both coexist.[43]

3.3 Bilateral Agreements

The European Union has concluded a number of agreements that address the protection of GIs with countries outside Europe. The first was the wine

---

consumers. In a recent decision on the indication 'Aceto Balsamico di Modena', the Mannheim District Court ruled that at least for German consumers the term 'Aceto Balsamico' was indicative of a provenance from Modena, although the term 'Aceto Balsamico' was not protected as a geographical indication in Italy. LG Mannheim 15 September 2015, 2O 187/14, http://lrbw.juris.de/cgi-bin/laender_rechtsprechung/document.py?Gericht=bw&nr=19891. The court did not rule on the question as to whether 'Aceto Balsamico aus Deutschland' was considered misleading for German consumers as to its geographical origin, an issue that would have to be argued under unfair competition prevention law. See infra Section 5. For further comments, see Christopher Heath, *Parmigiano Reggiano by Another Name – The ECJ's Parmesan Decision*, 39 INT'L REV. INTELL. PROP. & COMPETITION L. 951 (2008).

[41] EU-South Korea Free Trade Agreement, EU-S. Kor., 16 September 2010, 54 O.J. (L 127) 1, http://eur-lex.europa.eu/legal-content/EN/ALL/?uri=OJ:L:2011:127:TOC [hereinafter EU-South Korea FTA].

[42] Christopher Heath & Delphine Marie-Vivien, *Geographical Indications and the Principles of Trade Mark Law*, 46 INT'L REV. INTELL. PROP. & COMPETITION L. 819, 831 (2015).

[43] See art. 14(2), 2012 O.J. (L 343) 1. In practice, this provision will only apply to cases where the problem has not been envisaged at the stage of GI registration. In the notable case of Budějovický Budvar v. OHMI (Budweiser), Joined Cases T-53/04 to T-56/04, T-58/04, and T-59/04, Budweiser, 2007 E.C.R. II-57, the Czech indication 'Budweiser', although registered under the Lisbon Agreement for the Protection of Appellations of Origin and their International Registration (Lisbon Agreement), was permitted registration in the EU only in the Czech versions Budějovické pivo (PGI), Českobudějovické pivo (PGI) and Budějovický měšťanský var (PGI) so as to avoid trademark conflicts. Athens Accession Treaty to the European Union, Annex II art. 20 para. 18, 23 September 2003, 2003 O.J. (L 236) [hereinafter Treaty of Athens].

agreement concluded with Australia[44] in 1994. Subsequent agreements, specifically for wine, were concluded with South Africa[45] and the United States,[46] while the agreements with Canada,[47] Chile[48] and Mexico[49] contain GI protection only as part of a broader framework of free trade.[50]

The agreements vary in scope and approach, yet are generally guided by the principle of reciprocal protection of GIs contained in an annex to the agreement,[51] and protection against the expressions 'kind', 'type', 'style', 'imitation', 'method' or the like. Further, the use of conflicting trademarks must be ceased, an obligation that may give rise to conflicts not only with existing trademark rights but also with other bilateral FTAs that may envisage obligations that cannot be reconciled with each other.[52] As of yet, the European

---

[44] EC-Australia Wine Agreement, EC-Austl., 31 March 1994, 1994 O.J. (L 86) 3, now replaced by EC-Australia Wine Agreement, EC-Austl.,30 January 2009, 2009 O.J. (L 28) 3, which came into force 1 September 2010.

[45] Agreement between the European Community and the Republic of South Africa on trade in wine, EC-S. Afr., 30 January 2002, 2002 O.J. (L 28) 4; Agreement between the European Community and the Republic of South Africa on trade in spirits, EC-S. Afr., 30 January 2002, 2002 O.J. (L 28) 113.

[46] Agreement between the European Community and the United States of America on trade in wine, EC-US, 24 March 2006, 2006 O.J. (L 87) 2.

[47] Agreement between the European Community and Canada on trade in wines and spirit drinks, EC-Can., 6 February 2004, 2004 O.J. (L 35) 3.

[48] Agreement establishing an association between the European Community and its Member States, of the one part, and the Republic of Chile, of the other part, Annexes V and VI, 18 November 2002, 2002 O.J. (L 352) 3.

[49] Economic Partnership, Political Coordination and Cooperation Agreement between the European Community and its Member States, of the one part, and the United Mexican States, of the other part, 28 October 2000, 2000 O.J. (L 276) 45 (incorporating 1997 O.J. (L 152)16).

[50] *See Wine: Bilateral agreements with third countries*, EUR. COMM'N (23 May 2016), http://ec.europa.eu/agriculture/wine/third-countries/index_en.htm (providing an overview over all agreements currently in force).

[51] Such automatic protection without verifying whether such indication would be considered protectable under national law is also a characteristic of the Lisbon Agreement. *See* Lisbon Agreement for the Protection of Appellations of Origin and Their International Registration, 31 October 1958, *as revised* 14 July 1967, 923 U.N.T.S. 205 [hereinafter Lisbon Agreement]. *See also* David Vivas-Egui & Christoph Spennemann, *The Evolving Regime of Geographical Indications in WTO and in Free Trade Agreements*, *in* INTELLECTUAL PROPERTY AND INTERNATIONAL TRADE: THE TRIPS AGREEMENT 163, 188 (Carlos Correa & Abdulqawi Yusuf eds., 2nd edn. 2008).

[52] ANKE MOERLAND, WHY JAMAICA WANTS TO PROTECT CHAMPAGNE: INTELLECTUAL PROPERTY PROTECTION IN EU BILATERAL TRADE AGREEMENTS 159–66 (2013). The EU tries to avoid such conflicts when allowing protection for geographical indications without prejudice to existing trademarks. This was the case with the indication 'Budejovice Budvar' in the 2004 Treaty of Athens. *See* Treaty of Athens, *supra* note 43. A related problem may arise in case the same GI is protected for different countries, and conflicting obligations arise due to

Union has concluded one FTA with an Asian country – South Korea.[53] Under this agreement, in Annex 1 Part B, the European Union is obliged to protect sixty-three Korean indications of origin for food and one for an alcoholic drink.[54]

The scope of protection under bilateral agreements is normally stipulated in the agreement itself. Article 10.21 of the EU-South Korea FTA[55] extends the protection against 'type', 'style', etc. to all registered indications and provides safeguards against the use in transliteration.[56] While the extended scope of protection is limited to those indications expressly listed under the agreement, there is a provision that allows a regular update of this list.

Conflicts with registered trademarks are either solved in favour of the GI or, where this is not possible, by way of a coexistence (while problematic cases were filtered out during the negotiations).

3.4 International Multilateral Agreements

The Paris Convention for the Protection of Industrial Property (Paris Convention) in Article 1.3 lists GIs ('indications of source or appellations of origin') as one form of industrial rights.[57] Article 10 concerns a rather obsolete provision to prohibit the use of a false indication of origin when linked to a fictitious commercial name,[58] and Article 10*bis*, the general provision against all acts of unfair competition, requires protection against confusing or misleading use of an indication and thereby depends on the perception of domestic consumers.[59] These remedies have not proved very efficient.[60]

---

membership of these countries to different international or bilateral agreements. An example may be conflicts between North and South Korea based on the fact that North Korea is a member to the Lisbon Agreement (as are several European countries), and South Korea is part of the bilateral EU-South Korea FTA. While under the Lisbon Agreement, Kaesong Koryo Inasm (Ginseng from Kaesong) is protected (for North Korea), the FTA protects Koryo Insam Jepum (white Ginseng).

[53] EU-South Korea FTA, *supra* note 41.
[54] EU-South Korea FTA, *supra* note 41, Annex 1 pt. B.
[55] EU-South Korea FTA, *supra* note 41.
[56] For details on issues related to GIs in the EU's FTAs, see Tim Engelhardt, *Geographical Indications under Recent EU Free Trade Agreements*, 46 INT'L REV. INTELL. PROP. & COMPETITION L. 781 (2015).
[57] Paris Convention for the Protection of Industrial Property art. 1.3, March 20, 1883, *as revised* 14 July 1967, 21 U.S.T. 1583, 828 U.N.T.S. 305 [hereinafter Paris Convention].
[58] *See* Paris Convention art. 10 (regarding the seizure of products bearing false indications as to their sources).
[59] *See* Paris Convention art. 10*bis* (regarding the prohibition of acts of unfair competition).
[60] Albrecht Krieger, *Der internationale Schutz von geographischen Bezeichnungen aus deutscher Sicht*, GRUR INT'L 71, 72, 1984.

The same holds true for the provisions of the TRIPS Agreement (section 3)[61] that, although pretty detailed, ultimately does not offer protection that goes further than to prevent misleading use.[62] Protection beyond this is only offered for wines and spirits.[63]

The Madrid Agreement for the Repression of False or Deceptive Indications of Sources of Goods (Madrid Agreement)[64] protects against the use of false or misleading 'indirect' indications,[65] or false or misleading indications with such additions as 'system', 'type' or the like.[66] In Article 4, it also tries to contain the generic use of a foreign indication, yet leaves it to 'courts of each country'[67] to decide whether an indication has become generic:

> The position under which the tribunal of any country may decide that an appellation of origin has become generic creates insecurity and also contradiction. An appellation of origin protected by legislation or jurisprudence in a certain country may not be used by producers or manufacturers of such country and yet may be used freely by producers or manufacturers in a contracting country.[68]

---

[61] See TRIPS, *supra* note 13, sec. 3 (covering Articles 22–24 on GIs).

[62] TRIPS, *supra* note 13, art. 22(2) ('In respect of geographical indications, Members shall provide the legal means for interested parties to prevent: (a) the use of any means in the designation or presentation of a good that indicates or suggests that the good in question originates in a geographical area other than the true place of origin in a manner which misleads the public as to the geographical origin of the good; and (b) any use which constitutes an act of unfair competition within the meaning of Article 10*bis* of the Paris Convention (1967).').

[63] TRIPS, *supra* note 13, art. 22(3), provides additional protection for GIs, specifically for wines and spirits.

[64] See Madrid Agreement for the Repression of False and Deceptive Indications of Source on Goods, 14 April 1891, 828 U.N.T.S. 163 [hereinafter Madrid Agreement].

[65] An example would be the decision of the Japanese Patent Office to refuse registration of the mark 'Loreley' for wine products which bore no relation to Germany. Christopher Heath, *Geographical Indications: International, Bilateral and Regional Agreements*, *in* NEW FRONTIERS OF INTELLECTUAL PROPERTY LAW, IP AND CULTURAL HERITAGE – GEOGRAPHICAL INDICATIONS – ENFORCEMENT – OVERPROTECTION 99 n.4 (Christopher Heath & Anselm Kamperman eds., 2005).

[66] In almost all bilateral agreements on the protection of geographical indications, provisions can be found indicating that 'diluting' an indication by additions such as 'type', 'method', etc., is not permissible. See EU-South Korea FTA, *supra* note 41; Engelhardt, *supra* note 56, at 781.

[67] Madrid Agreement, *supra* note 64, art. 4 reads: 'The courts of each country shall decide what appellations, on account of their generic character, do not fall within the provisions of this Agreement, regional appellations concerning the source of products of the vine being, however, excluded from the reservation specified by this Article.'

[68] STEPHEN P. LADAS, PATENTS, TRADE MARKS, AND RELATED RIGHTS 1589(1975).

Membership to the Madrid Agreement is limited even amongst European countries, and the Agreement has never played any role in decisions concerning the protection of GIs.

The above weaknesses of the Madrid Agreement clarify the motives for concluding the subsequent Lisbon Agreement for the Protection of Appellations of Origin and their International Registration (Lisbon Agreement):[69]

(1) To prevent the tribunals of any member state from holding an indication generic. In other words, no indication of origin should be exempt from protection because it is considered generic.
(2) To set up a system whereby protection was not decided by the member whose indication was the object of a dispute, but by the member from which the indication originated.

Both conditions are vital for understanding the Lisbon Agreement, as both limit the competence of national courts. National courts ('tribunals') should neither be entitled to hold an indication generic nor should they be entitled to question the validity of an indication once that indication has been protected in the country of origin, communicated to the international bureau and examined by the other countries.

The Lisbon Agreement came into force in 1966 with the original member states of Cuba, Czechoslovakia, France, Haiti, Israel, Mexico and Portugal. Subsequently, the following countries acceded to the Agreement: Hungary (1967), Italy (1968), Algeria (1972), Tunisia (1973), Bulgaria (1975), Burkina Faso (1975), Gabon (1975), Togo (1975), Congo (1977), the Czech Republic and Slovakia (1993), Costa Rica (1997), Yugoslavia (1999, subsequently Serbia and Montenegro), Moldova (2001), Georgia (2004), North Korea (2004), Iran (2005), Peru (2005), Nicaragua (2006), Macedonia (2010) and Bosnia (2013).[70]

The protection under the Lisbon Agreement is of proprietary nature and works as follows:

> Every member state of the Paris Convention that also adheres to the agreement undertakes to protect in its own territory all appellations of origin of other member states for those products registered on the express condition that protection is also afforded in the home countries. The expression 'qualified' means that the right of an appellation of origin first of all needs to be recognised in the country of origin. The agreement thereby imposes on all member states a uniform set of rules, yet without separating this from

---

[69] See Lisbon Agreement, *supra* note 51.
[70] *WIPO-Administered Treaties*, WORLD INTELL. PROP. ORG., www.wipo.int/treaties/en/ShowResults.jsp?lang=en&treaty_id=10 (last visited 28 May 2016).

national rules ... Registration of an appellation of origin under the agreement can only be demanded by the country of origin ... Protection must thus be granted against all attacks of the exclusive rights given to those entitled to use the appellation, be it against the unlawful use ... be it against the fraudulent imitation of an appellation.[71]

Article 4[72] clarifies that an indication protected under the Agreement cannot be considered or become generic.

As of yet, the only country in East Asia that can profit from the protection offered under the Lisbon Agreement is North Korea, which (as of 1 January 2016) has registered six indications:[73]

No. Appellations

1.	866	개성고려인삼
2.	867	백두산
3.	881	고려신덕산샘물
4.	884	강서약수
5.	886	백두산들쭉술
6.	887	평양랭면

Table 8.1 Indications registered by North Korea

The Geneva Act of the Lisbon Agreement was agreed on 20 May 2015[74] by the twenty-seven Member States of the Lisbon Union and (as of 1 January 2016) signed by fourteen of these.[75] The Geneva Act provides different rules for indications considered generic in a Member State, and for the invalidation of a registered indication. Particularly, in the case of conflicting trademark rights, the courts of a Member State are entitled to an invalidation of the indication. Whether this is possible under the original Lisbon Agreement is disputed.[76]

---

[71] Actes de la Conference du Lisbonne 1958, Geneva 1963, 814/815.
[72] See Lisbon Agreement, *supra* note 51, art. 4.
[73] *Lisbon, The International System of Appellations of Origin*, WIPO, www.wipo.int/ipdl/en/se arch/lisbon/search-struct.jsp (last visited 28 May 2016) (providing the list of appellations of origin registered by North Korea).
[74] See Lisbon Agreement for the Protection of Appellations of Origin and Their International Registration, Geneva Act of the Lisbon Agreement on Appellations of Origin and Geographical Indications (as adopted on 20 May 2015), WORLD INTELL. PROP. ORG, www .wipo.int/wipolex/en/details.jsp?id=15625 (last visited 20 May 2015).
[75] *Contracting Parties, Lisbon Agreement*, WORLD INTELL. PROP. ORG., www.wipo.int/treaties/ en/ActResults.jsp?act_id=50 (last visited 28 May 2016).
[76] While the Italian Supreme Court affirmed that indications validly registered under the Lisbon Agreement could be invalidated at least for the national territory of a Member State, *Budweiser*, Italian Supreme Court, Decision of 21 May 2002, 34 IIC – INT'L REV. INTELL. PROP. & COMPETITION L. 676 (2003), the Israel Supreme Court denied such possibility

4 GEOGRAPHICAL INDICATIONS AND EUROPEAN TRADEMARK LAW

In contrast to GIs that confer a geographical origin, trademarks confer a commercial origin of an enterprise. The registration of names considered to indicate a geographical origin as a trademark should thus not be possible where such mark would be considered descriptive (of the geographical origin of the goods for which the mark is registered or applied) or misleading (as to its geographical origin). Such a bar to registration is also an important safeguard for all those using the name as an indication of geographical origin, and thus in a descriptive manner. Still, registrations of geographical names have been allowed in Europe either for goods or services different from those for which the geographical name is known ('Darjeeling lingerie', as elaborated below), in cases where the name is not known to consumers as conferring a geographical connotation (a significant problem for indications from Asia, as these tend not to be known) or (most questionable) where the applicant was an official body or even the state ('Sidamo', also as elaborated below). GIs can be registered as collective marks in Europe, however.

4.1 Registrability and Use of Geographical Terms for Ordinary Marks

First, it should be noted that trademarks 'which consist exclusively of signs or indications which may serve, in trade, to designate the ... geographical origin ... of the goods or services'[77] cannot be registered under European law. This provision expresses a general principle that a mark perceived to indicate a geographical origin cannot serve the trademark function to distinguish the goods or services of one enterprise from those of another. In other words, a geographical origin is not a commercial origin.

The leading case of the European Court of Justice (ECJ, now renamed Court of Justice of the European Union, CJEU), the decision in *Chiemsee*,[78] has interpreted the provision as follows:

---

where protection was valid in the country of origin. *Budweiser II*, Decision of 13 September 1992, 25 INT'L REV. INTELL. PROP. & COMPETITION L. 589 (1994).

[77] Directive 2008/95/EC, art. 3.1(c) of the European Parliament and of the Council of 22 October 2008 to approximate the laws of the Member States relating to trademarks, 2008 O.J. (L 299) 5 [hereinafter Trade Mark Directive].

[78] Joined cases C-108/97 & C-109/97, Windsurfing Chiemsee Produktions- und Vertriebs GmbH (WSC) v. Boots, 1999 E.C.R. I-2779.

25. Article 3(1)(c) of the Directive pursues an aim which is in the public interest, namely that descriptive signs or indications relating to the categories of goods or services in respect of which registration is applied for may be freely used by all, including as collective marks or as part of complex or graphic marks. Article 3(1)(c) therefore prevents such signs and indications from being reserved to one undertaking alone because they have been registered as trade marks.

26. As regards, more particularly, signs or indications which may serve to designate the geographical origin of the categories of goods in relation to which registration of the mark is applied for, especially geographical names, it is in the public interest that they remain available, not least because they may be an indication of the quality and other characteristics of the categories of goods concerned, and may also, in various ways, influence consumer tastes by, for instance, associating the goods with a place that may give rise to a favourable response.

29. Article 3(1)(c) of the Directive is not confined to prohibiting the registration of geographical names as trade marks solely where they designate specified geographical locations which are already famous, or are known for the category of goods concerned, and which are therefore associated with those goods in the mind of the relevant class of persons, that is to say in the trade and amongst average consumers of that category of goods in the territory in respect of which registration is applied for ... [but also for those indications which] designate(s) a place which is currently associated in the mind of the relevant class of persons with the category of goods concerned, or whether it is reasonable to assume that such an association may be established in the future.[79]

The Court thereby highlights a principle of public policy that geographical names should not become subject to private trademark rights. The provision is thus broad as regards the indication ('may serve to designate'; 'association may be established in the future'[80]). Yet it is at the same time narrow as it only concerns marks that *exclusively* consist of a geographical name. A combined word/device mark including a geographical name does not fall under this provision, and a disclaimer for the geographical term is not required. As elaborated below, this is important to notice and, for example, is allowed for the registration of 'Darjeeling' as a combined word and device mark.

However, as mentioned above, these principles are often not adhered to in practice. Evidence is the story of Sidamo, a coffee-growing area in Ethiopia, about which the World Intellectual Property Office (WIPO) (no less) reports:

---

[79] Joined cases C-108/97 & C-109/97, 1999 E.C.R. at para 25–26, 29. [80] See *supra* note 76.

The government of Ethiopia decided that instead of trying to protect Ethiopian coffee's geographical origin, it would be better to protect its commercial origin, which it would do through registering trade marks. This was seen as a more direct route of protection because it would grant the government of Ethiopia the legal right to exploit, license and use the trade marked names in relation to coffee goods to the exclusion of all other traders. Unlike a GI, a trade mark registration does not require a specific coffee to be produced in a specific region or have a particular quality in connection with that region. Using trade mark registrations, the government of Ethiopia could then produce greater quantities of specialty coffees from all over the country. Rural producers outside the Sidamo region could grow Sidamo coffee, as it would not need to have a characteristic that is unique to the Sidamo region.[81]

This summarises about everything that is legally wrong with registering geographical names as trademarks – the mark would inevitably be either descriptive[82] or deceptive[83] (or, as the text reads, both). Yet, the mark has been duly registered in Japan,[84] the European Union[85] and the United

---

[81] For an introduction, see *The Coffee War: Ethiopia and the Starbucks Story*, WORLD INTELL. PROP. ORG., www.wipo.int/ipadvantage/en/details.jsp?id=2621 (last visited 1 June 2015).

[82] A good example is the decision of the General Court in the October 2015 cases T 292/14 and T 293/14 where trademark registration for the indication 'Halloumi' for cheese was denied. Joined Cases 292 & 293/14, Republic of Cyprus v. OHIM (XAΛΛOYMI and HALLOUMI), 2015 O.J. (C 398) 52. The application had been made by the Cyprus government and was meant to protect the foremost geographical indication of Cyprus. *Id.* OHIM and the General Court held that the mark was descriptive for a certain product and thus incapable of identifying a commercial origin. *Id.*

[83] 'Deceptive' refers to marks that describe a geographic location and are applied to goods that do not originate from that place. Authority in Europe on this issue is the 'Cuvée Palomar' decision. Case T-237/08, Abadía Retuerta v. OHIM (CUVÉE PALOMAR), 2010 O.J. (C 179) 59.

[84] SIDAMO Registration No. 4955561 (Japan), www3.j-platpat.inpit.go.jp/cgi-bin/ET/TM_LIST_E.cgi?ITEM01=106&KEY01=Sidamo&OPT01=01&ITEM02=702&KEY02=&OPT02=01&ITEM03=402&KEY03=&OPT03=01&ITEM04=705&KEY04=&OPT04=01&STIME=1464563777364026431883 42&HITCNT=1&HITCNT3=1&S_FLAG=00&TERMOPT=02&PAGE=01. In Japan, the Ethiopian government also managed to invalidate a registration of 'Sidamo' owned by the Japan Coffee Association as misleading. Chiteki Zaisan Kōtō Saibansho [Intellectual Prop. High Ct.] 29 March 2010, 2009 (Gyo-Ke) no. 10227, Saibansho saibanrei jōhō [Saibansho Web] 1, www.ip.courts.go.jp/app/files/hanrei_en/160/000160.pdf. The court held that the mark could not be considered descriptive as to a lack of recognition amongst consumers that 'Sidamo' was a place name. *Id.* at 2. However, consumers would associate the term with high-quality coffee. *Id.*

[85] SIDAMO, Registration No. 004348751 (EUIPO). The registration is inconsistent with the above *Chiemsee* decision in that 'Sidamo' 'designate(s) a place which is currently associated in the mind of the relevant class of persons with the category of goods concerned, or whether it is reasonable to assume that such an association may be established in the future'. Joined Cases C-108/97 & C-109/97, Windsurfing Chiemsee, 1999 E.C.R. I-2779, para. 31.

States[86] and applied for in Canada.[87] Another example is the registration of 'Tabasco' for chilli sauce on behalf of a US enterprise.[88] After all, Tabasco is a Mexican state where chilli is widely cultivated, and the product or its ingredients do not even originate from Mexico.

Last, but not least, the protection against the use of misleading indications comes into play both at the stage of registration and at the stage of use (independent of whether the indication has been registered or not). In the long-running *Budweiser* battle,[89] the Italian Supreme Court[90] held that a registration of 'Budweiser' on behalf of Anheuser Busch (a US company) could cause Italian consumers to assume that the beer came from Bohemia (Budweis is the German name of what is now Ceske Budejovice, a town with a renowned tradition for brewing beer):

> After all, for a trade mark that consists of a geographical indication to be considered misleading it is sufficient that there exists a link between the indicated place and the quality of the labeled products. Only if this is not the case, the geographical mark would simply be of imaginary nature and therefore legitimate. According to the facts of this case, such connection is undeniable here.

The importance of this decision also lies in the fact that protection against misleading use and registration is not limited to official place names, but any place name associated by the public with a certain geographical origin. This may find application for Asian place names such as 'Ceylon' (nowadays Sri Lanka), 'Bangkok' (officially Krung Thep) or 'Saigon' (officially Ho-Chi Minh City).

4.2 Scope of Protection

The scope of protection for European trademarks is determined by Article 9(1) Community Trade Mark Regulation (CTMR),[91] and for similar signs and/or

---

[86] SIDAMO, Registration No. 78589307.   [87] SIDAMO, Application No. 0916800 (Can.).

[88] There are a number of word marks such as 'Tabasco' registered in Europe on behalf of the US company McIlhenny starting with Community mark 001126176. *eSearch plus, The EUIPO's database*, EUIPO, https://euipo.europa.eu/eSearch/#details/owners/51748 (last visited 29 May 2016).

[89] This was a dispute involving several dozens of jurisdictions. Christopher Heath, *The Budweiser cases: A brewing conflict*, in LANDMARK INTELLECTUAL PROPERTY CASES AND THEIR LEGACY 181 (Christopher Heath & Anselm Kamperman Sanders eds., 2011).

[90] '*Budweiser V*,' *Decision of the Supreme Court 19 September 2013 – Case No. 21472/13*, 46 INT'L REV. INTELL. PROP. & COMPETITION L. 891 (2015).

[91] *See* Community Trade Mark Regulation, Council Regulation (EC) 207/2009 of 26 February 2009 on the Community trademark, art. 9(1), 2009 O.J. (L 78) 1 [hereinafter Community Trade Mark Regulation].

similar goods, infringement requires a showing of confusion. In particular, an infringement can only be established once the allegedly infringing sign is perceived as an indication of commercial origin. In fact, use of a registered trademark as a geographical origin is a defence to trademark infringement under Article 12 CTMR, as long as it is used in accordance with honest practices.[92]

In this respect, reference is made to the above observations for possible conflicts with (earlier or subsequent) registrations of GIs.[93]

4.3 Collective Marks

Apart from the registration of ordinary trademarks, EU law also allows for the registration of collective marks. Different from ordinary marks, registration is also possible for geographically descriptive names:

> Article 66 of Regulation No 207/2009 provides for the possibility of registering Community collective marks. According to Article 66(1) of that regulation, 'a Community trade mark which is described as such when the mark is applied for and is capable of distinguishing the goods or services of the members of the association which is the proprietor of the mark from those of other undertakings' may constitute such a mark. That provision states that such marks may be applied for by '[a]ssociations of manufacturers, producers, suppliers of services, or traders which, under the terms of the law governing them, have the capacity in their own name to have rights and obligations of all kinds, to make contracts or accomplish other legal acts and to sue and be sued, as well as legal persons governed by public law'. Article 66(3) of Regulation No 207/2009 also states that the provisions of that regulation are to apply to Community collective marks, 'unless Articles 67 to 74 [thereof] provide otherwise'.
>
> Article 66(2) of Regulation No 207/2009 allows 'signs or indications which may serve, in trade, to designate the geographical origin of the goods or services' to be registered as Community collective marks within the meaning of Article 66(1) of that regulation, in derogation from Article 7(1)(c) thereof, pursuant to which trade marks consisting exclusively of such signs or indications are not to be registered.

---

[92] See Community Trade Mark Regulation, art. 12, which, according to the European Court of Justice, decision of 19 November 2004, case C-245/02, means 'an expression of the duty to act fairly in relation to the legitimate interests of the trade-mark proprietor'. The decision concerned use of the geographical term 'Budweiser' for beer in a situation where 'Budweiser' was registered on behalf of a US company for beer.

[93] See supra Section 4.1.

It follows from case-law that, under the provisions of Article 8(1)(b) of Regulation No 207/2009, in conjunction with Article 66(3) of that regulation, a Community collective mark, like any other Community trade mark, enjoys protection against any infringement resulting from the registration of a Community trade mark that involves a likelihood of confusion.[94]

One prominent example of a registered collective mark is 'Darjeeling', registered as No. 4312718 on 31 March 2006.[95] In a long-running dispute, the question arose whether this mark could be successfully invoked against the registration of 'Darjeeling' for lingerie and telecommunications. While these goods or services were undoubtedly dissimilar to tea, the Indian Tea Board argued that the scope of a collective mark should also extend to a protection of geographical origins, and consumers should in such case be protected against geographical misconceptions. Essentially, although the goods or services were different, registration should be denied where the goods or services did not originate or were not linked to the geographical notion conferred by the mark. The General Court of the CJEU rejected such an interpretation:[96]

> In the present case, it is not disputed that the word element 'darjeeling' may serve, in trade, to designate the geographical origin of the product covered by the earlier trade marks. That finding cannot be undermined by OHIM's argument based on the possible perception of that word by part of the public, which would not recognise 'darjeeling' as a geographical name. However, while it is true – as the applicant rightly argues – that the essential function of a geographical indication is to guarantee to consumers the geographical origin of goods and the special qualities inherent in them (see, to that effect, judgment of 29 March 2011 in *Anheuser-Busch v Budějovický Budvar*, C-96/09 P, ECR, EU:C:2011:189, paragraph 147), the same cannot be said of the essential function of a Community collective mark. The fact that the latter consists of an indication which may serve to designate the geographical origin of the goods covered does not affect the essential function of all collective marks as stated in Article 66(1) of Regulation No 207/2009, which is to distinguish the goods or services of the members of the association which is the proprietor of that mark from those of other associations or undertakings (see, to that effect, judgment in *RIOJAVINA*, cited in paragraph 32 above, EU:T:2010:226, paragraphs 26 and 27). Consequently, the function of a Community collective mark is not altered as a result of its registration under Article 66(2) of Regulation No 207/2009. More specifically,

---

[94] Case T-624/13, The Tea Board v. OHIM – Delta Lingerie (*Darjeeling*), 2015 EUR-Lex CELEX LEXIS 743 (2 October 2015).
[95] Id.   [96] Id. at para. 41.

a Community collective mark is a sign allowing goods or services to be distinguished according to which association is the proprietor of the mark and not according to their geographical origin.[97]

The above interpretation confirms that collective marks are treated as ordinary trademarks unless specific provisions apply (namely the possibility of registering geographical terms). In particular, the language of Article 66 (3) expressly states so.[98]

Following the reasoning of the Court, the possibility of registering geographical terms would thus not mean that geographical connotations are part of the function of a collective mark. The Tea Board, on the other hand, had argued that 'similarity' in the case of collective marks should be affirmed where the goods could be of the same geographical origin. The latter argument may find some justification in the specific provision of Article 66(2) of the CTMR,[99] which is a special safeguard for third parties who use the geographical mark in accordance with honest practices, namely where the goods indeed originate from such place. It is not clear why such provision should have been inserted over and above the exceptions in Article 9 of the CTMR,[100] if the scope of a collective mark, particularly with regard to geographical connotations, was the same as for ordinary trademarks. In addition, the decision is a narrow reading of the above *Chiemsee* decision:

> The mere possibility that the average consumer might believe that the services in question, namely the retail services offered under the trade mark Darjeeling, are connected with goods originating in the geographical area of the same name, or that the telecommunications services provided under the same trade mark are connected with, or will offer information about, that geographical area is not sufficient to establish a similarity between the services covered by the mark applied for and the product covered by the earlier trade marks.[101]

The case is currently under appeal before the CJEU.[102]

---

[97] *Id.* The Tea Board in this case did not rely on its registered GI in order to oppose Delta's trademark registration. The case does not shade any light as to why this was so.

[98] *See* Community Trade Mark Regulation, art. 66(3) ('The provisions of this Regulation shall apply to Community collective marks, unless Articles 67 to 74 provide otherwise.').

[99] Community Trade Mark Regulation, art. 66(2).

[100] *See* Community Trade Mark Regulation, art. 9 (providing rights conferred by a Community trademark).

[101] Case T-624/13, The Tea Board v. OHIM – Delta Lingerie (*Darjeeling*), 2015 EUR-Lex CELEX LEXIS 743, at para. 53 (2 October 2015).

[102] *See* the status of The Tea Board v. OHIM – Delta Lingerie, Case C673/15, at *InfoCuria – Case-law of the Court of Justice*, CURIA, http://curia.europa.eu/juris/liste.jsf?num=C-673/15&language=en (last visited 29 May 2016).

4.4 Protection as a Well-Known Trademark or Geographical Indication

European law allows for an extended protection of a trademark against dissimilar goods in case the mark has obtained a reputation under Article 9(1) of the CTMR.[103] In particular, it is necessary for the trademark owner to show reputation, and for the use of the trademark to take unfair advantage of or be detrimental to the distinctive character or repute of the registered mark. This provision has been tested at national level in two French cases concerning the GI 'Darjeeling'.

Notably, there are two *Darjeeling* decisions regarding the protection against the registration of the term for dissimilar products that should be discussed in this context. One is the more recent decision of the TGI Paris of 30 May 2013,[104] while the other, also a French decision, dates back to the year 2006.[105] These decisions reached opposite conclusions. The earlier one did not allow a third party to register 'Darjeeling' for communication products/services, while the second one allowed the registration for insurance products.

In the earlier case, the Tea Board of India requested the cancellation of a semi-figurative trademark composed of the name 'Darjeeling' and the design of a teapot, filed on 14 November 2002, by Jean-Luc Dusong, for editing- and communication-related products. At first instance, the TGI[106] rejected the claim based on the absence of confusion due to the difference between the products. This decision was overturned by the Court of Appeal,[107] which considered that it mattered little if the products in question were different, but rather, whether through the adoption of this denomination associated with the teapot design, Jean-Luc Dusong had sought to profit from the reputation attached to the Darjeeling indication that, according to the Court of Appeal, identifies in the perception of the public a tea originating from the region of Darjeeling, synonymous with excellence and refinement, and the savoir-faire of the Tea Board in promoting this product, which has been exploited free of cost.

It is important to note that, in this case, the trademark of Jean-Luc Dusong included not only the denomination Darjeeling but also the drawing of a teapot and was used together with the slogan 'Communication is our cup

---

[103] *See* Community Trade Mark Regulation, art. 9(1).
[104] Tribunal de grande instance [TGI] [High Court] Paris, 30 May 2013, RG 2010/01706.
[105] Cour d'appel [CA] [Court of Appeal] Paris, 4th Chamber, 22 November 2006, 05/20050.
[106] Tribunal de grande instance [TGI] [High Court] Paris, 6 July 2005, 03/11092.
[107] Cour d'appel [CA] [Court of Appeal] Paris, 4th Chamber, 22 November 2006, 05/20050.

of tea'. The Court established that the trademark undeniably evoked the tea 'Darjeeling'. It was further established that in order to promote its trademark, Jean-Luc Dusong regularly made reference to the world of tea. According to the Court of Appeal:

> It matters little that the products referred to are different from tea, since by adopting the name associated with a teapot drawing, Jean-Luc Dusong sought to take advantage of the reputation attached to that geographical indication which identifies in the mind of the public tea native of this region, synonymous with excellence and refinement, and of the expertise of the Tea Board to promote this product, borrowing its image without cost; that such use for products other than tea harms this prestigious geographical indication that only The Tea Board can exploit, by vulgarising and diluting its distinctive character.[108]

The Court of Appeal thus overturned the decision of the TGI of 2005 which only looked at the dissimilarity of goods to decide that

> the reputation of a tea label cannot be of benefit to publishing products; that the trade mark application does not characterize any willingness to appropriate the reputation and is not likely to result in a dilution or weakening of the indication of origin 'Darjeeling'; and that, moreover, the conditions of exploitation of the trademark can neither be faulted nor are they likely to cause any damage, because they are limited to the registered class and mainly to editing.[109]

Conversely, in the more recent *Darjeeling* case, the French tribunal[110] affirmed Placement Direct's argument that it did not use the reputation of Darjeeling for the marketing of its life insurance contract, and held that Placement Direct did not profit from the reputation of Darjeeling. As such, there was no wrong attributable to Placement Direct. The TGI considered that the trademark of Placement Direct made no reference to the world of tea, and considered that even if the green colour was used, this did not directly make reference to the world of tea, because green was a common colour.[111]

---

[108] Heath & Marie-Vivien, *supra* note 42, at 833 (Delphine Marie-Vivien providing translated portion of the court's opinion).
[109] *Id.*
[110] Tribunal de grande instance [TGI] [High Court] Paris, May 30, 2013, RG 2010/01706.
[111] 'Darjeeling', Decision of the Paris District Court (Tribunal de grande instance) 30 May 2013 – Case No. RG 2010/01706, 46 INT'L REV. INTELL. PROP. & COMPETITION L. 868, 871 (2015) [hereinafter *Darjeeling*].

More questionable is the argument of the Tribunal that the choice of the name 'Moka' for another contract could not constitute any evidence against Placement Direct, since the name 'Moka' also denoted a town in Yemen, and Darjeeling was the name of a town situated in the province of the same name, as well as the name of a train connecting the valley with that town.[112] Indeed, before becoming generic, Moka was an indication of origin famous for coffee – so famous that in many countries it became synonymous for the product itself. Therefore, Moka is not just any city but a place of origin famous for a product very similar to tea. And the colour of the Moka trademark on the website of Placement Direct is as brown as coffee. *Honi soit qui mal y pense!*

The question is thus whether the two decisions can be reconciled given that in one case 'Darjeeling' was protected against a registration for dissimilar goods, while in the other it was not. The key difference between the two cases seems to be the fact that in one reference was made to the world the product belonged to, while this was not so in the other case. In the earlier, the mark featured a teapot and an advertisement that made an allusion to the world of tea, while in the second the connection between 'Darjeeling' and tea was absent. Yet such an allusion seems to be a condition for affirming the risk of dilution of the reputation and thus for denying registrability. In the first case, the trademark of Jean-Luc Dusong was revoked because it made reference to tea, which was not the case of the trademark of Placement Direct. In conclusion, it appears that the existence of the reputation of the GI is not enough to prevent registration or use of marks for dissimilar goods. Rather, a reference to the world the GI belongs to is necessary.

A further argument in the second case was that in a Google search for the term 'Darjeeling', the results confirm that this expression has been used to denote products and services different from tea, mainly products of lingerie which have been marketed for several years under the Community mark 'Darjeeling'.[113] According to Placement Direct, such use demonstrates that the term 'Darjeeling' is used in France in contexts different from the one of tea.

There is one argument of the Tribunal that requires some digestion: 'Darjeeling tea is a product coming from a precisely defined Indian region, it is, however, not proved that consumers consider it as equivalent to an exceptional beverage, for the reason that it is a consumer product sold by

---

[112] *Id.*
[113] DARJEELING, Registration Nos. 009468463, 009466228, 009466269, 009468521; DARJEELING LINGERIE Registration No. 004189742 (Fr.).

Unilever in supermarkets under the Lipton brand."[114] Whether it is taken to be correct or not, it confers an important message. Often, the reputation of GIs is dependent upon those who market rather than those who produce. Manufacturers abroad may thus be dependent upon European distributors for the reputation of the indication.

5 NON-PROPRIETARY PROTECTION

As has been explained in the previous two sections, proprietary protection of geographical terms, be it as GIs or trademarks, limits the possibility of third parties wishing to use the term. This is one of the reasons why the registration of geographical terms as a GI requires proper structures of control and supervision in order to make sure that all those entitled to make use of the geographical term can do so. In the case of trademarks, registrability of geographical terms is limited so as to guarantee the freedom to operate of those who can legitimately use the term[115] and in order to avoid misperceptions in trade.

The absence of proprietary protection first of all ensures the freedom to operate. Importers of 'Kobe beef' are not prevented from importing meat under this denomination due to third-party rights. Still, in cases where Kobe beef does not originate from Kobe (or even from Japan), Japanese importers have an interest to limit such denomination to beef from Kobe (or Japan). Whether they can successfully do so in the absence of proprietary rights depends on consumer perception. If Kobe beef is regarded as a purely generic term, or is completely unknown to those in the trade,[116] there is no cause of

---

[114] *Darjeeling*, supra note 111, at 870.
[115] An example could be cupuaçu, a Brazilian fruit that can be processed to fruit juice as well as butter. The company Asahi Foods developed a process for the manufacture of chocolate from cupuaçu and registered (or attempted to register) the term for fruit juice. Thanks to the NGO Amazonlink, the trademark was invalidated in *Japan: Decision of the Japanese Patent Office, 18 February 2004*, 37 INT'L REV. INTELL. PROP. & COMPETITION L. 98 (2006).w. comment by Edson Beas Rodrigues; withdrawn in the US, CUPUACU, Registration No. 2729413, while at OHIM, an application on behalf of the Body Shop was withdrawn, and the registered mark on behalf of Asahi Foods was invalidated. *eSearch plus, The EUIPO's database*, EUIPO, https://euipo.europa.eu/eSearch/#basic/1+1+1+1/50+50+50+50/CUPUACU (last visited 29 May 2016). The Japanese Patent Office reasoned that the term was either descriptive of the product (if used for cupuaçu), or misleading (if used for anything different).
[116] If an indication is unknown, there can be no case for confusion or misperception. Yet in a world of globalised trade, it is important to properly determine the relevant public, which should include immigrant communities and importers: Christopher Heath & Tiffany Prüfer, *Fremdsprachige Bezeichnungen als Marke*, in FESTSCHRIFT FÜR GERHARD SCHRICKER 791, 797 (2005).

action. If Kobe beef is considered as indicating certain qualities, then there is a case against misleading use if beef of a different quality is sold under this name.[117] The same is true if Kobe beef is considered as originating from Kobe (or Japan), and beef of a different origin is sold. Remedies in such cases depend on national law. These may be administrative (by competition or consumer authorities) or civil (by consumer associations, or competitors). As there is no uniform European law on this matter, the following three examples from three different jurisdictions should give the reader some idea in this respect.

The English decision *Greek Yoghurt*[118] affirmed consumer misperception for the use (not registration) of the term 'Greek Yoghurt' for yoghurt not originating from Greece. In the absence of a proper implementation of Article 10*bis* section 3(iii) of the Paris Convention,[119] the plaintiff in the United Kingdom must show confusion by proving goodwill and misappropriation,[120] which is different from most other European countries where a case under unfair competition prevention law requires a misleading use but not a wide recognition of the indication. The action was brought by a major Greek producer of yoghurt.

The Italian decision *Salame Felino* rendered by the Supreme Court[121] dealt with the question whether use of this term by producers outside the area of Felino was an actionable case of unfair competition (initiated by the producer association of Salame Felino). The Supreme Court ultimately rejected this, while the previous instances had affirmed. The reason lay more in the rather complicated interplay between national and EU law on the protection of GIs, however. 'Salame Felino' has meanwhile been registered as a European GI.[122]

---

[117] This was expressly affirmed by the Italian Supreme Court in the 'Salame Felino' decision. Cass. Sez.Un., 12 Febbraio 2015, n. 2828, 2015 RIVISTA DI DIRITTO INDUSTRIALE 251. However, the plaintiff, the Association of Salame Felino, had not argued the case of consumer deception.

[118] Fage UK Ltd. v. Chobani UK Ltd. [2014] EWCA 5 (Civ).

[119] *See* Paris Convention, 10*bis*(3)(3) ('[T]he following in particular shall be prohibited: 3. indications or allegations the use of which in the course of trade is liable to mislead the public as to the nature, the manufacturing process, the characteristics, the suitability for their purpose, or the quantity, of the goods.').

[120] This is of course a serious hurdle and may lead to consumers being confused without any remedy at hand. Anheuser-Busch Inc v. Budejovicky Budvar NP [1984] F.S.R. 413 (CA).

[121] C, Cass., Sez. Un. [Court of Cassation, Grand Chamber], 12 Febbraio 2015, n. 2828, 2015 RIVISTA DI DIRITTO INDUSTRIALE 251.

[122] Commission Regulation 186/2013, 2013 O.J. (L 62) 4.

The German decision *Aceto Balsamico* rendered by the Mannheim District Court[123] dealt with the question whether the use of the term 'Aceto Balsamico' for vinegar that originated in Germany was infringing the registered indication 'Aceto Balsamico di Modena', or, even if not, was misleading as to the origin of the product (the latter being an unfair competition claim). As the court had already affirmed the former under Article 13 of the Regulation 1152/2012,[124] there was no need to decide on the latter. But even for the first claim, the court held that at least according to German consumer perception, 'Aceto Balsamico' was perceived to come from Modena despite the fact that 'Aceto Balsamico' was registered only with the addition 'Modena', and was perhaps perceived to be generic in Italy.

[123] LG Mannheim 15 September 2015, 2O 187/14, http://lrbw.juris.de/cgi-bin/laender_rechtsprechung/document.py?Gericht=bw&nr=19891.

[124] Regulation 1152/2012 of the European Parliament and of the Council of 21 November 2012, Amending Council Regulation 2371/2002 on the Conservation and Sustainable Exploitation of Fisheries Resources under the Common Fisheries Policy art. 13, 2012 O.J. (L 343) 30, states:

1. Registered names shall be protected against:
   (a) any direct or indirect commercial use of a registered name in respect of products not covered by the registration where those products are comparable to the products registered under that name or where using the name exploits the reputation of the protected name, including when those products are used as an ingredient;
   (b) any misuse, imitation or evocation, even if the true origin of the products or services is indicated or if the protected name is translated or accompanied by an expression such as 'style', 'type,' 'method,' 'as produced in,' 'imitation' or similar, including when those products are used as an ingredient;
   (c) any other false or misleading indication as to the provenance, origin, nature or essential qualities of the product that is used on the inner or outer packaging, advertising material or documents relating to the product concerned, and the packing of the product in a container liable to convey a false impression as to its origin;
   (d) any other practice liable to mislead the consumer as to the true origin of the product.

   Where a protected designation of origin or a protected geographical indication contains within it the name of a product which is considered to be generic, the use of that generic name shall not be considered to be contrary to points (a) or (b) of the first subparagraph.
2. Protected designations of origin and protected geographical indications shall not become generic.
3. Member States shall take appropriate administrative and judicial steps to prevent or stop the unlawful use of protected designations of origin and protected geographical indications, as referred to in paragraph 1, that are produced or marketed in that Member State.

   To that end Member States shall designate the authorities that are responsible for taking these steps in accordance with procedures determined by each individual Member State.

   These authorities shall offer adequate guarantees of objectivity and impartiality, and shall have at their disposal the qualified staff and resources necessary to carry out their functions.

6 CONCLUSION

The protection of Asian GIs in Europe is an uphill battle. Most Asian indications face the problem of being latecomers; thus, they have to deal with prior trademark rights, with ignorance or with the perception that they are generic. The easiest way for proprietary protection might be through bilateral trade agreements. Alternative ways are registration under the Lisbon Agreement or the European Regulation on GIs that is limited to food products and requires the GI to contain the name of a region or locality.[125]

The administrative burden of monitoring quality and geographical scope can be onerous. The alternative of applying for trademark protection is dubious on legal grounds, and is not meant to indicate a geographical origin. The latter is also true for collective marks that are available for geographical terms. The minimum that should be achieved is the freedom to operate, for which it may be necessary either to oppose conflicting trademark applications or to sue against generic or misleading use. But a word of caution is necessary – many of the cases that have been litigated took years until a final decision could be obtained, as in the cases mentioned previously, and required considerable financial investment and a long-term perspective. This sounds a bit like the little steam locomotive that winds its way up from Colombo to Nuwara Eliya (a paradise for tea lovers); always an uphill struggle, but worth it.

---

[125] Council Regulation 510/2006 of 20 March 2006, on the Protection of Geographical Indications and Designations of Origin for Agricultural Products and Foodstuffs, 2006 O.J. (L93) 12 (EC).

9

Looking Beyond the Known Story: How the Prehistory of Protection of Geographical Indications in the Americas Provides an Alternate Approach

Christine Haight Farley[*]

1 INTRODUCTION

The current divide within the international community over the appropriate level of protection for geographical indications (GIs) is epitomized by the conflict between the European Union (EU) and the United States (US) in the context of the Transatlantic Trade and Investment Partnership Agreement (TTIP).[1] While GIs receive extensive protections that go beyond international treaty standards within the EU, the US (along with other "New World" countries) has repeatedly opposed strengthening the existing international GI protections.

The US's resistance to strong protection of GIs has become a popularized account. The history of the US's interest in GI protection, however, is more complex. Since 1929, the US has been bound by a little-known international convention that ensures strong protection of GIs: the General Inter-American Convention for Trade Mark and Commercial Protection (Inter-American Convention).[2] The Inter-American Convention is a regional agreement that was instituted by the US with several countries in the Americas. At the time in which the Convention went into force, the provisions on GIs in the Inter-American Convention were the most developed and strongest protections

---

[*] Professor of Law, American University Washington College of Law.
[1] Lina Monten, *Geographical Indications of Origin: Should They Be Protected and Why? An Analysis of the Issue from the U.S. and EU Perspectives*, 22 SANTA CLARA HIGH TECH. L.J. 315, 315 (2005) (noting how the members of the World Trade Organization who ultimately enact the laws proposed by the treaties are split between the EU and the "Old World" in favor of enhanced protection of GIs and the US and the "New World" in favor of limited protection, if any).
[2] General Inter-American Convention for Trade-mark and Commercial Protection, February 20, 1929, 46 Stat. 2907, 124 L.N.T.S. 357 (hereinafter Inter-American Convention) (being referred to as both the Inter-American Convention and the Pan American Convention).

available in any international agreement. And remarkably, these provisions were developed by the US.

This history of the protection of GIs in the US remains enigmatic. Few scholars and lawyers are aware of the Inter-American Convention, let alone its chapter on GI protection. Why was such a chapter included, and why were similar provisions not included in the 1946 Trademark Act or subsequent international agreements? The treatment of GIs both in this convention and in the US Trademark Act is largely the result of the work of Edward Rogers and Stephen Ladas, two of the leading practitioners of US trademark law in the twentieth century. These two men had as sophisticated an understanding of US common law and international obligations as anyone at that time. The resulting texts of the Inter-American Convention and the Trademark Act – both of which they were instrumental in drafting – were no accident.

As the Inter-American Convention is still in force, it indicates the minimum standards for the protection of GIs in the US, at least with respect to beneficiaries of the Convention. It is also arguably a self-executing treaty in the US. Understanding this agreement therefore offers more than historical insight; it may offer an alternate approach to the protection of GIs. The Inter-American Convention also offers lessons for developing GI protection standards in other regions, such as Asia. One reason for the Convention's inconspicuousness is that it was primarily intended to be used by US business in Latin America; it was not designed for the equal benefit of all member states. In addition, it was negotiated without the benefit of any experience protecting GIs on the part of the Latin American trading partners. Perhaps, it is not surprising then that the largely theoretical origins of the protections have resulted in the absence of a robust practice of applying them.

While the focus of this book is to consider GIs in Asia, this chapter will examine a particular historical moment in the legal protection of GIs that will expose a different view of the American approach to the protection of GIs. The reason to introduce this history is to offer policy makers in this region alternative approaches to GI protection beyond the current models advanced by the EU and the US. The short story is that the EU favors strengthening the current protections of GIs – it is said to be one of their greatest assets[3] – while

---

[3] Catherine Saez, *WIPO Design Treaty Fate Left to Assembly, Despite Shift on Technical Assistance*, INTELL. PROP. WATCH (March 21, 2013), www.ip-watch.org/2014/03/21/wipo-design-treaty-fate-left-to-assembly-despite-shift-on-technical-assistance/ (citing to a letter written by EU Parliament President Martin Schulz to members of the Internet Corporation for Assigned Names and Numbers (ICANN) expressing concern over the misuse of European GIs as domain names).

the US disfavors the development of additional protection for GIs beyond those offered by trademark law. The Inter-American Convention certainly complicates this story and provides a possible alternate approach.

2 THE 1929 GENERAL INTER-AMERICAN CONVENTION ON TRADE MARKS AND COMMERCIAL PROTECTION

The US experience with the international protection of GIs began with the 1929 Inter-American Convention on Trademarks and Unfair Competition. This relatively unknown Convention is still in force in all of the ten member states that were original parties to the Convention.[4] The Convention came out of the Pan-American movement, in which the US asserted its dominance in the region over British and European rivals in the postcolonial era. The Convention was an instance of the US effort to replace militarism with institutionalism. The US recognized that Latin America had much to offer in terms of a supply of raw materials and a potential market for US finished products. As a result, there was then an ambitious effort to unite the Americas through innovations such as the creation of a railway system, a customs union, and a common currency.[5] A harmonized intellectual

---

[4] The 1929 Convention included nineteen signatory countries. STEPHEN P. LADAS, THE INTERNATIONAL PROTECTION OF TRADE MARKS BY THE AMERICAN REPUBLICS 11 (1929) (stating the signatories to the Convention were Bolivia, Brazil, Chile, Colombia, Costa Rica, Cuba, the Dominican Republic, Ecuador, Guatemala, Haiti, Honduras, Mexico, Nicaragua, Panama, Paraguay, Peru, the United States, Uruguay, and Venezuela). The Convention entered into force on April 2, 1930, and became effective in the United States, by Presidential proclamation, on February 27, 1931. Ten states ultimately ratified the Convention: Colombia, Cuba, Guatemala, Haiti, Honduras, Nicaragua, Panama, Paraguay, Peru, and the United States. The Convention remains in force today in every one of the original member states. See *Contracting Parties/Signatories: General Inter-American Convention for Trade-Mark and Commercial Protection*, WIPO www.wipo.int/wipolex/en/other_treaties/parties.jsp?treaty_id=353&group_id=21 (last visited April 10, 2015).

[5] PAN AMERICAN UNION, FIFTH INTERNATIONAL CONFERENCE OF AMERICAN STATES, SPECIAL HANDBOOK FOR THE USE OF THE DELEGATES 6 (1922) ("The first International Conference was held at the city of Washington from October 2, 1889, to April 19, 1890. Invitation to this Conference was authorized by an act of the Congress of the United States, promulgated May 24, 1888, directing the President of the United States to invite the Republics of Mexico, Central and South America, Haiti, the Dominican Republic, and Empire of Brazil to meet in conference with United States. The same act sets forth the topics which the Conference was called upon to consider, which were as follows:

1. To preserve the peace and promote the prosperity of the American states.
2. Formation of an American customs union.
3. Establishment of regular and frequent communication between the American States.
4. Establishment of a uniform system of customs regulations.

property law was just one of the many attempts to create a regional market. The 1929 treaty was the last of six treaties concluded by the Pan-American Union that addressed trademarks.[6]

The text, which was evidently prepared by the US delegation,[7] included, and still includes, some startlingly innovative provisions. Among these[8] is an entire chapter, Chapter V, devoted to "the Repression of False Indications of Origin or Source."[9] The legal concept captured by the phrase "indications of origin or source" is not the equivalent of "geographical indication." Although the concept is not defined in the Inter-American Convention, indications of source generally do not demand a link to the geographical area, nor do they demand a reputation of the area for the goods.[10] Therefore, this chapter can be understood to address the use of geographic terms generally.[11] As a result, it actually offers protection to a broader category of geographical terms than the protection offered to GIs under the Agreement on Trade-Related Aspects to Intellectual Property Rights (TRIPS

---

5. Adoption of a uniform system of weights and measures, and laws to protect patents, copyrights, and trademarks.
6. Adoption of a common silver coin.
7. Agreement upon the recommendation for adoption to their Governments of a definite plan of arbitration.
8. Consideration of other matters relating to the welfare of the several countries, which may be presented at the Conference.").

[6] Six conventions were ratified between 1889 and 1929. All of these conventions are still in force, but more recent conventions supersede previous one for those parties who sign both. Since Brazil and the US both ratified the 1923 convention, but only the US ratified the 1929 Convention, the 1923 Convention remains in force as between the US and Brazil.

[7] Just prior to the conference, Stephen Ladas published an influential book titled *The International Protection of Trade Marks by the American Republics* in an effort to "facilitate the work of the conference of trade mark experts and specialists of the American countries, meeting at Washington, February 11, 1929." LADAS, *supra* note 4, at v. In this book, Ladas offered his own draft of the treaty. In a footnote in another book he published later, Ladas referred to "preparatory work" done by US trademark experts – including him – that seems to have been the basis of his draft text. STEPHEN P. LADAS, PATENTS, TRADEMARKS AND RELATED RIGHTS: NATIONAL AND INTERNATIONAL PROTECTION 1754 n.40 (1975) [hereinafter LADAS, PATENTS, TRADEMARKS AND RELATED RIGHTS].

[8] See generally Christine Haight Farley, *The Pan-American Trademark Convention of 1929: A Bold Vision of Extraterritorial Meets Current Realities*, in TRADEMARK PROTECTION AND TERRITORIALITY: CHALLENGES IN THE GLOBAL ECONOMY (Irene Calboli & Edward Lee eds., 2014) (discussing novel priority provisions of the Convention).

[9] Inter-American Convention, *supra* note 2, ch. V.

[10] Paris Convention for the Protection of Industrial Property, March 20, 1883, *as revised* July 14, 1967, 21 U.S.T. 1583, 828 U.N.T.S. 305 [hereinafter Paris Convention].

[11] *Id.*

Agreement).[12] Ultimately, the Inter-American Convention's protections are sweepingly broad.

For instance, Article 23 prohibits as "fraudulent and illegal" "any indication of geographical origin or source which does not actually correspond to the place in which the article, product or merchandise was fabricated, manufactured, produced or harvested."[13] This language would seem to indicate that any false use of a geographical source is prohibited whether or not it is misleading.[14] Thus, Article 23 of the Inter-American Convention mirrors the strict standard of Article 23 of the TRIPS Agreement, but, significantly, it is not limited to wines and spirits.[15] In addition, the Inter-American Convention limits the use of generic terms.[16] Article 27 indicates that the exception for generic terms does not include "regional indication of origins of industrial or agricultural products, the quality and reputation of which, to the consuming public, depends on the production of origin."[17] This article also indicates that "industrial" products are protected along with "agricultural products."

Moreover, the chapter on geographical names in the Inter-American Convention not only prohibits the false use of geographical terms; it also limits the acquisition of trademark rights over geographical terms. Article 25 flatly states that "geographical names are not susceptible to individual appropriation."[18] Depending on the interpretation given to "geographical names," this restriction may prohibit any geographical term from being protected as a trademark in any of the member states.

In addition to a chapter on geographical names, another chapter of the Inter-American Convention, Chapter IV, is devoted to unfair competition and, in turn, applies to unfair competition-related uses of geographical

---

[12] Agreement on Trade-Related Aspects of Intellectual Property Rights arts. 22–24, April 15, 1994, Marrakesh Agreement Establishing the World Trade Organization, Annex 1C, 1869 U.N.T.S. 299 [hereinafter TRIPS].
[13] Inter-American Convention, *supra* note 2, art. 23.
[14] *See* LADAS, PATENTS, TRADEMARKS AND RELATED RIGHTS, *supra* note 7, at 1581 (explaining that the only two requirements are that the term is understood as a geographic place and that the goods are not from that place); *see also* Amy P. Cotton, *123 Years at the Negotiating Table and Still No Dessert? The Case in Support of TRIPS Geographical Indication Protections*, 82 CHI.-KENT L. REV. 1295, 1300–01 (2007) (discussing the requirement of deception in GI protection under the Madrid and Lisbon Agreements).
[15] *Compare* Inter-American Convention, *supra* note 2, art. 23, *with* TRIPS, *supra* note 12, art. 23.
[16] Interestingly, the original draft had limitations on the use of generic terms within Article 23. Somewhere along the way the qualification was removed and now only appears in Article 27.
[17] Inter-American Convention, *supra* note 2, art. 27.   [18] *Id.* at art. 25.

names.[19] In particular, two of the five acts of unfair competition delineated in this chapter explicitly address the use of geographical terms.[20] In notable contrast to the chapter on geographical terms, this chapter of the Inter-American Convention unmistakably addresses the *deceptive* use of geographical terms. Under this chapter, the use of a geographical term in a deceptive manner constitutes a prohibited act of unfair competition.[21] The fact that this chapter requires deception suggests that unfair competition protection is different from the protections in the chapter on geographical terms. This is further reason not to read in an implied deception requirement in the chapter on geographical terms. To do so would mean that the provisions in the unfair competition chapter are duplicative.

---

[19] See Inter-American Convention, *supra* note 2, ch. IV, which provides:

Article 20. Every act or deed contrary to commercial good faith or to the normal and honorable development of industrial or business activities shall be considered as unfair competition and, therefore, unjust and prohibited.

Article 21. The following are declared to be acts of unfair competition and unless otherwise effectively dealt with under the domestic laws of the Contracting States shall be repressed under the provisions of this Convention:

(a) Acts calculated directly or indirectly to represent that the goods or business of a manufacturer, industrialist, merchant or agriculturist are the goods or business of another manufacturer, industrialist, merchant or agriculturist of any of the other Contracting States, whether such representation be made by the appropriation or simulation of trade marks, symbols, distinctive names, the imitation of labels, wrappers, containers, commercial names, or other means of identification;

(b) The use of false descriptions of goods, by words, symbols or other means tending to deceive the public in the country where the acts occur, with respect to the nature, quality, or utility of the goods;

(c) The use of false indications of geographical origin or source of goods, by words, symbols, or other means which tend in that respect to deceive the public in the country in which these acts occur;

(d) To sell, or offer for sale to the public an article, product or merchandise of such form or appearance that even though it does not bear directly or indirectly an indication of origin or source, gives or produces, either by pictures, ornaments, or language employed in the text, the impression of being a product, article or commodity originating, manufactured or produced in one of the other Contracting States;

(e) Any other act or deed contrary to good faith in industrial, commercial or agricultural matters which, because of its nature or purpose, may be considered analogous or similar to those above mentioned.

Article 22. The Contracting States which may not yet have enacted legislation repressing the acts of unfair competition mentioned in this chapter, shall apply to such acts the penalties contained in their legislation on trade marks or in any other statutes, and shall grant relief by way of injunction against the continuance of said acts at the request of any party injured; those causing such injury shall also be answerable in damages to the injured party.

[20] Id. [21] Id.

2.1 Creating New Standards

The above-mentioned provisions do not seem to reflect any then existing international legal standards to which the US was obligated.[22] Moreover, there is no evidence that any Latin American states had corresponding protections at that time.[23] The GI protection standards in the Inter-American Convention also do not appear to reflect a contemporary understanding of then existing US statutory or common law.

Consider, for example, the case of "Tabasco." Tabasco is a state in Mexico, where a particular chili pepper is grown and known as "Tabasco" pepper.[24] "TABASCO," however, is also a trademark registered in the US since 1927 for a certain chili sauce.[25] "Tabasco" brand sauce is made from the type of pepper that is known as "Tabasco" pepper in Mexico, although not from peppers grown in Mexico. Interestingly, the TABASCO trademark was the object of several US federal court cases in the two decades preceding the ratification of the Inter-American Convention. In *Gaidry v. McIlhenny Co.*,[26] decided in 1918, the court recognized McIlhenny as the exclusive holder of the right to sell pepper sauce with the mark "Tabasco." In particular, the court found that, despite the geographic descriptiveness of the word Tabasco, it had acquired a secondary meaning to the public as a source identifier for McIlhenny's chili sauce. Likewise, in *McIlhenny Co. v. Ed. Bulliard*, decided in 1920, the Tabasco trademark was upheld as signifying the brand and not the place.[27] The court stated as fact that since 1868 McIlhenny had been making a sauce from peppers he grew from the seeds of peppers from the State of Tabasco, Mexico. The court stated that "McIlhenny gave his sauce the *distinctive* name 'Tabasco Pepper Sauce.'"[28]

It is intriguing then that the press release published by the US delegation announcing the US ratification of the Inter-American Convention stated

---

[22] In 1929, the US was a party to the Paris Convention, which addressed both indications of source and unfair competition, but neither provision corresponded to the standards set out in the Inter-American Convention. See *supra* notes 10–21 and accompanying text.
[23] See *infra* notes 24–29 and accompanying text.
[24] *Tabasco*, ENCYCLOPÆDIA BRITANNICA, https://global.britannica.com/place/Tabasco-state-Mexico (last visited June 30, 2016).
[25] TABASCO, Registration No. 223310 (U.S.).
[26] McIlhenny Co. v. Gaidry, 253 F. 613 (5th Cir. 1918).
[27] McIlhenny Co. v. Ed. Bulliard, 10 TRADEMARK REP. 213, 215 (W.D. La. 1920) ("At this time these peppers were grown in the State of Tabasco, Mexico and elsewhere in Mexico, and were known as Mexican or Chili peppers – not as Tabasco peppers.").
[28] *Id.* (emphasis added). Interestingly, the first brand name he used was "Petite Anse Sauce," "Petite Anse" being the French name for the island on which he lived. Hence both names had a geographical significance, which was likely common for merchants at that time.

that Chapter V was derived from US principles. Notably, the document stated that

> Chapter V extends through Latin American common law principles of honest trading which have been enforced in the United States for forty years under the elastic jurisdiction of our equity courts. It has always been the law in this country that the application of geographical terms to merchandise not originating in the geographical district indicated, is unfair and unlawful. This chapter extends that salutary doctrine throughout Latin America.[29]

Whether the Inter-American Convention drafters truly understood themselves to be codifying existing principles or creating new legal standards probably will never be known.

The timing of the Inter-American Convention is noteworthy. Ratified in 1929, the Inter-American Convention was one of the earliest international conventions to address geographical terms along with the Paris Convention[30] and the Madrid Agreement.[31] The Inter-American Convention also preceded the 1958 Lisbon Agreement by almost three decades, and it was adopted earlier than most of the domestic legislation that was enacted in the European countries.[32] The Convention then was significant as a very early recognition of the protection of geographical terms in an international agreement.

---

[29] Press Release, U.S. Delegation to the Inter-American Convention, The Advantages Accruing to American Citizens from the General Convention for Trademark and Commercial Protection 2 (February 11, 1929).

[30] Paris Convention, *supra* note 10, *as revised* at The Hague, November 6, 1925, 47 Stat. 1789, T.S. No. 834..

[31] According to the Madrid Agreement for the Repression of False and Deceptive Indications of Source on Goods, April 14, 1891, 828 U.N.T.S. 163 [hereinafter Madrid Agreement], all goods bearing a false or deceptive indication of source, by which one of the Contracting States, or a place situated therein, is directly or indirectly indicated as being the country or place of origin, must be seized on importation, or such importation must be prohibited, or other actions and sanctions must be applied in connection with such importation.

[32] It was not until 1935 – six years after the Inter-American Convention – that the Institut National des Appellations d'Origine (INAO) was created, the same year that French law established a special category of AOC for wine and spirits. Champagne was not granted an AOC until the following year. Décret 47–1331 du 16 Juillet 1947 Fixant La Composition du Comite National des Appellations D'origine [Law 47–1331 of July 16, 1947, Determining the Composition of the National Committee of Origin], JOURNAL OFFICIEL DE LA RÉPUBLIQUE FRANÇAISE [J.O.] [OFFICIAL GAZETTE OF FRANCE], July 19, 1947, p. 6948. Judicial decisions produced uncertainty, so the French government created an official body to both establish and protect appellations of origin. This new regime recognized the importance of both origin *and* quality. DEV GANGJEE, RELOCATING THE LAW OF GEOGRAPHICAL INDICATIONS 109 (2012).

2.2 Understanding the Objective

Yet, what was the objective of including these provisions on the protection of geographical terms in the Inter-American Convention? Were the US drafters seeking to extend US legal principles across the Americas, or were they on a mission to create new rights?

As mentioned above, the individuals most responsible for the Convention's text were two of the most revered figures in US trademark law: Edward Rogers and Stephen Ladas. Perhaps, only the authors of trademark treatises had as sophisticated understanding of US trademark law as these practitioners. Rogers, who is best known as the drafter of the US Trademark Act,[33] litigated many of the Supreme Court and other trademark and unfair competition cases that the treatise authors studied.[34] Ladas, the named partner in Ladas & Parry LLP and the author of an important trademark treatise himself,[35] later represented the US at the 1958 revisions to the Paris Convention. As well as being fully informed of the existing state of US common law with regard to the protection of geographical terms, Rogers and Ladas were also well aware of international developments in trademark law.[36] Likewise, both experts had followed and written extensively on the delineation of specific acts of unfair competition in comparative jurisprudence during the first decades of the twentieth century.[37] The Inter-American Convention came along at an opportune time for these experts to articulate what they deduced was a developing set of principles, as well as to refine and further that agenda.

Still, as part of the history of the Inter-American Convention, there are hints that there was also a sense of developing conflict over protection standards for geographical terms. Later in his career, Ladas pointedly referred to the GI

---

[33] See Edward S. Rogers, *The Lanham Act and the Social Function of Trademarks*, 14 LAW & CONTEMP. PROBS. 173, 180 (1949) (recounting how he drafted what was introduced by Congressman Lanham in 1938 as the original bill based on ABA committee meetings).

[34] See generally Stephen P. Ladas, *Latin American Economic Integration and Industrial Property*, 62 TRADEMARK REP. 1 (1972).

[35] See LADAS, PATENTS, TRADEMARKS AND RELATED RIGHTS, *supra* note 7.

[36] Ladas reflected in 1930 that few countries regulated place names in their domestic legislation and that domestic and international standards were occurring simultaneously. STEPHEN LADAS, THE INTERNATIONAL PROTECTION OF INDUSTRIAL PROPERTY 658–59 (Cambridge Press 1930).

[37] Rogers, for instance, drafted a "Uniform Code dealing with Unfair Competition," which was an effort not only to distil the rules from US common law, but also to incorporate international developments into enumerated acts of unfair competition. See Edward S. Rogers, *Business Good-Will and Trade-Marks Nationally and Internationally Considered*, 34 TRADEMARK REP. 281 (1939).

chapter in the Inter-American Convention as an "amelioration" of the Madrid Agreement,[38] which was revised in 1925, just four years prior to the Inter-American Convention. Perhaps, Ladas had in mind Article 4 of the Madrid Agreement, which prescribed protection for products of the vine according to the country of origin.[39] Yet the Inter-American Convention did not privilege wines and spirits, or even agricultural products.[40]

3 LESSONS TO BE DRAWN FROM THE INTER-AMERICAN CONVENTION

Many lessons can be drawn from illuminating this little-known chapter on international GI protection in the Inter-American Convention. Many of these lessons are cautionary, but the primary lesson is that the US GI tradition is a bit more complicated than many have thought.

In particular, the Inter-American Convention represents an alternative approach, and one generated by the US. Moreover, the Inter-American Convention represented an early example of a regional approach to IP protection. Interestingly, this early twentieth-century attempt at regionalism in the Americas, much like recent regional agreements, was motivated in part by a strategy of forum shifting. More specifically, the Inter-American Convention was an attempt by the US to create a regional alternative to the Paris Convention, which at that time was dominated by European countries with few Latin American signatories.[41]

Also in common with more recent examples, we see in the Inter-American Convention one country imposing its interests on the other, weaker states and trading partners. In this respect, the Inter-American Convention appeared to be primarily intended to benefit US firms conducting business in Latin America. In contrast, almost nothing in the Convention would have benefited Latin American firms at the time. Ladas admitted as much when he noted that Latin American "countries rarely register any trademarks in US, and the problem of protection of their trademarks is hardly existing."[42] Thus, the objective of the Inter-American Convention was to protect US businesses; it was never even anticipated that it would be used by another signatory as

---

[38] LADAS, PATENTS, TRADEMARKS AND RELATED RIGHTS, *supra* note 7, at 1754.
[39] Madrid Agreement, *supra* note 31, art. 4.
[40] See *supra* notes 10–21 and accompanying text.
[41] Ladas, *supra* note 4, at 11. In addition to addressing the meager participation of Latin American states in the Paris Union, it appears that the drafters of the Inter-American Convention were interested in dealing with the perceived issues in the region with greater focus.
[42] Ladas, *supra* note 4, at 32.

a beneficiary of the provisions of the Convention in a US court. So not only was the Inter-American Convention an example of an imbalance of expertise in negotiating positions, but it was also problematic as a regional agreement where, other than desiring trade relations, the signatories did not have much else in common.

Ultimately, as a result of the dominant interests and negotiating position of the US, the Inter-American Convention was drafted without the benefit of any experience protecting GIs on the part of the Latin American signatories. In other words, rather than developing out of a tradition of protecting GIs steeped in practice, the Inter-American Convention's provisions had more of a theoretical origin. The lack of correspondence of the protections to a practice may in part explain why the Inter-American Convention fell into disuse in many of the member states and has been largely forgotten. Certain of the provisions, however, have continued to be used and taken advantage of by US trademark owners in Latin America.

Still, as obvious as it may sound, countries should endeavor not to forget a convention that obligates them. Moreover, just as efforts to engage in regional trade partnerships have continued since 1929, so too have developments in the international protection of GIs. In fact, the US has since signed six separate free trade agreements (FTAs) with countries that are members of the Inter-American Convention in the intervening years.[43] Perversely, the Inter-American Convention was not explicitly referred to in any of these agreements even as these FTAs incorporated by reference other international agreements.[44] In addition, the standards of protection for GIs in these more recent agreements are not consistent with the standards in the Inter-American Convention described above. These FTAs did not commence from the foundation set by the Inter-American Convention, but rather began from a blank slate as if there had been no agreement in place already. In this respect, it would have been useful to take account of the rights that have already been agreed to before moving forward with different standards.

---

[43] See United States-Colombia Trade Promotion Agreement, U.S.-Colom., November 22, 2006 (2012), https://ustr.gov/trade-agreements/free-trade-agreements/colombia-fta/final-text; United States-Panama Trade Promotion Agreement, U.S.-Pan., June 28, 2007, https://ustr.gov/trade-agreements/free-trade-agreements/panama-tpa/final-text (entered into force October 31, 2012); Central America Free Trade Agreement (2006) (Guatemala, Honduras, Nicaragua) Dominican Republic-Central America-United States Free Trade Agreement (CAFTA-DR), U.S.-Cent. Am.-Dom. Repub., May 28, 2004, 43 I.L.M. 514; Peru Trade Promotion Agreement, April 12, 2006, Temp. State Dep't No. 09–54, KAV 8674.

[44] See supra note 43.

In light of this, as I have suggested elsewhere, there is a real possibility that the Inter-American Convention is today a sleeping treaty.[45] Were private parties to take notice of the Convention and make greater use of it as a basis for bringing individual claims in US courts, the US may be compelled to consider its obligations under it.

Notably, not only do countries not have the option to forget their obligations under treaties, but in this case there is a strong basis for resurrecting it in a US court. In 1940, the US Supreme Court pronounced the Inter-American Convention a self-executing treaty, and as such, the law of the land without the need for implementing legislation.[46] In fact, the Inter-American Convention was drafted in such a manner as to anticipate its provisions being used directly as operable law. For instance, under Article 28, the final article in the chapter on GIs, parties are authorized to make a claim and seek a remedy under existing domestic trademark laws in the event that no local law exists implementing the Convention's protections.[47]

Although there is some case law rejecting the assertion of rights under the Convention,[48] the Trademark Trial and Appeal Board (TTAB), a body within the United States Patent and Trademark Office (USPTO), has ruled in a few cases, beginning in the year 2000, that the Convention is a self-executing treaty. First in *British-American Tobacco v. Philip Morris*,[49] the TTAB concluded that the Inter-American Convention has the same force of law as the Trademark Act, is independent of the Trademark Act, and it grants the USPTO jurisdiction to cancel registrations when it is alleged that there is

---

[45] See Christine Haight Farley, *The Pan-American Trademark Convention of 1929: A Bold Vision of Extraterritorial Meets Current Realities*, in TRADEMARK PROTECTION AND TERRITORIALITY: CHALLENGES IN THE GLOBAL ECONOMY (Irene Calboli & Edward Lee eds., 2014); Christine Haight Farley, *The Protection of Geographical Indications in the Inter-American Convention on Trademarks*, 6 WIPO J. 68 (2014).
[46] Bacardi v. Domenech, 311 U.S. 150, 161 (1940).
[47] Inter-American Convention, *supra* note 2, art. 28 ("In the absence of any special remedies insuring the repression of false indications of geographical origin or source, remedies provided by the domestic sanitary laws, laws dealing with misbranding and the laws relating to trade marks or trade names, shall be applicable in the Contracting States.").
[48] In Havana Club Holding v. Galleon, the Second Circuit Court of Appeals wrestled with the question of the applicability of this treaty and held that it was not applicable because a party must assert rights under the Inter-American Convention "pursuant to § 44(b) of the Lanham Act." Havana Club Holding v. Galleon, 203 F.3d 116 (2d Cir. 2000). In other words, it must make a claim for relief under the Trademark Act. Thus, the Second Circuit did not consider it as providing an independent basis of jurisdiction. See also Empresa Cubana Del Tabaco v. Culbro Corp., 399 F. 3d 462 (2d Cir. 2005).
[49] British-American Tobacco Company Limited and Tabacalera Istmena, S.A. v. Philip Morris USA, Inc., 55 U.S.P.Q.2d 1585 (T.T.A.B. 2000).

a violation of the Convention.[50] Only one of these TTAB cases involved the false use of a geographical term, but this case happened to be brought under a different provision of the Convention.[51] As a result, we do not have an application of the GI provisions of the Convention in a US tribunal.

As the international community moves forward with the development of GI protections, it may be that considering the strengths and weaknesses of the Inter-American Convention proves helpful. But at a minimum, the Convention certainly serves to complicate the story about the US's position on the protection of GIs, and demonstrates that the anti-GI narrative is of a more recent origin in the US.

4 UNITED STATES V. EUROPEAN UNION: TWO DIFFERENT VIEWS AND OBJECTIVES FOR THE PROTECTION OF GEOGRAPHICAL INDICATIONS

Despite the US's complex history regarding the protection of GIs,[52] it appears that today's US approach on GIs is generally referred to as the anti-EU approach. As is well known, the US and the EU have very different views about how GIs should be protected and to what extent they should be protected, and are referred to as being on opposite sides of the debate.[53]

The opposing views of the US and the EU on GIs were well documented in the negotiations leading to the adoption of the GI provisions in TRIPS, and later in the gridlock of the multilateral negotiations under the built-in TRIPS agenda and the Doha Development Agenda under the Doha Ministerial Declaration.[54] More recently, the US and the EU have been engaged in

---

[50] Id.
[51] The case of Cor Cimex S.A. v. DM Enterprises & Distributors, No. 91178943, 2008 WL 5078739 (T.T.A.B. November 17, 2008), was simply brought as a trademark case in 2008. The Cuban brand was successful in preventing the registration of Cubita for this other party.
[52] *See* Christine Haight Farley, *The Protection of Geographical Indications in the Inter-American Convention*, 6 W.I.P.O. J. 68, 69 (2014) (highlighting that the Inter-American Convention had some of the strongest GI protections in any international agreement even though the US has never been a strong supporter of GI protection).
[53] *See* Philippe Zylberg, *Geographical Indications v. Trademarks: The Lisbon Agreement: A Violation of Trips?*, 11 U. BALT. INTELL. PROP. L.J. 1, 1 (2003) (noting that the US and EU are the main contributors to the GI debate).
[54] World Trade Organization, Ministerial Declaration of November 14, 2001, WTO Doc. WT/MIN(01)/DEC/1, ¶ 18, 41 ILM 746 (2002) [hereinafter Doha Declaration]. For a detailed analysis of the Doha Declaration, see *TRIPS: Issues, Geographical Indications*, WORLD TRADE ORG., http://wto.org/english/tratop_e/trips_e/gi_e.htm (last visited November 20, 2015).

a contest to see whose vision of GI protection will prevail as part of the negotiations for bilateral and plurilateral FTAs with third countries, including with countries in Asia.[55] As several experts have noted, the two positions – from the US's and the EU's points of view – seem to be incompatible and thus a contest (and a race to lock in trading partners with the preferred view) has expectedly ensued.[56] At present, Asia is certainly a main battleground, especially in light of the recently concluded Trans-Pacific Partnership Agreement (TPP), and the many bilateral agreements that the US and EU have respectively concluded or are negotiating in Asia.[57] An example of this battle is Korea, who recently signed FTAs with both the US and EU and thus agreeing to incompatible protections for GIs.[58]

In particular, the EU supports a strong protection of GIs to safeguard its economic interest in goods such as wine and cheese, which strategically rely on GIs to distinguish themselves from nonlocal competitors.[59] In the EU, GI protection is efficiently handled administratively by the EU Commission based on several EU Regulations.[60] As part of the registration process,

---

[55] For a detailed review of these agreements, see Susy Frankel, *Geographical Indications and Mega-Regional Trade Agreements and Negotiations*, and Anselm Kamperman Sanders, *Geographical Indications as Property: European Union Association Agreements and Investor–State Provisions*, in this Volume.

[56] See Bernard O'Connor, *The European Union & the United States: Conflicting Agendas on Geographical Indications – What's Happening in Asia?*, 9 GLOBAL TRADE & CUSTOMS J. 66, 66 (2014).

[57] See, e.g., Trans-Pacific Partnership, ch. 18, Intellectual Property, October 5, 2015, https://ustr.gov/sites/default/files/TPP-Final-Text-Intellectual-Property.pdf [hereinafter TPP, Intellectual Property Chapter]; United States-South Korea Free Trade Agreement, U.S.-S. Kor., June 30, 2007, https://ustr.gov/trade-agreements/free-trade-agreements/korus-fta; United States-Singapore Free Trade Agreement, U.S.-Sing., May 6, 2003, Temp. State Dep't No. 04–36, KAV 6376; United States-Oman Free Trade Agreement, U.S.-Oman, January 19, 2006, Temp. State Dep't No.09–53, KAV 8673; EU-Vietnam Free Trade Agreement, EU-Viet., August 5, 2015, http://trade.ec.europa.eu/doclib/docs/2015/august/tradoc_153674.pdf; EU-Singapore Free Trade Agreement, EU-Sing., September 20, 2013, http://ec.europa.eu/trade/policy/countries-and-regions/countries/singapore/; EU-South Korea Free Trade Agreement, EU-S. Kor., September 16, 2010, 54 O.J. (L 127) 1, 46–47, http://eur-lex.europa.eu/legal-content/en/ALL/?uri=OJ:L:2011:127:TOC .

[58] See *supra* note 57.

[59] Zylberg, *supra* note 53 (noting that the US and EU are the main contributors to the GI debate).

[60] See Regulation 1151/2012, of the European Parliament and of the Council of November 21, 2012, on Quality Schemes for Agricultural Products and Foodstuff, 2012 O.J. (L 343) 1 [hereinafter EU Agricultural Products and Foodstuff Regulation]; Council Regulation 479/2008 of April 29, 2008 on the Common Organization of the Market in Wine, Amending Regulations 1493/1999, 1782/2003, 1290/2005, 3/2008 and Repealing Regulations (EEC) 2392/86 and 1493/1999, 2008 O.J. (L 148) 1 [hereinafter EU Wine Regulation]; Regulation 110/2008,

applicants need to identify both the internal and the external entities that will enforce quality control for the GI products.

A crucial component of the EU GI protection is that GIs are categorically protected from becoming generic terms (even in the case that consumers may refer to the product generically in practice),[61] which means that GIs cannot fall into the public domain and be used as generic terms.[62] In this way, EU law aims at preserving the advantages that historic regional industries have against competitors who may claim (as they do in the US) that a term has become generic. For instance, if Tabasco were a GI in the EU, the protection received under EU law would ensure that the name continued to signify a place and not a type of product. I refer to this objective of EU law as a type of protection against the dilution of registered GIs because it seeks to maintain the significance and reputation of GIs in the same way that trademark dilution protection seeks to maintain the significance and reputation of a famous mark against free riders who attempt to take advantage by creating an association with the mark.

These strong protections are partially balanced in EU law by restricting GI protection to a circumscribed subject area. Under current EU law at least, GI protection only applies to foodstuffs, wines, and spirits.[63] Thus, manufactured products and services are excluded from protection, even though the EU is currently considering extending GI protection to nonagricultural products.[64]

The more recent position of the US with respect to GI protection is seemingly incompatible with the EU approach. In principle, the US appears to be against the enhancement of GI protection. Like the EU, the US position

---

of the European Parliament and of the Council of January 15, 2008, on the Definition, Description, Presentation, Labeling and the Protection of Geographical Indications of Spirits Drinks and Repealing Council Regulation (EEC) 1576/89, 2008 O.J. (L 39) 16 [hereinafter EU Spirits Regulation].

[61] In Italy, for example, many consumers use the word "parmigiano" to refer to the grated cheese used on their pastas, yet only the producers associated with the Consorzio del Parmigiano Reggiano can use the term "Parmigiano" on their products. Case C-132/05, Comm'n v. Federal Republic of Germany (Parmesan), 2008 E.C.R. I-957.

[62] Zylberg, *supra* note 53, at 3 (2003) (noting that the US and EU are the main contributors to the GI debate).

[63] See *supra* note 62.

[64] On September 22, 2015, the European Parliament also considered the issue in a plenary session following the opinions of several of its committees, and called "on the Commission to propose without delay a legislative proposal with the aim of establishing a single European system of protection of geographical indications for non-agricultural products." Comm. on Legal Affairs, Report on the Possible Extension of Geographical Indication Protection of the European Union to Non-Agricultural Products, EUR. PARL. DOC. A8-0259, at 6/26 ¶ 3 (2015).

corresponds to economic realities, namely its interest in protecting its large food producers, who frequently use European names based on the claim that these names are generic terms.[65]

The fundamental difference, however, can be reduced to the legal approach taken by both the EU and the US. Notably, while the EU favors a *sui generis* approach based on the administrative requirement of GI registration, the US strenuously advocates addressing GI protection through trademark law exclusively.[66] As a result, the source of GI protection in the US is not a registration system per se (even though GIs are protected primarily as registered trademarks), but a market understanding.[67] Moreover, in order for US trademark law to protect a geographical name/GI as an ordinary trademark, the name must have acquired secondary meaning.[68] Like other trademarks, a distinctive sign can also lose its source-identifying significance over time through generic use. Furthermore, US trademark law does not protect geographical terms against dilution; instead, it is incumbent on the producers from that region to maintain the meaning.[69] Still, it should be noted that many GIs are protected in the US as certification and collective marks,[70] and that the conditions to be satisfied in order to obtain this protection – which is granted to a collectivity of producers and not to individual undertakings – resemble, to a considerable extent, the process to be followed in order to obtain a GI registration under a *sui generis* system.

Relatedly, US trademark law leaves enforcement to interested parties. For example, although the term "ROQUEFORT" is registered with the USPTO as a certification mark for cheese produced in the Roquefort region in France,[71] if a producer of cheese not from that region were to use this designation on its products in the US market, it would be incumbent on the

---

[65] U.S. Dairy Industry Drives Home Concerns on Geographical Indications and Common Food Name Issues During TTIP Stakeholders Forum, CONSORTIUM FOR COMMON FOOD NAMES (February 4, 2015), www.commonfoodnames.com/u-s-dairy-industry-drives-home-concerns-on-geographical-indications-and-common-food-name-issues-during-ttip-stakeholders-forum/ (last visited July 12, 2016) (relating the dairy industry opposition to EU pressure for protection of geographical indications).

[66] See, e.g., United States-Australia Free Trade Agreement, U.S.-Austl., art. 17.2.1, May 18, 2004, Temp. State Dep't No. 05–074, KAV 7141 ("Each Party shall provide that marks shall include marks in respect of goods and services, collective marks, and certification marks. Each Party shall also provide that geographical indications are eligible for protection as marks.").

[67] Zylberg, *supra* note 53, at 6, 15. [68] *Id.* at 15.

[69] *See generally* Trademark Dilution Revision Act of 2006, Pub. L. No. 109–312, § 2, 120 Stat. 1730 (to be codified at 15 U.S.C. § 1125(c)(2)(A)).

[70] *See, e.g.*, GROWN IN IDAHO, Registration No. 2,914,307 (U.S.).

[71] *See* ROQUEFORT, Registration No. 571,798 (U.S.).

registrant to bring a private lawsuit in a federal court.[72] Finally, as US trademark law loosely follows consumer understanding of signs, it is possible for geographical terms to be protected for any type of product whether agricultural or manufactured. In addition, it is possible to achieve protection in the US based on use without first obtaining a registration. For instance, common-law certification marks such as "COGNAC" have been recognized by US courts.[73]

In sum, the EU and the US advocate for considerably diverging approaches to GI protection with the key features of these systems corresponding to different objectives. The EU system seeks to achieve a form of dilution protection through an administrative system. In contrast, the US system seeks to achieve a form of unfair competition protection limited by the contours of trademark law.[74]

5 AN ALTERNATE APPROACH

Presented with these two diverging approaches, Asian countries, such as Korea, find themselves in the unenviable position of navigating between the EU and the US in deciding their national systems of GI protection. In this respect, the model embodied in the Inter-American Convention, with its provisions on GIs and unfair competition principles described above, could represent a distinct alternate approach.

First, the Inter-American Convention offers an alternative to the strict public law–private law divide between the EU and the US as member states can meet their obligations to protect GIs through either method so long as they agree to the broadly stated standards.[75]

---

[72] UNITED STATES PATENT AND TRADEMARK OFFICE, GEOGRAPHICAL INDICATION PROTECTION IN THE UNITED STATES 4 (2016), www.uspto.gov/sites/default/files/web/offices/dcom/olia/globalip/pdf/gi_system.pdf (explaining that "with respect to protection of geographical indication certification marks, affected parties can oppose registration or seek to cancel registrations, all within the existing trademark regime in the United States").
[73] Institut National Des Appellations D'Origine v. Brown-Forman Corp., 47 U.S.P.Q.2d 1875 (T.T.A.B. 1998) (holding "COGNAC" to be a geographical indication for brandy from France).
[74] But see Irene Calboli, Time to Say Local Cheese and Smile at Geographical Indications of Origin? International Trade and Local Development in the United States, 53 HOUS. L. REV. 373 (2015) (pointing out that the US protects appellations for wines with a sui generis system, and that the controversy between the US in the EU is primarily driven by diverging business interests; thus, consensus can be found when these interests overlaps, such as in the case of wines).
[75] See generally Inter-American Convention, supra note 2.

Second, both the EU and US approaches seem to work best at the national level (the regional level in the EU, in which GI protection is based on EU law). The Inter-American Convention approach, however, works best at a regional level (not strongly integrated as in the EU). As noted above, the Inter-American Convention was precisely an attempt to extend developing norms of unfair competition protection at the regional level among countries in the Americas. At the time when the Inter-American Convention was negotiated, the protection of GIs under US trademark law was not so well developed (and the current trademark act had not yet been adopted), and, thus, the convention aimed at (also) filling this gap.

Third, a model based on the Inter-American Convention may be better suited to address the conflicts that could possibly arise with respect to generic terms within a region. In particular, the generic exception – that is, the right to use foreign GIs on the basis that they are generic in the jurisdictions in question – is limited in the Inter-American Convention. As countries within a specific region – in Asia as much as in the Americas – may be more likely to share generic language and have awareness of the geographical meaning and reputations of GI regions and GI products from neighboring countries, the Inter-American Convention could represent a viable model for Asian countries to adopt a system of GI protection, which would take into account GIs registered in other countries in the same region.[76] In other words, a dilution-like GI protection such as that is applied in the EU could be achieved in Asia by adopting a system similar to the Inter-American Convention.

Another possible and positive consequence of adopting a model of GI protection having its source in unfair competition law, as in the Inter-American Convention, is the breadth of subject matter that can be protected under this model. In particular, because unfair competition law seeks to protect the reputation of a good, this type of GI protection can be used to protect agricultural products as much as nonagricultural products. This is explicitly the case in the Inter-American Convention text. Such possibility is of particular relevance in Asian countries, as many of these countries are rich in

---

[76] In this respect it could be mentioned that the revised text of the Lisbon Agreement for the Protection of Appellations of Origin and their International Registration that was adopted following a Diplomatic Conference was convened in Geneva, Switzerland, in May 2015 includes the possibility to register the same GI in two different countries through an application for a "trans-border area." *See Diplomatic Conference for the Adoption of a New Act of the Lisbon Agreement for the Protection of Appellations of Origin and Their International Registration*, WORLD INTELL. PROP. ORG., www.wipo.int/meetings/en/details.jsp?meeting_id=35202 [hereinafter Geneva Act] (last visited July 28, 2016)

traditional handicrafts and several of them already provide for GI protection for nonagricultural products.[77]

6 PROTECTION FOR GEOGRAPHICAL INDICATIONS IN ASIA

Considering GI protection in the Asian region allows us to open the discussion beyond GI protection from the perspective of the EU or the US. This discussion is important because the objectives in protecting GIs in other regions may not exactly mirror those of the EU and the US, as several of the chapters in this volume also demonstrate. In particular, the inflexibility of the models presented by the EU and US regimes limits regional experimentalism, and the Inter-American Convention may present a suitable alternative.

To date, several Asian countries have implemented or are considering primarily national systems of *sui generis* protection modeled after the EU regime. In addition, several countries in the region have negotiated or are negotiating FTAs with the EU or ad hoc agreements for GI protection. For instance, the EU and China have reached certain agreements where they reciprocate recognition of certain GIs (so far ten from China and ten from the EU) in the model of EU law. From the EU side, this includes "Grana Padano" cheese, "Prosciutto di Parma" ham, and "Stilton" blue-veined cheese – all these products are protected as *sui generis* GIs in China today.[78] In reciprocation, the EU has agreed to recognize GIs for Chinese products such as "Pinggu da Tau" peaches and "Dongshan Bai Lu Sun" asparagus. It is debatable whether this reciprocal agreement is of equal benefit for both parties. Christopher Heath's chapter in this volume indicates, for example, that seventeen Asian GIs are registered in the EU, yet none of which will likely be familiar to Europeans (at least to date).[79]

Of course, many Asian GIs are well known to consumers outside of Asia. For instance, "Basmati" rice and "Darjeeling" tea are two Indian GIs that are

---

[77] See various examples in this respect in Part III of this volume.
[78] *EU-China Geographical Indications – "10 plus 10" Project Is Now Completed*, EUR. COMM'N (November 30, 2012), http://europa.eu/rapid/press-release_IP-12-1297_en.htm (discussing the pilot program between the EU and China and listing the ten GIs to which both sides committed to register and protect); *Geographical Indications*, E.U.-CHINA TRADE PROJECT (II), www.euctp.org/index.php/en/agriculture-food-safety/geographical-indications-gi.html (last visited November 20, 2015) (supporting GI registration in the EU and China).
[79] See Christopher Heath, *How Would Geographical Indications from Asia Fare in Europe?*, in this volume.

recognized around the world for agricultural products from India.[80] Yet, the recognition and the rights to be recognized to each of these GIs have been legally tested under the EU and US GI regimes with mixed results for the GIs. In short, these GIs have not fared as well as desired by their owners, showing the still existing problems for the protection of foreign GIs under the US and EU systems.

The legal saga of "Basmati" in the US is well known to GI experts. "Basmati" is an Indian GI for aromatic, long-grain rice that grows in the Punjab region in northern India and across the Pakistani border.[81] India has repeatedly claimed that the distinctive characteristics of basmati rice are a byproduct of the Indian soil that is irrigated by the Himalayan Rivers.[82] India is the largest exporter of basmati rice in the world. The word "basmati," however, has been used generically in the US for decades referring to aromatic long grain rice without regard to where the rice is grown. This US generic use predated any legal protection for "Basmati" in India. In the late 1990s, a US company provoked the ire of the Indian government by not only using brand names such as "American Basmati" and registering the trademark "Texmati,"[83] but also attempting to patent its production of this rice.[84] Moreover, in the US, the term "Basmati" is also used in connection with goods other than rice. Several "Basmati" marks have been registered, such as "Basmati Bus," which is a registered service mark for food truck services.[85] These registrations are generally not related to goods or services originating from India.

Furthermore, while the Indian government succeeded in invalidating the patents covering basmati rice, it could not prevent the US company from using the trademark "Texmati." This episode angered the Indian public who believed that the use of the word "basmati" was pirating their indigenous product.[86] Indian nongovernmental organizations have insisted that the

[80] *But see* Michelle Agdomar, *Removing the Greek from Feta and Adding Korbel to Champagne: The Paradox of Geographical Indications in International Law*, 18 FORDHAM INTELL. PROP. MEDIA & ENT. L.J. 541, 582–84 (2008) (explaining the legal battle over the "Basmati" GI in the US).

[81] Saritha Rai, *India-U.S. Fight on Basmati Rice is Mostly Settled*, N.Y. TIMES (August 25, 2001), www.nytimes.com/2001/08/25/business/india-us-fight-on-basmati-rice-is-mostly-settled.html.

[82] *Id.*

[83] *See* TEXMATI, Registration No. 1,859,875 (U.S.); Utsav Mukherjee, A STUDY OF THE BASMATI CASE (INDIA-US BASMATI RICE DISPUTE): GEOGRAPHICAL INDICATION PERSPECTIVE (National Law University Jodhpur, 2008) http://papers.ssrn.com/sol3/papers .cfm?abstract_id=1143209.

[84] U.S. Patent No. 5,663,484 (filed August 7, 1994); *see also* Rai, *supra* note 81.

[85] *See* U.S. Trademark Application Serial No. 86557496 (filed March 9, 2015).

[86] Rai, *supra* note 81.

US change its rice standards so that only rice grown in India and Pakistan can be branded with the word "basmati."[87] This dispute may have prompted the Indian government to protect basmati rice as a GI for the regions where it is being grown in India. However, this attempt was met with spirited opposition both from a state within India that produces basmati rice but had been excluded from the "Basmati region,"[88] as well as the Basmati Growers Association of Pakistan, who protested that basmati rice is grown in both India and Pakistan.[89]

Similarly, the name "Darjeeling" has been the subject of several abuses, and legal challenges both in the US and the EU. The "Darjeeling" GI protects tea that is cultivated and grown in the Darjeeling region of West Bengal in India.[90] The distinctive quality and flavor of Darjeeling tea has been globally recognized for over a century.[91] The distinctiveness of Darjeeling tea is said to be due to two main factors: the tea's geographic origin, and the process by which the tea is made.[92] The tea is grown in tea gardens located 2,000 meters above sea level, and the environment at that particular elevation is said to add to the uniqueness of the tea.[93] In addition to these two factors, the Tea Board of India's quality control mechanisms ensure that the product maintains its high quality and that the tea originates only from the GI region.[94]

Hence, there have been several controversies around the use of the term "Darjeeling" for non-tea products outside India in recent years. For instance, the Tea Board of India disputed the use of "Darjeeling" as a mark by a French company for intimate lingerie.[95] In this case, the Tea Board ultimately succeeded in protecting the name under EU trademark law, as Darjeeling was first registered as a mark in the EU,[96] and only subsequently was registered

---

[87] Mukherjee, *supra* note 83.
[88] The State of Madhya Pradesh filed an opposition on the grounds that the application for "Basmati" as a GI had excluded thirteen territories of Madhya Pradesh (MP) where Basmati rice is grown.
[89] If the evidence of opposition were not filed within the prescribed time, the application would be deemed to be abandoned.
[90] S. C. Srivastava, *Protecting the Geographical Indication for Darjeeling Tea*, WORLD TRADE ORGANIZATION, www.wto.org/english/res_e/booksp_e/casestudies_e/case16_e.htm.
[91] *Id.*   [92] *Id.*   [93] *Id.*
[94] See the Chapter by Yogesh Pai & Tania Singla, *"Vanity GIs": India's GI Legislation and the Missing Regulatory Framework*, in this volume.
[95] *The Darjeeling Question: What's Your Cup of Tea – a T-bag or a G-string?*, THE IPKAT (October 14, 2015), http://ipkitten.blogspot.com/2015/10/the-darjeeling-question-whats-your-cup.html.
[96] The Tea Board's trademark is DARJEELING, Registration No. 004325718 (EU). The opposed marks were DARJEELING collection de lingerie, Trade Mark No. 009466228 (EU) and DARJEELING, Trade Mark No. 009466269 (EU).

as a *sui generis* GI.[97] Still, in another dispute in France, an insurance company used "Darjeeling" as a mark for its services.[98] In response, however, the French courts concluded that because Lipton marketed "Darjeeling" in French supermarkets, that the term did not have enough of a distinctive reputation to receive dilution protection under trademark law in France.[99]

In the US, several "Darjeeling" trademarks have been registered for non-tea products, again by parties unrelated to the producers of Darjeeling tea in India. For instance, "THE DARJEELING BAGS" is registered for luggage products.[100] Additionally, "DARJEELING" is registered to a company that sells shirts, shorts, dresses, and ladies undergarments.[101] These registrations are still in force and it does not seem that it would be possible to obtain their cancelation based on US trademark law.

Under an unfair competition approach, such as the one that is embodied in the Inter-American Convention, GI protection is justified not only to ensure that consumers are not deceived, but also to protect producers from the region referenced. For example, out of fairness to consumers and producers, countries interested in combating unfair competition would not want companies to use "Basmati" on rice that does not come from that region. But, this justification for protection does not apply in situations where non-rice products are marketed with "Basmati" marks because there is no threat to competition. Thus, while the mark "Texmati" would probably not withstand a legal challenge under a provision similar to the Inter-American Convention, the use of "Darjeeling" for non-similar goods or service would unlikely be prohibited.

7 CONCLUSION

As I have elaborated in this chapter, the US history with respect to GI protection is a little more complex than most assume. In particular, the US has not consistently shied away from GI protection nor has it always relied upon a trademark system to achieve GI protection. In 1929, in drafting and ratifying the Inter-American Convention, the US forged a different

---

[97] Commission Implementing Regulation No 1050/2011 of October 20, 2011, entering a name in the register of protected designations of origin and protected geographical indications (Darjeeling (PGI)), 2011 O.J. (L276) 5; DOOR, *Denomination Information*, Eur. Comm'n, http://ec.europa.eu/agriculture/quality/door/registeredName.html?denominationId=1900.

[98] *See* the chapter by Christopher Heath, *How would Geographical Indications from Asia fare in Europe?*, in this volume.

[99] *Id.*   [100] THE DARJEELING BAGS, Registration No. 4855286 (U.S.).

[101] DARJEELING, Registration No. 2043112 (U.S.).

approach to GI protection to be applied in several countries in the Americas. The Inter-American Convention offered a broader, more comprehensive system of protection to GIs compared to the systems of protection achieved in any other treaty at that time. While the US may no longer officially follow this (still in force) approach today, and many in the US may barely have been aware of the Inter-American Convention, a similar system may be interesting for Asia, and for other regional blocks of countries coming into this discussion, as a model to consider. Ultimately, the Inter-American Convention offers the international community an alternate approach, or a middle path between the current US and EU models, with its unfair competition foundation. At a minimum, the Inter-American Convention offers a variant to the *sui generis* system today applied in the EU and the trademark approach of the US.

10

European Union-Singapore Free Trade Agreement: A New Chapter for Geographical Indications in Singapore

Susanna H.S. Leong*

1 INTRODUCTION

As a signatory to the Agreement on Trade-Related Aspects of Intellectual Property Rights (TRIPS),[1] Singapore is obliged to confer protection to geographical indications (GIs). For the past fifteen years, the relevant legislation in Singapore has been the Geographical Indications Act (GI Act 1999),[2] which came into force on 15 January 1999. However, with the successful conclusion of negotiations of the European Union (EU) and Singapore Free Trade Agreement (EU-Singapore FTA)[3] in 2013, the law on GIs in Singapore is set to change. One key takeaway from the EU-Singapore FTA Intellectual Property Chapter is that the EU and Singapore reached an agreement and Singapore will enhance its existing regime for the protection of GIs. Consequently, a new Geographical Indications Act (GI Act 2014) for Singapore has been passed by Parliament on 14 April 2014.[4] The new GI Act 2014 will replace the current GI Act 1999 once it is brought into force (as at the date of this writing and as of February 2017, just before this book goes to press, the GI Act 2014 has still not been brought into force in Singapore). Under the

---

* Professor and Vice Dean (Graduate Studies), NUS Business School, National University of Singapore.
[1] See Agreement on Trade-Related Aspects of Intellectual Property Rights, 15 April 1994, Marrakesh Agreement Establishing the World Trade Organization, Annex 1C, Legal Instrument – Result of the Uruguay Rounds Vol. 31, 33 I.L.M. 83, 1869 UNTS 299 (1994) [hereinafter TRIPS].
[2] Geographical Indications Act (Cap 117B, 1999 Rev. Ed.) (Sing.) [hereinafter GI Act 1999].
[3] See EU-Singapore Free Trade Agreement, EU-Sing., June 29, 2015 [hereinafter EU-Singapore FTA], http://trade.ec.europa.eu/doclib/press/index.cfm?id=961.
[4] Geographical Indications Act (No. 19 of 2014) (Sing.) [hereinafter GI Act 2014].

GI Act 2014, Singapore will strengthen its current protection by establishing an ad hoc register for GIs,[5] and a new chapter will begin for the protection of GIs.

In particular, the new GI Act 2014 heralds an enhanced protection regime for GIs in Singapore, and the provisions of the new Act will come into operation in several stages in tandem with the general ratification process of the EU-Singapore FTA. The first stage of implementation of the FTA will involve the establishment of the GI Registry.[6] However, the Registry will be established only when the EU ratifies the EU-Singapore FTA.[7] Likewise, the enhanced regime under the GI Act 2014 will be applicable only when the EU-Singapore FTA is implemented in the EU and Singapore. Furthermore, as part of this process, amendments related to the protection of GIs will have to be made to the current provisions of the Trade Marks Act 1998.[8] The final stage of implementation is supposed to take place within three years of entry into force of the EU-Singapore FTA. The same time frame will apply to the implementation of improved border enforcement measures with respect to registered GIs, as these measures will need to be adopted as part of Singapore's obligations in the FTA. The staged approach adopted by the Singapore Parliament aims at ensuring that companies and government organizations will have sufficient time to adjust to the impact of the new GI protection regime in Singapore.

As Singapore moves into the next phase of legislative development on GIs with the enactment of GI Act 2014, this chapter examines and assesses the protection accorded to GIs in Singapore, but with a specific interest in the provisions of the new GI Act 2014. The chapter begins with a broad overview of the protection of GIs in Singapore under the GI Act 1999. It then addresses the adoption of the GI Act 2014. Next, the chapter focuses on the relevant provisions of the newly adopted (but not yet entered into force at the time of this writing) GI Act 2014 and discusses the legal issues as well as business implications that may be raised by the new GI provisions.

---

[5] *See* GI Act 2014 pt. IV, §§ 17–37.   [6] *See id.*

[7] EU-Singapore FTA, art. 11.17 ('(2) The systems referred to in paragraph 1 shall contain elements such as ... (a) a domestic register.') The Intellectual Property Chapter of the EU-Singapore FTA is available at http://trade.ec.europa.eu/doclib/docs/2013/september/tradoc_151761.pdf.

[8] Singapore Trade Marks Act (Cap 332, 2005 Rev Ed) [hereinafter Trade Marks Act 1998].

2 LEGAL PROTECTION OF GEOGRAPHICAL INDICATIONS IN SINGAPORE

2.1 The Law Prior to the Geographical Indications Act of 1999

Once upon a time, under the old Trade Marks Act 1938,[9] it was difficult to register and protect a word which, according to its ordinary signification, is a geographical name, as it was not considered to be distinctive or adapted to distinguish the proprietor's goods from the goods of any other trader.[10]

During those times, marks which were geographical names were protected in Singapore under the common-law action for passing off, provided that the three elements of goodwill, misrepresentation and likelihood of damage are satisfied. Accordingly, owners of (generally foreign) GIs could take action in passing off against unauthorized use of their GIs by third parties in Singapore. However, the challenge remained, and still remains under a passing-off action in Singapore, that a GI which is protected in another country may not enjoy goodwill in Singapore because it is possible that the public in Singapore does not associate goods bearing the GI with the special qualities and characteristics attributable to the geographical region indicated in the GI. Another difficulty pertains to the second element of misrepresentation, which requires proof of a likelihood of confusion amongst the public. If the public in Singapore, on seeing a GI, understands that the goods do not originate from the geographical region as indicated in the GI (for example, if the GI, when applied, is accompanied with words such as 'kind', 'type', 'style', 'limitation' or 'the like'[11]), there is no confusion and passing off is not established, which may add to the chagrin of GI owners, as they would not be able to protect their GIs.

Starting in 1999, with the repeal of the Trade Marks Act 1938 and the enactment of the Trade Marks Act 1998 on 15 January 1999,[12] the owners of GIs that are used to identify products are permitted to register their GIs as a trademark under the Trade Marks Act 1998 if the GIs fall within the ambit of the statutory requirements for trademark registration.[13] It should be noted that trademark laws in Singapore do not prohibit the registration of GIs per se.

---

[9] Singapore Trade Marks Act (Cap 332, 1992 Rev Ed) [hereinafter Trade Marks Act 1938]. For more than half a century since 1 February 1939, the Trade Marks Act 1938 was the operative statute and cornerstone of trademark protection in Singapore. After Singapore became a signatory to TRIPS on 15 April 1994, the Trade Marks Act 1938 was repealed and the Trade Marks Act 1998 came into force on 15 January 1999.
[10] Trade Marks Act 1938 at § 10(1)(d).   [11] TRIPS, arts. 22–24.
[12] See Trade Marks Act 1998.
[13] See Trade Marks Act 1998 §§ 7–9, which cover the grounds of refusal of registration of trademarks.

Nevertheless, GI owners can prevent registration of a GI as a trademark which is not authorized by them. For example, Section 7(4)(b) of the Trade Marks Act 1998 provides that 'a trade mark shall not be registered if it is ... of such a nature as to deceive the public for instance as to the nature, quality or *geographical origin* of the goods or service'.[14] Furthermore, Section 7(7) of the Trade Marks Act 1998 stipulates that a 'trade mark shall not be registered if it contains or consists of a GI in respect of a wine or spirit and the trade mark is used or intended to be used in relation to a wine or spirit not originating from the place indicated in the GI'.[15] The prohibition against registration remains

> whether or not the trade mark has, or is accompanied by, an indication of the true geographical origin of the wine or spirit, as the case may be, or an expression such as 'kind', 'type', 'style', 'imitation' or the like, and irrespective of the language of the geographical indication is expressed in that trade mark.[16]

Under the Trade Marks Act 1998, GIs may also be registered as collective or certification marks.[17] However, a GI which is a generic term to the public in Singapore cannot be registered as a collective or certification mark.[18] Beyond trademark laws, the use or application of a false trade description on goods including their place of origin is prohibited and constitutes an offence under the consumer protection legislation.[19]

As a whole, it may be said that legal protection for GIs at that stage of Singapore's IP infrastructure developments did not meet Singapore's obligations under TRIPS,[20] and a change in the law was hence considered necessary.

2.2 The Law Post–Geographical Indications Act 1999

To meet Singapore's international obligations to provide protection for GIs as stipulated in TRIPS, the Singapore Parliament enacted the GI Act 1999,[21] which came into force on 15 January 1999. Thus, for the past fifteen years, the GI Act 1999 has been the relevant legislation which laid down the basic

---

[14] *See id.* § 7(4)(b) ('(4) A trade mark shall not be registered if it is: ... (b) of such a nature as to deceive the public (for instance as to the nature, quality or geographical origin of the goods or service.')).

[15] *See id.* § 7(7) ('A trade mark shall not be registered if it contains or consists of a GI in respect of a wine or spirit and the trade mark is used or intended to be used in relation to a wine or spirit not originating from the place indicated in the geographical indication'.).

[16] *Id.* § 7(8). [17] *See id.* pt. VIII, §§ 60–61. [18] *See* Trade Marks Act 1998, scheds. 1–2.

[19] Consumer Protection (Trade Description and Safety Requirements) Act (Cap 53, 1985 Rev Ed).

[20] *See* TRIPS, arts. 22–24. [21] GI Act 1999.

framework for GI protection in Singapore. The GI Act 1999 is a short Act with only twelve sections.[22]

Under GI Act 1999, a GI is defined as

> any indication used in trade to identify goods as originating from a place, provided that -
> (a) the place is a qualifying country or region or locality in the qualifying country; and
> (b) a given quality, reputation or other characteristics of the goods is essentially attributable to that place[.][23]

According to this definition, not all GIs are protected in Singapore. Indeed, only GIs of a country which is a member of the World Trade Organization (WTO),[24] a party to the Paris Convention for the Protection of Industrial Property (Paris Convention)[25] or a country designated by the Singapore government as a qualifying country can be protected.[26]

Furthermore, the GI Act 1999 does not provide a registration system for GIs in Singapore. Instead, protection for GIs is granted automatically if the criteria set forth in the GI Act 1999 are met.[27] A producer or trader of goods identified by GIs could institute civil proceedings against a person for committing an act prohibited under the GI Act 1999 if he is able to prove that he is entitled to protection for the GI in question.

The following uses are prohibited under the GI Act 1999:[28]

1. Use of the GI on goods which do not originate in the place indicated in the GI, in a manner *which misleads the public as to the geographical origin* of the goods
2. Use of the GI which constitutes an act of unfair competition within the meaning of Article 10*bis* of the Paris Convention[29]
3. For wines and spirits, there is an additional level of protection[30] – its use on wines or spirits not originating from the place indicated in the GI is prohibited whether or not
   (i) the true geographical origin of the second-mentioned wine is used together with the GI;
   (ii) the GI is used in translation; or
   (iii) the GI is accompanied by any of the words 'kind', 'type', 'style', 'imitation', or any similar word or expression.

---

[22] *See id.* §§ 1–12.   [23] *See id.* § 2.   [24] *See* TRIPS, art. 22(2).
[25] Paris Convention for the Protection of Industrial Property, 20 March 1883, 21 U.S.T. 1583, 828 U.N.T.S. 305 (revised 1967) [hereinafter Paris Convention].
[26] *Compare* GI Act 1999 § 2 *with* GI Act 1999 § 11.   [27] *See id.* §§ 2–3.   [28] *See id.* § 3(2).
[29] *See* Paris Convention, art. 10*bis*.   [30] *See* GI Act 1999 § 3(2)(c).

Essentially, the GI Act 1999 has adopted a two-tier approach in granting protection to GIs, which is consistent with TRIPS.[31] At a more basic level, the GI Act 1999 provides a general protection for GIs based on wrongful use resulting in misrepresentation or unfair competition. An enhanced level of protection is accorded to wines and spirits in that the protection approximates that of a dilution-type remedy, which is not premised on a likelihood of confusion on the part of the public.[32]

Singapore did not, and still does not, have a list of GIs or her own GIs for which protection is sought. Thus, the legal framework provided under the GI Act 1999 was initially considered to be adequate as far as GI protection in Singapore was concerned, at least as the first step after the implementation of TRIPS in Singapore.[33] In this respect, it may be said that the main inadequacy of the GI Act 1999 lies in the fact that it does not provide for the establishment of a registration system. As a result, filing a claim in the Singapore courts for infringement of a GI under the GI Act 1999 requires that the GI owners first establish that they are entitled to protection for the GI in question.[34] Essentially, in practice, this means that GI owners are required to go before a court to prove conclusively that their GIs are entitled to be protected in Singapore. This would be considered as unsatisfactory and inadequate protection to most GI owners in general, in particular those who enjoy comprehensive protection in a *sui generis* system such as the EU.[35]

The successful conclusion of the EU-Singapore FTA in 2013 has provided the impetus for change in the law of GIs,[36] and it is to the substantive provisions in the GI Act 2014 that we shall now turn.

3 THE NEW LAW TO BE IN SINGAPORE: SALIENT FEATURES OF THE GEOGRAPHICAL INDICATIONS ACT 2014

The GI Act 2014 will repeal and re-enact with amendments the old GI Act 1999. Compared to the GI Act 1999, the number of provisions in the GI Act

---

[31] TRIPS, art. 23. [32] See, e.g., TRIPS, arts. 22–24.
[33] The language used in TRIPS for prescribing the standard of protection for GIs is fairly wide and it is clear that TRIPS does not make protection of GIs contingent on registration. See TRIPS, art. 22(2)(a)–(b).
[34] See GI Act 1999 § 3(1).
[35] The European Union protects GIs through an extensive Register which encompasses over 1,400 food and agricultural products and over 3,000 wines and spirits. See 'E-bacchus', a database consisting of the Register, which is available at http://ec.europa.eu/agriculture/markets/wine/e-bacchus/. See also the DOOR Databases for foodstuff and agricultural GIs, which is available at http://ec.europa.eu/agriculture/quality/door/list.html.
[36] See EU-Singapore FTA, art. 11.17(1)–(2).

2014 has significantly expanded from twelve to ninety.[37] In broad terms, the GI Act 2014 is significant in three areas: (a) the establishment of a GI Registry;[38] (b) the conferment of enhanced protection of GIs in Singapore;[39] and (c) the provision of improved border enforcement measures for GIs.[40]

3.1 The Establishment of a Geographical Indications Registry in Singapore

Part IV of the GI Act 2014[41] establishes a system of registration for GIs in Singapore. This new GI Registry will reside within the Intellectual Property Office of Singapore (IPOS). Once established, the GI Registry will examine applications for GI registration in respect of wines, spirits, selected categories of foodstuffs and agricultural products such as cheese, meat and seafood.[42] The registration process of GIs mirrors that of the trademark registration system in Singapore,[43] which essentially comprises three main stages: (a) application;[44] (b) examination;[45] and (c) publication and opposition.[46]

Only certain categories of persons are entitled to file an application for registration of a GI.[47] They include 'persons who are carrying on an activity as a producer in the geographical area specified in the application with respect to the goods specified in the application'[48] and 'an association of such persons',[49] as well as competent authorities having responsibility for the geographical indication for which registrations are sought.[50]

Section 39 of the GI Act 2014[51] provides that an application for registration of a GI must be done in the prescribed manner and shall specify details such as the name, address and nationality of the applicant; the capacity in which the applicant is applying for registration; the GI for which registration is sought; the goods to which the GI applies; the geographical area to which the GI applies; and the quality, reputation or other characteristics of the goods and how they are attributable to the geographical origin. Registration of a GI may only be made in respect of prescribed categories of goods as set out in the Schedule of the GI Act 2014.[52]

---

[37] See GI Act 2014.   [38] See id. pt. IV, §§ 17–37.   [39] See id. pt. II.
[40] See GI Act 2014 pt. VI.   [41] See id. pt. IV, §§ 17–37.
[42] See GI Act 2014, sched. (listing wines, spirits, beers, cheese, meat and meat products, seafood, edible oils, non-edible oils, fruits, vegetables, spices and condiments, confectionery and baked goods, flowers and parts of flowers, and natural gum).
[43] See Trade Marks Act 1998 pt. II.   [44] Id. §§ 5–6A.   [45] Id. § 12.   [46] Id. § 13.
[47] GI Act 2014 § 38.   [48] Id. § 38(a).   [49] Id. § 38(b).   [50] Id. § 38(c).   [51] Id. § 39(1).
[52] See id., sched.

The GI Act 2014 implements a system of substantive examination of the application for registration of a GI in Singapore. In particular, the GI Act 2014 establishes that, after the submission of an application to register a GI, the Registrar will conduct an examination of the application[53] to determine whether the application for registration of a GI satisfies all the requirements of the GI Act 2014. To do so, the Registrar may (and likely will) carry out a search of earlier trademarks[54] and earlier GIs.[55] The Registrar may refuse to register a GI based on any of the grounds set out in Section 41 of the GI Act 2014.[56] These grounds of refusal of registration of a GI fall broadly into two categories. The first category pertains to objections associated with the innate attributes or qualities of the GI under consideration for registration such as:[57]

(a) If the indication does not fall within the meaning of 'geographical indication'[58] as defined in Section 2 of the GI Act 2014
(b) If the GI identifies goods which do not fall within any of the categories of goods set out in the Schedule of the GI Act 2014
(c) If the GI is contrary to public policy or morality
(d) If the GI is not or has ceased to be protected in its country or territory of origin
(e) If the GI is identical to the common name of any goods in Singapore, where registration of the GI is sought in relation to those goods
(f) If the GI contains the name of a plant variety or an animal breed and is likely to mislead the consumer as to the true origin of the product.

This set of grounds for refusal for registration of a GI in Section 41(1) of the GI Act 2014 resembles the absolute grounds for refusal of registration of

---

[53] Id. § 43.
[54] See id. § 43(7) ('An "earlier trademark" means (a) a registered trademark or an international trademark (Singapore), the application for registration of which was made earlier than the application for registration of the geographical indication in general, taking into account (where appropriate) the priorities claimed in respect of the trademark under the Trade Marks Act 1998; or (b) a trademark which, at the date of application for registration of the geographical indication in question, was a well-known trademark'.).
[55] See id. § 2(1) ('An "earlier geographical indication," ... means a geographical indication (a) which has been registered under section 48; or (b) an application for registration of which has been made under section 39, before the date of application in question'.).
[56] See id. § 41.   [57] Id. § 41(1)(a)–(f).
[58] The definition of a 'geographical indication' in the GI Act 2014 is the same as that in GI Act 1999. Section 2(1) of the GI Act 2014 defines a 'geographical indication' to mean 'any indication used in trade to identify goods as originating from a place, provided that (a) the place is a qualifying country or a region or locality in a qualifying country; and (b) a given quality, reputation or other characteristic of the goods is essentially attributable to that place'. GI Act 2014 § 2(1).

a trademark under Section 7 of the Trade Marks Act 1998. In particular, these grounds for refusal include the lack of distinctiveness[59] and/or other obstacles such as bad faith[60] or being against public policy.[61] Both sets of grounds of refusal for registration of a GI and a trademark focus on the innate ability of the GI or the trademark to distinguish goods or services in the marketplace. In the case of a GI, the inquiry is whether GIs distinguish the goods that originate from the particular geographical location from goods that do not; in the case of a trademark, the inquiry is whether the trademarks distinguish goods that are associated with one trader from those of other traders. It is anticipated that given the close relationship between a GI and a trademark, the principles developed in trademark law, in particular those used to determine whether a sign or indication has 'become customary in current language or bona fide and established practices of trade',[62] would certainly help inform the calibration of whether a GI may be considered 'identical to the common name of any goods in Singapore'[63] under Section 41(1)(e) of the GI Act 2014 and consequently must be refused registration. It should be noted that in this regard Section 41(2) of the GI Act 2014 provides that in determining whether a GI is 'identical to the common name of any goods in Singapore' under Section 41(1)(e), any marketing material in Singapore which uses a GI shall be relevant evidence to show that the GI is *not* the common name of any goods in Singapore, if the marketing material suggests in a misleading manner that the goods to which the marketing material relates originate in the geographical origin of the GI, when in fact those goods originate elsewhere.[64] This may be done through using either words or pictures.

The other set of grounds for refusal of registration of a GI may be referred to as the relative grounds for refusal of registration because the objections lie essentially in that if the proposed GI is registered, its use will conflict with an 'earlier GI'[65] or an 'earlier trademark'.[66] These relative grounds for refusal of registration of a GI under Sections 41(3) to (6) may be summarized as follows:

(a) A GI shall not be registered if there exists a likelihood of confusion on the part of the public because the GI is identical with or similar to, and has the same geographical origin as, an earlier GI.[67] An exception to this

---

[59] Trade Marks Act 1998 § 7(1)(b).   [60] *Id.* § 7(6).   [61] *Id.* § 7(4)(a).
[62] *See id.* § 7(1)(d). See also Wing Joo Loong Ginseng (S) Ltd v. Qinghai Xinyuan Foreign Trade Co Ltd [2009] 2 SLR 814, in which the SGCA suggested that trademarks which are generic descriptions of the goods in question are caught by section 7(1)(d) of the Trade Marks Act 1998. Both Trade Marks Act 1998 § 7(1)(d) and GI Act 2014 § 41(1)(e) are targeted at generic terms.
[63] GI Act 2014 § 41(1)(e).   [64] *Id.* § 41(2).   [65] *Id.* § 41(3).   [66] *Id.* § 41(4)–(5).
[67] *Id.* § 41(3).

ground for refusal of registration is the registration of homonymous GIs under Section 42 of the GI Act 2014.[68] A homonymous GI refers to a GI 'that, in part or in whole, has the same spelling as, or sounds the same as, a GI for any goods having a different geographical origin'.[69] The Registrar may register homonymous GIs subject to the imposition of practical conditions so as to differentiate the homonymous GIs from the earlier GI.[70] In doing so, the Registrar shall have regard to factors such as (i) the need to ensure equitable treatment of all the interested parties concerned; (ii) the need to ensure that consumers are not misled; and (iii) the views and submissions of the applicant for registration of the homonymous GI and of the applicant for registration or registrant of the earlier GI.[71]

(b) A GI shall not be registered if there exists a likelihood of confusion on the part of the public because (i) the GI is identical with or similar to a trademark;[72] and (ii) the trademark is a *registered trademark* – the application or registration for which was before the date of application for the GI in Singapore and the application or registration of the said trademark was in good faith – or that the trademark has been *used* in good faith in Singapore in the course of trade before the date of application for registration of the GI in Singapore.[73]

(c) A GI shall not be registered if it is identical with or similar to a trademark that is, before the date of application for registration of the GI in Singapore, a well-known trademark in Singapore and registration of the GI is liable to mislead consumers as to the true identity of the goods identified by that GI.[74]

If there are no objections from the Registrar or if the objections have been successfully overcome, the application will be accepted and the Registrar shall cause the application to be published in the prescribed manner.[75] Thereafter, any person may within the prescribed time commence opposition proceedings against the registration of the GI.[76] If the opposition is successful, the application for registration of the GI will be refused. On the other hand, if the opposition is unsuccessful or if there is no opposition, the GI will be registered and a certificate of registration will be issued to the applicant.[77] The GI will be registered for a period of ten years from the date of registration,[78] and may be renewed for further periods of ten years in respect of each renewal.[79]

---

[68] *Id.* § 42.   [69] *Id.* § 2.   [70] *Id.* § 42(2).
[71] *Id.* § 42(3); see also TRIPS, art. 23(2), covering the refusal of registration of trademarks for wines containing homonymous indications.
[72] GI Act 2014 § 41(4).   [73] *Id.* § 41(5).   [74] *Id.* § 41(6).   [75] *Id.* § 45(1).   [76] *Id.* § 45(2).
[77] *Id.* § 48.   [78] *Id.* § 50.   [79] *Id.* §§ 50–51.

Post-registration, a registered GI may be cancelled by either the Registrar upon an application by the registrant or by the court or Registrar upon an application by any other person on any of the grounds stipulated in Section 52(2) of the GI Act 2014.[80] These grounds include:[81]

(a) that the GI was registered in breach of Section 41[82] of the GI Act 2014;
(b) that the registration was obtained fraudulently or by misrepresentation;
(c) that the GI has ceased to be protected in its country or territory of origin;
(d) that there has been a failure to maintain, in Singapore, any commercial activity or interest in relation to the GI, including commercialization, promotion or market monitory;
(e) that, in consequence of a lack of any activity by any interested party of goods identified by a registered GI, the GI has become the common name of those goods in Singapore.

If the GI is cancelled upon application of the registrant, the rights conferred by the registration on any interested party of goods identified by the GI shall cease to exist with effect from the date of cancellation of the registration.[83]

In the event that a GI is cancelled based on the grounds that it has been registered in breach of Section 41 of the GI Act 2014[84] or that the registration was obtained fraudulently or by misrepresentation, the GI shall be deemed never to have been registered.[85]

If the GI is cancelled based on any of the other grounds, it shall cease to exist with effect from the date of application for cancellation or if the Registrar or the court is satisfied that the ground existed at an earlier date.[86]

3.2 Enhanced Protection of Geographical Indications in Singapore

The new GI Act 2014, when brought into force, will establish a *sui generis* system of protection for GI in Singapore. Both unregistered and registered GIs are set to be protected under the GI Act 2014.

In respect of unregistered GIs, the protection is the same as that provided under the GI Act 1999.[87] Essentially, this means a trader or an association of producers or traders may bring action against any person for the use of an unregistered GI in relation to any goods which did not originate in the place indicated by the GI, in a manner which misleads the public as to the

---

[80] *Id.* § 52(1)–(2). [81] *Id.* § 52(2)(a)–(e).
[82] *Id.* § 41 (stating the grounds for refusal of registration). [83] *Id.* § 52(5). [84] *See id.* § 41.
[85] *Id.* § 52(6). [86] *Id.* § 52(7). [87] GI Act 1999 §§ 2, 3(2).

geographical origin of the goods or if the use of the unregistered GI constitutes an act of unfair competition within the meaning of Article 10bis of the Paris Convention.[88]

The protection accorded to GIs which identify wines and spirits as conferred under the GI Act 1999 remains unchanged under the GI Act 2014. The use of GIs on wines or spirits not originating from the place indicated in the GI is prohibited whether or not

(i) the true geographical origin of the second-mentioned wine is used together with the GI;
(ii) the GI is used in translation; or
(iii) the GI is accompanied by any of the words 'kind', 'type', 'style', 'imitation' or any similar word or expression.[89]

This enhanced level of protection formerly accorded only to wines and spirits under the repealed GI Act 1999 is now extended to registered GIs for selected categories of agricultural products and foodstuff as stated in the Schedule of the GI Act 2014.[90] Protection is conferred on GIs of these selected agricultural products and foodstuff even if consumers are not misled as to the products' true geographical origin.[91]

3.3 Improved Border Enforcement Measures for Geographical Indications

Under Part VI of the GI Act 2014,[92] owners of a registered GI will have access to a suite of improved border enforcement measures. One such improved border enforcement measure is that an interested party of goods identified by a registered GI may request the customs authorities in Singapore to detain suspected infringing goods and restrict the importation or exportation of such goods.[93]

These improved border enforcement measures will only be implemented within three years after the EU-Singapore FTA comes into force.[94] Substantial resources will have to be allocated to enhance the capabilities of Singapore customs authorities so as to undertake effective GI enforcement actions.

---

[88] Compare GI Act 2014 §4(2)(a)–(b) with Paris Convention, art. 10bis.
[89] GI Act 2014 § 4(2)(c)–(d).   [90] See id., sched.   [91] Id. § 4(6).
[92] See id. pt. VI, §§ 55–74.   [93] Id. § 56.
[94] Sing. Parl. Deb., Official Rep. (14 April 2014) vol. 91 (Indranee Rajah, Senior Minister of State for Education and Law).

4 ISSUES AND IMPLICATIONS OF THE NEW GEOGRAPHICAL INDICATIONS REGIME IN SINGAPORE

4.1 Establishing a Registration System for Geographical Indications in Singapore

The new GI Registry[95] to be established under the GI Act 2014[96] will commence receiving applications for registration of GIs after the EU-Singapore FTA is ratified by the European Parliament. The examination of applications for registration of GIs is a major undertaking of the new GI Registry and it will require the establishment of substantial institutional capabilities and resources to facilitate and support it.

Under Article 11.17 of the EU-Singapore FTA,[97] both the EU and Singapore have agreed to subject the names listed under Annex 11-A of the EU-Singapore FTA[98] to their respective domestic registration processes to determine the registrability of these names as GIs.[99] Thereafter, both parties to the EU-Singapore FTA will convene to adopt a decision in the Trade Committee regarding the list of names that are to be protected as GIs in Singapore and the EU.[100] Yet, it is noteworthy that under the EU-Singapore FTA, Singapore did not accept to grant automatic recognition and protection to a limited list of key GIs from the EU. There are altogether 196 names from the EU to be examined and to be verified by the Registrar that they identify goods originating in territories of the EU or a region or locality in the EU, where a given quality, reputation or other characteristic of the goods is essentially attributable to their geographical origin.[101] In contrast, Singapore has no list of its own GIs for which it wants protection in the EU. The Singapore position is noteworthy because several other countries that have concluded FTAs with the EU have accepted to protect the same or a similar list of EU GIs automatically (i.e. without a substantive examination), even though some exceptions have been carved for certain names in some of these countries.[102]

---

[95] *See* GI Act 2014 §§ 17–20.   [96] *See id.* pt. IV, §§ 17–37.
[97] EU-Singapore FTA art. 11.17.   [98] *See* EU-Singapore FTA, Annex 11-A.
[99] Article 11.17(3), EU-Singapore FTA.   [100] *Id.*   [101] GI Act 2014, Annex 11-A.
[102] *See, e.g.*, EU-South Korea Free Trade Agreement, EU-S. Kor., 16 September 2010, 2011 O.J. (L 127) 47, art. 10.21, http://eur-lex.europa.eu/legal-content/EN/TXT/PDF/?uri=CELEX:22011A0514(01)&rid=8; *see also* EU-Vietnam Free Trade Agreement, EU-Viet., 5 August 2015, http://trade.ec.europa.eu/doclib/docs/2015/august/tradoc_153674.pdf; Comprehensive Trade and Economic Agreement, Can.-EU, Consolidated CETA Text, ch. 22, Intellectual Property, 26 September 2014, http://trade.ec.europa.eu/doclib/docs/2014/september/tradoc_152806.pdf.

Nevertheless, in order to expedite the processing of a list of priority EU GIs,[103] the Singapore government has agreed to take fully into account the fact that the GIs have been evaluated and registered in the EU when carrying out the examination of EU GIs. This includes the possibility of rationalizing the volume of information to be submitted, based on the fact that the EU legislation has been examined and on the principle of recognition of GI systems. Nevertheless, given the volume of examination of names to be registered as GIs that must be undertaken in Singapore by a relatively new and inexperienced Registry, the learning curve for those in charge of the Registry is expected to be steep.[104]

Further delays may be expected as a result of third-party opposition proceedings,[105] in particular if there are objections raised that the EU-recognized GIs should be refused registration on the basis that they have become generic names in Singapore, or conflict with prior registered trademarks in Singapore.[106] In opposition proceedings based on the generic nature of the products, only evidence of genericness within Singapore will be relevant.[107]

As Singapore has few local agricultural, foodstuff or wine producers,[108] it is anticipated that opposition to registration of GIs in Singapore is likely to be mainly initiated by producers in other major agricultural export countries such as the United States, Canada, Australia, New Zealand, India, China and Japan, just to name a few, whose produce is marketed and sold in the Singapore market. In this regard, it is noteworthy that to secure stronger protection for its GIs through bilateral trade agreements, affected industries in the United States have come together to establish the Consortium for Common Food Names.[109] The Consortium is an international initiative based in Washington, DC, and it seeks to foster the adoption of an appropriate

---

[103] See letter from Mr Lim Hng Kiang, Singapore Minister for Trade and Industry, addressed to Mr Karel De Gucht, Member of the European Commission (21 January 2013), http://trade.ec.europa.eu/doclib/docs/2013/september/tradoc_151779.pdf. However, it is unclear from the Minister's letter whether priority is to be given to *all* 196 GIs from the EU in the list, or just some of them.

[104] See id. [105] GI Act 2014 §§ 45, 48.

[106] See Trans-Pacific Partnership (TPP), arts. 18.20, 18.32, https://ustr.gov/sites/default/files/TPP-Final-Text-Intellectual-Property.pdf. These provisions in the TPP uphold the principle that prior use and existing rights of a trademark could prevent the registration of a GI.

[107] See GI Act 2014 § 41(1)(e).

[108] Central Intelligence Agency, *Singapore*, THE WORLD FACTBOOK (5 May 2016), www.cia.gov/library/publications/the-world-factbook/geos/sn.html.

[109] The Consortium for Common Food Names is an international initiative to preserve the right to use generic food names; see CONSORTIUM FOR COMMON FOOD NAMES, www.commonfoodnames.com/ (last visited 12 May 2016).

model for protecting both legitimate geographical indications and generic food names.[110]

Be that as it may, Singapore is a small market of approximately 5.4 million people,[111] and it remains to be seen whether there will be a large number of opposition proceedings against the registration of EU-recognized GIs in Singapore from affected third-party producers.

4.2 Interrelationships between Owners of Registered Geographical Indications and Other Existing Right Holders

With the new GI protection regime coming into force in Singapore, one area of concern is the interrelationships between registered GI owners and existing GI holders, registered trademark owners as well as users of signs identical with or similar to the registered GIs. The government is mindful of the impact that the new GI registration system will have on the rights of existing GI holders and trademark owners. In the Second Reading speech on the Geographical Indications Bill on April 14, 2014,[112] Senior Minister of State for Law Indranee Rajah SC explained the relationship between the existing GI protection regime and the new Bill:

> When the new GI protection regime comes into force, it will *not* over-ride or undermine any rights which GI holders already have under the existing regime. These rights will co-exist with those under the new regime.[113]

---

[110] The Consortium for Common Food Names has a set of guidelines which it hopes will be adopted by national governments and international organizations in their efforts to establish a fair model for the protection of both common names and legitimate food-related geographical indications. The guidelines include the following: (a) requiring that a geographical indication include the name of the region or sub-region where the product is produced, and a second term that describes the product (e.g. 'Camembert de Normandie', 'Idaho Potatoes', etc.); (b) maintaining a strong tie to the full original geographical indication by protecting the term only in its original language and in transliteration (e.g. 'Parmigiano Reggiano'); (c) establishing reference points for identifying common names, such as existence of a Codex standard or other international standards; use of the term in dictionaries, newspapers, product descriptions in tariff schedules or in explanatory notes; levels and diffusion of global production; international trade; etc.; (d) providing the opportunity for stakeholders around the world to comment on geographical indication applications to ensure that officials have fully considered the request and its impact on other farmers and food producers. See CONSORTIUM FOR COMMON FOOD NAMES, www.commonfoodnames.com/the-issue/our-mission/ (last visited May 12, 2016).

[111] Department of Statistics Singapore, Singapore in Figures (2015), www.singstat.gov.sg/docs/default-source/default-document-library/publications/publications_and_papers/reference/sif2015.pdf.

[112] Sing. Parl. Deb., Official Rep. (14 April 2014) vol. 91 (Indranee Rajah, Senior Minister of State for Education and Law).

[113] *Id.* (emphasis added).

Thus, the legislative framework in the GI Act 2014 preserves the 'first-in-time, first-in-right' principle in managing the conflicting interests of various stakeholders in the protection and enforcement of GIs in Singapore. Essentially, this means that 'a new application for a GI registration may not invalidate a prior conflicting GI or trademark which already exists'.[114]

4.2.1 Registered or Protected Geographical Indications Owners under Geographical Indications Act 2014 and Existing Geographical Indications Holders

Section 12(1) of GI Act 2014[115] makes provisions for a prior user (who is a qualified person[116]) of a GI, being a GI identifying a wine or spirit in relation to any goods or services if he or his predecessors in title have continuously used in Singapore that GI in relation to those goods or services or related goods or services either (a) for at least ten years preceding 15 April 1994[117] or (b) in good faith preceding that date.[118]

By this provision, the law recognizes that for reasons of business efficacy, there is a need to allow the co-existence of a GI (whether registered or unregistered) used in relation to a wine or spirit with another GI used in relation to any goods or services in the marketplace when the duration of such use meets the requisite length (ten years) or that its use precedes the said wine or spirit GI in good faith. To avail himself of this exception, the prior user of a GI must also show to the satisfaction of the courts that he has 'continuously used' the earlier GI.[119] It should be noted that the concept of 'continuous use' is also found in Section 28(2) of Trade Marks Act 1998,[120] which provides for a similar prior use defence to a defendant sued for trademark infringement. It is submitted that principles developed in trademark law in relation to the concept of 'continuous use' are relevant and may be applied in interpreting the phrase 'continuously used' in Section 12(1) of the GI Act 2014. Thus, concepts such as 'genuine commercial use' developed by the courts in trademark cases[121] under the old law[122] would also be relevant. Hence, the prior use exception under Section 12(1) of GI Act 2014[123] should not be available

---

[114] *Id.*   [115] *See* GI Act 2014 § 12(1).
[116] A 'qualified person' means (a) a citizen of Singapore or an individual resident in Singapore; (b) a body corporate incorporated under any written law in Singapore; or (c) any other person who has a real and effective industrial or commercial establishment in Singapore. *See id.* § 12(3).
[117] *Id.* § 12(1)(a).   [118] *Id.* GI Act 2014 § 12(1)(b).   [119] *Id.* § 12(1)–(2).
[120] *See* Trade Mark Act 1998 § 28(2).
[121] *See* Electrolux Ltd v. Electrix Ltd [1954] 71 RPC 23 (CA); Imperial Group Ltd v. Philip Morris & Co Ltd [1982] FSR 72 (CA).
[122] *See* Trade Marks Act 1938.   [123] *See* I Act 2014 § 12(1).

where it is clear that the use demonstrated was made merely for the purpose of securing the exception with no intent for genuine use of the earlier GI in Singapore.

4.2.2 Registered or Protected Geographical Indications Owners under Geographical Indications Act 2014 and Existing Registered Trademark Owners

GIs and trademarks are similar in that both are badges of origin and they convey important information to the ultimate consumers about the products to which they are attached. Trademarks are source indicators of commercial origins in that they inform the consumers about the manufacturers or producers of the goods or services. GIs, on the other hand, do not identify a specific manufacturer or producer but make reference to a geographical location and the special attribute or reputation which is associated with that product by virtue of that geographical location. GIs and trademarks are, however, very different in the following aspects:

(i) Trademarks are personal property and are owned by individual commercial enterprises.[124] They may be assigned, licenced and pledged as collaterals to raise funds. In contrast, GIs are collectively owned by the producers in a demarcated geographical location who have the right to use them in relation to their products.[125] Thus, GIs are not personal property and cannot be dealt with in the same manner as trademarks.

(ii) Trademarks co-exist with the business enterprises that own them. If the business ceases, the trademarks are unlikely to be renewed. Furthermore, trademarks may be revoked if they fall into non-use.[126] On the other hand, GIs continue to exist for as long as the geographical locations to which the products owe their special qualities and reputation also exist.

The relationship between trademarks and GIs is an interesting one. Traditionally, trademark laws disallow signs denoting geographical locations to be registered on the grounds of public interest to ensure that such signs may be freely used by all and to prevent traders seeking to monopolize terms which are already common names in the public domain.[127] In the same vein, trademark laws provide as a defence to infringement the use of a sign 'to indicate the kind, quality, quantity, intended purpose, value, geographical origin or other

---

[124] See Trade Marks Act 1998 § 4.
[125] See NG-LOY WEE LOON, LAW OF INTELLECTUAL PROPERTY OF SINGAPORE [28.0.3] (2nd edn. 2014).
[126] Trade Marks Act 1998 § 22(1).   [127] Trade Marks Act 1938 § 10(1)(d).

characteristic of goods or services, the time of production of goods or of the rendering of services, subject to the condition that the use must be in accordance with honest practices in industrial or commercial matters'.[128] Recent exceptions to these trademark rules are collective marks,[129] certification marks[130] and GIs.

When the GI Act 2014 comes into force in Singapore, the interplay between the GI registration system and the trademark registration system may be summarized as follows:

1. Cumulative protection for a GI under the GI Act 2014 and the Trade Marks Act 1998 is possible. Thus, producers and associations with GIs will have an option as to whether to register their GIs under the GI Registry or as certification or collective marks under the Trade Marks Act 1998.
2. The registration of a GI may be refused if it is identical with or similar to (i) a *registered* trademark which was applied for or registered in good faith, or (ii) a trademark which was used in good faith in Singapore in the course of trade before the date of application for registration of the GI, where there exists a likelihood of confusion on the part of the public.[131]
3. The registration of a GI may also be refused if it is identical or similar to a trademark and the trademark is, before the date of application for registration of the GI in Singapore, a well-known trademark in Singapore and registration of the GI is liable to mislead consumers as to the true identity of the goods identified by that GI.[132]
4. In general, a mark which consists of an indication of a geographical origin of the goods or services should not be the monopoly of any particular trader, and by virtue of Section 7(1)(c) of the Trade Marks Act 1998,[133] such a mark is not registrable unless it has in fact acquired a distinctive character as a result of the use made of it. However, when the new GI registration system comes into force, the Trade Marks Act 1998 will be amended to include a new Section 7(10A) that precludes a trademark

---

[128] Trade Marks Act 1998 § 7(1)(c).
[129] A collective mark is a sign used, or intended to be used, in relation to goods or service dealt with or provided in the course of trade by members of an association to distinguish those goods or services from goods or services so dealt with or provided by persons who are not members of the association. See id. § 60(1).
[130] A certification mark is a sign used, or intended to be used, to distinguish goods or services (a) dealt with or provided in the course of trade; and (b) certified by the proprietor of the certification mark in relation to origin, material, mode of manufacture of goods or performance of services, quality, accuracy or other characteristics, from other goods or services dealt with or provided in the course of trade but not so certified. See id. § 61(1).
[131] See GI Act 2014 § 41(4)–(5).   [132] See id. § 41(6).   [133] Trade Marks Act 1998 § 7(1)(c).

which has acquired a distinctive character as a result of the use made of it before the date of application for registration from being registered if (a) it contains or consists of a GI which is registered or in respect of which an application has been made before the date of application of the trademark; and (b) the goods for which the trademark is sought to be registered are identical or similar to that for which the GI is registered or sought to be registered, and do not originate in the place indicated by the GI.[134]

5. A mark which consists of an indication of geographical origin of the goods or services may be registered as a collective mark under Section 60 of the Trade Marks Act 1998.[135] Registrability of a collective mark is subject to the same absolute and relative grounds for refusal in Sections 7 and 8 of the Trade Marks Act 1998 as for 'ordinary' trademarks.[136] However, the proprietor of such a mark is not entitled to prohibit the use of the signs or indications in accordance with honest practices in industrial or commercial matters, in particular by a person who is entitled to use a geographical name.[137]

6. Registrability of certification marks is also subject to the same absolute and relative grounds for refusal in Sections 7 and 8 of the Trade Marks Act 1998 for 'ordinary' trademarks.[138] An exception to Section 7(1)(c) of the Trade Marks Act 1998 has been created in the case of a certification mark,[139] just like that of collective marks, such that even if the certification mark may consist of an indication of a geographical origin of the goods or services, it may nevertheless be so registered. However, the registration does not entitle the proprietor of a certification mark to prohibit the use of the sign by a third party in accordance with honest practices in industrial or commercial matters.[140]

4.2.3 Registered or Protected Geographical Indications Owners under Geographical Indications Act 2014 and Users of Signs Identical with or Similar to These Geographical Indications

Under Section 4 of the GI Act 2014, the use of a registered GI or a GI protected under the Act such as one which identifies a wine or spirit is prohibited, and any interested party may take legal action against such unauthorized use. The remedies for infringement of a registered GI or a GI protected under the GI Act 2014 include injunctions and damages or an account of profits.[141]

---

[134] *See* GI Act 2014 § 90(c). [135] Trade Marks Act 1998 § 60.
[136] *Id.*, §§ 7–8 which cover grounds of refusal of registration. [137] *See id.* sched. 1, para. 3(2).
[138] *Id.* § 60. [139] *See id.* sched. 2, § 3(1). [140] *See* sched. 2, § 3(2). [141] GI Act 2014 § 5.

The use of a GI includes the use of a trademark which contains or consists of the GI in question.[142]

However, an exception is created in the case of a prior user of a trademark which is identical or similar to a GI if the prior user has continuously used that trademark in good faith before 15 January 1999 or before the GI in question is protected in its country or territory of origin.[143]

5 CONCLUSION

Undoubtedly, Singapore's ratification of several significant international IP treaties and conventions is an important driving force in the rapid development of Singapore's IP legal infrastructure. At the same time, free trade agreements to which Singapore is a signatory have also played a significant role in shaping Singapore's IP legal landscape in recent years. We have seen the impact of free trade agreements on IP laws since the conclusion of the US-Singapore Free Trade Agreement in 2003 (US-Singapore FTA).[144] As a result of the US-Singapore FTA, the regulatory framework for IP protection in Singapore has undergone substantial reforms in 2004,[145] spanning across areas of copyrights and trademarks. Pursuant to her obligations under the US-Singapore FTA, Singapore has basically subscribed to a framework of protection of GIs which allows registration of signs including words associated with GIs as trademarks (subject to certain restrictions),[146] and the person who registers the trademark associated with the GI first in time and who has successfully overcome opposition proceedings, if any, shall have the right to be protected.

A decade later in 2013, when Singapore concluded the negotiations on the EU-Singapore FTA, the stage was set once again for changes in IP laws with the most significant changes taking place in the area of GIs. The EU protects GIs with a specialized and extensive registration system that offers an enhanced protection. In the free trade agreements which the EU has previously entered into with South Korea and Canada, detailed provisions on the establishment of a registration system and various aspects of enhanced protection to be accorded to wines, spirits and other agricultural products can be found in the intellectual

---

[142] *See* GI Act 2014 § 4(4).   [143] *See* GI Act 2014 § 12(2).

[144] United State-Singapore Free Trade Agreement, U.S.-Sing., May 6, 2003, [hereinafter US-Singapore FTA], https://ustr.gov/sites/default/files/uploads/agreements/fta/singapore/asset_upload_file708_4036.pdf.

[145] For example, the Trade Marks (Amendment) Act 2004 introduced several important changes to the Trade Marks Act 1998, including the concept of trademark dilution in the case of trademarks well known to the public at large in Singapore.

[146] *See* US-Singapore FTA, art. 16.2.

property chapters. The EU-Singapore FTA is no exception and Singapore has agreed to establish a Registry for GIs even though Singapore does not have any GIs of her own for which protection is sought.[147] Before the adoption of the GI Act 2014, protection for GIs in Singapore was comparable to the level set out in TRIPS even in the absence of a registration system. Once the GI Act 2014 is brought into force, protection for GIs in Singapore will be significantly enhanced with the establishment of a dedicated GI Registry.

Admittedly, the registration of GIs in Singapore, in particular the automatic recognition and protection to a list of key EU GIs if accepted, would have a far-reaching impact on existing GI users and trademark owners. However, to minimize the impact of the change brought forth by the new law on GI protection, the Singapore government negotiated the EU-Singapore FTA and secured the agreement from the EU that there will be no automatic recognition and protection to a list of key EU GIs but that Singapore will be allowed to develop its own GI registration system. The list of key EU GIs will be subject to examination by the new GI Registry, and third parties who object to their registrations on the grounds of genericness would be given the opportunity to do so under the law. This may be seen as a significant break-through in trade negotiations on GIs, and may offer a 'middle way' in the resolution of divergent attitudes towards GI protection amongst countries. The Singapore government should be commended for her attempts to create a fair model of protection which, it is hoped, will better balance the interests of GI owners and legitimate GI users in general. Be that as it may, it should also be noted that the Singapore model is, however, the exception rather than the norm and that the arrangements of the EU-Singapore FTA for GIs 'reflect the fact that Singapore's legislation does not permit direct protection of geographical indications via the Agreement, and underlines that this does not constitute *a precedent*'.[148]

The implementation of the changes brought forth by the GI Act 2014 is unfortunately delayed as the EU-Singapore FTA is still awaiting ratification by the EU Parliament.[149] In a recent report in July 2015,[150] Prime Minister Lee

---

[147] See *supra* note 103.

[148] See *id*. (emphasis added) (explicitly stating the EU's stance on this matter).

[149] Although the EU and Singapore concluded the FTA in October 2014, there is uncertainty as to how the legal agreement should be classified. More importantly, an opinion of the Court of Justice of the European Union (CJEU) needs to clarify whether it is an agreement which the EU has exclusive competence to sign and to ratify or whether it is a 'mixed agreement' which requires the approval of every single parliament in every single Member State before the agreement can be ratified. The EU Commission has since made a request for a CJEU legal opinion on the precise legal status of the EU-Singapore FTA. See Council Directive C332/45, 2015 O.J. C 332 45–46. The CJEU's opinion will be awaited with interest.

[150] Jamie Lee, *Ratification of EU-Singapore FTA Would Encourage EU-ASEAN Trade Deal: PM Lee*, BUSINESS TIMES (29 July 2015 3:48 PM), www.businesstimes.com.sg/government-economy/ratification-of-eu-singapore-fta-would-encourage-eu-asean-trade-deal-pm-lee.

Hsien Loong was of the view that a ratification of the EU-Singapore FTA would encourage an ASEAN-EU FTA deal, and he was quoted to say 'Singapore is the *bellwether*. If you can do one with Singapore, I think that will encourage other deals to come in, including the ASEAN-EU deal.'[151] Of course, it remains to be seen whether the Singapore model on the protection of GIs will be accepted by the EU through the ratification of the EU-Singapore FTA and whether it will pave the way for a middle-ground approach where countries of differing views on GI protection may agree to meet each other half way.

---

[151] *Transcript of Prime Minister Lee Hsien Loong's Remarks at the Joint Press Conference with UK Prime Minister David Cameron on 29 July 2015*, PRIME MINISTER'S OFFICE, www.pmo.gov.sg/mediacentre/transcript-prime-minister-lee-hsien-loongs-remarks-joint-press-conference-uk-prime (last visited 9 October 2015).

PART III

THE PROMISE AND PROBLEMS OF GEOGRAPHICAL INDICATIONS FOR LOCAL AND RURAL DEVELOPMENT

11

Sunshine in a Bottle? Geographical Indications, the Australian Wine Industry, and the Promise of Rural Development

Peter Drahos*

1 INTRODUCTION

Running through the various detailed justifications for intellectual property is a grand promise. By enacting laws that confer some degree of exclusivity over intangibles such as knowledge, data, and information, a country is promised a better future. In the case of geographical indications (GIs) the promise is of rural development. The recitals to a 1992 Council Regulation of the European Community, which set up a framework for registering GIs relating to agricultural products and foodstuffs, imply this promise, suggesting that GIs could improve farmer income and help keep people in 'less-favoured or remote areas'.[1]

A regulatory tool that promises to improve the lot of the poor, especially the rural poor, deserves serious attention. With more and more of the world's population moving into cities, governments everywhere are interested in policy ideas that will help keep some people in agricultural production. In the case of the European Union's (EU) twenty-eight members, some 23 per cent of the population live in rural regions.[2] More and more people, and not just Europeans, are looking to participate in the economic life of cities. More of us are drawn to shopping malls than barns.

---

* Professor, RegNet School of Regulation and Global Governance, Australian National University; Chair in Intellectual Property, Queen Mary University of London.
[1] *See* Council Regulation (EEC) No 2081/92 of 14 July 1992 on the Protection of Geographical Indications and Designations of Origin for Agricultural Products and Foodstuffs, 1992 O.J. (L 208) 1.
[2] *Urban-intermediate-rural Regions*, EUROSTAT PRESS OFFICE (30 March 2012), http://ec.euro pa.eu/eurostat/documents/2995521/5150318/1-30032012-BP-EN.PDF.

The EU's advocacy for more international protection for GIs is well known. It was the EU that put forward draft text for the protection of GIs at the beginning of the negotiations of what became the Agreement on Trade-Related Aspects of Intellectual Property Rights (TRIPS) 1994.[3] Since then, the EU has continued to pursue protection for its GIs through preferential trade negotiations.[4]

One of the first countries to negotiate with the EU over protection of its wine GIs was Australia. After long negotiations that began in the 1980s, Australia and the EU signed an agreement in 1994 to regulate the wine trade between them (1994 Agreement).[5] A replacement agreement was signed in 2008, coming into force in 2010.[6] These agreements were entered into because Australia needed better access to the EU's wine market and in particular wanted to provide consumers with more information on wine labels relating to matters of vintage, variety, and production.[7] Australia enacted legislation in 1993 that would protect the wine GIs of EU countries, as well as allow Australian wine producers to apply for GIs.[8]

At the time of the negotiations, many on the Australian side, especially those in government, saw national GI systems in Europe as part of the protectionist agricultural policies of the EU. During this time, Australia was one of the leaders of the Cairns Group, the group that was leading the charge to liberalize trade in agriculture in the Uruguay Round of multilateral trade negotiations.[9] The belief that GIs were examples of a larger picture of the over-regulation of the EU wine sector is understandable keeping in mind that since 1962 more than 2,000 directives, regulations, and decisions concerning wine in the EU

---

[3] UNCTAD-ICTSD, RESOURCE BOOK ON TRIPS AND DEVELOPMENT 279 (2005) (ebook).
[4] *See, e.g.*, Comprehensive Economic and Trade Agreement, Can.-EU, Consolidated CETA Text, ch. 22, Intellectual Property, 26 September 2014, http://trade.ec.europa.eu/doclib/docs/2014/september/tradoc_152806.pdf; *see also* Irene Calboli, *Expanding the Protection of Geographical Indications of Origin under TRIPS: 'Old' Debate or 'New' Opportunity?*, 10 MARQ. INTELL. PROP. L. REV. 181 (2006).
[5] Agreement between Australia and the European Community on Trade in Wine, and Protocol, Austl.-EU, *opened for signature* 26 January 1994, 1820 U.N.T.C. 3 (entered into force 1 March 1994).
[6] Agreement between Australia and the European Community on Trade in Wine, Austl.-EU, 1 December 2008, [2010] A.T.S. 19 (entered into force 1 September 2010).
[7] Explanatory Memorandum, Australian Wine and Brandy Corporation Amendment Bill 1993 (Cth) 2.
[8] The *Australian Wine and Brandy Corporation Act 1980* was amended in 1993 to provide a system of protection for GIs. See *Australian Wine and Brandy Corporation Amendment Act 1993 (Cth)*.
[9] DONALD KENYON & DAVID LEE, THE STRUGGLE FOR TRADE LIBERALISATION IN AGRICULTURE: AUSTRALIA AND THE CAIRNS GROUP IN THE URUGUAY ROUND (2006).

have been published.[10] At the same time, the trade incentives for Australia to continue negotiating with the EU over GIs were and remain strong. For example, in 2007–2008 the European Community accounted for about 50 per cent of Australia's wine exports, worth about $1.3 billion.[11]

In any case, Australia's enactment of a wine GI system did set up a natural experiment in which Australia's wine regions would become test sites for whether or not GIs contribute to regional development. By definition, natural experiments are not run under laboratory conditions. Australia did not copy a European GI model but rather, taking into account the circumstances of the Australian wine industry, it developed its own model of protection. Perhaps the most important aspect of those circumstances was that an export boom had begun in the late 1980s, well and truly before Australia's GI legislation came into operation in 1994.[12] As we will see, Australia's wine GI system represents an experiment with a minimalist model of GI regulation: one that can be contrasted with a French command-and-control model.

Little attention has been paid thus far as to whether or not Australia's wine GI system has contributed to Australia's regional economies. One might argue that it was not designed to, but this does not necessarily mean that it has not had such effects in practice. In this chapter, I present the results of interview data with actors from the wine industry, including winemakers, wine associations, tourist associations, government officials (federal and state), and regulators. The interviews with winemakers took place in some of Australia's premium wine growing regions (Tasmania and the Yarra Valley in Victoria) as well as regions that were generally not regarded as such (e.g. Southern Queensland). The data are part of a bigger project carried out with William van Caenegem and Jen Cleary that examined the issue of whether Australia should enact a GI system for food.[13] However, in this chapter I am concerned with the narrower question of whether there is evidence of regional developmental benefits that might be attributed to Australia's wine GI system.

---

[10] Giulia Meloni & Johan Swinnen, *The Political Economy of European Wine Regulations* 3 (LICOS Ctr. for Insts. & Econ. Performance, Discussion Paper 320/2012, 2012) https://feb.ku leuven.be/drc/licos/publications/dp/dp320.pdf.
[11] *See* Parliament of Australia, *Bills Digest*, No 21 of 2009–2010, 22 June 2009.
[12] *See* ROBERT OSMOND & KYM ANDERSON, TRENDS AND CYCLES IN THE AUSTRALIAN WINE INDUSTRY, 1850–2000 (1998), www.adelaide.edu.au/wine-econ/papers/Aust_Wine_Trends_ and_Cycles_1998.pdf.
[13] *See* WILLIAM VAN CAENEGEM ET AL., PROVENANCE OF AUSTRALIAN FOOD PRODUCTS: IS THERE A PLACE FOR GEOGRAPHICAL INDICATIONS? (2015), https://rirdc.infoservices.com.au/ items/15-060.

This is very much a micro-study, one grounded in the idea that there is merit in getting actors steeped in industry experience to exercise the wisdom of hindsight on critical issues such as the regional benefits of GIs. As with all micro-studies, there are limitations about its generalizability, but then I would argue that this is precisely the broader conclusion that one should come to about intellectual property. Its universal prescription as development medicine for countries sits at odds with the fact that it is an intervention into organic and local systems that respond very differently to the same medicine. The present case study does not point to regional development benefits, but rather it reveals the existence of mechanisms that explain how GIs might function to deliver regional benefits. Whether or not these mechanisms will operate is, as we will see, a matter of complex causal context. For example, lack of trust in a rural region can spoil the best-designed GI system. Wine has economic characteristics that many other products do not have, setting another potential limitation on what might be inferred from the present study.

The remainder of this chapter sets out the Australian GI scheme, including its costs and enforcement. If one were to summarize the Australian system in tweetable form, it is that 'flexibility rules'. After the sections on the GI scheme, there follows a section on how various actors in the wine industry view GIs. The remaining sections discuss the link between GIs and regional development, identifying two mechanisms – reciprocal spillovers and group identity – that suggest how a GI might help regional development.

2 AUSTRALIA'S SYSTEM OF GEOGRAPHICAL INDICATIONS FOR WINE

The wine industry in Australia is the only industry that has the option of registering a GI under legislation specially dedicated to that purpose, namely Part VIB of the *Australian Grape and Wine Authority Act 2013* (AGWA Act). Under the AGWA Act, the Geographical Indications Committee (GIC) has powers of determination to decide applications for GIs.[14] The Act lists organizations that may apply for a GI and it specifies that a winemaker or grower of grapes may make an application. The detailed criteria for

---

[14] See Australian Grape and Wine Authority Act 2013 (Cth) ss 40P–40Q [hereinafter AGWA Act 2013]. Sub-section 40Q(1) gives the GIC the power to 'determine a geographical indication'. The same sub-section allows the GIC to determine a GI 'on its own initiative'. In determining a GI, the GIC has to identify the boundaries of the GI area, decide on the indication, and, if relevant, set conditions of use. See AGWA Act 2013, s 40T(1).

determination are prescribed in the relevant regulations.[15] These criteria include geological, climatological, cultural, and historical factors.[16]

Lying at the heart of a GI system is the delineation of the boundaries of an area and the decision on the indication to be used in relation to that area. Boundaries have to be described as accurately as possible because these descriptions would be included in the Register of Protected GIs and would become the legal basis for deciding whether, for example, someone has made a false claim on a wine label.[17] By way of example, the description on the GI Register for 'South Eastern Australia' is as follows:

> The beginning point of the boundary is located at the intersection of the Tropic of Capricorn and the eastern coastline of Australia and proceeds thence in a generally south west direction in a straight line to the intersection of the Queensland / New South Wales State borders with the State border of South Australia at the location identified on the map as 'Cameron Corner', and proceeds thence in a generally south west direction in a straight line to the intersection of the South Australia coastline with the Great Australian Bight (Southern Ocean) passing through the centre of the township of Ceduna in South Australia.
>
> The area so enclosed includes all of the State of New South Wales, all of the State of Victoria, all of the State of Tasmania, all of the Australian Capital Territory, and those parts of the State of Queensland lying to the south and the east of the described boundary, and those parts of the State of South Australia lying to the south and the east of the described boundary, and all of those off-shore islands under Australian Government control lying to the south and east of the described boundary.[18]

There is something else to note about this GI: its extraordinary size. It includes, for example, the State of New South Wales, a state bigger than France in terms of square kilometres (800,642 square kilometres compared to 549,087).[19] The State of New South Wales is itself a registered GI and within

---

[15] See, e.g., Australian Grape and Wine Authority Regulations 1981 (Cth) reg. 25 [hereinafter AGWA Regulations 1981].

[16] See id.

[17] The offence of false description is dealt with in sections 40C and 40D of the AGWA Act.

[18] Section 40ZB requires the Registrar to keep a Register of Protected Geographical Indications and Other Terms. The register can be searched electronically. See Register of Protected GIs and Other Terms, WINE AUSTRALIA, www.wineaustralia.com/en/Production%2oand%20Exporting/Register%20of%20Protected%20GIs%20and%20Other%20Terms.aspx [hereinafter Register].

[19] Land Areas of States and Territories, AUSTRALIAN GOVERNMENT: GEOSCIENCE AUSTRALIA, www.ga.gov.au/scientific-topics/national-location-information/dimensions/area-of-australia-states-and-territories (figure for New South Wales); Surface Area, THE WORLD BANK, http://data.worldbank.org/indicator/AG.SRF.TOTL.K2 (figure for France).

New South Wales there are a number of registered GIs, the most well-known being the Hunter Valley.[20] With GIs that enclose areas the size of large European countries, there is little plausibility to the claim that there is a distinctive set of qualities imparted by the locality to a particular wine. The system was not designed to bring *terroir* into a close regulatory association with the production of wine, but rather had a market-access goal. This is clear from the Explanatory Memorandum to the *Australian Wine and Brandy Corporation Amendment Act 1993* when it states that in order 'to enable wine labelled by region to be marketed in the EC, the boundaries of Australian geographical indications concerned must be defined'.[21] The fact that large country-like GIs of the size of 'South Eastern Australia' were created meant that no Australian wine producers would be left out of a GI region and therefore access to the EC market.

The rules that govern the use of a wine GI registered in Australia are straightforward compared to those found in many European systems, especially the French appellation system appellation d'origine contrôlée (AOC). The French system allows obligatory rules to be prescribed for many things, including allowable grape varieties within a region, minimum levels of alcohol, production methods, maximum yield levels, and methods of harvesting.[22] The purpose behind this detailed prescription is to ensure the production of a wine of good quality from grapes that best fit the *terroir* of the area. The regulation of yield in the French system is one important element of a scheme aimed at maintaining a standard of quality. Regulating yield was probably one of the last things on the minds of the Australian designers of the GI system in the boom years of the 1990s. The Australian wine GI system is a simple system concerned with the regional designation of grapes and is silent on processes about which the French system is vocal. The principal regulatory tool in Australia is a Label Integrity Program[23] (LIP) that includes GI labelling but with the GI system not specifying standards aimed at quality.

In Australia there is no obligation to use a GI, but where a single GI such as 'McClaren Vale' is used, at least 85 per cent of the wine must have come from grapes grown in the region defined by the registered GI.[24] Multiple GIs can

---

[20] See Register, *supra* note 18.   [21] See Explanatory Memorandum, *supra* note 7, at para 5.
[22] See William van Caenegem, *Registered Geographical Indications: Between Intellectual Property and Rural Policy* – Part I, 6 J. OF WORLD INTELL. PROP. 699–719 (2003); *see also* William van Caenegem, *Registered Geographical Indications: Between Intellectual Property and Rural Policy* – Part II, 6 J. OF WORLD INTELL. PROP. 861–874 (2003).
[23] See AGWA Act 2013, *supra* note 14, pt. VIA.
[24] See AGWA Regulations 1981, *supra* note 15, reg. 21.

also be claimed, though only up to a maximum of three in total.[25] In the case of multiple claims, the basic rule is that 95 per cent of the wine must have come from grapes grown in those regions, with at least 5 per cent of the wine coming from each region.[26]

The Australian GI system takes a strict bright-line approach to GIs, its aim being to contribute to the greater goal of ensuring 'the truth, and the reputation for truthfulness, of statements made on wine labels'.[27] For example, the Australian Grape and Wine Authority's guide to labelling with GIs makes clear that

> [s]tatements such as 'our winery is situated in McLaren Vale' when the particular wine in question is not from McLaren Vale are not permitted, even if true and even if supplemented by clarifying information.[28]

The 85 per cent rule means that there is some flexibility in terms of sourcing grapes since, if required, up to 15 per cent can come from outside the region. If so, there is no requirement for this to be mentioned on the label. Similarly, there is no obligation under GI rules to process the grapes in the region in which they are grown.[29]

The Australian wine GI system, because it relies only on rules of origin and imposes no other standards, does set up a potential free-rider problem. A small group of winemakers within a region may work hard to create a reputation for quality through the adoption of best-practice methods and drawing on the strong innovation base of the industry. In the absence of detailed prescribed standards, there is nothing to stop someone from buying into the region, making a lower-quality wine, but being able to use the GI to market the wine because they have sourced 85 per cent of the grapes from the region. It is clear from the interviews that at least some winemakers see the reputation of a region as depending on a small pool of excellent producers: 'Six out of 50 wineries are excellent [in the region], there are about 10 other wineries that are good' (Respondent #16).

At the time the rules of the Australian GI system were being talked about, the industry produced wines of varying quality and price. A number of interviewees pointed out that in order to accommodate this diversity a 'keep it simple' approach was adopted. The GI system was not intended to be a barrier

---

[25] See id.   [26] See id.   [27] See AGWA Act 2013, *supra* note 14, s 39A.
[28] See, e.g., *Labelling*, WINE AUSTRALIA, www.wineaustralia.com/en/Production%20and%20E xporting/Labelling.aspx.
[29] This follows from the fact that neither the AGWA Act 2013 nor its regulations require processing within a GI region.

to entry into the industry. Rather than using formal rules and sanctions to set a standard of wine production in a region, the industry has pursued quality in other ways. For example, the interviews showed that important to the drive for quality at the regional level have been informal social mechanisms such as tasting groups organized by winemakers – places where they can have an 'honest conversation about the quality issue' (Respondent #15). Such groups provide new entrants into a region with information, constructive feedback, support, and the opportunity to win recognition through competing for prizes. The aim has been to socialize those who are interested into a culture of quality production rather than prescribe it through law. According to our interviewees, the Australian approach to GIs has helped the industry to grow. A highly prescriptive system might have functioned as a deterrent. In the words of one interviewee:

> How would it have been if people were allowed to say 'mate you're not good enough to get into this even though you grow your fruit here'? (Respondent #94)

3 ENFORCEMENT

As we have seen, the regulatory footprint of Australia's GI system, in terms of rules, is light. Nevertheless, if a GI system is to win the trust of consumers, producers have to follow its rules. This is something well understood by the Australian wine industry. In the words of the industry regulator, the Australian Grape and Wine Authority (AGWA):

> Australia is increasingly recognised as an abundant source of regionally distinctive wines made from an array of both traditional and recently introduced grape varieties. Maintaining the integrity of region and variety claims has, therefore, never been more important.[30]

This in turn raises questions about how compliance with the rules is best achieved, how breaches of the rules are to be detected, and what the strategies for enforcement should be. AGWA provides information and educational services to the wine industry about its labelling obligations. It also has responsibility for monitoring compliance with the LIP, GI claims forming part of that program.[31] The LIP imposes record-keeping obligations on those in the wine supply chain.[32] In addition, AGWA has a range of sanctions available under

---

[30] See *Regulatory Services*, WINE AUSTRALIA.
[31] Part VIA of the AGWA Act 2013 contains provisions relating to the Label Integrity Program.
[32] AGWA Act 2013, *supra* note 14, s 39F.

the law, including the suspension or cancellation of an export licence, as well as terms of imprisonment and/or fines.[33]

Compliance with the LIP is monitored by a small group of auditors (a total of four at the time of the interviews).[34] This audit team aims to cover all Australian wine producers once every three to four years. Audits may be done via cold-calls or by appointment. Wine producers are obliged to keep detailed records that help to ensure full traceability because traceability is one of the things that compliance inspectors comment on in their audit reports. Auditors appear to follow what is known in the regulatory literature as an enforcement pyramid. The key idea behind the pyramid is that punishment and persuasion should be linked in a certain sequence that always begins with dialogue and persuasion at the base of the pyramid and ends with the most punitive sanction at the apex of the pyramid.[35] At the time of the interviews, approximately 400 audits were being carried out annually. Resorting to coercive levels of the enforcement pyramid by the regulator appeared to be rare, with few licence suspensions and only two prosecutions in the last fifteen years (Respondent #104). Only one of those prosecutions related to alleged breaches of provisions relating to GIs (Respondent #104). A lot of the effort invested in obtaining compliance takes the form of presentations, advice, and the provision of manuals and templates to wine producers and exporters.

4 COSTS

There is a range of costs that accompanies the wine GI system: the costs of application, the costs of running the system, and the ongoing costs of compliance. The costs begin with a group's time in putting together an application for the determination of a GI. These costs include a fee and those arising from assembling the evidence/information required as part of the application

---

[33] AGWA Regulations 1981, *supra* note 15, reg 9 (dealing with the suspension and cancellation of licences). Offences along with their respective penalties and/or fines are in the case of the LIP contained in Part VIA of the AGWA Act 2013 and in Part VIB in the case of the misuse of GIs.

[34] The information in this paragraph concerning the operation of the audit system was obtained from interviewing members of AGWA. Details of the audit system are also available from Wine Australia. *Regulatory Services Quality Manual*, WINE AUSTRALIA (June 2015), www.wineaustralia.com/en/~/media/ooooIndustry%20Site/Documents/Production%20and%20Exporting/Label%20Integrity%20Program/Regulatory%20Services%20Quality%20Manual%20June%202015.ashx.

[35] IAN AYRES AND JOHN BRAITHWAITE, RESPONSIVE REGULATION: TRANSCENDING THE DEREGULATION DEBATE 35–38 (1992).

process. The application fee is currently set at $27,500, a fee that approximates the average cost of the GIC hearing an application (Respondents #103 and #104). The fees for wine GIs have changed over time. Initially they were met out of industry levies and then were kept at a low rate (Respondent #104). The potentially deterrent effect of the present fee was seen as a desirable consequence by many interviewees.

The real costs of application, however, lie in the evidence that is required to convince the GIC that it should determine the boundaries of a GI. The applicant has to provide evidence on matters such as the history of an area, its discreteness, and homogeneity by reference to attributes such as climate and geology, all of which require expert evidence (Respondent #94). Estimates from the interviews suggest that such costs amount to tens of thousands of dollars. Costs might rise to a six-figure sum if, for example, there is opposition to the GI from a trademark owner. This sum might be larger still if, as in the case of the dispute over the determination of the boundary for the Coonawarra GI in South Australia, the matter ends up before the Federal Court with many years of legal expenses having to be met.

The Coonawarra saga is a spectacular example of a bitter and prolonged dispute over a GI boundary, but it is also something of an outlier.[36] Settling GI boundaries has been a story of consensus rather than conflict. Most other Australian GI boundaries were determined without recourse to battalions of lawyers and appeals to the Federal Court (Respondent #94). One reason may be that before the introduction of the formal GI system, some winemakers in Australia were organizing themselves on a regional basis and so perhaps there was, at least in some regions, a customary sense of boundaries. For example, there were about six regional wine associations in Victoria in the 1980s (Respondent #151). Also in the 1980s some winemakers had organized an appellation program in Tasmania (Respondent #128).

5 PERCEPTIONS OF GEOGRAPHICAL INDICATIONS

As the quote from AGWA in Section 3 suggests, many people in the wine industry believe that GI regions are important. How important turns out to be difficult to say, and the reasons vary among regions and participants. Two perspectives on wine GIs emerged from the interviews. One was a winemaker's perspective that, not surprisingly, looked to the role of GIs in helping to define

---

[36] See Gary Edmond, *Disorder with Law: Determining the Geographical Indication for the Coonawarra Wine Region*, 27 ADEL. L. REV. 59 (2006).

and communicate the connection between the region and the wine. The other was a marketing perspective in which assessing the value of GIs comes down to answering one simple question about them: 'does the consumer care?' (Respondent #128).

If we look to consumer preferences as a guide to the importance of GIs, separating the influence of region from a range of other purchasing influences such as age, awards, brand, expert or other recommendation, price, previous experience, and so on, it is not clear where region sits in a ranking exercise. Studies suggest that region is probably recurrently important, but how important is difficult to isolate.[37] The answer is likely to vary depending on which segment of the consumer market is being studied.

Those interviewed tended to think that GIs were needed above a certain price point: 'From $15.00 onwards you need a region' (Respondent #158). Others nominated higher price levels. GIs had a 'halo effect' that 'helped 5%–10% of the export market' for Australian producers (Respondent #151). The importance of GIs in export markets was linked to the increase in value of the Australian dollar: '[We] got priced out of the low-end market because of the rise in the dollar. [We] make more on a £10 bottle and there the "Yarra Valley" region makes the difference' (Respondent #163).

The interviews with those in the wine industry who took a marketing perspective on GIs tended to confirm the difficulty of isolating the effects of regions on consumer purchasing decisions. Some interviewees made the point that industry surveys showed that the recall by Australian consumers of even high-profile GIs, such as the Barossa, the Hunter Valley, and Coonawarra, is weak and essentially non-existent for many lesser Australian GIs. Amongst consumers in international markets there is also very little recall of Australian GIs. The survey results reported by interviewees (internal and not published) would have many winemakers reaching for antidepressants. There is 'massive ignorance and confusion out there' when it comes to GIs with consumers, according to one survey, thinking that Chardonnay and Jacobs were GIs (Respondents #103, #104, and #171). In Europe, consumer awareness of the European GI scheme was also reported as being very low, with only 8 per cent of consumers recognizing the relevant symbols.[38] This is a telling example, as it shows how difficult it is to familiarize consumers with new GI label

---

[37] Steve Goodman et al., *Wine Marketing: What Influences Consumer Selection in the Retail Store?*, THE AUSTRALIAN & NEW ZEALAND GRAPEGROWER & WINEMAKER, December 2006, at 61–63, www.adelaide.edu.au/wine-future/research/fields/consumer_knowledge/Goodman_Lockshin_Cohen_GW_2006.pdf.

[38] Eur. Ct. of Auditors, *Do the Design and Management of the Geographical Indications Scheme Allow It to Be Effective?*, Special report No 11/ 2011 (15 November 2011).

categories (in this case, the protected designation of origin (PDO) and protected geographical indication (PGI) symbols). Extolling the virtues of GIs is much easier if one is growing one's grapes in Burgundy.

The interviews also suggested that the export success of Australia's wine industry in the 1990s was built around the application of modern brand-building techniques that allowed the winemakers of the New World to communicate with European consumers in ways that caused the Old World to sniff with disdain. At the core of this marketing success was the image of Australia itself: a place that could pour sunshine into wine bottles from where it could be released like a genie to brighten the gloomiest European day.[39] The marketing of Yellow Tail wines is a good example of the kind of creative strategy that was employed. Yellow Tail is reported to sell more in the US market than all French producers combined.[40]

Australian GIs were not central to this marketing strategy. The Australian wine export figures for the period 1989–1998 show remarkable growth, with an average increase of 26 per cent per year.[41] They also show that Australia's export success was occurring well before the introduction of the GI system. GIs functioned as a Trojan horse allowing the Australian industry to gain greater access to European consumers. Once in the market, the combination of quality, price, and marketing of Australian wine did the rest.

It is probably also fair to say that GIs became progressively more important in the wine industry's thinking as it considered its future. One interviewee, a winemaker and leader within the wine industry, referred to the 1996 publication *Strategy 2025*, describing it as a long-term vision for the Australian industry that included an important role for GIs. In his words, 'We didn't want to be the wool industry. If we'd taken the path of the wool industry we'd be shipping tankards of fermented grape juice' (Respondent #151).

Some eleven years later, the growing emphasis on GIs and regions can be seen in the AGWA's 2007 publication *Directions to 2025*:

> Today, Australian wine is rightly best known for its Brand Champions. We will be able to consider the job near-done when we can say the same for our

---

[39] The story of this marketing success is entertainingly told in the ABC documentary *Chateau Chunder. Chateau Chunder*, ABC TELEVISION (17 December 2015), www.abc.net.au/tv/programs/chateauchunder.htm.

[40] Mike Veseth, *[Yellow Tail] Tales*, THE WINE ECONOMIST (26 February 2008), http://wineeconomist.com/2008/02/26/the-yellow-tail-tale/.

[41] Andy Hira & David Aylward, *Australia as a Triple Helix Exemplar: Built upon a Foundation of Resource and Institutional Coordination and Strategic Consensus*, 31 PROMETHEUS 399, 402 (2013).

Regional Heroes – wines which reflect the remarkable number of successful combinations of classic grape varieties with Australian wine regions.[42]

And even more recently, AGWA, outlining its strategic plan for 2015–2020 in a discussion paper, indicated that 'increasing the demand and premium paid for Australian wine' was a key strategic priority to be underpinned by research into 'Australia's unique terroirs' and compliance with its labelling laws.[43]

There was a strongly held view amongst interviewees that having too many new GIs could create marketing problems. Australia's well-known GIs were reputable wine regions before they became GIs. The Barossa Valley, McLaren Vale, the Hunter Valley, the Yarra Valley, and Rutherglen grew in prominence as wine regions throughout the twentieth century. These regions progressively changed from an exclusive reliance on producing cheap fortified wine and bulk wine to making improved quality table wine, particularly as better grape varieties were developed and the industry placed more emphasis on technological innovation of all kinds.[44] When Australia adopted the GI system, these regions had the benefit of sunk reputational costs. Taking a largely unknown region and turning it into a consumer brand is a much more difficult and expensive exercise irrespective of whether or not the region is defined by a GI. Some GIs were described as 'unwieldy and impossible' (Respondent #171). Thinking about how to lift some of Australia's GIs out of anonymity remains a marketing challenge for the wine industry.

Interviewees, whether speaking from a winemaker's perspective or a marketing perspective, were generally not in favour of a further sub-delineation of Australia's existing wine GIs. For example, Tasmania has been a registered GI since 1994 with no sub-regions appearing on the register. The Tasmanian winemakers interviewed saw no gains in the creation of GI sub-regions. They saw Tasmania as a strong and recognizable brand. They characterized their industry as a small industry that had to work together in order to grow and keep the focus on producing quality wines. Their worry was that sub-regional GIs might have a splintering effect on an industry that could not at this point in its evolution lose the cooperation it had achieved: 'At this stage of our maturity

---

[42] See Winemakers' Federation of Australia & Wine Australia, *Directions to 2025: An Industry Strategy for Sustainable Success* 14 (May 2007), www.wfa.org.au/assets/strategies-plans/pdfs/Directions-to-2025.pdf.

[43] Austl. Grape & Wine Auth., *Strategic Plan 2015–2020* 8 (Discussion Paper, 9 December 2014), http://research.wineaustralia.com/wp-content/uploads/2014/12/AGWA-Strategic-Plan-2015–2020-Discussion-Paper.pdf.

[44] Hira & Aylward, *supra* note 41, at 401.

we've got more to lose than to gain by going our own separate ways' (Respondent #128).

The wariness about sub-regional GIs was not confined to Tasmania. The view that Australia had enough wine GIs was reported by our interviewees to be a general view within the industry. That said, some interviewees in Tasmania and elsewhere did hint at the desire of some smaller winemakers to have their own identity, suggesting that there is at least some debate within the industry about sub-regional GIs. An overall view from the interviewees was that while sub-regions could certainly be identified, something not surprising given the size of Australia's wine GIs and the diversity of soils within those GIs, at this stage of the industry's growth it was better not to formalize those boundaries. Many winemakers saw themselves as still being in a learning and experimental phase: 'There's a lot of learning to identify the perfect single vineyard for growing grapes – it can take 100 years to work it all out.'

The more general lesson here is that if an industry is to work successfully with a GI system, it will have to arrive at a general consensus about its use, avoid its potentially destabilizing effects, and make it an ongoing part of its planning conversations. The Australian wine industry has many levels and institutional actors from the public, private, and research sectors that produce internal circles of deliberation and debate about its future.[45] From those internal circles it has been able to forge common strategic objectives that at first did not heavily prioritize GIs in the export boom years of the 1990s, but now with the boom well and truly over, do include a greater emphasis on GIs.

6 GEOGRAPHICAL INDICATIONS AND REGIONAL BENEFITS

Even if, as seems likely, GIs will come to play a more important role in the Australian wine industry in terms of marketing, more sales will not necessarily translate into significantly more income or benefits for a wine GI region in Australia. The test of the development benefits of a GI system, as the Council regulation referred to in the introduction makes clear, is encouraging people in rural areas to stay and improving their income. In the case of the Australian wine GI system there is no obligation to process the wine within the region. Continued mechanization and automation in the Australian wine industry will also affect local employment opportunities. Industry structure matters to

---

[45] Id. at 399.

the likelihood of regional benefits. Australia's wine companies are export-oriented, as well as part of global ownership structures.[46] Investment decisions by large wine companies are likely to be determined by a global-market perspective rather than a regional perspective. For example, Accolade Wines, Australia's largest wine company, has a presence in 115 countries and a business model based on brand investment and contracting with grape growers.[47]

The extent to which a GI improves the income of a wine region will also be deeply affected by market structures concerning distribution. For example, two supermarkets in Australia, Coles and Woolworths, dominate the retail grocery market and together account for some 70 per cent of domestic wine sales.[48] This structure makes for hard bargaining when it comes to winemakers selling their wine to these supermarkets. In the words of one of Australia's largest winemakers, 'they just taste and check with their calculators'. These retailers are also creating their own private label wines, placing even more pressure on the capacity of winemakers to improve their margins.[49] Even if some wine GIs result in a willingness by consumers to pay more for the wine, players other than individual winemakers may end up capturing those greater margins.

The Australian GI system was designed so as not to disturb the flexibility and diversity of the industry. Australia's GIs are, as pointed out earlier, like a set of very large Russian nesting dolls giving large wine companies a lot of flexibility when it comes to sourcing grapes and using GIs to indicate the source of the grapes. Large wine companies in Australia own about 20 per cent of the national vineyard estate, with the remainder in the hands of specialist grape growers and some small wineries.[50] In a recent submission to the Australian Senate, the Wine Grape Growers Association of Australia argued that the returns to their industry, which is most directly involved in regional

---

[46] Sixty-two per cent of industry volume is exported. See CENTAURUS PARTNERS, WINE INDUSTRY REPORT: EXPERT REPORT ON THE PROFITABILITY AND DYNAMICS OF THE AUSTRALIAN WINE INDUSTRY 5 (2013), www.wfa.org.au/assets/noticeboard/Expert-Review-Report.pdf. On the impact of globalization on the Australian industry, see D. K. Aylward & Michael Zanko, *Emerging Interorganizational Structures in the Australian Wine Industry: Implications for SMEs*, UNIV. OF WOLLONGONG RESEARCH ONLINE (2006), http://ro.uow.edu.au/cgi/viewcontent.cgi?article=1076&context=commpapers.

[47] See Accolade Wines, Submission No 26 to the Senate Standing Committees on Rural and Regional Affairs and Transport References, Parliament of Australia, *Inquiry into the Australian Grape and Wine Industry*, May 2015.

[48] CENTAURUS PARTNERS, *supra* note 46, at 26.   [49] See id.

[50] KIRI-GANAI RESEARCH PTY LTD, THE AUSTRALIAN WINE GRAPE INDUSTRY TAKING STOCK AND SETTING DIRECTIONS FINAL REPORT 49 (2006), http://wgga.com.au/wp-content/uploads/TSSD-final-report_27Dec2006.pdf.

employment, were affected by their members' relative lack of bargaining power with large wine companies.[51] GIs, one suspects, have made little impact on who gains how much out of the wine supply chain.

On the question of GIs and regional benefits, the interviews suggested two possible mechanisms that might help to answer the question of how a region might benefit from a GI. For convenience we can label these the reciprocal spillover mechanism and the group identity mechanism. The next two sections discuss each in turn.

7 RECIPROCAL SPILLOVERS

One wine region in which a number of interviews took place was in the Granite Belt (a registered GI), Queensland. Wine GIs do not commonly occur in Australia's north, but the Granite Belt, because of its elevation (600–1,000 metres) and soils, is quite suitable for viticulture. Centred on the town of Stanthorpe in Southern Queensland, the Granite Belt case study suggests that a registered GI may create regional development benefits beyond that of other more generic, region-specific, provenance branding options.

Queensland does not have a great or even good reputation for wine because its tropical and sub-tropical climate and soils are largely unsuitable for growing wine grapes, with the granite soils around the Stanthorpe area being an exception. The problem for the winemakers in the region was the reputation of Queensland wine; as long as they were under the banner of 'Queensland wine', success was limited. Queensland was simply not known as a traditional grape-growing area. Winemakers had to be skilled in creating interest in their product first and not mentioning Queensland in their marketing. One winemaker described how they explained the location of their winery in the Granite Belt to customers, commenting, 'notice how I don't use the word Queensland' (Respondent #18). The registration of the Granite Belt GI in 2002 was seen as an important breakthrough: 'it's given us our own identity' (Respondent #18).

In the interviews, the winemakers were very clear that it was the registration of a GI that had been crucial to their success. It created the opportunity for them to escape the poor reputation of Queensland wines. The Granite Belt GI became the basis for a marketing strategy for wine that allowed

---

[51] See Wine Grape Growers Australia, Submission No 30 to Senate Standing Committees on Rural and Regional Affairs and Transport, Parliament of Australia, *Inquiry into the Australian Grape and Wine Industry*, 18 June 2015.

winemakers to distinguish their wine from the rest of Queensland. It also became the basis for creating a broader identity for the region as a tourist destination. Importantly, there was an organizational vehicle that helped to back the promotion of the Granite Belt in the form of Granite Belt Wine and Tourism (GBWT), a peak local body representing wineries and other tourist operations.

According to interviewees, the GBWT works with the GI boundary as a guide for its promotional activities. These activities are funded from member levies and fees, with businesses being able to buy different promotional packages. Critical to the stability of the GBWT has been finding a fee structure acceptable to the different types of businesses involved. Establishing a regional identity was described as a 'slog' (Respondent #20). The challenges include settling on an identity, since there are always options, alternatives, and a diversity of views.

The Granite Belt wine GI seems to have played an important role in the region's growth by helping winemakers gain an independent identity and allowing them the opportunity to forge a reputation for the quality of their wines that was not distorted by an association with Queensland. As the region's wines began to achieve recognition for their quality, tourists became more interested in visiting the region. This in turn generated demand for food and accommodation services, services that both drew on the success of the wine industry and contributed to its drawing power. In this particular case, the GI was integral to a process of reciprocal spillovers in which the benefits of the wine GI spilled over into various other food and tourist ventures, which in turn created benefits for the local wine industry. This process of reciprocal spillovers has continued to intensify with the establishment of the Queensland College of Wine Tourism in the region, a specialist education and training provider relating to the wine tourism industry.

The Granite Belt case suggests that a GI may, under a set of conditions, help a region gain the benefits of reciprocal spillovers that might not otherwise occur. In the case of the Granite Belt two conditions emerged as crucial: distance to a large urban centre (Brisbane is three hours away by road) and the creation of an owner-operated regional marketing organization (the GBWT). In terms of the proximity to Brisbane, what emerged from the interviews was that the marketing focused upon the Granite Belt as a weekend destination rather than a day-trip destination. This had important implications for the accommodation businesses in the region. Without a regional marketing body the Granite Belt region would have enjoyed much less success. As one non-wine producer who was paying $1600 to GBWT pointed out, 'where would $1600 go if we had to market ourselves?' (Respondent #12).

Proximity to tourism was mentioned as a factor in other interviews in other regions. In the Yarra Valley one winemaker pointed out that Yarra Valley Shiraz grapes commanded a higher price than Grampian Shiraz grapes (the difference being in the range of $400–$600 per tonne), despite the excellence of the Grampian grapes (Respondent #164). He attributed this to the fact that the Grampians did not get the tourist exposure of the Yarra Valley. Conversely, if we consider the situation where no Granite Belt GI was registered and the winemakers in the region continued to operate under a Queensland identity, then on their own account they would have continued to struggle and the region would have attracted fewer tourists. The GI was important rather than some other marketing strategy based on a certification mark because of the precise in/out group effect of the GI, which is discussed in the next section.

The Granite Belt case study points to the possibility of a GI triggering or accelerating a process of reciprocal spillovers. It is not the only case study where the spillover process was observed. In the Yarra Valley an interviewee from a dairy observed that the success of Yarra Valley wine in China had also triggered an interest in other Yarra Valley products such as cheese.

One important issue is whether a product other than wine can trigger this spillover process. Wine is a complex cultural product. It can be a bulk commodity (beverage wine), as well as a Veblen good (a wine of excellent or superexcellent reputation), a term used by economists to describe the purchase of goods that are linked to social status. In the case of goods with Veblen attributes, consumers are prepared to pay more because these goods have status and cultural effects. More is being satisfied in the consumption of such goods than simply thirst or hunger. People are prepared to pay for wine-tour holidays and tell their friends about them, whereas apple-eating tours would perhaps not generate the same pattern of social reporting. The number of food products like wine that can generate strong reciprocal spillover effects may be quite restricted. The interviews revealed that the Granite Belt region does have a reputation for producing good apples, but it would be unlikely that a GI for Granite Belt apples would generate a process of reciprocal spillovers of the same intensity as one for wine. The mechanism of reciprocal spillovers, which explains how other businesses in a region both benefit from and contribute benefits to a GI area, depends critically on the possession of a signature or iconic GI.

8 FROM GROUPS TO COMMUNITIES OF SHARED COMMERCIAL FATE: INVESTING IN QUALITY

The certainty that GIs bring to the placement of boundaries appears to be playing an important contributory role in attracting investment into a GI region. Wine GIs in Australia, as they are subject only to rules of origin and not additional quality standards, do not of themselves trigger an interest in the production of quality wines. As indicated earlier, investment in quality in Australia's traditional wine-growing areas was occurring well before the advent of the GI system. A GI by virtue of its precise delineation creates a simple group identity based on geographic lines. For example, the Barossa Valley GI enables one to claim the identity of being a Barossa Valley winemaker. The GI can be thought of as creating a minimal group identity: a formal right to be counted as part of a group. But, of course, groups once constituted may evolve in all sorts of ways; this evolution itself is affected by variables such as trust and leadership. In those GI regions where a sufficient number of winemakers have committed to investing in quality and in improvement, the GI does not simply define a geographical group but also defines who is potentially a part of a community of shared commercial fate. A winemaker who produces a poor-quality wine and who is in a region known for its quality wine generates a negative externality for the region. A winemaker who wins prizes generates a positive externality for their region. The interviews with winemakers from regions with a reputation for premium wines indicated that all were sensitive to the negative and positive effects that individuals could have on a region's reputation.

Informal mechanisms and practices have evolved amongst winemakers to try to ensure that the production of wine in a GI region that is associated with wines of a particular quality continues to meet or improve on those standards of quality. A common practice is the use of tasting groups or clusters in which winemakers bring along samples for evaluation by their peers. The goal is constructive criticism aimed at improving the wine prior to bottling (Respondents #18 and #123). Wine competitions also seem to play a role in creating a culture of quality. Winemakers care about winning prizes. The esteem in which they are held by their peers and the broader industry matters to them. There are also the more obvious benefits that accrue from winning prizes – the capacity to price accordingly. Wine competitions are important networking sites where they can find out from judges in informal conversation why they did not win a place and how they might improve. The leadership of more established wineries in a region, such as a Josef Chromy in Tasmania, is also important. These wineries keep a weather eye out for newcomers, finding ways to give them advice about what works best in the region. The response is generally positive: 'nobody wants to make bad wine – they jump on board immediately' (Respondent #123).

Where a region has committed to quality, the GI boundary creates certainty for future investors. They know precisely where they must buy in order to gain the benefit of the GI. Winemakers who want to expand their business into premium wines benefit from having precisely defined regions that are associated with quality winemaking. A wine company such as De Bortoli, which has its headquarters in Griffith (an area not associated with premium wines), has expanded into the Yarra Valley as part of a strategy to increase its production of premium wines. The Yarra Valley GI is seen as generating an important halo effect.

The group identity that a GI system creates through its precise boundary delineation function helps winemakers who are interested in investing in quality to identify those who they must work with if they are to create a community with a sense of shared commercial fate within a region. If a group of winemakers makes the transition to quality wine production, then other effects such as greater investment in the region are likely to follow. The group-identity mechanism that operates as a result of the Australian wine GI system makes a modest but important contribution by defining who is in an area and who is not. This is simply a start. What happens after that depends heavily on leadership and the inclinations of people to work together.

9 CONCLUSION

There are two points that come from the negotiating phase of Australia's experience with GIs that are worth emphasizing. Australia's 1994 Agreement with the EU was an agreement that was specific to trade in wine. In other words, unlike in the case of a preferential trade deal that covers many industries and therefore sets up many possible trade-offs and complexities, the negotiations focused solely on the wine industry. This does raise the issue of whether it is better to negotiate GIs outside of a preferential trade agreement. The answer to this question will depend on whether one is negotiating with the EU or some other major trading partner such as the United States or China, but the point here is that the option of attempting to negotiate a specific agreement on GIs outside of a preferential trade agreement should at least be evaluated.

At the time of Australia's introduction of a wine GI system, the relationship between trademarks and GIs in Australia did not prove a problem, one reason being that Australia was not party to preferential trade agreements that contained provisions on the issue. Like other countries, Australia has gone down the preferential trade agreement path concluding in 2004 the *Australia-United States Free Trade Agreement*. Amongst other things, this agreement led to provisions in Australian law that allow for objections to the determination of a GI based on pre-existing trademark rights.[52] For example, Rothbury Wines were able to use these provisions to object successfully to the determination of a 'Rothbury' GI, citing the existence of a suite of registered, pending, and common-law trademarks.[53] As countries become parties to more and more preferential trade agreements, they will have to introduce much more procedural complexity into the design of any domestic GI scheme. At a more fundamental level, if a trademark office has allowed many trademark registrations over the country's valuable agricultural place names to creep onto the register, it may have created a huge practical obstacle to introducing a GI system.

Turning now to the issue of regional development, Australia's GI system was introduced at a time when the Australian wine industry was in the greatest export boom period of its history. The dominant regulatory principle of this system was truth in labelling, but it was also a principle that was bent to serve the interests of the wine industry in flexibility. Truth had to accommodate the demand for flexibility in production and processing. A consumer buying a bottle of wine with the GI 'South Eastern Australia' on it is being told that the grapes come from an area the size of several large European countries. The Australian industry is now in one of its bust cycles, and there is much more talk about concentrating on quality, suggesting that the GIs linked to Australia's premium wine regions will perhaps gain more attention from marketers. It is also important to keep in mind that Australia's experience with GIs is a little more than two decades old, whereas the Australian wine industry itself has a history of boom–bust cycles going back to the 1850s. It would be fair to say that the industry is still in something of a learning period with GIs. The future of wine GIs in Australia and globally is more likely to be influenced by decisions in the designer boardrooms of multinationals than in the cramped offices of the many hundreds of small wine producers in Australia, 75 per cent of whom crush less than 100 tonnes per year.[54] Of Australia's 2,573 wine companies, the top four account for 48 per cent of the national crush.

---

[52] See *US Free Trade Agreement Implementation Act 2004 (Cth)* sch 3 (Austl.).
[53] Rothbury Wines Pty Ltd v. Tyrrell [2008] ATMOGI 1 (13 June 2008) (Austl.).
[54] *Wine Industry Statistics – Wine Producers*, WINETITLES MEDIA WINE INDUSTRY SOLUTIONS, www.winebiz.com.au/statistics/wineries.asp (last visited 16 February 2016).

The Granite Belt GI does point to the mechanisms of reciprocal spillovers and group identity that help to explain how a GI could contribute to regional growth. However, for reciprocal spillovers, the case of the Granite Belt shows that proximity to a large city (Brisbane) matters. The same is true for the Yarra Valley with its close proximity to Melbourne. A wine GI may help a region in terms of jobs and growth by being able to entice city dwellers to visit. Regions with iconic GIs need cities to tango. Wine has that allure. Apples do not. For those interested in a GI system that truly serves poor and remote regions, the Australian wine GI model is almost certainly not the answer. But then perhaps no GI model could serve in that way.

12

Legal Protection of Geographical Indications as a Means to Foster Social and Economic Development in Malaysia

Tay Pek San[*]

1 INTRODUCTION

The concept of a geographical indication (GI) as a badge of origin that performs the function of identifying the geographical source of a product and its unique characteristics or quality that results from its geographical origin is a fairly recent development in the landscape of Malaysian intellectual property law. GIs were only formally recognised in Malaysia as a distinct type of intellectual property right when the Geographical Indications Act 2000 (GIA 2000)[1] was enacted. The Act, which came into force on 15 August 2001, was Malaysia's response to its international obligations to protect GIs under the Agreement on Trade-Related Aspects of Intellectual Property Rights (TRIPS Agreement).[2] At that time, there was relatively little understanding of the benefits and potential impact of a system of protection of GIs on the socio-economic development of the country, particularly with regard to sustainable rural development. Even though there is currently no specific study that has been conducted in Malaysia on the impact of GI protection on the country's socio-economic development, it is safe to say that at the present moment there is a general perception among stakeholders of intellectual property rights that GIs have a potentially positive impact on the generation of income, creation of local employment and, implicitly, the country's social

---

[*] Associate Professor, Faculty of Law, University of Malaya. The author gratefully acknowledges the research assistance of Tay Jia Jen in the preparation of this paper. All errors remain mine.
[1] Geographical Indications Act 2000 (Act No. 602/2000) (Malay) (as amended by Geographical Indications (Amendment) Act 2002).
[2] Agreement on Trade-Related Aspects of Intellectual Property Rights, 15 April, 1994, Marrakesh Agreement Establishing the World Trade Organization, Annex 1C, 1869 U.N.T.S. 299 [hereinafter TRIPS].

and economic development.³ This is because consumers often place value on products that they associate with a certain geographical origin and GIs are potentially effective marketing tools of great economic value.⁴ GIs are able to link products to their geographical regions, which oftentimes are in rural areas, and connect consumers to the producers.

As GIs were not perceived as a distinct form of intellectual property prior to the GIA 2000, it is not surprising that no applications were made to the Intellectual Property Corporation of Malaysia for the registration of geographical indications until the year 2003. Even then, there was only one application for registration made in that year.⁵ The number soon escalated, and in the year 2015 alone there were thirty-one new applications filed to register GIs in Malaysia.⁶ Of these, twenty-nine applications were by Malaysian applicants while two were by foreigners. Needless to say, not all applications were successful because they lacked the necessary requirements, but it suffices to note that by the end of 2015 there were in total fifty-nine registered GIs on the Register of Geographical Indications set up under the Act.⁷ These registered GIs belong primarily to products related to agriculture-intensive industries as well as to producers in the handicraft and food sectors, which possess historical and cultural links between the geographical area of the GI-denominated products and the respective groups of producers.⁸ For example, in the agriculture industry, producers of pepper, tea, coffee, rice, ginger, mangoes, groundnuts and durians have obtained registration of their GIs under the Act.⁹ Producers of handicrafts such as *songket* (a handwoven fabric), batik and wood-carving have also registered their GIs for protection.¹⁰ Similarly, GIs have been registered by producers of food items such as *belacan* (shrimp paste), cheese and

---

³ WORLD INTELL. PROP. ORG., GEOGRAPHICAL INDICATIONS: AN INTRODUCTION 17, www.wipo.int/edocs/pubdocs/en/geographical/952/wipo_pub_952.pdf.
⁴ DWIJEN RANGNEKAR, THE SOCIO-ECONOMICS OF GEOGRAPHICAL INDICATIONS: A REVIEW OF EMPIRICAL EVIDENCE FROM EUROPE (2004), www.iprsonline.org/unctadictsd/docs/CS_Rangnekar2.pdf.
⁵ *See Geographical Indications Statistics*, INTELL. PROP. CORP. OF MALAY., www.myipo.gov.my/web/guest/geo-statistik (last visited 8 March 2016).
⁶ *Id.*   ⁷ *Id.*   ⁸ *Id.*
⁹ *Geographical Indication – Search*, INTELL. PROP. CORP. OF MALAY. ONLINE SEARCH & FILING SYS., https://iponline.myipo.gov.my/ipo/main/search.cfm [hereinafter *GI Registry*]. See the following registrations: Sarawak Pepper (GI03-00001), Sabah Tea (GI06-00001), Tenom Coffee (GI06-00005), Bario Rice (GI08-00001), Tambunan Ginger (GI09-00003), Mangga Harumanis Perlis (GI2011-00004), Kacang Goreng Sempalit (GI2013-00004) and Durian Nyekak Sarawak (GI2013-00002).
¹⁰ *Id.* See the following registrations: Songket Terengganu (GI2013-00007), Sabah Batik (GI2013-00008) and Ukiran Kayu Besut (GI2014-00004).

biscuits.[11] The increase in the number of applications for registration of GIs over the relatively short span of time suggests that producers are aware of the importance of adequate legal protection of GIs in contributing to the commercial success of their products.

Starting from the premise that GIs play an important role as a tool in marketing strategies to advance the commercial and economic interests of GI producers,[12] this chapter discusses whether the current legal protection of GIs in Malaysia is adequate to prevent third parties from free-riding on the reputation of a GI. Adequate legal protection is necessary to prevent the unauthorised use of a GI by a third party for the purpose of misleading or confusing the public as to the geographical origin of a product, particularly when the product does not comply with the specific conditions of manufacture or does not originate from the geographical area. Apart from that, widespread unauthorised use of a GI could eventually result in the GI becoming a generic term. The unauthorised use of a GI in trade is detrimental to the legitimate interests of consumers and producers and, ultimately, will negatively impact the economic success of the industry that markets its products using the GI. In particular, the first part of the chapter provides an overview of the importance of GIs in the marketplace and describes two scenarios, both at a supranational level involving Malaysia, where GIs were at issue. The second part of the chapter discusses the scope of protection conferred on GIs pursuant to the GIA 2000 and the extent to which the Act promotes the use of GIs in trade. This is then followed by a discussion of the role played by the law of passing off in protecting GIs, particularly prior to the enactment of the GIA 2000. Subsequently, the provisions of the Trade Marks Act 1976 (TMA 1976),[13] the Consumer Protection Act 1999 (CPA 1999)[14] and the Trade Descriptions Act 2011 (TDA 2011)[15] that are relevant to the protection of GIs are briefly mentioned. Finally, the chapter analyses whether the current regime for protection of GIs in Malaysia creates a suitable legal

---

[11] *Id.* See the following registrations: Belacan Bintulu (GI2011-00005), Langkawi Cheese (GI2011-00002) and Biskut Dan San Sungai Lembing (GI2012-00007).

[12] IRENE CALBOLI & DANIEL GERVAIS, SOCIO-ECONOMIC ASPECTS OF GEOGRAPHICAL INDICATIONS (2015), www.wipo.int/edocs/mdocs/geoind/en/wipo_geo_bud_15/wipo_geo_bud_15_9.pdf; CERKIA BRAMLEY ET AL., THE ECONOMICS OF GEOGRAPHICAL INDICATIONS: TOWARDS A CONCEPTUAL FRAMEWORK FOR GEOGRAPHICAL INDICATION RESEARCH IN DEVELOPING COUNTRIES 116 (2009), www.wipo.int/export/sites/www/ip-development/en/economics/pdf/wo_1012_e_ch_4.pdf.

[13] Trade Marks Act 1976 (Act No. 175/1976) (Malay).

[14] Consumer Protection Act 1999 (Act No. 599/1999) (Malay).

[15] Trade Descriptions Act 2011 (Act No. 730/2011) (Malay).

environment that enables holders of GIs to prevent their unauthorised use by third parties in the marketplace.

2 GEOGRAPHICAL INDICATIONS AS AN IMPORTANT TOOL IN TRADE

The notion of a GI hinges on the link that exists between the product, its geographical origin and its quality or other unique characteristics that are attributed to the geographical source. The particular quality, trait or unique characteristics result from natural geographic advantages such as climate, soil, raw materials, manufacturing skills or food processing techniques local to a region. Essentially, the reputation that is associated with a GI is the intrinsic element that sells the product and contributes to the success of the industry that uses the GI. The geographical area of origin is therefore at the heart of all GIs and represents the normative basis for GI protection.[16]

As mentioned earlier, the increase in the number of applications for GI registration in Malaysia suggests the growing importance of GIs for trade in the country. A number of reasons may be proffered for the increase in the number of GIs registered each year with the Intellectual Property Office of Malaysia (IP Office). First, with the public awareness campaigns conducted by the IP Office, the relevant industries and stakeholders, there is now a significant conscious awareness among the public in Malaysia of the functions of GIs and their utility in the course of trade, as well as the legal benefits of seeking GI registration. Second, with a clearer understanding that GIs enable producers to differentiate their offerings from those of other producers because of the unique quality and characteristics that are attributed to production in a particular location of the country, producers are better equipped to use their GIs as a basis for branding and promotion of their products. Accordingly, GI producers are able to gain competitive advantages in the marketplace, thanks to the value added by identifying their products with GIs. Third, with the perceived or actual quality differences imbued in the public mind between GI-denominated products and generic products, GI producers are able to command premium pricing for their products.

The importance of GIs as assets of great value in trade may be demonstrated through the following two illustrations: The first illustration concerns disputes that arose between Malaysia and Indonesia a few years ago over allegations that Malaysia had asserted ownership of some GIs and cultural icons that

---

[16] BRAMLEY ET AL., *supra* note 12, at 111.

Indonesia claimed it owned.[17] For instance, Indonesia had claimed ownership over the textile art of batik, which involved the practice of dyeing cloth through wax-resistant methods. At the same time, the batik industry is also an important part of Malaysian cultural heritage, which has garnered widespread popularity. In Malaysia, the batik industry is a bustling commercial activity and an important source of commercial income for those involved in the industry.[18] Another example is the registration of *Bario* rice under the GIA 2000 by an agency of the Sarawak state government. Indonesia claimed that the rice was originally known as *Beras Adan* and had originated from the local rice area of Malinau in East Kalimantan.[19] During the same period of time, tension had also arisen over Indonesia's claim that Malaysia had asserted ownership of some of their cultural icons, such as the sacred Balinese temple dance known as the *pendet* dance, the shadow puppet theatre known as the *wayang kulit*, the folksong *Rasa Sayang*, the ceremonial dagger known as the *kris* and the meat dish known as *rendang*.[20] While these cultural icons are not registered as GIs, the disputes show that the controversies over the geographical origin of a product, which also embodies an important part of national or local cultural heritage, can potentially create barriers to trade and raise issues regarding the importance of elements of national culture, as disputes over these elements can result in creating tension in international relations.

The second illustration concerns the inclusion of issues related to GI protection in free trade agreements, namely those signed by Malaysia with other countries. In particular, in the Malaysia-Chile Free Trade Agreement, which was concluded in 2010, Malaysia was required to recognise the *Chilean Pisco* GI, but without prejudice to Malaysia's right to also recognise the *Pisco* GI from Peru. Similarly, the ASEAN-Australia-New Zealand Free Trade

---

[17] See MARSHALL CLARK & JULIET PIETSCH, INDONESIA-MALAYSIA RELATIONS: CULTURAL HERITAGE, POLITICS AND LABOUR MIGRATION 78–79 (2014).

[18] See Rohaida Nordin & Siti Safina Abu Bakar, *Malaysian Batik Industry: Protecting Local Batik Design by Copyright and Industrial Design Laws*, 13 INT'L J. OF BUS. & SOC'Y 117 (2012), www.wbiconpro.com/448-Dewi.pdf; Mohd Zulkifli Mokhtar & Wan Nur Syahida Wan-Ismail, *Marketing Strategies and the Difference Level of Sales and Profits Performance of the Batik SMEs in Malaysia*, 7 INT'L J. OF BUS. & MGMT. 96 (2012), www.ccsenet.org/journal/index.php/ijbm/article/view/19648/14380.

[19] See Iman Sjahputra, *The Protection of Indonesian Native Products Is Weak*, IMAN SJAHPUTRA & PARTNERS (29 April 2011), http://imansjahputra.com/articles-and-publications/r/the-protection-of-indonesian-native-products-is-weak.

[20] Jinn Winn Chong, 'Mine, Yours or Ours?': *The Indonesia-Malaysia Disputes over Shared Cultural Heritage*, 27 SOJOURN: J. OF SOC. ISSUES IN SE. ASIA 1 (2012); Wahyu Sasongko, *The Legal Protection of Geographical Indications in Indonesia Towards the ASEAN Economic Community*, 1 INT'L CONF. ON L., BUS. & GOVERNANCE 56 (2013).

Agreement requires signatory parties to recognise that GIs may be protected through a trademark system. In addition, parties are also to recognise that where a trademark predates a GI within the jurisdiction, parties are required to continue to protect that trademark over the GI.[21] Currently, Malaysia is engaged in negotiations with the European Union (EU) on the Malaysia-European Union Free Trade Agreement (MEUFTA), whose negotiations started in 2010. One of the issues at the negotiating table amongst other intellectual property rights is precisely the legal protection of GIs.[22] Although the final content of the agreement has yet to take some form, it is likely that insofar as GI issues are concerned, Malaysia's obligations on the protection of GIs will closely resemble that found in the European Union-Singapore Free Trade Agreement (EUSFTA).[23] To a large extent, the EUSFTA shares many similar obligations with the South Korea-European Union Free Trade Agreement.[24] Assuming that the MEUFTA's provisions on GIs will parallel that of the Singapore and South Korea counterparts, it would appear that the enhanced level of protection currently granted to wines and spirits under the GIA 2000 will be extended to a broader category of goods in Malaysia, such as agricultural products and foodstuffs. In addition, it is likely that the MEUFTA will include specific provisions in the event of conflicts between trademarks and GIs, namely it may require that a GI is not to be protected if such protection would result in conflict arising with an existing well-known trademark, and consumers would be misled as to the true identity of the product. Apart from that, rightholders may be obliged to maintain minimal commercial activity of their GIs for continued protection and also to put in place control provisions for production of the goods.

3 CURRENT LEGAL PROTECTION OF GEOGRAPHICAL INDICATIONS IN MALAYSIA

Since the TRIPS Agreement does not mandate any specific system for the protection of GIs, Malaysia had opted to adopt a *sui generis* regime for the

---

[21] For a discussion of the intellectual property issues in the free trade agreements which Malaysia has signed, see Heng Gee Lim, *Free Trade Agreements and the Effects of Existing Agreements on Malaysian Intellectual Property Laws*, in INTELLECTUAL PROPERTY AND FREE TRADE AGREEMENTS IN THE ASIA-PACIFIC REGION 387 (Christoph Antons & Reto M. Hilty eds., 2015).

[22] *Malaysia-European Union Free Trade Agreement*, MINISTRY OF INT'L TRADE & INDUS., www.miti.gov.my/index.php/pages/view/content8066.html (last visited 21 March 2016).

[23] *European Union-Singapore Free Trade Agreement*, EUR. COMM'N, http://trade.ec.europa.eu/doclib/press/index.cfm?id=961 (last visited 12 May 2016).

[24] Free Trade Agreement, E.U.-S. Kor., 16 September 2010, 2011 O.J. (L 127) 1.

protection of GIs rather than make changes to its existing intellectual property laws. Although the notion of GIs as a distinct type of intellectual property right with its own content and characteristics was statutorily embodied in Malaysia only fifteen years ago with the adoption of the GIA 2000, prior to that date a patchwork of different laws existed that could be invoked to protect GIs. The more significant laws in this respect are the law of passing off, the TMA 1976,[25] the CPA 1999[26] and the law on trade descriptions.[27] Nevertheless, the only reported court decision prior to the enactment of the GIA 2000 where a GI was contested was *The Scotch Whisky Association & Anor v. Ewein Winery (M) Sdn Bhd*,[28] and it was argued solely on the basis of the law of passing off without reference to any of the other areas of law. The case demonstrates that GIs, though not a defined category of intellectual property right at that time, were already perceived by industries as meriting some form of legal protection.

3.1 Protection under the Geographical Indications Act of 2000

The GIA 2000[29] was enacted for the express purpose of providing protection for GIs in Malaysia. A 'GI' is defined in section 2 of the GIA 2000 as 'an indication which identifies any goods as originating in a country or territory, or a region or locality in that country or territory, where a given quality, reputation, or other characteristic of the goods is essentially attributable to their geographical origin'.[30] This reproduces the definition of a GI in Article 22(1) of the TRIPS Agreement and underscores the triple association between the goods, their quality or other characteristics and the geographical origin.[31] Section 2 of the GIA 2000 defines 'goods' as 'any natural or agricultural product or any product of handicraft or industry'. It follows from this definition that services do not fall within the meaning of a GI and are accordingly excluded from the protection of this regime.

---

[25] Trade Marks Act 1976 (Act No. 175/1976) (Malay).
[26] Consumer Protection Act 1999 (Act No. 599/1999) (Malay).
[27] Prior to the enactment of the Geographical Indications Act 2000, the Trade Descriptions Act 1972 applied, but this statute was subsequently repealed and replaced with the Trade Descriptions Act 2011 (Act No. 730/2011) (Malay).
[28] *The Scotch Whisky Association & Anor v. Ewein Winery (M) Sdn Bhd* [1999] 6 M.L.J. 280.
[29] The Geographical Indications Act 2000 was amended once in 2002 to deal with administrative changes consequent upon the establishment of the Intellectual Property Corporation of Malaysia and to introduce new provisions on the renewal as well as restoration of a registration.
[30] Geographical Indications Act 2000 (Act No. 602/2000), § 2 (Malay).
[31] TRIPS, *supra* note 2, art. 22(1).

The GIA 2000 also creates a system for the registration of GIs, but it does not make registration mandatory as a precondition for entitlement to the protection afforded by it. Instead, the GIA 2000 provides that the same scope of protection is conferred on both registered and unregistered GIs. This is made clear in section 3(1)(a), which states that protection under the Act shall be given to a GI regardless of whether or not it is registered.[32] However, although registration is not a prerequisite for protection, there are benefits a proprietor of a registered GI enjoys that are not available in the case of unregistered GIs. Pursuant to section 20(1), a registered GI shall, in any proceeding, raise a presumption that the indication is a GI within the meaning of the Act.[33] Apart from this, section 20(2) provides that a certificate of registration shall be prima facie evidence of the facts stated in the certificate and of the validity of the registration.[34] Also, pursuant to section 21(1), only producers carrying on their activity in the geographical area specified in the Register shall have the right to use a registered GI in the course of trade.[35]

Overall, the GIA 2000 deals with two main aspects of GI protection: First, Parts II and VI of the GIA 2000 translate Malaysia's obligations under Articles 22,[36] 23[37] and 24[38] of the TRIPS Agreement into domestic law. Second,

---

[32] Geographical Indications Act 2000 (Act No. 602/2000), § 3(1)(A) (Malay). [33] Id. § 20(1).
[34] Id. § 20(2). [35] Id. § 21(2).
[36] Article 22(2) of TRIPS requires WTO Members to provide the legal means for interested parties to prevent the use of GIs that indicate that the goods in question originate in a geographical area other than the true place of origin in a manner that misleads the public. In addition, it also requires WTO Members to have in place legal means to prevent any use that constitutes an act of unfair competition within the meaning of Article 10bis of the Paris Convention (1967). See TRIPS, supra note 2, art. 22(2). Article 22(3) of TRIPS provides for the ex officio refusal or invalidation of trademarks that contain or consist of a GI in the situations spelt out in the article. See id. art. 22(3). Article 22(4) of TRIPS requires protection to be given to a GI against another GI that, although literally true as to the area in which the goods originate, falsely represents to the public that the goods originate in another area. See id. art. 22(4).
[37] Article 23 provides for additional protection of GIs in respect to wines and spirits. Article 23(1) requires WTO Members to prohibit the use of GIs identifying wines and spirits not originating in that geographical area, even where the true origin of the goods is indicated or the GI used is accompanied by expressions such as 'kind', 'type', 'style', 'imitation' or the like. See id. art. 23(1). Article 23(2) requires Members to refuse or invalidate a trademark that contains or consists of a GI identifying wines and spirits where the product does not originate from the geographical area indicated, regardless of whether the public is misled. See id. art. 23(2). Article 23(3) provides a further protection for wines in that it obliges Members to protect homonymous GIs for wines and requires Members to determine the conditions under which the homonymous indications will be differentiated from each other. See id. art. 23(3).
[38] Article 24 provides that WTO Members have agreed to enter into negotiations concerning the establishment of a multilateral system of notification and registration of GIs for wines. It also lays out a number of exceptions to the protection of GIs. See id. art. 24.

Parts III, IV, V and VII of the GIA 2000 deal with the registration of GIs and matters pertaining to GI registration, such as the administration of the registration system, the procedure for registration and opposition, renewal of registration, cancellation and rectification of the Register, and exceptions to the right to use a GI. In this respect, the GIA 2000 effectively created a *sui generis* system for GI protection in Malaysia, which paved the way for many GI registrations and for the growing acceptance of GIs as important tools to secure exclusive rights on geographical names for producers in various sectors of the Malaysian economy.

3.1.1 Protectable Geographical Indications

The GIs that are protectable in Malaysia are specified in section 3 of the GIA 2000,[39] and include all GIs that satisfy the definition of a GI in section 2.[40] In addition, section 3(b) provides that protection is also granted to a GI as against another GI which, although literally true as to the geographical area of origin, falsely represents to the public that the goods originate in another geographical country, territory, region or locality.[41] With regard to homonymous GIs for wines, section 7(1) states that protection shall be accorded to each indication, but the Registrar of Geographical Indications shall determine the conditions under which the homonymous GIs will be differentiated from each other so as to ensure the producers enjoy equal treatment and the public is not misled.[42]

Section 4 excludes four types of GIs from protection under the GIA 2000, although these may in appropriate cases be protected by other areas of law such as the law of passing off.[43] These are GIs that do not correspond to the meaning of a 'GI' as defined in section 2,[44] GIs that are contrary to public order or morality,[45] GIs that are not or have ceased to be protected in their country or territory of origin[46] and GIs that have fallen into disuse in their country or territory of origin.[47]

3.1.2 The Registration System for Geographical Indications in Malaysia

The administration of the registration system in Malaysia is overseen by the Registrar of Geographical Indications who is assisted by Deputy Registrars of Geographical Indications and Assistant Registrars of Geographical Indications.[48] For the purpose of registration of GIs,

---

[39] Geographical Indications Act 2000 (Act No. 602/2000), § 3 (Malay).   [40] *Id.* § 2.
[41] *Id.* § 3(b).   [42] *Id.* § 7(1).   [43] *Id.* § 4.   [44] *Id.* § 4(a).   [45] *Id.* § 4(b).   [46] *Id.* § 4(c).
[47] *Id.* § 4(d).   [48] *Id.* § 8.

a Central Geographical Indications Office[49] was set up and a Register of Geographical Indications was created to record relevant particulars pertaining to registered GIs.[50]

Pursuant to section 11(1) of the GIA 2000, an application for the registration of a GI may be made by any person (or group of persons) who is a producer of goods in the specified geographical area, a competent authority or a trade organisation or association.[51] In this respect, the term 'producer' encompasses a number of different entities. Section 2 defines a 'producer' as any producer or trader of agricultural products, any person or trader exploiting natural products and any manufacturer or trader of products of handicraft or industry. A 'competent authority' is defined as 'any government or statutory body carrying out the functions of, on behalf of, or sanctioned by, the Government'.[52]

When applying for registration, the applicant submits his personal particulars,[53] the GI for which registration is sought,[54] the geographical area and goods for which the GI applies,[55] and the quality, reputation or other characteristic of the goods for which the GI is used.[56] If the applicant complies with these formality requirements and the Registrar is satisfied that the GI is not contrary to public order and morality, the Registrar shall advertise the application in the Gazette.

Any 'interested person', who is defined as a person entitled to file an application for the registration of a GI laid down in section 11(1), may oppose the application only on one of the following four grounds: where the GI does not fall within the meaning of a GI under the GIA 2000,[57] where the GI is contrary to public order or morality,[58] where the GI is not or has ceased to be protected in its country of origin[59] or where the GI has fallen into disuse in its country of origin.[60] The GIA 2000 lays out a procedure for reply by the applicant and a subsequent response to that reply by the opponent. Based on the parties' submissions, the Registrar makes a decision either to refuse the registration or to register the GI with or without conditions or limitations imposed.[61] The GIA 2000 provides an avenue of appeal to the High Court from the Registrar's decision,[62] and no further appeal is allowed from the High Court's decision.[63]

---

[49] Id. § 9(1). Apart from the Central Geographical Indications Office, which is based in Kuala Lumpur, there are six other branches, which are located in Sarawak, Sabah, Johor Bahru, Kuantan, Penang and Melaka.
[50] Id. § 10(1).   [51] Id. § 11(1).   [52] Id. § 2.   [53] Id. § 12(1)(a).   [54] Id. § 12(1)(b).
[55] Id. § 12(1)(c)–(d).   [56] Id. § 12(1)(e).   [57] Id. § 14(1)(a).   [58] Id. § 14(1)(b).
[59] Id. § 14(1)(c).   [60] Id. § 14(1)(d).   [61] Id. § 16(4).   [62] Id. § 18(1).   [63] Id. § 31.

The period of registration of a GI is ten years from the date of filing,[64] and registration is renewable for a period of ten years each.[65] There is no limit to the number of renewals that may be made, which endorses the function of GIs as identifiers that link a product to a particular origin and, accordingly, the right of producers in the geographical region to use the GI in perpetuity. However, the failure to renew a GI will result in its removal from the Register.[66] But this does not diminish the right of the producers to use the GI concerned. The removal from the Register simply means that the GI will not be accorded the rights accrued to registered holders of GIs under the Act – namely the endorsement that the identifier used by the producers is a GI and the evidential benefit of registration. Nevertheless, the Registrar may restore a GI that has been removed from the Register if an application for restoration is made within twelve months from the date of expiry.[67] The application for restoration will only be granted if the Registrar is satisfied that there has been no use in bad faith of the GI during the year immediately preceding its removal, and no deception or confusion is likely to arise from the use of the GI by reason of its previous use.[68]

The Act also provides for the possibility of cancellation and rectification of a registration. Any 'interested person' may request the cancellation of a GI on the ground that it does not qualify for protection because it is excluded from protection under section 4.[69] An application for the rectification of the registration of a GI may be made on the ground that the geographical area specified in the registration does not correspond to the GI, the indication of the products for which the GI is used is missing or the indication of the quality, reputation or other characteristic of the products is unsatisfactory.[70] In its plain and ordinary meaning, 'cancellation' refers to the expungement of the whole of a GI from the Register, while 'rectification' denotes the varying or correcting of an entry or the imposition by the Registrar of limitations.

3.1.3 Rights Conferred upon Registration and Exceptions

Upon registration, section 21(1) of the GIA 2000 provides that only producers carrying on their activity in the geographical area specified in the Register shall have the right to use a registered GI in the course of trade.[71] In this respect, GIs do not grant a monopoly right akin to that of a patent, a registered trademark or a registered industrial design because the right to use a registered GI belongs jointly to the producers carrying on their activity in the

---

[64] *Id.* § 19(2).　[65] *Id.* § 19A(4).　[66] *Id.* § 19A(7).　[67] *Id.* § 19B(a).　[68] *Id.* § 19B(b).
[69] *Id.* § 22(1)(a).　[70] *Id.* § 22(1)(b).　[71] *Id.* § 21(1).

geographical area specified in the Register and is not limited to any particular enterprise. Essentially, GIs grant an exclusive right that aims at protecting the collective reputation that is embedded in the GI and is shared by, as well as accrues to, all enterprises in the geographical area that meet the requirements for use of the indication. It is this reputation revolving around a GI that helps to reduce consumers' search costs. This is because in a market marked by asymmetry of information, the valuable information intrinsic in a GI sends signals to consumers about the quality of a product. While benefiting consumers by providing them with accurate information that links a product with its qualities and geographical origin, GI protection also benefits the producers of the goods by protecting them against the unauthorised use of GIs by third parties.[72]

Pursuant to section 21(2) of the GIA 2000, the right to use a GI is confined to the products specified in the Register in accordance with the specified quality, reputation or characteristics.[73] Section 20(1) states that a registered GI shall raise a presumption that the indication is a GI within the meaning of section 2, which provides the rightholder with some degree of certainty.[74] In addition, by section 20(2), a certificate of registration shall be prima facie evidence of the facts stated in the certificate and of the validity of the registration.[75]

The rights conferred upon registration are circumscribed in the situations mentioned in sections 27(2), 28 and 29 of the GIA 2000.[76] Essentially, these are defences that may be raised in an action against any person who infringes the rightholder's exclusive right. Pursuant to section 27(2), no legal proceedings shall be brought under the Act against another person in respect to his/her use of a GI prior to the commencement of the GIA 2000, that is, 15 August 2001.[77] Section 28 provides for the right to the continued use of a GI in respect of wines[78] and spirits where the use had commenced prior to certain specified dates.[79] According to section 28(1), where a GI of another country identifying wines or spirits has been used in connection with goods or services by any national or domiciliary of Malaysia and that use has been in a continuous manner with regard to the same or related goods or services in Malaysia either for at least ten years before 15 April 1994,[80] or in good faith before that date, the

---

[72] See Malobika Banerji, *Geographical Indications: Which Way Should ASEAN Go?*, B.C. INTELL. PROP. & TECH. F. 1, 4 (2012). *But see* CALBOLI & GERVAIS, *supra* note 12.
[73] Geographical Indications Act 2000 (Act No. 602/2000), § 21(2) (Malay). [74] *Id.* § 20(1).
[75] *Id.* § 20(2). [76] *Id.* §§ 27(2), 28 & 29. [77] *Id.* § 27(2). [78] *Id.* § 28(1).
[79] *Id.* § 28(2).
[80] 15 April 1994 is the date the TRIPS Agreement was concluded. *See Agreement on Trade-Related Aspects of Intellectual Property Rights*, WORLD TRADE ORG., www.wto.org/english/tratop_e/trips_e/t_agm0_e.htm (last visited 10 March 2016).

user has the right to continue with the use in Malaysia.[81] Apart from this, section 28(2) allows for the continued use or registration of a trademark that is identical with or similar to a GI where the use of the trademark or its registration took place before the commencement of the GIA 2000 (that is, 15 August 2001) or before the GI became protected in its country of origin.[82] This is consistent with the 'first in time, first in right' principle, which is supported by countries such as the United States (US) and provides that pre-existing trademarks should not be cancelled due to the subsequent registration of a foreign GI. Pursuant to section 28(3) of the GIA 2000, where a GI is identical with a generic word in Malaysia for the goods concerned, no protection will be granted to the GI under the Act.[83] A final exception to the rights given upon registration is provided in section 29, which allows any person to use his name in the course of trade unless the use is in such a manner as to mislead the public.[84]

3.1.4 Institution of Proceedings to Prevent the Unlawful Use of a GI

According to section 5(1) of the GIA 2000, any 'interested person' may institute proceedings in the court to prevent the unlawful use of a GI, irrespective of whether the GI is registered or otherwise.[85] As mentioned earlier, an 'interested person' is defined in section 11 as either a producer of the goods in the geographical area concerned, a competent authority or a trade organisation or association.[86] From a commercial perspective, by explicitly providing for the institution of legal proceedings to curb the unauthorised use of a GI, section 5(1) ensures that the authenticity of the origin of a product is preserved. In some cases, the producers of a GI product become members of a trade association or society that is entrusted with the promotion of their rights and interests and protects them against the unauthorised use of the GI by third parties. For instance, in *The Scotch Whisky Association & Anor v. Ewein Winery (M) Sdn Bhd*[87] and *Chocosuisse Union des Fabricants Suisses de Chocolat & Ors v. Maestro Swiss Chocolate Sdn Bhd & Ors*,[88] which are discussed later in this chapter, the actions were instituted by the respective

---

[81] Geographical Indications Act 2000 (Act No. 602/2000), § 28(1) (Malay). [82] Id. § 28(2).
[83] Id. § 28(3). [84] Id. § 29. [85] Id. § 5(1). [86] Id. § 11.
[87] *The Scotch Whisky Association & Anor v. Ewein Winery (M) Sdn Bhd* [1999] 6 M.L.J. 280.
[88] *Chocosuisse Union des Fabricants Suisses de Chocolat & Ors v. Maestro Swiss Chocolate Sdn Bhd & Ors* [2010] 5 C.L.J. 794 [hereinafter *Chocosuisse v. Maestro* (HC)]; *Chocosuisse Union des Fabricants Suisses de Chocolat & Ors v. Maestro Swiss Chocolate Sdn Bhd & Ors* [2013] 6 C.L.J. 53 [hereinafter *Chocosuisse v. Maestro* (CA)]; *Maestro Swiss Chocolate Sdn Bhd & 3 Ors v. Chocosuisse Union des Fabricants Suisses de Chocolate & 2 Ors (and Another Appeal)* [2016] A.M.E.J. 0250 [hereinafter *Maestro v. Chocosuisse* (FC)].

trade associations together with a few other producers having the right to use the GI to defend the reputation of the respective GIs.

Section 5(1) of the GIA 2000 spells out four situations in which the use of a GI, whether registered or otherwise, is deemed to be unlawful. First, under section 5(1)(a), the use of a GI is unlawful if in the course of trade its use in the designation or presentation of any goods suggests that the goods originate in a geographical area other than the true place of origin and this has the effect of misleading the public.[89] This is a basic level of protection conferred on all GI products. Second, under section 5(1)(b), it is unlawful for any GI to be used in the course of trade if the use constitutes an act of unfair competition within the meaning of Article 10*bis* of the Paris Convention for the Protection of Industrial Property (1967).[90] Third, pursuant to section 5(1)(c), it is unlawful to use in the course of trade a GI which, although literally true as to the geographical area in which the goods originate, falsely represents to the public that the goods originate in another geographical area.[91] Fourth, in the case of wines and spirits, section 5(1)(d) provides that it is unlawful in the course of trade to use a GI if the wine or spirit does not originate in the place indicated by the GI in question. The use remains unlawful even where the true origin of the wines or spirits is indicated or the GI is accompanied by expressions such as 'kind', 'type', 'style' or 'imitation'.[92] There is no necessity to demonstrate that consumers might be misled or that the use constitutes unfair competition. A distinction is thus made between the levels of protection accorded to goods generally on the one hand and wines and spirits on the other. Wines and spirits enjoy an enhanced level of protection compared to other GI products. This is in line with the requirement laid out in Article 23 of the TRIPS Agreement.[93]

Pursuant to section 7(1) of the GIA 2000, in the case of homonymous GIs for wines, protection shall be accorded to each indication.[94] In such a case, section 7(2) requires the Registrar to determine the practical conditions under which the homonymous GIs in question will be differentiated from each other.[95] This would entail taking into account the need to ensure

---

[89] Geographical Indications Act 2000 (Act No. 602/2000), § 5(1)(a) (Malay).
[90] *Id.* § 5(1)(b); Paris Convention for the Protection of Industrial Property of 20 March 1883, as revised at Brussels on 14 December 1900, at Washington on 2 June 1911, at The Hague on 6 November 1925, at London on 2 June 1934, at Lisbon on 31 October 1958 and at Stockholm on 14 July 1967, 21 U.S.T. 1583, 828 U.N.T.S. 305, art. 10*bis*.
[91] Geographical Indications Act 2000 (Act No. 602/2000), § 5(1)(c) (Malay). [92] *Id.* § 5(1)(d).
[93] TRIPS, *supra* note 2, art. 23.
[94] Geographical Indications Act 2000 (Act No. 602/2000), § 7(1) (Malay). [95] *Id.* § 7(2).

equitable treatment of the producers affected and the concern that the public not be misled.

The court may grant an injunction to prevent any unlawful use of a GI, award any damages or grant other legal remedy as it deems fit.[96] Where a legal proceeding brought under section 5 is to prevent the use of a trademark which contains or consists of a GI, a time limit to commence the action is set by section 6.[97] Pursuant to section 6, unless bad faith is involved, no action shall be brought after the expiry of five years from the date the use of the trademark containing the GI has become generally known in Malaysia or from the date of registration of the trademark under the TMA 1976, whichever is earlier.[98] In the case of bad faith use or registration, no time limit for bringing an action is imposed.[99]

Where a GI exists before the coming into force of the GIA 2000, section 27(2) provides that no legal proceedings shall be brought for anything done before the coming into force of the Act.[100] Section 27(2) was applied recently in the Federal Court case *Maestro v. Chocosuisse*.[101] In this case, the plaintiffs, who were the respondents before the Federal Court, were Swiss chocolate manufacturers (except for the first respondent who was a trade association for Switzerland-based chocolate manufacturers). The respondents sued the appellants for passing off and infringement of GIs because the latter had used the mark 'Maestro Swiss' on the packaging of their chocolates and chocolate products. Both the Federal Court and Court of Appeal allowed the respondents' claim for passing off. However, the Federal Court disagreed with the Court of Appeal's finding that the respondents' claim under the GIA 2000 should be dismissed. The Federal Court opined that the Court of Appeal had erred when it held that section 27(2) of the Act applied in the case and therefore precluded any action brought for anything done prior to the commencement of the Act. The arguments based on passing off are discussed below, but insofar as the arguments based on the Act are concerned, the Federal Court held that the word 'Swiss' for chocolates and chocolate-related products satisfied the definition of a GI under section 2 of the GIA 2000 in that it signified that the chocolates were made in Switzerland and of high quality. According to the Federal Court, the purpose of the respondents' claim was to prevent the appellants from continuing to use the mark after the GIA 2000 came into force and 'not so much *for "anything done before the commencement of the Act."* '.[102] The Federal Court held that if the decision of the Court of Appeal in allowing the application of section 27(2) was upheld, it

[96] *Id.* § 5(2).   [97] *Id.* § 6.   [98] *Id.* § 6(1).   [99] *Id.* § 6(2).   [100] *Id.* § 27(2).
[101] *Maestro v. Chocosuisse* (FC).   [102] *Id.* at 77 (emphasis in original).

would mean that the appellants could continue to use the mark despite the court's finding that there had not been a bona fide use by the appellants of the respondents' mark.[103] Another matter made clear by the case was that although there is a certain degree of overlap between an action brought pursuant to section 5(1) and one that is commenced under the law of passing off, section 5(1) does not preclude the application of the law of passing off.[104] Indeed, as *Chocosuisse Union* demonstrates, an action may be brought concurrently for passing off and infringement of GIs.

3.2 Other Forms of Legal Protection for Geographical Indications

3.2.1 Protection under the Law of Passing Off

Even with the enactment of the GIA 2000, passing-off law remains available to prevent the unauthorised use of a GI. Indeed, it is usual for a plaintiff to invoke the law of passing off and the protection under GIA 2000 in an action to prevent the unauthorised use of a GI. To demonstrate the continued importance passing-off law plays in protecting GIs, two decided cases that were argued primarily on passing-off law are discussed in this section.

The first case, *The Scotch Whisky Association & Anor v. Ewein Winery (M) Sdn Bhd*,[105] was decided before the enactment of the GIA 2000 and was argued solely on the basis of the law of passing off. The second case, *Maestro v. Chocosuisse*,[106] was decided after the GIA 2000 came into force and was argued largely on the basis of the law of passing off as the main contention and, to a lesser extent, on infringement of a GI under the Act. The latter case is useful to demonstrate the continued relevance of the law of passing off as a form of protection for GIs even after the enactment of the GIA 2000.

In *The Scotch Whisky Association*, the second plaintiffs were distillers, blenders and exporters of Scotch Whisky, being whisky distilled and matured in Scotland. The first plaintiff was a trade association that was concerned with the protection of the interest of the Scotch Whisky trade worldwide. The phrase 'Scotch Whisky' had acquired considerable international reputation and goodwill because of the intrinsic quality and characteristic of the product. The plaintiffs claimed that the defendants, who carried on the business of processors and bottlers of liquor in Penang, had passed off their

---

[103] *Id.* at 78. [104] Geographical Indications Act 2000 (Act No. 602/2000), § 5(1) (Malay).
[105] *The Whisky Association & Anor v. Ewein Winery (M) Sdn Bhd* [1999] 6 M.L.J. 280.
[106] *Maestro v. Chocosuisse* (FC).

spirits, which were not distilled in Scotland, as and for Scotch Whisky. The alleged acts of passing off included the defendants' use of features of get-up with visual representations and labels suggesting Scottish origin, such as the prominent use of the words 'Compounded Scotch Whisky' and 'Imported Scotch Whisky Distilled in Scotland under British Government Supervision' on the packaging of their products. In determining whether the defendants had committed acts of passing off, the court applied the test laid down by Lord Diplock in *Erven Warnink BV v. Townend & Sons (Hull) Ltd*.[107] In this case, it was held that the plaintiff in a passing-off action was required to show, first, the existence of a misrepresentation; second, that was made by a trader in the course of trade; third, to prospective customers; fourth, that is calculated to injure the business or goodwill of another trader; and finally, that causes actual damage to a business or goodwill of the trader by whom the action is brought. In applying this test, the court found against the defendant for extended passing off and, accordingly, granted an order for an injunction and account of profits.

The factual matrix of the second case, *Maestro v. Chocosuisse*,[108] bears many similarities with the decision in *The Scotch Whisky Association*.[109] As mentioned earlier, the respondents, who were entities interested in the 'Swiss' GI when used in relation to chocolates or chocolate products, sued the appellants for using the name 'Maestro Swiss' on the packaging of their chocolates and chocolate-related products. In addition, the word 'Swiss' appeared in bold white colour against a red rectangular box emulating the white and red colours of the Swiss flag. The respondents argued that the appellants had deliberately used the word 'Swiss' together with the red and white colours to deceive or mislead the public into thinking that the appellants' products originated in Switzerland.[110] At first instance, the trial judge rejected the market survey evidence conducted by the respondents, which indicated that there was confusion among members of the public that the words 'Maestro Swiss' denoted chocolates that originated in Switzerland. The reasons for the rejection were that the survey failed to represent a true cross-section of the chocolate-buying public in Malaysia, the questionnaire contained leading questions and the survey was conducted only four years after the filing of the action. The trial judge found that the appellants' use of the words 'Maestro Swiss' instead of 'Swiss chocolates' did not create any false

---

[107] *Erven Warnink BV v. Townend & Sons (Hull) Ltd* [1980] R.P.C. 31.
[108] *Maestro v. Chocosuisse* (FC).
[109] *The Scotch Whisky Association & Anor v. Ewein Winery (M) Sdn Bhd* [1999] 6 M.L.J. 280.
[110] *Chocosuisse v. Maestro* (HC)] at 5–14 (particularly at 12).

impression that the chocolates were made in Switzerland.[111] In addition, the trial judge opined that the appellants' packaging was sufficiently distinctive so much so that no reasonable person would be led to think that the chocolates were made in Switzerland.[112] On appeal, the Court of Appeal, while agreeing that the court should be cautious in accepting survey evidence, held that the trial judge had erred in not giving any consideration at all to the results of the survey.[113] Contrary to the trial judge's decision, the appellate court relied on the outcome of the survey and concluded that there was likelihood of confusion in the minds of some members of the public that the appellants' chocolates were made in Switzerland.[114] This point on the admissibility of survey evidence was affirmed by the Federal Court. Importantly, the Federal Court emphasised that the case was one of extended passing off instead of passing off in its classical form because the respondents had misrepresented that their products were of the kind that enjoyed the reputation and goodwill attached to chocolates made in Switzerland.[115] Unlike extended passing off, passing off in its classical form is concerned with the protection of the goodwill of a particular trader's business.

A final important point, which the Federal Court clarified, concerned the *locus standi* of the first respondent in bringing a passing-off action against the appellants. The first respondent was a trade association that, *inter alia*, had the responsibility of protecting the designation 'Swiss Chocolates' or words that indicated that the chocolates had Swiss origin. The trial judge held that since the first respondent neither sold nor manufactured chocolates, they did not have any goodwill in the chocolate business and, accordingly, did not have any *locus standi* to bring the passing-off action.[116] However, the Court of Appeal overturned this finding and instead held that the first respondent, being a trade association, shared a common interest with its members in protecting the designation 'Swiss chocolate' and the goodwill associated with chocolates of Swiss origin.[117] The court also found support from two earlier decisions, the English case of *Chocosuisse Union des Fabricants Suisse de Chocolat and Others v. Cadbury*[118] and the above-mentioned case *The Scotch Whisky*

---

[111] *Id.* at 65. [112] *Id.* at 56.
[113] *Chocosuisse v. Maestro* (CA) at 48–58. On appeal, the Federal Court agreed with the Court of Appeal's findings in *Maestro v. Chocosuisse* (FC) at 59–62.
[114] *Chocosuisse v. Maestro* (CA) at 64; *Maestro v. Chocosuisse* (FC) at 63.
[115] *Chocosuisse v. Maestro* (CA) at 36; *Maestro v. Chocosuisse* (FC) at 37–57.
[116] *Chocosuisse v. Maestro* (HC) at 30.
[117] *Chocosuisse v. Maestro* (CA) at 24–28; *Maestro v Chocosuisse* (FC) at 36.
[118] *Chocosuisse Union des Fabricants Suisse de Chocolat & Others v. Cadbury* [1998] R.P.C. 117 at 149.

Association,[119] which accepted without controversy, the *locus standi* of trade associations to bring passing-off actions to protect the interests of their members. The Federal Court disagreed with the Court of Appeal and found that the trial judge was correct in holding that the first respondent did not have any *locus standi* to commence the passing-off action because it did not have any business interest or goodwill which it was entitled to protect by way of passing off in Malaysia.[120] The position differs with regard to the action under the GIA 2000. The Federal Court agreed with the Court of Appeal that the first respondent qualified as an 'interested person' within section 11 of the GIA 2000 and fell within the categories of persons entitled to register a GI. Accordingly, the Court held that the first respondent had *locus standi* to bring an action under the GIA 2000.[121]

The importance of the law of passing off in resolving disputes that essentially are attempts to protect the geographical origins of products continues even after the enactment of the GIA 2000, as is evident from the case of *Maestro v. Chocosuisse*.[122] Passing-off law prevents misrepresentation to be made to third parties in the course of trade as to the geographical origin of a product and, as such, is aptly suitable to be added as a cause of action in legal proceedings apart from that provided under the GIA 2000.

3.2.2 Protection under the Trade Marks Act 1976

There are provisions under the TMA 1976[123] that are sufficiently broad to offer some degree of protection of GIs, even though some of these were not enacted for the specific purpose of protecting such indications. Section 56 of the TMA 1976 provides that a mark is registrable as a certification mark if it is used in relation to goods or services for the purpose of distinguishing in the course of trade such goods or services in respect to origin, material, mode of manufacture, quality, accuracy or other characteristics from goods or services not so certified.[124] Certification marks thus indicate that the goods or services that use the marks have specific characteristics or originate from certain geographical regions.

Sections 14(1)(f) and 14(1)(g) were inserted by the Trade Marks (Amendment) Act 2000 in response to Malaysia's obligations under the TRIPS Agreement to protect GIs.[125] Pursuant to section 14(1)(f), the registration of any trademark that contains or consists of a GI with respect to goods not

---

[119] *The Scotch Whisky Association & Anor v. Ewein Winery (M) Sdn Bhd* [1994] 3 C.L.J. 509 at 4.
[120] *Maestro v. Chocosuisse* (FC) at 33.
[121] *Chocosuisse v. Maestro* (CA) at 28; *Maestro v. Chocosuisse* (FC) at 36.
[122] *Maestro v. Chocosuisse* (FC).   [123] Trade Marks Act 1976 (Act No. 175/1976) (Malay).
[124] *Id.* § 56(1).   [125] Trade Marks (Amendment) Act 2002 (Malay).

originating in the territory indicated is prohibited if its use in Malaysia is of such a nature as to mislead the public as to the true place of origin of the goods.[126] Section 14(1)(g) prohibits the registration of a mark for wines or spirits that do not originate in the place indicated by the GI even if the mark does not mislead the public.[127] Exceptions to section 14(1)(f) and section 14(1)(g) are made in the case of good-faith use or where the registration of the trademark took place either before the commencement of the GIA 2000 or before the GI was protected in the country of origin.[128]

Apart from the above provisions, section 14(1)(a), which prohibits the registration of a trademark that is likely to deceive or cause confusion to the public, has also been successfully invoked to remove from the Register a registered trademark comprising a GI.[129] In *The Agricultural and Processed Food Products Export Development Authority of India (APEDA) & Ors v. Syarikat Faiza Sdn Bhd*,[130] the respondent had applied for registration of the word 'Ponni' for rice prior to the coming into force of the GIA 2000. The application was successful and the word 'Ponni' was registered in the respondent's name. Subsequently, the applicants applied to expunge the respondent's trademark on the ground that 'Ponni' denoted a particular variety of rice cultivated in the Ponni region in Tamil Nadu, India. The rice is known for its benefits to diabetic patients. The court held that the word 'Ponni' was not a distinctive mark that denoted that the rice originated from any particular trader but rather was a word that denoted a particular variety of rice from the Tamil Nadu region. Accordingly, the court held that the respondent was not entitled to the registration of the 'Ponni' trademark.[131] In addition, relying on section 14(1)(a) of the TMA 1976, the court held that the use of 'Ponni' as a trademark for rice not originating in the Tamil Nadu region was likely to mislead the public. The respondent's mark was held to be an entry wrongly made and wrongly remaining in the Register and, thus, was ordered to be removed from the Register.[132]

3.2.3 Protection under the Trade Descriptions Act 2011

The TDA 2011 states that it is an offence to use false trade descriptions in relation to the supply of goods.[133] As a trade description is defined to include an indication of the place of production of any goods[134] and the TDA 2011

---

[126] Trade Marks Act 1976 (Act No. 175/1976) § 14(1)(f) (Malay). [127] *Id.* § 14(1)(g).
[128] *Id.* § 14A. [129] *Id.* § 14(1)(a).
[130] *The Agricultural and Processed Food Products Export Development Authority of India (APEDA) & Ors v. Syarikat Faiza Sdn Bhd* [2011] 2 M.L.J. 768.
[131] *Id.* at 26. [132] *Id.* at 25.
[133] Trade Descriptions Act 2011 (Act No. 730/2011) § 5(1)(b)–(c) (Malay). [134] *Id.* § 6(1)(m).

makes it an offence to apply a false trade description to any goods,[135] the TDA 2011 is an additional mechanism to protect GIs.

3.2.4 Protection under the Consumer Protection Act 1999

Section 10(1)(l) of the CPA 1999 prohibits any person from making a false or misleading representation that concerns the place of origin of the goods.[136] A representation that a product originates from a geographical area when it does not is a criminal offence under section 25.[137] Nevertheless, in the light of the fact that the purpose of the Act is to protect consumers and not the producers of goods,[138] it would appear that the applicability of the CPA 1999 in the context of protection of GIs is of incidental relevance only.

4 IS THE SCOPE PROTECTION FOR GEOGRAPHICAL INDICATIONS IN MALAYSIA ADEQUATE?

As discussed above, the principal area of law that protects GIs is the GIA 2000, which provides for a registration system but does not make registration mandatory for protection in Malaysia. Nevertheless, GI registration is beneficial because only producers carrying on activities in the geographical area specified in the Register are entitled to exclusively use the GI in the course of trade. By the same token, producers of the same type of product from another geographical region are not permitted to use the same GI. Moreover, registration raises a presumption that the indication is a GI, thereby giving producers more confidence when using their distinguishing indicia as a marketing tool. Likewise, consumers can confidently place their trust in a product bearing a GI mark since they are assured of the geographical origin of the product. Further, registration is prima facie evidence that the registered GI is indeed a GI, which also means that in legal proceedings the burden lies with the party challenging the legitimacy of the GI to prove his case.

Overall, the framework of the GIA 2000 provides a satisfactory scope of protection for GIs in Malaysia, particularly with respect to the provisions regarding the types of GIs that may be registered, the persons who qualify to

---

[135] *Id.* § 5(1)(a).   [136] Consumer Protection Act 1999 (Act No. 599/1999) § 10(1)(l) (Malay).
[137] *Id.* § 25.
[138] *Id.* § 2. The Act will only apply in respect to all goods and services that are offered or supplied to one or more consumers in trade.

apply for registration, the rights acquired by the registered holder upon registration, the procedure for registration, the institution of legal proceedings for the unlawful use of a GI, the defences in an action for the infringement of a registered GI and the rectification of the Register. In fact, the framework closely mirrors the general layout of the other, more established intellectual property statutes, such as the TMA 1976,[139] the Patents Act 1983[140] and the Industrial Designs Act 1996.[141]

Be that as it may, it is suggested that there is scope for further improvements to the GIA 2000 in order to have in place a more robust regime for the protection of GIs in Malaysia.

First, as consumers have come to expect that GIs connote a certain level of product quality, it is proposed that provisions be inserted in the Act to preserve the producer-quality-geographical region link by requiring rightholders to maintain a minimum level of quality in their products. Second, rightholders should be required to ensure that at least a minimal level of commercial activity is carried out in relation to the registered GI. Third, pursuant to section 13 of the GIA 2000, in an application for registration, the Registrar is currently only required to conduct an examination of the formal requirements of the Act. The formal requirements are spelt out in section 12(1), and these include stating the particulars of the applicant,[142] the GI and geographical area for which registration is sought,[143] the goods for which the GI applies,[144] the quality or other characteristic of the goods for which the GI is used[145] and any other particulars which may be prescribed by the Minister under section 32 of the Act.[146] If these requirements are complied with and the GI is not contrary to public order or morality, the Registrar shall advertise the application. In addition to this formal examination, it is recommended that the Registrar additionally conduct a substantive examination of the application, particularly to ensure that the indication applied for meets the definition of a GI and genuinely embodies the characteristics claimed for a product originating from the geographical region. This may require the assistance of expert assessors, which may be costly. However, a substantive examination is increasingly important to guarantee the actual quality and quality control of the GI-denominated products. Also, through a substantive examination, the examiner should check for possible conflict with existing trademarks, whether registered or not.

[139] Trade Marks Act 1976 (Act No. 175/1976) (Malay).
[140] Patents Act 1983 (Act No. 291/1983) (Malay).
[141] Trade Descriptions Act 2011 (Act No. 730/2011) (Malay).
[142] Geographical Indications Act 2000 (Act No. 602/2000) § 12(1)(a) (Malay).
[143] Id. § 12(1)(b) and (c). [144] Id. § 12(1)(d). [145] Id. § 12(1)(e). [146] Id. § 12(1)(f).

Fourth, under the TMA 1976, there are provisions for border enforcement measures to combat trademark-counterfeiting activities at the borders of the country through the seizure of counterfeit goods.[147] A parallel system could be put in place for GI protection for the same purpose. The final suggestion relates to an ambiguity that arises from a reading of section 3 of the GIA 2000. As mentioned earlier, section 3 states that protection under the GIA 2000 shall be given to a GI regardless of whether or not it is registered under the Act.[148] Yet, section 21(1), which spells out the exclusive right of a rightholder, states that '[i]n the case of registered geographical indications, only producers carrying on their activity in the geographical area specified in the Register shall have the right to use a registered geographical indication in the course of trade'.[149] This section is amenable to two possible interpretations: On the one hand, by section 3 extending the protection granted under the Act to all unregistered GIs, it may be argued that the exclusive right under section 21(1) applies equally to unregistered GIs. On the other hand, the opening words of section 21(1) appear to qualify the applicability of the section only to registered GIs, which would mean that only registered GIs enjoy the exclusive right under the section. This apparent ambiguity should be addressed by Parliament, which should clarify that only registered GIs enjoy the exclusive rights provided under the Act.

5 CONCLUSION

It is not an exaggeration to explicitly state that a GI is a singular marketing tool that encapsulates important information about the triple association that exists between a product, its quality or other unique characteristic, and its geographical origin. As GI products often command premium prices, they play an important role in the development of rural areas, which are usually the regions that produce such products and, by extension, are able to contribute to the social and economic development of a country. The valuable information embodied in a GI renders it a valuable commercial asset, which merits legal protection against the unauthorised use by third parties. The discussion above has examined the scope of protection of GIs in Malaysia, emphasising the *sui generis* protection under the GIA 2000 and outlining the protection under the common law of passing off as well as the statutory protection under the TMA 1976, the TDA 2011, and the CPA 1999. Based on the earlier

---

[147] Trade Marks Act 1976 (Act No. 175/1976) pt. XIVA (Malay).
[148] Geographical Indications Act 2000 (Act No. 602/2000) § 3 (Malay). [149] *Id.* § 21(1).

discussion, it may be surmised that as a whole, the overall scope of protection for GIs in Malaysia creates a suitable environment for the protection of GIs. Nevertheless, as recommended above, there is room for improvement of the GIA 2000 in order to provide a more comprehensive scope of GI protection under the law in Malaysia.

13

The Use of Geographical Indications in Vietnam: A Promising Tool for Socioeconomic Development?

Barbara Pick,[*] Delphine Marie-Vivien,[**] and Dong Bui Kim[***]

1 INTRODUCTION

This chapter seeks to investigate the way in which the system of protection of geographical indications (GI) has developed in the legal, policy, and socioeconomic context of an emerging country such as Vietnam. Vietnam has over fifteen years of experience in GI protection, and GIs are considered an important tool for socio-economic development in the country. Vietnam also recently completed the negotiations of two international free trade agreements, which include specific provisions on GIs: one with the European Union, the European Union-Vietnam Free Trade Agreement,[1] and the other one with twelve countries of the Pacific (including the United States), the Trans-Pacific Partnership Agreement (TPP).[2] Our analysis in this chapter aims at providing useful insights on the law and practice of GIs in Vietnam, which could also be relevant with respect to other countries in the region, as several countries in South East Asia are currently considering reforms to their existing laws or are implementing new provisions in the areas of GIs.

---

[*] PhD Candidate, Law Department, London School of Economics and Political Science, University of London.
[**] Researcher, International Agricultural Research for Development (CIRAD), UMR Innovation, Montpellier, France/Malica Research Platform, Hanoi, Vietnam; guest lecturer at the Foreign Trade University, the Vietnam National University of Hanoi.
[***] Researcher, Center for Agrarian Systems Research and Development (CASRAD), Hanoi, Vietnam. All the interviews referred to in this chapter have been conducted by the authors, and the transcripts of each interview are on file with the authors.
[1] *See EU-Vietnam Free Trade Agreement*, EUR. COMM'N, http://trade.ec.europa.eu/doclib/press/index.cfm?id=1437 (last visited 16 May 2016).
[2] *Trans-Pacific Partnership*, OFF. OF THE U.S. TRADE REPRESENTATIVE, https://ustr.gov/tpp/ (last visited 22 March 2016).

First established in 1995 through the system of appellations of origin brought by the French, the Vietnamese legal framework for the protection of GIs provides for a State-driven, top-down management of GIs that is supported by strong public policies. Indeed, beyond the strict legal scope, GIs have recently attracted an increasingly growing interest within the country as a promising tool for 'socio-economic development ... to eliminate hunger and reduce poverty'[3] and for the preservation of the 'cultural values and traditional knowledge of the nation'.[4] Yet despite the political will to promote GIs, the impact of GIs for socio-economic development in Vietnam in practice is facing two challenges. First, the number of registered GIs is still very low compared to that of geographical names registered as trademarks (TMs). Second, the use of the registered GIs on products for sale in Vietnam is still very limited. As this chapter will uncover, the reasons for the limited registration and use of GIs in Vietnam are due to a range of institutional, socio-economic, and organizational factors.

The existing literature, referring to origin labelling as 'branding from below'[5] or 'development from within',[6] has embraced GIs as an instrument of socio-economic development owing to the link with the origin. Indeed, while the primary functions of GIs relate to competition rules and market regulation,[7] a large body of scholarship has built upon the market utility of GIs to claim that they may also contribute to local development by advancing the economic and commercial interests of local farmers, producers, and other stakeholders along the supply chain. In line with the economics of product differentiation,[8] it is contended that GIs – by exhibiting the very characteristics of a specific *terroir*[9] – help producers get out of the 'commodity trap of

---

[3] Annual Report of the National Office of Intellectual Property, NAT'L OFF. INTELL. PROP. (NOIP) 1, at 23 (2012).

[4] See NAT'L OFF. INTELL. PROP., www.noip.gov.vn/web/noip/home/en?proxyUrl=/noip/cms_en.nsf/(agntDisplayContent)?OpenAgent&UNID=49BC1C4511A1FFCA4725767F00377FAD (last visited 22 September 2015).

[5] Maria Cecilia Mancini, Geographical Indications in Latin America Value Chains: A 'Branding from Below' Strategy or a Mechanism Excluding the Poorest?, 32 J. OF RURAL STUD. 295, 296 (2013).

[6] Sarah Bowen, Development from Within? The Potential for Geographical Indications in the Global South, 13 J. OF WORLD INTELL. PROP. 231, 231 (2010).

[7] PETRA VAN DE KOP ET AL., ORIGIN-BASED PRODUCTS: LESSONS FOR PRO-POOR MARKET DEVELOPMENT (Paul Mundy & Bergisch Gladbach eds., 2006).

[8] CERKIA BRAMLEY, A REVIEW OF THE SOCIO-ECONOMIC IMPACT OF GEOGRAPHICAL INDICATIONS: CONSIDERATIONS FOR THE DEVELOPING WORLD 3–5 (2011), www.wipo.int/e docs/mdocs/geoind/en/wipo_geo_lim_11/wipo_geo_lim_11_9.pdf.

[9] The French concept of *terroir*, which has been traditionally associated with the wine industry, conveys the idea that the unique qualities or characteristics of an agricultural product are determined by the ecological environment of the place from which it comes, including the

numerous similar and undifferentiated products trading primarily on price'.[10] Pursuant to this, a number of food sociologists have described the emergence of a 'wider Renaissance of "alternative agro-food networks" and "quality discourse" '[11] in which GIs fit in reaction to the hyper-industrialization, mass production, and standardization of 'placeless' food, as well as the failure to impose safety criteria, as illustrated by the spread of mad cow disease.[12]

In this context, it has been argued that the successful marketing of a product based on the link between its specific origin and its unique quality, characteristic, or reputation[13] may allow GI producers to increase their access to new or existing markets, gain a competitive advantage, and make a profit from the product differentiation.[14] The capturing of price premiums by producers is 'often one of the first aims of supporting a strategy for an origin-linked product'.[15] It is further suggested that the economic benefits derived from the successful marketing of GIs may also foster trust, social cohesion, and

---

soil, climate, and local varieties, as expressed through local know-how and human practices. *See* Laurence Bérard & Philippe Marchenay, LES PROCÉDURES DE PATRIMONIALISATION DU VIVANT ET LEURS CONSÉQUENCES, PATRIMOINE ET MODERNITÉ 159, 162–65 (Dominique Poulot ed., 1998).

[10] DANIELE GIOVANNUCCI ET AL., GUIDE TO GEOGRAPHICAL INDICATIONS: LINKING PRODUCTS AND THEIR ORIGINS 8 (2009), www.origin-gi.com/images/stories/PDFs/English/E-Library/geographical_indications.pdf.

[11] GIOVANNI BELLETTI & ANDREA MARESCOTTI, GI SOCIAL AND ECONOMIC ISSUES 15 (2006), www.origin-food.org/2005/upload/SIN%20-%20WP2%20FinalReport%20DEF.pdf.

[12] David Goodman, *Rural Europe Redux? Reflections on Alternative Agro-Food Networks and Paradigm Change*, 44 SOCIOLOGIA RURALIS 3 (2004); Jonathan Murdoch et al., *Quality, Nature, and Embeddedness: Some Theoretical Considerations in the Context of the Food Sector*, 76 ECON. GEOGRAPHY 107, 107–08 (2000); Henk Renting et al., *Understanding Alternative Food Networks: Exploring the Role of Short Food Supply Chains in Rural Development*, 35 ENV'T & PLAN. A 393, 395–98 (2003); Jan Douwe van der Ploeg et al., *Rural Development: From Practices and Policies towards Theory*, 40 SOCIOLOGIA RURALIS 391, 399 (2000).

[13] Felix Addor & Alexandra Grazioli, *Geographical Indications beyond Wines and Spirits: A Roadmap for a Better Protection for Geographical Indications in the WTO/TRIPS Agreement*, 5 J. OF WORLD INTELL. PROP. 865, 870 (2002).

[14] BRAMLEY, *supra* note 8, at 3–5; Food & Agric. Org. of United Nations, *Promotion of Traditional Regional Agricultural Products and Food: A Further Step Towards Sustainable Rural Development*, in REPORT OF THE FAO REGIONAL CONFERENCE FOR EUROPE 36 (26–27 June 2008), ftp://ftp.fao.org/docrep/fao/meeting/014/k3400E.pdf (last visited 18 May, 2016); Sophie Réviron et al., *Geographical Indications: Creation and Distribution of Economic Value in Developing Countries* 10–15 (NCCR Trade Regulation Working Paper No. 14, 2009), http://phase1.nccr-trade.org/images/stories/publications/IP5/report_IP5_GI_Value_2009.pdf.

[15] EMILIE VANDECANDELAERE ET AL., LINKING PEOPLE, PLACES AND PRODUCTS: A GUIDE FOR PROMOTING QUALITY LINKED TO GEOGRAPHICAL ORIGIN AND SUSTAINABLE GEOGRAPHICAL INDICATIONS 20 (2nd edn., 2009–2010), www.fao.org/docrep/013/i1760e/i1760e00.pdf.

solidarity since operators need to cooperate and exchange information.[16] This is particularly true in Europe, where there is a long history of producer-led GI collectives. There, the *sui generis* system of protected designations of origin and protected geographical indications requires the formation of a producers' association and a code of practice at the application stage. This arguably fosters collective action and collaboration among local stakeholders.[17]

In contrast, a number of authors have pointed out that in developing and emerging countries, GI initiatives are often driven by outside actors such as the State or development agencies. Hence, not enough GI-related activity, leading to the organization of producers and registration of GIs, is developed at the local level and within local producers.[18] Yet, as recalled by Biénabe and Marie-Vivien, what makes GIs peculiar and valuable instruments from a social development standpoint is the capacity of GIs to embody the link with the geographical origin where the product's reputation is built, which accounts for public considerations by the State and national governments, while still retaining private considerations insomuch as GIs are used by private stakeholders to identify products destined to consumers.[19]

However, while the literature holds promises of GIs as tools for socio-economic development, it has been noted that empirical data in this respect are lacking, especially from emerging and developing countries.[20] In particular, it has been noted that some context-specific factors may facilitate or hinder the ability of GIs to effectively promote such development.[21] This

---

[16] Rachael Marie Williams, Do Geographical Indications Promote Sustainable Rural Development? Two UK Case Studies and Implications for New Zealand Rural Development Policy 47 (2007) (unpublished Master thesis, Lincoln University) (on file with Lincoln University), https://researcharchive.lincoln.ac.nz/bitstream/handle/10182/585/william s_mnrmee.pdf?sequence=1.

[17] Erik Thévenod-Mottet & Delphine Marie-Vivien, *Legal Debates Surrounding Geographical Indications*, in LABELS OF ORIGIN FOR FOOD: LOCAL DEVELOPMENT, GLOBAL RECOGNITION 13 (Elizabeth Barham & Bertil Sylvander eds., 2011); Marie-Vivien, *The Role of the State in the Protection of Geographical Indications: From Disengagement in France/Europe to Significant Involvement in India*, 13 J. OF WORLD INTELL. PROP. 121, 141 (2009).

[18] See Marie-Vivien, *supra* note 17, at 140–42; *see also* Réviron et al., *supra* note 14, at 19–21.

[19] Estelle Biénabe & Delphine Marie-Vivien, *Institutionalising GIs in Southern Countries: Lessons Learned from Basmati and Rooibos*, WORLD DEV., at 6–7 (2016), doi:10.1016/j.worlddev.2015.04.004.

[20] Indeed, most of the data available so far in relation to GIs have been collected in Europe. See JUSTIN HUGHES, COFFEE AND CHOCOLATE – CAN WE HELP DEVELOPING COUNTRY FARMERS THROUGH GEOGRAPHICAL INDICATIONS? 32–36 (2009) (report prepared for the International Intellectual Property Institute).

[21] Dominique Barjolle & Bertil Sylvander, *Some Factors of Success for 'Origin Labelled Products' in Agri-food Supply Chains in Europe: Market, Internal Resources and Institutions*, 36 ECONOMIES ET SOCIÉTÉS 1441, 1435–37 (2002); Sophie Réviron & Marguerite Paus, *Special*

conclusion seems to be reflected also in the existing empirical research conducted so far. This research has in fact yielded inconclusive results of the effect of GIs on economic development and demonstrated that the impacts of GIs essentially vary on a case-by-case basis.[22] Even with respect to successful GIs, particularly in Europe, economists such as Belletti and Marescotti have drawn attention to the risk that only the largest processing and distribution firms that sell in international markets or use modern and long marketing channels might capture the additional earnings that can be obtained due to GIs.[23] Overall, it remains difficult to measure the extent to which the price premium that is commanded often by GI products is directly attributable to the legal protection granted to GIs only or whether other factors can also contribute to such premium, for example, the long-established reputation of certain products or the existence of subsidies and private investments in certain sectors of the economy.[24] Ultimately, what has emerged as a consensus among researchers is that GI legal protection alone is a necessary but insufficient condition to bring the desired effects.[25] In this regard, Hughes contends that '[t]he argument that substantially stronger GI protection will benefit developing countries simply mistakes the piling up of laws for the piling up of capital investment'.[26]

Yet there is a need for research as to what an enabling legal and institutional GI framework is, or should be, in the context of an emerging country. In addition, it seems that a combination of other enabling factors is required for a GI framework to positively impact socio-economic development.[27] For example, commentators have pointed to the need for substantial investments in

---

Report: Impact Analysis Methods. WP2, Social and Economic Issues. SINER-GI Project. European Commission – Sixth framework program, February 2006, 29–46.

[22] Cerkia Bramley & Estelle Biénabe, *Developments and Considerations Around Geographical Indications in the Developing World*, 2 QUEEN MARY J. OF INTELL. PROP. 14, 26–33 (2012); Ramona Teuber et al., *The Economics of Geographical Indications: Welfare Implications* 12–17 (SPAA Network, Working paper No. 2011–6, 2011), www.ualberta.ca/~langinie/papers/Lit-Ov erview_GI_Paper_04_2011.pdf; Webster D. McBride, *GI Joe? Coffee, Location, and Regulatory Accountability*, 85 N.Y.U. L. REV. 2138, 2158–66 (2010); HUGHES, *supra* note 20, at 28–37.

[23] Giovanni Belletti & Andrea Marescotti, *Origin Products, Geographical Indications and Rural Development*, in LABELS OF ORIGIN FOR FOOD: LOCAL DEVELOPMENT, GLOBAL RECOGNITION 75, at 81–82 (Elizabeth Barham & Bertil Sylvander eds., 2011).

[24] GIOVANNUCCI ET AL., *supra* note 10, at 116–19.

[25] See, e.g., Sarah Bowen & Ana Valenzuela Zapata, *Geographical Indications, Terroir, and Socioeconomic and Ecological Sustainability: The Case of Tequila*, 1 J. RURAL STUD. 108, 117–18 (2009).

[26] Justin Hughes, *Champagne, Feta and Bourbon: The Spirited Debate About Geographical Indications*, 58 HASTINGS L. J. 299, 370 (2006).

[27] Barjolle & Sylvander, *supra* note 21, at 1456–57.

advertising and marketing to develop a product's image and reputation[28] as well as to establish quality control, monitoring, and enforcement mechanisms aimed at building consumer trust in the product's quality.[29] However, while Albisu cautions that 'marketing of many OLPs [Origin Labelled Products] is often one of the weakest links in the chain',[30] Zografos notes that the costs involved might be considerable for small farmers in developing countries, especially given the low reputation of many GI products.[31] Notably, the collective action dynamics involved in the GI initiatives, which tie local actors 'in a lattice of interdependence',[32] have also emerged as critical factors for directing their effects.[33] According to Barjolle and Sylvander, the effectiveness of the collective action depends on the ability of each local actor to 'appropriate the collective process'[34] – an act that may be undermined by dominant market positions, local power relations, and supply chain inequalities.[35] In this regard, Larson stresses the need for an enabling institutional environment and collective organization with strong institutional mechanisms and governance systems.[36]

This chapter offers additional insights on GIs and socio-economic development from the perspective of an emerging country, namely Vietnam. In particular, our study seeks to identify some of the factors that are limiting the use of both the GI registration system and the registered GI labels on the

---

[28] HUGHES, *supra* note 20, at 80–81; Daphne Zografos, *Geographical Indications and Socio-economic Development* 13 (IQSensato Working Paper No. 3, December 2008), http://papers.ssrn.com/sol3/papers.cfm?abstract_id=1628534.

[29] HUGHES, *supra* note 20, at 97; Williams, *supra* note 16, at 59; CIRAD, THE CHALLENGES RELATING TO GEOGRAPHICAL INDICATIONS (GIS) FOR ACP COUNTRIES (Joint CTA, AFD, and CIRAD Workshop Report CD-ROM, March 2009).

[30] LUIS MIGUEL ALBISU, SYNTHESIS WP 2 LINK BETWEEN ORIGIN LABELLED PRODUCTS AND LOCAL PRODUCTION SYSTEMS, SUPPLY CHAIN ANALYSIS FINAL REPORT 4, 9 (July 2002), www.origin-food.org/pdf/wp2/wp2-1.pdf.

[31] Zografos, *supra* note 28, at 12–13.

[32] DWIJEN RANGNEKAR, GEOGRAPHICAL INDICATIONS AND LOCALISATION: A CASE STUDY OF FENI 17 (2009), http://papers.ssrn.com/sol3/papers.cfm?abstract_id=1564624.

[33] *See* ORG. FOR ECON. COOPERATION & DEV. (OECD), APPELLATIONS OF ORIGIN AND GEOGRAPHICAL INDICATIONS IN OECD MEMBER COUNTRIES: ECONOMIC AND LEGAL IMPLICATIONS 15 (21 December 2000); Sophie Réviron & Jean-Marc Chappuis, *Geographical Indications: Collective Organization and Management*, *in* LABELS OF ORIGIN FOR FOOD: LOCAL DEVELOPMENT, GLOBAL RECOGNITION 45 (Elizabeth Barham & Bertil Sylvander eds., 2011); Réviron et al., *supra* note 14, at 16–21.

[34] Barjolle & Sylvander, *supra* note 21, at 10.

[35] JORGE LARSON, RELEVANCE OF GEOGRAPHICAL INDICATIONS AND DESIGNATIONS OF ORIGIN FOR THE SUSTAINABLE USE OF GENETIC RESOURCES 56–58 (2007) (this study was prepared for the Global Facilitation Unit for Underutilized Species); *see* Réviron et al., *supra* note 14, at 16–21; GIOVANNUCCI ET AL., *supra* note 10, at 94–95.

[36] CIRAD, *supra* note 29; LARSON, *supra* note 35, at 58–59; Bowen, *supra* note 6, at 243–44.

products themselves. In this respect, our chapter seeks to provide useful empirical data that could assist in better understanding the use of GIs in practice in an emerging country in Asia. The chapter proceeds as follows. After a description of the methodology in Section 2, we provide a thorough analysis of the legal and policy framework for the protection of GIs in Vietnam in Section 3. Subsequently, we present two GI case studies – the fried calamari from Hạ Long and the star anise from Lạng Sơn – with a particular focus on the commercial and marketing strategies of these GI initiatives in Section 4, which will lead to our discussion in Section 5.

To conclude, we highlight the following three points: first, despite the increasing number of registered GIs in Vietnam, which is explained by a strong top-down involvement by the State in the identification and registration of GIs, the success of the registration process remains mixed due to the extremely strict criteria for demonstrating the link with the origin. Second, the commercial and marketing aspects have an impact on whether the use of GI labels is promoted or hindered. These factors determine the success of GIs from a socio-economic development perspective; it depends especially on whether it is a domestic or an export-marketing channel, and a processed or raw product. Third, the commercial and marketing channels also influence the negotiation skills of local farmers and producers, which in turn affect the way the GI labels are used in trade, as well as the extent to which they may contribute to building the product's reputation and fostering local economic development.

2 METHODOLOGY

Our methodology in this chapter is primarily qualitative. We used a variety of methods to generate data. First, in order to provide a thorough understanding of the Vietnamese legal and policy framework for GIs, secondary data were generated through the analysis of legal and policy documents, including the Vietnamese Intellectual Property Law[37] (Vietnam IP Law), its circulars and decrees, and other sources of law such as GI codes of practice. Second, we conducted a number of interviews with officials of the National Office of Intellectual Property (NOIP) and experts on intellectual property law to strengthen our analysis of legal documents. Third, we adopted a comparative case study approach to assess the impact of the commercial and marketing channels, and compared two GI initiatives with contrasting commercial and

---

[37] *Luat Sua Đoi, Bo Sung Mot So Đieu Cua Luat So Huu Tri Tue* [Law on Intellectual Property of Vietnam], No. 50/2005/QH11 (1 July 2005) [hereinafter IP Law].

marketing strategies. This approach led us to study the fried calamari from Hạ Long, which has a very strong local market, and the star anise from Lạng Sơn, which is an export-oriented product. The contrast between these two GI initiatives allows us to analyse whether, and why, different marketing strategies may affect the success of GIs from a socio-economic development perspective.

For the purposes of the two case studies, we collected primary data through a combination of semi-structured interviews with public authorities and stakeholders in the supply chain, including farmers and processors; distributors and traders; and leaders of farmers' associations and cooperatives. The interviews were conducted in Vietnam between March and May 2014. Overall, we conducted 6–8 semi-structured interviews for each GI product under investigation. Furthermore, official documents relating to the establishment and organization of the GI initiatives, including charters, bylaws, and board regulations, and internal documents, such as meeting reports, project reports, and annual statements collected from the interviewees, have provided valuable information on the operation and management of the GI initiatives under study. Finally, data were also sourced from development projects funded by international agencies in which we had previously been involved.

3 LIMITED NUMBER OF REGISTRATIONS DESPITE A COMPLETE LEGAL AND POLICY FRAMEWORK FOR GEOGRAPHICAL INDICATIONS IN VIETNAM

3.1 Demanding Criteria for the Registration of Geographical Indications

The actual *sui generis* legal framework for protecting geographical names that designate the origin of products in Vietnam was created in 1995 with the introduction of the protection of 'appellation of origin' in the Civil Code of Vietnam,[38] which contained all provisions regarding intellectual property, following a cooperation between France and Vietnam.[39]

According to Article 786 of the Civil Code of Vietnam of 1995, an 'appellation of origin is a geographical name of a country or locality that is used to indicate the origin of the goods as being in that country or locality, provided that the goods have characteristics or qualities that reflect the specific and advantageous geographical conditions of a natural or human character or the

---

[38] *Bo Luat Dan Su* [Civil Code of Vietnam] (1995) art. 786 (Vietnam).
[39] TRONG BINH VU & DUY HUAN DAO, GEOGRAPHICAL INDICATION AND APPELLATION OF ORIGIN IN VIETNAM: REALITY, POLICY, AND PERSPECTIVE 176 (2006), www.fao.org/filead min/templates/olq/documents/documents/GI%20and%20AO%20in%20Vietnam.pdf.

combination of thereof. Interestingly, the Vietnamese definition does not seem to provide for the combination of 'human and natural factors' that could be said is included in the definition of 'appellation of origin' as provided by the 1958 Lisbon Agreement for the Protection of Appellation of Origin.[40] Still, the definition requires proof of a strong link between a product's quality or characteristics and its origin for the definition of a geographical name to be an 'appellation of origin' under the Civil Code.

In 2001, with technical assistance from France, Vietnam registered the first two appellations of origin for Phu Quoc fish sauce[41] and Moc Chau Shan Tuyet tea[42] following the definition in the Civil Code.[43] In January 2007, Vietnam joined the World Trade Organization (WTO) and, as part of the accession process, adopted a new Intellectual Property Law (IP Law) in 2005. In this new IP Law, Vietnam introduced the same definition of GIs as in Article 22 of the Agreement on Trade Related Aspects of Intellectual Property Rights (TRIPS Agreement).[44] This definition is partially less strict than the previous definition of appellation of origin under the Vietnam Civil Code of 1995. In particular, Article 79 of the IP Law provides that a GI product must originate from the area, locality, territory, or country corresponding to the related GI and must also have the reputation, quality, or characteristics essentially attributable to the geographical conditions of the area. According to Article 81 of the IP Law, this criterion of reputation is based on consumer trust in the product. However, in practice, the criterion of 'reputation', or reputation-based GIs, has not been used on its own so far in Vietnam. Instead, the registration of all forty-nine GIs that are currently registered in Vietnam

---

[40] Lisbon Agreement for the Protection of Appellations of Origin and their International Registration (with Regulations for Carrying Out the Said Agreement and Official English Translation) art. 2(1), 31 October 1958, 923 U.N.T.S. 189 (appellations of origin refer to 'the geographical name of a country, region or locality which serves to designate a product originating therein, the quality and characteristics of which are due exclusively or essentially to the geographical environment, including natural and human factors').

[41] GI Registration No. 001. See Phu Quoc, ECAP III GEOGRAPHICAL INDICATION FICHE, www.asean-gidatabase.org/sites/default/files/gidocs/VNGI006-2001–0001-en.pdf [hereinafter *Phu Quoc Fish Sauce GI*].

[42] GI Registration No. 002. See Shan Tuyet Moc Chau, ECAP III GEOGRAPHICAL INDICATION FICHE, www.asean-gidatabase.org/sites/default/files/gidocs/VNGI000000000002-en.pdf [hereinafter *Shan Tuyet Moc Chau Tea GI*]. See the list of GIs on NOIP's website. NAT'L OFF. INTELL. PROP. VIETNAM, www.noip.gov.vn/web/noip/home/vn?proxyUrl=/noip/cms_vn.nsf/(agntDisplayContent)?OpenAgent&UNID=55E27823B4B0DFCD47257BB8000F954 C (updated as of 26 July 2013) (last visited 11 April 2016).

[43] The process of GI registration in Vietnam is outlined in NOIP's website. See NAT'L OFF. INTELL. PROP. VIETNAM, www.noip.gov.vn (last visited 15 March 2016).

[44] Michael Blakeney, *Geographical Indications and TRIPS*, QUAKER UNITED NATIONS OFF. (2001).

was granted upon demonstration that the relevant geographical area conferred on the product specific quality and characteristics as defined by one or several qualitative, quantitative, or physical, chemical, microbiological perceptible norms. These characteristics had to have the ability to be tested by technical means or by experts with appropriate testing methods.[45]

Moreover, Article 82 of the IP Law requires that the characteristics of the GI-denominated products that are derived from geographical conditions include both 'natural factors[46] *and*[47] human factors'.[48] This language directly suggests a mandatory combination of human and natural factors to justify GI registration in Vietnam,[49] which is much stricter than the definition of GIs that is provided in TRIPS regarding the strength of the link between a product and its geographical origin.[50] Ultimately, it can be said that GIs in Vietnam are still considered 'appellations of origin' under the original definition that is provided in the Vietnam Civil Code since the criterion of proving the link between the quality of products and their respective geographical environments must still be met. Evidence of this is the length of the GI dossiers – around twenty pages each – including the demonstration of the link between the products and their geographical origins. As mentioned earlier, so far no GI registration has been issued in Vietnam based on the criterion of reputation alone.

3.2 Type of Products Designated as Registered Geographical Indications in Vietnam

Table 13.1 lists all registered GIs in Vietnam as of March 2017. It lists the GIs and divides them per type of products. As the readers may easily notice, GI-designated products in Vietnam are currently still primarily raw materials, including fruits, vegetables, and materials used in processed products (79 per cent of registered GIs). These materials tend to have low economic value despite the economic and cultural importance for the country of processed

---

[45] IP Law art. 81.2.
[46] 'Natural factors' include climate, hydrograph, geology, terrain, ecological systems, and other natural conditions.
[47] Emphasis added by authors.
[48] 'Human factors' includes the skill and expertise of producers, and other traditional production processes within the locality. See IP Law art. 82 (emphasis added).
[49] This language was not included in the Vietnamese definition of appellation of origin; it recalls the international definition of 'appellation of origin' as set out in the Lisbon Agreement.
[50] Delphine Marie-Vivien, *The Protection of Geographical Indications for Handicrafts: How to Apply the Concepts of Natural and Human Factors to All Products*, 4 WIPO J. 191 (2013).

TABLE 13.1. *List of protected GIs of Vietnam (not included foreign GIs)[51] as of March 2017*

Registration certificate No	GI	Product	Date of issuance
00001	PHÚ QUỐC	Fish sauce	01.06.2001
00002	MỘC CHÂU	Tea shan tuyet	06.06.2001
00004	BUÔN MA THUỘT	Coffee	14.10.2005
00005	ĐOAN HÙNG	Grapefruit	08.02.2006
00006	BÌNH THUẬN	Dragon fruit	15.11.2006
00007	LẠNG SƠN	Anise	15.2.2007
00009	THANH HÀ	Litchi	25.5.2007
00010	PHAN THIẾT	Fish sauce	30.5.2007
00011	HẢI HẬU	Eight oval rice	31.5.2007
00012	VINH	Orange	31.5.2007
00013	TÂN CƯƠNG	Tea	20.9.2007
00014	HỒNG DÂN	Rice	26.6.2008
00015	LỤC NGẠN	Litchi	26.6.2008
00016	HÒA LỘC	Mango	30.9.2009
00017	ĐẠI HOÀNG	Banana	30.9.2009
00018	VĂN YÊN	Cinnamon	7.01.2010
00019	HẬU LỘC	Shrimp paste	25.6.2010
00020	HUẾ	Conical leaf hat	19.7.2010
00021	BẮC KAN	Kaki Seedless	8.9.2010
00022	PHÚC TRẠCH	Grapefruit	9.11.2010
00024	TIÊN LÃNG	Pipe tobacco	19.11.2010
00025	BẢY NÚI	Eight oval rice	10.10.2011
00026	TRÙNG KHÁNH	Chestnut	21.3.2011
00027	BÀ ĐEN	Mat	10.8.2011
00028	NGA SƠN	Sedge	13.10.2011
00029	TRÀ MY	Cinnamon	13.10.2011
00030	NINH THUẬN	Grapes	7.2.2012
00031	TÂN TRIỀU	Grapefruit	14.11.2012
00032	BẢO LÂM	Red Seedless	14.11.2012
00033	BẮC KAN	Tangerine	14.11.2012
00034	YÊN CHÂU	Mango round	30.11.2012
00035	MÈO VẠC	Honey	1.3.2013
00036	BÌNH MINH	Pomelo	29.8.2013
00037	HẠ LONG	Fried squid	12.12.2013
00038	BẠC LIÊU	Salt	12.12.2013

[51] The foreign GIs registered in Vietnam are Cognac, Spirits (Republic of France), GI Registration No. 003; Pisco, Liquor (Republic of Peru), GI registration No. 008; Scotch Whisky, Spirits (Scotland), GI Registration No. 023; Isan Thailand Yarn, Silk (Thailand), GI Registration No. 042; Kampong Speu, Sugar cane (Cambodia), GI registration No. 053; and Kampot, Pepper (Cambodia), GI Registration No. 054.

TABLE 13.1. *Cont*

Registration certificate No	GI	Product	Date of issuance
00039	LUẬN VĂN	Grapefruit	18.12.2013
00040	YÊN TỬ	Yellow apricot flowers	18.12.2013
00041	QUẢNG NINH	Ngan (a type of shellfish)	19.3.2014
00043	ĐIỆN BIÊN	Rice	25.09.2014
00044	VĨNH KIM	Fruit milk	28.10.2014
00045	QUẢNG TRỊ	Pepper	28.10.2014
00046	CAO PHONG	Oranges	5.11.2014
00047	VAN DON	Peanut worm	
00048	LONG KHÁNH	Rambutan fruit	Unknown
00049	NGỌC LINH	Medicinal herb	Unknown
00050	VĨNH BẢO	Pipe tobacco	Unknown
00051	THƯỜNG XUÂN	Cinnamon	Unknown
00052	HÀ GIANG	Orange	Unknown
00055	HƯNG YÊN	Longan fruit	Unknown

Source: NOIP, 2017

products and handicrafts. In turn, this may account for the limited impact of GI protection on socio-economic development in Vietnam.

3.3 A State-Driven Top-down Registration and Management Process

The governance of GIs in Vietnam is characterized by the State's top-down registration and management process. In particular, Vietnam's GI system is characterized by the division of rights between (a) the right to own the GI; (b) the right to register the GI, which means the right to decide on the content of the code of practices, including the geographical area; (c) the right to manage the GI, which relates to managing the granting of the right of use and of control procedures; and (d) the right to use the GI.

Some of those rights can be delegated to others as shown below:

(a) In Vietnam, geographical indications are owned by the State.[52] Therefore, this ownership cannot be transferred as GIs are considered a part of Vietnam's national heritage.
(b) The State, as owner of GIs, has the right to register GIs. This right may be delegated to
    – producers, organizations, and individuals;
    – collective organizations representing individuals; or
    – administrative authorities of the locality.

---

[52] IP Law art. 121.4.

(c) As the owner, the State has the right to manage GIs. It may delegate this right to[53]
- the People's Committee of the province or city where the product comes from;
- any agency or organization assigned by the People's Committee of provinces and cities if it represents all organizations and individuals using the GIs, and if that agency or organization represents all other organizations or individuals granted with the right to use geographical indications.[54]

(d) Producers have the right to use the GI,[55] including organizations and individuals authorized by the managing authority (point (c) above).

In practice, GIs are always registered by local authorities, such as the provincial Departments of Science and Technology (DOST), or People Committees (PC) of provinces, districts, or cities.[56] Even though they are legally permitted, no applications or registrations of GIs are made by producers or collective organizations representing individuals.[57] Once the GI is registered by the relevant authority, the latter promulgates a regulation for its management, where either the same authority or a different one (either a sub-department or a sub-region) is designated to manage the GI. In very rare cases (such as the conical hat from Hué GI),[58] the management agency is not a public authority but an association (the Women's Union).[59]

Legal use of GIs has been slow, with many GIs completing the 'experimental period' of the distribution and use of stickers and labels on the packaging of the products. For example, in the case of the GI Moc Chau Shan Tuyet Tea,[60] the association of producers launched a special packaging with the name of the GI. Additionally, in the case of the Nuoc Mam Phu Quoc fish sauce,[61] no fewer than eighty-three out of eighty-six producers are

---

[53] NGHỊ ĐỊNH Quy định chi tiết và hướng dẫn thi hành một số điều của Luật Sở hữu trí tuệ về sở hữu công nghiệp [Decree Detailing and Guiding the Implementation of a Number of Articles of the Law on Intellectual Property Regarding Industrial Property] Decree 103/2006/ND-CP art. 19 (22 September 2006) (Vietnam).
[54] IP Law art. 121.4. [55] Id.
[56] NOIP, Document presented at AsiaGI2016 (28 March 2016) (on file with Authors). [57] Id.
[58] GI registration No. 00020. See Hue Palm-Leaf Conical Hat, ECAP III GEOGRAPHICAL INDICATION FICHE, www.asean-gidatabase.org/sites/default/files/gidocs/VNGI00000000020-en.pdf [hereinafter Hue Conical Hat GI].
[59] See Decision of Promulgating the Regulation of 'Hue' Geographical Indication Management for Conical Hat in Thua Thien Hue Province (20 October 2010) (on file with authors).
[60] Shan Tuyet Moc Chau Tea GI, supra note 42.
[61] GI Registration No. 0001. See table published by NOIP. NAT'L OFF. INTELL. PROP. VIETNAM, www.noip.gov.vn/web/noip/home/vn?proxyUrl=/noip/cms_vn.nsf/(agntDisplayContent)?OpenAgent&UNID=55E27823B4B0DFCD47257BB8000F954C (last visited 11 April 2016).

members of the association, among whom sixty-six have been granted the right to use the GI, but only eight are actually using the GI label.[62]

As we elaborate below, for example, with respect to one of the case studies below (the Lang Son star anise GI),[63] the management of GIs also includes quality-control activities, which are supposed to be carried out by STAMEQ (Standards, Metrology, and Quality Department) at the provincial level.[64] However, in practice, these activities are not always implemented.[65]

3.4 Strong Public Policies to Aid in the Identification and Registration of Geographical Indications

Since 2005, several programs have been launched in Vietnam to support the protection of GIs. According to Decree 122/2010/ND-CP,[66] the Ministry of Agriculture and Rural Development and the Ministry of Industry and Trade shall assume prime responsibility for, and shall coordinate with People's Committees of provinces or centrally run cities in, identifying specialties, features of products, and processes of production of specialties bearing GIs that are managed by ministries, branches, or localities.[67] In this context, the Ministry of Sciences and Technology launched the first phase of the national 'Program 68' in 2008 aimed at identifying specialty products that could benefit from intellectual property protection, either as a GI or as a collective/certification TM.[68] Program 68 runs throughout Vietnam on a quota system of three products per province. The Program includes one product to be protected as a GI, the second product as a collective TM, and the third product as a

---

[62] Interview with Ngo Sy Dat Rural Development Center (RUDEC) (March 2015).
[63] GI Registration No. 00010. *See Lang Son Star Anise*, ECAP III GEOGRAPHICAL INDICATION FICHE, www.asean-gidatabase.org/sites/default/files/gidocs/VNGI0000000000007-en.pdf [hereinafter *Lang Son Star Anise GI*].
[64] This is the case, for example, for GIs Phu Quoc fish sauce, Hué conical hats, Lang Son star anise according to the regulation for the management of each GI. *See Phu Quoc Fish Sauce GI, supra* note 41; *Hue Conical Hat GI, supra* note 58; *Lang Son Star Anise GI, supra* note 63. *See also* DELPHINE MARIE-VIVIEN ET AL., STUDY (DIAGNOSTIC AND RECOMMENDATIONS) TO ASSESS NATIONAL GEOGRAPHICAL INDICATION CONTROL/CERTIFICATION SYSTEMS AND IDENTIFY CERTIFICATION OPTIONS AT NATIONAL/REGIONAL LEVELS 105 (2015) (report on file with authors).
[65] Interview with Luu Duc Thanh, Director of the Department of GIs at NOIP (May 21, 2014).
[66] NGHỊ ĐỊNH Sửa đổi, bổ sung một số điều của Nghị định số 103/2006/NĐ-CP ngày 22 tháng 9 năm 2006 của Chính phủ quy định chi tiết và hướng dẫn thi hành một số điều của Luật Sở hữu trí tuệ về sở hữu công nghiệp [Decree No. 122/2010/ND-CP of December 31, 2010, Amending and Supplementing a Number of Articles of the Government's Decree No. 103/2006/ND-CP of September 22, 2006, Detailing and Guiding a Number of Articles of the Law on Intellectual Property Regarding Industrial Property] Decree No. 122/2010/ND-CP (31 December 2010), www.wipo.int/edocs/lexdocs/laws/en/vn/vn071en.pdf.
[67] Decree, *supra* note 66, at art. 1.2. [68] *Id.*

certification TM.[69] While the first phase of Program 68 led to the registration of GIs and TMs, the second phase dealt with the management of GIs, i.e., post-registration issues and the issuance of regulations for the management and control of the use of GIs.

A number of programs that run at the provincial and district levels also aim to support the registration of GIs and TMs, such as the program run by the Province of Quang Ninh, which has aided in registering nine GIs/TMs since 2010.[70] International projects funded by the International Fund for Agricultural Development (IFAD) or the French government have supported particular GIs with the aim of reinforcing the value chain and small producers.[71] For all those programs, the Vietnamese authorities enlisted the expertise of national research institutes such as CASRAD, the Institute of Policy and Strategy for Agriculture and Rural Development (IPSARD), and private consulting agencies to develop the GI application dossier and prepare the management documents and regulations.[72]

Vietnam has also been very active in the GI debate at the international level. The Government of Vietnam represents the interests of GI producers when negotiating bilateral agreements in order to get international protection for their GIs. In particular, Vietnam has negotiated FTAs with Europe and several countries in the Pacific, including the United States, notwithstanding the fact that the European Union and the United States do not share the same vision for GIs.[73]

The Government of Vietnam has also acted to facilitate the registration of national GIs outside Vietnam. For example, the denomination Nuoc Mam Phu Quoc fish sauce was registered as a protected denomination of origin in the European Union in 2012.[74] In October 2012, Vietnam and the European Union signed the Framework Agreement on Comprehensive Partnership and Cooperation between Vietnam and the European Union in order to promote the mutual recognition of their respective GIs.[75] In 2015, Vietnam and the

---

[69] Interview with Nguyễn Văn Quyền, Department of Science and Technology (DOST), Province of Yen Bai (October 2013).

[70] Interview with Dinh Sy Nguyen, Head of IP Division of the Department of Science and Technology (DOST), Province of Quang Ninh (March 2014).

[71] See, for example, the support for the protection of Nuoc Mam Phu Quoc from various GI experts from France. Interview with Denis Sautier, Cirad (25 April 2015).

[72] Interview with expert of CASRAD and Rudec (18 April 2014).

[73] Tim Josling, *The War on Terroir: Geographical Indications as a Transatlantic Trade Conflict*, 57 J. AGRIC. ECON. 337 (2006).

[74] *Phu Quoc VN/PDO/0005/0788*, EUR. COMM'N AGRIC. & RURAL DEV., http://ec.europa.eu/agriculture/quality/door/registeredName.html?denominationId=2356 (last visited 18 2016).

[75] *Framework Agreement on Comprehensive Partnership and Cooperation Between the European Union and Its Member States, of the One Part, and the Socialist Republic of Vietnam, of the Other Part*, DELEGATION OF EU TO VIETNAM, http://eeas.europa.eu/delegations/vietnam/documents/eu_vietnam/pca.pdf.

European Union also completed the negotiations for an FTA providing, among other provisions, for the mutual recognition of 39 Vietnamese GIs in the European Union and the protection of 171 EU GIs in Vietnam.[76]

In conclusion, the concept of appellation of origin was certainly first introduced into the Civil Code of Vietnam as a result of the collaboration between Vietnam and the French government. Later, Vietnam introduced the concept of GIs as part of Vietnam's obligations in order to join the WTO. Still, Vietnamese policy-makers at both national and regional levels have gone far beyond the mere enactment of a legal framework establishing the protections of GIs as an international obligation. In particular, Vietnam has actively promoted a series of public policies for increasing the number of GI registrations and educating GI producers and stakeholders to correctly manage GIs. This has led to a positive dynamic and an increase in GI protection of four to five GIs per year in Vietnam over the past several years.

Yet, while this State-driven process has led to the registration of forty-nine GIs so far and has resulted in the promulgation of forty regulations for the management of GIs in Vietnam, there has been little use of GIs in practice so far, as illustrated by the two case studies in the following section. This again indicates the partial dichotomy between the existing legal protection of GIs in Vietnam and the actual (still limited) impact of these GIs on socio-economic development in Vietnam.

4 CASE STUDIES ON THE USE OF GEOGRAPHICAL INDICATIONS AND THEIR CONTRIBUTION TO SOCIO-ECONOMIC DEVELOPMENT IN VIETNAM

Bearing in mind the stated development policy goals attached to GIs,[77] this section reviews two cases studies. First, it presents the case study of the GI-denominated fried calamari from Hạ Long, a product that is characterized by a strong local market and local consumption in Vietnam. Second, it presents the case study of the GI-denominated star anise from Lạng Sơn, a product that is instead primarily export-oriented. By presenting these two case studies, we seek to show the extent to which the actual use of GI labels on local products in Vietnam may be impacted by the commercial and marketing strategies of local actors and how such strategies may generate different socio-economic development outcomes.

---

[76] *EU-Vietnam Free Trade Agreement: Agreed Text as of January 2016*, EUR. COMM'N, http://trade.ec.europa.eu/doclib/press/index.cfm?id=1437 (last visited 18 May 2016).

[77] *Annual Report*, *supra* note 3; NAT'L OFF. INTELL. PROP., *supra* note 4.

4.1 The Fried Calamari from Hạ Long: Strong Local Market and Short Marketing Channels

The fried calamari from Hạ Long (Hạ Long fried calamari) is a typical product of Hạ Long City, in Quảng Ninh Province (Northeast Vietnam). Hạ Long fried calamari have been produced by traditional family units since 1946[78] and derive specific taste and characteristics from both the high quality of the calamari found in the Gulf of Tonkin and the technical know-how of the processors/producers. As a typical product listed among the fifty most delicious dishes in Vietnam in 2012 and the one hundred most delicious dishes in Asia in 2013,[79] Hạ Long fried calamari have long enjoyed a very good reputation among local consumers, and the producers benefit from the millions of tourists that the nearby Hạ Long Bay (a United Nations Educational, Scientific and Cultural Organization (UNESCO) World Heritage Site) draws to the region every year.[80]

Proof of the reputation of the fried calamari from Hạ Long is not only the mass consumption of up to 1,500 kg/day in Hạ Long City but also the widespread misuse of the name on squid products that do not come from Hạ Long, as it happened particularly in the Quang Yên Province.[81] Initially, the first objective of the calamari producers was in fact to stop, or at least counter, the misuse of the product name – Hạ Long – and promote the specific quality and characteristics of genuine products to consumers inside and outside the Hạ Long region. In December 2013, in order to protect the Hạ Long name, the People's Committee of Hạ Long City (at the District level) registered the GI Hạ Long for fried calamari.[82] Subsequently the Committee delegated the right

---

[78] This statistic was taken from a survey conducted in 2012 in Hạ Long City among calamari producers. See Code of Practice of the Geographical Indication 'Hạ Long' for the Fried Calamari from Hạ Long City § 3.1.3, 3 (the Codes of Practice are not available online nor in any Official Gazette but have been transmitted to the authors by the management authority of the GI, and a copy is on file with authors; personal translation).

[79] Tourism in Vietnam grew from 1.2 million tourists in 2002 to approximately 3.9 million in 2014. See VIETNAM BOOK OF RECORDS (2012); see also ASIAN BOOK OF RECORDS (2013).

[80] CENTER FOR AGRARIAN SYSTEMS RESEARCH AND DEVELOPMENT (CASRAD), BUILDING AND DEVELOPING THE GEOGRAPHICAL INDICATION 'HẠ LONG' FOR THE FRIED CALAMARI FROM HẠ LONG CITY 16–17 (2014). See also Hạ Long Bay Site World Heritage Description, IUCN WORLD HERITAGE OUTLOOK, www.worldheritageoutlook.iucn.org (last visited 20 February 2016).

[81] CASRAD, supra note 80, at 18.

[82] GI Registration No. 00037. See Hạ Long Fried Calamari, ECAP III GEOGRAPHICAL INDICATION FICHE, www.asean-gidatabase.org/sites/default/files/gidocs/VNG I000000000037-en.pdf [hereinafter Hạ Long Fried Calamari GI].

to manage the GI to the District's Economic Department,[83] following the establishment of the association of producers/traders of fried calamari in the region. In order to use the GIs, producers have to become members of the association. As part of their obligations as members of the association, producers have to abide by the conditions set forth by the association and reflected in the GI specification. This includes, among others, the location of the processing and production facilities in Hạ Long City and a minimum of three years of experience in the production and trade of fried squid.[84]

The whole project – including surveys, mapping activities, determination of the quality of the raw material, establishment of the association, and registration of the GI – benefited from public funding from the Quảng Ninh Province (80 per cent of the total budget amounting to about 90,000 USD) and the Hạ Long City District (20 per cent of the total budget). It is worth mentioning that the project initially involved educational trips to Phu Quoc Island for producers/traders of the Hạ Long fried calamari to learn from the experience of the producers/traders of the Phu Quoc fish sauce; however, this trip was cancelled due to lack of funding.[85] Interestingly enough, both the Phu Quoc fish sauce and Hạ Long fried calamari GI initiatives exclude the fishermen who provide the raw materials for the processing of the GI products even though the geographical area in which fish must be caught is strictly defined in both cases.[86] As a result, the association of producers/traders of the Hạ Long fried calamari is rather small and gathers producers/traders only, with a total membership of twenty-three trader families.[87] Among them, three 'pilot families', who have the largest processing facilities, have been testing the use of the GI label since its registration in December 2013. As of September 2015,

---

[83] Regulation of the management and use of the GI 'Hạ Long Fried Calamari' art. 11 (the Regulation is not available online but has been transmitted to the authors by the management authority of the GI, and a copy is on file with authors).

[84] Regulation of the management and use of the GI 'Hạ Long Fried Calamari' art. 4.5.

[85] CASRAD, *supra* note 80, at 123.

[86] See Regulations of Use of the Geographical Indication of the Geographical Indication 'Halong' for the Fried Calamari from Hạ Long City art. 5 ('Any individual, organization and enterprise involved in the *processing* of the fried calamari in Hạ Long city, Quang Ninh province, has the right to use the GI "Halong" subject to the following conditions ...' (emphasis added)) (document on file with authors; transmitted by the management authority of the GI; personal translation); see also Code of Practice of the Geographical Indication 'Halong' for the Fried Calamari from Hạ Long City art. 4.1 (October 2013) ('The right to use the geographical indication can be granted only to establishments that comply with the requirements for *materials and processing techniques* as detailed in this document' (emphasis added)) (document on file with authors; transmitted by the management authority of the GI; personal translation).

[87] CASRAD, *supra* note 80, at 130.

a total of fifteen families were granted the right to use the Hạ Long GI by the District's Economic Department upon payment of the prescribed use fees (around 53 USD for a three-year period).[88]

Taking a closer look at the commercial and marketing aspects of the Hạ Long fried calamari, it is noteworthy that all members of the association are involved in short marketing circuits in the two markets in Hạ Long City ('Hạ Long I market' and 'Hạ Long II market', respectively). These markets are overwhelmingly and traditionally local, with about 95 per cent of the volume of traded fried calamari from Hạ Long being sold locally, either through direct sales to final consumers in the two main markets of Hạ Long City with no middlemen involved (50 per cent of the total trading volume) or to restaurants, hotels, and retailers located in Hạ Long City via short marketing channels involving middlemen (about 45 per cent of the total trading volume).[89] The remaining 5 per cent of the trading volume of Hạ Long fried squid is sold to final consumers in big cities of other provinces (such as Ho Chi Minh City and Hanoi, where two shops sell this product) through a number of middlemen and distributors such as supermarkets, food stores, and retailers in urban areas, which leads to lower profit margins for producers.[90]

While the high concentration of traders in the two markets of Hạ Long City has led to fierce competition among producers – which has discouraged some producers who are not members of the association from conducting business there[91] – direct sales and contact with consumers have contributed to building the reputation of the product while providing producers with more flexibility in setting selling prices. This is shown in the higher prices charged by the producers who sell directly on the markets with no middlemen (about 14–15 USD/kg in December 2014; up from less than 9 USD/kg in 2007) compared to the lower prices charged by the producers who are involved in longer marketing channels with middlemen (about 13 USD/kg).[92] Among those producers who sell directly on the market, it is of particular interest that the use of the GI label by the three pilot families has resulted in an increase in their selling price by about 15 per cent to 17 per cent USD/kg in December 2014, thereby contributing to higher incomes.[93] In contrast, the price of the fried calamari that incorrectly

---

[88] Interview with the Vice-President of the Association of Producers and Traders of the Fried Calamari from Hạ Long City (March 2014). Data was last updated by CASRAD in September 2015, see email exchange between the authors and the Project Leader from CASRAD on 1 September 2015 (on file with authors).
[89] CASRAD, *supra* note 80, at 104–05.   [90] *Id.* at 106.
[91] Three interviews with producers who are not members of the Association (Mar. 2014).
[92] CASRAD, *supra* note 80, at 268. This was confirmed by interviews with producers of fried calamari from Hạ Long City (March 2014) [hereinafter Hạ Long City Producers' Interviews].
[93] *Id.*

used the name 'Hạ Long' for calamari not produced in Hạ Long is about 9.5 USD/kg.[94]

Besides, the GI initiative seems to have benefited from the communication strategy implemented by the Department of Culture, Sports, and Tourism at the provincial level in 2013.[95] This strategy intended to raise consumers' awareness of the Hạ Long fried calamari by organizing tourist visits to the markets, mentioning fried calamari in guide books, participating in fairs and exhibitions, and broadcasting daily on local radio and TV promotion programs about the specific quality and characteristics of the Hạ Long fried calamari.[96]

As a result, according to a number of interviewees, consumers' demand for Hạ Long fried calamari has greatly increased over the past few years.[97] Although higher demand by consumers will undoubtedly be welcomed, as an increase in sales volume will lead to higher incomes for local producers/traders, it might also negatively impact the sustainability of primary raw material (i.e., calamari) from the Gulf of Tonkin, where, according to the GI code of practice, at least 70 per cent of calamari should be fished.[98] Indeed, a number of interviewees reported that the supply of calamari is quickly decreasing due to greater consumer demand and unsustainable fishing practices outside of the reproduction area.[99] Because of this, producers have been increasingly sourcing their calamari from Central Vietnam, China, Indonesia, and Malaysia, which may affect the quality of the fried calamari.[100] Yet if the 70 per cent minimum rule is not met, the fried calamari might be considered a fraud as it will not meet the requirements of the code of practice.

4.2 The Star Anise from Lạng Sơn: Export-Oriented Product with Long Market Access Chains

Star anise is a dark-grey spice that has six to eight equal, separate petals arranged in a star shape. The Province of Lạng Sơn in Northern Vietnam, located on the border of the Guangxi Province in China, is a very important production site of star anise, occupying a total of 35,575 hectares out of a total production area of 58,500 hectares within the whole country, about 60 per

---

[94] Id.
[95] Interview with Mr Tuan, Deputy Head of the Department of Culture and Tourism of Hạ Long City (March 2014).
[96] Id.   [97] Hạ Long City Producers' Interviews, *supra* note 92.
[98] Article 3.3.1 of the Code of Practice, *supra* note 72.
[99] Hạ Long City Producers' Interviews, *supra* note 92.   [100] Id.

cent of the total cultivated area.[101] The total production output is estimated to be between 6,000 and 10,000 tons/year.[102] Additionally, there are two value chains: the production of dry star anise and star anise oil. The process of planting and harvesting star anise is based mainly on traditional know-how and experience, including manual techniques.

In February 2007, the appellation of origin was granted to the People's Committee of Lạng Sơn Province with funding from the government program 'Program 68'.[103] The Province later delegated the right to manage the appellation of origin to its Department of Science and Technology. Subsequently, in 2008, the association for the production and marketing of star anise from Lạng Sơn was established. In contrast to the association for the production of Hạ Long fried calamari, membership to the Lang Son star anise association is not a requirement for the right to use the GI.[104] Still, compared to the relatively small association for the Hạ Long fried calamari, the association for the Lạng Sơn star anise is open to farmers, processors, collectors, and traders and has a large membership; about 700 out of a few thousand households are engaged in the production and trade of star anise in the Lạng Sơn Province. However, its actual activities were reported to be very limited and most members are not even aware of the very existence of the GI.[105] Surprisingly, compared to the high number of households involved in the production and trading of the star anise, only two export companies have been granted the right to use the GI so far, Aforex Co., Ltd. and Vinaspaex Co., Ltd.[106] Moreover, only one of them has been using the GI label. Also, there has been no observable difference in the selling prices of star anise grown in GI-protected areas and non-protected areas (between 1.3 and 2.7 USD/kg in May 2014, depending on the quality of the star anise). Neither has there been proof of economic benefit from the use of the GI label.[107]

The very limited use of the GI label in practice may be explained by a number of factors, including low awareness and lack of interest by local stakeholders in the GI value, as well as the absence of involvement by local

---

[101] CATHOLIC ORGANISATION FOR RELIEF AND DEVELOPMENT AID (CORDAID) & SNV NETHERLANDS DEVELOPMENT ORGANISATION, LEVERAGING THE SPICE SECTOR FOR POVERTY REDUCTION IN NORTHERN VIETNAM 32 (February 2013).
[102] Interview with Luong Dang Ninh, Director of the Department of Science and Technology (DOST) of the Lạng Sơn Province (May 2014).
[103] Id.   [104] Id.
[105] Interview with Mr Kien, President of the Association of Producers and Traders of Star Anise from Lạng Sơn (May 2014).
[106] Interview with the Director of DOST, *supra* note 102.
[107] Outcome of various interviews conducted with producers of star anise from Lạng Sơn conducted by the authors (May 2014) [hereinafter Lang Son producers' interviews].

authorities in the promotion of the GI and GI products.[108] All these factors seem to be connected to the lack of collective action, cohesion, and collaboration amongst the high number of farmers, processors, collectors, and traders involved in the production and trading of the Lạng Sơn star anise. But most impactful are the GIs' marketing channels, as will be explained below.

In actual figures, only 15 per cent of the total production of Lạng Sơn star anise is sold on the domestic market. Instead, about 80 per cent of the products are estimated to be exported to China (as star anise oil) and India (as dry star anise). Both countries use star anise for culinary and medicinal purposes.[109] The remaining 5 per cent of the products are exported to other countries such as Indonesia, Malaysia, and Thailand. Star anise is also exported to European countries such as France, Germany, and Belgium, where the spice is used to improve the flavour of wine and other beverage products.[110] Therefore, the marketing channels for star anise are characterized by a very large number of middlemen and long chains of intermediaries at the regional and international levels.

There are a number of reasons for China and India's prominent roles in the trade of the Lạng Sơn star anise. On the one hand, China and Vietnam are the two largest producers of star anise in the world. However, unlike Vietnam, where the domestic demand is very low and the majority of its production output is exported, China is the largest consumer of star anise in the world and exports only 5 per cent of what it produces.[111] Because its domestic production does not meet its domestic demand, China relies extensively on imports of star anise from Vietnam, which are estimated to be thousands of tons per year.[112] According to a number of interviewees, a large part of this trade takes place through unofficial exchanges at the border between farmers, where the transaction is completed without written contracts or certificates of quality.[113]

On the other hand, star anise is widely used in Indian cuisine. It is a major component of *garam masala*: an aromatic mixture of ground spices used as a base in many Indian dishes. However, because the production of star anise in India is limited to a part of the Arunachal Pradesh State in the northeast, India has become the largest importer of star anise, accounting for 50 per cent of world imports from production countries, such as Vietnam and

---

[108] Id. [109] Interview with the Director of DOST, *supra* note 102.
[110] Precise data on production and turnover for star anise are difficult to collect because they are usually mixed with data for similar spices. Furthermore, official information on the star anise trade between Vietnam and China is not comprehensive due to the large number of informal commercial transactions occurring between the two countries.
[111] CORDAID & SNV, *supra* note 101. [112] Id.
[113] Id. This point was confirmed in Lang Son producers' interview, *supra* note 107.

China.[114] Because the free trade agreement between India and Vietnam, which came into force on 1 January 2014, requires the removal of all import-export taxes (following the signing of the ASEAN-India Trade in Goods in 2009), Indian importers have become more interested in importing star anise from Vietnam rather than China, which still imposes a 30 per cent export tax duty.[115]

Given this situation, the value and utility of the GI label is practically non-existent. According to the interviewees, importers who buy star anise from the two export companies with the right to use the GI seem to deliberately opt out of using the label for a number of interesting reasons: Chinese traders want their customers to think that the star anise was grown in China, so they re-package star anise from Lạng Sơn with a Chinese logo, and Indian traders want to hide the origin of star anise from their own competitors to keep their supply sources a secret.[116] The export companies with the right to use the GI label also explained that when they tried to negotiate the use of the GI label, their customers threatened to find other suppliers.[117] Thus, the use of the GI label is useful only within the domestic market.[118]

However, between these two export companies, one exports its entire production to foreign markets and thus does not use the GI at all, while the other company exports about 90 per cent and sells the rest in its local shop, resulting in a very limited use of the GI label.[119] Ironically, when visiting this one shop, the GI logo had been affixed to not only the star anise's packaging but also the cinnamon's packaging. The sales manager of this company explained that the use of the GI logo on the cinnamon packaging was meant to identify the commercial origin of its products – regardless of whether the product was in fact cinnamon or star anise – and promote the image of the company as if the GI were owned solely by this company.[120]

5 DISCUSSION

So far, our study has examined the use of the GI registration scheme and two particular GI labels in the context of an emerging country, Vietnam, which actively promotes GIs as a socio-economic development tool. The analysis in

---

[114] CORDAID & SNV, *supra* note 101. This point was confirmed in an interview with a trader from India who requested to remain anonymous (May 2014).
[115] *Id.*
[116] Outcomes of interviews with Nguyen Thi Huyen, Sales Manager of Aforex Co, Ltd. and Que Anh, Director of Vinaspaex Co., Ltd. (May 2014).
[117] *Id.*   [118] *Id.*   [119] *Id.*
[120] Interview with Nguyen Thi Huyen, Sales Manager of Aforex Co, Ltd. (May 2014).

this section hopes to provide valuable insights into an important issue, namely identifying the legal and other contextual factors that may hinder the positive impact of a GI system in an emerging country. In particular, from the case studies above, our research suggests several impediments at three separate but interdependent levels: (a) the legal and institutional framework, (b) the commercial and marketing channels, and (c) the collective action of producers within the GI initiatives.

5.1 Legal and Institutional Framework

First, with respect to the legal and institutional framework, our analysis shows that the definition of GIs and its application in practice in Vietnam are more in line with the definition of the appellation of origin in the Lisbon Agreement than with the definition of GIs in TRIPS, as Vietnam law requires a very strong link to the origin of products. In other words, this criterion is a considerably demanding criterion for registering GIs in Vietnam.

Perhaps because of this stringent criterion, the overwhelming majority of registered names of local products are protected through a collective or certification TM comprised of the relevant geographical name. There were about 116 collective and 72 certification TMs registered as of May 2013, compared with only 43 GIs.[121] These trademarks were registered following the same top-down process with State agencies, which own the certification trademarks or, at the initiative of the creation of the associations, the collective trademarks.[122] Furthermore, while there is no need to demonstrate a link with the place of origin for TMs, and although in other jurisdictions such as the European Union, the scope of protection is weaker for TMs than for GIs, the law in Vietnam allows for the registration of geographical names as collective TMs and certification TMs.

Second, the quota system under Program 68 to support GIs and TMs has resulted in some geographical designations being registered as TMs and not GIs, even if the link with the origin is very strong. For example, Shan tuyết tea from Moc Chau[123] has been registered as a GI, but the Shan tuyết tea from Suối Giàng in the Province of Yen Bai,[124] though described with as many

---

[121] Data transmitted by NOIP (May 2013) (on file with authors).
[122] Delphine Marie-Vivien et al., Geographical Indications and Trademarks in Vietnam: Confusion or Real Difference? Agriculture in an Urbanizing Society, Rome (14–15 September 2015).
[123] *Shan Tuyet Moc Chau Tea GI*, supra note 42.
[124] Certification TM No. 4201209301, information transmitted by NOIP (on file with authors).

details as the GI Moc Chau Tea, is protected as a certification TM because there was already one GI in the same province as the cinnamon of Van Yen.[125]

Third, and most importantly, the State-driven process has been successful in registering forty-nine GIs and in having them protected in the European Union. The government also remains in charge of enforcing GIs. In 2013, the Vietnamese government also successfully managed to obtain the cancellation of a Chinese trademark[126] comprising the designation Buon Ma Thuot Coffee, a GI registered in Vietnam since 2005.[127]

Yet this top-down approach may also negatively impact and ultimately jeopardize the initiative and involvement of the producers in seeking GI registration and later in managing the GI. This top-down approach also will inevitably impact various operators in the supply chain who use the GI (technically, the *right* to use the GI, as the State remains the holder of most rights related to the GI). This can also impact the management of GIs and GI-denominated products. Certainly, the rights that belong to the State can be delegated to the collectives of producers, as provided by the Vietnam IP Law.[128] But subsequent decrees have given more power to the State. For example, Article 4 of the Decree 122/2010/ND-CP[129] provides that 'People's Committees of provinces or centrally run cities shall file applications for registration and organize the management of GIs used for local specialties and license the registration of collective marks or certification marks for geographical names and other signs indicating the geographical origin of local specialties.'

Finally, even though the Vietnamese legal framework for GI protection certainly is on par with all other WTO countries, legal protection is not sufficient in itself to turn GIs into successful tools for socio-economic development. Legal protection is a necessary condition for the success of a GI system. However, so are a number of market- and product-specific conditions, as will be shown below. In other words, the success or failure of a GI-system to unleash the potential for GI protection for the purpose of socio-economic development remains heavily dependent on context-specific conditions.

---

[125] GI Registration No. 00018. See *Van Yen Cinnamon*, ECAP III GEOGRAPHICAL INDICATION FICHE, www.asean-gidatabase.org/sites/default/files/gidocs/VNGI000000000018-en.pdf.
[126] See *Abolishing China's Buon Me Thuot Coffee Trademark*, VOICE OF VIETNAM (March 2, 2014) http://english.vov.vn/economy/abolishing-chinas-buon-me-thuot-coffee-trademark-273778.vov.
[127] GI Registration No. 004. See *Buon Ma Thuot Coffee*, ECAP III GEOGRAPHICAL INDICATION FICHE, www.asean-gidatabase.org/sites/default/files/gidocs/VNGI000000000004-en.pdf.
[128] IP Law art. 121.4.   [129] Decree, *supra* note 66.

5.2 Relevance of Commercial and Marketing Channels

A number of context-specific issues have emerged as particularly relevant in explaining both the 'success' and 'failure' of GI initiatives. At the operations level, by contrasting the cases of the Hạ Long fried calamari and Lạng Sơn star anise, we see the importance of taking the commercial and marketing channels into account when analysing the extent to which GI labels are actually used in an emerging country.

First, our empirical findings suggest that, especially in the case of the Hạ Long fried calamari, a strong local market with traditional short marketing circuits is important factors for building the reputation of a local product and empowering local producers who are able to set prices more easily. This is shown by the higher selling prices that the use of the GI label has allowed. In contrast, the domestic market for the Lạng Sơn star anise is virtually non-existent and the use of the label is very limited, thus not affecting selling price or sale volume. However, we do not suggest that the findings of this case study extend to other export GI products from emerging countries. For instance, both *Darjeeling*[130] tea and *Café de Colombia*[131] are successful emblematic GI products with a strong export focus, which should thus lead us to make more nuanced considerations. In reality, the penetration into the market for a labelled GI product also depends strongly on the producers' collective organization and its knowledge and skills about GIs, as will be shown in Section 3.5 below.

Second, we have found that the marketing channel that is adopted may be linked to the nature of the product. The Hạ Long fried calamari is a processed food product sold locally, whereas the star anise from Lạng Sơn is a raw product, usually processed into oil before being sold in export markets without the GI label. The case study of the Lạng Sơn star anise demonstrates the need to 'decommodify' this product, and other spices, at the global level in order to better value the spices' origin, as has been done for coffee, tea, pepper, or more recently, salt.[132] A 'de-commodification' process would allow the GI value to increase in the international market, as the GI would gain recognition with customers, which would allow for price premiums[133] as well as higher earnings due to the non-applicability of tariffs for commodity products.[134]

---

[130] Deepthi Elizabeth Kolady et al., *The Economic Effects of Geographical Indications on Developing Country Producers: A Comparison of Darjeeling and Oolong Teas*, 2 WIPO J. 157 (2011).

[131] Xiomara Quiñones-Ruiz et al., *Can Origin Labels Re-shape Relationships Along International Supply Chains? – The Case of Café de Colombia*, 9 INT'L J. COMMONS 416 (2015).

[132] On this aspect, see HUGHES, *supra* note 20, at 152.

[133] See Réviron et al., *supra* note 14, at 13. [134] Williams, *supra* note 16, at 42.

5.3 Importance of Collective Actions by Producers

Finally, we argue that the commercial and marketing channels of these two products have largely affected the opportunities for producers to take ownership of the GI initiatives. Whereas the producers of fried calamari sell their products to customers in traditional local markets at a price set by them, the producers of the Lạng Sơn star anise cannot control where the product is eventually sold nor its final packaging, considering that 85 per cent of the production is sold to traders who re-sell the product in their own country or to other countries. Moreover, the fact that the two export companies with the right to use the GIs have not managed to impose the use of the GI label clearly illustrates the one-sidedness of the negotiations and the Vietnamese producers' lack of negotiation skills. To go deeper into the issue, even though the right to use the GI was granted by a State agency, it is, in reality, simply denied by importers at the transaction level. This leads to a situation in which importers expropriate the legal right from Vietnamese producers and traders to use the GI, which impedes the potential of the GI initiative to bring about economic benefits. Therefore, we argue that an intervention by the State to restore the right to use the GI would be welcomed.

By supporting the right to use the GI labels, producers would become more aware of the utility of the GI label and actually understand its implications. For example, while producers of fried calamari actively promote the GI label to get a higher selling price, most producers of the star anise are not aware of the very existence of the GI logo. Furthermore, the only company utilizing it in the domestic market affixes the GI logo on other products, such as cinnamon, in order to promote the image of the company. This clearly demonstrates a lack of understanding of the very meaning of a GI, not to mention the inefficiency or lack of quality control and product inspection due to a shortage of funding and equipment. Once again, some level of State intervention would be useful to increase awareness of the meaning of a GI and its value as well as to strengthen quality control of the GI product.

6 CONCLUSION

In conclusion, in light of the above, the highest priority in Vietnam should be to empower local farmers and producers to use the GI system and the GI labels beyond the current status quo. Undoubtedly, this is a challenge in the context of a State-driven economy in which GI policies are developed through top-down governance. Still, the law in Vietnam permits that the right to register and manage GIs can be delegated to collectives of producers. Such a management model could be applied more often in order for producers and producer associations to play a more prominent role in the GI landscape than they do today. Naturally, Vietnam continues to go through a learning process regarding the use of the GIs, after a first successful step of registration of GIs, as many other countries of the region. Still, GI protection can have a beneficial impact on economic development in many areas of the economy in Vietnam, and thus producers should learn to use the GI system to a fuller extent to capture more of its promises.

14

'Vanity GIs': India's Legislation on Geographical Indications and the Missing Regulatory Framework

Yogesh Pai[*] and Tania Singla[**]

1 INTRODUCTION

A walk through the narrow winding lanes of Bari Bazaar in India's holy city of Varanasi (popularly known as Benaras or Kashi) is captivating for several reasons. Located in one of the oldest continually inhabited cities in the world, Bari Bazaar is a popular hub for producers and sellers of Banarasi silk sarees and brocades. The region represents an epitome of syncretism in India's diverse cultural setting. As the river Ganges silently flows through the city, Varanasi today has emerged as a confluence of products protected by geographical indications (GIs) with five GI registrations assigned to this region alone.[1]

But there is also a crisis of survival. Today, one of the most important challenges facing Banarasi saree producers is that cheaper synthetic imitations are produced in the textile city of Surat, which is located in the Western Indian state of Gujarat. It has also been reported that traders frequently import Chinese silk cloth and sell them in the Indian markets as Banarasi sarees.[2] This illegal trade negatively impacts Banarasi producers, since Surat-made synthetic sarees

---

[*] Assistant Professor of Law and Co-Director, Centre for Innovation, Intellectual Property and Competition, National Law University, Delhi, India.
[**] LL.B., National Law University, Delhi; Ms Singla previously worked as a student fellow with the Centre for Innovation, IP and Competition (CIIPC) at National Law University, Delhi. This chapter continues our ongoing research in this area and adapts and updates an article previously published as *Post-Registration Quality Control for Geographical Indications in India: the Way Forward*, 7 INDIAN J. INTELL. PROP. L. 103 (2014–2015).
[1] Binay Singh, *Varanasi Emerges As a Hub of GI Products*, TIMES OF INDIA (17 April 17, 2015 6:31 PM), http://timesofindia.indiatimes.com/city/varanasi/Varanasi-emerges-as-a-hub-of-GI-products/articleshow/46959699.cms.
[2] Shefalee Vasudev, *Ground Report | The Banaras Bind*, LIVE MINT (23 November 2013 12:04 AM), www.livemint.com/Leisure/5h1lnyORjhtn9ProZ4wiXL/Ground-Report-The-Banaras-bind.html [hereinafter Shefalee Vasudev, *The Banaras Bind*].

333

and Chinese-made sarees are regularly passed off as Banarasi products in different markets across India.[3] Not only are the motifs and patterns of Banarasi sarees ripped-off, and their best weavers poached by producers in Surat; much more problematically, these 'Surat-made Banarasi-style sarees' are produced at a fraction of the cost (due to the use of synthetic materials and polyester) in comparison to an 'authentic' silk Banarasi saree.[4] It is quite intriguing that Banarasi saree producers have, so far, not contemplated legal action against producers, or traders, of Surat-made or Chinese-made Banarasi-style sarees for infringing on their registered GI. Instead, several Banarasi weavers are also seeking access to cheaper raw materials for their sarees on the basis of and assumption that, by reducing their production costs, they could better fend off the competition by producing cheaper replicas of their sarees. Moreover, these producers seek to reduce costs to compete against the other legitimate producers of GI-denominated Banarasi sarees.

However, this situation begs several questions: Why are (several) Banarasi saree producers choosing to compete in a race to the bottom rather than turning to the legal enforcement of their GI and encashing the premium value of their products protected by the GI? Moreover, what implications will this strategy of lowering the quality of the authentic Banarasi sarees have on those producers who may continue to use silk fibres and not choose to compete by diluting the brand? In other words, what are the obligations of GI producers in India and does the Indian GIs system protect GI producers against those members of the GI producers' community who decide to turn to a lesser quality relying on the historical reputation of the GI products, that is, those who become 'free-riders from within?'

Overall, the existence of a GI registration on a product is meant to enable producers within a collective group to capture a premium for their products by (also) preventing members of the group from arbitrarily changing the product quality. In this respect, a GI registration also aims at preventing members of the collective group from deciding to lower the quality of the products to compete with other GI producers, or producers of similar products outside the GI-denominated market, especially when consumers are agnostic or unaware about those distinctions. Hence, the case of Banarasi sarees reveals that (at least a considerable number of) GI holders are often not concerned about the

---

[3] Rajiv Dikshit, *Narendra Modi's Dilemma: Surat vs Banarasi Saris*, TIMES OF INDIA (27 March 2014 1:20 AM), http://timesofindia.indiatimes.com/news/Narendra-Modis-dilemma-Surat-vs-Banarasi-saris/articleshow/32742485.cms.

[4] *Id.*; see also *Banarasi Sarees in Surat*, EXPORTERSINDIA.NET, www.exportersindia.net/surat/banarasi-sarees.html (last visited 7 March 2016) (providing a list of exporters of Banarasi sarees in Surat).

loss of combined reputation of their GIs resulting from compromise on the distinctive quality. Unfortunately, such instances are not unique to Banarasi sarees in India.[5] This sense of lack of agency among GI holders highlights the collective action problem that goes deep into the ambiguity surrounding what makes a particular GI unique and the lack of adequate quality control on the ground amongst many GI producers in India. Interestingly, some may argue that changing the composition of raw materials by a few entrepreneurial members of a GI club could be seen as innovation. Yet, when that innovation includes turning to cheaper materials and to synthetic fabrics for sarees historically woven with silk, it should more likely be regarded as a compromise of GI-product quality and a (self)dilution of the GI's distinctiveness.[6]

Essentially, this debate comes down to the quality and characteristics that GI-denominated products are supposed to possess and that GIs are supposed to purport to consumers. Presently, however, almost all of the GI awareness campaigns in India seem to be focused only on the registration component of GIs.[7] Even though the branding and promotion of GI products has started receiving some attention both on the domestic and international fronts,[8] the Indian government and the surrounding legal and policy discourse on Indian GIs have, at least until now, completely ignored the introduction of quality-control and maintenance measures for goods produced under the GI tag. In many ways, it could be said that the Indian GIs regime promotes a system of 'Vanity GIs' where the registration of GIs is seen as an end in itself and a measure for brand promotion, with little attention being paid to the deep linkages between the registration of GIs and the quality control that should follow the registration. Instead, quality control – and in turn the function of GIs as guarantors of and symbols assuring product quality – is central to the success of the Indian GIs regime, and this chapter seeks to fortify this claim by identifying how the consumer perception of quality has a sharp influence on the economics of GIs.

Accordingly, this chapter focuses on the post-registration quality-control regulatory measures for GIs in India. First, this chapter identifies the problem

---

[5] Recently, studies conducted on Assam's Muga silk have also faced similar issues. Kiran George, *When the Tezpur University Came to GI Tagged Muga Silk of Assam's Rescue*, SpicyIP (28 April 2015), http://spicyip.com/2015/04/when-the-tezpur-university-came-to-gi-tagged-muga-silk-of-assams-rescue.html.

[6] Amit Basole, *Authenticity, Innovation and the Geographical Indication in an Artisanal Industry: The Case of the Banarasi Sari* (Department of Economics, University of Massachusetts, Working Paper No. 2014-09), http://repec.umb.edu/RePEc/files/2014_09.pdf.

[7] Vrunda Kulkarni & Viren Konde, *Pre- and Post- Geographical Indications Measures for Handicrafts in India*, 16 J. Int'l Prop. Rts. 463, 467 (2011).

[8] Winson Thomas, *Economic Competitiveness through Geographic Indications*, 2 Int'l J. Mktg., Fin. Servs. & Mgmt. Res. 182, 183 (2013).

involving the interface between GIs as collective intellectual property (IP) rights and their linkages with quality and product/process standards. Second, it briefly discusses the experiences of two comparative jurisdictions – the United States (US) and the European Union (EU) – regarding the linkages between the GIs framework and the corresponding regulatory framework for quality control. Third, the chapter explores the missing regulatory framework in India and discusses the limitations of Indian GI law in this regard. A few short case studies are presented to highlight the various combinations of statutory and self-voluntary mechanisms associated with different GI products in India. The objective is to show how different mechanisms for quality control have led to either preservation or dilution of the collective reputation of GI. This chapter concludes by elaborating on the reasons for failure of the Indian GIs regime on issues of quality control and suggests that decentralized mechanisms for different GIs, which are nevertheless governed by a uniform statutory framework, are the way forward to restore the credibility of many GIs and promote a successful system of GI protection in India.

2 THE RELEVANCE OF QUALITY FOR GEOGRAPHICAL INDICATIONS

GIs do not serve merely as indications of their origin. In their simplest form, GIs also signify a connection between 'a product's reputation, quality or characteristic and its geographical origin'.[9] In the marketplace, consumers often find it difficult to assess product quality without searches or experience and normally possess limited information about the valuable attributes of the product.[10] The producers, however, possess full information about the product's attributes and quality relative to other goods in the market.[11] This results in the 'natural chaos' of asymmetrical information. Such information asymmetry can negatively impact the market, or the purchasing choice of consumers, when it is exploited by certain producers who may be inclined to lower the quality of the goods supplied precisely because consumers lack complete information, as is often the case.[12] In such a scenario, GIs can help restore the symmetry in information by offering consumers additional information on the products' quality and reputation so that they are not adversely placed against producers. In his model on reputation, Shapiro suggested that reputation

---

[9] Cerkia Bramley, A *Review of the Socio-Economic Impact of Geographical Indications: Considerations for the Developing World*, WIPO Worldwide Symposium on Geographical Indications 1 (2011).
[10] *Id.* at 2.   [11] *Id.*   [12] *Id.*

operates as a signalling device, which transmits information about a certain quality to the consumers, thereby reducing the consumer's search costs.[13] The operation of GIs is quite similar and therefore GIs could have a direct impact on consumer welfare by leading consumers towards goods of a higher quality.[14]

One of the prime motives behind obtaining a GI registration is in fact to create a distinct reputation for the product bearing the GI label so that consumers will eventually move from the point of brand awareness, in this case GI-awareness, about the product to brand preference, in this case GI preference, where they are willing to pay a higher price ('premium') for the GI-denominated product and, at the same time, refuse to accept other alternatives.[15] In this regard, surveys conducted by the United Nations Conference on Trade and Development (UNCTAD) among EU consumers provide good insights. These surveys show that for GI-registered agricultural products consumers are willing to pay a premium of up to 10 to 15 per cent, whereas for non-agricultural products the premium could range anywhere between 5 and 10 per cent.[16] In particular, most consumers expect GI products to be of a higher quality than non-GI products.[17] The findings of certain empirical studies show that in case of foodstuffs. Even though labelling of GIs does not operate as the most important quality attribute,[18] GIs are frequently associated with higher quality control and consumers highly value food safety inspection. Thus, GIs remain an important indicator of quality in the marketplace.[19] Consumer

---

[13] Carl Shapiro, *Premiums to High Quality Products as Returns to Reputation*, 98 THE Q. J. ECON., 659, 670–72 (1983).

[14] Thierry Coulet, *Assessing the Economic Impact of GI Protection*, in EXTENDING THE PROTECTION OF GEOGRAPHICAL INDICATIONS: CASE STUDIES OF AGRICULTURAL PRODUCTS IN AFRICA 101, 103 (Michael Blakeney et al. eds., 2013); Luisa Menapace & Gian Carlo Moschini, *Quality Certification by Geographical Indications, Trademarks and Firm Reputation*, 39 EUR. REV. AGRIC. ECON. 539, 539–49 (2012).

[15] Amarjit Singh, *The Role of Collective Marks, Certification Marks and Geographical Indications*, WORLD INTELLECTUAL PROPERTY ORGANIZATION (2007), www.wipo.int/meetings/en/doc_details.jsp?doc_id=81475.

[16] Shashikant B. Bagade & Deven B. Metha, *Geographical Indications in India: Hitherto and Challenges*, 5 RES. J. PHARM., BIOLOGICAL & CHEM. SCIS. (2014), www.rjpbcs.com/pdf/2014_5%282%29/[146].pdf.

[17] Ramona Teuber, Sven Anders & Corinne Langinier, *The Economics of Geographical Indications: Welfare Implications* (Structure and Performance of Agriculture and Agri-products industry Network, Working Paper No. 2011–16), http://ageconsearch.umn.edu/bitstream/103262/2/Lit-Overview_GI_Paper_04_2011.pdf.

[18] Wim Verbeke, *Food Quality Policies and Consumer Interests in the EU*, in CONSUMER ATTITUDES TO FOOD QUALITY PRODUCTS: EMPHASIS ON SOUTHERN EUROPE 13, 17 (Marija Klopčič, Abele Kuipers & Jean-Francois Hocquette eds., 2013).

[19] *Id.*

perception regarding GI labels thus has important economic implications as it directly influences consumer preferences for the product.[20] For example, Louriero and McCluskey have concluded that Spanish consumers are more inclined to pay a premium for fresh meat products labelled with a protected geographical indication (PGI) label – Galician Veal, which is regulated by the European Union – because the consumer perception associates the certification directly with food safety in addition to quality.[21]

But it would be incorrect to claim that the association of reputation with quality is unique to GIs. Trademarks also operate as useful information tools for consumers by allowing them to equate the quality of a good with a distinct brand and business, thereby reducing consumer confusion and their search costs.[22] Consequently, trademark protection offers a natural incentive for every business to produce and maintain a 'consistent quality over time and across consumers'.[23] This encourages the firm to invest in quality (as expected by the customers) and brand value, lest it lose customer loyalty and of course sales.[24]

Despite these similar tendencies, unfortunately, the incentive to maintain quality does not arise in the case of GIs in the same way it does in the case of trademarks. GIs are collective public or 'club' goods and, as such, are more prone to the classic 'free-rider' problem compared to other distinctive signs like trademarks.[25] In particular, the link between the GI as a collective mark and its owners (i.e. association of producers) is not as direct as in the case of trademark owners protecting their marks. Moreover, not only do GIs identify the quality and the characteristics of the GI-denominated products, but they also embody the *collective* reputation that consumers place on the association or group of producers in a

---

[20] John M. Crespi & Stéphan Marette, *Some Economic Implications of Public Labeling*, FARM FOUNDATION (2003), www.farmfoundation.org/projects/03-65CrespiMarettepaper.htm.

[21] Maria L. Loureiro & Jill J. McCluskey, *Assessing Consumer Response to Protected Geographical Identification Labeling*, 16 AGRIBUSINESS 309, 314 (2000).

[22] Gian Carlo Moschini, Luisa Menapace, & Daniel Pick, *Geographical Indications and the Competitive Provision of Quality in Agricultural Markets*, 90 AM. J. AGRIC. ECON. 794, 794 (2008).

[23] William M. Landes & Richard A. Posner, *The Economics of Trademark Law*, 78 TRADEMARK REP. 267 (1988).

[24] World Intellectual Property Organization, *The Economics of Trademarks in Brands And Reputation in the Global Marketplace*, in 2013 WORLD INTELLECTUAL PROPERTY REPORT 81, No. 944E/2013, www.wipo.int/edocs/pubdocs/en/intproperty/944/wipo_pub_944_2013.pdf.

[25] Lina Monten, *Geographical Indications of Origin: Should They Be Protected and Why? An Analysis of the Issue from the U.S. and EU Perspectives*, 22 SANTA CLARA HIGH TECH. L. J. 315, 315 (2005).

certain region (who participate in the production of the GI product) and which is carried forward through tradition over time.[26] Therefore, while conducting a realistic assessment of GIs one must take into account and tackle the possibility of free-riding from within, i.e. by insiders.[27] These insiders are individual producers that operate within the collective group of GI producers, are legally entitled to produce GI-denominated products (as a registered proprietor or authorized user), but have succumbed to producing goods of inferior quality in a bid for higher profit margins. In order to prevent this unwelcome phenomenon, the regulation structure that is at the basis of GI protection needs to provide for specific procedures, which must account not only for the verification of the geographical origin and manufacturing source of the products but also for specific quality certification to ensure that the GI-denominated products ascribe to the registered GI specifications.

3 HOW CAN GEOGRAPHICAL INDICATIONS BE REGULATED? THE EUROPEAN AND AMERICAN EXPERIENCE

Presently, there are two dominant models of formal regulatory mechanisms for quality control and maintenance for GI-denominated products operating in different socio-economic and political contexts across the world: (a) the European-style *sui generis* quality scheme; and (b) the American-style quality scheme based on certification marks, which is not specifically a *sui generis* system for GIs but nonetheless includes relevant provisions with respect to quality control.

3.1 The Sui Generis *Protection and Related Quality Scheme in the European Union*

It is not surprising that the European Union, which was among the demanders of GI protection during the Uruguay Round TRIPS negotiations, has robust mechanisms for issues pertaining to quality control of GI products. The European Union maintains a distinct approach and position on the issue of GI protection when compared with the United States on the other side of the

---

[26] Bramley, *supra* note 9; Menapace & Moschini, *supra* note 14.
[27] Daniela Benavente, *The Economics of Geographical Indications: GIs Modeled as Club Assets* (Graduate Institute of International and Development Studies, Working Paper No: 10/2010), http://graduateinstitute.ch/files/live/sites/iheid/files/sites/international_economics/shared/int ernational_economics/publications/working%20papers/2010/HEIDWP10-2010.pdf.

Atlantic. Unlike the United States, European national laws and the European Community's IP law recognize GIs as *sui generis* rights.[28] The European Union has passed a number of regulations to govern the grant and operation of GIs, the most significant of which is the Council Regulation 2081/92 '*on the protection of geographical indications and designations for agricultural products and foodstuffs*' and its subsequent amendments.[29] The Regulation was then repealed in 2006 and replaced by Regulation 510/2006. The 2006 Regulation was later amended and replaced in 2012 with Regulation 1151/2012, which is the current community legal instrument that governs the protection of GIs for agricultural products and foodstuffs in the European Union.[30] In addition, there is a separate set of Regulations that governs the regulation of GIs for wines and spirits.[31]

Presently, the European Union only grants GI protection for agriculture-related products, even though the European Commission is currently contemplating extending such protection to non-agricultural products.[32] The EU Green Paper published in 2014 on this possible extension of GI protection highlights the difficulties that one may encounter in cases of the protection of non-agricultural products, which base their claims on given reputations derived by virtue of long usage rather than more specific product

---

[28] Johann Robert Basedow & Davide Bonvicini, *The EU-US Trade Dispute on Geographical Indications: Two Scorpions in a Bottle?* (Graduate Institute of International and Development Studies, Working Paper), http://graduateinstitute.ch/files/live/sites/iheid/files/sites/mia/users/Imene_Ajala/public/WTO%20Seminar%202009/Basedow,_Bonvicini_-_The_EU-US_trade_dispute_on_Geographical_Indications.pdf (last visited 7 March 2016).

[29] Council Regulation 2081/92 of 14 July 1992 on the protection of geographical indications and designations of origin for agricultural products and foodstuffs, 1992 O.J. (L 208) 1, as amended by 1997 O.J. (L 83) 3 & 2003 O.J. (L 99) 1 (emphasis added).

[30] Regulation 1151/2012 of the European Parliament and of the Council of 21 November 2012 on Quality Schemes for Agricultural Products and Foodstuff, 2012 O.J. (L 343) 1 [hereinafter Regulation (EU) No. 1151/2012]. For an overall survey of the EU protection of GIs, see MICHAEL BLAKENEY, THE PROTECTION OF GEOGRAPHICAL INDICATIONS: LAW AND PRACTICE (2014).

[31] Commission Regulation 479/2008 on the common organization of the market in wine, amending Regulations No. 1493/1999, 1782/2003, 1290/2005, 3/2008 and repealing Regulations (EEC) No. 2392/1986 and 1493/1999, O.J. (L 148) 1; Regulation 110/2008 of the European Parliament and of the Council of 15 January 2008 on the definition, description, presentation, labeling and the protection of geographical indications of spirits drinks and repealing Council Regulation (EEC) No. 1576/1989, 2008 O.J. (L 39) 16.

[32] *Making the Most Out of Europe's Traditional Know-How: A Possible Extension of Geographical Indication Protection of the European Union to Non-Agricultural Products*, COM (2014) 469 final (15 July 2014), http://eur-lex.europa.eu/legal-content/EN/TXT/PDF/?uri=CELEX:52014DC0469&from=EN.

characteristics.[33] A study commissioned on the same topic and published the previous year specifically notes that a given reputation is 'only quoted in the definition [of GI] and there is no specific criteria established to determine whether or not a product has acquired a specific reputation'.[34] Yet, the European Union has been careful not to sideline quality in its drive to expand GI protection and continues to require, in its various Regulations, conformity with the quality schemes for each product and compliance with the specifications.

In this respect, the EU standards go far beyond the protection envisaged for GIs under the Agreement on Trade-Related Aspects of Intellectual Property (TRIPS Agreement). Notably, Article 22 of the TRIPS Agreement envisages a basic level of protection for a GI and does not require a particular standard or quality control to be associated with a GI-denominated product.[35] Rather, the provision only contemplates an intrinsically higher-than-generic quality level for which the supply is limited due to the geographical confinement of production. It is not surprising that the European Union has adopted stringent standards because the GI provisions in the TRIPS Agreement arose largely due to the efforts and insistence of the European Union.[36]

In particular, EU law lays down stringent standards under quality schemes for guaranteeing the quality of all European products.[37] These standards are enforced through competent authorities designated by Member States (Competent Authorities) responsible for official controls carried out to verify compliance with the legal requirements relating to the quality schemes.[38] Reports of the control activities of these Competent Authorities must be included within the multi-annual and annual national control plans submitted by every Member State to the European Union.[39] At the time of registration of a protected designation of origin ('PDO') and a PGI, the

---

[33] *Id.* at 17. The paper notes:

> Requiring the description of product features ensures stable product quality, but does not require a particular level of quality. This can only be achieved by requiring a minimum quality level. However, identifying a meaningful quality benchmark may not work for all products, and setting a particular level of quality requires an element of discretion.

Id.

[34] *Study on Geographical Indications Protection for Non-Agricultural Products in the Internal Market*, EUROPEAN COMMISSION (18 February 2013), http://ec.europa.eu/internal_market/in dprop/docs/geo-indications/130322_geo-indications-non-agri-study_en.pdf.

[35] Agreement on Trade-Related Aspects of Intellectual Property Rights, 15 April 1994, Marrakesh Agreement Establishing the World Trade Organization, Annex 1C, 1869 U.N.T.S. 299, 33 I.L. M. 1197 (1994) art. 22(1).

[36] Monten, *supra* note 25.   [37] Regulation (EU) No. 1151/2012, *supra* note 30.

[38] *See, e.g., id.* art. 36.   [39] *Id.* art. 40.

applicant group is required to identify one or more certification bodies, which will ensure that the product specifications associated with the GI products are met before the goods are placed on the market.[40] They are required to comply with and, as of 1 May 2010, be accredited in accordance with European standard EN 45011 or ISO/IEC Guide 65.[41] The operation of certification bodies is, in turn, scrutinized by the Competent Authorities.[42] Thus, a system of checks and balances has been integrated within the GI mechanism of the European Union.

3.2 The Trademark-Style Protection Adopted in the United States for Geographical Names

The United States provides a different approach owing to the fact that they lack penchant for GIs. Yet, the regulatory model for quality certification and enforcement is notable. Under the current US law, there is no *sui generis* protection available for products on the basis of their geographical origin.[43] The only exception to this is the protection afforded to appellation for wines, which are protected both at the federal and state levels under a system that could be defined as a *sui generis* system.[44] Hence, the principal method by which geographical indicators can be protected under US law is by means of trademark protection, namely certification marks under the aegis of the Lanham Act, the federal trademark law currently in force in the United States.[45] Trademarks also form part of US unfair competition law, within which the Lanham Act is the primary statute governing GIs protection of agricultural produce and foodstuffs.[46] Under the US Lanham Act,

---

[40] Regulation (EU) No. 1151/2012, *supra* note 30; Irena Kireeva, *European Legislation on Protection of Geographical Indications: Overview of the EU Member States' Legal Framework for Protection of Geographical Indications*, IPR2 (February 2011), www.ipkey.org/en/resources/ip-information-centre/19-geographical-indications/1947-european-legislation-on-protection-of-geographical-indications-overview-of-the-eu-member-states-legal-framework-for-protection-of-geographical-indications.

[41] Regulation (EU) No. 1151/2012, *supra* note 30, art. 39.2.   [42] *Id.* art. 38, 39.

[43] Bruce A. Babcock & Roxanne Clemens, *Geographical Indications and Property Rights: Protecting Value-Added Agricultural Products*, MATRIC Briefing Paper 04-MBP 7 (May 2004).

[44] On this point, see Irene Calboli, *Time to Say Local Cheese and Smile at Geographical Indications of Origin? International Trade and Local Development in the United States*, 53 Hous. L. Rev. 373, 394–95 (2015).

[45] Inessa Shalevich, *Protection of Trademarks and Geographical Indications*, 6 Buff. Intell. Prop. L. J. 67, 73 (2008).

[46] 15 U.S.C. § 1052(e) (2006); Justin M. Waggoner, *Acquiring a European Taste for Geographical Indications*, 33 Brook. J. Int'l L. 569, 581 (2008).

Certification Trademarks are used to indicate '(1) regional or national origin; (2) material, mode of manufacture, quality, accuracy or other characteristics of the goods/services; or (3) that the work or labour on the goods/services was performed by a member of a union or other organization'.[47] In general, geographic indicators would not pass muster as trademarks or collective marks in the United States because they are geographically descriptive. However, an applicant can still register them as certification trademarks without showing any sign of acquired distinctiveness.[48] Several other kinds of distinctive names, which are otherwise protected under the rubric of *sui generis* GIs in different countries, are protected through several mechanisms, including certification trademarks, trademarks or by way of a common law remedy of passing off.[49]

Even though there is no separate recognition granted to geographical indicators under US law, the US government plays an active role in ensuring that the value of the quality associated with a certified product is not diluted due to 'insiders'. Notably, in most instances, the authority that registers and consequently exercises control over the use of a geographical term as a certification mark is a governmental body or a body operating with governmental authorization.[50] The US government has separate inspectors for various agricultural types of food and beverages in order to ensure quality maintenance and control post-registration for geographical Certification Trademarks.[51] Consumers and competitors are presumed to have the highest interest in maintaining accuracy and certified standards and therefore can file an opposition or cancellation proceeding against the certification mark or bring an action in the federal court if the prescribed standards are not met.[52] Overall, even though the United States remains different, at large, from the EU system of protecting GIs, the two systems are not so opposite and, in both systems, quality control represents one of the most important components of the systems in order to safeguard consumers and the long-term quality of the products. The US approach focuses on promoting competition and innovation based on the premise that GIs could be harmful to the economy 'as they are deemed to be untradeable, collective and conserve old-fashioned production methods'.[53]

---

[47] U.S. Patent & Trademark Office, *Geographical Indication Protection in the United States*, www.uspto.gov/sites/default/files/web/offices/dcom/olia/globalip/pdf/gi_system.pdf (last visited 7 March 2016).
[48] *Id.* [49] *Id.* [50] *Id.* [51] *Id.* [52] *Id.*
[53] Basedow & Bonvicini, *supra* note 28, at 6; *but see* Calboli, *supra* note 44, at 389–99 (noting that the US protects appellations of origin for wines under a *sui generis* system under the Treasury Department Alcohol and Tobacco Tax and Trade Bureau).

4 CASE STUDIES REFLECTING DIFFERENT EXPERIENCES WITH GEOGRAPHICAL INDICATIONS IN INDIA

In India, GI protection is available through a *sui generis* system operationalized through the Geographical Indications of Goods (Registration & Protection) Act of 1999 ('GI Act').[54] The GI Act was followed by the Geographical Indications of Goods (Registration and Protection) Rules of 2002 ('GI Rules').[55] The Intellectual Property Office in Chennai is in charge of the GI Registry for India. As of today, the Registry has been able to successfully register around 237 Indian GIs involving agricultural products, handicrafts and manufactured products.[56]

Under the GI Act, the definition of 'geographical indication' adopted states that a GI is

> an indication which identifies such goods as *agricultural goods, natural goods or manufactured goods* as originating, or manufactured in the territory of a country, or a region or locality in that territory, where a *given quality, reputation or other characteristic of such goods is essentially attributable to its geographical origin.*[57]

But under the Act, names that do not denote the name of a country or region or locality can still be considered for registration as long as they relate to a specific geographical area and are used in relation to goods originating from that region.[58] This provides the leeway for extending protection to other famous symbols such as 'Alphonso mangoes'[59] and 'Basmati Rice'.[60] It is emphasized that this is not unique to India and the same practice is used in several other

---

[54] The Geographical Indications of Goods (Registration & Protection) Act, No. 48 of 1999.
[55] Biswajit Dhar & Kasturi Das, *Operationalization of GI Protection in India: A Preliminary Exploration* (2007), www2.warwick.ac.uk/fac/soc/csgr/events/conferences/conference2007/papers/das.pdf.
[56] Geographical Indication Registry, *State Wise Registration Details of G.I. Applications*, http://ipindia.nic.in/girindia/ (last visited 7 March 2016).
[57] The Geographical Indications of Goods (Registration & Protection) Act, No. 48 of 1999 ch. 1 § 2(e) (emphasis added).
[58] *Id. See* Explanation appended to Section 2 (e) in the Indian GI Act.
[59] Alphonso Mango has not been formally registered as a GI but the application for its registration is currently pending before the GI registry. *See* Geographical Indications Registry, *Application Details*, http://ipindiaservices.gov.in/GirPublic/ViewApplicationDetails.aspx?AppNo=139&index=1&pIndex=0&status=0 (last visited 8 March 2016) [hereinafter Alphonso Mango Registration Application].
[60] Basmati has not been formally registered as a GI, but the application for its registration is currently pending before the GI registry. *See* Geographical Indications Registry, *Application Details*, http://ipindiaservices.gov.in/GirPublic/ViewApplicationDetails.aspx?AppNo=14&index=1&pIndex=0&status=0 (last visited 8 March 2016).

countries, including the European Union – Feta is not a region of Greece, for example.

Several scholars have suggested that the collective-action problems that can derive from the misuse of GIs with regard to quality maintenance can be alleviated to a certain extent by the adoption of 'some regulatory process that polices quality and technique among producers within the GI'.[61] However, despite the stakes involved for consumers in this respect, not much attention has been paid to post-registration quality-control measures exclusively for Indian GIs under the current system of GI protection under Indian law. A recent empirical study by an Indian scholar notes the absence of an inspection mechanism on the ground in the GI-denominated regions and calls for 'a stringent quality control mechanism in place to assure the consumer of the authenticity and quality for which she pays a premium price'.[62] The study notes that among the selected sample of GI producers, only 40 per cent indicated that quality checks were carried out for their GI products before these products were distributed to consumer and after.[63]

Still, despite the lack of quality control for GI-denominated products in practice, Indian law does provide for some measures guaranteeing quality control in language similar to that of European law. Notably, at the time of the application to register a GI under the GI Act, a combined reading of Section 11(2) of the Act and Form GI-1 suggests that the applicant group should identify an 'Inspection Body', which is responsible for quality control of the products within the GI.[64] In fact, Rule 32(1)(g) of the Geographical Indications of Goods (Registration and Protection) Rules, 2002 specifically requires 'particulars of the inspection structure, if any, to regulate the use of the geographical indication in respect of the goods for which application is made in the definite territory region or locality mentioned in the application'.[65] Still, it is important to note that the non-existence of an inspection structure will ultimately not be considered as a

---

[61] Kal Raustiala & Stephen R. Munzer, *The Global Struggle over Geographical Indications*, 18 EUR. J. INT'L L. 337, 360 (2007).

[62] Dr Ruppal W. Sharma & Shraddha Kulhari, *Marketing of GI Products: Unlocking Their Commercial Potential* (Centre for WTO Studies, Indian Institute of Foreign Trade, August 2015), http://wtocentre.iift.ac.in/Papers/Marketing%20of%20GI%20Products%20Unlocking%20their%20Commercial%20Potential.pdf.

[63] *Id.* at 92.

[64] Form GI-1, Application for the Registration of a Geographical Indication in Part A of the Register, GI Act s 11, GI Rules r 23, http://ipindia.nic.in/girindia/Form_GI1.pdf (last visited 8 March 2016).

[65] Geographical Indications of Goods (Registration and Protection) Rules, 2002.

sufficient ground for demonstrating the inadequacy of an application to register a GI for the final granting of the GI under Indian law.[66]

Moreover, in addition to referring to the Inspection Body suggested by the collective group, the law in India could be strengthened by also requiring that an independent neutral agency is also appointed to maintain the quality standards of the GI-denominated products post-registration of the GI.[67] It should also be noted that the current legislative framework has no teeth as there is no statutory liability imposed on Inspection Bodies under the current GI Act in the event that they fail to conduct periodic verification of compliance with the product specifications of the associated GI.[68] At present, if members of the collective group entitled to use the GI, or consumers, want to hold a member of the group accountable for not complying with the quality standards of the products, the only course of action available is under Section 27 of the GI Act, which provides the cancellation of registration of the non-complying member from the list of authorized GI producers.[69] This mechanism is not sufficient, however, and the fact that additional preventive regulatory mechanisms may be needed to ensure the quality control of the GI-denominated products in India is accentuated by reports that popular GI-denominated products are losing their markets to adulterated products that are sold by 'insiders'. Further, the availability of cheaper raw material imports is promoting the sale of inferior-quality products. These products are handed to the unaware consumers who still rely on the name of the GI-registered products and thus are lured into paying premium prices for products that no longer carry the same characteristics of the genuine GI-denominated products.

---

[66] Although section 11(6) of the GI Act states 'Subject to the provisions of this Act, the Registrar may refuse the application of accept it absolutely or subject to such amendments, modification. Conditions or limitations, if any, as he thinks fit.' However, the GI Act does not contain any specific provision that relates to insufficiency in GI application due to non-existence of inspection structures. The Geographical Indications of Goods (Registration & Protection) Act, No. 48 of 1999.

[67] Office of Controller General of Patents, Designs and Trade marks, *Draft Manual of Geographical Indications Practice and Procedure*, http://ipindia.nic.in/manuals/DraftManual_GI_PracticeProcedure_31March2011.pdf (last visited 8 March 2016).

[68] There is no legislation at present that governs the qualifications and the nature of responsibilities of Inspection Bodies and the liability that may be imposed on such Bodies for failure to act in accordance with their responsibilities. E.g., in the case of textiles, The Export Promotion and Quality Assurance Division of the Textiles Committee is the First Accredited Inspection Body in India under ISO 17020 (Type 'A' Inspection Body). The ISO 17020 standard specifies general criteria for the competence of impartial bodies performing inspection. However, these Inspection Bodies have not been made liable under the Act to secure given quality in the case of GI products.

[69] The Geographical Indications of Goods (Registration & Protection) Act, No. 48 of 1999, § 27.

In the following sub-sections, this chapter reviews four case studies of Indian GI-denominated products for which it seems that 'free-riding' by insiders has become the norm. As we elaborate in the reminder of this chapter, this has negatively impacted the market for other producers within the respective collective groups.

4.1 Sarees and Brocades from Banarasi

Since the Mughal era Banarasi sarees have enjoyed a distinguished reputation on account of their fine silk, gold or silver brocade or *zari*, and opulent embroidery.[70] Even today, they continue to be a popular item among the womenfolk in India. To protect the authenticity of the weaving tradition of the Banarasi sarees, several organizations – Banaras Bunkar Samiti, Human Welfare Association ('HWA'), joint director industries (eastern zone), director of handlooms and textiles Uttar Pradesh Handloom Fabrics Marketing Cooperative Federation, Eastern UP Exporters Association ('EUPEA'), Banarasi Vastra Udyog Sangh, Banaras Hath Kargha Vikas Samiti and Adarsh Silk Bunkar Sahkari Samiti – filed an application for GI registration for 'Banarasi' in 2007. They finally secured the GI in 2009.[71]

However, despite the considerable reputation that the industry enjoys in both the domestic and international markets,[72] and the GI registration, the weavers have been facing stiff competition from cheap silk fabric imports from China and Surat.[73] Notably, known for its unique gold-bordered designs and improvisations of medieval artistic patterns on its sarees and brocades, Banarasi sarees have been witness to fast changes and rapid industrialization. Particularly, power looms have scaled-up production and have been responsible for bringing intense competition to suit pockets of the highly segmented Indian consumer market.[74] Power-loom-based manufacturers are

---

[70] *Dream of Weaving: Study & Documentation of Banaras Sarees and Brocades*, TEXTILES COMMITTEE 36, http://textilescommittee.nic.in/writereaddata/files/banaras.pdf (last visited 8 March 2016).

[71] Binay Singh, *Banarasi Sarees Get Copyright Cover*, THE TIMES OF INDIA (18 September 2009 4:40 AM), http://articles.economictimes.indiatimes.com/2009-09-18/news/28410802_1_gi-sta tus-banarasi-silk-gi-registration.

[72] Statistics suggest that the annual turnover of the industry is Rs. 30,000 million (approximately $500 million). *See* Basole, *supra* note 6.

[73] *Id.*; *see also* Shefalee Vasudev, *The Banaras Bind*, *supra* note 2.

[74] Shefalee Vasudev, *The Powerloom Lobby is out to Destroy India's Handloom Advantage: Ashoke Chatterjee*, LIVE MINT (25 April 2015 1:39 AM), www.livemint.com/Industry/bA QbFuEgGCEFrrUGOm7zxJ/The-powerloom-lobby-is-out-to-destroy-Indias-handloom-adva n.html.

now seeking parity with producers of handloom in the Banarasi region.[75] Initially, handloom-based producers of Banarasi sarees hoped not to be affected by this competition as they cater to the higher-income markets – markets in which consumers still appreciate the techniques and materials that go into a handwoven saree. Still, new ideas have emerged in the attempt to popularize handloom Banarasi sarees as 'green products' to capture newer markets abroad.[76]

More problematically, studies show that, in order to compete with power-loom-based manufacturers, master weavers and artisans have also started to resort to strategies such as passing off synthetic fibres for silk and power-loom fabric as handloom. This, in turn, has compromised the quality of dyes and designs of the traditional sarees.[77] To date, the penetration of the markets by these inferior-quality products has reached a point where the ordinary Indian consumer can no longer be sure of the quality of the Banarasi saree she is buying. This uncertainty raises transaction costs for the consumer and unfortunately operates against the collective group of producers that have seen the sales of their artisans' products greatly reduced.[78] The tragedy of the situation is such that some Banarasi saree producers are now advocating that the government must support new spinning mills in Banaras that produce Banarasi sarees using synthetic materials, so as to compete with Surat-made Banarasi sarees. As an alternative, these producers are advocating that they should have access to cheaper imported silk yarns, which are still natural fibres.[79]

In theory, five inspection bodies were identified by the applicant group of producers in Banarasi in the GI application that was submitted to the GI Registry. These Inspections Bodies are the Department of Handlooms (Government of Uttar Pradesh), the Development Commissioner (Handlooms), the Weavers' Service Centre, Master Weavers' Self-Regulation and the Textiles Committee. The role of the Textiles Committee is arguably the most prominent in this respect, as the Committee is a statutory body whose main objective is *'to ensure the quality of textiles and textile machinery both for internal consumption and export*

---

[75] Id.
[76] Prashant Pandey, *'Green' plans for Banarasi Sarees to Take It Global*, THE INDIAN EXPRESS (16 September 2014 4:20 AM), http://indianexpress.com/article/cities/lucknow/green-plans-for-banarasi-sarees-to-take-it-global/.
[77] Basole, *supra* note 6.   [78] Shefalee Vasudev, *The Banaras Bind*, *supra* note 2.
[79] Rajeev Dikshit, *Silk Rivals Kashi, Surat Join Hands to Fight Crisis*, THE TIMES OF INDIA (16 February 2015 10:18 AM), http://timesofindia.indiatimes.com/city/varanasi/Silk-rivals-Kashi-Surat-join-hands-to-fight-crisis/articleshow/46378029.cms.

purposes'.[80] The Export Promotion and Quality Assurance division of the Textiles Committee is an Accredited Inspection body in India under ISO 17020[81] and provides a host of inspection services for importers/traders/exporters/manufacturers for textiles.[82] The Textiles Committee is also the implementation agency for the Handloom Mark, which certifies that the product being purchased is genuinely handwoven.[83] This presents a picture quite similar to the European model, where the certification bodies for agricultural produce are accredited in accordance with European standard EN 45011 or ISO/IEC Guide 65.[84]

However, until the present day, the Textiles Committee has focused its attention in the sphere of GIs almost entirely on the facilitation of the registration of GIs for unique textile products in India.[85] Besides facilitating the procedures related to GI registration, the Textile Committee does not oversee special quality or process certification schemes that are supposed to be in place for GI-denominated products, including those products which are listed as requiring an Inspection Body in the product specification, to ascertain whether the products are actually being produced in accordance with the registered specifications. Instead, at present, the Banarasi saree operates with a multitude of certification marks such as the Silk Mark and the Handloom Mark.[86] The Silk Mark Organization of India (SMOI), the registered owner of the SILK Mark, recently introduced a high-security nano-particle-embedded fusion label as a mark of purity for Banarasi silk to enable customers to verify the authenticity of the source of silk.[87] Beyond these external agencies, quality

---

[80] *About Us*, TEXTILES COMMITTEE, MINISTRY OF TEXTILES, GOVERNMENT OF INDIA (emphasis added), http://textilescommittee.nic.in/about-us/about-us (last visited 8 March 2016).

[81] The ISO 17020 standard specifies general criteria for the competence of impartial bodies performing inspection. It also specifies an independence criterion of Inspection Bodies.

[82] *Inspection*, TEXTILES COMMITTEE, MINISTRY OF TEXTILES, GOVERNMENT OF INDIA, http://textilescommittee.nic.in/services/services-0 (last visited 8 March 2016).

[83] *Handloom Mark*, TEXTILES COMMITTEE, MINISTRY OF TEXTILES, GOVERNMENT OF INDIA, http://textilescommittee.nic.in/about-us/handloom-mark (last visited 8 March 2016).

[84] Organic Research Centre, *The European Regulatory Framework and its implementation in Influencing Organic Inspection and Certification Systems in the EU* (Susanne Padel ed., 2010), http://certcost.org/Lib/CERTCOST/Deliverable/D14_D11.pdf.

[85] *Facilitation of IPR Protection through Geographical Indications*, TEXTILES COMMITTEE, MINISTRY OF TEXTILES, GOVERNMENT OF INDIA, http://textilescommittee.nic.in/services/geographical-indications (last visited 8 March 2016).

[86] Krishna Dwivedi & Souvik Bhattacharya, *Restore Glory of the Banarasi Sari*, THE HINDU BUSINESS LINE (21 December 2012), www.thehindubusinessline.com/opinion/restore-glory-of-the-banarasi-sari/article4226412.ece.

[87] Ajay Kumar, *Banarasi Silk Gets Nano Mark of Purity*, HINDUSTAN TIMES (30 May 2012 10:05 PM), www.hindustantimes.com/india-news/banarsi-silk-gets-nano-mark-of-purity/article1-863590.aspx.

control internally among the GI producers is especially difficult. Despite being aware of the negative impact of inferior-quality sarees, stakeholders in the industry are unable to take action due to the complex market dynamics involved.[88] It is also noteworthy that legitimate users of the Banarasi GI for sarees are not in the financial position to bear the cost of protracted litigation against traders involved in non-compliance with the product specification, which in turn diminishes the premium value that a consumer of Banarasi sarees would have ordinarily paid for the Banarasi GI due to inferior alternatives.

4.2 Pashmina from Kashmir

One of the most popular and sought-after craft items associated with Kashmir, the Kashmir Pashmina refers to the extremely soft woollen fabric with fibres spun out of the Pashmina goat called 'Capra Hiracus'.[89] The Kashmir Pashmina is known for its 'fineness, warmth, softness, desirable aesthetic value, and timelessness in fashion'.[90] The application for GI registration of the Kashmir Pashmina was an initiative undertaken by the Craft Development Institute (CDI) to secure protection for local artisans against the mushrooming power looms and fake pashminas flooding the markets in India (and abroad). The CDI only acted as a temporary registered proprietor of the GI since the GI was assigned to TAHAFUZ, an association that comprises a diverse group of Kashmiri artisans, when TAHAFUZ was registered under the Societies Act.[91] Similar to the Banarasi sarees, however, the traditional weavers in Kashmir are under severe strain due to the machine-made Semi Pashmina Shawls and imitations of the Kashmiri name that are being spun in Amritsar, located in the Indian province of Punjab (geographically close to the Indian state of Jammu and Kashmir), and China and that are sold to consumers, who are not aware of the geographical significance of the name Kashmir Pashmina and the traditional qualities associated with the authentic products.[92]

---

[88] The Energy and Resources Institute (TERI), *The Protection of Geographical Indications in India: Issues and Challenges* (March 2013), www.teriin.org/div/briefing_paper_GI.pdf.

[89] Ishrat Yaqoob, Asif H. Sofi, Sarfaraz A. Wani, FD Sheikh, & Nazir A. Bumla, Pashmina Shawl – A Traditional Way of Making in Kashmir, 11 INDIAN J. TRADITIONAL KNOWLEDGE 329, 329 (2012).

[90] Id.

[91] Form GI-1 (Pashmina), http://ipindiaservices.gov.in//GI_DOC/46/46%20-%20Form%20GI-1%20-%202009–12-2005.pdf (last visited 8 March 2016).

[92] Sanjiv Singh, *Geographical Indication; A Case Study of Kashmir Pashmina (Shawls)*, 1 NEWMAN INT'L J. MULTIDISCIPLINARY STUD. 96, 100 (2014).

Unfortunately, when the application for the GI was filed, the identification of an Inspection Body for the compliance of the products with the specification was suspended until a later time.[93] Eventually, the responsibility for ensuring quality control for the Kashmir Pashmina products was handed over to the Pashmina Testing and Quality Certification Centre ('PTQCC') in 2013.[94] The purpose of this body is to certify the quality of the products. Procedurally, authentic Kashmir Pashmina Shawls will receive the Kashmir Pashmina Mark (GI) by the PTQCC after verification of the weaving technology, the spinning method and the genuineness of the raw materials.[95] In order to ensure greater authenticity, a micro-chip known as the Secure Fusion Authentic Label ('SFAL') would be attached to the product with a unique number that could be read under infrared light.[96] To date, the effectiveness of the PTQCC in guaranteeing the quality of the GI-denominated products still needs to be proven, as the system is in a nascent stage. Yet, as a matter of policy, the creation of a more detailed system of control for the stages of production as well as the application of a tracking system for the products is believed to be a step in the right direction in order to guarantee product compliance with the standards required as per the GI specification.

In this respect, it is interesting to note that, unlike several other prominent GIs in India, there is no certification mark associated with the Kashmir Pashmina. This again may be due to the initial lack of organization of the group of producers in setting up a quality control system for their products, as certification marks also require a dedicated certifying authority that guarantees the conformity of the marked products with the standards set for the certification.

4.3 Tea from Darjeeling

Whether you are from India or abroad, if you are a tea-drinker, it is almost certain that you would have heard of the famous Darjeeling tea. Darjeeling tea

---

[93] Form GI-1 (Pashmina), *supra* note 91.
[94] Press Trust of India, *J&K Weaves Plan to Save Pashmina; Power Looms Fake*, THE INDIAN EXPRESS (13 July 2014 11:19 AM), http://indianexpress.com/article/india/india-others/jk-weaves-plan-to-save-pashmina-power-looms-fake/.
[95] Press Trust of India, *GI Mark for Handwoven Pashmina Shawls*, BUSINESS STANDARD (5 August 2013 8:39 PM), www.business-standard.com/article/pti-stories/gi-mark-for-handwoven-pashmina-shawls-113080501152_1.html.
[96] Masood Hussain, *Now Micro-chip Embedding into the Pashmina Shawls to Assure its Authenticity*, THE ECONOMIC TIMES (6 August 2013 5:53 AM), http://articles.economictimes.indiatimes.com/2013-08-06/news/41132034_1_pashmina-shawl-farooqui-crore.

contributes just over one per cent to the total tea production in India (10.85 million kilograms of Darjeeling tea as compared to 981 million kilograms of total tea production).[97] But the reputation of Darjeeling tea remains unparalleled due to its distinctive quality and flavour and in turn has made the region a hallmark for tea, underscoring the fact that the incomparable quality of the tea is largely attributable to its geographical origin.[98] Almost synonymous with Indian tea in foreign markets, Darjeeling tea is cultivated, grown and produced in the Darjeeling district of West Bengal. Interestingly, the tea has been produced in the region by the local population for over one and a half centuries and continues to remain one of the most coveted black teas in the world.[99]

In the sphere of GIs, the Darjeeling tea industry has set a milestone in Indian history. Darjeeling tea was the first GI to be registered in India after the enactment of the GI Act in 1999.[100] Even though the tea industry in India lies in the hands of the private sector, the Ministry of Commerce has exercised statutory control in maintaining the quality of Darjeeling tea since 1933 under various legislations (that culminated in the Tea Act in 1953) and the Tea Board.[101] The Tea Board, a statutory authority established in 1953 under the Tea Act, has administered the use of the Darjeeling logo for many years to maintain quality and ensure that the Darjeeling logo is applied only to the tea that has been certified by the Tea Board as conforming to the prescribed characteristics of Darjeeling tea.[102] Certification services are provided to the Tea Board by Intertek Agri Services, a private entity that conducts testing and possesses inspection expertise for agricultural commodities, foods and related products.[103]

To ensure genuineness in the exports of Darjeeling tea, a system of certification for the authenticity of the exported Darjeeling tea by the Board was

---

[97] WORLD INTELLECTUAL PROPERTY ORGANIZATION, *Managing the Challenges of the Protection and Enforcement of Intellectual Property Rights*, www.wipo.int/ipadvantage/en/details.jsp?id=2540 (last visited 8 March 2016).
[98] *Id.*   [99] *Id.*
[100] Sudhir Ravindran & Arya Mathew, *The Protection of Geographical Indication in India – Case Study on 'Darjeeling Tea'*, PROPERTY RIGHTS ALLIANCE (2009), www.altacit.com/wp-content/uploads/2015/03/The-Protection-of-Geographical-Indication-in-India-Case-Study-on-Darjeeling-Tea.pdf.
[101] S. C. Srivasatava, *Protecting the Geographical Indication for Darjeeling Tea*, in MANAGING THE CHALLENGES OF WTO PARTICIPATION: 45 CASE STUDIES 231 (Peter Gallagher, Patrick Low & Andrew Stoler eds., 2005).
[102] Brief for Petitioner at 240, *In re* Tea Board, India (2003), http://ipindiaservices.gov.in//GI_DOC/1/1%20-%20Statement%20of%20Case%20-%2017-10-2003.pdf.
[103] *List of Inspection Agency Approved by Tea Board*, TEA BOARD OF INDIA (6 May 2005), www.teaboard.gov.in/pdf/policy/List_of_Insp_Ag_under_TDEC_05.pdf.

made mandatory under the Tea Act in 2003.[104] All dealers of Darjeeling tea are bound to enter into a licensing agreement with the Tea Board, which includes the payment of an annual licence fee. Under the agreement, dealers are required to furnish information regarding the production and manufacture of Darjeeling tea and its sale, through auction or otherwise.[105] On the basis of the information supplied, the Tea Board is thus able to track and compute the total volume of Darjeeling tea produced and sold in a particular period.[106] Certificates of origin are issued for export consignments under the Tea (Marketing and Distribution Control) Order of 2000 as read in conjunction with the Tea Act of 1953. These certificates are to be compulsorily cross-checked at all customs checkpoints in India.[107] This detailed series of measures to control the origin and characteristics of the tea ensures that the sale-chain integrity of Darjeeling tea is maintained until the consignments leave the country.[108] Under the authentication process that is supervised by the Tea Board, 171 companies dealing in Darjeeling tea have registered with the Tea Board, seventy-four of which are producer companies and ninety-seven of which are trader/exporter companies.[109]

As per the licensing agreement, every licensee is required to submit a sample of the tea sold by him to the Tea Board, to enable the Board to monitor the legitimacy and quality of Darjeeling tea produced by the licensees for exports *and* domestic markets.[110] Further, the Board reserves the right to inspect, prior to and after the grant of license, the premises of any licensee where tea is being processed, manufactured, packed or stored, to ensure that the standards laid down by the proprietor are being adhered to and complied with.[111] The Tea Board has also registered the 'Darjeeling Logo' and the word 'Darjeeling' as certification trademarks. These marks may be used by any of the dealers of Darjeeling tea as long as they have been granted licensee rights by the Tea Board.[112]

The initiatives taken by the Tea Board in the field of monitoring and quality assurance, in collaboration with the Darjeeling Planters' Association (which is the only producers' forum in Darjeeling), are the reason why Darjeeling tea continues to enjoy an untarnished reputation not just in India but across the

---

[104] Tea Marketing (Control) Order, 2003 § 3.
[105] Tea Marketing (Control) Order, 2003; Srivastava, *supra* note 101.
[106] Srivastava, *supra* note 101.   [107] *Id.* at 232.   [108] *Id.*
[109] WIPO, *Managing the Challenges of the Protection and Enforcement of Intellectual Property Rights, supra* note 97.
[110] *Id.* at 5.2.   [111] *Id.* at 5.3.
[112] The Tea Board of India, *Protection and Administration of Darjeeling in India* 1, www.teaboard.gov.in/pdf/policy/India.doc (last visited 8 March 2016).

globe. However, it has been noted that cheaper tea from Nepal is sourced by Indian blenders (due to open trade and porous borders with Nepal). This tea is very similar, in quality and characteristics, to the Darjeeling tea and unfortunately it can find its way into Indian markets sold as Darjeeling tea by traders that are not associated with the Tea Board.[113] Hence, only 100 per cent Darjeeling tea can be identified with the Darjeeling tea GI and all other tea mixtures have to be identified as blends. In this respect, it should be noted that the transitory norm that was applicable in the European Union, which allowed EU importers to blend 51 per cent Darjeeling tea with 49 per cent of any other tea, and still sell the final products as Darjeeling tea, has finally been repealed in 2016.[114] This may give an additional boost to Darjeeling tea exports from India into the European Union.

4.4 Alphonso Mango and the Related Controversy

Alphonso mango is a popular export variety mango grown in the coastal districts of Maharashtra, Goa, Karnataka and Gujarat.[115] In 2014, the European Union had imposed a temporary ban on the import of Alphonso mangoes and four other vegetables from India, causing a major upheaval in the EU-India bilateral trade ties because of the impact of this decision on the Indian farmers' annual estimates of profits.[116] The decision was taken by the EU Standing Committee on Plant Health because 207 consignments of

---

[113] Shaoli Chakrabarty, *Concern over Darjeeling Clone*, THE TELEGRAPH CALCUTTA, INDIA (13 April 2015), www.telegraphindia.com/1150413/jsp/business/story_14233.jsp#.VqYo3IV97IU.

[114] Regulation (EU) No. 1050/2011 of 20 October 2011 entering a name in the register of protected designations of origin and protected geographical indications (Darjeeling (PGI), O.J. (L 276); Mithun Dasgupta, *GI Tag in Place, Darjeeling Tea Growers Gear Up to Push Exports*, THE FINANCIAL EXPRESS (16 January 2016 3:32 AM), www.financialexpress.com/article/markets/commodities/gi-tag-in-place-darjeeling-tea-growers-gear-up-to-push-exports/195696/; combined cases in India: T-624/13, T-625/13, T-626/13, T-627/13, respectively entitled, The Tea Board v. OHMI – Delta Lingerie (Darjeeling), The Tea Board v. OHMI – Delta Lingerie (Darjeeling collection de lingerie), The Tea Board v. OHMI – Delta Lingerie (Darjeeling collection de lingerie), The Tea Board v. OHMI – Delta Lingerie (Darjeeling).

[115] G-1 Application Form for Alphonso Mango, http://164.100.176.36/GI_DOC/139/139%20-%20Form%20GI-1%20-%2022-09-2008.pdf (last visited March 8, 2016). This variety accounts for about 60 per cent of India's mango exports.

[116] *See* European Union Press Release, EU Stops Some Fruit and Vegetable Imports from India, to Protect EU Crops from Pests (1 May 2014), http://eeas.europa.eu/delegations/india/documents/press_release_eu_stops_some_fruit_and_vegetable_imports_from_india.pdf (last visited 8 March 2016); *see also EU Bans Indian Alphonso Mangoes, 4 Vegetables from May 1*, THE HINDU (28 April 2014), www.thehindu.com/news/international/world/eu-bans-indian-alphonso-mangoes-4-vegetables-from-may-1/article5956482.ece [hereinafter EU Bans Indian Alphonso Mangoes].

Alphonso mangoes and the other vegetables, which had been imported from India into the European Union, were found to be contaminated by pests such as fruit flies and other quarantine pests.[117] The ban was successively lifted by the European Union in January 2015.[118] At present, Alphonso mangoes are not formally registered as a GI in India, but an application to register the GI is pending before the GI Registry.[119] The news of the ban imposed by the European Union underscored the importance of quality certification for agricultural products. Accordingly, as a soon-to-be-registered GI with immense export potential,[120] the Alphonso mango certainly deserves our attention in this chapter.

The mandate of inspection and certification for agricultural food products in India has been entrusted to the Agricultural and Processed Food Products Export Development Authority ('APEDA'), a statutory body established by the Government of India in 1986.[121] APEDA fixes standards and specifications for agricultural products for the purpose of exports[122] and also has powers to carry out inspection at storage houses where such products are kept to ensure quality.[123] In this respect, state-of-the-art packaging houses have been set up in major production zones to ensure a uniform quality across export consignments in order to maintain the highest quality standards in mangoes.[124] APEDA has additionally put in place internationally recognized treatment facilities, like hot water treatment, vapour heat treatment and irradiation facilities at various places along the production belt.[125] These facilities are supplemented by a unique product identification system, supplemented by the traceability networking and Residue Monitoring Plan, which have been

---

[117] *Mango Ban: India Threatens to Drag EU to WTO*, THE HINDU (1 May 2014), www.thehindu.com/news/mango-ban-india-threatens-to-drag-eu-to-wto/article5970369.ece.

[118] *See* European Commission – Daily News, Plant Health: Experts Endorse the Lift of the Import Ban of Mango Fruits from India (20 January 2015), http://europa.eu/rapid/press-release_MEX-15-3523_en.htm.

[119] Alphonso Mango Registration Application, *supra* note 59.

[120] The United Kingdom alone imports nearly 16 million mangoes every year and the market for the fruit is nearly 6 million pounds annually. *See EU Bans Indian Alphonso Mangoes*, *supra* note 116.

[121] *About APEDA*, AGRICULTURAL AND PROCESSED FOOD PRODUCTS EXPORT DEVELOPMENT AUTHORITY (APEDA), http://apeda.gov.in/apedawebsite/about_apeda/About_apeda.htm (last visited 8 March 2016).

[122] The Agricultural and Processed Food Products Export Development Authority Act 1985, No. 2 of 1986 § 10(2)(c).

[123] *Id.* at 10(2)(d).

[124] *Mango*, APEDA, http://apeda.gov.in/apedawebsite/SubHead_Products/Mango.htm (last visited 8 March 2016).

[125] *Id.*

developed for consumer safety wherein APEDA can even issue a product recall in case of exigencies.[126]

Once the Alphonso mango would be registered as a GI, it would be important that, in addition to the requirement already in place under the system supervised by APEDA, all consignments of mangoes be subject to another layer of verification based on the quality control that would be required as part of the GI specification. In particular, the group of producers that has applied for the GI for Alphonso mango, Dr Balakrishna Sawant Konkan Krishi Vidyapeeth ('BSKKV') has stated that the BKSSV and the Department of Horticulture, College of Agriculture, will decide on a Standards and Quality Committee, which will operate as the Inspection Body and maintain high standards in the quality of the mango.[127] The success of this model of self-regulation can only be assessed once the GI is registered and the Committee begins to operate. However, the long-term success of the GIs and the producers of Alphonso mangoes certainly require a high level of product quality control and traceability of products from the producers to the market.

Moreover, even though quality control for export products has been successfully managed by regulators in certain cases,[128] the EU ban on Indian mangoes indicates that internal quality control mechanisms to protect a GI product have to be carefully coordinated with the specific requirements of applicable Sanitary and Phytosanitary ('SPS') measures in the country where the exports are destined. However, SPS measures may also be used in a discriminatory manner. For example, the abnormally high number of fruit flies present in the Alphonso mango shipments that arrived in the European Union turned out to be 22, as compared to 102 from Pakistan, 27 from Dominican Republic, 22 from Jamaica, 19 from Ivory Coast, and 16 from Kenya, which contained the same fruit flies.[129] Accordingly, the European Union may even have violated her obligations under the WTO Agreement on SPS in banning the mangoes from India.[130] Further, the European Union imposed a blanket ban on Indian mangoes, when it could have approved the mangoes sourced and authenticated by APEDA, thereby imposing a more

---

[126] Id. [127] Form GI-1, *supra* note 64.
[128] Sharma and Kulhari, *supra* note 63. As an example, the study notes that the Spice Board in India has developed mandatory pre-shipment inspection mechanisms to check for authenticity.
[129] Chinmay Deshmukh, *Pulp Friction: World Trade Organization Violations in the European Union's Ban of Indian Fruit Exports*, 2 CORNELL INT'L L. J. ONLINE 111 (2014), http://cornellilj.org/wp-content/uploads/2014/09/C.-Deshmukh-EU-Fruit-Ban.pdf.
[130] Id. at 113 (noting that it could violate Article 2.3 of the Sanitary and Phytosanitary (SPS) Agreement).

restrictive trade measure.[131] Similarly, a trade ban could not exclude GI-denominated products, despite stronger quality control and inspections, even though such inspections may contribute to avoiding possible bans since these bans negatively impact the collective reputation of the GI producers.

5 CONCLUSION

GIs must be able to create value for their products in order to be valuable to registered producers. The GI regime in India borrows heavily from the regulatory framework of trademarks. Consequently, it is highly trader-centric, focusing primarily on protecting GIs against the misuse of the names by unauthorized users. The GI Act does not account, however, or accounts considerably less for the producer-centric need to maintain the quality and reputation of the GI-denominated products. Perhaps, due to the lack of awareness and lack of enough incentives, producers have not been able to assure themselves of a premium market. Legitimate interests of consumers cannot, and should not, be ignored; providing quality assurance and promoting consumer welfare have been found to be central to the success of any GI regime across the world, especially the European model.

This chapter presented four different case studies highlighting both the successes and pitfalls of post-registration quality control of GIs in India. The case study of Banarasi sarees highlights the need for collective action among the traditional producers who are choosing to compete with the synthetic fabric producers – those who sell sarees made from synthetic fabrics under the GI names – and by producers belonging to the collective group who are entitled to use the Banarasi GI. However, by choosing to compete with subpar products, producers will only dilute the premium value of the GI-denominated products. The case study of Pashmina highlights how voluntary regulatory mechanism with the support of the government has the potential to strengthen quality control and provide assurance to consumers about the origin and characteristics of the products. The use of technology to track the products and certify quality throughout the manufacturing chain may assist producers in monitoring the production of the GI-denominated products. The world-famous Darjeeling tea GI is an interesting case study, where due to the establishment of inspection structures governed by the Tea Board, the supply chains have been foolproof. But this is only on account of historical factors responsible for the establishment of the Tea Board and subsequent strict

[131] Id. at 114.

compliance with quality norms by authorized users. And yet, it is only since 2016 that Darjeeling tea producers can take legal action against blended tea sellers in the European Union. Finally, the Alphonso mango case study, after the EU ban, highlights the need to incorporate the SPS standards of importing destinations into inspection structures by authorities in India. Due to the weak link in the GI Act, where inspection structures are not linked with compliance by GI authorized users, it remains to be seen how market dynamics will play out in this sector.

The Indian experience thus highlighted how the different mechanisms of regulation currently associated with some of the most prominent Indian GIs showcase a fragmented framework of quality-control structures across the country. This could perhaps be an advantage as GIs across the country face different issues. Yet, even though a decentralized mechanism with different approaches to the implementation of a system of quality control could be the way forward, it is also crucial that the legislature consider either the inclusion of a chapter on the responsibilities of Inspection Bodies within the GI Act or enact a separate statute altogether for the same purpose. Certainly, Indian policymakers can no longer afford to ignore quality-control debate in the policy discourse surrounding GIs as quality control is a key element to preserve the premium value of GIs as it ensures compliance with quality. To the contrary, the Indian GIs system, with its several registered GIs, will be called out for its vanity!

15

Protection of Geographical Indications in Taiwan: Turning a Legal Conundrum into a Policy Tool for Development

Szu-Yuan Wang*

1 INTRODUCTION

Intellectual property (IP) protection is nothing new to Taiwan. Prior to the 1980s, Taiwanese IP laws were criticized for their limited recognition and protection of intellectual property rights (IPRs), inadequate deterrence for infringements, and protectionist provisions. Foreign entities were denied the same treatment as nationals, and unrecognized foreign entities were often denied protection for their IPRs as well as the standing to seek redress for infringement.[1] Under the threat of trade retaliation by the United States (US), Taiwan began a major IP law reform in the 1980s.[2] The "crucial turning point" in the development of Taiwanese IP law occurred when Taiwan realized the political and economic importance of its accession to the World Trade Organization (WTO) and its accompanying obligation to protect IP.[3] This particular goal drove Taiwan to implement more IP reforms. By 1998, one commentator was able to proudly claim that "Taiwan's statutory regime for intellectual property protection now by and large complies with the Agreement on Trade Related Aspects of Intellectual Property Rights (TRIPS Agreement).[4] In some areas, the regime reaches beyond the TRIPS

---

* Assistant Professor, Graduate Institute for Intellectual Property Rights, Shih Hsin University, Taiwan.
[1] Yeh Kurt Chang, *Special 301 and Taiwan: A Case Study of Protecting United States Intellectual Property in Foreign Countries*, 15 Nw. J. INT'L L. & BUS. 206, 217 (1994).
[2] Kung-Chung Liu, *The Protection of Well-Known Marks in Taiwan: From Case Study to General Theory*, 90 TMR 866, 867 (2000); Chang, *supra* note 1, at 217–18.
[3] Liu, *supra* note 2, at 867.
[4] Agreement on Trade-Related Aspects of Intellectual Property Rights, April 15, 1994, Marrakesh Agreement Establishing the World Trade Organization, Annex 1C, Legal Instruments – Result of the Uruguay Rounds vol. 31, 33 I.L.M. 81 (1994) [hereinafter TRIPS].

Agreement's threshold."[5] Others also found no difference between Taiwan's IP law and the standards under the TRIPS Agreement.[6]

However, it is a completely different picture when it comes to geographical indications (GIs). GI protection officially originated in 2002 when Taiwan became the 144th member of the WTO[7] and it has been viewed as a new IP issue. One commentator even described GIs as a "purely transplanted norm for Taiwan."[8] The Taiwan Intellectual Property Office (TIPO), the government agency in charge of policymaking and administration of IP,[9] claims that GIs are a brand-new legal norm introduced into Taiwan as a result of the implementation of TRIPS obligations:

> After having joined the WTO, we have to implement the TRIPS obligations regarding geographical indications, but geographical indication is brand new norm that our people are not familiar with. What is a geographical indication? What is the scope of protection? How to claim the protection? These are all foreign to us.[10]

However, unfamiliarity did not prevent Taiwanese policymakers from promptly developing a legal regime for the protection of GIs. In its 2004

---

[5] Andy Y. Sun, *From Pirate King to Jungle King: Transformation of Taiwan's Intellectual Property Protection*, 9 FORDHAM INTELL. PROP. MEDIA & ENT. L.J 67, 83 (1998).

[6] JIN-MEI CHAO ET AL., INTRODUCTION TO INTELLECTUAL PROPERTY LAW 378 (7th edn. 2010).

[7] Taiwan was formally approved to be a member of the WTO on November 11, 2001, when the Ministerial Conference in Doha, Qatar, endorsed the island's accession protocol. Chinese Taipei (Taiwan) has been a member of WTO since January 1, 2002. Further background information on Taiwan's WTO membership, see Steve Charnovitz, *Taiwan's WTO Membership and Its International Implications*, 1 ASIAN J. WTO & INT'L HEALTH L. & POL'Y 401(2006).

[8] Min-Chiuan Wang, *The Asian Consciousness and Interests in Geographical Indications*, 96 TMR 906, 934 (2006).

[9] Taiwan Intellectual Property Office (TIPO), *Overview of Taiwan Intellectual Property Office* (September 6, 2011) www.tipo.gov.tw/mp.asp?mp=2.

[10] Wang, *supra* note 8. Here, Wang also notes that before Taiwan's accession to the WTO in 2002, geographical indication laws were used mostly to protect European wine and spirit GIs:

> In the early days of Taiwan's geographical indication laws, they were used mostly to protect the geographical indications for European wines and spirits. During the consultation stage when Taiwan was joining the WTO, the Ministry of France, at the request of the European Union that the European geographical indications for wines be protected, promised to incorporate this protection into the Tobacco and Alcohol Administration Act. There were numerous cases involving the misuse of GIs for Scottish whisky and French wines. In the Taiwan-EU bilateral agreement, signed in 1998, Taiwan also promised to protect whisky and other wines from Europe.
>
> *Id.*

Communication to the TRIPS Council,[11] the Taiwanese government enumerated the three elements of the Taiwanese GI regime as the Trade Mark Act,[12] the Fair Trade Act,[13] and the Tobacco and Alcohol Administration Act.[14] While the Fair Trade Act and the Tobacco and Alcohol Administration Act provide administrative regulation prohibiting the false or misleading representation of GIs, the heart of the Taiwanese GI regime is the Trademark Act. Apart from "negative protection," which prevents geographical terms from being registered as trademarks, the Trademark Act also provides for the "positive protection" of GIs, namely, the registration of geographical terms as certification marks.[15] Later in 2007, collective trademarks were added as a means of positive protection.[16]

Taiwan has also been an active participant in international GI negotiations. The inclusion of GIs in the Uruguay Round Negotiations was initiated by the EU and resisted by the United States, Canada, Australia,[17] and some Latin American countries.[18] This disagreement was described as the "North-North division,"[19] "New World v. Old World,"[20] or "immigrant v. emigrant countries."[21] This struggle continues even after the conclusion of the TRIPS Agreement.

---

[11] See WORLD TRADE ORGANIZATION, REVIEW UNDER ARTICLE 24.2 OF THE APPLICATION OF THE PROVISIONS OF THE SECTION OF THE TRIPS AGREEMENT ON GEOGRAPHICAL INDICATIONS, WTO Doc. IP/C/W/117/Add.30 (June 16, 2004).

[12] Trademark Act 2003 (Taiwan) [hereinafter Trademark Act 2003].

[13] Fair Trade Act of 2011 (Taiwan).

[14] The Tobacco and Alcohol Administration Act 2013 (Taiwan).

[15] WORLD TRADE ORGANIZATION, supra note 11.

[16] TIPO, Examination Guidelines on Certification Marks, Collective Trademarks and Collective Membership Marks (July 25, 2007) www.intellektus.com/upload/editor/Examination_Guidelines_on_Certification_Marks.pdf [hereinafter Examination Guidelines].

[17] Stacy D. Goldberg, Who Will Raise the White Flag? The Battle between the United States and the European Union over the Protection of Geographical Indications, 22 U. PA. J. INT'L ECON. L. 107, 109–110 (2001).

[18] Julie Chasen Ross & Jessica A. Wasserman, Trade-Related Aspects of Intellectual Property Rights, in THE GATT URUGUAY ROUND: A NEGOTIATING HISTORY (1986–1992) VOLUME II: COMMENTARY 2245–2333 (Terence P. Steward ed., 2003).

[19] Albrecht Conrad, The Protection of Geographical Indications in the TRIPS Agreement, 86 TMR 11, 29–31 (1996).

[20] Kevin M. Murphy, Conflict, Confusion, and Bias under TRIPs Articles 22–24, 19 AM. U. INT'L L. REV. 1181, 1186 (2004); Lina Montén, Geographical Indications of Origin: Should They Be Protected and Why? – An Analysis of the Issue from the U.S. and EU Perspectives, 22 SANTA CLARA COMPUTER & HIGH TECH. L. J. 315, 315 (2006); Justin Hughes, Champagne, Feta, and Bourbon: The Spirited Debate about Geographical Indications, 58 HASTINGS L. J. 299, 301–302 (2006).

[21] José Manuel Cortés Martín, TRIPS Agreement: Towards a Better Protection for Geographical Indications?, 30 BROOK. J. INT'L L. 117, 127 (2004).

In 2002, Taiwan joined Argentina, Australia, Canada, Chile, the Dominican Republic, El Salvador, Guatemala, New Zealand, Paraguay, the Philippines, and the United States in opposing the extension of the higher level of GI protection for wines and spirits to all goods.[22] According to TIPO, the reason for this was that "after thoughtful review, we have concluded that extension will not provide meaningful benefits but will instead create new difficulties."[23] Furthermore, on March 11, 2005, Taiwan joined the New World countries, including Argentina, Australia, Canada, Chile, Ecuador, Mexico, New Zealand, and the United States, in supporting the establishment of a nonbinding and voluntary multilateral register for wine GIs.[24] This group of countries proposed that the TRIPS Council set up a voluntary system where GI holders could register their GIs in a database. The governments who choose to participate in the system would then have to consult the database when making decisions regarding GI protection in their own countries. Nonparticipating members would be "encouraged" but "not obliged" to consult the database.[25]

Judging from the façade, Taiwanese GI law seems to represent just another successful example of legal transplantation. However, as it will be revealed in this chapter, this tranquility is misleading, if not deceiving. The truth is that GI-protection issues have been a legal conundrum for Taiwanese policymakers and the history of Taiwanese GI law has been characterized by dereistic policy premises, perennial overhauls, doctrinal dilemmas, and atavistic evolution. This chapter aims to reveal and decipher Taiwan's GI conundrum and provide strategies to turn this conundrum into a tool for policy development.

2 DEREISTIC POLICY PREMISES

Dereism is a psychological term that refers to mental activities that do not accord with reality or logic.[26] This term is used here, in the abstract, to

---

[22] See WORLD TRADE ORGANIZATION, IMPLICATIONS OF ARTICLE 23 EXTENSION, WTO Doc. IP/C/W/386 (November 8, 2002).

[23] Id. ¶ 1.

[24] WORLD TRADE ORGANIZATION, PROPOSED DRAFT TRIPS COUNCIL DECISION ON THE ESTABLISHMENT OF A MULTILATERAL SYSTEM OF NOTIFICATION AND REGISTRATION OF GEOGRAPHICAL INDICATIONS FOR WINES AND SPIRITS, WTO Doc. TN/IP/W/10/Rev.2 (July 24, 2008).

[25] WORLD TRADE ORGANIZATION, GEOGRAPHICAL INDICATIONS – BACKGROUND AND THE CURRENT SITUATION, www.wto.org/english/tratop_e/trips_e/gi_background_e.htm#wines_spirits (last visited April 10, 2016).

[26] RAYMOND CORSINI, THE DICTIONARY OF PSYCHOLOGY 267 (2002).

describe the nature of the policy premises on which Taiwanese GI law has been based. This section identifies and explores three such policy premises, including the misidentification of policy context in which GIs are protected, misinterpretation of the GI–trademark relation, and opportunistic distortion of the meaning of protection.

2.1 An Intellectual Property-Centerd Policy on Geographical Indications

As we have seen, Taiwanese GI law was enacted in response to a new IP obligation imposed by the TRIPS Agreement. This IP-centered premise has not changed since 2003. The policy interests for GIs becoming a separate form of IP at the national and regional levels, thus causing international problems, have not been considered by Taiwanese policymakers. Problems with such a premise for policymaking are twofold. At the general level, it contravenes the economic rationales behind IP protection. It has been argued that IP protection is a form of government intervention in the economy. Such an intervention is not the end per se but rather an instrument for the achievement of other policy goals.[27] Thus, protecting IP simply for the sake of doing so, without identifying the proper policy context in which it operates, as the Taiwanese GI law has done, is to put the cart before the horse. More specifically, failing to identify the specific policy interests that GIs are intended to address, such as rural development or food quality control,[28] has turned the development of Taiwanese GI law into a Hamlet without the Prince of Demark.[29]

2.2 Interpreting Geographical Indications as Trademarks

Another policy premise that has guided the development of Taiwanese GI law is that GIs are equivalent, or at least similar, to trademarks. According to TIPO, the adoption of this "trademark approach" was inspired by existing international paradigms. Taiwan's policymakers and commentators identified

---

[27] See, e.g., Herbert Hovenkamp, *Antitrust and the Regulatory Enterprise*, COLUM. BUS. L. REV. 335, 336 (2004); Mark A. Lemley, *Property, Intellectual Property, and Free Riding*, 83 TEX. L. REV. 1031, 1073–74 (2005).

[28] See, e.g., Elizabeth Barham, *Translating Terroir: The Global Challenge of French AOC Labelling*, 19 J. RURAL STUD. 127 (2003); DANIELE GIOVANNUCCI ET AL., GUIDE TO GEOGRAPHICAL INDICATIONS: LINKING PRODUCTS AND THEIR ORIGINS 90 (2009).

[29] THE OXFORD ENGLISH DICTIONARY VOLUME VI 1056 (2nd edn. 1989) (This phrase is used to refer to "a performance without the chief actor or a proceeding without the central figure").

two types of GI protection: the EU's *sui generis* model and the trademark model in the United States. The former recognizes GIs as a form of intellectual property in its own right and protects GIs through the *sui generis* legislation, whereas the latter views GIs as a subset of trademarks and thus protects them under existing trademark law.[30] Taiwan's reasons for adopting the trademark approach are twofold. First, in the eyes of Taiwan's policymakers, GIs are similar to trademarks. This is because GIs, as "commercially valuable source-identifiers," are similar to trademarks in terms of function and value. They are also similar in terms of the rationales behind their legal protection – consumer protection and the prevention of unfair competition. In the case of GIs, misuse may be detrimental to the interests of consumers and thus constitute unfair competition between producers. Secondly, subsuming GIs under existing trademark law is easy and convenient.[31] Therefore, to Taiwanese policymakers, the two GI protection models differed on a technical basis rather than substantive basis.

However, this interpretation completely disregards the fact that under the TRIPS Agreement, GIs and trademarks are two separate categories of IPR. Under the TRIPS Agreement, GIs are "indications which identify a good as originating in the territory of a Member, or a region or locality in that territory, where a given quality, reputation or other characteristic of the good is essentially attributable to its geographical origin."[32] As the WTO explained, GIs are names of places or words associated with a place "used to identify the origin and quality, reputation or other characteristics of products."[33] Moreover, differences between GIs and trademarks are obvious as the TRIPS Agreement defines trademarks as "[a]ny sign, or any combination of signs, capable of distinguishing the goods or services of one undertaking from those of other undertakings."[34] The ability to distinguish goods and services of undertakings is the universal requirement for a sign to be protected as a trademark.[35]

---

[30] Szu-Yuan Wang, Geographical indications as Intellectual Property: In Search of Explanations of Taiwan's GI Conundrum 2–3 (February 2013) (unpublished Doctoral Dissertation, Newcastle University, on file with author).

[31] *Id.* at 3 (stating that Taiwanese scholars also hold this view); *see* Wang, *supra* note 8, at 914 ("Among these models, two major ones are the trademark model, associated primarily with the United States, and the French appellation of origin model ... these models ... are all oriented toward a twofold purpose: on the one hand, preventing misleading use and misappropriation of collective goodwill, and hence, on the other, protecting consumers").

[32] *See* TRIPS, *supra* note 4, art. 22.1.   [33] WORLD TRADE ORGANIZATION, *supra* note 25.

[34] *See* TRIPS, *supra* note 4, art. 15.

[35] Dev Gangjee, *Protecting Geographical Indications as Collective Trademarks: The Prospects and Pitfalls*, in IIP BULLETIN 112, 114 (2006).

As to the rationales behind protection, the TRIPS Agreement provides two levels of protection for GIs. TIPO's interpretation only acknowledges protection for GIs for all goods, which is based on consumer protection and the prevention of unfair competition rationales. It ignores the additional level of protection for wine and spirits. Furthermore, although they claim to have been inspired by both the United Statess and EU's models, TIPO's interpretation is in fact a faithful reflection of that of the United States Patent and Trademark Office's (USPTO)[36] regime, and a total ignorance or misunderstanding of the EU's concept of GIs. Under EU law, a GI is "the name of a region, a specific place or, in exceptional cases, a country, used to describe an agricultural product or a foodstuff."[37] Such terms would normally be considered generic or descriptive under the trademark doctrine.[38]

2.3 Distinction between Positive Protection and Negative Protection

Since GIs are treated as trademarks, the policymaker's task has been to absorb GIs into the existing trademark law. This approach faces an immediate challenge because under the trademark doctrine GIs are normally not considered distinctive and thus they are not protectable.[39] Hence, Taiwanese

---

[36] UNITED STATES PATENT AND TRADEMARK OFFICE (USPTO), *Geographical Indication Protection in the United States*, available at www.uspto.gov/web/offices/dcom/olia/globalip/pdf/gi_system.pdf.

[37] Council Regulation 510/2006 of March 20, 2006, On the Protection of Geographical Indications and Designations of Origin for Agricultural Products and Foodstuffs, 2006 O.J. (L. 93/12) arts. 2.1(a)–(b).

[38] Commission Regulation No 1898/2006 of December 14, 2006, Laying Down Detailed Rules of Implementation of Council Regulation (EC) No. 510/2006 on the Protection of Geographical Indications and Designations of Origin for Agricultural Products and Foodstuffs, 2006 O.J. (L369/1) art. 3.1 (further sets qualifications for eligible names: (i) "Only a name that is in use in commerce or in common language, or which has been used historically to refer to the specific agricultural product or foodstuff, may be registered." (ii) "Only a name that is used, whether in commerce or in common language, to refer to the specific agricultural product or foodstuff may be registered."); For information about the generic and descriptive nature of GIs, *see also*, Xuan-Thao N. Nguyen, *Nationalizing Trademarks: A New International Trademark Jurisprudence?*, 39 WAKE FOREST L. REV. 729, 757 (2004); Felix Addor & Alexandra Grazioli, *Geographical Indications beyond Wines and Spirits: A Roadmap for a Better Protection for Geographical Indications in the WTO TRIPS Agreement*, 5 J. WORLD INTELL. PROP. 865, 871 (2002); Emily Nation, *Geographical Indications: The International Debate over Intellectual Property Rights for Local Producers*, 82 U. COLO. L. REV. 959, 975 (2011).

[39] *See, e.g.*, Felix Addor & Alexandra Grazioli, *supra* note 38.; Dev Gangjee, *Quibbling Siblings: Conflicts between Trademarks and Geographical Indications* 82 CHI-KENT L. REV. 1253, 1255 (2007); SHUBA GHOSH ET AL., INTELLECTUAL PROPERTY: PRIVATE RIGHTS, THE PUBLIC INTERESTS, AND THE REGULATION OF CREATIVITY ACTIVITY 491 (2007); MARSHA

policymakers have adopted an opportunistic strategy to overcome this apparent and inherent difficulty by widening the meaning of trademark protection to include "negative protection."

Trademark protection under the Taiwanese Trademark Act is based on the "registration protection principle." This means that "protection" refers to the acquisition of trademark rights through registration.[40] In order to be registered and protected, the mark in question must meet three statutory requirements. A failure to comply with any of the requirements will result in registration being refused and thus no protection for the mark. The requirements are that (i) the mark in question must "be composed of a word, figure, symbol, colour, sound, three-dimensional shape or a combination thereof,"[41] (ii) the mark in question must be capable of being "expressed in a visually perceptible representation,"[42] (iii) the mark must be "distinctive enough for relevant consumers of the goods or services to recognize it as identification to that goods or services and to differentiate such goods or services from those offered by others."[43] However, nondistinctive elements may be included in a registered trademark on the condition that "the applicant disclaims the exclusive right for using the said feature."[44]

A registered trademark confers on its proprietor the right to exclude others from using that particular sign in relation to specified commercial activities.[45] This exclusive right may be infringed by someone using the trademark in Taiwan without the proprietor's consent.[46] The proprietor of a registered trademark may also license,[47] assign,[48] create a pledge over,[49] or abandon[50] his trademark rights. Additionally, the proprietor has the rights to customs and border measures.[51] Upon successful registration, the trademark is protected for ten years, starting from the date of publication.[52] Thereafter, registration may be renewed for another ten years.[53] However, the proprietor's exclusive right to a registered trademark may not be infringed by use in Taiwan without his consent in the following instances: (i) *bona fide* and fair use of one's own name or title or the name, shape, quality, function, place of origin, or other description of goods or services, provided that the use is for non-trademark purposes;[54]

A. ECHOLS, GEOGRAPHICAL INDICATIONS FOR FOOD PRODUCTS: INTERNATIONAL LEGAL AND REGULATORY PERSPECTIVES 242 (2008).

[40] TIPO, What Are the Advantages of Trademark Registration? (updated, March 19, 2013) www.tipo.gov.tw/ct.asp?xItem=214845&ctNode=7078&mp=1; DU-TSUEN WANG, TRADEMARK LAW 6 (2nd edn., Wunan 2011); CHOU-FU LIN, TRADEMARK 39 (2nd edn., Wunan 2009).
[41] Trademark Act 2003, *supra* note 12. [42] *Id.* at art. 17.1. [43] *Id.* at art. 5.2.
[44] *Id.* at art. 19. [45] *Id.* at art. 29.1. [46] *Id.* at art. 29.2.
[47] Trademark Act 2003, *supra* note 12, at art. 33. [48] *Id.* at art. 35. [49] *Id.* at art. 37.
[50] *Id.* at art. 38. [51] *Id.* at art. 65. [52] *Id.* at art. 27.1.
[53] Trademark Act 2003, *supra* note 12, at art. 27.2. [54] *Id.* at art. 30.1(1).

(ii) a three-dimensional shape of a good or package "indispensable for performing its intended functions";[55] (iii) *bona fide* use prior to the filing date of a registered trademark;[56] (iv) if the goods bearing the registered trademark are traded or circulated in the marketplace by the proprietor or an authorized person, or are offered for auction or disposal by a relevant agency, then the proprietor shall not claim infringement of his trademark on the said goods.[57]

Interestingly, the concept of "negative protection" was previously unheard of in Taiwanese trademark jurisprudence. According to TIPO, the basis for "negative protection" for GIs can be found in Articles 23.1(11) and 23.1(18) of the Trademark Act 2003. Article 23.1(11) provides for the refusal of an application for trademark registration if the proposed mark is "likely to mislead the public with respect to the nature, quality, or place of origin of the designated goods or services."[58] Additionally, Article 23.1(18) provides for the refusal of a mark "that is identical or similar to a geographical indication of wines and spirits of a country or region that mutually protects trademark with Taiwan, and is designated for use on wines and spirits."[59] Thus, negative protection actually refers to the refusal of registration. However, by distinguishing negative protection from positive protection, TIPO is now able to claim that GIs are protected as trademarks under Taiwanese trademark law. Thus, the sophistry of negative protection is not only a euphemism for the refusal of protection but also a form of deception to allow the policymaker to ignore the obvious incompatibility between GIs and trademarks.

3 POSITIVE PROTECTION: PERENNIAL OVERHAULS, DOCTRINAL DILEMMAS, AND ATAVISTIC EVOLUTION

Positive protection, which is the registration of GIs as certification marks and collective trademarks, has been characterized by perennial overhauls, doctrinal dilemma, and atavistic evolution. Although the Trademark Act 2003 was the first official response to the GI-protecting obligations, it simply added the words "place of origin" to the categories of qualities certifiable by certification marks. Later in 2004, TIPO introduced a whole new administrative mechanism for "the registration of geographical indications as certification marks."[60]

---

[55] *Id.* at art. 30.1(2).　[56] *Id.* at art. 30.1(3).　[57] *Id.* at art. 30.2.　[58] *Id.* at art. 23.1(11).
[59] Trademark Act 2003, *supra* note 12, at art. 23.1(18).
[60] The Main Points for the Registration of Geographical Indications as Certification Marks 2004, available at www.tipo.gov.tw/lp.asp?ctNode=7051&CtUnit=3495&BaseDSD=7&mp=1&qpsubmit=5949.8&htx_topCat=&htx_xpostDate_S=&htx_xpostDate_E=&htx_stitle=%E5%9C%B0%E7%90%86%E6%A8%99%E7%A4%BA&htx_xbody=&htx_xurl [hereinafter GI Registration Points].

It incorporated the TRIPS Agreement's definition of GIs and established procedures to ensure the existence of a required link between the product and the place of origin.[61] It also introduced a decision-making process through which the decision to grant GI protection was a joint decision by TIPO and the relevant government authorities in charge of the products identified by the GI, such as Ministry of Agriculture and Ministry of Treasury.[62] However, this mechanism was abolished in 2007 when TIPO introduced the registration of "geographical certification marks" and "geographical collective trademarks." At the heart of this new mechanism was the requirement of distinctiveness of the geographical term – a link between the product and place was no longer required. The TIPO was now the sole authority for granting GI protection. Further change came in mid-2011 with the enactment of the Trademark Act 2012 (TMA 2012),[63] which codified the terms "geographical certification mark" and "geographical collective mark." In doing so, the TRIPS definition of GIs was formally incorporated into the definition of "geographical certification marks" and "geographical collective marks." Surprisingly, the requirement of distinctiveness was abolished and a joint decision-making process was reintroduced – not to qualify the product but to qualify the applicant.

3.1 Trademark Act of 2003

The Trademark Act 2003, the first official response to GI obligation, simply added "place of origin" to the categories certifiable by certification marks. Under Taiwanese trademark law, a "certification mark is used to certify the characteristics, quality, precision, place of origin or other matters of another person's goods or services shall apply for certification mark registration."[64] This means that, unlike general trademarks, a certification mark is not used to indicate a single business source. Instead, it is "used by multiple people who comply with the labelling requirements in connection with their respective goods or services."[65] Only "a juristic person, an organization or a government agency capable of certifying another person's goods or services" is eligible to apply for a certification mark.[66] However, the owner of a certification mark is not allowed to use the mark. Rather, he is obliged to "control the use of the mark, supervise the authorized users' use, and ensure that the certified goods

---

[61] GI Registration Points, *supra* note 60, at 2.1.   [62] *Id.* at 4.1.
[63] TMA 2012 was scheduled to enter into force in 2012 and thus termed the Trademark Act 2012.
[64] Trademark Act 2003, *supra* note 12, at art. 72.1.
[65] Examination Guidelines, *supra* note 16, at 2.1.
[66] Trademark Act 2003, *supra* note 12, at art. 72.2.

or services meet the articles governing use."[67] Also, the owner of a certification mark must allow any person who complies with the requirements to apply to use the certification mark.[68] The year 2003 saw the registration of what the TIPO claims to be the first geographical certification mark: "池上米" (Chinese characters for "Chi-Shang rice").[69] This certification mark was registered by the Chi-Shang Township Office of Taitung County to certify rice originating from the Chi-Shang Township of Taitung County, and that its quality met the "Criteria Governing Chi-Shang Rice quality rice logo" that was established by the owner of the mark.[70]

The main effect of registration of a geographical certification mark is that, after such registration, any application to register the same "geographical name" as a trademark would be rejected pursuant to Article 23–1(11) of the Trademark Act 2003 because the latter application might mislead the public with respect to the quality, nature, or place of origin of the goods that the second mark would identify, if registered. In other words, after "池上米" is registered, another person's application to register the same geographical name as part of a trademark, which is likely to mislead the public with respect to the place of origin, shall be rejected. However, any registered trademark acquired prior to the registration of the corresponding geographical certification mark is not affected. Furthermore, the owner of the geographical certification mark would not have the right to prohibit the owner of the trademark from using that geographical name in good faith and in a reasonable manner.[71]

However, it is noteworthy that TIPO's narrative does not entirely align with reality. Certification marks were first included under TMA 1993. Under the TMA 1993, certification marks are used to certify characteristics, quality, precision, or other matters of goods or services.[72] It has been pointed out that this provision is broad enough to cover even the "place of origin."[73] Moreover, a survey of TIPO's trademark register also confirms that there were certification marks registered before the TMA 2003 came into force on November 28, 2003, which may certify the place of origin of products. Some examples include the following: the mark "CALIFORNIA" with a device to certify that the cling peach products it identifies originated from California, US, and that they comply with the quality standards set by the proprietor of the mark (the certifier);[74] the mark "QUALITY USA" with

---

[67] Examination Guidelines, *supra* note 16, at 2.1.   [68] *Id.*
[69] *See* Wang, *supra* note 8, at 935.   [70] Examination Guidelines, *supra* note 16, at 3(1).
[71] *Id.* at 2.4.4.   [72] Trademark Act 2003, *supra* note 12, at art. 73.1.
[73] WEN-YIN CHEN, TRADEMARK LAW 17–19 (Sanmin 1998).
[74] California, Registration No. 00000002 (April 16, 1995).

a device that certifies "the certified peanut products are absolutely originated in the USA and comply the relevant US Federal standards and regulations";[75] the mark "IQF EDAMAME OF TAIWAN" with a map of Taiwan to certify that their edamames originate from Taiwan and that their quality and sanitation methods comply with the standards set by the certifier;[76] and the mark "JAMAICA BLUE MOUNTAIN" that certifies that the coffee beans identified by the mark originate from the Jamaican Blue Mountain area and that their storage, processing, and packaging comply with the requirements of the certifier.[77]

Thus, it is argued that listing the words "place of origin" in the TMA 2003 does not create a new legal right. It is only a declaratory gesture used to express Taiwan's determination to implement its TRIPS obligations.[78]

3.2 Main Points for the Registration of Geographical Indications of 2004

In September 2004, TIPO adopted the "Main Points for the Registration of Geographical Indications as Certification Marks" (GI Registration Points 2004).[79] The GI Registration Points 2004 established a whole new administrative mechanism for the registration of GIs as certification marks and has three main features.

First, the GI Registration Point 2004 incorporated the TRIPS Agreement's definition of GIs.[80] TIPO further refined this definition into three elements: (i) the indication must be a geographical name, a picture, or word related to that geographical term which identifies the nexus between a particular good and that geographical area; (ii) the geographical area in question may encompass a WTO Member's entire territory, or a single administrative unit, a combination of several administrative units, or a specific area where the raw materials grow or processing takes place; and (iii) there must be a nexus between a given quality, reputation, or other characteristic of the good and that geographical area.[81]

Second, it established procedures to verify the existence of a link between the product and the place of origin. TIPO set out three alternative criteria to determine the existence of the product–place nexus. First, all stages of production (growth of raw materials, processing, and packaging) must take place

---

[75] Quality USA, Registration No. 00000075 (November 1, 2002).
[76] IQF Edamame Of Taiwan, Registration No. 00000104 (September 16, 2003).
[77] Jamaica Blue Mountain, Registration No. 00000095 (July 1, 2003).
[78] WEN-YIN CHEN, TRADEMARK LAW 29 (3rd edn. 2005).
[79] GI Registration Points, *supra* note 60.   [80] *Id.* at 2.1.   [81] *Id.* at 2.2.

within the designated area. Second, the main raw materials (tea leaves, for example) must originate from the designated area and only a small portion of raw materials may be supplied from other areas; or, third, the production stage which gives the product its distinctive feature must take place within the designated area.[82] The applicant must also submit a product specification with the following information: (i) definition of the geographical area; (ii) raw materials and their place of origin; (iii) description of the raw materials, including physical, chemical, microbiological, sensual characters and evidence of such characters; (iv) description of methods of production, including the local conventional or unvarying methods; and (v) description and evidence of the specific facts or factors in relation to the geographical environment, such as the soil, climate, wind, water quality, altitudes, humidity, and their connection to the product.[83]

Third, it also introduced a joint decision-making process by the TIPO and relevant government authorities in charge of the products identified by the GI, such as Ministry of Agriculture and Ministry of Treasury, for the granting of GI protection. Generally, an application to register a GI as a certification mark will be examined by TIPO under the normal procedures for certification marks. However, the GI Registration Points indirectly indicated that TIPO might not be in the best position to judge the product–place nexus. Hence, the "Main Points" obliged TIPO to seek professional opinion from the Council of Agriculture where the agricultural product in question was not wine or alcohol, or the Treasury of the Ministry of Finance if the product concerned was wine or alcohol.[84]

Thus, the GI Registration Points 2004 represents an attempt to absorb GIs into the trademark law by grafting the branch of EU-styled *sui generis* GI law onto the stem of trademark law.

3.3 *The Examination Guidelines of 2007*

In 2007, the GI Registration Points 2004 were abolished when TIPO introduced the "Examination Guidelines on Certification Marks, Collective Trademarks and Collective Membership Marks" (the Examination Guidelines 2007). The Examination Guidelines marked the beginning of a new phase of Taiwanese GI law. Instead of using the term "geographical indications," it adopted the terms "geographical certification mark" (產地證明標章)[85] and "geographical collective trademark" (產地團體商標).[86] Most importantly,

---

[82] *Id.* at 2.3. [83] *Id.* at 3.2.2.2(2). [84] *Id.* at 4.1.
[85] Examination Guidelines, *supra* note 16, at 2.2.3.2. [86] *Id.* at 3.3.2.

"distinctiveness" of the mark was now the *sine qua non* condition for the registration of geographical certification marks and geographical collective trademarks. The product-place nexus was no longer required and TIPO became the sole authority in charge of the examination of registration applications for geographical certification marks and geographical collective trademarks.

Similar to individual trademarks, distinctiveness is an essential condition for the registration of geographical certification marks. TIPO expounds the meaning of distinctiveness of a geographical certification mark as follows:

> A "geographical certification mark" mainly comprises a geographical name and differs from a generally descriptive "indication of source." A general "indication of source" only describes the place where the goods or services are manufactured, produced or provided, for instance, "台灣製造" (meaning "made in Taiwan") and "made in Taiwan." On the other hand, a "geographical certification mark" is used to certify that one's goods or services originate in a certain geographical region and the certified goods or services have a certain quality, reputation or other features attributed to the specific natural or human factors of its geographical environment. In other words, because the geographical name has garnered certain reputation due to its use over time, consumers would immediately associate the geographical name with the certified goods or services as soon as they encounter it; therefore, the geographical indication may be granted registration because of distinctiveness.[87]

A collective trademark is "mainly used by the members of a collective group in order to identify the goods or services operated or offered by its members."[88] This means that a collective trademark allows the consumer to distinguish goods or services provided by a member of a collective group from those offered by nonmembers. Only a "business association, social organization, or any other group that exists as a juristic person" may be eligible to apply for a collective trademark.[89] Furthermore, it was also mentioned that "[c]ollective trademarks are still trademarks by nature. While ordinary trademarks are used to identify a single source of goods or services, collective trademarks are used by the members of a given group on the goods or services provided by the members of that group."[90] Thus, a collective trademark is similar to a general trademark in the sense that both are used to indicate the business source of goods or services.[91]

---

[87] *Id.* at 2.4.1.2. [88] Trademark Act 2003, *supra* note 12, at art. 77.
[89] Examination Guidelines, *supra* note 16, at 3.1. [90] WANG, *supra* note 40, at 20.
[91] Examination Guidelines, *supra* note 16, at 3.1.

According to TIPO, the main difference between these two categories of marks lies in their respective relations to their users. A general trademark is only used by the owner himself, if he does not license it out. However, a collective trademark is jointly used by the members of a group on the goods or services of the respective members. But if the owner wants to launch advertising campaigns for its members, it may use the collective trademark to promote the goods or services offered by its members.[92] Under Taiwanese trademark law, the main difference between a collective trademark and a certification mark is that the former is exclusive to the owner, but the latter is open to the public. In other words, whereas a collective trademark is used only by the members of its collective group, anyone who complies with the prescribed requirements to use a certification mark must be allowed to use it.[93]

Like trademarks, a geographical collective trademark is not registrable if it is considered descriptive.[94] However, a geographical collective mark becomes registrable if it "has acquired distinctiveness as specified in Article 23–4 of the Trademark Act."[95] TIPO envisaged the process in which a geographical name may acquire distinctiveness as follows:

> Unlike an "indication of source" with a general descriptive nature, a "geographical collective mark" not only denotes the place where the goods or services are manufactured, produced or provided, but also signifies that the goods or services identified thereunder have certain quality, reputation or other characteristics attributable to the natural or human factors of that geographical region. Therefore, a geographical collective trademark identifies the goods or services originating in a particular region that has certain quality or characteristics. In other words, as the geographical name has acquired certain reputation after a long-term use, consumers can immediately associate it with the designated goods or services. Such geographical collective trademark may be registered because it meets the distinctiveness requirements of a geographical collective trademark.[96]

Given the importance of distinctiveness, TIPO provided a series of definitions to clarify the concept of distinctiveness under the Trademark Act of 2003. For individual trademarks, "distinctiveness of a trademark relates to how it denotes the source of goods or services and distinguishes such goods or services from those of others."[97] A general collective trademark is deemed distinctive "if it is able to distinguish the goods or services of the members of a collective

---

[92] Id. [93] Id. at 3.1. [94] Id. at 3.4.1.2. [95] Id. [96] Id.
[97] TIPO, *Examination Guidelines on Distinctiveness of Trademarks*, 2 (January 1, 2009).

group from those goods or services of non-member parties."[98] In TIPO's definition, the "distinctiveness of a general certification mark refers to the characteristics, quality, precision or other matters that is/are used to certify one's goods or services; the use of which on the certified goods or services is sufficient to distinguish them from the goods or services that are not certified."[99] However, this definition is ambiguous and elusive.

Thus, the Examination Guidelines 2007 represented a new approach to incorporate GIs into the existing trademark law. For this purpose, TIPO created a new concept of distinctiveness for geographical certification marks and geographical collective trademarks, which incorporated the TRIPS Agreement's definition of GIs.

Similar to that of certification marks, TIPO's narrative of adding geographical collective trademarks as a protective measure for GIs originated in some specific events. Collective trademarks, in general, were first added to Taiwan's trademark law in 2003.[100] However, the registration of "geographical collective trademarks" was not formally provided for under the TMA 2003. It was, instead, recognized under the Examination Guidelines 2007.[101] According to TIPO, in 2007, the government decided to enhance the protection of GIs by allowing the registration of "geographical collective marks"[102] as a response to the 2005 incident that the names of seven well-known Taiwanese tea production districts were registered as trademarks in China. In particular, TIPO treats the "geographical collective trademark" as a special type of collective trademarks. Section 3.1 of the 2007 Examination Guidelines states: "In addition to a general collective trademark, the applicant may apply to register a geographical name as a geographical collective trademark, which is jointly used by the members of a collective group incorporated within the defined geographical region to denote the source of goods or services they offer."[103] Therefore, the registration of geographical collective trademarks was only officially allowed under the Examination Guidelines 2007.

However, there were collective trademarks registered prior to 2007, which appear capable of performing the same functions as "geographical collective trademarks." For instance, the following marks were registered: YAMAGATA SAKE BREWERY ASSOCIATION (Japan) (山形縣酒造合作社日本) registered the collective trademark "山形讚香YAMAGATA SANGA" for Japanese

---

[98] Examination Guidelines *supra* note 16, at 3.4.1.1.   [99] *Id.* at 2.4.1.1.
[100] TIPO, *Comparative Study on the Examination and Infringement of Collective Trademark, Certification Mark and Collective Membership Mark* 7 (2006), available at www.tipo.gov.tw /lp.asp?CtNode=7069&CtUnit=3509&BaseDSD=7&mp=1.
[101] Examination Guidelines *supra* note 16, at 3.1.   [102] *Id.*   [103] *Id.*

wine and sake on December 16, 2005;[104] the Italian company CONSORZIO PRODUTTORI MARMO BOTTICINO CLASSICO registered "MARMO BOTTICINO CLASSICO" for marble products on September 1, 2006;[105] the Italian company CONSORZIO DEL PROSCIUTTO DI PARMA registered "PARMA" for ham as a collective trademark on July 16, 2007;[106] the Goat Farmer Association R.O.C. registered the collective trademark "國產優質生鮮羊肉TAIWAN FRESH GOAT MEAT (with picture)" for goat meat on October 1, 2006.[107]

3.4 Trademark Act of 2012

Further amendments to Taiwanese GI law were made in mid-2011 with the adoption of the Trademark Act 2012 (TMA 2012).[108] The TMA 2012 codifies the terms "geographical certification mark"[109] and "geographical collective mark."[110] Article 80.1 defines certification marks as a mark used by its proprietor to certify the specific quality, precision, materials, method of production, place of origin, or other matters of others' goods or services, and to distinguish the certified goods or services uncertified ones.[111] Article 80.2 further states that the good or service certified by a geographical certification mark must have "a given quality, reputation, or characteristic." However, there is no requirement for the essential nexus between the product and place of origin. For example, the place name "Taipei" (台北) cannot be registered as a geographical certification mark for rice noodles because it has no connotation of a given quality, reputation, or characteristic for rice noodles and simply describes the place of origin. On the other hand, since "Meinong" (美濃) is famous for the quality of its rice noodles, it fits the definition of a geographical certification mark.[112]

Article 88.2 defines a "geographical collective trademark" as a collective trademark, which "serves to indicate a specific place of origin of goods or services of a member, such goods or services from that geographical region shall have a given quality, reputation or other characteristic."[113] Applicants for registration of a collective trademark, including geographical collective

---

[104] 山形讚香Yamagata Sanga, Registration No. 01188326 (December 16, 2005).
[105] Marmo Botticino Classico, Registration No. 01227793 (September 1, 2006).
[106] Parma, Registration No. 01271826 (July 16, 2005).
[107] 國產優質生鮮羊肉Taiwan Fresh Goat Meat, Registration No. 01232137 (October 1, 2006).
[108] Trademark Act 2012 (Laws and Regulations Database of the Republic of China 全國法規資料庫英譯法規查詢系米, English) (L. & Reg. DB), available at http://law.moj.gov.tw/Eng/LawClass/LawContent.aspx?PCODE=J0070001 [hereinafter Trademark Act 2012].
[109] Id. at art. 80.1. [110] Id. at art. 88.2. [111] Id. at art. 80.1. [112] Id. at art. 80.
[113] Id. at art. 88.2.

trademark, must submit to the Registrar Office the regulations governing the use of the geographical collective trademark.[114] Article 89.3 requires the proprietor of a geographical collective mark to allow anyone whose good or service complies with the regulations[115] to become a member. As a result, the distinction between the geographical collective trademark and the geographical certification mark was eliminated and the former simply became the latter but with a different name. Articles 80.2 and 88.2 allow "a sign containing that geographical term or a sign capable of indicating that geographical area" to be registered as a geographical certification mark or geographical collective trademark respectively.[116] Interestingly, the distinctiveness requirement does not apply to the "geographical name" used in geographical certification marks or geographical collective trademarks.[117] More intriguing is the fact that it is not necessary to disclaim the geographical name in question.[118]

The TMA 2012 also contains provisions that explicitly deal with the effects of GI registration. As mentioned, TMA 2012 waives the requirement of distinctiveness for the registration of geographical names as geographical certification marks or collective trademarks. It further provides that it is not necessary to disclaim such geographical names.[119] The general rule for trademarks is that nondistinctive elements may be included in a registered trademark on the condition that "the applicant disclaims the exclusive right for using the said feature."[120] This seems to suggest that the registration of a geographical certification mark or geographical collective mark will confer on its owner exclusive rights despite the lack of distinctiveness. This becomes especially ambiguous when one reads the provision providing that the "proprietor of a geographical certification mark is not entitled to prohibit the use of the signs to indicate the geographic origin of their goods or services in according with honest practices in industrial or commercial matters."[121] On closer inspection, this provision is merely a reiteration of the fair use doctrine to trademark rights.[122] Under the fair use doctrine, the proprietor's exclusive rights to a registered trademark are not infringed by the use of the trademark in Taiwan without his consent if the use includes the use of one's own name or title, or the name, shape, quality, function, place of origin, or other description

---

[114] Trademark Act 2012, *supra* note 108, at art. 89.1. According to 89.2, the regulations shall specify (i) the qualifications of the members; (ii), the conditions on the use of the collective trademark; (iii) the methods of managing and supervising the use of the collective trademark; and (iv) the provisions against any violation of the regulations.
[115] *Id.* at art. 89.3.   [116] *Id.* at arts. 80.2, 88.2.   [117] *Id.* at arts. 84.1, 91.   [118] *Id.*   [119] *Id.*
[120] Trademark Act 2012, *supra* note 108, at art. 19.   [121] *Id.* at art. 84.2.   [122] *Id.* at art. 36.

of goods or services.[123] The purpose of adding this provision was to "safeguard the freedom of one's right to describe his goods or services."[124] As a result, no one's right to use the registered geographical name would be affected. Thus, the owner could not exclude anyone from using the registered geographical name to indicate the geographical origin of his goods or services.

Therefore, the evolution of Taiwanese GI law is an atavistic one.[125] By requiring the proprietor to admit anyone whose product complies with the set criteria as a member, the TMA 2012, in practice, makes geographical collective trademarks geographical certification marks. This means that under the TMA 2012, geographical collective trademarks are no different from geographical certification marks except in name, and thus Taiwanese trademark law ultimately only protects GIs as certification marks. As to the effect of protection, the emphasis on safeguarding the freedom of competitors to describe the origin of their products through the fair use doctrine represented the trademark doctrine's absolute victory. Thus, the enactment of the TMA 2012 actually brings Taiwanese GI law *status quo ante* 2003 and all the efforts and struggles have added nothing but new terminology.

4 MAKING GEOGRAPHICAL INDICATIONS WORK FOR DEVELOPMENT

Given what we have seen in the past, it is time to end the chaos and emancipate Taiwanese policymakers from their Sisyphean mission of designing an ideal positive protection mechanism for GIs under the existing trademark law. Surprisingly, the *manumissio*[126] required is actually rather obvious and straightforward. While Taiwan's GI conundrum is a result of perennial overhauls, doctrinal dilemmas, and atavistic evolution, the heart of the problem lies in its dereistic policy premises. Taiwanese policymakers' immediate task should be to escape the GI–TM confusion. To accomplish this task, policymakers must stop seeing GIs through the lens of the trademark doctrine, and acquire a genuine understanding of the long-ignored EU *sui generis* paradigm. Once the GI–TM muddle is cleared, there will no longer be

---

[123] *Id.* at art. 30.1(1).   [124] General Statement about Trademarks Act 2012.
[125] Atavism is a term use in biology to refer to a tendency to reproduce the ancestral type in animals or plants, *see* THE OXFORD ENGLISH DICTIONARY (2nd edn. 1989); THE RANDOM HOUSE DICTIONARY OF THE ENGLISH LANGUAGE (2nd edn. 1987). In the social sciences, atavism is a cultural tendency to revert to the ways of thinking and acting of a former time, *see Atavism*, DARWIN WAS RIGHT, www.darwinwasright.org/atavism.html (last visited October 15, 2015).
[126] The legal process under Roman law whereby a master freed his slave, *see* PAUL DU PLESSIS, BORKOWSKI'S TEXTBOOK ON ROMAN LAW 96 (4th edn. 2010).

a need to employ the sophistry of "negative protection" to belie the incompatibility between GIs and trademarks. Only then can the Sisyphean effort of designing an ideal "positive protection" mechanism for GIs within the Trademark Act be stopped.

Another matter left to be considered is whether it is advisable for Taiwan to shift from the trademark approach to a GI regime modeled on the EU *sui generis* paradigm. In order to answer this question, policymakers must first ask themselves what they want GIs to do for Taiwan. An example would be the name "阿里山" (Ali Shan, meaning Ali Mountain), one of the most prestigious tea production regions in Taiwan as well as in the Chinese-speaking world. The Chia-Yi County Council registered "嘉義縣阿里山高山茶" (Chia Yi County Alishan High Mountains Tea) as a geographical certification mark on December 16, 2006.[127] This certification mark is used to certify tea produced in six towns located around the Ali mountain area and that complies with government safety regulations in relation to the use of chemicals. Furthermore, the name "Ali Shan" is not disclaimed.[128] But despite the registration, a search of TIPO's database on April 10, 2011, displayed 104 entries containing the name "阿里山." Among the 104, 12 were pending applications and 92 were registered. Among the 92 registered, 37 were for tea products, and of the 37, 24 were registered after December 16, 2006, after the "阿里山" mark was registered. A search not too long ago revealed that registration of the name "阿里山" still continues despite the vicissitudes of law. A search of TIPO's trademark registry database on September 5, 2015, displayed 171 entries containing the name "阿里山." Among these results, 15 were pending applications and 156 were registered. Of the 156 registered, 43 were registered for tea products and among the 15 pending applications, 4 were for tea products.[129]

For those who are skeptical of the value of GIs as a form of IP in its own right and who seek to subsume GIs under trademark law, the coexistence of multiple applications and registrations is in line with the economic rationale behind trademark law and its doctrinal principle. On the contrary, for those who view GI as a valuable policy tool for rural development because of its potential to provide "measurable economic benefits to a wide portion of its stakeholders while enhancing, or at least not compromising, the social and

---

[127] 嘉義縣阿里山高山茶Registration No. 01242948 (December 16, 2006). [128] *Id.*
[129] A similar situation is also found in the name of another prestigious tea production region, namely, "凍頂" (Dong Ding) for Oolong tea. A search of the trademark registry database on September 5, 2015, displayed 30 entries containing the name "凍頂." All the 30 are registered. Among the 30 registered, 18 are registered for tea products.

environmental conditions there,"[130] this state constitutes a lamentable case of what Gangjee describes as the "hidden consequences" of protecting GIs as collective or certification marks:

> Protecting GIs as Collective or Certification marks is certainly a pragmatic compromise in countries where a separate protection regime does not exist, but there are hidden consequences. For a start, the US "Tequila" Certification mark ... has to coexist with 263 other live applications or registrations which include "Tequila," making the ability to communicate a clear message of Mexican origin doubtful.[131]

Thus, the proposition of constructing a meaningful GI regime is the predetermination of an unambiguous policy goal. Therefore, it is necessary for the policymaker to recontextualize Taiwanese GI law. By doing so, GIs will no more be merely an exogenous IP obligation imposed by the TRIPS Agreement. Instead, GIs will become a policy issue that has a real connection to Taiwan. It is in this new policy context that the policymaker will be able to adopt, after in-depth cost–benefit analyses, as components of Taiwanese GI law, legal measures not because they are IP but because they are necessary to achieve the policy goal.

5 CONCLUSION

Taiwan has been facing a GI conundrum, which is symptomized by the perennial overhauls, doctrinal dilemmas, and atavistic evolution. Roots of the conundrum lay in its dereistic premises, that is, the misidentification of policy contexts, misinterpretation of the GI–trademark relation, and the opportunistic distortion of the meaning of protection. To terminate the chaotic state the policymaker must stop seeing GIs through the lens of the trademark doctrine and acquire a genuine understanding of the long-ignored EU *sui generis* paradigm. To turn GIs into a policy tool for development, the policymaker must determine a clear policy goal in the first place.

---

[130] See GIOVANNUCCI, *supra* note 28.
[131] Dev Gangjee, *(Re)Locating Geographical Indications: A Response to Bronwyn Parry*, in TRADE MARKS AND BRANDS 381, 396 (Lionel Bently, Jennifer Davis, & Jane C. Ginsburg eds., 2008).

16

A Unique Type of Cocktail: Protection of Geographical Indications in China

Haiyan Zheng*

1 INTRODUCTION

China is a nation with a large population and vast territory with numerous products originating in specific parts of the country. The introduction of a geographical indication (GI) regime in China can assist in preserving the authenticity of these products, both in terms of their geographical origin and the characteristics.

The history of GI protection in China can be traced back to the mid-1980s when China joined the Paris Convention for the Protection of Industrial Property (Paris Convention).[1] Under the obligations of the Paris Convention, China started to protect indications of source and appellations of origin by way of administrative decrees. In 1989, the State Administration for Industry and Commerce (SAIC)[2] issued an administrative decree to protect the French GI 'Champagne' from being misused as a generic term for a type of

---

* Director of Examination Division I, Trade Mark Office, State Administration for Industry and Commerce (SAIC), P.R.China. This chapter draws on some material already published as Haiyan Zheng, *Geographical Indications Protection in China*, in RESEARCH HANDBOOK ON INTELLECTUAL PROPERTY AND GEOGRAPHICAL INDICATIONS 327 (Dev Gangjee ed., 2016).

[1] Paris Convention for the Protection of Industrial Property, *opened for signature*, 20 March 1883, 21 U.S.T. 1583, 828 U.N.T.S. 305 (revised at Brussels on 14 December 1900, at Washington on 2 June 1911, at The Hague on 6 November 1925, at London on 2 June 1934, at Lisbon on 31 October 1958, and at Stockholm on 14 July 1967, and as amended on 28 September 1979) [hereafter Paris Convention].

[2] SAIC is a ministerial-level government agency, which administers trademark registration and protection, company name registration, anti-unfair competition, consumer protection, and other market-related issues. The Trade Mark Office is under the umbrella of SAIC. *See* State Administration for Industry & Commerce of the People's Republic of China, *About Us*, SAIC, www.saic.gov.cn (last visited 15 June 2016).

sparkling wine in Chinese markets.[3] This was probably the first significant event in China regarding GI-related administrative protection. Since then, several legislative efforts have been made in this respect, and different government agencies have been involved in protecting GIs in China.

Still, China does not adopt a uniform approach in protecting GIs. In particular, both trademark protection and a *sui generis* regime are available for GI protection today. In addition, these types of protection are complemented by laws on unfair competition, consumer protection, and product quality. However, as this chapter elaborates, the parallel and sometimes conflicting different legal systems under which GIs can be protected in China today may also hamper the creation of a healthy and efficient system of GI protection.

Notably, this chapter offers an overview of how the GI legal system has evolved in China. It also compares the advantages and disadvantages of the different regimes currently available for GI protection, and concludes with specific suggestions for improvements to the existing arrangement.

2 PROTECTING GEOGRAPHICAL INDICATIONS UNDER THE CHINESE TRADEMARK SYSTEM

The philosophy of using trademarks to protect GIs is that GIs function quite similarly to trademarks. In particular, the primary purpose of a trademark regime is to protect the interests of consumers by way of the trademark's source-identifying function and the quality guarantee function. Moreover, trademark protection extends to protect the business interest of trademark owners, namely the trademark goodwill and the investments that trademark owners have in the marks, and the products. Generally speaking, a trademark is an identifier of one single producer or service provider.

Similar to trademarks, GIs also designate source, even though a geographical source guarantees specific qualities of the products that derive from the natural and human factors within the given geographical area, and protect the investment made by generations of local producers on the reputation that is associated with the GIs. In this sense, GIs can be understood as a subset of trademarks.[4] More specifically, a GI usually serves to identify

---

[3] *See* State Administration for Industry & Commerce of the People's Republic of China, *Notice of Stopping the Use of the Word 'Champagne' on Goods Classified as Alcoholic Drinks*, TRADE MARK OFFICE (25 October 1989).

[4] Lynne Beresford, *Geographical Indications: The Current Landscape*, 17 FORDHAM INTELL. PROP. MEDIA & ENT. L. J. 979, 980–81 (2007).

a group of producers who share something in common, that is, the producers' products possess a certain quality, reputation, or other characteristics which are essentially attributable to their geographical origin.[5]

Generally, GIs are protected as certification or collective marks in China, the two types of marks that best accommodate GI protection within the trademark system.[6] Notably, both certification marks and collective marks identify groups of users, instead of one single business entity, which best reflect the nature of GIs as collective rights and signs that guarantee specific (and certified) product quality and characteristics. Moreover, the ownership of certification marks or collective marks is for applicants which have a collective legal nature, usually in the form of an association of producers.[7] Again, this best corresponds to the collective nature of a GI registrant. Therefore, both certification marks and collective marks can be used to protect GIs under the trademark system in China.

2.1 Legislative History

Before 1993, it was not possible to protect GIs within the trademark system in China. However, Rules for the Implementation of the Trade Mark Law (1993 Revision) (TM Implementing Rules 1993)[8] introduced provisions for the protection of certification marks and collective marks. This made it possible to protect GIs as trademarks. In December 1994, based on the Trade Mark Law of 1993 (TM Law 1993)[9] and the TM Implementing Rules 1993, SAIC formulated and promulgated the Procedures for the Registration and Administration of Collective Marks and Certification

---

[5] *See* Daniele Giovannucci, Elizabeth Barham & Richard Pirog, *Defining and Marketing 'Local' Foods: Geographical Indications for US Products*, 13 J. WORLD INTELL. PROP. 94, 104 (2010).

[6] *See* Irina Kireeva, Xiaobing Wang & Yumin Zhang, *Comprehensive Feasibility Study for Possible Negotiations on a Geographical Indications Agreement between China and the EU*, 21 (2009), available at www.ipkey.org/en/resources/ip-information-centre/19-geographical-indications/1942-comprehensive-feasibility-study-for-possible-negotiations-on-a-geographical-indications-agreement-between-china-and-the-eu.

[7] In China, the government or its agencies cannot become trademark registrants due to certain restrictions on the eligibility of ownership.

[8] *See* Rules for the Implementation of the Trademark Law of the People's Republic of China (1993 Revision) (Approved by the State Council of People's Republic of China on January 3, 1988, and secondly revised and approved by the State Council on 15 July 1993), available at http://en.pkulaw.cn/display.aspx?cgid=6324&lib=law.

[9] *See* Trademark Law of the People's Republic of China (as amended by Decision of 22 February 1993, of the Standing Committee of the National People's Congress, on Revising the Trademark Law of the People's Republic of China), available at www.wipo.int/wipolex/en/text.jsp?file_id=181327 [hereinafter TM Law 1993].

Marks,[10] which provided that certification marks could be used to certify the place of origin, raw materials, method of production, quality, accuracy, or other characteristics of the said goods or services. This was the first administrative rule regarding the protection of a GI in the national legal system in China.[11]

Less than a decade later, in 2001, China made a commitment to introduce specific GI protection in its Trade Mark Law as part of its accession to the World Trade Organization (WTO). As a result, the concept of 'geographical indication' was officially introduced in the revised Trade Mark Law of 2001 (TM Law 2001).[12] This legislation elevated the legal basis for GI protection from administrative rule to national law.[13] However, the 2001 revision to the Trade Mark Law did not provide for a specific procedure to register a GI in China. Thus, a year later, in 2002, the State Council promulgated Regulations for the Implementation of the Trade Mark Law (TM Implementing Regulations 2002)[14] in order to create a system of registration.

In particular, Article 6.1 of the TM Implementing Regulations 2002 stipulates that 'for geographical indications referred to in Article 16 of the Trade Mark Law, applications may be filed to register them as certification marks or collective marks under the provisions of the Trade Mark Law and these Regulations'. Article 3 of TM Law 2001 was later confirmed in the same provision in the Trade Mark Law of 2013 (TM Law 2013),[15] which defines

---

[10] See Procedures for the Registration and Administration of Collective Marks and Certification Marks (issued by State Administration for Industry and Commerce, 30 December 1994, effective 1 March 1995, repealed 1 June 2003) (China), available at http://vip.chinalawinfo.com/newlaw2002/SLC/slc.asp?db=chl&gid=18688.

[11] Qinghu An, Speech at the International Symposium on Geographical Indications: Legal System on Geographical Indication Protection in China and Related Issues (25 June 2007), available at www.zjfw.org/xw-view.asp?bid=1&sid=2&id=504.

[12] See Trademark Law of the People's Republic of China (as amended up to Decision of 30 August 2013, of the Standing Committee of National People's Congress on Amendments to the Trademark Law of the People's Republic of China) art. 16(2), available at www.wipo.int/wipolex/en/text.jsp?file_id=341321 (English), http://sbj.saic.gov.cn/flfg1/flfg/201309/t20130903_137807.html (Chinese) [hereinafter TM Law 2013].

[13] See An, *supra* note 11.

[14] See Regulations for the Implementation of the Trademark Law of the People's Republic of China (promulgated by Order No. 358 of the State Council of the People's Republic of China on 3 August 2002; amended by order No. 651 of the Decision of the State Council on Amending the Regulations for the Implementation of the Trademark Law of the People's Republic of China on 29 April 2014), available at www.wipo.int/wipolex/en/details.jsp?id=15011 [hereinafter TM Implementing Regulations 2002].

[15] See Trademark Law of the People's Republic of China (as amended up to Decision of 27 October 2001, of the Standing Committee of National People's Congress Revising the Trademark Law of the People's Republic of China), available at www.wipo.int/wipolex/en/text.jsp?file_id=131395 [hereinafter TM Law 2001].

a collective mark as 'a mark registered in the name of a group, association, or any other organization and used by its members to indicate membership'.[16] It also goes on to define a certification mark as 'a mark which is owned by an organization that exercises supervision over a particular product or service and which is used to indicate that third-party goods or services meet certain standards pertaining to place of origin, raw materials, mode of manufacture, quality, or other characteristics.'"[17]

In 2003, SAIC issued the Measures for the Registration and Administration of Certification and Collective Marks[18] in response to the revised Trade Mark Law, making detailed provisions about the registration and administration of GIs. As a result, GIs can be registered and protected as collective marks or certification marks under the trademark regime with the Trade Mark Office under SAIC.

2.2 *Current Protection under the Chinese Trademark System*

Article 16 of the TM Law 2013 provides that geographical indication 'means that it is the place of origin on the goods at issue and that the special qualities, reputation or other characteristics of the goods are primarily determined by the natural conditions or other humanistic conditions of the geographical location involved'.[19]

2.2.1 What May be Registered as a Geographical Indication under the Trademark System

Under Chinese trademark law, a GI registered as a collective mark or a certification mark may be the name of the geographical region indicated or any other visual signs capable of indicating that a good originates from the region. The area of the region designated as the region from which GI products originate is not required to be fully consistent with the name or boundary of the administrative division of the same region.[20] In this respect, the scope of trademark protection is much wider than that of the *sui generis* protection for GIs, as the latter only allows for the registration of geographically accurate names.

---

[16] *Id.* art. 3. [17] *Id.*
[18] *See* Measures for the Registration and Administration of Collective Marks and Certification Marks (issued by State Administration for Industry and Commerce, 17 April 2003), available at www.wipo.int/wipolex/en/text.jsp?file_id=181612 (English), http://sbj.saic.gov.cn/flfg1/sbxzgz/200906/t20090603_60312.html (Chinese) [hereafter SAIC Measures 2003].
[19] TM Law 2013, *supra* note 12, at art. 16.
[20] SAIC Measures 2003, *supra* note 18, at art. 8.

2.2.2 Special Registration Requirements

Applicants should follow the general rules enacted to register collective or certification marks in order to register a GI as a trademark. In addition, in order to apply for registration, applicants have to present the following supporting documents or evidence:

(1) a document issued by the people's government which has jurisdiction over, or the competent authority of, the concerned industry approving the applicant's registration of the GI in question, for example, agricultural or fishery authorities;[21]
(2) a description of the GI including (i) the given quality, reputation, or any other characteristic of the goods indicated by the sign, (ii) the relation between the given quality, reputation, or any other characteristic of the goods and the natural and human factors of the region indicated by the GI, and (iii) the boundary of the region indicated by the GI;[22]
(3) detailed information of the professionals and special testing equipment of the applicant or of any other organization authorized by the applicant to show its capability of supervising the particular quality of the goods indicated;[23]
(4) the regulation governing the use of a collective mark or certification mark.[24] The registrant of a GI imposes control over the use of the GI mainly through the implementation of this regulation.

Foreign applicants should appoint a trademark agent to act for them in China,[25] and further present documents certifying that the GI being applied for is protected also in the country of origin, in addition to the documents mentioned in (2), (3), and (4) above.[26]

2.2.3 Use of Geographical Indications as Registered Certification or Collective Marks

Anyone within the specified geographical area who satisfies the prescribed standard can ask for permission to use the GI and the owner cannot refuse it. Therefore, the trademark system makes it possible that even small producers can share the benefits of the exclusive rights granted by GI protection.[27] If a qualified product meets the standards set by the owner of the certification mark, the producer must be permitted to use the mark fairly. Generally,

---

[21] Id. art. 6.1. [22] Id. art. 7. [23] Id. arts. 4, 5. [24] Id. arts. 10, 11.
[25] TM Law 2013, supra note 12, at art. 18.2.
[26] SAIC Measures 2003, supra note 18, at art. 6.2.
[27] TM Implementing Regulations 2002, supra note 14, at art. 4.2

certification trademarks are not held by private businesses but by certification bodies, who should be impartial towards producers.[28] These bodies must exercise legitimate control over the use of the marks, but may not discriminate against a producer who actually meets the standards. Therefore, collective use is open to all producers in the specified region who comply with the rules or specifications of the certification trademarks.

The difference between GIs as collective marks and certification marks lies in that only the members of the association that has registered the mark can use the former.[29] The bodies eligible for collective mark GI registration should be composed of members located within the regions designated by the GIs.[30] Anyone whose goods satisfy the conditions under which the GI is used may request membership from the collective mark registrant, and the registrant must accede to this request in accordance with its articles of association.[31] For those who do not request membership, fair use of the geographic name of the said GI must be allowed to describe the origin of their products.[32] This use constitutes a type of fair use exemption of a geographical mark under the trademark system in China.

2.2.4 Control and Supervision over Certification and Collective Marks

The registrants/trademark owners in accordance with the control and supervision system that is set for the products to which the collective or certification marks apply exercise the control of the use of GIs as certification or collective marks. This control and supervision system is specifically articulated in the regulation governing the use of the said marks, and is a required component of the application documents of these types of trademarks.[33] If the registrants/trademark owners of a collective or certification mark fail to exercise effective control over the use of the mark and, as a result, the goods to which the said mark applies fail to meet the requirements of the regulation governing the use of the mark, causing damage to consumers, the administrative authority for industry and commerce can order them to rectify the situation within a time

---

[28] A provision similar to US practice. *See* DANIELE GIOVANNUCCI, TIM JOSLING, WILLIAM KERR, BERNAD O'CONNOR & MAY T YEUNG, GUIDE TO GEOGRAPHICAL INDICATIONS: LINKING PRODUCTS AND THEIR ORIGINS 66 (2009); *see also* SAIC Measures 2003, *supra* note 18, at art. 20 (the registrant of a certification mark shall not use the certification mark on goods provided by himself or itself).

[29] TM Law 2013, *supra* note 12, at art. 3.   [30] SAIC Measures 2003, *supra* note 18, at art. 4.2.

[31] TM Implementing Regulations 2002, *supra* note 14, at art. 6.2.

[32] Article 6.2 of the TM Implementing Regulations 2002 provides for fair use of the GI, and Article 18 of the SAIC Measures 2003 modifies it to be fair use of the geographical name.

[33] TM Implementing Regulations 2002, *supra* note 14, at arts. 10, 11.

limit. If the registrants/trademark owners refuse to do so, they will be imposed a fine.[34]

2.2.5 Protection and Enforcement

Protecting GIs as certification or collective marks follows the general rule of ordinary product or service marks. Article 3.1 of TM Law 2013 provides that '[a] trademark registrant shall enjoy an exclusive right to use the trademark, which shall be protected by law'.[35] The statute also provides a list of the acts that constitute infringements of the exclusive right to use a registered trademark, which are also applicable to a registered certification or collective marks (used to protect the GIs).[36]

Under the Chinese trademark system, there is a twin-track system to enforce trademark rights. In particular, right holders may either institute legal proceedings in the people's court or request the administrative authorities for industry and commerce (AICs) to take action. The AICs are empowered by the TM Law 2013 to investigate and handle trademark infringement cases. The AICs can order the infringer to immediately stop the infringing act. Additionally, the AICs can confiscate and destroy the infringing goods and the tools that are used to manufacture the goods. The AICs can also impose a fine for counterfeiting the registered trademark.[37] If the case is so serious as to constitute a crime, the AICs shall transfer the case to the judicial authority for determination.[38] Alternatively, the interested party may directly bring a lawsuit to the people's court for trademark infringement.

3 PROTECTION OF GEOGRAPHICAL INDICATIONS UNDER THE SUI GENERIS REGIME

Meanwhile, there are two independent *sui generis* systems available in China for GI protection. These systems implement the ministerial rules on GIs by the General Administration of Quality Supervision, Inspection, and Quarantine (AQSIQ)[39] and the Ministry of Agriculture (MOA) respectively.

Under a *sui generis* system, the legal recognition and protection of GIs is based on a 'unique' approach, which is specifically dedicated to this type of intellectual property. With its close links to the specific geographical area, GIs belong to the region itself and not to individual producers located

---

[34] *Id.* art. 21. [35] TM Law 2013, *supra* note 12, at art. 3.1. [36] *Id.* art. 57. [37] *Id.* art. 53.
[38] *Id.* art. 61.
[39] Due to institutional reconstruction, AQSIQ was created in 2001 to incorporate the former State Bureau of Quality and Technical Supervision and the former State Administration for Entry-Exit Inspection and Quarantine.

therein. Because GIs grant collective rights, GI protection also sees a deep involvement of the public authorities. In particular, under a *sui generis* system, the definition of the GI area, the eligible users of the GIs, and the ability to enforce regulations often are driven, at least in part, by the public authorities. Moreover, governments intervene in terms of control and supervision on the quality and specific characteristics of the products marketed under GIs.[40] In this respect, *sui generis* protection puts more emphasis on the quality of GI products, which requires strict controls over their production processes.

3.1 First SUI GENERIS *Regime: General Administration of Quality Supervision, Inspection, and Quarantine Practice*

The AQSIQ rules in China have been heavily influenced by the appellation d'origine contrôlée (AOC) system of France. The former State Bureau of Quality and Technical Supervision, in close cooperation with the French Ministry of Agriculture, the Ministry of Finance, and the Bureau National Interprofessionnel Du Cognac, promulgated China's Provisions on Protection of Designations of Origin Products in 1999. This was also the first administrative regime specifying protection for designations of origin.[41] Two years later, the former State Administration for Entry-Exit Inspection and Quarantine promulgated the Provisions on the Administration of Marks of Origin in 2001. These two agencies then merged to form the AQSIQ in 2001. AQSIQ proceeded to promulgate the Provisions on the Protection of Geographical Indication Products (PPGIP)[42] in 2005, which replaced the above-mentioned two rules. All the rules mentioned above are administrative rules.

According to PPGIP, GI products are 'products that originate from a particular geographical region with the quality, reputation or other characteristics substantially attributable to the natural and human factors of the region, and denominated with the name of the region upon examination and approval'.[43] Products of GIs include (i) those grown or cultivated in the region;

---

[40] *See* Kireeva, Wang & Zhang, *supra* note 6, at 16.
[41] Jing Dai, 试论我国地理标志产品保护制度[*On the Protection System of Geographical Indication Products in China*], 3 MOD. BUS. 277 (2009).
[42] *See* Provisions on the Protection of Geographical Indication Products (promulgated by General Administration of Quality Supervision, Inspection and Quarantine, 16 May 2005, effective 15 July 2005), available at www.wipo.int/wipolex/en/text.jsp?file_id=181517 (English), www.gov.cn/gongbao/content/2006/content_292138.htm (Chinese) [hereinafter PPGIP].
[43] *Id.* art. 2.1.

and (ii) those made, wholly or partially, of the raw materials from the region and produced or processed with the particular techniques in the region.[44] The coverage of GI products under PPGIP is rather wide and includes agricultural products, handicraft works, spirits, and other products protected under the trademark regime.

3.1.1 Registration Procedures

As a starting point, there is a two-tier process for applicants to apply for registration of the GI products. First, registration of the GI needs to take place with provincial quality and inspection departments, then with the AQSIQ. After the GI has been registered, producers who intend to use the GIs for their products have to go through a similar two-tier process to get the approval to use the GI. The applicants can either be entities designated by local governments, enterprises, or associations accredited by local governments.[45] For GI products of exporting enterprises, applications should be made to entry-exit inspection and quarantine departments of the prescribed area. For other GI products, applications should be made to the local (that is at or above county level) quality supervision departments.[46]

3.1.2 Examination and Approval

Provincial quality supervision departments or entry-exit inspection and quarantine departments conduct the first level of examination for registering a GI. These departments draw up preliminary opinions on the application and then submit their report and application documents to AQSIQ.

At the second level, AQSIQ first conducts formal checks on the application, and will then publish a notice of acceptance in the AQSIQ Gazette, as well as on its website if the application satisfies the formality requirements.

If the application fails to meet the formality requirements, the AQSIQ will notify the applicant in writing.[47] Anyone who objects to the registration can file an opposition within two months after publication.[48]

For an application without opposition or where the opposition is unsuccessful, the AQSIQ will set up an expert examination panel according to the features of the products in question. The expert panel will then conduct a technical examination on the application and the AQSIQ will publish its approval of the application, if it passes the technical review by the expert panel.[49]

---

[44] *Id.* art. 2.2. [45] *Id.* art. 8. [46] *Id.* art. 11. [47] *Id.* art. 13.
[48] PPGIP, *supra* note 42, at art. 14. [49] *Id.* arts. 15, 16.

3.1.3 Application by the Producer to Use a Geographical Indication Product

Any producer within the geographical limits of the origin region who wishes to use the GI sign on its product first has to file an application with the local (provincial) quality supervision department or entry-exit inspection and quarantine departments. Successful applications will then be subject to review by the AQSIQ.

After the AQSIQ approves its application and publishes it in the AQSIQ Gazette, the producer will be eligible to use the sign in question.[50] The application process for hopeful users of GI products is quite similar to the registration system.[51]

3.1.4 Control and Supervision

Local quality inspection authorities exert routine control on the quality of the GI products and do so in a very detailed way. Their scope covers almost every aspect of production. This includes raw materials, production techniques, quality features, classifications of quality, quantity, packaging and labelling of GI products, as well as the printing, distribution, quantity, and use of the special signs of the product, manufacturing environment, production equipment, and conformity with standards of the product.[52]

3.1.5 Protection and Enforcement

The approved GI products are protected in accordance with PPGIP. There are three types of acts that can be categorized as infringing the legitimate rights of registrants:[53] (i) use without authorization or forging a GI and its specific marks; (ii) unauthorized use by producers within the protected regions who cannot obtain approval because their products fail the requirements; and (iii) use of signs that are so similar to the protected signs that consumers will be misled into believing the products are protected GI products.

According to PPGIP, the quality supervision and entry-exit inspection and quarantine departments are responsible for investigating the above-mentioned acts.[54] Similar to the trademark regime, interested parties can either lodge complaints with local quality supervision departments or bring lawsuits to the people's court. The quality supervision departments rely on China Law of

---

[50] *Id.* art. 20.2.
[51] *See* Bradley M. Bashaw, *Geographical Indications in China: Why Protect GIs with Both Trade Mark Law and AOC-type Legislation?* 17 Pac. Rim L. & Pol'y J. 73, 84 (2008).
[52] PPGIP, *supra* note 42, at art. 22.   [53] *Id.* art. 21.   [54] *Id.* art. 4.

the People's Republic of China on Product Quality,[55] Standardization Law of the People's Republic of China,[56] and Law of the People's Republic of China on Import and Export Commodity Inspection[57] to impose administrative penalties in dealing with cases of GI products.[58]

3.1.6 Protection of Foreign Geographical Indication Products

PPGIP provides that separate provisions are to be formulated for the registration of foreign GIs in China.[59] Yet, there are no such provisions available to date. In 2007, the European Union (EU) initiated a '10 plus 10' pilot project with AQSIQ, under which both sides presented a list of ten agricultural GIs, respectively, to seek protection in each other's territories – that is, ten GIs from China were protected in EU and ten GIs from the EU were protected in China under the pilot project.[60] In addition, AQSIQ accepted an application from the French GI 'Cognac' in June 2009. AQSIQ approved the application in December 2009 pursuant to the Memorandum of Understanding on Geographical Indications[61] signed by AQSIQ of China and the European Commission DG Trade, with reference to the PPGIP. 'Cognac' is the first foreign GI product protected by AQSIQ in China.

---

[55] See China Law of the People's Republic of China on Product Quality (adopted by the Standing Comm. Nat'l People's Cong., 22 February 1993, amended 8 July 2000), available at www.most.gov.cn/eng/policies/regulations/200501/t20050105_18422.htm.

[56] See Standardization Law of the People's Republic of China (adopted by the Standing Comm. Nat'l People's Cong., 29 December 1988, promulgated by the People's Rep. of China 29 December 1988), available at www.npc.gov.cn/englishnpc/Law/2007-12/12/content_1383927.htm.

[57] See Law of the People's Republic of China on Import and Export Commodity Inspection (adopted by the Standing Comm. Nat'l People's Cong., 21 February 1989, amended by the People's Rep. of China on Import and Export Commodity Inspection Standing Comm. Nat'l People's Cong., April 28, 2002), available at http://english.mofcom.gov.cn/article/policyrelease/Businessregulations/201303/20130300045852.shtml.

[58] PPGIP, supra note 42, at art. 24.   [59] Id. art. 26.

[60] The EU list is comprised of Grana Padano; Prosciutto di Parma; Roquefort; Pruneaux d'Agen/Pruneaux d'Agen mi-cuits; Priego de Cordóba; Sierra Mágina; Comté; White Stilton Cheese/Blue Stilton Cheese; Scottish Farmed Salmon; and West Country Farmhouse Cheddar. The Chinese AQSIQ list comprises of Dongshan Bai Lu Sun (asparagus), Guanxi Mi You (honey pomelo), Jinxiang Da Suan (garlic), Lixian Ma Shan Yao (yam), Longjing Cha (tea), Pinggu Da Tao (peach), Shaanxi Ping Guo (apple), Yancheng Long Xia (crayfish), Zhenjiang Xiang Cu (vinegar), and Longkou Fen Si (vermicelli). See European Commission, Agricultural and Rural Development, http://ec.europa.eu/agriculture/newsroom/26_en.htm (last visited 8 June 2016).

[61] See General Administration Quality Supervision, Inspection and Quarantine of the People's Republic of China, Notice on Protection for Products of Cognac Geographical Indication (No. 117 2009), available at http://kjs.aqsiq.gov.cn/dlbzcpbhwz/ggcx/201001/t20100106_134265.htm (last visited 8 June 2016).

3.2 Second SUI GENERIS Regime: Ministry of Agriculture Practice

In addition to AQSIQ, the MOA has also promulgated a set of administrative rules, namely the Measures for the Administration of Geographical Indications of Agricultural Products (MOA Measures),[62] in 2007 according to the Agriculture Law of the People's Republic of China and Law of the People's Republic of China on Agricultural Product Quality Safety. The MOA Measures entered into force in February 2008.

Article 2 of the MOA Measures defines 'agricultural products' as 'primary products sourced from agriculture, namely, plants, animals, microorganisms, and the products thereof obtained in agricultural activities'.[63] Among the three types of protection regimes (under Trade Mark law, the PPGIP, and MOA Measures), the scope of protected products under MOA Measures is the narrowest, only covering agricultural products.

3.2.1 Registration Procedures

The MOA Measures is quite similar to PPGIP in that the registration procedures also involve a two-level process – provincial and national – for an applicant to obtain registration.

Under the MOA Measures, agricultural product GIs are regarded as a collective right; accordingly, individuals or enterprises are not eligible to make applications. Eligible applicants include professional cooperative organizations of farmers and industrial associations determined by governments at or above the county level.

3.2.2 Examination and Approval

After receiving the application, provincial agricultural authorities will conduct on-site verification and propose their preliminary examination opinion. For applications that meet the requisite conditions, the authorities will send the filing documents and preliminary opinion to the Centre for Agri-food Quality and Safety (the Centre), operated under the MOA. For those that do not, the authorities will notify the applicant of their opinion.[64]

Within twenty working days after receiving the documents, the Centre will examine the application and organize expert examination. The expert

---

[62] *See* Measures for the Administration of Geographical Indications of Agricultural Product (issued by Ministry of Agriculture, 25 December 2007, effective 1 February, 2008) (China), available at www.wipo.int/wipolex/en/text.jsp?file_id=182476 (English), www.gov.cn/gongbao/content/2008/content_1071853.htm (Chinese) [hereinafter MOA Measures].

[63] *Id.* art. 2.   [64] *Id.* art. 10.

committee will then undertake the appraisal of the registration of GIs of agricultural products, work out appraisal conclusions independently, and be responsible for the conclusions.[65] If the expert committee is in favour of the application after appraisal, the Centre will publish an announcement approving the application on behalf of the MOA. Anyone who has an objection to the approval can file their opposition within twenty days with the Centre. If there are no objections, the MOA will make an announcement, issue a Certificate of People's Republic of China on the Registration of Geographical Indications of Agricultural Products, and publish the relevant technical regulations and standards. If the expert committee does not approve of the application, the MOA will make a decision not to register it and notify the applicant of the decision in writing.[66]

3.2.3 Application to Use Geographical Indications on Agricultural Product

Any producer who satisfies the following conditions may apply to the registration certificate holder for uses of the GI on suitable agricultural products. In particular, applicants will need to (1) have the capability to supervise and administer the GIs of agricultural products and the products thereof;[67] (2) have the capability to provide guidance for the production, processing, and marketing of agricultural products with GIs;[68] and (3) have the capacity to bear civil liabilities independently.[69]

3.2.4 Protection Term

Unlike GIs registered as collective marks or certification marks, which have to be renewed every ten years, the MOA registration of a GI for an agricultural product will remain valid permanently without need to be renewed.[70]

3.2.5 Control and Supervision

Moreover, the MOA *sui generis* regime emphasizes administrative supervision and control over the quality and source of products. Competent local agricultural authorities will be responsible for conducting regular inspections and administering the use of GI signs, as well as evaluating the boundary requirement of geographical origin.[71] The producers of agricultural products with GIs also shoulder some responsibility by establishing a quality control tracing system.[72]

---

[65] Id. art. 11.   [66] Id. art. 12.   [67] Id. art. 8.1.
[68] MOA Measures, *supra* note 62, at art. 8.2.   [69] Id. art. 8.3.   [70] Id. art. 13.
[71] Id. art. 18.   [72] Id. art. 19.

3.2.6 Protection and Enforcement

Forgery, use of GIs without authorization, or false claims regarding any registration certificates are considered to violate the MOA Measures.[73] Like the PPGIP, there is no direct provision in the MOA Measures concerning any administrative penalty. Rather, administrative punishment will be imposed according to the Law on Agricultural Product Quality Safety.[74]

3.2.7 Protection of Foreign Geographical Indications for Agricultural Products

Article 24 of the MOA Measures provides that the 'Ministry of Agriculture accepts applications for the registration of geographical indications of agricultural products from foreign countries, and protects them once they have been registered in China'.[75] However, the specific measures as to the application and registration of foreign GIs for agricultural products are yet to be formulated. As no such specific measures have been promulgated, no foreign GIs of agricultural products have been registered under the MOA regime so far.[76]

4 PROTECTING GEOGRAPHICAL INDICATIONS UNDER OTHER LAWS IN CHINA

In addition to be protected under the trademark system and a *sui generis* system, GIs can be protected in China (at least to a certain extent) under other laws. In particular, the Anti-Unfair Competition Law,[77] Product Quality Law,[78] and Law on Protection of Consumer Rights and Interests[79] were

---

[73] *Id.* art. 20.
[74] *See* MOA Measures, *supra* note 62, at art. 23. *See also* Law of the People's Republic of China on Quality and Safety of Agricultural Products (ordered by the People's Rep. of China, amended and adopted by the Standing Comm. Nat'l People's Cong., 29 April 2006, hereby promulgated and shall go into effect as of 1 November 2006), available at www.npc.gov.cn /englishnpc/Law/2008-01/02/content_1387986.htm.
[75] *See* MOA Measures, *supra* note 62, at art. 24.
[76] *See* Kireeva, Wang & Zhang, *supra* note 6, at 115.
[77] *See* Anti-Unfair Competition Law (PRC) (promulgated by the Standing Comm. Nat'l People's Cong., 2 September 1993, effective 1 December 1993) (China), available at www .lawinfochina.com/law/display.asp?id=648 [hereinafter Anti-Unfair Competition Law].
[78] *See* Product Quality Law (PRC) (promulgated by the Standing Comm. Nat'l People's Cong., 22 February 1993, effective 1 September 1993, revised for the first time 8 July 2000, revised for the second time 27 August 2009), available at www.lawinfochina.com/law/display.asp?id=615 [hereinafter Product Quality Law].
[79] *See* Law on Protection of Consumer Rights and Interests (PRC) (promulgated by Standing Comm. Nat'l People's Cong., 31 October 1993, effective 1 January 1994, revised 25 October 2013), available at www.lawtime.cn/faguizt/117.html [hereinafter Law on Protection of Consumer Rights and Interests].

enacted to protect producers and consumers. They only stipulate general rules, but can serve the purposes of GI protection.[80]

4.1 Unfair Competition

Under the Anti-Unfair Competition Law of China, falsely indicating the place of origin of commodities is a prohibited unfair competitive activity.[81] The Anti-Unfair Competition Law also prohibits business operators from using any false advertising or other means of false publicity in business activities regarding the origin of products.[82]

Accordingly, it is clear that the Anti-Unfair Competition Law does protect the concept of place of origin from the perspective of consumer and producer. However, the protection afforded to GIs under this law is directly finalized at safeguarding not GIs per se, but rather consumers and fairness in competition.[83]

4.2 Consumer Protection

The Law on Protection of Consumer Rights and Interests stipulates that consumers have the right to obtain genuine information on commodities or services, including information on place of origin. Business operators are therefore under the obligation to provide this information.[84] Providing false information on place of origin constitutes an offence under the Law.

4.3 Product Quality Protection

The Product Quality Law forbids the inaccurate use of the place of origin on products.[85] However, the products mentioned in the Product Quality Law refer to products processed and manufactured for the purpose of marketing.[86] A great number of GI products, namely primary agricultural products such as vegetables and fruits, are excluded from protection under this Law. Therefore, the scope of protection accorded by Product Quality Law to GI is rather inadequate.[87]

---

[80] See Bashaw, *supra* note 51, at 86.
[81] Anti-Unfair Competition Law, *supra* note 77, at art. 5(4). [82] *Id.* art. 9.
[83] See TIAN FURONG, 地理标志法律保护制度研究》 [STUDY ON THE LEGAL SYSTEM FOR PROTECTION OF GEOGRAPHICAL INDICATIONS] 272 (2009).
[84] Law on Protection of Consumer Rights and Interests, *supra* note 79, at arts. 8, 20.
[85] Product Quality Law, *supra* note 78, at art. 5. [86] *Id.* art. 2(1).
[87] See FURONG, *supra* note 83, at 273.

5 MAJOR CHALLENGES FOR THE PROTECTION OF GEOGRAPHICAL INDICATIONS IN CHINA

In conclusion, there are three parallel ways in which one may seek protection for GIs in China's legal system – within trademark law, under the PPGIP regimes administered by AQSIQ, and the MOA regime. Each of them is administered by different governmental agencies, with a distinct legal basis. There are also more general legal regimes which target misleading conduct in the marketplace and can thus protect GIs, namely, unfair competition regime (Anti-Unfair Competition Law), consumer protection regime (Law on Protection of Consumer Rights and Interests), and product quality regulation regime (Product Quality Law).

Still, GI protection in China faces many challenges. The most controversial issue is the concurrent operation of trademark and *sui generis* models, and this is made more complicated by the fact that there are two parallel *sui generis* models operated by AQSIQ and the Ministry of Agriculture. As previously noted, trademark protection falls within the jurisdiction of the SAIC, while protection of GI products in general and protection of agricultural products in particular come under the administration of AQSIQ and the Ministry of Agriculture respectively. Since there are three independent and parallel systems of GI protection in China, the same GIs may be simultaneously protected, potentially obtaining three independent kinds of protection.

Simultaneously, the possibility of registering place names qualified to be GIs as ordinary trademarks causes conflicts between individual trademarks and GIs-as-trademarks within the trademark regime. Therefore, there are two principal challenges: one is the conflict between ordinary trademarks containing geographical terms and geographical indications by means of certification or collective marks; and the other is the overlap and ensuing conflict arising from the co-existence of trademark and *sui generis* mechanisms.[88]

5.1 Conflicts between Trademarks and Geographical Indications within the Trademark Regime

5.1.1 Causes of Conflicts

In general, geographical terms, which are descriptive, cannot be registered as trademarks on the ground of lack of distinctiveness as they are unable to distinguish the goods or services of one undertaking from those of others,

---

[88] See ZHAO XIAOPING, 地理标志的法律保护研究 [STUDY ON LEGAL PROTECTION OF GEOGRAPHICAL INDICATIONS] 285 (2007).

a fundamental function of trademarks.[89] Meanwhile, this also prevents the possibility of the monopolization of geographical terms by a single entity.[90] Moreover, if the goods or services are not offered within the designated region, the geographically descriptive term could be misleading to consumers.

However, the Trade Mark Law in force before 1993 allowed registration of geographical names (even administrative place names at or above the county level) as ordinary trademarks. Today, even misleading trademarks indicating a false place of origin continue to be valid if they were previously registered under this law in good faith.[91] The 金华(JINHUA) trademark for ham is one such example. Notably, the proprietor of JINHUA for ham does not produce ham originating in Jinhua City. Rather, the proprietor of the mark is located in another city within the same province. Accordingly, the mark actually indicates a false origin for the products that it identifies, but remains valid because it was a bona fide registration before 1993. Moreover, it becomes a rather famous trademark due to the heavy long-term investments made by the trademark owner.

Another issue is that the TM Law 2013[92] only regulates the registration of geographical terms consisting of administrative regions as ordinary trademarks. However, geographical boundaries are determined by natural environment and human skills, which makes them not necessarily identical to administrative regions. The same is true with administrative place names under the county level. Such geographical terms, following Article 10.2 of the TM Law 2013, cannot be prevented from being registered as ordinary trademarks. As a consequence, many geographical names below the county level, or non-administrative place names, have been registered as ordinary marks and these privately held trademark rights may be used to prohibit the use of such place names by local producers situated within the indicated place.[93]

Thus, if there were a causal link between the geographical place and the quality, reputation, or other characteristics of goods originated from this place, such a geographical name would be eligible for GI protection. However, a prior registered trademark may obstruct the registration of such a GI.

---

[89] WORLD INTELL. PROP. ORG., MAKING A MARK: AN INTRODUCTION TO TRADEMARKS FOR SMALL AND MEDIUM-SIZED ENTERPRISES 4 (2006).

[90] See FURONG, supra note 83, at 248.

[91] Bashaw, supra note 51, at 79; see also Trade Mark Law 2013, supra note 12, at art. 16(1) (where a trademark contains a GI of the goods in respect of which the trademark is used, the goods are not from the region indicated therein, and it misleads the public, it shall be rejected for registration and prohibited from use; however, any trademark that has been registered in good faith shall remain valid).

[92] TM Law 2013, supra note 12.   [93] See XIAOPING, supra note 88, at 281.

5.1.2 Proposed Solutions

The conflict between ordinary trademarks containing geographical terms and GIs applied for as certification or collective marks may be solved within the trademark regime itself. The 'first in time, first in right' principle is often proposed as an optimal solution to addressing the problem.[94] But sometimes it is not as clear-cut an issue in practice.

The Jinhua Ham case is an exemplary case study of a situation where a rigid application of the priority principle would not produce satisfactory results. As mentioned above, JINHUA is a trademark used on ham owned by Zhejiang Jinhua Ham Co. Ltd.[95] After becoming aware that Jinhua Ham could qualify as a protected GI, the Office for Protecting Jinhua Ham Certification Trade Mark filed an application for Jinhua City Jinhua Ham as a certification mark with the Trade Mark Office in 2003. Normally, in accordance with the principle of priority, a subsequent confusingly similar sign (as is the case here) should be refused registration based on the prior registration of a mark which is used on identical or similar goods. However, sometimes one needs to settle such conflicts by taking historical factors as well as the interests of producers and consumers into consideration. While the proprietor of JINHUA is a company outside the boundary of Jinhua City, local Jinhua ham producers want Jinhua City Jinhua Ham to be registered as a GI so that its hams can be adequately protected. After difficult and lengthy negotiations and mediation, Jinhua City Jinhua Ham was published in the Trade Mark Gazette in 2009 and registered as a certification mark GI.[96] This has created a de facto co-existence of quite similar marks under the trademark system. Although co-existence is one solution for such conflicts, it should be subject to strict control and only allowed in exceptional cases. After all, intellectual property rights are generally subject to the principle of priority, which ensures exclusivity. Co-existence should be treated as an exception to this principle, only allowed under very limited circumstances because it has certain adverse effects on the right holders. If the system allows co-existence, the holder of a GI sometimes has to tolerate the use of the GI by third parties provided that the parties use it in accordance with honest practices in industrial and commercial matters. Otherwise, the owner of a prior trademark would need to take the risk of trademark dilution.

---

[94] Dev Gangjee, *Quibbling Siblings: Conflicts between Trademarks and Geographical Indications*, 82 CHICAGO-KENT L. REV. 1253, 1263 (2007).

[95] *See* Jinhua, Registration No. 130131, available at http://sbcx.saic.gov.cn:9080/tmois/wszhcx_pageZhcxMain.xhtml?type=reg&intcls=&regNum=130131&paiType=0.

[96] *See* Jinhua City Jinhua Ham, Registration No. 3779376, available at http://sbcx.saic.gov.cn:9080/tmois/wszhcx_pageZhcxMain.xhtml?type=reg&intcls=&regNum=3779376&paiType=0.

There is a suggestion that the TM Law 2013 be amended to allow for the cancellation of ordinary trademarks containing GIs or to disallow renewal of such trademarks. As a consequence there would not be any prior trademarks that could potentially conflict with a subsequent GI application.[97] However, it seems unrealistic to revise the TM Law 2013 along these lines because it will result in legal uncertainty and deprive the trademark holders of their investment, and probably lead to more confusion among consumers. This is particularly true for famous individually owned geographical trademarks, which are also eligible for GI protection. In such cases, it may be better to maintain the status quo because the trademark has earned itself a good reputation in the marketplace at the owner's expense. The owner has already considerably invested in the brand, so the potential cancellation of such famous regular trademarks or even co-existence between them and subsequent GIs would negatively impact upon the trademark owner. Furthermore, in the minds of consumers, after powerful presence of the brand in the marketplace for so many years, the geographical term would point to a specific producer rather than a region. Therefore, continuing to recognize the geographical term as an ordinary trademark would better serve the interests of consumers.

One case decided by the Trade Mark Review and Adjudication Board (TRAB)[98] reveals that the 'first in time, first in right' principle may not apply if the registered trademark has a GI nature, and the use of the trademark by the registrant might mislead the public as to the origin of its goods. In 2003, XIANG LIAN (literally meaning Hunan Lotus Seed) was registered by a Fujian-based company as an ordinary trademark on lotus seeds and other products. The Hunan Xiangtan Xianglian Association filed an application with TRAB to cancel this registration on the ground that Xianglian was in fact a GI, referring to lotus seeds produced in Hunan Province. In that case[99] the trademark owner defended itself by arguing that the disputed trademark has distinctiveness as an ordinary trademark. According to the evidence filed by the appellant, TRAB found that Xianglian is mainly produced in Hunan Province, and the lotus seeds have distinctive qualities, which are essentially attributable to the local temperature, humidity, soil, as well as the planting methods. 'Xianglian' had been in use for over 1400 years to refer to the lotus seeds produced in Hunan Province. It thus satisfied the conditions established

---

[97] See Bashaw, *supra* note 51, at 90.
[98] As an agency in parallel to the Trade Mark Office, TRAB is also under the administration of SAIC.
[99] See Xianglian, Registration No. 3023790, available at http://sbcx.saic.gov.cn:9080/tmois/wszhcx_pageZhcxMain.xhtml?type=reg&intcls=&regNum=3023790&paiType=0.

in Article 16.2 of the TM Law 2001.[100] Furthermore, TRAB found that the trademark owner engaged in lotus seed trade with producers in Hunan Province before its registration. The trademark owner thus knew that Xianglian referred to lotus seeds produced in Hunan Province but still applied for trademark registration, which was liable to mislead the public as to the quality and origin of its product. This act was in violation of the provision of Article 16.1 of the Trade Mark Law (providing 'where a trade mark contains a geographic indication of the goods in respect of which the trade mark is used, the goods are not from the region indicated therein and it misleads the public, it shall be rejected for registration and prohibited from use; however, any trade mark that has been registered in good faith shall remain valid').[101] Accordingly, TRAB cancelled the registration of the disputed trademark. In this case TRAB established that unregistered GIs in China could also be protected.[102] This is the first case where TRAB recognized and protected an unregistered GI in a trademark dispute case.

5.2 Priority Conflicts between SUI GENERIS GIs and Ordinary Trademarks

5.2.1 Causes for Conflicts

Conflicts will presumably not arise if GIs are owned by the same entities under different protection systems, though it might be regarded as a waste of time, money, or energy to seek parallel avenues for protecting the same GI. However, if the same GIs are pursued by more than one unrelated entity via different protection systems, it is likely that conflicts will occur.[103] Moreover, the co-existence of the systems confuses applicants as to which avenue to take. In the absence of clarification regarding their differences, many of them have opted for cumulative registrations in all three of the relevant agencies. If conflicts arise out of different ownership decided by different authorities, the parties have to go to court to resolve them, which could be expensive and time-consuming. The current regime is thus ineffective and creates uncertainty for GI stakeholders.

A given geographical name associated with a product may be protected as a GI under criteria set by one administration, but the same geographically significant term may be considered as having acquired distinctiveness under

---

[100] TM Law 2001, *supra* note 15, at art. 16.2.   [101] *Id.* art. 16.1.
[102] Xinzhang Shi, *Recognition and Protection of Geographical Indication in Trade Mark Dispute Cases for the First Time* (2009), available at www.saic.gov.cn/spw/cwtx/200904/t20 090409_55216.html.
[103] Kireeva, Wang & Zhang, *supra* note 6, at 147.

the TM Law 2013 and be eligible for registration as an ordinary trademark.[104] At present there are no explicit rules in either the TM Law 2013 or its related regulations, or the *sui generis* administrative rules of the AQSIQ and Ministry of Agriculture, which can resolve the conflict between rights granted under the trademark system and those granted under the *sui generis* systems.

The case of 金华火腿 (Jinhua Ham) is a milestone regarding the resolution of the conflict between *sui generis* GIs and trademarks in China.[105] As noted above, the trademark JINHUA and the GI 'Jinhua City Jinhua Ham' (registered as a certification mark) are concurrently valid under the trademark system. Yet, before the Jinhua City Jinhua Ham was able to obtain GI protection as a certification mark from SAIC, the Jinhua municipal authorities applied for a designation of origin (which later became a GI) for its ham and successfully obtained approval from the predecessor of AQSIQ. When the defendant, a company located in Jinhua, which is authorized to use the designation of origin, put Jinhua Ham on the packages of its products, the individual trademark proprietor sued him for infringement. So the dispute is in fact a conflict arising out of two protection systems, namely, trademark protection versus designations of origin (*sui generis* GIs). After a trial, the court decided that the trademark owner of Jinhua had the exclusive right but was not entitled to prohibit the fair use of a third party. The fact that the defendant was authorized to use the designation of origin Jinhua Ham, which was approved by another government agency, granted the defendant the fair-use exemption. Both parties enjoyed independent IP rights, namely a trademark right and a sui *generis* GI right, both of which were protected by law. The court also ruled that in order to guarantee that their acts were legal and justifiable both parties should respect each other's intellectual property rights and exercise their respective rights within the scope of protection, strictly following the relevant provisions.[106] Although the court decided the case by allowing coexistence of both sets of rights and the two parties accepted the judgment, the potential for clashes between the two systems remains the same.

5.2.2 Proposed Solutions

From the JINHUA judgment, one can see that clashes between trademark rights and GI rights could be settled based on principles of honest concurrent

---

[104] World Intellectual Prop. Org. (WIPO), *Geographical Indications and the Territoriality Principle*, WIPO Doc. SCT 9/5 (1 October 2002).

[105] *See* Zhejiang Food Co. Ltd. v. Shanghai Taikang Food Co. Ltd., Sup. People's Ct. Gaz. (Shanghai No.2 Interm. People's Ct., 25 December 2003) (unreported). *See also* Tian Furong, *supra* note 83, at 277–79.

[106] *See* Guoqiang Lv & Denglou Wu, 我国地理标志法律制度的完善 [*Optimization of China's Legal System of Geographical Indications*], 1 Leg. Sci. 154, 158 (2006).

use. For historical reasons relating to permissive legislation, many place names with potential GI significance have been registered as individual trademarks. The trademark owners have made tremendous efforts to enhance the reputation of the marks. On the other hand, the efforts and investment made by generations of local producers cannot be denied, either. Under such circumstances the law should protect both rights, provided that separate right holders use them fairly and honestly in the course of industrial and commercial activities.[107] However, co-existence is achieved at the price of compromises made by both trademark and GI right holders.

5.3 Conflicts between SUI GENERIS GIs and GIs Registered as Trademarks

Different administrative authorities may confer the same GI right on different entities, define different geographical boundaries, and enforce different quality standards. Take Shanxi Laochencu (literally meaning Old Vinegar in Shanxi) for example. AQSIQ recognized it as a protected product of designation of origin (now product of geographic indication) in 2004.[108] Then the Trade Mark Office registered it as a certification mark in 2010.[109] However, the production boundaries as well as the production standards determined by the two systems are so different that conflicts among the two right holders, as well as producers, would be unavoidable. Under such circumstances, it is difficult to coordinate the systems to achieve efficient GI protection.

6 COMPARISON BETWEEN THE TRADEMARK REGIME AND SUI GENERIS PROTECTION

As mentioned before, the most prominent problem is the co-existence of the trademark and *sui generis* systems for GI protection. By weighing the advantages and disadvantages of the two systems respectively, and taking into consideration the conflicts precipitated by the co-existence of the two systems, it is suggested that in China it would be better to maintain only one system. This should preferably be the trademark mechanism because it accommodates the rationale of GI protection better than *sui generis* mechanisms, bearing legal and economic considerations in mind.

---

[107] *Id.* at 159.
[108] Administration of Quality Supervision, Inspection and Quarantine, Product of Designation of Origin, Announcement No. 104, Protection of Shanxi Laochencu (1994).
[109] *See* Shanxi Laochencu, Registration No. 6173333, available at http://sbcx.saic.gov.cn:9080/tmois/wszhcx_pageZhcxMain.xhtml?type=reg&intcls=&regNum=6173333&paiType=0.

6.1 Costs

The trademark system is already in place to conduct GI examination (as collective or certification marks), whereas the *sui generis* system does not provide for protection for foreign GIs due to lack of procedural rules. It would be expensive to build up a comprehensive *sui generis* system to address international GI protection.

6.2 Obtaining Exclusive Rights

Despite the fact that in China it is usually government departments that set up the relevant association as the applicant to initiate the registration of a certification or collective mark GI, under the trademark regime it is the right holder who makes further decisions in seeking protection without government actions. On the international level, GIs as certification or collective marks can be applied for directly by the interested parties without an official government action being necessary, as is required under the Lisbon Agreement.[110] Trademark registration also involves less government intervention, as the standards for inspection and verification are set by the certification or collective mark owner, rather than the competent authorities. These government agencies are not expected to take on many roles that are supposedly taken on by private parties, such as market functions like defining the production or operating standards, managing verification of compliance, or controlling output.[111] Sometimes government agencies tend to be bureaucratic and demand complex procedures to be satisfied. The two-level examination and approval processes under both AQSIQ and MOA practices mirror the complexity of the procedures. From the producers' point of view, it is far more complicated to obtain *sui generis* GI registration.

6.3 Enforcement of Exclusive Rights

In cases where the use of a GI is not well regulated and monitored, or where misappropriation and abuses of GIs have become rampant, GI protection can hardly achieve its goal of protecting producers and consumers and promoting local development. In countries like China, the available practical benefits of

---

[110] *See* World Intellectual Prop. Org. (WIPO), *Document SCT/6/3 Rev. On Geographical Indications: Historical Background, Nature of Rights, Existing Systems for Protection and Obtaining Protection in Other Countries*, at 22, WIPO Doc. SCT/8/4 (2 April 2002).

[111] Giovannucci et al., *supra* note 28, at 53.

enforcement of GI protection are far more important than simply acquiring registered protection.

As far as the right holder is concerned, when facing misrepresentation or fraudulent use of GI, a private trademark owner can take immediate legal action to reduce the negative effect to a minimum. On the other hand, public authorities could be slow in reacting or responding due to bureaucratic procedures. Private owners will always try their best to maximize their profits and interests, whereas government agencies usually take other factors, such as political ends, into consideration when dealing with GI protection, and may not always treat the interests of producers as a top priority.[112] From the perspective of administrative enforcement, an expeditious and efficient means is already in place for trademark owners who want to lodge complaints against misuse and infringement of their exclusive right. Under the trademark regime, the nationwide administrative forces for industry and commerce (AICs) guarantee rapid, convenient, and effective enforcement against trademark infringement. In fact, the administrative protection enforced by AICs has an irreplaceable advantage in China.[113] Comparatively, AQSIQ administrative forces put more emphasis on product quality supervision in the production channels and inspection of imported or exported goods according to their defined functions by the State Council, mostly dealing with what happens in the workshops where processing and production take place and not in the circulation channel (market supervision is within the competence of SAIC).[114] Additionally, the Ministry of Agriculture does not have experienced forces to handle GI infringement issues.

7 LEGAL CONSIDERATIONS

7.1 *Trademark Law Ranks Higher Than Administrative* Sui Generis *Regimes*

The hierarchy of the Chinese national legal system, from the highest level, starts at the Constitution. The next tier would be national laws made by the National People's Congress or its Standing Committee, after which are administrative regulations made by the State Council based on the Constitution and national laws, followed by regional laws made by the provincial people's congress, and

---

[112] *Id.*
[113] *See* Jianli Su, 论我国商标权的行政保护 – – 以商标行政执法为中心 [*On the Administrative Protection of Trademark Right –Focusing on the Administrative Law Enforcement*], www.docin.com/p-472469996.html (last visited 16 June 2016).
[114] *See* Yumin Zhang, 地理标志的性质和保护模式选择 [*On Its Character & Mode Choice of Geographical Indications*] 6 LAW SCIENCE MAGAZINE 6, 11 (2007).

finally administrative rules made by ministries or provincial governments for the purpose of implementing national laws, administrative regulations, or regional laws.[115]

According to the classification, the TM Law 2013 is a national law promulgated by the Standing Committee of the National People's Congress. The PPGIP and MOA Measures are administrative rules promulgated and implemented by ministerial agencies, which are lower in the legal hierarchy than national laws.

7.2 International Protection

7.2.1 Protection Pursued by Domestic Right Holders

Trademark systems have been established for an extended period of time and are well accepted in most countries. GI right holders have the option to apply for trademark registration in those countries where protection for GIs as collective marks or certification marks is available.[116] Even absent the possibility of collective or certification marks, they can often rely on regular trademarks to protect GIs. In contrast, there has been no harmonized international system regarding GI protection up to now. The Lisbon Agreement has only twenty-eight contracting parties, and China is not one of them.[117]

Overseas GI protection can also be achieved by way of bilateral trade agreements or specific GI protection agreements via the provision of lists of protected GI terms in the annex, but this method relies heavily on the initiatives and efforts of governments and this takes time to negotiate and conclude. So far few such bilateral agreements have been reached between China and other countries.[118] By comparison, trademark protection is always available in other jurisdictions where GI producers have a market interest. While they can file the applications individually in these countries, the Madrid international registration system makes it much easier and cheaper to achieve the same goal. In particular, Rule 9(4)(x) of the Common

---

[115] See An, *supra* note 11.
[116] Paris Convention, *supra* note 1, at art. 7bis. (It sets a legal basis to make it possible to register GIs as collective marks in other countries and requires Member States to provide protection for collective marks. The obligation is incorporated into TRIPS Agreement by Article 2.1.)
[117] For a list of contracting parties to the Lisbon Agreement, *see* World Intellectual Prop. Org. (WIPO), *Contracting Parties – Lisbon Agreement*, WIPO, http://wipo.int/treaties/en/ShowResults.jsp?lang=en&treaty_id=10 (last visited 6 June 2016).
[118] One such bilateral agreement is the Free Trade Agreement between China and Peru. Meanwhile, China and the EU are still in the process of negotiating a possible agreement on GIs.

Regulations under the Madrid Agreement Concerning the International Registration of Marks and the Protocol Relating to that Agreement[119] stipulates that, where the basic application or the basic registration relates to a collective or certification mark, the international application should contain an indication to that effect.[120] Successful examples of Chinese GIs registered as certification trademarks include Zhangqiu Scallion[121] and Guanxi Sweet Shaddock[122] (also known as a pomelo). After commercial success on domestic markets, the trademark owners may exploit the commercial potential of the mark internationally by using the Madrid system to seek GI protection in overseas markets.[123]

7.2.2 Protection Pursued by Foreign Right Holders

At present it is difficult to register foreign GIs in China under the *sui generis* systems. As there is a lack in procedural rules, neither the PPGIP nor the MOA Measures can be used to register foreign GIs. So far, the AQSIQ has put several foreign GIs in its recording list, but these have been based on the conclusion of bilateral agreements, which are time-consuming and costly. The easiest way available is to register them as certification or collective marks under the trademark regime.[124] Therefore, only the trademark mechanism fully complies with the TRIPS requirement in terms of national treatment and enforcement.

7.3 Administrative Appeal and Judicial Review

The TM Law 2013 allows judicial review of administrative decisions made by the TRAB on refusal of registration, opposition, cancellation, revocation, as well as the administrative penalties such as fines made by AICs.[125] This is

---

[119] See Common Regulations under the Madrid Agreement Concerning the International Registration of Marks and the Protocol Relating to that Agreement (as in force 1 April 2016), available at www.wipo.int/wipolex/en/treaties/text.jsp?file_id=397995.

[120] World Intellectual Prop. Org. (WIPO), *Addendum to Document SCT/6/3 Rev. on Geographical Indications: Historical Background, Nature of Rights, Existing Systems for Protection and Obtaining Protection in Other Countries*, at 10, WIPO Doc. SCT 8/5 (2 April 2002).

[121] See Zhangqiu Scallion, Registration No. 1299947, available at http://sbcx.saic.gov.cn:9080/tmois/wszhcx_pageZhcxMain.xhtml?type=reg&intcls=&regNum=1299947&paiType=0.

[122] See Guanxi Sweet Shaddock, Registration No. 1388988, available at http://sbcx.saic.gov.cn:9080/tmois/wszhcx_pageZhcxMain.xhtml?type=reg&intcls=&regNum=1388988&paiType=0.

[123] See Shiping Chen, 平和琯溪蜜柚品牌效益凸显》 [*Brand Effects Obvious of Pinghe 'Guanxi Sweet Shaddock'*] 2 CHINA FRUIT NEWS 37, 37–38 (2009).

[124] *Id.* at 109.   [125] See TM Mark Law 2013, *supra* note 12, at arts. 34, 35, 45, 54.

particularly important for the fulfilment of the TRIPS Agreement. By contrast, neither the *sui generis* AQSIQ nor the MOA rules explicitly provide for the rights of administrative appeal or judicial review.[126] If the application fails to be accepted by the administrative agency, there is no remedy to correct the application form or any other administrative appeal procedures. Nor is there any judicial review for opposition, cancellation, or revocation decisions. The TRIPS Agreement requires Member States to provide for judicial remedies for any intellectual property in their legislation.[127] From this aspect, only the trademark regime enables China to fulfil its WTO obligations.

At present there are some Chinese scholars who advocate protecting GIs as an independent commercial sign in parallel with trademarks, certification marks, and collective marks under the Trade Mark Law.[128] As noted by other scholars,[129] this is also a common legislative practice adopted in some countries, such as Indonesia (Law on Marks)[130] and Russia (Federal Law on Trademarks, Service Marks and Appellations of Origin of Goods).[131] The advantages of such a model include granting a rather straightforward and definite protection on GIs without the necessity of framing a separate new law. In addition, it facilitates the determination of priority and classification of products if both trademarks and GIs are subject to examination under the Trade Mark Office,[132] which is not available under the current dual system.

The separation of GIs from certification or collective trademarks is certainly a big change which needs discrete analysis and scrutiny. In view of the fact that a *sui generis* system under AQSIQ and the Ministry of Agriculture is

---

[126] See Bashaw, *supra* note 51, at 100.
[127] Agreement on Trade-Related Aspects of Intellectual Property Rights, 15 April 1994, Marrakesh Agreement Establishing the World Trade Organization, Annex 1C, Legal Instruments – Result of the Uruguay Rounds vol. 31, 33 I.L.M. 81, at art. 41.4 (1994) (Parties to a proceeding shall have an opportunity for review by a judicial authority of final administrative decisions and, subject to jurisdictional provisions in a Member's law concerning the importance of a case, of at least the legal aspects of initial judicial decisions on the merits of a case. However, there shall be no obligation to provide an opportunity for review of acquittals in criminal case).
[128] See Xiaoxia Li, 地理标志商标法保护模式的重构 [*On the Reconstruction of Protecting Model of Geographical Indications by Trade Mark Law*], 1 J. XINYANG NORMAL UNIV. 95, 97 (2009).
[129] See BERNARD O'CONNOR ET AL., GEOGRAPHICAL INDICATIONS AND TRIPS: 10 YEARS LATER Part II – PROTECTION OF GEOGRAPHICAL INDICATIONS IN 160 COUNTRIES AROUND THE WORLD (2007).
[130] See Law No. 15 of 1 August, 2001, regarding Marks (Indonesia).
[131] See Trademark Law #3520–1 of 23 September 1992, as amended by the federal law 166-FL on 11 December 2002 (Russia).
[132] See Li, *supra* note 128, at 97.

still in operation, it seems too early to categorize GI as an independent sign under the trademark system. Otherwise it may make GI protection more complicated and confusing. Nevertheless, it is a direction for Chinese legislators to undertake further consideration on the method of GI protection in China.

In conclusion, this chapter discusses various approaches of GI protection in China, compares their advantages and disadvantages, and presents the challenges. It concludes that the unique type of cocktail is not as tasty as imagined and changes are needed to achieve more effective GI protection in China.

17

The Potentials, and Current Challenges, of Protecting Geographical Indications in Sri Lanka

Naazima Kamardeen[*]

1 INTRODUCTION

In a country like Sri Lanka, the importance of obtaining protection for unique products can hardly be overstated. Sri Lanka is a small nation, both in size and in production capacity. Still, Sri Lanka is known globally for its tea, in particular, Ceylon Tea. Although China and Kenya produce more tea than Sri Lanka,[1] Sri Lanka remains one of the largest global exporters of tea.[2] This has been achieved partly due to the fact that the name of its famous tea, Ceylon Tea, is protected as a registered certification mark[3] and under the regime for the protection of geographical indications (GIs),[4] as is the logo identifying the "Ceylon Tea."[5] Sri Lanka is also famous for its "true cinnamon," the Ceylon Cinnamon,[6] which is also widely exported, and which also enjoys protection as a certification mark and under the current GI regime.

But what if Sri Lanka could make better use of its existing protection for geographical names and protect additional products coming from specific geographical areas in the country? For example, Sri Lanka is famous for Ceylon Sapphires, Dumbara Mats, and Beeralu Lace – just to name a few products. Yet, the producers of these products have not been successful at

---

[*] Senior Lecturer, Faculty of Law, University of Colombo, Sri Lanka.
[1] Food and Agriculture Organization of the United Nations [FAO], *World Tea Production and Trade – Current and Future Development*, at 4, U.N. Doc. I4480E/1/03.15 (2015), available at www.fao.org/3/a-i4480e.pdf.
[2] *Id.* at 5.   [3] *See* discussion *infra* Section 5.   [4] *See* discussion *infra* Section 4.
[5] *See* RAVINDRA A. YATAWARA & AMRIT RAJAPAKSE, GAINING COMPETITIVE ADVANTAGE THROUGH THE PROTECTION OF GEOGRAPHICAL INDICATIONS: AN ANALYSIS OF THE TEA, SAPPHIRES AND CINNAMON INDUSTRIES OF SRI LANKA (2006).
[6] *See* discussion *infra* Section 4.

marketing them internationally, or at least, to the extent of renown enjoyed by Ceylon Tea and Ceylon Cinnamon. The reason for this lies in both gaps in the legal protection for these products and the unawareness among many producers of the potential returns that might be yielded from the further sales that could be promoted by a higher degree of legal protection and marketing of the products.

In particular, there is one major hurdle in the protection of GIs in Sri Lanka to date, namely, there is no registration-based system for GIs under the Sri Lankan GI regime. Instead, producers have to turn to the trademark system to obtain a trademark registration through which they can protect their geographical names. Generally, this involves applying for a certification or collective trademark under Sri Lankan trademark law. The lack of a registration-based system under the Sri Lankan GI regime has attracted criticism and raised concerns about the functionality, enforcement procedures, and level of protection and has prompted a call for an update to ensure that Sri Lankan products enjoy fuller protection.

This chapter first examines the legal protection that is currently afforded to GIs and will proceed to analyze the deficiencies of the current system. It will then evaluate the international system of GI protection and assess Sri Lanka's position within this system. Based on the findings gathered, this chapter will then offer some suggestions that could be undertaken in order to ensure that an effective regime for GI protection is put in place so that Sri Lankan producers may benefit meaningfully from GI protection. In particular, the primary suggestion offered in this chapter is that Sri Lanka could, and perhaps should, consider improving its current GI regime by implementing a national GI registry. In particular, creating a registration-based scheme for GI protection in Sri Lanka could offer additional certainty to GI producers, and in turn competitors and other interested parties who could be made aware of existing GI registrations. In turn, this greater certainty could lead to a greater willingness to invest in marketing and promoting the registered GIs. Still, this chapter concludes that, even with a GI registry, the actual success of any GI product in Sri Lanka would ultimately depend on wise management, product quality, and marketing.

2 GEOGRAPHICAL INDICATIONS DEFINED

The earliest mention of protecting signs indicating "source," including geographical source, can be found in the 1883 Paris Convention for the Protection of Industrial Property (Paris Convention), even though the Paris Convention does not protect geographical names per se.[7] The first international agreement that mentioned and protected GIs was the 1981 Madrid Agreement for the Repression of False and Deceptive Indications of Source (Madrid Agreement).[8] The next international agreement to focus specifically on the protection of "appellations of origin" was the Lisbon Agreement for the Protection of Appellations of Origin and their International Registration (Lisbon Agreement), which was adopted in 1958, subsequently revised in Stockholm in 1967, and most recently revised in 2015.[9] Neither the Madrid Agreement nor the Lisbon Agreement had a large membership, however, which made their impact limited at the international level.

It was only in 1994 that GI protection became a more global, and globally contested, issue with the adoption of the Agreement on Trade-Related Aspects of Intellectual Property Rights 1994 (TRIPS),[10] which was adopted as part of the creation of the World Trade Organization (WTO). In particular, TRIPS defines the term "geographical indications" as

> [I]ndications which identify a good as originating in the territory of a Member, or a region or locality in that territory, where a given quality, reputation or other characteristic of the good is essentially attributable to its geographical origin.[11]

TRIPS also provides for a minimum standard of protection for GIs that all WTO Members have to implement into their national laws,[12] even though TRIPS leaves WTO Members to implement this protection as they

---

[7] Paris Convention for the Protection of Industrial Property, March 20, 1883, 21 U.S.T. 1583, 828 U.N.T.S. 305 [hereinafter Paris Convention].

[8] Madrid Agreement for the Repression of False and Deceptive Indications of Source on Goods, April 14, 1891, 828 U.N.T.S. 163.

[9] The Lisbon Agreement for the Protection of Appellations of Origin and their International Registration, October 31, 1958, *as revised* July 14, 1967, 923 U.N.T.S. 205 [hereinafter Lisbon Agreement]. Art 2(1) adopted the French definition of "appellation of origin" as signs identifying products "exclusively or essentially" originating from a certain geographical region. In May 2015, a Diplomatic Conference was convened to review the Lisbon Agreement in Geneva, Switzerland. *See* Diplomatic Conference for the Adoption of a New Act of the Lisbon Agreement for the Protection of Appellations of Origin and Their International Registration, WORLD INTELL. PROP. ORG., (May 20, 2015), available at www.wipo.int/meetings/diplomatic_conferences/2015/en/ [hereinafter Geneva Act of Lisbon Agreement]. Sri Lanka is not a signatory to the Lisbon Agreement (in its original version nor any of the revised versions) and therefore is not technically able to register any geographical names in the Lisbon Registry administered by the World Intellectual Property Organization (WIPO).

[10] Agreement on Trade-Related Aspects of Intellectual Property Rights, April 15, 1994, Marrakesh Agreement Establishing the World Trade Organization, Annex 1C, Legal Instruments – Result of the Uruguay Rounds vol. 31, 33 LL.M. 81 (1994) [hereinafter TRIPS Agreement].

[11] *Id.* art. 22(1). [12] *Id.* arts. 22–24.

prefer – generally through existing unfair competition rules, trademark laws, or via the adoption of ad hoc *sui generis* protection.[13]

As has been observed by several scholars, GI protection is generally justified by the fact that GIs perform the function of identifying goods, and they are used to distinguish goods as having certain properties or a reputation attributable to a particular geographic area.[14] In this respect, GI protection aims at protecting the information function of GIs with respect to these properties and reputation. In particular, the distinguishing qualities of the product may be due to local geological factors (such as climate and soil) and/or to human factors present at the location (such as a traditional manufacturing method or any particular manufacturing technique).[15] The GI may also consist of a combination of both these factors, that is, the geological and the human factors that contribute to the uniqueness of the GI products. The inclusion of the human factor as part of the definition of GIs is useful when considering the viability of GI protection for certain types of products such as artisanal products in addition to purely agricultural products. Because GIs identify local products, GI protection is commonly justified based on the assertion that GIs can promote and protect local and rural developments in the GI-denominated areas.[16]

3 DIFFERENT TYPES OF PROTECTION AND THEIR IMPLICATIONS

A survey conducted by the World Trade Organization (WTO) in 2003 established that WTO Members use any of the following three possible methods to protect GIs (intended as geographical names or names indicating products coming from a specific geographical region).[17] The first method is to protect GIs through laws focusing on business practices and consumer protection based on the template provided by the Paris Convention. The second is to achieve protection through the law which protects trademarks – a position

---

[13] *Id.* art. 22. *See* discussion *infra* Section 3.
[14] Irene Calboli & Daniel Gervais, *Socio-Economic Aspects of Geographical Indications*, WORLD INTELL. PROP. ORG. (2015), available at www.wipo.int/edocs/mdocs/geoind/en/wipo_geo_bud_15/wipo_geo_bud_15_9-annex1.pdf.
[15] YATAWARA & RAJAPAKSE, *supra* note 5, at 1; Calboli & Gervais, *supra* note 14, at 1–4.
[16] Calboli & Gervais, *supra* note 14, at 1–4.
[17] Council for Trade-Related Aspects of Intellectual Property Rights, *Note by the Secretariat: Review under Article 24.2 of the Application of the Provisions of the Section of the TRIPS Agreement on Geographical Indications: Summary of the Responses to the Checklist of Questions (IP/C/13 AND ADD.1)*, WTO Doc. IP/C/W/253/Rev.1. (November 24, 2003) [hereinafter WTO Review].

supported by the United States (US) and several common-law countries. The third, and most significant, is to create a special *sui generis* system of protection for GIs.

It is important to note that TRIPS does not impose any system of protection for GIs for WTO Members. As mentioned in Section 2, TRIPS merely provides a minimum standard of protection that all WTO Members should implement with the legal means that they see most appropriate for their individual legal systems.[18]

With respect to the first type of protection, the laws focusing on business practices are laws that have not been enacted with the specific purpose of protecting GIs but which nevertheless do so through the broader objective of regulating business practices or consumer protection. Some examples of such legislation are those which deal with unfair competition, consumer protection, trade descriptions, food standards, and the common-law action for passing off. These could be used to protect GIs when the misuse of a GI in a particular situation falls within the conduct regulated by such laws. For example, the false use of a GI that misleads consumers as to the origin or qualities of the goods would be actionable. Quite often these laws are a good alternative to a *sui generis* law because firstly these laws are available in most legal systems, and secondly they are usually familiar to business lawyers. On the downside, these laws are not specifically geared for GI protection, and hence may not be useful in more complex situations involving GIs.

Under the second type of protection, trademark protection, GIs are generally protected and registered under a special category of trademarks – collective marks and certification marks. In particular, collective marks identify a mark as belonging to a group of enterprises, such as a union of producers in a particular area. Certification marks identify the goods of an enterprise as having met certain standards or having certain qualities, such as a particular geographical origin. Prominent scholars have observed that, of these categories, certification marks are the most suitable to protect GIs because they can underpin the requisite product origin and quality and/or characteristics that are embodied in the GI product.[19]

---

[18] Article 22 of the TRIPS Agreement only requires that member states provide the legal means for interested parties to prevent (a) the use of any means in the designation or presentation of a good that indicates or suggests that the good in question originates in a geographical area other than the true place of origin in a manner which misleads the public as to the geographical origin of the good and (b) any use which constitutes an act of unfair competition within the meaning of Article 10bis of the Paris Convention (1967). *See* TRIPS Agreement, *supra* note 10, at art. 22.

[19] YATAWARA & RAJAPAKSE, *supra* note 5, at 1.

A collective mark is usually owned by the association of enterprises, while a certification or guarantee mark is owned either by an association of enterprises or by a separate entity. In order to avoid a conflict of interest, it is usually provided that the owner of a certification or guarantee mark may not itself use the mark or carry on a business in the kind of goods or services certified. Registration of this type of mark has to be accompanied by registration of the conditions governing the eligibility of interested parties to use the mark. If the interested party meets the requirements listed in the certification, then that party may then use the mark. The mark owner is also obliged to monitor compliance with the conditions of use by mark users.[20] Compared to the first system (laws focusing on general business practices), trademark protection appears to be better suited to protect GIs as it contains more precise rules related to the geographical and quality standards of the products.

The third system of GI protection is that of a *sui generis* GI regime, that is, the adoption of a specialized regime for GI protection listing the specific requirements for and the rights granted as part of this protection. Frequently, a *sui generis* system for GI protection is also based on a national registration system under which GIs are registered in a national registry administered by the national authorities. In addition to the general rules set by TRIPS, individual countries may set administrative procedures for the national protection and registration of GIs.[21] In the EU, *sui generis* GI protection applies at the EU level, as GIs are protected and registered as a matter of EU law. Interestingly, countries that have traditionally opposed or been resistant to GI protection also protect some types of GIs with their own unique GI regime. This includes Australia and the US, which protects GIs for wines with *sui generis* protection, while other geographical names are currently protected under the trademarks regime, the unfair competition regime, or passing off.[22]

Where a *sui generis* system includes the registration of GIs, the necessary criteria to be satisfied for such registration generally include the definition of the geographical area; the link between the geographical area and the product (e.g., that all stages of production, or a particular stage, take place in the particular geographical area); the indication of the particular quality, reputation, or other characteristic of the product; and the inspection requirements to

---

[20] *Id.* at 9.   [21] *Id.*
[22] The US protection for appellations for wines is detailed in Irene Calboli, *Time to Say Local Cheese and Smile at Geographical Indications? International Trade and Local Development in the United States*, 53 HOUS. L. REV. 373, 396–97 (2015).

be put in place, including the control bodies in charge of certifying and controlling the quality of the products. In addition, the applicant should be able to demonstrate that it has a legal interest in the GI or is in a position to control the use of the GI.[23] Overall, a *sui generis* GI regime certainly offers the most comprehensive protection for GIs, but also requires considerable investments – financially and administratively – from the applicants (the collective of GI producers).

As elaborated in the various chapters in this volume, the majority of WTO Members have adopted a combination of the three types of systems that have been described. Still, as noted by scholars, important differences continue to exist with respect to national eligibility requirements, and the scope of protection.[24] These differences undoubtedly make the international protection of GIs cumbersome and increase costs when an enterprise seeks to develop and manage international marketing strategies for their GI products, which may have a bigger impact on developing countries as compared to developed countries.

4 PROTECTION FOR GEOGRAPHICAL INDICATIONS CURRENTLY AVAILABLE IN SRI LANKA

The Sri Lankan legal framework for protecting GIs includes the three types of protection identified above. Each of these types of protection will be discussed briefly below.

4.1 Laws Focusing on Business Practices or Consumer Protection

In this category, there are four separate types of protection that can be used to protect GIs in Sri Lanka under different legal provision or doctrines.

First, is the unfair competition provision set out in section 160 of the Intellectual Property Act, No. 36 of 2003 (IP Act of 2003).[25] This provision defines acts of unfair competition as any acts that are contrary to honest practices,[26] and those that are misleading as to the GIs of the goods or services

---

[23] WTO Review, *supra* note 17.
[24] Ludwig Bäumer, *Protection of Geographical Indications under WIPO Treaties and Questions Concerning the Relationship between Those Treaties and the TRIPS Agreement, in* SYMPOSIUM ON THE INTERNATIONAL PROTECTION OF GEOGRAPHICAL INDICATIONS IN THE WORLDWIDE CONTEXT 9–38 (1997), available at www.wipo.int/edocs/pubdocs/en/geographical/760/wipo_pub_760.pdf.
[25] Intellectual Property Act, No. 36 of 2003, § 160 [hereinafter IP Act of 2003].
[26] *Id.* § 160(1) (a).

concerned.[27] In the case of infringement, possible remedies include injunction and damages.[28]

Second, the consumer protection law, embodied in the Consumer Affairs Authority Act, No. 9 of 2003 (CAA Act of 2003),[29] is also applicable under this category. In particular, if a GI is used to mislead or deceive consumers by conveying a message that is not truthful about the origin or quality of the products, the State or the Consumer Affairs Authority has the right to sue the offender on the basis of a complaint lodged by the affected consumer.[30] Penalties in this case are more severe than under the unfair competition law and include the possibility of a fine and/or imprisonment for the offenders.[31]

Third is the false trade descriptions law that is contained in section 186(1) (d) of the IP Act of 2003.[32] Under section 186(1) (d) of the IP Act of 2003, it is an offense to apply for a false trade description to goods, unless it can be proved that the act was committed without intention to defraud.[33] A false trade description includes, among others, any indication as to the origin of any goods, which is false or misleading in a material respect.[34] Therefore, this provision can be used to counter false or misleading uses of a GI. Affected parties should alert the authorities, who will initiate proceedings.[35] The infringer may be fined, imprisoned,[36] and/or may face an order for destruction or forfeiture of the offending goods.[37]

Fourth, and last, the common-law action for passing off is also available and applicable to the misuses of GIs in Sri Lanka. The elements of the action, as outlined in the case of *Reckitt & Colman v. Borden*,[38] are as follows: (a) the claimant should have goodwill;[39] (b) the defendant should have made a misrepresentation that is likely to deceive the public;[40] and (c) the plaintiff must demonstrate that he has suffered or is likely to suffer damage due to the misrepresentation.[41] The passing-off action is used widely in the United Kingdom (UK), where GIs have often been protected through this avenue.[42]

---

[27] *Id.* § 160(4).   [28] *Id.* § 160(8) (a).

[29] Consumer Affairs Authority Act, No.9 of 2003, § 30 [hereinafter CAA Act of 2003], notes that "no trader shall, in the course of a trade or business, engage in any type of conduct that is misleading or deceptive or is likely to mislead or deceive the consumer or any other trader." CAA Act of 2003, § 31(c) provides that no trader shall represent that goods or services have characteristics they do not have.

[30] *Id.* §§ 12–13.   [31] *Id.* § 13(6).   [32] IP Act of 2003, *supra* note 25, at § 186(1)(d).

[33] *Id.* at § 186(1).   [34] *Id.* at § 189(1).   [35] *Id.* at § 170.   [36] *Id.* at § 186(4).

[37] *Id.* at § 186(5).   [38] *Reckitt & Colman Ltd.* v. *Borden Inc.* [1990] 1 WRL 491 (HL)

[39] *Id.* at p. 499 (Lord Oliver of Alymerton, concurring).   [40] *Id.*   [41] *Id.*

[42] Some notable cases are *Bollinger v. Costa Brava* [1959] 1 WRL 277 (related to the name "Champagne"), *Vine Products Ltd v. Mackenzie & Co* [1969] RPC 1 (related to the name

Additionally, the origin of Sri Lanka's passing-off action derived from the UK legal system.[43] Under an action for passing off, the remedy is an injunction and/or damages for loss.[44]

4.2 Trademark Law

The relationship between the Sri Lankan trademark regime and its interaction with the protection of GIs is complex.

At the outset, section 102(3) of the IP Act of 2003 provides that a trademark may consist of, inter alia, geographical names.[45] Accordingly, it would seem that GIs can be registered as ordinary marks under the language of this section. However, section 103(1) (h) of the IP Act of 2003 states that a mark cannot be registered if it is, according to its ordinary meaning, a geographical name.[46] If we compare the two sections, it thus seems that, under the IP Act of 2003, a GI can be registered as a trademark only where the name no longer identifies the geographical origin of the good in that it has acquired a secondary meaning; in other words, it has become distinctive of the source of the products in terms of the products' manufacturer rather than their geographical origin.[47]

Rather than registering GIs as ordinary trademarks, an easier option is to protect GIs as a certification mark or collective mark, as is the case in many other countries. In particular, the IP Act of 2003 allows the registration of geographical names as certification or collective marks. The relevant legal provision for certification marks is contained in section 142 of the IP Act of 2003,[48] and those which relate to collective marks are contained in sections

---

"Sherry"), *John Walker & Sons Ltd v. Henry Ost & Co Ltd* [1970] RPC 489 (related to the name "Scotch Whisky"), and *Taittinger v. Allbev* [1994] 4 All ER 75 (related to "Elderflower Champagne"). The claimants in each case were associations of producers in the area denoted by the GI.

[43] IP Act of 2003, *supra* note 25, at § 200(1). [44] *Id.* at § 170. [45] *Id.* at § 102(3).
[46] *Id.* at § 103(1) (h).
[47] For example, section 3(1) (c) of the Trade Marks Act 1994 in the United Kingdom does not allow geographical names to be registered as trademarks. "The following shall not be registered – ... (c) trade marks which consist exclusively of signs or indications which may serve, in trade, to designate the kind, quality, quantity, intended purpose, value, *geographical origin*, the time of production of goods or of rendering of services, or other characteristics of goods or services" (emphasis added). *See* Trade Marks Act 1994 (U.K). The reason for this prohibition is that such names should be free for all to use; to allow someone a monopoly over the name of a place or city would have an unfair effect on the surrounding producers and businesses in the area. Several other trademark legislations in the EU and other countries include a similar provision. *See also* YATAWARA & RAJAPAKSE, *supra* note 5, at 13.
[48] IP Act of 2003, *supra* note 25, at § 142.

138–141.[49] The registration of a collective mark or certification mark grants the exclusive right of use of such mark to the applicants, who are generally a collective group of producers in the state. Notably, third parties, without the consent of the mark owners, are prohibited from the following:

> Section 121(2) (a) – Use of the mark, or of a sign resembling it in such a way as to be likely to mislead the public, for goods or services in respect of which the mark is registered or for similar goods or services in connection with which the use of the mark or sign is likely to mislead the public.[50]
>
> Section 121(2)(b) – Use of the mark, or of a sign or trade name resembling it, without just cause and in conditions likely to be prejudicial to the interests of the registered owner of the mark.[51]

Still, under Sri Lankan trademark law, third parties cannot be precluded from using a name that is a geographical name even when the name is registered either as a certification mark or a collective mark if (1) they are entitled to use the geographical name, and (2) they are acting according to honest practice.[52] Similarly, the rights of a registered owner of a mark that is comprised of a geographical name do not include the power to prevent other parties from using the name in good faith and descriptively to indicate the place of origin of their goods or services.[53]

In addition to names that are purely geographical names, the following names can be registered as a collective mark under section 138(3) of the IP Act of 2003: "indication[s] which may serve in trade to designate the geographical origin of the goods."[54] The same type of indications can also be registered as certification marks under section 142(2) of the IP Act of 2003.[55] This includes, as elaborated in the following paragraphs, the most famous Sri Lankan GIs – Ceylon Tea and Ceylon Cinnamon – which are registered as certification marks, even though the name "Ceylon" is no longer a geographical name in Sri Lanka. Notably, the word "Ceylon," the name that the British had given to Sri Lanka when it was a British colony, is no longer officially used to describe

---

[49] Id. at §§ 138–41.   [50] Id. at § 121(2) (a).   [51] Id. at § 121(2) (b).
[52] Id. at § 138(3).
> Notwithstanding the provisions of section 103 a collective mark may be registered which consists of a sign or indication which may serve, in trade, to indicate the geographical origin of the goods or services:
>> Provided, however, the owner of such a mark shall not be entitled to prohibit the use of such sign or indication in accordance with honest practices in industrial or commercial matters and in particular, by a person who is entitled to use a geographical name. IP Act of 2003, sec. 142(3) contains the same restrictions in relation to the use of a certification mark.

[53] Id. at § 122(a).   [54] IP Act of 2003, supra note 25, at § 138(3).   [55] Id. at § 142(2).

the island nation, and Sri Lanka officially changed its name in 1972. Still, the name "Ceylon" clearly refers to the geographical origin of the products that it identifies – tea and cinnamon that originate from Sri Lanka – and thus can be validly registered as a certification mark under the IP Act of 2003.

However, differently than certification marks that are comprised of indications which are actual geographical names, certification marks that are comprised of indications which are no longer proper geographical names enjoy a broader scope of protection. In particular, the owners of these marks can prevent any use of these marks also where a third party seeks to use the name descriptively.[56] For example, the Sri Lanka Tea Board (SLTB), the owner of the certification mark "Ceylon Tea," can prevent the use of any identical and similar signs sought to be used, even if the party who would like to use it would use the term "Ceylon" descriptively. Instead, every interested party would be entitled to use the term "Sri Lankan Tea" to indicate geographical origin.[57] Accordingly, the name Ceylon receives a stronger protection under Sri Lankan trademark law than the term Sri Lanka.

4.3 Sui Generis *Protection*

The provisions relating to Sri Lanka's *sui generis* GI system are contained in Chapter XXXIII of the IP Act of 2003, which repeats and expands the definition of "geographical indications" provided in TRIPS.[58] In particular, unlike TRIPS, the definition of "geographical indications" under the IP Act of 2003 extends beyond goods to include services.[59] Moreover, the Chapter goes even further than TRIPS in its scope of protection and extends the higher level of protection granted by TRIPS to GIs for wines and spirits to GIs for all products in Sri Lanka.[60] The rationale for extending this enhanced protection to all GIs originates from the fact that Sri Lanka does not produce wines and spirits but rather other products. Protection for homonymous indications is also made available to all GIs, which under TRIPS is limited to GIs for wines. Any "interested party" is given standing to file action under this Chapter.[61] The relief available includes injunction, damages, and destruction of infringing goods.[62]

---

[56] *Id.* at § 161(2).   [57] YATAWARA & RAJAPAKSE, *supra* note 5, at 13.
[58] IP Act of 2003 *supra* note 25, at § 161(5), § 101.
[59] *Id.* at § 101. The definition of "certification mark" and "collective mark" expressly includes marks used in relation to goods and services.
[60] *Id.* at § 161(3).   [61] *Id.* at § 161(1).   [62] *Id.* at §§ 161(4), 170.

However, one of the most problematic aspects of the GI regime in Sri Lanka is that, unlike most other GI regimes, Sri Lanka has not opted for a registration system. In turn, this has raised concerns about the effectiveness, enforcement procedures, and level of protection in practice for GIs under the current GI regime.[63] Instead, the enforcement of rights in relation to GIs in Sri Lanka is based on establishing the statutory eligibility criteria.[64]

Still, section 191(b) of the IP Act of 2003 provides for a special prohibition against any use of the terms "Ceylon Tea" and "Ceylon Cinnamon."[65] Notably, the provision states that "any person who makes a false declaration in respect of [a] geographical indication inclusive of Ceylon Tea and Ceylon Cinnamon" shall be guilty of an offense.[66] This provision was originally inserted into the IP Act of 2003 because, at the time of the enactment of the IP Act of 2003, neither Ceylon Tea nor Ceylon Cinnamon were registered as a certification mark. Accordingly, both terms were granted indirect GI protection under the IP Act of 2003, even in the absence of a GI registration system, because of their existing economic importance in Sri Lanka. Remedies for infringement of Ceylon Tea and Ceylon Cinnamon under the *sui generis* GI protection include a fine,[67] injunction, damages, and destruction of infringing goods.[68]

As noted before, the system of *sui generis* protection contained in Part IX, Chapter XXXIII of the IP Act of 2003 applies to GIs that identify any type of product, including artisanal products and handicrafts.[69] In addition, special legislation regulating particular national, regional, or local industries or sectors often confer power on the relevant minister or statutory authority to adopt regulations for the purpose of carrying out the objects and purposes of the *sui generis* GI protection in the IP Act of 2003. This can provide a means for the implementation of ad hoc systems of protection for GIs in the particular industry or sector covered by these legislations.[70]

4.4 Relative Weaknesses of the Current System

As discussed above, the major flaw of the current *sui generis* GI regime in Sri Lanka is that it does not allow for the registration of GIs in a national registry.

---

[63] YATAWARA & RAJAPAKSE, *supra* note 5, at 14, 40–42.
[64] IP Act 2003, *supra* note 25, at § 191(b).   [65] *Id.* at § 191(b).   [66] *Id.*   [67] *Id.*
[68] *Id.* at § 170.   [69] *Id.* at § 161(1) (ii), § 160.
[70] *See* YATAWARA & RAJAPAKSE, *supra* note 5, at 13.

Accordingly, in order obtain a registration for a geographical name – or a name that indicates a geographical region – in Sri Lanka, producers have to still register that name as a certification or collective trademark. As also noted above, the protection of geographical names under the trademark system too has flaws, as it confers only a limited exclusivity and cannot prevent third parties from using these names descriptively. Only the names that are not a purely geographical term – as it is the case with respect to Ceylon Tea and Ceylon Cinnamon – are granted heightened protection under the trademark system in Sri Lanka.

5 PRODUCTS CURRENTLY PROTECTED IN SRI LANKA: CEYLON TEA AND CEYLON CINNAMON

Even though Sri Lanka has been famous for its spices from time immemorial,[71] the protection of these products' geographical names is a recent phenomenon. As highlighted above, the most relevant examples of protection in Sri Lanka today are for the names "Ceylon Tea" and "Ceylon Cinnamon." These names are registered as certification marks and are also protected under the current GI system.[72] The specific details of the protection granted to each of these products will be discussed in the following sections.

5.1 Ceylon Tea

Considering the success and fame of Ceylon Tea, it may be remarkable to learn that tea is not a plant native to Sri Lanka. In fact, coffee was the main crop grown in the country for most of the 1800s. In the 1820s, experiments with the cultivation of coffee in Ceylon (the current Sri Lanka) began and by 1848 coffee cultivation was the backbone of the Ceylon economy. However, in the 1870s, a fungus devastated the coffee monoculture and the coffee industry in Ceylon turned bleak.[73] Eventually, and in response, tea was cultivated instead.[74] Since then, Sri Lanka has never looked back and has instead

---

[71] The flagship products from Sri Lanka are well known abroad. In particular, the main export markets for Sri Lanka products are the US and EU markets. Additional markets include the Middle East for tea and some Latin American countries for spices.

[72] Any false declarations in respect of "Ceylon Tea" are considered to be offenses under § 191(b) of the IP Act of 2003 and any false declarations in respect of "Ceylon Cinnamon" are considered to be offenses under § 191(b) of the IP Act of 2003.

[73] ROLAND WENZLHUEMER, FROM COFFEE TO TEA CULTIVATION IN CEYLON, 1880–1900 AN ECONOMIC AND SOCIAL HISTORY 31 (2008).

[74] Id. at 75–89.

embraced the production of tea aided by the perfect climatic conditions of the hill country to grow this herb. Tea has since become synonymous with this tiny island nation.

Still, locals refused to work in the tea plantations, complaining that the conditions were hazardous, the work too strenuous, and the wages were too low. Accordingly, the British brought workers from South India to Sri Lanka to work in the tea estates.[75] It cannot, therefore, be stated that Ceylon Tea is a GI, in the sense that a GI reflects some local custom, culture, or tradition. Ceylon Tea is, instead, a commercial product that acquired a GI status because of its internationally recognized quality. Be that as it may, it is now an undeniable fact that Ceylon Tea is here to stay.

The SLTB[76] was at the forefront of the efforts to obtain exclusive protection for Sri Lankan tea. The term "Ceylon Tea" had been promoted by Sri Lanka globally for decades, and the SLTB had spent a substantial amount of funding on this exercise.[77] As Ceylon Tea became synonymous with high quality, counterfeiting and misuse of the term became rampant. It became imperative that these acts be stopped if the brand was to maintain its reputation. A year after the introduction of the IP Act of 2003, the SLTB attempted to register "Ceylon Tea" as a certification mark. However, it was not until 2010 that the SLTB managed to obtain Home Registration for "Ceylon Tea" as a certification mark.[78]

The SLTB has also obtained a certification mark for a special type of tea grown in an ozone-friendly manner. Historically, the use of the chemical methyl bromide (MB) was widespread in the tea sector. The industry had set a target date of January 1, 2015, for the phase out of this chemical, which was harmful to the environment. The tea sector in Sri Lanka phased out the use of MB well before the target date. In 2011, the "Ozone Friendly Pure Ceylon

---

[75] After the British left when Sri Lanka gained independence, these workers found themselves being discriminated against as they were denied citizenship in Sri Lanka. This was done through the Citizenship Act of 1948, which disenfranchised the estate Tamils.

[76] A body incorporated under the provisions of the Sri Lanka Tea Board Law No. 14 of 1975, which aims to promote the tea industry in Sri Lanka.

[77] As can be seen from the filings for the mark around the world: CEYLON TEA SYMBOL OF QUALITY, Registration No. 3753672 (U.S.); CEYLON TEA SYMBOL OF QUALITY, Registration No. 005751227 (EU); CEYLON (with device), Registration No. T0211757J (Singapore); CEYLON TEA SYMBOL OF QUALITY, Registration No. 4-0052528-000 (Vietnam).

[78] In addition, in 2011, the SLTB was successful in obtaining separate certification trademark registration for the seven major agro-climatic regional teas where Ceylon Tea is grown. The seven agro-climatic regions for tea in Sri Lanka are Nuwara Eliya, Dimbula, Uva, Uda Pussellawa, Kandy, Ruhuna, and Sabaragamuwa.

Tea" logo was launched as a certification mark.[79] This logo certifies that the teas cultivated are grown or manufactured in tea gardens and factories in the tea growing districts of Sri Lanka without the use of any ozone depletion substances. The "Ozone Friendly Pure Ceylon Tea" logo is thus a valuable addition to the island's best-known export product. It is also expected that the ozone-friendly logo will help Ceylon Tea gain a competitive advantage in the global markets, as environmentally responsible products are gaining value in markets all over the world. Through the new logo, the Ceylon Tea industry has marketed the tea as a premium product in and outside Sri Lanka.

5.2 Ceylon Cinnamon

Ceylon Cinnamon is also called "true cinnamon," as there are many other types of cinnamon which originate from other countries. The spice found in the Ceylon Cinnamon is the dried bark of *Cinnamomum zealanicum*, which is indigenous to Sri Lanka (as denoted by the word "zealanicum," which has reference to the word "Ceylon"). This spice has its origins in the central hills, in places such as Kandy, Matale, Belihuloya, Haputale, and the Sinharaja forest range. Today, the cinnamon plantations are concentrated along the coastal belt stretching along from Kalutara to Matara, but cultivations of cinnamon have made inroads also to the areas of Ambalangoda and Ratnapura – areas between the coast and mountain.

In 2013, land used for cinnamon cultivation in Sri Lanka had expanded to reach a total of 31,278 ha.[80] Sri Lanka is also the largest producer of Ceylon Cinnamon, with an estimated annual production of over 16,000 metric tons in 2013.[81] The unique method of processing and curing of cinnamon has resulted in a unique flavor, which results in a taste unlike any other variety of the same plant. A key part of the process is the preparation of the cinnamon quills. This involves a combination of art and skill unique to Sri Lankans, as the knowledge of these skills has been handed down from generation to generation over

---

[79] The mark is also protected in Malaysia: OZONE FRIENDLY PURE CEYLON TEA, Registration No. 2012007431 (Malaysia). But it should be noted that the application for registration for the mark in the US (Trademark: 85590777) has been suspended.

[80] K.H.K.L. Piyasiri & M. Wijeratne, *Comparison of the Cultivated Area and the Production Trends of Ceylon Cinnamon with the Main Competitors in the Worlds' Total Cinnamon Market*, 6(1) INT'L J. SCI. & RES. PUBLICATIONS 476, 477 (2016), available at www.ijsrp.org/research-paper-0116/ijsrp-p4973.pdf.

[81] *Id.* at 478.

centuries. At present, Sri Lanka is the world's largest exporter of true cinnamon, with 97 percent of the global market.[82]

In order to ward off competition from inferior varieties of cinnamon such as Cassia, the Spice Council of Sri Lanka, together with the Sri Lanka Exports Development Board, has engaged in efforts to protect locally grown cinnamon. The result was the registration of the name "Pure Ceylon Cinnamon" as a certification mark. The mark can be used on any products made using cinnamon from Sri Lanka.[83] The Sri Lanka Export Development Board, which is the registered owner of the mark, has developed comprehensive guidelines for the mark's use, including listing out product categories, as well as producers, who are entitled to apply for the mark.[84] The mark has also been registered in a few key foreign markets including the US, the EU, Peru, and Colombia.[85]

6 PRODUCTS THAT COULD BENEFIT FROM ADDITIONAL PROTECTION FOR GEOGRAPHICAL INDICATIONS IN SRI LANKA

Boasting a long and proud history and a rich and diverse heritage, Sri Lanka is home to many products that could also benefit from stronger GI protection. A few of these products are outlined in the following paragraphs. To date, these products are not registered as certification or collective trademarks in Sri Lanka and, in the absence of a registration system for *sui generis* GI protection, cannot be registered as *sui generis* GIs. Thus, they can only be protected under the current language for GI protection in the IP Act of 2003 and with a possible action for passing off in the event of misuse of these names. Moreover, some of these products have also suffered from a lack of patronage, or have not been able to withstand the march of global development. Still other products have

---

[82] Embassy of Sri Lanka, Washington DC, *A Development Oriented Budget for All Citizens in 2015*, NEWS SRI LANKA (November 2014), http://slembassyusa.org/NewsLetter/201411/NL201411.pdf.
[83] PURE CEYLON CINNAMON, http://pureceyloncinnamon.srilankabusiness.com/index.html (last visited August 2, 2016).
[84] Sri Lanka Export Development Board, *Guidelines for the Use of "Pure Ceylon Cinnamon" Logo*, EDS http://pureceyloncinnamon.srilankabusiness.com/docs/guidelines.pdf (last visited August 2, 2016).
[85] Press Communiqué, Ministry of Industry and Commerce, Sri Lanka, World's First Official True Cinnamon Pass Now Live (August 10, 2014) (on file with author), available at http://pureceyloncinnamon.srilankabusiness.com/docs/cinnamon_live.pdf. For the trademark registrations, see the following: Pure Ceylon Cinnamon, Registration No. 4643497 (U.S.); Pure Ceylon Cinnamon, Registration No. 010353092 (EU).

been noticed by the global markets and have been subsequently revived by producers that have managed to survive into the twenty-first century as small cottage industries.

17.6.1 Ceylon Sapphires

Sri Lanka has a proud and long history relating to gemstones in general and sapphires in particular.[86] Sapphires are part of the Corundum gem family and are reported to be a royal gem with extreme hardness. Ceylon Sapphires are mined in Sri Lanka and are known for their unique color.[87] Ceylon Sapphires are very famous among both locals and foreigners. Generally, the gem industry in Sri Lanka is heavily regulated by the government to ensure minimal environmental impact. This has the potential to become a point of concern because of the traditional mining methods that are still used.

Not surprisingly, the popularity of the Ceylon Sapphire has led to other types of sapphires being passed off as Ceylon Sapphires. In order to curb this problem, the Gem and Jewellery Authority of Sri Lanka has been engaged in efforts to register Ceylon Sapphires as a certification mark. Based on the success of Ceylon Tea and Ceylon Cinnamon in registering their respective certification marks, it is expected that this registration will be granted in the near future.[88] This would allow the producers of Ceylon Sapphires to protect their sapphires against others traders who misuse the name "Ceylon."

Today, Ceylon Sapphires seems to have been recognized as a GI by the Intellectual Property Office of Sri Lanka.[89] However, if Sri Lanka would create a national GI registry, so that Ceylon Sapphires could be registered as

---

[86] It is reported that Marco Polo wrote that the island had the best sapphires, topazes, amethysts, and other gems in the world. Ptolemy, the second-century astronomer, is supposed to have recorded that beryl and sapphire were the mainstay of Sri Lanka's gem industry. Records from sailors that visited the island state that they brought back "jewels of Serendib." Serendib was the ancient name given to the island by middle-eastern and Persian traders that crossed the Indian Ocean to trade gems from Sri Lanka to the East during the fourth and fifth centuries. This proves that the gem industry in Sri Lanka has ancient roots. See John Pinkerton, *The Curious and Remarkable Voyages and Travels of Marco Polo, A Gentleman of Venice*, in A GENERAL COLLECTION OF THE VOYAGES AND TRAVELS IN ALL PARTS OF THE WORLD 101 (1811).

[87] Peter C. Zwann, *Sri Lanka: The Gem Island*, 18 GEMS & GEMMOLOGY 62, 66 (1982).

[88] Ajith Perera, *Sri Lanka World's Sapphire Capital*, DAILY NEWS (May 17, 2010), http://archives.dailynews.lk/2010/05/17/bus25.asp.

[89] Ceylon Sapphires are listed as an example of geographical indications on the website of the National Intellectual Property Office of Sri Lanka, see National Intellectual Property Office if Sri Lanka, *Geographical Indicators (GI)*, www.nipo.gov.lk/gi.htm (last visited August 2, 2016).

a GI, this would promote greater certainty and hence better protection for this name due to the advantages of a system based on registration. The name "Ceylon Sapphires" could also be registered as a certification mark, as this could afford the same, stronger protection that Ceylon Tea and Ceylon Cinnamon enjoy today. In addition, it would be beneficial to protect the name "Ceylon Sapphires" in foreign jurisdictions either as a *sui generis* GI system or as a trademark to prevent misuse of the name outside Sri Lanka. Finally, it is important to note that the Ceylon Chamber of Commerce had been instrumental in advocating for the higher level of protection offered to GIs for wines and spirits under TRIPS to be extended to all products carrying the name Ceylon in Sri Lanka.[90] The IP Act of 2003 went a step further and granted the additional protection to all products. This heightened protection for the name "Ceylon Sapphires" can offer protection against confusing and misleading uses of the name as well as provide relief against misappropriation also in the absence of consumer confusion.

6.2 *Ruhunu Curd*

Ruhuna is the traditional name for the southern part of Sri Lanka. Historically, this area has been famous for its curd, made primarily from buffalo milk. Buffaloes were the traditional source of labor in the paddy fields; hence, buffalo milk was once plentifully available. However, changes in society and the times have brought this once-thriving industry to its knees.

A study done by Ulluwishewa of the University of Sri Jayewardenepura identifies several reasons for this decline. The replacement of buffaloes with tractors and modern farm equipment resulted in lowering the demand for buffaloes, which were then sold as meat instead of being retained for labor. Further, the reduction of grassland, as well as the reduction of female labor, required for curd production also contributed to the problem.[91] As far back as 2005, it was reported that the Ruhunu Curd industry was facing a downturn, with many cattle farmers deciding to leave the industry for good.[92] This is one

---

[90] Dwijen Rangnekar, *The International Protection of Geographical Indications: The Asian Experience*, UNCTAD / ICTSD Regional Dialogue, University of Hong Kong, P.R.C., at 14 (November 8–10, 2004), available at www.ictsd.org/downloads/2008/09/rangnekar_2004-11-08.pdf.

[91] Rohana Ulluwishewa, *Crisis of Dairy Farming in Ruhuna – An Overview*, 5 VIDYODAYA J. Soc. Sci. 17 (1991), available at http://dl.sjp.ac.lk/dspace/bitstream/123456789/477/1/Crisis%20of%20Dairy%20Farming.pdf.

[92] *Id.*

of the examples of a traditional product from a specific region of Sri Lanka possibly disappearing due to changes in society and the modern economy.

Today, Ruhunu Curd can only be protected under the current language of the IP Act of 2003 as a GI. As illustrated extensively in the chapter, however, the IP Act of 2003, grants limited protection to GIs in the absence of a registration system. Still, in Sri Lanka, GIs are currently granted the higher level of protection provided by TRIPS, which implies that the name "Ruhunu Curd" can enjoy protection against confusing as well as misappropriating uses of the name in Sri Lanka. The name could also be registered as a certification mark, even though the protection for this mark could not extend to the descriptive use of the name "Ruhunu" as mentioned above. Hence, it is admitted that it cannot be affirmatively concluded that protecting Ruhunu Curd by registering it as a certification mark, or as a registered *sui generis* GI should a national GI registry be implemented in Sri Lanka, necessarily saves the industry from its current downfall. Given the experience of other traditional products, which are dependent on local culture, traditions, and raw materials[93] and are protected as GIs or trademarks in other countries, it could nonetheless be argued that this protection (and in turn the possibly following extra attention to the product) could positively impact the Ruhunu Curd industry and help to keep it afloat.[94]

6.3 *Dumbara Mats*

Dumbara mats are woven in the village of Henawela, located in the Dumbara valley, in the city of Kandy, in the central province of Sri Lanka.[95] Weaving the mats is an activity performed mainly by women, though some men are also experts at mat weaving. The leaves used for these mats are found in the valley itself, and after the pulp of the leaf is stripped, the remaining fiber is boiled and mixed with local dyes to form the colorful strips used in these eye-catching mats.[96] The mats themselves are used more as ornaments than as utility items.

---

[93] There have been similar calls in India to protect the Indian Chilika curd. *See* Dhiraj Kumar Nanda et al., *Indian Chilika Curd – A Potential Dairy Product for Geographical Indication Registration*, 12 INDIAN J. TRADITIONAL KNOWLEDGE 707 (2013).

[94] W.A. Sanath Sameera Wijesinghe, *The Protection on Geographical Indications in Developing Countries: The Case of Ceylon Tea*, 1 BALANCE–MULTIDISCIPLINARY L. J. 11 (2015), available at www.slsh.edu.in/assets/balancepdf/sanath-geographical%20indicators.pdf.

[95] Laksala Sri Lanka, *Dumbara Mats*, http://laksalasl.weebly.com/dumbara-mats.html (last visited August 2, 2016).

[96] ARNOLD WRIGHT, TWENTIETH CENTURY IMPRESSIONS OF CEYLON: ITS HISTORY, PEOPLE, COMMERCE, INDUSTRIES AND RESOURCES 186–87 (1907, reprinted 1999).

In the past, mat weaving in the Dumbara valley was considered a necessary craft to be practiced by every female villager. Today, the region largely functions as a cottage industry with few established sales outlets. Weavers generally market their mats at festivals, fairs, and pilgrimage sites.

A recent article titled "The Waning Weave" highlights the problems faced by the Dumbara mat weavers. In the past, these weavers enjoyed royal patronage, but today only about ten to fifteen families are still engaged in this craft. The craft has declined due to several reasons. Firstly, the Niyanda leaf used to make the mats has reached near extinction, and weavers are forced to turn to the less delicate hemp leaf. Unfortunately, this leaf is also difficult to access. Secondly, this craft was passed down traditionally from parents to children, but it has found little favor with the younger generation, as this generation is not interested in the hard hours of labor required to turn out a single mat. Thirdly, and most importantly, the income derived from these mats is not sufficient for many people to sustain on mat weaving as a livelihood option. The National Craft Council of Sri Lanka has attempted to assist the weavers by advertising and marketing Dumbara mats, which has partially helped. The council has also advised the weavers on trying out new and more practical items such as book covers, bags, mobile phone covers, tablemats, cushion covers, and handbags, as opposed to the more traditional items such as mats and wall hangings that they were previously confined to.[97]

As with the case of the Ruhunu Curd, the Dumbara Mat appears to be recognized as a GI, and thus enjoys, at least in writing, the higher level of protection granted to GIs under the IP Act of 2003, despite the absence of a GI registry.[98] Here again, the name Dumbara Mat could also be registered as a certification mark. However, protecting the name "Dumbara Mats" via the registration as a certification mark, or in the future possibly as a registered GI, may not necessarily assist this industry's recovery due to the fact that the industry's problems rest primarily on its need to modernize and find new customers that could support the industry and the weavers.

6.4 Ambalangoda Masks

Ambalangoda is a coastal town in the Galle District, famous for traditional wooden masks and puppets. The traditional masks are carved from light balsa-

---

[97] Hiranthi Fernando, *The Waning Weave*, SUNDAY TIMES (October 17, 2010), www.sundaytimes.lk/101017/Plus/plus_01.html.
[98] Wijesinghe, *supra* note 94, at 11.

like kaduru wood, the trees of which grow in the marshy lands that border paddy fields. Before being crafted on, the wood is smoke-dried for a week in preparation. The hand-carved and hand-painted masks are then used in traditional dance dramas that are both vibrant and colorful.

There are three different types of dancing rituals, and accordingly three different types of masks: the "Kolam" masks, the "Sanni" masks, and the "Raksha" masks. The "Kolam" masks are used in a Kolam, which is a comic folk play, set in a rural setting, with dances, mimes, and dialogues. The types of masks range from devils and animals to humans and human royalty.[99] The "Sanni" masks are used in the Sanni Yakuma, which is an exorcism ritual. The wearers of the "Sanni" mask would represent the different types of Sanni (diseases).[100] The belief was that the ritual would, as depicted in the ritual with the exorcists ridding the Sanni, rid people of diseases.[101] Finally, there are "Raksha" masks, which are used in festivals and processions. The Naga Raksha (Cobra demon) mask of the "Raksha Kolama" (demon dance) is particularly famous and consists of a ferocious face with bulging, popping eyes, a carnivorous tongue, and protruding hood-distended cobras.[102]

These masks were highly popular for many decades, due to their attractive nature and perceived powers. The Kolam dances were the primary recreational outlet for villagers, and prior to the advent of television, highly popular in the villages. Belief in devils and other spirits persisted, and the Sanni masks were used in exorcism ceremonies, also termed as "devil dancing ceremonies." The low-country tradition of dancing also uses masks, and the Raksha masks were used in this type of dancing as well as for the processions that were also an integral part of community life in the village. All this meant that there was a steady source of demand for the masks for many years.

In recent times, however, demand for the masks has changed. As television has changed viewer preferences, viewership of Kolam dances has also dropped. Similarly, festivals and processions are also not as popular as they used to be, and to add to these problems, the low-country dance form is practiced by very few. In addition, devil dancing is not perceived as the most

---

[99] Richard Boyle, *Masks Unmasked*, SRILANKAN (February 2013), http://serendib.btoptions.lk/article.php?id=968&issueId=38.

[100] Mark S. Bailey & H Janaka de Silva, *Sri Lankan Sanni Masks: An Ancient Classification of Disease*, 333 BMJ 1327–28 (2006), *available at* www.bmj.com/content/333/7582/1327.

[101] Alan Pate, *Devil Dance Masks of Sri Lanka*, L'ASIE EXOTIQUE (September 1998), www.lasieexotique.com/mag_masks/mag_masks.html.

[102] Boyle, *supra* note 99.

efficient remedy for ailments, as it used to be in the past. Accordingly, demand for the masks has diminished.[103] Still, masks have become popular as ornaments in recent years, and both locals and foreigners seek them as decorations. Mask-making has thus become a cottage industry in Ambalangoda, though there are also a few large-scale mask-making enterprises in the region. There are also museums dedicated to this craft.[104] For all these reasons, Ambalangoda masks could benefit from protection, both as a certification mark and as a *sui generis* registered GI should a GI registry be created in Sri Lanka. Today, as with the other examples mentioned above, Ambalangoda masks can be protected as GIs under the current protection offered under the IP Act of 2003.

6.5 *Moratuwa Furniture*

Moratuwa is a town to the South of Colombo, which is well known for its skilled wood craftsmen and beautifully crafted furniture. The town houses many furniture shops, and any online search on the term Moratuwa will inevitably yield information about these shops and furniture galleries. Moratuwa has been referred to as the "heart of quality furniture products in Sri Lanka."[105] Moratuwa craftsmen are skilled in the manufacture of older Sri Lankan designs, which are characterized by intricate carvings, but they are also able to create the more modern pieces that the market craves.

Unlike some of the other products discussed in this section, the Moratuwa furniture industry has thrived and has managed to survive the ravages of time and changing tastes. To a large extent, this is due to the fact that the industry has been able to market their products effectively. Further, even though furniture designs may have evolved in modern society, the need for furniture is a basic need for most people, and furniture remains a useful and necessary item to purchase as opposed to other crafts that may not be equally necessary.

Perhaps also relevant is the fact that Moratuwa artisans are largely male, and thus the primary care providers for many families. In turn, this may have pushed these artisans to update their designs and business models in order to continue selling their products. As described below, the same has not been the

---

[103] *The Ambalangoda Mask Museum*, ARIYAPALA & SONS, www.masksariyapalasl.com/mask_museum.htm (last visited August 3, 2016).

[104] For example, there is an Ambalangoda Mask Factory & Museum located in Thoranagama, Hikkaduwa.

[105] *About us*, ARATUWA WOOD WORKS, www.furnituresrilanka.com/about-furniture-sri-lanka.html (last visited August 6, 2016).

case for other crafts such as Beeralu lace, which is almost exclusively carried out by women.

As in the case of the Ambalangoda masks and the other cases above, this industry could benefit from protection of the name "Moratuwa furniture" both as a certification mark and as a *sui generis* registered GI in addition to the protection that is granted to the name under the current GI provisions in the IP Act of 2003.

6.6 Beeralu Lace

Beeralu lace refers to the lace made in the southern region of Sri Lanka, most notably in the Galle District. Introduced originally by the Portuguese, lace-making flourished as an industry in the sixteenth and seventeenth centuries. Many women engaged in making lace for pleasure or profit. Traditionally, there was good local as well as foreign demand for Beeralu lace.[106] However, with the advent of the open economic policy in 1977, women began to abandon their homes and crafts for more profitable day jobs. In addition, the lace industry saw the rise of intermediaries, which resulted in reduced profits for producers.[107] These factors reduced Beeralu lace-making into a hobby practiced by very few. Today, a few organizations have sought to support the industry, at least as a cottage industry.[108] Still, many of the weavers are old, face poverty, and have difficulties in addressing the threat of competition from mass-produced items and cheaper imports.[109] Moreover, Beeralu lace-making is a time-consuming activity, which results in the final products being fairly expensive, which may, in turn, affect consumer demand.

Similar to Ceylon today, and unlike Ruhuna, Moratuwa, and Dumbara, the term "Beeralu" is not a geographical name. The word comes from the term used to describe the wooden bobbins that are used to weave a single piece of lace. However, the term has become synonymous with the region where the lace is made. Accordingly, the name "Beeralu" could be registered as a certification mark as well as could be registered as *sui generis* GI should Sri Lanka implement a national registry. Instead, today, the name "Beeralu" can only be protected under the current GI regime, which does not include

---

[106] Sassanka, *The Beauty of Beeralu Lace*, LANKA HELP MAGAZINE (September 4, 2011, 7:38 PM), http://magazine.lankahelp.com/2011/09/04/the-beauty-of-beeralu-lace/.
[107] Id.
[108] Aysha Aseef, *Living in the Shadows: The Lace Makers of Galle*, THE SUNDAY TIMES (February 15, 2009), www.sundaytimes.lk/090215/Plus/sundaytimesplus_03.html.
[109] Id.

a registration system. In particular, even though it does not seem that competitors are misusing the name to date, it cannot be excluded that producers of mass-produced lace may decide to use a similar name for their lace in order to create an association with the more famous Beeralu lace. Some producers of Beeralu lace have also called for the government to support the export of this product in order to protect the dying trade.[110] In this respect, Beeralu lace does appear to have global popularity, as can be seen by its showcase at the London Asia House Design 2016.[111] Thus, the possibility exists that getting protection for the heritage of Beeralu lace could increase the price and consequently the survivability of the Beeralu lace industry as well.

7 COMPARATIVE ANALYSIS: SHOULD SRI LANKA ADOPT AN INDIAN-STYLE PROTECTION FOR GEOGRAPHICAL INDICATIONS?

As I mentioned in Section 4, the current standard of protection for GIs in Sri Lanka, particularly with respect to the *sui generis* GI regime, is unsatisfactory and could be improved. In this respect, it could be useful to look at the approach adopted in India. India is Sri Lanka's closest neighbor and shares many similarities with Sri Lanka in terms of culture and traditions. However, India has been more proactive than Sri Lanka in protecting its cultural and traditional items.[112] In particular, India enacted a *sui generis* system for GI protection in 1999, which includes a registration-based system – the Geographical Indications of Goods (Registration & Protection) Act (India GI Act) – after its accession to the World Trade Organization (WTO).[113] This law came into force with effect from September 15, 2003.

Notably, section 8 of the India GI Act provides that a GI can be registered for any of the goods listed in the GI registry.[114] The India GI Act extends

---

[110] Ananda Kannangara, *Beeralu Sustained as a Cottage Industry*, SUNDAY OBSERVER (March 18, 2012), www.sundayobserver.lk/2012/03/18/fea04.asp.

[111] See *Beeralu Lace, Handicrafts Showcased at London Asia House Design 2016*, DAILY FT (March 16, 2016), www.ft.lk/article/531324/Beeralu-lace-handicrafts-showcased-at-London-Asia-House-Design-2016.

[112] For example, India has put in place a traditional knowledge digital library that records all the uses of traditional knowledge, in order to defeat the novelty aspect of patent applications made using pirated Indian traditional knowledge.

[113] Geographical Indications of Goods (Registration & Protection) Act 48 of 1999 (India) [hereinafter Indian GI Act].

[114] The reasons for which a GI registration will be denied are described in Section 9 of the Indian GI Act.

GI protection to all types of goods and thus covers a spectrum of goods from handicrafts to agricultural products. The India GI Act further lists out the procedure to be followed. Interestingly, and unlike the case in Sri Lanka, section 25 of the India GI Act prohibits the registration of a GI as a trademark (other than a certification mark under the Indian Trade Mark Act, 1999).[115]

The first GI registered in India was Darjeeling tea in 2004, and to date 236 GIs have been registered in India. Initially, GIs were registered primarily for handicrafts, but recent GI registrations have been made in favor of agricultural products, which include types of litchi, mandarins, and lemons.[116]

At this time, it remains unclear if the system of GI protection in India and the GI registrations have, in fact, improved the financial viability of any of the industries for which GI protection was obtained. Still, it remains a fact that the large number of registrations have been granted, and that these registrations represent a vehicle that can help producers in advertising the GI products. Moreover, producers have to agree on common standards and product quality control as part of the application for GI registration. This process alone can assist in motivating producers in a particular area to invest in the quality of their products and in promoting their products in the national and international markets.

Thus, even though Sri Lanka may need some more time before it can implement a system of GI registration similar to India, it should be noted that the system in India does allow for GI registration and, in turn, GI producers can enjoy the full protection of a *sui generis* GI protection system. In contrast, the only avenue for producers in Sri Lanka to register their geographical names is through the trademark system.

8 CONCLUSION

As described above, the current status of GI protection in Sri Lanka is still a work in progress. To date, the strongest form of protection is found in the trademark system, as geographical names can be registered as certification

---

[115] See the full text of the Indian GI Act, *available at* http://ipindia.nic.in/girindia/GI_Act.pdf (last visited August 3, 2016).

[116] The following GI registrations can be found in the Geographical Indications Registry, published by Intellectual Property India: Tezpur Litchi, Registration No. 438 (India); Khasi Mandarin, Registration No. 465 (India); Temple Jewellery of Nagercoil, Registration No. 36 (India); Kachai Lemon, Registration No. 466 (India). *See Registered GIs*, GEOGRAPHICAL INDICATIONS REGISTRY, http://ipindia.nic.in/girindia/ (last visited August 3, 2016).

and collective marks, as in the case of Ceylon Tea, Ceylon Cinnamon, and (likely) Ceylon Sapphires. In contrast, the *sui generis* Sri Lankan GI regime does not include a registration system; thus, it offers a less comprehensive level of protection. In particular, even though a system without registration still grants protection to the GIs, a registration-based scheme can provide additional certainty for producers (and competitors who can be made aware of GI registrations). In turn, this greater certainty may lead to a greater willingness to invest in marketing and promoting the registered GIs on the part of GI producers and other interested parties.

As indicated in this chapter, several products from Sri Lanka could benefit from a more comprehensive system of protection and the creation of a GI registry similar to the one operating in India and in several other countries today. As it has been the case with Ceylon Tea and Ceylon Cinnamon, the primary consideration in seeking protection for geographical names is to prevent the misuse of these names by third parties that are not authorized to use them and, in turn, ward off competition from cheap product imitations. Still, while Ceylon Tea and Ceylon Cinnamon are protected today through the trademark system, and also enjoy (the so far limited in Sri Lanka) GI protection, several other products do not enjoy any form of meaningful protection, as these products are not registered marks and so far enjoy only limited protection under the current *sui generis* GI regimes. Hence, the producers of these products also have concerns about cheap alternatives, as could become the case with respect to Beeralu lace.

Naturally, the creation of a GI registry would not become a panacea for protecting traditional products in Sri Lanka. In fact, the mere fact of having a system of GI registration may not help an industry that is already unprofitable or for which there is no consumer demand. However, if the industry at issue already has a good target market, and consumers are interested in the products, then GI registration has the potential to position the products more meaningfully within that market. In particular, granting exclusive rights through GI protection (and more meaningfully GI registration) would likely serve to incentivize producers to invest and capitalize in the GI name, which could potentially lead to greater returns. Moreover, many of the industries that rely on culture and traditions in Sri Lanka (such as Dumbara mats and Ruhunu Curd) could also benefit from some intervention and assistance, either by the State or by other public or private entities.

In this respect, it should be noted that the intervention of the State is an important component of the process of registering GIs under the current *sui generis* GI regime. Furthermore, the registration process requires identifying ad hoc entities in charge of controlling the quality of products. Again, this series of controls could benefit several traditional products in Sri Lanka. Finally, the State and these entities could further assist producers in marketing and managing the GI products in the national and international markets.

Finally, while repeating that a registration system could be beneficial from Sri Lanka, we must note that moving into a registration system and then maintaining it can be a relatively costly endeavor. Thus, in order for this to be a successful change in the current system, it would be important that a considerable number of products be registered as GI. It would also be important that, in addition to seeking GI registration, producers work toward maintaining the quality of GI products and managing the GIs wisely. For example, should a GI gain popularity, GI producers should be mindful and not try to increase production unsustainably. Product quality should not be sacrificed for quantity. Overall, it is important to remember that GI protection is a useful tool for local and rural development, but the proper managing of GIs remains the primary strategy for potential long-term success of these products in Sri Lanka, as it is with the rest of the world.

PART IV

THE SHIFTING RELATIONSHIP BETWEEN GEOGRAPHICAL INDICATIONS, TRADITIONAL KNOWLEDGE, AND CULTURAL HERITAGE

18

The Geographical Indication Act 2013: Protection of Traditional Knowledge in Bangladesh with Special Reference to *Jamdani*

Mahua Zahur[*]

1 INTRODUCTION

Geographical indications (GIs) refer to signs or symbols that are used to denote a product, the distinctive characteristics of which are linked to its place of origin. GIs are different from other intellectual property rights because of their unique characteristics, namely, the fact that they can be collectively owned by a group of producers. Additionally, GIs have a connection to the territory from which the products originate, both in terms of geographical origin as well as quality and characteristics of the products.[1] The inclusion of GIs in the provisions of the Agreement on Trade-Related Aspects of Intellectual Property Rights (TRIPS)[2] was controversial precisely due to the differences between "old world" and "new world" countries, with respect to some of the theories supporting GI protection.

After a long debate, GI protection was nevertheless introduced into TRIPS, and subsequently had to be protected in most countries worldwide.[3] Nevertheless, although TRIPS requires for the protection of GIs, it does not provide for the specific mechanism that members of TRIPS should adopt to protect GIs under their national laws.[4] Consequently, individual countries

---

[*] Senior Lecturer, Department of Law, East West Univrsity.
[1] *See generally* Steve Stern, *Are GIs IP?*, 29 Eur. Intell. Prop. Rev. 39–42 (2007).
[2] Agreement on Trade-Related Aspects of Intellectual Property Rights, April 15, 1994, Marrakesh Agreement Establishing the World Trade Organization, Annex 1C, 1869 U.N.T.S. 299 [hereinafter TRIPS].
[3] Elizabeth Barham, *Translating Terroir: The Global Challenge of French AOC Labeling*, 19 J. Rural Stud. 127, 128–129 (2003); Irene Calboli, *Of Markets, Culture and Terroir: The Unique Economic and Culture Related Benefits of Geographical Indications of Origin*, in International Intellectual Property: A Handbook of Contemporary Research 433 (Daniel J. Gervais ed., 2015).
[4] TRIPS, *supra* note 2, at art. 22.2.

439

have chosen their own modality for the protection of GIs within their domestic system. Some countries have preferred to protect GIs under their existing trademarks law, whereas others have enacted a *sui generis* mechanism for GI protection, largely based upon the system currently adopted by the European Union (EU). In response to TRIPS' obligations, many Asian nations have also enacted ad hoc legislations for the protection of GIs, keeping in mind the socioeconomic conditions of their countries.[5]

In this respect, Bangladesh has recently enacted the Geographical Indication (Registration and Protection) Act 2013 (GI Act of 2013) (Act No. 54 of 2013).[6] Law makers and relevant business sectors hoped that through the enactment of the GI Act of 2013, Bangladesh would be able to protect traditional domestic goods that utilize the intellectual ingenuity and traditional knowledge of local producers, which previously fell outside the conventional type of intellectual property protection in Bangladesh.

This chapter aims to analyze GI protection from a Bangladeshi perspective. Furthermore, Section 2 will briefly revisit the provisions which relate to GI protection under TRIPS and how the notion of GIs is articulated within TRIPS' construction. Section 3 will project light upon the background of the newly enacted GI Act of 2013 and the practicalities of GI protection in Bangladesh. Briefly, the GI Act of 2013 is designed to conform to TRIPS while simultaneously seeking to accommodate the domestic needs of the country with respect to GI protection. Building on Section 3, Section 4 will review the salient features of the GI Act of 2013. This section will also mention some of the provisions of the Trademarks Act of Bangladesh of 2009 (TM Act of 2009) (Act No. 19 of 2009)[7] that provide indirect protection to GIs. The TM Act of 2009 was the only law applicable to GIs in Bangladesh before the passing of the GI Act of 2013.

Bangladesh is the home of many traditional place-based products. The GI Act of 2013 thus represents the normative framework for a potentially beneficial new model for the protection of domestic place-based local products. Among many other traditional products, one geographical name that has garnered particular attention in Bangladesh is *Jamdani*. The name *Jamdani* refers to an intricate woven fabric that has historically been associated with

---

[5] See generally N.S. Gopalakrishnan, Prabha S. Nair, & Aravind K. Babu, *Exploring the Relationship between Geographical Indications and Traditional Knowledge: An Analysis of the Legal Tools for the Protection of Geographical Indications in Asia* (Geneva: International Centre for Trade and Sustainable Development, Working Paper, 2007).

[6] The Geographical Indication (Registration and Protection) Act 2013 (Bangladesh) [hereinafter GI Act 2013].

[7] Trademarks Act 2009 (Bangladesh).

a particular region of Bangladesh. The process by which the fabric is created has also been recognized as an intangible cultural heritage of humanity by the United Nations Educational, Scientific, and Cultural Organization (UNESCO).[8] In November 2016, *Jamdani* became the first GI to be registered in Bangladesh under the GI Act of 2013. Section 5 of this chapter will explore the history of this woven tradition and will argue that *Jamdani* deserved be protected as a GI in Bangladesh. It is recognized, however, that the long-term protection of *Jamdani* and other traditional goods of Bangladesh does not only depend on the registration of their names as GIs under the GI Act of 2013. Instead, building an effective framework for GI protection in practice also requires that GIs are managed wisely by their producers and the communities. Only in this way can Bangladesh reap the benefits of the adoption of GI protection.

2 TRIPS AND GEOGRAPHICAL INDICATIONS: A BRIEF REVISIT

In 1994, the protection of GIs became globally accepted due to its inclusion into the widely ratified TRIPS agreement.[9] Nevertheless, this development did not come easily. During TRIPS' negotiations, the United States (US), Canada, Japan, and Australia opposed the inclusion of GI protection within TRIPS. However, the EU came forward to support GI protection as it had a strong interest to protect traditional foods and wine in the international market.[10] Notably, various similar concepts, aimed at protecting "indications of origin" and "appellations of origin," had previously been incorporated in other international agreements, but with less success than TRIPS.[11]

---

[8] United Nations Educational, Scientific and Cultural Organization (UNESCO), www.unesco.org/culture/ich/index.php?RL=00879 (last visited April 15, 2016). Inscribed in 2013 on the Representative list of the Intangible Cultural Heritage of Humanity.

[9] Irene Calboli, *Expanding the Protection of Geographical Indications of Origin under TRIPS: "Old" Debates or "New" Opportunity?*, 10 MARQ. INTELL. PROP. L. REV. 182, 189 (2006).

[10] Stacy D. Goldberg, *Who Will Raise the White Flag? The Battle between the United States and the European Union over the Protection of Geographical Indications*, 22 U. PENN. J. INT'L. L. 107, 109 (2001).

[11] Irene Calboli, *supra* note 9, at 189; *see* Paris Convention for the Protection of Industrial Property, March 20, 1883, *as revised* July 14, 1967, 21 U.S.T. 1583, 828 U.N.T.S. 305 [hereinafter Paris Convention]; Madrid Agreement for the Repression of False or Deceptive Indications of Source on Goods, April 14, 1891, 828 U.N.T.S. 163 [hereinafter Madrid Agreement]; Lisbon Agreement for the Protection of Appellations of Origin and their International Registration, October 31, 1958, *as revised* July 14, 1967, 923 U.N.T.S. 205 [hereinafter Lisbon Agreement]. In May 2015, a Diplomatic Conference was convened in Geneva, Switzerland, to review the Lisbon Agreement. *See* WIPO, *Diplomatic Conference for the Adoption of a New Act of the Lisbon Agreement – The Geneva Act of the Lisbon Agreement on Appellations of Origin and Geographical Indications* (2015), www.wipo.int/meetings/diplomatic_conferences/2015/en/. The Geneva Act of the Lisbon Agreement on

One of the most relevant aspects of TRIPS is that it provides a detailed definition of GIs. This is a step forward from the vague and ambiguity-ridden definitions one may find in the predecessors of the TRIPS agreement.[12] TRIPS defines GIs in Article 22(1) in the following terms:

Appellations of Origin and Geographical Indications, May 20, 2015, WIPO Lex. No. TRT/LISBON/009, available at www.wipo.int/wipolex/en/details.jsp?id=15625 [hereinafter Geneva Act]. The term "indication of source" is used in the Paris Convention and in the Madrid Agreement, even though the term is not defined in neither agreement. *See also* David Vivas Eugui, *Negotiations on Geographical Indications in the TRIPS Council and Their Effect on the WTO Agricultural Negotiations: Implications for Developing Countries and the Case of Venezuela*, 4 J. WORLD INTELL. PROP. 703, 704, 705 (2001). Generally, the term "indication of source" does not require that the products have any unique quality, characteristic, or reputation attributable to its place of origin, but nevertheless includes within the definition also the geographical origin of the products. On the other side, Article 2.1 of the Lisbon Agreement defines "appellation of origin" as "the geographical denomination of a country, region, or locality which serves to designate a product originating therein, the quality and characteristics of which are due exclusively or essentially to the geographical environment, including natural and human factors." This definition clarified that products not only have to originate from a specific place but must have the quality and characteristics that are due exclusively or essentially to the geographical environment inclusive of natural and human factors. Mere "reputation" is not sufficient to get protection through "appellations of origin"; specific qualities and characteristics need to be proved in the particular product. They stand for direct geographical names of countries, regions, or localities and any symbols or emblems indirectly signifying geographical origin are not enough. However, Article 2 of the Geneva Act regarding the definition of "appellations of origin and geographical indications" defines "denominations of origin" as "any denomination protected in the Contracting Party of Origin consisting of or containing the name of a geographical area, or another denomination known as referring to such area, which serves to designate a good as originating in that geographical area, where the quality or characteristics of the good are due exclusively or essentially to the geographical environment, including natural and human factors, and which has given the good its reputation." The same provision defines "geographical indications" as "any indication protected in the Contracting Party of Origin consisting of or containing the name of a geographical area, or another indication known as referring to such area, which identifies a good as originating in that geographical area, where a given quality, reputation or other characteristic of the good is essentially attributable to its geographical origin." Geneva Act, at art. 2(1).

[12] *See* Felix Addor & Alexandra Grazioli, *Geographical Indications beyond Wines and Spirits: A Roadmap for a Better Protection for Geographical Indications in the WTO/TRIPS Agreement*, 5 J. WORLD INTELL. PROP. 865, 868 (2002). The expression "geographical indication" used in TRIPS includes "appellations of origin" but in a wider scope. TRIPS allows "reputation" to be an independent criterion, sufficient to grant protection under the GI regime. TRIPS emphasizes the significance of a geographical area, as opposed to the name of the area, to be eligible for GI protection and requires the applicant to establish a link between the product and its particular characteristics, quality, or reputation attributable to the place of origin of the product. TRIPS does not necessitate that all these conditions should be coexisting. It is sufficient to prove only one of the above conditions. The expression "other characteristics of goods" connotes that the designated goods have some distinctive features from other related products in their characteristics. Natural factor is not the only test for the "indication" to be protected. Indications can qualify for GI protection if quality, reputation, or other

Geographical indications are, for the purpose of this Agreement, indications which identify a good as originating in the territory of a Member, or a region or locality in that territory, where a given quality, reputation or other characteristic of the good is essentially attributable to its geographical origin.

Article 22(2) of TRIPS[13] provides a general threshold against the use of GIs that would result in consumers being misled or which may amount to unfair competition. This general rule, however, finds an exception in the case of GIs for wines and spirits, for which a higher standard is required. Notably, TRIPS protects these GIs also when unauthorized uses of these GIs or similar terms do not mislead the public. Moreover, Article 23 of TRIPS[14] prohibits the use of these GIs in association with expressions like "kind," "type," "style," or other similar expressions.

This differentiated treatment was an issue of debate within the World Trade Organization (WTO) as many WTO members requested the same "higher" level of protection to products beyond wines and spirits. However, a group of countries led by the US opposed such an extension.[15] These countries opined that the GIs other than wines and spirits were already sufficiently protected[16] under Articles 22 and 24 of TRIPS.[17] The reason for their objection against equal treatment of all GI products was, *inter alia*, that developing countries would not be able to bear the cost of implementing a higher level of GI protection for all products.[18]

Nevertheless, Article 24 of TRIPS[19] provides for a built-in agenda for future GI negotiations precisely to discuss the possibility of extending a higher level of GI protection beyond wines and spirits. As of this date, there has been no international consensus as to the expansion of higher level of protection to all other products that are currently given to wines and spirits;[20] the creation of

---

characteristics of a product is the contribution of other factors, namely, human factors, quality of the materials, etc. Gopalakrishnan, Nair & Babu, *supra* note 5, at 15.

[13] TRIPS, *supra* note 2, at art. 22.2.   [14] TRIPS, *supra* note 2, at art. 23.
[15] Ritika Banerjee & Mohar Majumdar, *In the Mood to Compromise? Extended Protection of Geographical Indications under TRIPS Article 23*, 6 J. INTELL. PROP. L. & PRAC. 657, 659 (2011).
[16] Gail E. Evans & Michael Blakeney, *The Protection of Geographical Indications after Doha: Quo Vadis?*, J. INT'L ECON. L. 575, 578 (2006).
[17] TRIPS, *supra* note 2, at arts. 22, 24.
[18] Marsha A. Echols, *Geographical Indications for Foods, TRIPS, and the Doha Development Agenda*, 47 J. AFR. L. 199, 208 (2003).
[19] TRIPS, *supra* note 2, at art. 24.
[20] *Members "Not Ready to Move Forward Yet" on Wines and Spirits Register Negotiations*, WORLD TRADE ORG. (April 14, 2014), www.wto.org/english/news_e/news14_e/trip_01apr14_e.htm.

a multilateral registry for GIs also seems unlikely to take place in the near future.[21] However, most international negotiations on GIs are currently taking place outside the TRIPS/WTO framework, and a new generation of TRIPS-plus GI standards has been negotiated through regional and bilateral international free trade agreements (FTAs).[22]

Despite these stated controversies, TRIPS is still praiseworthy for defining GIs beyond all ambiguities, its wide acceptance throughout the world,[23] providing provisions relating to interplay between trademarks and GIs,[24] and paving the way for future negotiations toward increasing protection of GIs bilaterally or multilaterally.[25] Still, while TRIPS mandates for specific minimum standards for GI protection, it does not provide for a single particular mechanism of protection. Accordingly, TRIPS members are at liberty to protect GIs within their national boundaries by adopting *sui generis* law or through trademarks law or under unfair competition law. In this respect, Bangladesh, a member of the WTO since 1995, has decided to adopt a *sui generis* system of protection for GIs. The outcome of this decision is the enactment of the Geographical Indication (Registration and Protection) Act 2013.[26]

3 THE RATIONALE FOR PROTECTING GEOGRAPHICAL INDICATIONS IN BANGLADESH

Theoretically, the fundamental rationale for protecting GIs within an intellectual property regime is akin to that of trademark, that is, to protect signs that link products to certain places of origin or products that have certain characteristics. Protecting GIs will thus prevent consumers from being misled by third parties not authorized to use the GIs. In turn, this protection will grant legitimate producers the right to prevent the misappropriation of their valuable property.[27] GIs can also potentially play a relevant role in promoting development for local (generally small) communities as well as preserving local culture. These pro-development and pro-culture arguments have attracted the attention of GI scholars,[28] and have been brought to the forefront

---

[21] Banerjee & Majumdar, *supra* note 15, at 659. [22] *See* chapters cited *supra* Section 2.
[23] There are 161 members to TRIPS as of April 2015. World Trade Org., List of Members and Observers www.wto.org/english/thewto_e/whatis_e/tif_e/org6_e.htm (last visited May 23, 2016).
[24] TRIPS, *supra* note 2, at arts. 22.3, 24.5; *see also infra* Section 4.3.
[25] *See* TRIPS, *supra* note 2, at art. 24. [26] GI Act of 2013, *supra* note 6.
[27] Dev S. Gangjee, *Geographical Indications and Cultural Heritage*, 4 WIPO J. 92 (2012).
[28] *See generally* Calboli, *supra* note 3.

of the international debates – even though many remain doubtful.[29] Even though these arguments in support of GI protection may be beyond the practical reasons proffered for the protection of GIs at the domestic level, it is important to consider these arguments to better understand the reasons why GI protection can benefit national economies.

Yet, the arguments related to the value of GIs for community development and the preservation of cultural heritage did not appear to be as important during the discussion on GI protection as part of the adoption of TRIPS. Instead, GIs have been viewed, for a long time, as a European phenomenon within the TRIPS negotiations. The EU possesses most of the GI registrations, even outside wines and spirits,[30] and had argued strongly for the inclusion of GI protection within TRIPS.[31] In particular, the EU took the stance that GI-denominated products should be protected for their unique characteristics, while the US, Australia, and other countries opposed GI protection saying that, *inter alia*, most products can be replicated anywhere in the globe today by virtue of technological advances. In essence, this apparently theoretical debate was prompted from the respective trade interests of the "old world" and the "new world." GI protection was finally included into TRIPS as a trade compromise between these nations.[32] These nations also agreed on a higher level of GI protection for wines and spirits because they shared considerable economic interests in this area as producers and exporters of wines and spirits.

In the Asian context, this trade-based reality is not as clear as in the West. Nevertheless, the recent years have witnessed the proliferation of *sui generis* legislative endeavor toward GI protection in Asia.[33] Asian countries mostly relied on culture-based justifications to support the protection of GIs at the domestic level.[34] For example, India currently possesses more than two hundred registered GIs for different ranges of products, including foodstuff, fabric, jewelry, and furniture,[35] the trade importance of which is yet to be established.

---

[29] Gangjee, *supra* note 27, at 92.
[30] Massimo Vittori, *The International Debate on Geographical Indications (GIs): The Point of View of the Global Coalition of GI Producers-origin*, 13 J. WORLD INTELL. PROP. 304, 306 (2010).
[31] Tomer Broude, *Taking "Trade and Culture" Seriously: Geographical Indications and Cultural Protection in the WTO*, 26 U. PENN. J. INT'L ECON. L. 623, 627 (2005).
[32] Barnum, *supra* note 3, at 128–29.
[33] In recent years, many Asian countries, such as India, Malaysia, Thailand, and Sri Lanka, have adopted *sui generis* legislative protection within their domestic legal systems.
[34] *See generally* Gopalakrishnan, Nair, & Babu, *supra* note 5.
[35] GI registrations listed in this article can be found in the Geographical Indications Registry, published by Intellectual Property India, available at http://ipindia.nic.in/girindia/ (last visited May 19, 2016). Hyderabad Haleem, Registration No. 132; Sandur Lambani

It goes without saying that if the rationale for GIs was *solely* to preserve culture, such justification would simply be impractical. In this regard, the approach of Singapore is worth a mention. Initially, Singapore enacted GI laws which provided for automatic protection of GIs without any need for registration.[36] The law was designed in accordance with TRIPS.[37] However, in April 2014 the parliament of Singapore passed the new Geographical Indications Act which, when it comes into force, will replace the earlier Act.[38] This new enactment provides for the registration of GIs, in pursuance of EU-Singapore Free Trade Agreement.[39] This new enactment provides that a registry for GIs be set up.[40] Consequently, there would be an increase of costs required to set up and maintain this registry. If Singapore does not rely on strong domestic culture-based justification like most other Asian countries, then why is Singapore willing to shoulder this additional economic burden? Perhaps future trade implications under its trade agreements with the EU have persuaded Singapore to enact this new piece of law. In general, the practical rationale of protecting GIs at a domestic level may differ from place to place.

What prompted Bangladesh to enact the GI Act of 2013? Bangladesh can be viewed as the home of various agricultural and traditional products. Its GI legislation can thus be rationalized by cultural justification, which is the justification that most Asian developing nations cite as justification for GI protection. As per one research, 73 products have been identified, including foodstuffs, handicrafts, and weaving patterns from Bangladesh as having the traits linked to their place of origin.[41] Alongside this reason is the pragmatic rationale that Bangladesh, as a member of TRIPS, is under an obligation to implement the bulk of TRIPS' minimum standard. This international obligation has caused Bangladesh to replace their old trademark and copyright laws with new enactments in accordance with TRIPS. As a "least developed country," Bangladesh was originally granted a concession of ten years, which

---

Embroidery, Registration No. 128; Temple Jewellery of Nagercoil, Registration No. 36; Kashmir Walnut Wood Carving, Registration No. 162.

[36] Interested parties may bring actions under section 3 of the act without registration. Geographical Indications Act 1999 (Singapore).

[37] *Id.*

[38] Dedar Singh Gill & Yvonne Tang, *Singapore – Geographical Indications Act 2014 to Enhance Protection for Businesses and Consumers*, COVENTUS LAW (June 24, 2014), www.conventuslaw.com/archive/singapore-geographical-indications-act-2014-to-enhance-protection-for-businesses-and-consumers/.

[39] EU-Singapore Free Trade Agreement, available at http://trade.ec.europa.eu/doclib/press/index.cfm?id=961.

[40] Geographical Indications Bill 2014 (Singapore), Part IV §§ 17–20.

[41] A.B.M. Hamidul Mishbah, *Time to Enact Geographical Indication Act*, THE DAILY STAR (December 6, 2012), http://archive.thedailystar.net/newDesign/news-details.php?nid=260032.

was extended twice, up to 2021.[42] However, it fulfilled its obligation in 2013 with the enactment of the GI Act of 2013.[43]

On a related issue, it is a matter of concern whether Bangladesh can shoulder the economic expense of setting up the registry provided under the newly enacted GI Act of 2013. Unless GIs are proven to be economically viable at a domestic level (which must be assessed in the reality of every individual country), the adoption of GI protection may prove to be futile. In Bangladesh, the extent to which GIs may contribute toward the development of small communities and protection of cultural heritage can only be assessed once the newly enacted GI Act of 2013 law will come to its successful implementation. It may therefore be too early to reach an opinion on this particular matter.

It is worth mentioning the background that led to the enactment of the GI Act of 2013. In 2012, some location-based products of Bangladesh, such as *Jamdani*,[44] *Fazli* mango,[45] and *NakshiKantha*[46] (a weaving pattern) were registered as GIs in India under Indian GI law. As these products are generally regarded as flag bearers of the Bangladeshi national identity, the fact that these names had been registered as Indian GIs on the Indian GI Registry led to the fear of misappropriation of Bangladeshi cultural distinctiveness by other countries. Particularly, this event raised resentment among the stakeholders of the location-based products in Bangladesh. The *Jamdani* weavers along with other concerned parties claimed that this represented a cultural misappropriation. This incident may thus have contributed to the enactment of the GI Act of 2013 in Bangladesh.[47] In other words, policy makers may have found that this enactment was the only available option to "console" the resentment among local producers as opposition to the registration of GIs in other countries has to be based on the fact that these GIs are protected in their country of origin under the principles of TRIPS.

Generally, GI proponents have always supported that GI protection constitutes a system of protection that can promote the development of small communities in developing countries. If Bangladesh confines the use of the

---

[42] *Responding to Least Developed Countries' Special Needs in Intellectual Property*, WORLD TRADE ORG. (October 16, 2013), www.wto.org/english/tratop_e/trips_e/ldc_e.htm.
[43] GI Act 2013, *supra* note 6.   [44] UppadaJamdani Sarees, Registration No. 106 (India).
[45] Fazli Mango grown in the district of Malda, Registration No. 96 (India).
[46] NakshiKantha, Registration No. 49 (India).
[47] India's stance in registering these products is not judged here as legal or otherwise; rather this chapter focuses on the reaction which came after the registration of the above-named products which may have, to some extent, contributed to the prompt adoption of the GI Act of 2013. *Dhaka to Contest India's GI Claim over Jamdani Sarees, Fazli Mangoes*, BUSINESS LINE (November 30, 2012) www.thehindubusinessline.com/news/dhaka-to-contest-indias-gi-claim-over-jamdani-sarees-fazli-mangoes/article4150532.ece.

GIs only for the prevention of misappropriation of their cultural goods, the spirit of the GI Act of 2013 may be undermined. Accordingly, we should not concentrate all our attention to these three products. Instead, it is important to assess the overall benefits that GIs may bring about for Bangladesh in general.

As a matter of clarification, I do not seek to use this platform to hold India or Bangladesh as having done any wrong to each other. As a proponent of GI protection myself, my contention is that GIs must be appreciated for their features as a general matter, in the hope that GI protection will have a positive impact on national development. Thus, as Bangladesh now has laws protecting GIs, I look forward to seeing the benefits that GIs may bring in future to local and national development in Bangladesh.

4 SALIENT FEATURES OF THE GEOGRAPHICAL INDICATION ACT 2013 AND ITS COMPATIBILITY WITH TRIPS

The GI Act 2013[48] has recently been adopted in Bangladesh. Over the course of the last few years, especially in 2012–2013, GI protection for local products has become one of the most discussed issues in Bangladesh. As mentioned in the previous section, the debate started when Bangladesh started to fear that its traditional goods might not be able to get protection abroad considering the cross-border journey of these well-reputed products, especially *Jamdani*. The protection of other goods was also pertinent for similar reasons.[49]

4.1 The Definition of Geographical Indications

In accordance with the definition of GIs given in TRIPS, the GI Act of 2013 states that GIs can be used to denote the origin of goods where the quality, reputation, or other characteristics of such goods is essentially attributable to the place of origin of the said goods.[50] As per the definition, agricultural and natural goods can be protected as GIs, where the soil and climate play the key roles for the distinctive characteristics of the goods. The definition under the GI Act of 2013 goes beyond the TRIPS and specifically states that GIs can be used to designate manufactured goods as well.[51] It is thus implied that GIs can be used to designate a product, even where the characteristics of the product are the *sole* outcome of human factors, as long as it has developed reputation from

---

[48] GI Act 2013, *supra* note 6.
[49] Mishbah, *supra* note 41; Mahua Zahur, *GIs Protection: Where Do We Stand Legally?*, THE DAILY STAR(August 5, 2013), www.thedailystar.net/news/gis-protection-where-do-we-stand-legally.
[50] GI Act of 2013, *supra* note 6, ch. I § 2(9). [51] Id.

a particular place. For the protection of GIs that relate to manufactured goods, any of the activities relating to the production, processing, or preparation of the designated goods must take place in a particular territory and the reputation and the characteristics of those products should be attributable to that territory.[52]

4.2 Protection of Geographical Indications under the Geographical Indication of Goods (Registration and Protection) Act 2013 in Bangladesh

TRIPS requires that members provide legal means to prevent the use of GIs in a way that can mislead the public as to the geographical origin of the goods,[53] but it does not suggest the means of protection. As was mentioned earlier, the members of TRIPS may comply with this obligation by adopting various measures, such as through the adoption of a *sui generis* system,[54] through the adoption of provisions under trademark laws that have the effect of protecting GIs,[55] or through unfair competition law.[56]

---

[52] Section 2(9) of the GI Act of 2013 reads:

> [G]eographical indication of goods means any agricultural, natural and manufactured goods having geographical indication that indicates that such goods is originated or manufactured in a country or territory or a locality or region of such country or territory, where a given quality, reputation or other characteristics of such goods is essentially attributable to its geographical origin and in case such goods is manufactured goods one of the activities of either the production, processing or preparation of such goods takes place in such territory, region or locality.

> Section 2(8) of the GI Act of 2013 reads: "Goods mean any agricultural or natural goods or goods of handicraft and industry and includes food stuff."

[53] Article 22.2 of TRIPS reads,

> In respect of geographical indications, Members shall provide the legal means for interested parties to prevent: (a) the use of any means in the designation and presentation of a good that indicates or suggests that the good in question originates in a geographical area other than the true place of origin in a manner which misleads the public as to the geographical origin of the good.TRIPS, *supra* note 2, art. 22.2.

[54] The term *sui generis* is not defined in the TRIPS agreement. It literally means "of its own kind" and consists of a set of laws and ways recognized nationally for the protection of intellectual property rights. The definition and implementation of *sui generis* systems may vary from country to country. STEPHEN A HANSEN & JUSTIN W. VANFLEET, TRADITIONAL KNOWLEDGE AND INTELLECTUAL PROPERTY: A HANDBOOK ON ISSUES AND OPTIONS FOR TRADITIONAL KNOWLEDGE HOLDERS IN PROTECTING THEIR INTELLECTUAL PROPERTY AND MAINTAINING BIOLOGICAL DIVERSITY (2003). Many Asian countries have adopted *sui generis* systems for the protection of geographical indications within their municipal system. For example, see the relevant laws of India, Malaysia, Singapore, Thailand, and Sri Lanka.

[55] Some countries protect geographical indications under trademark law as collective marks or certification marks. For example, see the trademark laws of China, Australia, Canada, and the United States of America.

[56] *See* Unfair Competition Prevention Act of Japan 1993.

The GI Act of 2013 provides for registration as a means of protection of GIs under Chapter IV of the Act, but unregistered GIs are also protected under the GI Act if the indication is true as to its place of origin.[57] The registration of geographical indications may be sought by the producers of the goods or any association, institution, government body, or authority of any group which represents the interest of persons producing geographical indication of goods.[58] Any individual or group of individuals that are related to the production, collection, preparation, or processing of the goods registered under the Act may also be registered as authorized users of the goods so indicated.[59] The term of registration is for five years,[60] subject to renewal.[61] Compared to the GI laws of other Asian countries, this initial term of protection appears to be shorter.[62] To my mind, this provision may discourage the registration of many goods as the registration process is complex and requires intense scrutiny. However, if this provision was intended by legislators to ensure consistent quality of a given product before renewal, then it should nevertheless be appreciated.

Once validly registered, an authorized user of the registered geographical indication is entitled to use it in connection with his goods. He is also entitled to the remedies provided under the Act for the infringement of geographical indication.[63] However, the rights acquired through registration cannot be alienated in a way of transmission, assignment, licensing, etc.[64]

The GI Act of 2013 does not provide for any "misleading test" as a condition for registration or protection of GIs within the Act. The GI Act provides for equal levels of protection to all products for which GIs can be used. In other words, it does not provide for any enhanced level of protection to any particular products like wines, spirits, etc. However, the provision for the protection of homonymous[65] GIs has been incorporated within the Act following TRIPS,[66] but with a wider scope. The GI Act makes provision for the

---

[57] GI Act of 2013, *supra* note 6, ch. I § 6(1).   [58] *Id.*, ch. I § 9.   [59] *Id.*, ch. I § 10.
[60] *Id.*, ch. I § 16(2).   [61] *Id.*, ch. I § 16(3)–(4).
[62] See Section 18(1) of the Geographical Indication of Goods (Registration and Protection) Act of 1999 (India); *see also* Section 19(2) of the Geographical Indications Act of 2000 (Malaysia).
[63] GI Act of 2013, *supra* note 6, ch. I § 18.   [64] *Id.*, ch. I § 19(1).
[65] Section 2(16) of the GI Act of 2013 defines homonymous geographical indications as the geographical indications of those goods which have the similar names.
[66] TRIPS, *supra* note 2, at art. 23.3. This provision provides for the protection of homonymous geographical indications for wines only. In this regard Members shall determine the practical conditions under which the homonymous indications in question will be differentiated from each other, taking into account the need to ensure equitable treatment of the producers concerned and that consumers are not mislead. An identical provision is spelled out in section 7 of the GI Act of 2013, but unlike TRIPS, such protection has been extended past wines and spirits and applies to all products.

registration of homonymous GIs for all products.[67] So it follows that, unlike TRIPS, the protection of homonymous GIs is not limited to wine or any other particular product. However, the registration of certain GIs is prohibited under the GI Act. Consumer deception or confusion and public morality, *inter alia*, are set as criteria for which the registration of GIs is prohibited.[68] The GI Act also prohibits the registration of GIs that are generic, or that are not protected or ceased to be protected or have fallen into disuse in the country of origin.[69] This provision is enshrined within the GI Act in consonance with Articles 24.6 and 24.9 of TRIPS. Article 24.9 provides that

> [t]here shall be no obligation under this agreement to protect geographical indications which are not or ceased to be protected in their country of origin, or which have fallen into disuse in that country.

This provision implies that a member state of TRIPS cannot protect its GIs in the territory of other WTO members, unless the GIs are protected in their country of origin.[70] Accordingly, this provision may lead many countries to adopt their own GI protection regime, within their municipal law, for the purpose of reciprocal protection of GIs in international level. By the virtue of this provision, Bangladesh is now in a position to claim protection of its protected GIs in foreign territories and vice versa.

Apart from the reasons mentioned above, for which registration is prohibited within the GI Act of 2013, protection may also be denied if a third party can prove that the proposed registration should not be proceeded with for any justifiable cause spelled out in the GI Act of 2013.[71] This part of the Act is designed to provide for procedural safeguards so that the rights of all concerned are not impaired. At this stage, the Registrar is empowered with the discretion to either allow or deny the registration. The GI Act of 2013 is silent as to whether any party aggrieved from the Registrar's decision can move to the court of law following the dissonance. Thus, it may reasonably be inferred that the conclusion that the Registrar arrives at is final. This feature of the Act may thus curtail the possibility of judicial scrutiny, and should therefore be a point of reconsideration for the legislature.

As a means of protecting the interests of legitimate right holders, the GI Act of 2013 enables the same to institute infringement actions against any illegal use of GIs. The Act defines certain acts as infringement of GIs for which imprisonment and monetary fine is provided as punitive punishment.[72] Any

---

[67] GI Act of 2013, *supra* note 6, ch. I § 7. [68] *Id.*, ch. III § 8, (b), (d). [69] *Id.*, ch. I § 8(g).
[70] TRIPS, *supra* note 2, at art. 24.9. [71] GI Act of 2013, *supra* note 6, ch. I §§ 13, 14.
[72] *See* details accompanying GI Act of 2013, *supra* note 6.

use of GI that causes confusion among the consumers regarding its true origin[73] or any act of unfair competition or passing off[74] would constitute infringement under the Act. The use of GI in translation of the true place of origin or GI accompanied by expression such as "kind," "type," "imitation," or like expression would also constitute infringement.[75] All of these provisions encompassed in the GI Act of 2013 are in line with the provisions of article 22.2 (a), 22.2(b), and article 23.1 of TRIPS. Within TRIPS, unfair competition is an act that constitutes unfair competition as per article 10*bis* of the Paris Convention.[76] The present Act provides the definition of unfair competition with a list of activities that constitute unfair competition, in line with the relevant provisions of the Paris Convention.[77] The scope of section 28(d) of the GI Act of 2013[78] is wider than article 23.1 of TRIPS.[79] Unlike TRIPS, the section does not provide for any discrepancy among the type of products in evaluating the infringement of GIs, even if they are accompanied with expressions like "kind," "type," "style," etc. In other words, the enhanced protection that is granted to wines and spirits only within TRIPS is extended to all products under the Act.

4.3 Relationship of Geographical Indications with Trademarks

Following the adoption of TRIPS, GIs are recognized as an intellectual property right and are on the same footing with other branches of intellectual property, namely, patent, trademark, copyright, etc. This includes that GI protection is subjected to the application of the general provisions of TRIPS,

---

[73] *Id.*, ch. I § 28(1)(a).   [74] *Id.*, ch. I § 28(1)(b).   [75] *Id.*, ch. I § 28(1)(d).

[76] Article 21.2 of TRIPS reads, "members shall provide the legal means for interested parties to prevent: . . . (b) any use which constitutes an act of unfair competition within the meaning of Article 10*bis* of the Paris Convention (1967)."

[77] Section 28 (2) of the GI Act of 2013 defines the term "unfair competition" as any act of competition contrary to honest practices in relation to industrial and commercial matters. The following acts will be considered as unfair competition, namely:

(a) any act of such a nature as to create confusion among the public by any means whatever with the establishment, the goods, the industrial or the commercial activities of the competitor;

(b) false allegation in the course of trade of such a nature as to discredit the establishment, the goods or the industrial or commercial activities, of a competitor;

(c) geographical indications, the use of which in the course of trade is liable to mislead public as to the quantity, the nature, the manufacturing process, the characteristics, the suitability of their purpose, of the goods;

The Paris Convention under article 10*bis* (3) provides an identical list of activities that constitute unfair competition in connection to GIs.

[78] GI Act of 2013, *supra* note 6, ch. I § 28(1)(d).   [79] TRIPS, *supra* note 2, art. 23.1.

and thus to the principles of "national treatment"[80] and "most favored nation treatment."[81] In general, GIs can be protected with *sui generis* rights or through trademark protection as indicated in TRIPS, or rather due to the silence in TRIPS, as the means to protect GIs. Yet, despite the similar nature of trademarks[82] and GIs, the relationship between these two types of protection is contentious.[83]

In Bangladesh, the GI Act of 2013 redefines their relationship between the two types of intellectual property rights, but, of course, in a very narrow way. It provides that the registration of certain trademarks may be canceled or denied if they are in conflict with the GIs, and if the said trademark is comprised of a GI and the goods or services so indicated are not produced in the place they indicate,[84] or, the trademark is used in such a manner that

---

[80] National treatment is one of the fundamental principles in the international conventions protecting intellectual property. The principle is enshrined in most of the important treaties dealing with intellectual property, namely the Paris Convention, the Rome Convention, the Berne Convention, the Universal Copyright Convention, TRIPS, etc. It means that a treaty member must accord nationals of other member states the same treatment it accords to its own nationals. Ulrich Loewenheim, *The Principle of National Treatment in the International Conventions Protecting Intellectual Property*, in PATENTS AND TECHNOLOGICAL PROGRESS IN A GLOBALIZED WORLD (Straus ed., 2009). Within TRIPS the provision of national treatment is incorporated under Article 3. Article 3(1) provides that "Each member shall accord to the nationals of other members treatment no less favourable than that it accord to its own nationals with regard to the protection of intellectual property . . ." TRIPS Part I – General Provisions and Basic Principles, WORLD TRADE ORG., www.wto.org/english/tratop_e/trips_e/t_agm2_e.htm (last visited May 19, 2016).

[81] Under WTO Agreements, countries cannot normally discriminate between their trading partners. A member state has to treat all other WTO members equally. This principle is generally known as the "most favoured nation treatment." This principle has been incorporated in many WTO agreements including GATT, TRIPS, etc. but it is noted that the principle is handled slightly differently in the various instruments. This principle is incorporated in TRIPS Agreement under Article 4. Article 4 provides that "With regard to the protection of intellectual property, any advantage, favour, privilege or immunity granted by a member to the nationals of any other country shall be accorded immediately and unconditionally to the national of all other members . . ." *Principles of the Trading System*, WORLD TRADE ORG., www.wto.org/english/thewto_e/whatis_e/tif_e/fact2_e.htm (last visited May 19, 2016).

[82] Article 15(1) of TRIPS defines trademarks as "any sign and any combination of signs capable of distinguishing the goods or services of one undertaking from those of other undertakings, shall be capable of constituting a trademark." This definition of trademark necessitates that the distinguishing feature of a sign makes it capable to serve as a trademark, whereas the definition of GIs as stipulated in TRIPS emphasizes the identifying feature of the GI for being so capable. For the consumers, both these distinctive signs serve as source identifiers. Trademark identifies the source in a sense that it indicates the trade source from which the goods come. GI indicates the place of origin of the goods. *See* Dev S. Gangjee, *Quibbling Siblings: Conflicts between Trademarks and Geographical indications*, 82 CHICAGO-KENT L. REV. 1253, 1254.

[83] *See* Gangjee, *supra* note 82.   [84] GI Act of 2013, *supra* note 6, ch. I § 21(1)(a).

can create confusion among the consumers as to the place of origin of the goods or services.[85] The equivalent of this section in TRIPS is Article 22.3,[86] which requires that members refuse and invalidate the registration of the trademarks consisting of GI relating to goods, if the trademark is used in a way that misleads the public. The members will be required to do so either at the request of the interested party, or in any manner which is provided for in the legislation of the member.[87] Before the enactment of the GI Act, a similar sort of protection was granted to GIs against trademarks under the Trademark Act of 2009, where it is said that a trademark shall not be registered if the word proposed as a trademark is a geographical name.[88]

However, TRIPS does not bind members to protect GIs against identical or similar trademarks in a way that is unilaterally advantageous to the GIs and to the detriment of trademarks. As a result, under the GI Act of 2013, trademarks have been given protection against GIs under certain circumstances. In particular, the GI Act provides that the registration or validation or the right to use a trademark consisting of GIs will not be prejudiced if the said trademark is registered or used with bona fide belief before the GI Act came into being or before an application for registration of a GI in question is submitted. These provisions for the protection of trademarks embody the so-called principle of "first in time, first in right" in light of Article 24 of TRIPS. Article 24.5 of TRIPS[89] states that where a trademark has been applied for or registered in good faith, or where rights to a trademark have been acquired through use in good faith, the validity, registration, or a right to use a trademark should not be prejudiced on the basis of it being identical or similar to a GI. Article 24.8 of TRIPS[90] also protects the right of a person to use his name or the name of his predecessor in the course of trade. Accordingly, the GI Act of 2013 follows the TRIPS' provision and provides that GI protection does not prejudice the right of a person to use his personal name or the name of his predecessor in connection with his business, unless such use is misleading.[91]

---

[85] *Id.*, ch. I § 21(1)(b).   [86] TRIPS, *supra* note 2, at art. 22.3.
[87] Article 22.3 of TRIPS reads

> A Member shall, *ex officio* if its legislation so permits or at the request of the interested party, refuse or invalidate the registration of a trademark which contains or consists of a geographical indication with respect to goods not originating in the territory indicated, if use of the indication in the trademark for such goods in that member is of such a nature as to mislead the public as to the true place of origin.

[88] Section 6 of the Trademark Act 2009 provides that "A trademark shall not be registered in the Register, unless it contains or consists of (d) one or more words ... not being ... a geographical name.."
[89] TRIPS, *supra* note 2, art. 24.5.   [90] *Id.* at art. 24.8.
[91] GI Act of 2013, *supra* note 6, ch. I § 22.

5 PROTECTING JAMDANI AS TRADITIONAL KNOWLEDGE

At the international level, the possibility to protect traditional knowledge (TK) through GI protection has been recognized[92] by some scholars who have pointed out that TK and GIs both share a common characteristic, namely, the connection to a given territory. This connection is often articulated in the notion of *"terroir,"* a concept that was originally born in France and refers to a terrain, place, or soil of a particular region that contributes to the unique characteristics of the products originating from the region. In particular, these unique characteristics linked to the *terroir* are the biophysical features of a particular place as well as the contribution of the people who are traditionally associated with the place and who have preserved and nurtured knowledge relating to the place, and in turn the place–quality relationship with respect to the products manufactured in the place.[93]

Nevertheless, despite the positions supporting that GI protection could serve to also protect TK, some doubts have been expressed as to whether GIs are a suitable mechanism to ensure this protection.[94] In particular, it has been said that TK is a generic notion, which covers traditional cultural expression, folklore, etc. It stands for the knowledge, skill, know-how, and practices that have been developed, sustained, and passed on from generation to generation within a community. To a large extent, TK is a reflection of a given community's cultural identity and can be found in a variety of contexts, such as agricultural, scientific, technical, etc.[95] Instead, the protection legally granted to GIs only extends to protect the name or the symbol that identifies the components of TK and is based on characteristics, knowledge, and skill intertwined in the *terroir* of the GI-denominated region.[96]

Still, by extending the definition of GIs to include the quality, characteristics, or reputation of the products in the alternate as the distinct qualifier for GI protection, TRIPS has nonetheless paved the ground for using GI protection to protect TK.[97] The reputation or characteristics embodied in any GI-

---

[92] *See generally* Marion Pannizon, *Traditional Knowledge and Geographical Indications: Foundation, Interests and Negotiating Positions*, Trade Regulation (National Centre of Competence in Research (NCCR), Working Paper No.2005/1, 2006); Teshager W. Dagne, *The Identity of Geographical Indications and Their Relationship to Traditional Knowledge in Intellectual Property Law*, 5 WIPO J. 137, 143 (2014).

[93] Elizabeth Barham, *supra* note 3, at 131.

[94] *See generally* Susy Frankel, *The Mismatch of Geographical Indications and Innovative Traditional Knowledge*, 29 PROMETHEUS 253 (2011).

[95] *Traditional Knowledge*, WORLD TRADE ORG., www.wipo.int/tk/en/tk/ (last visited May 19, 2016).

[96] Frankel, *supra* note 94, at 6.   [97] Dagne, *supra* note 92, at 147.

denominated product is in fact the result of the association of the TK associated with the GI-denominated region and the natural factors of the region. In this context, it is to be evaluated whether *Jamdani*, a form of fabric that reflects the skill and knowledge of a given community associated with a particular territory, can be protected under GI regime within TRIPS.

As noted earlier, *Jamdani* is perhaps the most sought-after fabric from Bangladesh. Its uniqueness has similarly caught the attention of fashion lovers from all over the world.[98] The exact etymological origin of the word *Jamdani* is not known, and there are divergent opinions as to its original meaning. According to one authority, the word *Jamdani* is the combination of two words, "*jam*," which in the Persian language refers to a superior-quality alcoholic beverage, and "*dani*," which refers to an artistic serving dish. The proponent of this view holds that the fine quality of *Jamdani* could only be compared to something that was also adored for its supreme quality.[99] Others opine that the word originated from a Persian word *jam-dar* that means flowered or embossed.[100] *Muslin*,[101] the finest fabric of the history, is believed to be the ancestor of *Jamdani*. *Jamdani* was considered best among all the forms of *Muslin*. The patterns and motifs of *Jamdani* are floral and geometrical and are believed to have strong Persian influences.[102] Commonly, *Jamdani* patterns are geometric representations of trees, flowers, animals, etc.

The historical value of *Jamdani* is established from the fact that it has been chronicled in various historical documents as a fabric favored by emperors and kings.[103] The mention of *Jamdani* as an industry is found in *Kautilya's Arthashastra* (book of economics), where it is mentioned that this finest fabric was made in, what was then, Bengal and *Pundra* (now Bangladesh).[104] Although exact statistics are not known, *Jamdani* fabrics are now woven in Bangladesh in almost 150 villages from the adjacent areas of Dhaka like Rupgonj, Sonargaon, Sidhirgonj, etc.[105] Historically, *Jamdani* had been associated with this particular area due to the availability of superior-quality

---

[98] Desi Amin, *Fashion Designer Gaurang Sets Trend for "Made In Jamdani" Women's Wear*, DESIMAG, www.desimag.co.uk/fashion-designer-gaurang-sets-trend-made-jamdani-womens-wear/ (last visited May 19, 2016).

[99] Chandra Shekhar Saha, *Bangladesher Boyon Gourab*, CANVAS 18 (August 2007).

[100] Sayyada R. Ghuznavi, *Jamdani: The Legend and the Legacy*, in TEXTILE TRADITION OF BANGLADESH 44 (Haque ed., 2006).

[101] Muslin is a translucent fabric which was known for its fine quality. It is chronicled in the history as the finest fabric from Bengal. See Ghuznavi, *supra* note 100, at 37.

[102] *Id.* at 44.   [103] See Ghuznavi, *supra* note 100.

[104] Shumon Sengupta, *Poetry in Thread: The Jamdani of Dhaka*, THE DAILY STAR (April 9, 2011) www.thedailystar.net/news-detail-180989.

[105] Saha, *supra* note 99, at 19.

cotton, which is the raw material of *Jamdani*. Today, the *Jamdani* industry is still confined to these particular villages. Although there have been several instances of *Jamdani*-like imitations in other areas of the country, such imitations have failed to achieve *Jamdani*'s level of prominence.[106]

In addition, to use certain specific designs, *Jamdani* fabrics are woven following a particular traditional process. The weaving instructions are given by the master weaver to the apprentices verbally through poetic recitation known as *buli* or *sloka*. In this way, the knowledge of weaving patterns and processes are passed from masters to apprentices, that is, from generation to generation verbally.[107] Generally, members of the same family are involved in various activities of the weaving process. Currently, almost all weavers are either uneducated or have received little education. Nevertheless, all weavers have a very keen, perhaps intuitive, mathematical sense and mathematical skills as they have to understand the instruction of the weaving patterns, however complicated they are, from the *bulis* memorized by the masters.[108]

Historical analysis shows that *muslin*, the predecessor of *Jamdani* as traditional fabric, was patronized by the contemporary rulers, including the royal Mughals, for its sophistication. However, the industry of hand-woven fabrics (including both *muslin* and *Jamdani*) fell into decline following the separation of India and the Liberation War of Bangladesh in 1971. This decline persisted until the 1980s. At that time, the industry of hand-woven fabrics experienced a revival, thanks to a number of craft development organizations, non-governmental organizations (NGOs), and individuals who came forward to rescue the industry through economic patronization.[109] This intervention expanded the use of the fabrics with respect to other clothes. For example, conventionally, the use of *Jamdani* was limited only to *sarees*. Instead, today the *Jamdani* fabric is widely used as a dress material and for making various products, including home décor. *Jamdani* products are also exported to various countries of the world, thereby contributing greatly to the Bangladesh economy.

Because of this "success," however, designers have recently begun changing the traditional designs of the *Jamdani* in the name of modernization. Moreover, it is also feared that the originality and simplicity of *Jamdani* may be destroyed in the guise of value addition through the curse of globalization.[110]

Based on the above, *Jamdani* was certainly a name that qualified to be protected as a GI in Bangladesh. Even though GIs are used predominantly for the protection of agricultural goods, the use of GIs is not limited to agricultural

---

[106] Ghuznavi, *supra* note 100, at 44. [107] *Id.* at 48. [108] Saha, *supra* note 99, at 20.
[109] Ghuznavi, *supra* note 100, at 49. [110] *Id.* at 56.

products. Instead, GIs can be protected also when they identify products whose special qualities are the outcome of human factors like manufacturing skills and traditions, and not necessarily geological and other natural factors.[111] In other words, even though the unique characteristics of *Jamdani* are unlikely to be rooted in the climatic factors and other factors directly dependent from the soil and the land as other products, particularly agricultural products, usually are, *Jamdani* products also carry inimitable characteristics. These characteristics can be essentially attributable to the know-how and the human-factor-based traditions that are rooted in the geographical area where the *Jamdani* fabrics are woven.

Recently, research has been conducted to reconstruct the history of *Jamdani*. After examining historical documents, the researcher has revealed that the overall environment of the area around the river *Shitalakhya* has significantly contributed to the quality of cotton that is used as a raw material of *Jamdani* fabric. In his paper, the researcher has opined that this is perhaps the reason why *Jamdani* has developed in this particular area.[112] Thus, there is no denying of the fact that *Jamdani* has developed its reputation from its place of origin. Accordingly, even though *Jamdani* does not fit into that group of GIs for which natural factors – i.e. the land, the air, and the climate – have an impact on the distinctive qualities of the products, it clearly fits in with the TRIPS' definition based on "other characteristics" and "reputation." In particular, *Jamdani* fabrics derive their characteristics and reputation only from a particular place or territory in Bangladesh.

Another question might be whether GI protection should be extended only to names that are also the names of a place or territory. Famous examples in this respect include Darjeeling tea, Thai silk, Parmesan cheese, etc. The current law on GI protection, however, does not require that the GI names correspond to a geographical name, so long as the GI-denominated products originate from a clearly defined region. Examples in this respect include Vinho Verde, Cava, and Argan oil.[113] By making reputation an independent criterion for GI protection, TRIPS implies that it is not the

---

[111] World Intellectual Property Organization (WIPO), *Geographical Indications: An Introduction*, 10, WIPO Doc. 952(E).

[112] Iftekhar Iqbal, A Research Report on Protection of "Jamdani" as a Geographical Indication in Bangladesh, 2–6 (March 28, 2014), available at https://scarydriver.files.wordpress.com/2015/03/gi-study-report-final-revised-28-march-2014.pdf. This paper was a collaborative initiative of the Centre for Policy Dialogue (CPD) and the National Crafts council of Bangladesh (NCCB). It presented the dialogue on Protecting Geographical Indication Products in the Context of Bangladesh and Way forward.

[113] WIPO, *supra* note 111, at 9.

name of the geographical area but the significance of the geographical area as it attaches to the name of the products that has to be considered.[114] Here again, the GI Act of 2013 supports this interpretation,[115] which paved the way to protecting *Jamdani* as a GI in Bangladesh.

Ultimately, in November 2016, *Jamdani* was registered as the first GI of Bangladesh under the GI Act of 2013.[116] Bangladesh Small and Cottage Industries Corporation (BSCIC) applied for the registration of *Jamdani* in class 25(cloth) for *saree*, which is the traditional wear of Bangladeshi women. BSCIC submitted several documents to get the registration. These documents reveal historical and geographical facts and evidence to establish the nexus between the fabric and the place where it is produced.[117] The authority concerned, Department of Patents, Designs and Trade Marks (DPDT), after conducting a meticulous examination of the submitted documents, finally registered *Jamdani* on November 18, 2016, and the certificate of the registration was handed to the chairman of BSCIC.[118]

6 CONCLUSION

It goes without saying that the adoption of the GI Act of 2013 in Bangladesh has paved the way for the protection of traditional products nationally and possibly abroad, if Bangladeshi GIs could be registered in other countries. However, the enactment of the GI Act of 2013 is merely the first step in a longer process of recognition, commercialization, and management of Bangladeshi GIs and GI-denominated products. Moreover, alone, the GI Act may not be adequate to successfully protect the cultural heritage of Bangladesh. In any event, in order to preserve the cultural heritage of Bangladesh, the first task to be undertaken is to identify products that can be protected as GIs. These products, and the GIs that identify them, should then be brought under the registration mechanism now put into place by the GI Act of 2013 as has been the case with the registration of *Jamdani* in November 2016.

To make this possible, however, a vigorous campaign may be needed to alert stakeholders and make them sensitive to the importance of GI registration. Still, we may have to wait several years to adequately determine the

---

[114] Gopalakrishnan, Nair & Babu, *supra* note 5, at 14.
[115] GI Act of 2013, *supra* note 6, ch. II §§4–5.
[116] The Daily Star, *Jamdani Finally Gets Recognition*, at 1 (November 19 2016).
[117] Department of Patents, Designs and Trade Marks, The Geographical Indication (GI) Journal, Journal No 1, (March 2016).
[118] The Daily Star, *supra* note 116, at 1.

success of the GI Act of 2013 in relation to an effective protection of GIs in Bangladesh. Certainly, the enactment of the GI Act is aligning the legal system in Bangladesh with countries that have a tradition of protecting GIs, and this in turn creates the legal conditions for creating an effective system for the protection of cultural heritage and tradition of Bangladesh. An effective protection for Bagladeshi products can only come, however, from long-term wise management of national products and their names, and not only from GI registration.

19

From Chianti to Kimchi: Geographical Indications, Intangible Cultural Heritage, and Their Unsettled Relationship with Cultural Diversity

Tomer Broude[*]

1 INTRODUCTION

This chapter provides a critical perspective on the impact of two particular international legal constructs – geographical indications (GIs) and intangible cultural heritage (ICH) – on cultural diversity, with a focus on culinary culture. International law increasingly comprises a broad range of direct and indirect interactions with cultural diversity, such as international trade law, international human rights law, and cultural heritage law itself.[1]

The law of GIs, the form of intellectual property protection that is the main topic of this edited volume, is certainly relevant in this respect, and GIs are often casually mentioned as being potentially useful in the promotion and protection of cultural diversity.[2] So is the evolving law of ICH, a concept that

---

[*] Sylvan M. Cohen Chair in Law and Academic Director, Minerva Center for Human Rights, Faculty of Law and Department of International Relations, Hebrew University of Jerusalem. This chapter, with the exception of section IV(b) (on Kimchi-making), builds on and adapts a previously published chapter, Tomer Broude, A *Diet Too Far? Intangible Cultural Heritage, Cultural Diversity, and Culinary Practices*, in DIVERSITY IN INTELLECTUAL PROPERTY: IDENTITIES, INTERESTS, AND INTERSECTIONS 472 (Irene Calboli & Srividhya Ragavan eds., 2015).

[1] *See* JANET BLAKE, INTERNATIONAL CULTURAL HERITAGE LAW (2015); CULTURAL DIVERSITY IN INTERNATIONAL LAW: THE EFFECTIVENESS OF THE UNESCO CONVENTION ON THE PROTECTION AND PROMOTION OF THE DIVERSITY OF CULTURAL EXPRESSIONS (Lilian Richieri Hanania ed., 2014); JINGXIA SHI, FREE TRADE AND CULTURAL DIVERSITY IN INTERNATIONAL LAW (2013); CULTURAL HERITAGE, CULTURAL RIGHTS, CULTURAL DIVERSITY: NEW DEVELOPMENTS IN IN INTERNATIONAL LAW (Silvia Borelli & Federico Lenzerini eds., 2012); TANIA VOON, CULTURAL PRODUCTS AND THE WORLD TRADE ORGANIZATION (2007).

[2] *See* Tomer Broude, *Taking "Trade and Culture" Seriously: GIs and Cultural Protection in WTO Law*, 26 PENN. J. INT'L L. 623 (2005) (providing some examples and critical analysis) [hereinafter Broude, *Trade and Culture*].

can overlap, and in certain circumstances may even conflict[3] with traditional intellectual property rights,[4] although in formal senses it is distinct from intellectual property. The 2003 Convention for the Safeguarding of the Intangible Cultural Heritage (CSICH), adopted under the auspices of the United Nations Educational, Scientific, and Cultural Organization (UNESCO), does not in itself establish intellectual property rights, whether individual or collective,[5] and indeed carefully distances itself from internationally recognized intellectual property disciplines, such as GIs.[6] Moreover, ICH is "not necessarily original or unique"[7] – hardly the makings of classical intellectual property rights. Yet like GIs, ICH also unmistakably interacts with cultural diversity – the CSICH itself goes so far as to state that ICH, with all its uncertainties, is "a mainspring of cultural diversity."[8]

Similarly, both GIs and ICH have a special, though far from exclusive, affinity with culinary cultural practices. GIs are certainly assigned to various nonfood products, but are most clearly associated with agricultural products, as the ongoing debate (especially in Europe) on the extension of GI protection to nonagricultural products demonstrates.[9] As for ICH, the "Representative List of the Intangible Cultural Heritage of Humanity" under Article 16 of the CSICH[10] (the "Representative List") and the "List of Intangible Cultural

---

[3] See, e.g., E. Wanda George, *Intangible Cultural Heritage, Ownership, Copyrights and Tourism*, 4 INT'L J. OF CULTURE, TOURISM & HOSPITALITY RES. 376 (2010) (discussing potential conflicts with copyright law).

[4] See LUCAS LIXINSKI, INTANGIBLE CULTURAL HERITAGE IN INTERNATIONAL LAW 175 (2013) (providing an extensive discussion of intellectual property tools for addressing ICH) [hereinafter LIXINSKI, INTANGIBLE CULTURAL HERITAGE].

[5] UNESCO Convention for the Safeguarding of the Intangible Cultural Heritage, October 17, 2003, 2368 U.N.T.S. 1 [hereinafter CSICH]. The CSICH does not grant property rights, although "ownership" of ICH, in a social, non-property law sense, is implicit through repeated references to State Parties, communities (indigenous communities in particular), groups, and "in some cases, individuals" as creators and bearers of ICH.

[6] See CSICH, art. 3: "Nothing in this Convention may be interpreted as: [...] (b) affecting the rights and obligations of States Parties deriving from any international instrument relating to intellectual property rights ..." Id.

[7] *2003 Convention for the Safeguarding of the Intangible Cultural Heritage – Media Kit*, UNESCO (2014), www.unesco.org/culture/ich/doc/src/18440-EN.pdf [hereinafter UNESCO, Media Kit].

[8] See CSICH, 2nd Preambular Recital.

[9] See, e.g., *Making the Most out of Europe's Traditional Know-How: A Possible Extension of Geographical Indication Protection of the European Union to Non-Agricultural Products*, COM (2014) 469 final (July 15, 2014).

[10] See CSICH, art. 16(1) ("In order to ensure better visibility of the intangible cultural heritage and awareness of its significance, and to encourage dialogue which respects cultural diversity, the Committee, upon the proposal of the States Parties concerned, shall establish, keep up to date and publish a Representative List ...").

Heritage in Need of Urgent Safeguarding" under Article 17 of the same Convention[11] (the "Urgent Safeguarding List") now include a broad variety of over 300 "elements" from all around the world, ranging from Madagascan wood-carving[12] to Karabakh horse-riding games.[13] The lion's share of these is not related to food, but some of these elements relate, directly or indirectly, to culinary practices – food, beverage, and culinary customs can surely be "cultural," whether in their production or consumption or their social representations of identities,[14] even if they are often in need of special, apologetic, justification.

Just as GIs include Champagne, Darjeeling, and Parmigiano Reggiano, inscribed ICH elements include culinary ones such as the *Mediterranean Diet*,[15] the *Gastronomic Meal of the French*,[16] and *Traditional Mexican Cuisine – Ancestral, Ongoing Community Culture, the Michoacán Paradigm*,[17] and *Kimjang, Making and Sharing Kimchi in the Republic of Korea*.[18] Thus, both GIs and ICH lie at the intersection between cultural diversity and culinary practice. In this chapter I will discuss whether GIs and the legalized mechanisms of the CSICH can contribute to the protection and promotion of cultural diversity. My partial focus is on culinary practices, but the analytical framework is not specifically tailored to them, so that the analysis and discussion can certainly be extended to other types of GIs and ICH. Generally, my view of the effectiveness of GIs and ICH in this respect is

---

[11] *See Id.*, art. 17(1) ("With a view to taking appropriate safeguarding measures, the Committee shall establish, keep up to date and publish a List of Intangible Cultural Heritage in Need of Urgent Safeguarding, and shall inscribe such heritage on the List at the request of the State Party concerned.").

[12] *See Woodcrafting Knowledge of the Zafimaniry*, UNESCO, www.unesco.org/culture/ich/en/RL/woodcrafting-knowledge-of-the-zafimaniry-00080 (last visited March 21, 2016); U.N. Educ., Sci., & Cultural Org., Convention for the Safeguarding of the Intangible Cultural Heritage, Intergovernmental Committee for the Safeguarding of Intangible Cultural Heritage, November 8, 2008, U.N. Doc. ITH/08/3.COM/CONF.203/1, www.unesco.org/culture/ich/en/Decisions/3.COM/1 [hereinafter "ICSICH"].

[13] *See Chovqan, a Traditional Karabakh Horse-Riding Game in the Republic of Azerbaijan*, UNESCO, www.unesco.org/culture/ich/en/USL/chovqan-a-traditional-karabakh-horse-riding-game-in-the-republic-of-azerbaijan-00905 (last visited March 21, 2016); U.N. Educ., Sci., & Cultural Org., Convention for the Safeguarding of the Intangible Cultural Heritage, Intergovernmental Committee for the Safeguarding of the Intangible Cultural Heritage, December 7, 2013, U.N. Doc. ITH/13/8.COM/Decisions, www.unesco.org/culture/ich/en/8com.

[14] *See* Broude, *Trade and Culture, supra* note 2, at 642–44.   [15] *Id.*

[16] U.N. Educ., Sci., & Cultural Org., Convention for the Safeguarding of the Intangible Cultural Heritage, Intergovernmental Committee for the Safeguarding of the Intangible Cultural Heritage, November 19, 2010, U.N. Doc. ITH/10/5.COM/CONF.202/Decisions, www.unesco.org/culture/ich/en/5com.

[17] *Id.*   [18] *Id.*

critical, even skeptical, because their impact on cultural diversity will be uncertain and inconsistent, if not perverse.

Given the focus of this book, an exposition of GIs is not required here. However, it is necessary to dwell on the main legal and institutional elements of ICH and the CSICH, and this will be done in Section 2. In Section 3, I will discuss the relationship between the concepts of ICH and cultural diversity, taking into account the respective legal contexts of the CSICH and UNESCO cultural diversity law, primarily the 2005 Convention on the Promotion and Protection of the Diversity of Cultural Expressions (the CCD).[19] The section builds on a positive framework I have previously developed elsewhere[20] with respect to GIs as a point of reference for the purpose of critically assessing the effectiveness of legal measures ostensibly aimed at the protection and promotion of cultural diversity. Section 4 loosely applies this framework to two culinary practices inscribed as ICH: the *Mediterranean Diet*, and (as a more specific example from Asia) *Kimjang, Making and Sharing Kimchi in the Republic of Korea*. Section 5 concludes with general observations on the prospects and pitfalls of applying legal frameworks to the dynamics of cultural diversity.

2 INTANGIBLE CULTURAL HERITAGE AND THE CONVENTION FOR THE SAFEGUARDING OF THE INTANGIBLE CULTURAL HERITAGE: A CRITICAL PRIMER

In this section, I shall neither provide a detailed exposition of the concept of ICH nor a full commentary on the CSICH. These are already available, mainly through the work of scholars and experts who were close to the drafting process of the CSICH.[21] Instead, I will merely survey some fundamentals that

---

[19] UNESCO Convention on the Protection and Promotion of the Diversity of Cultural Expressions (Diversity Convention) art. 2(1), October 20, 2005 [hereinafter CCD], www.unesco.org/fileadmin/MULTIMEDIA/HQ/CLT/CLT/pdf/conventiontext_og_civilsociety_en.pdf.

[20] See, e.g., Broude, Trade and Culture, supra note 2.

[21] See, e.g., Mohammed Bedjaoui, The Convention for the Safeguarding of the Intangible Cultural Heritage: The Legal Framework and Universally Recognized Principles, 56 MUSEUM INT'L 150 (2004); Toshiyuki Kono & Julia Cornett, What is Intangible Cultural Heritage? An Analysis of the Convention for Safeguarding of Intangible Cultural Heritage and the Requirement of Compatibility with Human Rights, in SAFEGUARDING INTANGIBLE CULTURAL HERITAGE: CHALLENGES AND APPROACHES: A COLLECTION OF ESSAYS (Janet Blake ed., 2007); JANET BLAKE, COMMENTARY ON THE 2003 UNESCO CONVENTION ON THE SAFEGUARDING OF THE INTANGIBLE CULTURAL HERITAGE (2006); but see, e.g., Federico Lenzerini, Intangible Cultural Heritage: The Living Culture of Peoples, 22 EUR. J. OF INT'L L. 101 (2011); and LIXINSKI, INTANGIBLE CULTURAL HERITAGE, supra note 4.

are necessary for an analysis of the potential impact of the CSICH on cultural diversity in culinary practices.

In the most general of terms, the CSICH reflects the understanding that significant dimensions of humanity's cultural heritage are encapsulated not in physical and inanimate (i.e., tangible) artifacts, monuments, or sites but rather in living practice and knowledge. Furthermore, the CSICH is explicitly driven by the fear that "the processes of globalization and social transformation" give rise to "grave threats of deterioration, disappearance and destruction" of ICH.[22]

Article 2(2) of the CSICH refers to a non-exhaustive list of five "domains" in which ICH is revealed: oral traditions and expressions (including language); performing arts; social practices, rituals, and festive events; knowledge and practices concerning nature and the universe; and traditional craftsmanship.[23] This very broad range of ICH manifestations is amplified by the even broader overarching definition: "Intangible Cultural Heritage" means "the practices, representations, expressions, knowledge, skills – as well as the instruments, objects, artefacts and cultural spaces associated therewith – that communities, groups and, in some cases, individuals recognize as part of their cultural heritage."[24]

Despite the best efforts of the drafters of the CSICH (or not),[25] these definitions raise significant problems of legal application and operationalization, if taken seriously. First, they seem exceedingly broad, with no clear outer limits. In this respect, it is not very helpful to observe that "not all human cultural activity is defined as [ICH]."[26] The drafters of the CSICH may have assumed that ICH is first and foremost limited to "traditional" culture, as opposed to new, contemporary, or modern cultural expressions, but this is not effectively reflected in the text,[27] which is ultimately very inclusive. Indeed,

---

[22] See CSICH, *supra* note 5, 2nd Preambular Recital. [23] See *Id.*, art. 2(2).
[24] See *Id.*, art. 2(1).
[25] See Lucas Lixinski, *Selecting Heritage: The Interplay of Art, Politics and Identity*, 22 EUR. J. OF INT'L L. 81, 94 (2011) (noting that there was resistance among drafters toward establishing specific legal obligations of protection in the CSICH).
[26] See Richard Kurin, *Safeguarding Intangible Cultural Heritage in the 2003 UNESCO Convention: A Critical Appraisal*, 56 MUSEUM INT'L 66, 69 (2004).
[27] See CSICH, *supra* note 5, art. 2(1). Article 2(1) does refer to ICH as being "transmitted from generation to generation," implying a requirement of some intergenerational history and tradition, and indeed most applications for inscription in the Representative List allude to such transmission. But arguably, contemporary traditions would also qualify as ICH, even "invented traditions," as elaborated by Hobsbawm. See Eric Hobsbawm, *Introduction: Inventing Traditions*, in THE INVENTION OF TRADITION 1–14 (Eric Hobsbawm & Terence Ranger eds., 1983).

UNESCO prides itself on the inclusiveness of the CSICH.[28] Thus, to the extent that the CSICH establishes rights and obligations of states parties to it, the scope of application appears to be both very far-reaching and inadequately delimited.

Second, the general definition of ICH seems to be particularly wooly. Indeed, on its face, it appears to be utterly tautological and self-selecting: ICH is what someone "recognize[s] as part of their cultural heritage."[29] It is not clear in what sense the word "recognize" is employed here – is it declarative or constitutive, objective or subjective, or some combination thereof? Some commentators have embraced this "self-identification" character of ICH, citing it as an indication of a significant "philosophical" rationale of the CSICH that distinguishes it from the 1972 World Heritage Convention, making ICH totally dependent upon the "subjective perspective of its creators and bearers."[30] In theory, such unchecked self-selection is problematic. In practice, it is disingenuous. While it applies to ICH in general, the more robust inscription and listing processes under Articles 16 and 17 CSICH,[31] discussed below as the hardcore of CSICH substance, ultimately require institutional, political, non-idiosyncratic approval.

Third, in one fell swoop, tangible elements are clearly incorporated into the intangible realm of cultural heritage. Indeed, by any account, the tangible and intangible components of cultural heritage are difficult, if not impossible, to disentangle.[32] But the CSICH only glosses over this connection, leaving open operative questions relating to the degree of dependence of ICH on tangible components and vice versa.

Fourth, none of the constituent terms (such as "practices," "representations," "artefacts," "cultural spaces,"[33] etc.) is defined anywhere. These are terms whose meanings are gradually being filled post hoc and ad hoc through the work of expert and/or intergovernmental bodies at UNESCO, but whose forward-looking and conduct-defining capacities are a priori limited. Indeed,

---

[28] UNESCO, *Media Kit*. [29] *See* CSICH, art. 2(1). [30] Lenzerini, *supra* note 21, at 108.
[31] *See* CSICH, arts. 16(2), 17(2) (prescribing that "[t]he Committee shall draw up and submit to the General Assembly for approval the criteria for the establishment, updating and publication of this Representative List").
[32] *See, e.g.*, Mounir Bouchenaki, *The Interdependency of the Tangible and Intangible Cultural Heritage*, in 14th ICOMOS General Assembly and International Symposium, *Place, Memory, Meaning: Preserving Intangible Values in Monuments and Sites*, October 27–31, 2003, http://openarchive.icomos.org/468/; *see also* CSICH, 1st Preambular Recital (referring to the "deep-seated interdependence" between the tangible and intangible cultural heritage).
[33] *See* CSICH, art. 2(1).

even the Operational Directives prepared and adopted under the CSICH do not add formal clarity in this respect.[34]

Fifth, the relationship between the safeguarding of ICH, on the one hand, and other potentially overriding public policy considerations, on the other hand, is not sufficiently clarified in the CSICH, to say the least. The anthropological definition of culture is broad enough to include "almost all aspects of human behavior," including practices that violate human rights[35] or even Female Genital Mutilation.[36] The drafters of the CSICH were well aware of such potential conflicts, and attempted to embed ICH within a human rights context. Already the 1st recital of the CSICH refers to "international human rights instruments,"[37] alluding not only to economic, social, and cultural rights but also to civil and political rights. Article 2(1) CSICH, in its third sentence, provides that the Convention will consider ICH only if it "is compatible with existing international human rights instruments, as well as with the requirements of mutual respect among communities, groups and individuals, and of sustainable development."[38] As far as human rights are concerned, this clearly raises the problem of cultural relativism, and no less importantly, of cultural politics.[39] The phrasing of the relevant part of Article 2 CSICH is fuzzy, much less resolute than its corollary in Article 2(1) CCD, which clearly provides that no one may invoke the CCD in order "to infringe human rights and fundamental freedoms as enshrined in the Universal Declaration of Human Rights or guaranteed by international law, or to limit the scope thereof."[40] But in any case, the potential for conflict is considerable, entering dangerous and politically sensitive waters.

The above are general definitional problems regarding the CSICH. What of its substance? The purposes of the CSICH under Article 1 include "safeguarding" ICH, "ensur[ing] respect" for ICH, "raising awareness" of the importance of ICH, and providing for international cooperation and assistance.[41]

---

[34] See UNESCO (2012), *for the Implementation of the Convention for the Safeguarding of the Intangible Cultural Heritage*, adopted by the General Assembly of the States Parties to the Convention at its second ordinary session (Paris, France, June 16–19, 2008), amended at its third session (Paris, France, June 22–24, 2010), at its fourth session (Paris, France, June 4–8, 2012), and its fifth session (Paris, France, June 2–4, 2014) [hereinafter UNESCO, *Operational Directives*].

[35] See William S. Logan, *Closing Pandora's Box: Human Rights Conundrums in Cultural Heritage Protection*, in CULTURAL HERITAGE AND HUMAN RIGHTS 33 (Helaine Silverman & D. Fairchild Ruggles eds. 2007) (using the Ku Klux Klan rituals as an example).

[36] Kurin, *supra* note 26, at 70.   [37] CSICH, 1st Recital.   [38] See CSICH, art. 2(1).

[39] Logan, *supra* note 35, at 39 (showing the most scathing critique of the political and indeed hegemonic nature of cultural heritage, which can be found in her exposition of "Authorized Heritage Discourse"); *see* LAURAJANE SMITH, USES OF HERITAGE (2006).

[40] CCD, *supra* note 19, art. 2.   [41] CISCH, art. 1.

Safeguarding is perhaps the most important of these operative purposes, and is defined very broadly in Article 2(3) CSICH as "measures aimed at ensuring the viability of the [ICH]," including softer yet more technical measures such as identification, documentation, research, and education, but also harder and potentially much broader measures such as "preservation, promotion, enhancement, [and] transmission."[42]

How does the CSICH translate these goals into concrete rights and obligations? At the national level (Title III, CSICH),[43] states parties are subject to a broad obligation to take "necessary measures to ensure the safeguarding of ICH present in [their] territory."[44] These measures consist mainly of drawing up inventories, submitting periodic reports to the CSICH Committee, adopting policies for promoting ICH in society, establishing institutions, fostering research, and adopting other measures, including financial ones to this end.[45] States parties also endeavor to ensure education, awareness, and capacity building, all with participation of communities, groups, and where appropriate, individuals who are creators and bearers of ICH.[46] In short, the obligations are very general, discretionary, policy-oriented, and lacking in terms of enforceability and accountability. This is not to say that the provisions on safeguarding of ICH at the national level may not have any legal consequences whatsoever, e.g., in the justification of measures taken in provisional violation of other international obligations (such as under trade and investment agreements), but I will not address this potential here.

At the international level, under Title IV of the CSICH,[47] legal commitment is even less apparent. The central construct of the CSICH is the establishment of the Representative List, the Urgent Safeguarding List, and a list of programs, projects, and activities, as articulated in Article 18.[48] Although the drawing up of these lists constitutes the bulk of the institutional and procedural work under the CSICH (and their political highlight), it bears emphasizing that the convention itself does not appear to produce any explicit legal consequences to inscription in them. The Representative List has been established merely to "ensure better visibility," etc., as reflected in Article 16(1) of the CSICH,[49] and the Urgent Safeguarding List exists only "with a view to taking appropriate safeguarding measures" (Article 17(1) CSICH),[50] although nothing seems to prevent states parties from taking such measures notwithstanding inscriptive status of a particular item. Again,

---

[42] Id., art. 2(3).　[43] Id., arts. 11–15.　[44] Id., art. 11.　[45] See CSICH, art. 13.
[46] See Id., art. 15.　[47] See Id., arts. 16–18.　[48] See Id., art. 18.　[49] See Id., art. 16(1).
[50] See Id., art. 17(1).

inclusion in the lists may have evidentiary or indirect legal implications in other normative systems, but the absence of express legal consequences in the CSICH is striking.

3 LAW'S UNCERTAIN IMPACT ON CULTURAL DIVERSITY: FROM INTANGIBLE CULTURAL HERITAGE TO GEOGRAPHICAL INDICATIONS AND BACK AGAIN

With these general critical comments on the CSICH as an international legal instrument in mind, what indeed is the purported relationship between ICH and cultural diversity, writ large? As already mentioned, in its 2nd preambular recital, the CSICH denotes ICH as "a mainspring of cultural diversity."[51] What does this mean, at least in theory? Indeed, this very phrase might be cause for concern and confusion. In English, "mainspring" refers to the driving force of a mechanical device. Yet in the other equally authoritative language texts of the CSICH (as per Article 39),[52] the word employed is quite different (e.g., *Creuset* in French, *Crisol* in Spanish) – meaning "crucible" or "melting pot[.]"[53] Cultural diversity is surely not a mechanical device, and melting pots (indeed a culinary phrase) produce uniformity, not diversity, the very term strongly associated with assimilationist and homogenizing (even "Americanizing") approaches to immigrant cultures.[54]

This suboptimal clarity in the formulation of the relationship between ICH and cultural diversity in the CSICH's very preamble, I would suggest, is not merely textual, or (only) a matter of drafting, but rather stems from the essential dialectics and conceptual differences underlying the interlocking projects of safeguarding ICH and protecting and promoting cultural diversity. It is also a reflection of the inherent tensions between socio-anthropological conceptions of culture as fluid, dynamic, and "living" (a term which inevitably implies also the possibility of extinguishment, and "dying," although this is rarely, if ever, acknowledged), on the one hand, and advocacy tendencies to agitate for positive, legalized protection, on the

---

[51] *Id.*, 2nd Preambular Recital.   [52] *Id.*, art. 39.
[53] It is rare, though not unheard of, for different authentic language texts of treaties to have such widely discrepant meanings. *See* Bradly J. Condon, *Lost in Translation: Plurilingual Interpretation of WTO Law*, 1 J. OF INT'L DISPUTE SETTLEMENT 191 (2010).
[54] *See, e.g.,* Horace M. Kallen, *Democracy Versus the Melting Pot: A Study of American Nationality*, THE NATION, February 25, 1915 (critiquing cultural diversity in immigrant cultures).

other hand. It also casts more than a shadow of doubt on the very need and justification for the CSICH, and their nature, to begin with.

Having said that, and without any conviction that these tensions can or should be reconciled in an international institutional manner, I would make the following proposition regarding the structural and interpretative relationship between ICH and cultural diversity, which is consistent with both the CSICH and the CCD. Simpliciter, the CSICH at least aims to do exactly what it says it will do, namely, "safeguard"[55] ICH (a term that in itself encapsulates the tension between the dynamic nature of culture and the more static nature of legal protection). Thus, for example, the knowledge of following a particular culinary recipe or method – say, Tiramisu, Bresaola, or Biltong – might be an ICH "item." However, ICH – as an abstract concept, and as a collection of particular ICH "items" – is not a goal unto itself; rather, the aim is the protection and promotion of cultural diversity. The 2nd preambular recital of the CSICH indeed refers to the dangers of the "deterioration, disappearance and destruction" of ICH, but it does so in the broader context of cultural diversity.[56] The traditional making of each of Tiramisu, Bresaola, and Biltong, as we know them today, may each deteriorate and disappear, as many other traditional practices have died out over the centuries. The threat to be countered is not this dynamic process of change and recreation, but the fear that "the rich cultural variety of humanity is progressively and dangerously tending towards uniformity[,]"[57] i.e., not the disappearance of ICH expressions as such, but the erosion of cultural diversity, as an overarching value.

If this understanding of the role of ICH in cultural diversity (including culinary aspects) indeed manifests the deeper teleology of the CSICH, how is it expressed in the operational strategy(ies) of the conventions?

One approach would be a "kitchen sink" attitude to diversity in ICH, the-more-the-merrier. Anything remotely resembling ICH (e.g., any culinary or dietary dimension) is worthy, non-judgmentally, of safeguarding and promotive of diversity. This possibility is evident, for example, in Article 7 of the 2001 UNESCO Universal Declaration on Cultural Diversity, noting that "heritage in all its forms must be preserved, enhanced and handed on to future generations ...,"[58] as well as in Article 13 of the UNESCO 2003 Main Lines of an Action Plan for the Implementation of [the Declaration], which referred to the formulation of policies and strategies for the "preservation and

---

[55] CSICH, art. 2.   [56] *Id.*, 2nd Preambular Recital.   [57] Lenzerini, *supra* note 21, at 103.
[58] *See* UNESCO *Universal Declaration on Cultural Diversity*, UNESCO, art. 7, http://unesdoc.unesco.org/images/0012/001271/127162e.pdf.

enhancement" of "notably the oral and intangible cultural heritage."[59] This would amount to a *laissez-faire* approach in cultural terms, an approach that would cover anything that could fit a very broad definition of ICH, neither creating nor helpful to legal regulation based on a given set of established priorities.

In this respect, an alternative approach could be to be much more selective in deciding the relevance of ICH expressions for safeguarding because of its contribution to cultural diversity. Inclusion could thus be subject to criteria that promote policy goals, such as cultural diversity (for example, the need for "a better thematic, cultural and geographical balance" in cultural heritage).[60] Taken to an extreme, expressions of ICH would have to be selected for safeguarding according to predefined criteria. This appears, in fact, to be the unspoken strategy of the CSICH. Inscription in the Representative List (or Urgent Safeguarding List) reflects an understanding whereby listing (i.e., inclusion in the lists) makes a positive contribution to the safeguarding of ICH, which in turn makes a contribution to cultural diversity. Inscription in the lists therefore seems to be the crux (if not crucible) of the matter. And hence, the criteria for inscription become crucial, although they are not defined in the CSICH itself, and have instead been elaborated through expert and intergovernmental decisions and ultimately in the Operational Directives.[61]

Turning to the inscription criteria themselves, the first criterion merely requires that the "element" constitute ICH,[62] adding nothing to the Article 2 CSICH definition. The second criterion is that inscription will contribute to visibility and awareness toward ICH, a purely discretionary call.[63] The third criterion requires a program for protection and promotion of the element – but demands no accountability from those who would promote and preserve under such a program.[64] The fourth criterion requires community/group/individual support for the element's nomination, as a possible counterweight to institutional biases, but is certainly not difficult to satisfy.[65] And the fifth criterion requires some sovereign commitment by the states in whose territory the ICH is present – again, not a tall order, by any measure.[66] These criteria

---

[59] See UNESCO, *Main Lines of an Action Plan for the Implementation of the UNESCO Declaration on Cultural Diversity*, art. 13.

[60] See Marie-Theres Albert, *World Heritage and Cultural Diversity: What Do they Have in Common?*, in WORLD HERITAGE AND CULTURAL DIVERSITY 17, 18 (Dieter Offenhäußer et al. eds., 2010).

[61] UNESCO, *Operational Directives*, supra note 34.   [62] See Id., ch. I.1: U.1.

[63] See Id., ch. I.1: U.2.   [64] See Id., ch. I.1: U.3.

[65] See Id., ch. I.1: U.4; see, e.g., Lixinski supra note 25.

[66] See UNESCO, *Operational Directives*, supra note 34, ch. I.1: U.5.

seem quite meaningless in a normative sense – perhaps especially so, when dealt with in the culinary field.

Thus, it would appear, between the inoperability of full inclusiveness, on the one hand, and the impossibility and nonpolitical correctness of substantive cultural criteria, the CSICH follows the poorest possible path, subjecting inclusion in the ICH lists to political and diplomatic decision-making, while paying some lip-service to non-sovereign community expressions of concern. The gnawing doubts remain. Can, and should, such a legal and institutional structure safeguard ICH? Can it protect and promote cultural diversity, any more than conventional intellectual property may? Does it have any real relevance to cultural expressions?

In a previous study,[67] I asked very similar questions with respect to the purported role of GIs in cultural diversity. This was undertaken in the particular context of GIs for food and wine products, as beneficiaries of enhanced international legal protection under the Agreement on Trade Related Aspects of Intellectual Property Rights ("TRIPS Agreement"),[68] with distinct effects on the regulation and indeed restriction of international trade.[69] My conclusions were unequivocal: GIs "as legal mechanisms ... evidently do not have the independent capacity to protect local cultures ... or to prevent the erosion of cultural diversity. Market forces inevitably induce changes in local production methods and consumption preferences, in spite of the [GIs] that should, in theory, play a role in preserving them."[70] Thus, the goal of cultural diversity, in itself, cannot justify the special commercial advantages granted by GIs as intellectual property (or quasi-intellectual property) rights to certain food products. There may be other justifications, but it does not seem that the protection and promotion of cultural diversity is one of them.

Moreover, there does not appear to have emerged any countervailing logic or evidence over the last decade. In this respect, it is in fact worth clarifying and emphasizing that at no point does the argument against the utility and effectiveness of legal protections of culinary cultural diversity – whether through GIs, or the concept of ICH, for that matter – target

---

[67] Broude, *Trade and Culture*, supra note 2.
[68] Agreement on Trade-Related Aspects of Intellectual Property Rights, April 15, 1994, Marrakesh Agreement Establishing the World Trade Organization, Annex 1C, LEGAL INSTRUMENTS – RESULT OF THE URUGUAY ROUNDS vol. 31, 33 I.L.M. 81 (1994) [hereinafter TRIPS].
[69] In the present chapter, focused as it is on ICH and culinary practices, I will ignore the potential implications of the CSICH, for all its normative "softness," in the arena of international trade regulation.
[70] Broude, *Trade and Culture*, supra note 2, at 678.

"a preservationist notion of cultural heritage[,]" or rely upon the drawing of "binary distinctions between tradition and innovation[.]"[71] To be sure, as already discussed, such static/preservationist notions do exist in both scholarly work and legal formulations, often in tension with the more fluid and dynamic concepts of culture, which I most certainly share. However, the analysis of the irrefutably immense and fundamental changes in the substantive content of (model) protected GIs (such as the wine Appellations of Origin of Chianti Classico or St. Joseph, as mere cases in point)[72] does not just describe the occurrence of these changes, and certainly does not decry them as such. Rather, the critique seeks to explain these changes as primarily driven by markets, local and global, and/or by regulatory capture, despite legal protection. It is these important attributes of the process of change in cultural expressions in the shadow of legal regulation that often negate deep-seated traditions and heritages *of* innovation and cultural evolution. Thus, the values underlying the cultural heritage and diversity discourse are not meaningfully promoted by the legal frameworks that have ostensibly been constructed around them. To belabor the point somewhat, tradition and innovation are mutually conducive, not exclusive, and cultural diversity is a value nourished by both. It is, however, less than clear – rationally and empirically – that legal frameworks, of intellectual property rights or their ilk, truly protect or promote either one or the other.

Moreover, the framework of analysis applied to the cultural impacts of GIs can also relate, *mutatis mutandis*, to the international legal "safeguarding" of ICH. I refer to three dimensions of culture relevant to GIs: the culture of production, in which the process of creating a good – the way in which it is made – endows it with "cultureness"; the culture of consumption, in which a good gains cultural value "by virtue of the context in which it is consumed";[73] and the culture of identity, in which a good is somehow representative of a group's cultural identity. To be sure, with respect to GIs, the focus of these dimensions is on tangible goods – a type of cheese, a wine from a particular region, a cut of beef. Thus, one might ask, how do they apply to ICH? It is always the intangible traditions that endow goods with cultural value: the method of production (how the cheese is made, in which conditions, from which materials), the context of consumption (the cultural preference for one type of wine over another, the ceremonial dimensions of

---

[71] Dev S. Gangjee, *GIs and Cultural Heritage*, 4 WIPO J. 85, 94 (2014).
[72] *See* Broude, *Trade and Culture*, *supra* note 2, at 662–78 (providing several more examples).
[73] *Id.*, at 640.

drinking it, and pairing it with food and social environments), and identity-related recognition (the association of a type of beef with a regional or otherwise group identity). It is these intangible dimensions that culture informs and changes over time and place, but also that markets inevitably apply pressure upon to change, become diluted, even to homogenize, regardless of culture. And it is with respect to these dimensions that we must ask whether legal protections can contribute to the safeguarding, protection, or promotion of culinary cultural diversity.

4 INTANGIBLE CULTURAL HERITAGE, CULTURAL DIVERSITY, AND CULINARY PRACTICES: TWO CASE STUDIES

4.1 The Mediterranean Diet

The *Mediterranean Diet* was inscribed on the Representative List in 2010,[74] at the nomination of Greece, Italy, Morocco, and Spain.[75] In 2013, the supporting parties and geographical range of the item were amended and expanded to include additional "emblematic" communities in Cyprus, Croatia, and Portugal.[76] There are significant differences between the nomination documents in 2010 and 2013 that are worthy of scrutiny, most notably the removal of all references to the nutritional characteristics of the diet.[77] The 2013 resolution defines the *Mediterranean Diet* as "the set of skills, knowledge, rituals, symbols and traditions, ranging from the landscape to the table, which in the Mediterranean basin concerns the crops, harvesting, picking, fishing, animal

---

[74] U.N. Educ., Sci., & Cultural Org., Convention for the Safeguarding of the Intangible Cultural Heritage, Intergovernmental Committee for the Safeguarding of Intangible Cultural Heritage, November 19, 2010, U.N. Doc. ITH/10/5.COM/CONF.202/Decisions [hereinafter 5.COM, 2010].

[75] U.N. Educ., Sci., & Cultural Org., Convention for the Safeguarding of the Intangible Cultural Heritage, Intergovernmental Committee for the Safeguarding of Intangible Cultural Heritage, November 2010, Nomination File No. 00394 [hereinafter UNESCO, CSICH, 5.COM].

[76] U.N. Educ., Sci., & Cultural Org., Convention for the Safeguarding of the Intangible Cultural Heritage, Intergovernmental Committee for the Safeguarding of Intangible Cultural Heritage, December 2013, Nomination File No. 00884 [hereinafter UNESCO, CSICH, 8.COM].

[77] The nomination documents submitted in 2010 included the following definition for the Mediterranean diet: "[A] nutritional model that has remained constant over time and space, consisting mainly of olive oil, cereals, fresh or dried fruit and vegetables, a moderate amount of fish, dairy and meat, and many condiments and spices, all accompanied by wine or infusions, always respecting beliefs of each community." *See* UNESCO, CSICH, 5.COM; U.N. Educ., Sci., & Cultural Org., Convention for the Safeguarding of the Intangible Cultural Heritage, Intergovernmental Committee for the Safeguarding of Intangible Cultural Heritage, October 6, 2010, U.N. Doc. ITH/10/5.COM/CONF.202/6, 52.

husbandry, conservation, processing, cooking, and particularly sharing and consuming the cuisine[.]"[78]

This definition is incredibly broad, almost generic, but for its geographical delimitation.[79] One could substitute the word "Mediterranean" with practically any regional denomination, leaving the rest of the phrasing untouched, and we would have the makings of another equally valid element of ICH. The definition is, of course, somehow augmented by more detailed descriptions – referring, for example, to the importance of ceramic plates and glasses, then to the role of women, families, and various local festivals, as well as passing cultural references to Plutarch and Juvenal and the health and sustainability benefits of the diet, only generally referring to Ancel Keys' seminal studies from which the very term "Mediterranean Diet" emerged.[80] Yet these descriptions are surprisingly paltry, given the wealth of knowledge available on Mediterranean culinary culture.[81] One is struck by the vagueness and all-inclusiveness of the definition of the element to be safeguarded – especially following the removal of reference to the "nutritional model" of the diet, which is its main claim to fame.

Indeed, one might wonder whether such a broadly defined culinary concept as a "diet" (or "meal," or "cuisine") even formally qualifies as ICH. The question is not trivial from legal perspectives. In the context of the CCD, for example, Pulkowski is of the opinion that "in the absence of an element of representation, food items and their protected GIs should not enjoy protection [as cultural expressions]."[82] According to this narrow view, food becomes cultural for the purposes of the CCD only if it expresses a cultural identity. Moreover, until 2008, UNESCO parties and officials displayed negative views on the possibility of inscribing culinary heritage.[83]

---

[78] UNESCO, CSICH, 8.COM, at 6.
[79] The geographical definition is in itself problematic; the Mediterranean diet (or diets) has migrated with "Mediterraneans" to distant corners of the earth, and has also been adopted outside the region due to its purported health effects. See Anne Noah & Arthur Stewart Truswell, *There are Many Mediterranean Diets*, 10 Asia Pac. J. of Clinical Nutrition 2 (2001).
[80] Ancel B. Keys et al., Seven Countries: A Multivariate Analysis of Death and Coronary Heart Disease (1980); Ancel B. Keys & Margaret Keys, How to Eat Well and Stay Well the Mediterranean Way (1975).
[81] See, e.g., MediTERRA 2012: The Mediterranean Diet for Sustainable Regional Development (2012) (including bibliographies).
[82] Dirk Pulkowski, The Law and Politics of International Regime Conflict 163 (2014).
[83] Morgan Figuers, *Monuments, Mountains and ... the Mediterranean Diet? Potential for UNESCO's World Culinary Heritage Inscriptions to Positively Affect Sustainable Agriculture*, 24 Colo. Nat. Res., Energy and Envtl. L. Rev. 419, 440 (2013).

However, the approach followed by the CSICH (and I would venture that also by the CCD, *contra* the above position) clearly emphasizes cultures of production and consumption, perhaps even more than identity. Culinary practices and traditions, therefore, should certainly not be excluded a priori. But in examining the formal descriptions of the *Mediterranean Diet*, one senses such a high degree of generalization that more than a shadow of doubt is cast regarding the prudence and value of this particular inscription. We have already seen the generality of the definition, but what is the *Mediterranean Diet* as a domain of ICH? In its nomination documents for the Representative List, the *Mediterranean Diet* was noted as an oral tradition and expression; a social practice, ritual, and social event; knowledge and practice concerning nature and the universe; and traditional craftsmanship[84] – all the enumerated ICH domains except performing arts. This lack of precision stems, to begin with, from the absence of a recognized ICH domain of culinary heritage, but it also appears to reflect an inability or perhaps unwillingness (or some combination thereof) to clearly define what it actually is that is being inscribed. Clearly, in order to expand the group of CSICH parties supporting the nomination and to avoid alienating others, definitional compromise was required; lowest common denominators were resorted to, with the resultant low level of resolution.

To be sure, the point here is not to question the validity of the claim that there is such a thing as a *Mediterranean Diet* in the cultural or nutritional senses – although some experts do not hesitate to do so,[85] and even some of the *Mediterranean Diet*'s main champions make clear that "despite a long list of shared foods, the Mediterranean is a plural and diverse world, and its food habits could not be otherwise[.]"[86] The critique here is primarily from the perspectives of legal determinacy and functional effectiveness, and relates *in*

---

[84] UNESCO, CSICH, 8.COM, *supra* note 76, at 5.

[85] See, e.g., Noah & Truswell, *supra* note 79 (providing an interview-based research finding that there are important differences in food habits between Mediterranean countries and at least four distinct categories of diets in the Mediterranean basin); Artemis P. Simopoulos, *The Mediterranean Diets: What Is So Special about the Diet of Greece? The Scientific Evidence*, 131 THE J. OF NUTRITION 3065 (2001) (explaining that "[t]he term 'Mediterranean diet,' implying that all Mediterranean people have the same diet, is a misnomer. The countries around the Mediterranean basin have different diets, religions and cultures."

[86] See Isabel González Turmo, *The Mediterranean Diet: Consumption, Cuisine and Food Habits*, in MEDITERRA 2012: THE MEDITERRANEAN DIET FOR SUSTAINABLE REGIONAL DEVELOPMENT 115 (2012) (subsequently listing no fewer than 29 "core typologies," ranging from "cold or warm soups or broths, made with bread, oil, garlic or other spicy or sharp condiments" to "cooked or sweet-fried nuts").

concreto to the previous discussion of the internal and external limits of ICH as a legal and institutional system aimed at promoting and protecting cultural diversity. At minimum, it is difficult to understand how such a vaguely and broadly defined element of ICH can serve as the basis for effective safeguarding. Indeed, in the light of the social, economic, and political sea changes that the Euro-Mediterranean regions have witnessed, even just over the last decade,[87] it seems either tremendously naïve or disingenuous to think that such a vaguely defined item can have any genuine safeguarding effects. Despite the commonalities between them, the inclusion of such different culinary traditions as the Moroccan, Spanish, Italian, Greek, Cypriot, Croatian, and Portuguese under the same *Mare Nostrum* umbrella at least raises the fear that these distinct cultures will indeed be thrown into a melting pot, at the risk of cultural dilution and caricaturization. Proponents of the *Mediterranean Diet* are not oblivious to the additional concern that the inscription will be commercialized and commoditized,[88] but as in the case of GIs, this seems quite likely to happen, whether with respect to products or to food tourism.[89] How this will affect the safeguarding of ICH and the promotion and protection of cultural diversity is impossible to predict.

What is clearer, however, is that the advent of the *Mediterranean Diet* – in 2010, but even more so with its amendments in 2013 – is a child of the new "culinary diplomacy" or "gastrodiplomacy,"[90] reflecting in high relief the fears of both the politicization and the expert reductionism of ICH – with little to show for an effective protection and promotion of cultural diversity.

---

[87] See Senén Florensa & Xavier Aragall, *Mutations in Mediterranean Societies*, in MEDITERRA 2012: THE MEDITERRANEAN DIET FOR SUSTAINABLE REGIONAL DEVELOPMENT 91 (2012), for an excellent big-picture review of social trends (or "mutations" as they call them), some associated with "globalization" others not: changes in values, new lifestyles, religiosity vs. secularization, increased tourism and emigration, and intra-society demographic transitions.

[88] See González Turmo, *supra* note 86, at 115 (noting that "[t]his nomination cannot stand as a mere brandname that can be attached to food products, events and publications").

[89] See Ricardo Mazátlan Páramo, *Gastronomic Heritage and Cultural Tourism: An Exploration of the Notion of Risk in Traditional Mexican Food and the Gastronomic System*, 6 ESSEX GRADUATE J. OF SOCIOLOGY (2006) (discussing the potentially negative impacts of tourism on safeguarding of culinary cultural heritage, in the context of traditional Mexican food).

[90] See Sam Chapple-Sokol, *Culinary Diplomacy: Breaking Bread to Win Hearts and Minds*, 8 THE HAGUE J. OF DIPL. 161 (2013) (exploring the use of foods in diplomacy and international politics); Juyan Zhang, *The Food of the Worlds: Mapping and Comparing Gastrodiplomacy Campaigns*, 9 INT'L J. OF COMMC'N 568 (2015) (comparing and evaluating state campaigns to market national foods internationally, with specific reference to Korean Kimchi, discussed in section IV(b), *infra*).

4.2 Kimjang, Making and Sharing Kimchi in the Republic of Korea

The problems noted above with regard to the ICH inscription of the *Mediterranean Diet* as far as the protection and promotion of cultural diversity are concerned may be in significant part attributed to the highly, indeed overgeneralized and diluted nature of the inscription itself. What, then, of more specific and specialized culinary inscriptions that address particular foods? *Kimjang, Making and Sharing Kimchi in the Republic of Korea* is a noteworthy example. It was inscribed on the Representative List in 2013,[91] at the nomination of the Republic of Korea (South Korea).[92] Kimchi, as a distinct type of food, is defined (indeed, much more specifically than the *Mediterranean Diet*) as "Korean-style[93] preserved vegetables seasoned with local spices and fermented seafood."[94] Notably, the inscribed item reflects both a culture of production (the making of Kimchi) and a culture of consumption (its sharing). Kimchi serves as an omnipresent side-dish in Korean cuisine, and the Nomination File expounds on the long-lasting and pervasive tradition of making Kimchi.[95]

Beyond consumption and production, the ICH item of *Kimjang*, the traditional making of Kimchi, claims to reflect a culture of identity that is much more pronounced than the *Mediterranean Diet*. In Korean eyes, Kimchi is utterly Korean, reflective of a constructed "national spirit." The typical Korean *Kimjang* narrative refers to the geographical seclusion of the Korean peninsula and evokes its long winters and harsh terrain, its twentieth-century poverty, its reliance on the fruit of the sea, and its people's resilience.[96] National pride in

---

[91] U.N. Educ., Sci., & Cultural Org., Convention for the Safeguarding of the Intangible Cultural Heritage, Intergovernmental Committee for the Safeguarding of Intangible Cultural Heritage, December 7, 2013, U.N. Doc. ITH/13/8.COM/Decisions [hereinafter 8. COM, 2013].

[92] U.N. Educ., Sci., & Cultural Org., Convention for the Safeguarding of the Intangible Cultural Heritage, Intergovernmental Committee for the Safeguarding of Intangible Cultural Heritage, December 2013, Nomination File No. 00881 [hereinafter Nomination File].

[93] The qualification Korean-*style* is important. On the one hand, it excludes foods that are not produced in a Korean fashion (as set out in more detail in the Nomination File; *see Id.*). On the other hand, while the inscription relates to *Kimjang* in the Republic of Korea, the qualification recognizes the practice of Kimjang outside of South Korea, such as by Korean diasporas; on the importance of kimchi in Korean ethnic communities in Germany, *see* Gin-Young Song, *Kimchi – Geschmack und Migration: Zur Nahrungskultur von Koreanern in Deutschland* (Studien und Materialien des Ludwig-Uhland-Instituts der Universität Tübingen, 2012).

[94] Nomination File, *supra* note 92, at 3.   [95] *Id.*, at 3–4.

[96] *See* Suk-Heung Oh, Kye Won Park, James W. Daily III & Young-Eun Lee, *Preserving the Legacy of Healthy Korean Food*, 17 J. OF MEDICINAL FOOD 1 (2014).

the purported uniqueness of Kimchi and its effects has even led to the establishment of a governmental "World Institute of Kimchi" that presents an ethos whereby "Kimchi is the soul of Korean cuisine."[97] Outsiders acknowledge Kimchi as "the nearest thing to a culinary national treasure[.]"[98] And there are other talking points, relating to society, health, and gender. Traditional Kimchi-making is praised as "familial and emotionally resonant[.]"[99] Moreover, Kimchi has been associated with positive health effects, including the relative absence of obesity among Koreans,[100] although causality in this respect is uncertain. In social terms we are told that "[A]ll Koreans are [thus] part of one large [K]imjang community, which transcends regional and socio-economic boundaries within Korean society[.]"[101] National pride in Kimchi and its making has gone a long way – indeed as far as outer space.[102] Notably, in the ICH Nomination File, South Korea only applied two ICH domains ("social practices," etc., and "practices concerning nature") – leaving out "traditional craftsmanship" – thus, perhaps, emphasizing the social aspects of *Kimjang* rather than the specificities of traditional production. Driving home the importance of *Kimjang* in Korean society, the Nomination File cites a survey according to which "95.7 percent of Koreans reported regularly eating homemade kimchi either prepared within their households, or supplied by other family members or acquaintances. Only 4.3 percent acknowledged purchasing factory-made kimchi[.]"[103]

---

[97] See *World Institute of Kimchi as Leading Global Institute of Fermented Foods*, 8 BIOTECHNOLOGY J. 759, 760 (2013).

[98] See *The Kimchi Wars*, THE ECONOMIST, November 17, 2005.

[99] See Laurel Kendall, *Introduction: Material Modernity, Consumable Tradition*, in CONSUMING KOREAN TRADITION IN EARLY AND LATE MODERNITY: COMMODIFICATION, TOURISM, AND PERFORMANCE 14 (Laurel Kendall ed., 2010) [hereinafter Kendall, CONSUMING KOREAN TRADITION] (referring to Kyung-Koo Hang, *The "Kimchi Wars" in Globalizing East Asia: Consuming Class, Gender, Health, and National Identity*, in Kendall, CONSUMING KOREAN TRADITION, at 149).

[100] See Oh et al. *supra* note 96; *see* Kun-Young Park, Ji-Kang Jeong, Young-Eun Lee & James W. Daily III, *Health Benefits of Kimchi (Korean Fermented Vegetables) as a Probiotic Food*, 17 J. OF MEDICINAL FOOD 6 (2014); Meizi Cui, Hee-Young Kim, Kyung Hee Lee, Ji-Kang Jeong, Ji-Hee Hwang, Kyu-Young Yeo, Byung-Hee Ryu, Jung-Ho Choi & Kun-Young Park, *Antiobesity Effects of Kimchi in Diet-Induced Obese Mice*, 2 J. OF ETHNIC FOODS 137 (2015).

[101] Nomination File, supra note 92, at 2.

[102] See Choe Sang-Hun, *Kimchi Goes to Space, along with First Korean Astronaut*, NEW YORK TIMES (February 22, 2008), www.nytimes.com/2008/02/22/world/asia/22iht-kimchi.1.10302283.html?_r=0.

[103] Nomination File *supra* note 92, at 8.

This is all very impressive from social, cultural, and culinary perspectives, and on the record of these facts there should be little doubt that *Kimjang* is indeed worthy of ICH inscription. More worryingly, however, there is also little doubt that traditional kimchi-making is under threat and in need of safeguarding. In fact, the Nomination File belies the current crisis of Korean kimchi, which is characterized by significantly reduced consumption,[104] and a huge rise in the importation of commercially produced kimchi made in China.[105] The survey data cited in the Nomination File[106] do not take into account the large amounts of kimchi eaten in restaurants, which is often Chinese industrial kimchi. Whereas the Nomination File cites a 2011 study by the Korea Rural Economic Institute (KREI), according to which only 6.8 percent of kimchi consumed in Korea is commercially produced,[107] more recent data from the World Kimchi Institute suggest that Chinese commercially produced kimchi alone accounts for as much as 13 percent of national consumption.[108] Moreover, the KREI itself suggests a much higher proportion of industrial kimchi in overall consumption, both at the Korean household level and in the catering and restaurant industry (including governmental and military).[109] This is borne out by earlier studies as well.[110]

---

[104] " 'Domestic consumption has dropped dramatically' Why? People are eating out more, are eating less salty foods, and have developed a taste for Western foods. '[P]eople don't tend to eat kimchi with spaghetti.' " See Lucy Williamson, *Kimchi: South Korea's Efforts to Boost Its National Dish*, BBC NEWS (February 4, 2014), www.bbc.com/news/world-asia-25840493?ocid=socialflow_twitter. According to one source, kimchi consumption in Korea has dropped over the last decade from 100 grams a day (per person) to only 60 grams. See Jonah M. Kessel, *Preserving Korea's Kimchi*, NEW YORK TIMES (July 29, 2015), www.nytimes.com/video/business/100000003736899/kimchis-identity-crisis.html?action=click&gtype=vhs&version=vhs-heading&module=vhs&region=title-area.

[105] Alexandra Stevenson, *Uncertain Trade Path for South Korea's Kimchi*, NEW YORK TIMES (July 29, 2015), www.nytimes.com/2015/07/30/business/international/chinese-trade-rules-put-south-koreas-kimchi-industry-in-a-pickle.html.

[106] Nomination File, *supra* note 92.   [107] *Id.*

[108] See Gwynn Guilford, *The Kimchi War between South Korea and China is Getting Extra Spicy*, QUARTZ (February 5, 2014), http://qz.com/173722/the-kimchi-war-between-south-korea-and-china-is-getting-extra-spicy/. In financial terms, Chinese imports constitute about 5 percent of the Korean market for kimchi, indicating the relatively low cost, and the wholesale nature of the market for Chinese imports. See Yusun Lee, *Kimchi – No Longer Solely Korea's*, 51 FIN. & DEV. 32 (2014).

[109] See Yong-Sun Lee et al., *Survey and Research on the Consumption of Kimchi by Households and Foodservice Industry*, Korea Rural Economic Institute (December 30, 2011), http://library.krei.re.kr/dl_images/001/034/C2011_50.pdf.

[110] See Kun-Young Park & Hong-Sik Cheigh, *Kimchi*, in HANDBOOK OF FOOD AND BEVERAGE FERMENTATION TECHNOLOGY 714, 747 (Y.H. Hui et al., eds., 2005) (referring to data from 1997 showing that 27.1 percent of Korean kimchi consumption was sourced from commercial production).

These trends and their influence on *Kimjang* raise fears relating to erosion of cultural diversity. In this chapter, my concern, however, is with the effectiveness of international legal measures, such as GIs and ICH, that purport to directly protect and promote cultural diversity. More specifically, the question is whether from a legal perspective the ICH inscription or anything within it has the potential to safeguard traditional *Kimjang* in the face of commercial pressures and political interests abound with respect to kimchi.

In addressing this question, it is important to first recognize that the ICH inscription is not kimchi's first engagement with international law, and that South Korea has in fact been employing international legal measures to influence kimchi's domestic and international position for the last two decades, in ways that are more related to trade interests than to cultural diversity. In the second half of the 1990s, South Korea became troubled by the rising popularity of a Japanese, nontraditional version of Kimchi (called "Kimuchi," as a pronunciation of kimchi), which typically does not involve fermentation processes.[111] This led South Korea to campaign for the adoption of an international *Codex Alimentarius* standard for kimchi, which was ultimately approved in 2001.[112] The *Codex* standard emphasizes that kimchi must be fermented. It has, however, another interesting qualification that is far less traditional. Under the *Codex* standard, kimchi must be based on Chinese cabbage.[113] Cabbage kimchi (*paechu*) is indeed probably the most popular type of kimchi in South Korea, but it is rivaled by Daikon (*mu*) radish kimchi (*Kkakdugi*); moreover, kimchi, as a cultural culinary product, is highly diverse, with hundreds of types of kimchi utilizing many different basic ingredients, with numerous regional (Korean) styles.[114] Yet the *Codex Alimentarius* promoted by South Korea requires, as an exclusive basis, Chinese cabbage. The *Kimjang* Nomination File also refers many times to

---

[111] See Calvin Sims, *Cabbage Is Cabbage? Not to Kimchi Lovers; Koreans Take Issue With a Rendition Of Their National Dish Made in Japan*, THE NEW YORK TIMES (February 5, 2000), www.nytimes.com/2000/02/05/business/cabbage-cabbage-not-kimchi-lovers-koreans-take-issue-with-rendition-their.html?pagewanted=all. The Korea/Japan "kimchi/kimuchi" tension apparently arose from a Japanese proposal to designate kimuchi an official food of the 1996 Atlanta Olympics. See Agence France-Presse, *S.Korea, Japan in Struggle for Sovereignty over Pickled Cabbage* (March 16, 2000).

[112] See *Codex Standard for Kimchi* (Codex Stan 223–2001) (2001).

[113] *Id.*; see *Codex*, defining kimchi as the product "prepared from varieties of Chinese cabbage, Brassica pekinensis Rupr."

[114] See Mei Chin, *The Art of Kimchi*, SAVEUR (October 14, 2009). This principle is confirmed by the *Kimjang* Nomination File itself. See Nomination File *supra* note 92.

cabbage.[115] Although the Nomination File, as already noted, is much more particular and culturally sensitive than the superficiality of the *Mediterranean Diet*, a similar issue arises here. Can any legal, formal instrument, standard, item, capture the full richness of ICH without reducing and degrading it?

Furthermore, a relevant factor in understanding this incongruity is, perhaps, that Chinese cabbage is the predominant basis for *industrial* kimchi, and that South Korea is among the world's top five producers of Chinese cabbage, with the highest per capita production among the major producers.[116] South Korea also pursues simple trade policies to protect Chinese cabbage production, such as high tariffs and subsidies, within its generally protectionist agricultural policy. This clearly implicates economic and commercial interests, in this case perversely at the expense of cultural and culinary diversity. Protection has its cultural costs, of course – there have indeed been situations in which shortages on cabbage supply have harmed traditional *Kimjang*.[117]

South Korea has also had recourse to international law to protect its international export and import kimchi trade interests vis-à-vis China,[118] and this has predominantly related to industrial, wholesale kimchi.[119] Similarly, South Korea has attempted to promote legal protection through a very broad GI listing of "Korean Kimchi" in at least one bilateral trade agreement (with Chile),[120] with no notable effect. "Changnyeong Onion" – onions used in some localized kimchi-making, coming from a particular locale in South Korea – has reportedly been listed as a GI in South Korea, and recognized as a GI under the Korea-EU Association Agreement.[121]

---

[115] Nomination File *supra* note 92.

[116] See Food and Agricultural Organization of the United Nations statistical database, http://faostat3.fao.org/home/E.

[117] See Mark McDonald, *Rising Cost of Kimchi Alarms Koreans*, THE NEW YORK TIMES (October 14, 2010), www.nytimes.com/2010/10/15/world/asia/15kimchi.html.

[118] Both China and South Korea imposed restrictions on imports of kimchi having found parasite eggs in each other's kimchi products. See Scott Snyder & See-Won Byun, *China-ROK Disputes and Implications for Managing Security Relations*, 5 KOR. ECO. INST. – ACAD. PAPER SERIES (2010).

[119] See *The Kimchi Wars: South Korea and China Duel over Pickled Cabbage*, THE ECONOMIST (November 17, 2005).

[120] See *Protection of GIs in the Republic of Korea*, Italian Intellectual Property Rights DESK, 2010; Annex 16.4.3, *Free Trade Agreement between the Republic of Korea and the Republic of Chile*, signed February 15, 2003, entered into force April 1, 2004.

[121] See Annex 10-A, Part B, *Free Trade Agreement between the European Union and its Member States, of the one part, and the Republic of Korea, of the other part*, entered into force July 1, 2011.

Against this backdrop, both the raw economic interests involved and the various international legal experiences and attempts, it is extremely difficult to seriously envision how ICH inscription would protect or promote traditional *Kimjang*. The only significant measures the inscription refers to are entirely domestically South Korean, and not contingent on the CSICH or on ICH inscription – including subsidized public festivals, school programs, agricultural land allocations in urban areas, research programs, financial support, and more.[122] Indeed, as evident from the inscription itself, these have all existed in South Korea well before inscription. Moreover, not all these domestic efforts are focused on traditional *Kimjang*. For example, the World Institute of Kimchi is mainly engaged in research and development of industrial kimchi products, with a view to exports and adjusting the product to foreign market preferences: "[t]he institute's goal is to develop the domestic kimchi-making industry into the country's strategic export market[.]"[123]

For good measure, a recent development in UNESCO itself is indicative of the risks of politicization of legalized cultural heritage also in culinary fields. Only two years after the nomination of *Kimjang* by South Korea, in 2015 the Democratic People's Republic of Korea (North Korea) countered with a nomination of its own, the *Tradition of Kimchi-Making*.[124] At this point in time, it is unclear what the motivation of North Korea is, and whether this competing nomination will trigger debates about high politics, national prestige, cultural "authenticity," or trade.[125] It does, however, demonstrate again that the politicization of culinary culture in the institutional and softly legalized setting of the CSICH does not necessarily hold cultural diversity in its sights. Interestingly, the North Korean Nomination File does not mention cabbage even once.

---

[122] Nomination File *supra* note 92, at 6–9.

[123] See *World Institute of Kimchi: Finding the Essence of Kimchi*, KOREA.NET (April 5, 2010) www.korea.net/NewsFocus/Society/view?articleId=80769 (quoting Mr. Park Wan-soo, Director of the Institute).

[124] U.N. Educ., Sci., & Cultural Org., Convention for the Safeguarding of the Intangible Cultural Heritage, Intergovernmental Committee for the Safeguarding of Intangible Cultural Heritage, December 2015, U.N. Doc. ITH/15/10.COM/Decisions, Nomination File No. 01063.

[125] See Lucas Lixinski, *A Tale of Two Heritages: Claims of Ownership over Intangible Cultural Heritage and the Myth of "Authenticity,"* 11 TRANSNAT'L DIS. MGMT. 1 (2014) (providing a critical assessment of the concept of "authenticity" in cultural heritage, relating to not dissimilar circumstances (differences between China and South Korea over the "Dragon Boat Festival"). Lixinski concludes that authenticity is "a socially, historically and culturally contingent concept that should have no place in an international heritage system that seeks to enhance cross-cultural dialogue and promote the 'common heritage of mankind' ").

5 CONCLUSION

The prospects of "safeguarding" cultural items, and the protection and promotion of cultural diversity, are extremely thorny, not only in legal terms, but especially in their political, social, and economic dimensions. There is more than a modicum of hubris – or naïveté – in the claims that international legal constructs such as GIs and ICH can have any structured normative and beneficial effects in this respect. The advent of culinary GIs and ICH, such as in the form of the inscriptions of the *Mediterranean Diet* and *Kimjang*, pushes the envelope and tests the internal and external boundaries of these legal concepts and their interactions with cultural diversity.

In this chapter, I have tried to show mainly that despite mounds of sociological, anthropological, and ethnographical knowledge and wisdom relating to culinary traditions, there appears to be little systematic understanding – or justification – for international legal intervention for the sake of cultural diversity in these fields. This has been borne out in the intellectual property area of GIs, and by analogy, extension, and specific analysis seems to apply to the soft, quasi-intellectual property concept of ICH. Indeed, as I have argued, the scope for political and commercial capture, as well as inconsistent, if not potentially negative or at least incoherent, effects on cultural diversity is significant, probably more significant than the benefits that such protection aims to achieve. In this context, the inscription of the *Mediterranean Diet*, as an early harvest of culinary ICH – and in that respect a genuine achievement for its proponents – seems to be a particularly problematic item, due to its generality and vagueness. The inscription of *Kimjang*, much more justified on its own cultural merits, is nevertheless problematic as well, given the complex of economic and political considerations relating to kimchi production that ultimately have nothing to do with culture. As with GIs, ICH stakeholders should avoid rushing toward new and additional inscriptions of culinary ICH, and carefully consider the definition and scope of what it is they would wish for.

20

Geographical Indications, Heritage, and Decentralization Policies: The Case of Indonesia

Christoph Antons[*]

1 INTRODUCTION: GEOGRAPHICAL INDICATIONS, DEVELOPMENT, AND HERITAGE

Over the years, enthusiasts of geographical indication (GI) protection have often asserted its benefits for developing countries. It has been said that GIs can assist with the promotion of rural and regional development;[1] support the emerging creative industries; help to protect traditional cultural expressions;[2] ensure that the exploitation of traditional knowledge would recognize sacred beliefs and practices of traditional peoples;[3] safeguard cultural heritage;[4] promote environmentally sustainable

---

[*] Professor of Law, Newcastle Law School, Faculty of Business and Law, University of Newcastle, Australia; Affiliated Fellow, Max Planck Institute for Innovation and Competition, Munich; Senior Fellow, Center for Development Research, University of Bonn. This research was supported under the Australian Research Council's Discovery Projects funding scheme (Project No. DP130100213).

[1] Graham Dutfield, *Geographical Indications and Agricultural Community Development: Is the European Model Appropriate for Developing Countries?*, in THE INTELLECTUAL PROPERTY AND FOOD PROJECT: FROM REWARDING INNOVATION AND CREATION TO FEEDING THE WORLD 175, 176 (Charles Lawson and Jay Sanderson eds., 2013); Sarah Bowen, *Development from Within? The Potential for Geographical Indications in the Global South*, 13 J. WORLD INTELL. PROP. 231, 233–35 (2010).

[2] Tzen Wong & Claudia Fernandini, *Traditional Cultural Expressions: Preservation and Innovation*, in INTELLECTUAL PROPERTY AND HUMAN DEVELOPMENT: CURRENT TRENDS AND FUTURE SCENARIOS 175, 193–96 (Tzen Wong & Graham Dutfield eds., 2010).

[3] Michael Blakeney, *Protection of Traditional Knowledge by Geographical Indications*, in TRADITIONAL KNOWLEDGE, TRADITIONAL CULTURAL EXPRESSIONS AND INTELLECTUAL PROPERTY LAW IN THE ASIA-PACIFIC REGION 87, 87–108 (Christoph Antons ed., 2009).

[4] Dev S. Gangjee, *Geographical Indications and Cultural Heritage*, 4 WIPO J. 92, 92–102 (2012).

development;[5] and indirectly contribute to an increase in tourism.[6] Such laudable goals have also been mentioned in the Preamble of the Official Government Explanation introducing the relevant Government Regulation in Indonesia in 2007.[7] The Preamble speaks about using GIs for conserving the environment, empowering natural and human resources in the regions, and preventing migration to the cities by creating opportunities for work in these regions.[8]

Indonesia introduced a completely new Law on Trade Marks and Geographical Indications in November 2016.[9] The new Law No. 20 of 2016 invalidates the former Trade Marks Act of 2001, including its provisions on GI (Article 107 of Law No.20/2016). However, as happens frequently with new legislation in Indonesia,[10] Article 106 of the new law leaves all implementing regulations issued for the previous law in force as long as they are not in conflict with the new Law No.20/2016. As Government Regulation No. 51 of 2007 was issued to implement the GI provisions of the previous law (Article 56(9) of Law No. 15 of 2001 on Trade Marks),[11] this regulation remains in force. The new law of 2016 is similarly upbeat about GI protection in Indonesia. The official government explanation accompanying the draft of the Preamble[12] stresses the national potential for GIs to become superior commodities in domestic and international trade. The Government explains further that the increasing relevance of

---

[5] Rosemary J. Coombe, Sarah Ives & Daniel Huizenga, *Geographical Indications: The Promise, Perils and Politics of Protecting Place-Based Products*, in SAGE HANDBOOK ON INTELLECTUAL PROPERTY, 207, 207–23 (Deborah Halbert & Matthew David eds., 2014).
[6] Surip Mawardi, *Advantages, Constraints and Key Success Factors in Establishing Origin- and Tradition-Linked Quality Signs: The Case of Kintamani Bali Arabica Coffee Geographical Indication, Indonesia, Case Study on Quality Products Linked to Geographical Origin in Asia Carried Out for FAO* (May 25, 2009), http://eiado.prevision.com.au/supplementary-reports/annotated-bibliography/advantages-constraints-and-key-success-factors; Kasturi Das, *Prospects and Challenges of Geographical Indications in India*, 13 J. WORLD INTELL. PROP. 148, 180 (2010).
[7] *Penjelasan Atas Peraturan Pemerintah Republik Indonesia Nomor 51 Tahun 2007 Tentang Indikasi-Geografis.*
[8] For a specific example from the Krayan region in Kalimantan, see *Beras Adan Resmi Dipatenkan*, KOMPAS (January 15, 2012), http://regional.kompas.com/read/2012/01/15/18453496/Beras.Adan.Resmi.Dipatenkan.
[9] Undang-Undang Republik Indonesia Nomor 20 Tahun 2016 tentang Merek dan Indikasi Geografis
[10] Christoph Antons, *Indonesia*, in INTELLECTUAL PROPERTY IN ASIA; LAW, ECONOMICS, HISTORY AND POLITICS (Paul Goldstein and Joseph Straus eds., 2009), 101–102.
[11] Undang-Undang Republik Indonesia Nomor 15 Tahun 2001 tentang Merek.
[12] Penjelasan Rancangan Undang-Undang Republik Indonesia Nomor 20 Tahun 2016 tentang Merek dan Indikasi Geografis.

GIs is also visible from the fact that they are now included in the title of the law.

Although many developing countries introduced GI protection initially because of TRIPS pressures,[13] or because they were influenced by EU technical assistance programs,[14] reports of carefully selected pilot projects sponsored by the United Nations Food and Agriculture Organization (FAO) relating to newly registered GIs have suggested positive results.[15] Nevertheless, critical observers have pointed out that such positive results cannot be taken for granted. Using the case study of tequila in Mexico, Sarah Bowen finds that "influential actors have manipulated production standards and certification policies in ways that contradict the theoretical concept of a GI and negatively affect the overall quality of tequila."[16] Graham Dutfield, discussing the same example, has pointed to the potentially negative impact on biodiversity if production standards require the growing of only one variety at the expense of others.[17] Using the example of Pisco, a GI claimed by both Peru and Chile and registered by either in various countries, Dutfield also shows the cross-boundary issues that arise if two or more countries claim the same indication on the basis of the same or similar traditions.[18] Amit Basole, commenting on GIs used for weaving in Banaras, sees a preservationist paradigm at work that "freezes culture." Instead of adopting a preservationist view centered on the content of knowledge, he proposes a political economy perspective focused on the processes that create and sustain knowledge.[19] Rosemary Coombe et al. find that the "social imaginary" of GI protection for Rooibos tea in South Africa, for instance, obscures complex historical relationships in an environment

---

[13] See Das, *supra* note 6, at 148 (discussing India as an example of a country introducing GI protection because of TRIPS).

[14] Dutfield, *supra* note 1; Michael Blakeney, *The Pacific Solution: The European Union's Intellectual Property Rights Activism in Australia's and New Zealand's Sphere of Influence*, in INDIGENOUS PEOPLES' INNOVATION: INTELLECTUAL PROPERTY PATHWAYS TO DEVELOPMENT 165–88 (Peter Drahos & Susy Frankel eds., 2012).

[15] Mawardi, *supra* note 6 (discussing the "Quality Linked to Geographical Origin" program of FAO); *see also* Bowen, *supra* note 1, at 232.

[16] Bowen, *supra* note 1, at 235.   [17] Dutfield, *supra* note 1, at 188.

[18] *Id.* at 189–90. *See generally* Christoph Antons, *Epistemic Communities and the "People without History": The Contribution of Intellectual Property Law to the "Safeguarding" of Intangible Cultural Heritage*, in DIVERSITY IN INTELLECTUAL PROPERTY: IDENTITIES, INTERESTS AND INTERSECTIONS 453, 467–69 (Irene Calboli & Srividhya Ragavan eds., 2015) (highlighting that this is an increasingly widespread issue in the registration of heritage).

[19] Amit Basole, *Authenticity, Innovation and the Geographical Indication in an Artisanal Industry: The Case of the Banarasi Sari*, 18 J. WORLD INTELL. PROP. 127, 143 (2015).

"characterized by histories of racialized dispossession under apartheid rule, ongoing contestations over land, and shifting identity politics."[20]

In this chapter, I build upon these existing critiques and examine GIs in a "contested environment," with particular focus on Indonesia, i.e., in an environment characterized by Indonesia's extremely complex decentralization policies. Notably, I will show that decentralization in Indonesia leads to sometimes difficult bargaining processes among the central government, regional governments, and producer communities about the nature and use of intellectual property (IP) laws relating to tradition and heritage, including GIs. I will then examine the GI registration process and show that it is ultimately central government-controlled with relatively limited roles for regional players. The important questions in a country that has encouraged large-scale transmigration for many decades are who will be allowed to operate in the "cultural spaces" that GIs demarcate for purposes of development and to enjoy increased profits from local products as well as how the social and economic benefits will be defined. Decision-makers at the national, regional, and local levels may well have different ideas in this regard. Finally, I will examine in detail two examples of registered GIs and ask to what extent they will be able to fulfill some of the high hopes that the government has with regard to their economic and social benefits.

2 THE CONTEXT OF INDONESIA'S DECENTRALIZATION POLICIES

I would like to begin with a basic explanation of the context of Indonesian decentralization policies in which regional development and use of GIs have to be viewed.

The Indonesian coat of arms bears the Sanskrit motto *Bhineka Tunggal Ika*, which means "unity in diversity." For much of the country's history, successive governments have had different views of how to find the right balance between the two. During centuries of Dutch colonial rule, the Netherlands East Indies were formed around the main island of Java and already during colonial times it was common to refer to the rest of the Indonesian archipelago as the "outer islands." After independence, Indonesia recognized *Bahasa Indonesia*, which originated in Sumatra, as

---

[20] Rosemary J. Coombe, Sarah Ives & Daniel Huizenga, *The Social Imaginary of Geographical Indicators in Contested Environments: The Politicized Heritage and the Racialized Landscapes of South African Rooibos Tea*, in SAGE HANDBOOK ON INTELLECTUAL PROPERTY 224–37 (Deborah Halbert & Matthew David eds., 2014).

its national language, but politics and administration were centered in Java and the capital Jakarta. This led to tensions and even armed uprisings on some of the "outer islands" during the 1950s. Centralization reached its highpoint during the many years of rule of the autocratic and military-backed Suharto government. During the widespread unrest following the end of Suharto's rule in 1998, Suharto's successor Habibie introduced laws on local autonomy that gave the districts substantial powers in administrative and financial matters.[21] This initiated a move toward decentralization, which coincided with the promotion of decentralization policies and community-based natural resource management in developing countries more generally by many donor agencies and non-governmental organizations (NGOs).[22] Although there are generally high expectations with regard to democratization and local empowerment, Vandergeest and Wittayapak have pointed out that it is important to distinguish between administrative and political decentralization. Administrative decentralization shifts power to regional or local bureaucracies that remain upwardly accountable to central headquarters, whereas political decentralization transfers power to authorities who are downwardly accountable to local people.[23] They point to research on Southeast Asian countries that "decentralization had the effect of increasing state presence, power, and control at the local level, often through making local institutions responsible for monitoring and enforcing regulations in places where states previously had little influence over the everyday use of resources."[24]

The Indonesian laws on local autonomy were revised in 2004 and completely new legislation was introduced in 2014.[25] Decentralization was also incorporated into the revised Indonesian Constitution in Chapter VI on Regional Government.[26] Interestingly and unusually by international standards, Indonesia undertook its efforts at decentralization as a unitary and not as a

---

[21] TAUFIK ABDULLAH, INDONESIA: TOWARDS DEMOCRACY 536 (2009).
[22] *See* THE POLITICS OF DECENTRALIZATION: NATURAL RESOURCE MANAGEMENT IN ASIA (Chusak Wittayapak & Peter Vandergeest eds., 2010); COMMUNITIES AND CONSERVATION: HISTORIES AND POLITICS OF COMMUNITY-BASED NATURAL RESOURCE MANAGEMENT (J. Peter Brosius, Anna Lowenhaupt Tsing & Charles Zerner eds., 2005).
[23] Peter Vandergeest & Chusak Wittayapak, *Decentralization and Politics*, in THE POLITICS OF DECENTRALIZATION: NATURAL RESOURCE MANAGEMENT IN ASIA 1, 4 (Chusak Wittayapak & Peter Vandergeest eds., 2010).
[24] *Id.* at 11.
[25] Law No. 23 of 2014 on Regional Government Administration (Undang-Undang No. 23 Tahun 2014 tentang Pemerintahan Daerah).
[26] INDON. CONST. arts. 18-18B, 1945.

federated state.[27] The reasons for this approach are to be found in history. A struggle for independence against the returning Dutch after the end of Japanese occupation in World War II ended with the formal recognition of a federated "United States of Indonesia" by the Netherlands. However, Dutch influence and interference in the affairs of some of the states brought a swift end to this federated structure barely nine months later.[28] The Indonesian political elite has been deeply distrustful of federalism ever since.[29]

As a consequence of decentralization, Article 18 of the Constitution provides for local government at the respective levels of a province, *Kabupaten* (regency), and city in accordance with the principles of autonomy and with the task to provide assistance. Again unusual for such constitutional arrangements, but not unusual for Indonesia, Article 18A refers to further laws for details on how administrative competences, finance, services, natural resources, and other resources are to be divided between the central government and the various regional governments. Article 18B recognizes local governments, but also and importantly the unity of *masyarakat hukum adat* (customary law communities) and these communities' traditional rights "as long as they are still in existence and in accordance with the development of society and the principles of the unitary Republic of Indonesia regulated by law." Although heavily qualified, Article 18B(2) recognizes in principle many traditionally living communities, including forest dwellers that would be referred to as "indigenous peoples" elsewhere.[30] A similarly qualified recognition is to be found in Article 28I(3) in a newly introduced part on human rights. Accordingly, the cultural identity and rights of traditional communities are respected "in accordance with the development of the times and civilization."[31]

Obviously, the text of these constitutional provisions leaves much room for discretion and debate. However, it has encouraged the representatives of forest-dwelling "customary law communities," commonly referred to in Indonesia as

---

[27] INDON. CONST. art. 1(1) (stating that "[t]he State of Indonesia is a unitary state in the form of a republic").

[28] ABDULLAH, *supra* note 21, at 191–99.

[29] VEDI R. HADIZ, LOCALISING POWER IN POST-AUTHORITARIAN INDONESIA: A SOUTHEAST ASIA PERSPECTIVE (2010).

[30] On the difficulties with the use of this term in countries like Indonesia, see Anna Lowenhaupt Tsing, *Adat/Indigenous: Indigineity in Motion*, in WORDS IN MOTION: TOWARDS A GLOBAL LEXICON 40–64 (Carol Gluck & Anna Lowenhaupt Tsing eds., 2009); Gerard Persoon, "Being Indigenous" in Indonesia and the Philippines, in TRADITIONAL KNOWLEDGE, TRADITIONAL CULTURAL EXPRESSIONS AND INTELLECTUAL PROPERTY LAW IN THE ASIA-PACIFIC REGION 195–216 (Christoph Antons ed., 2009).

[31] INDON. CONST. art. 28I(3), 1945.

adat communities, to fight for their rights to their traditional forest environment under the national Forestry Law and these rights have been recognized in a landmark decision by the Indonesian Constitutional Court in 2012.[32] To understand GIs in the context of decentralization policies in Indonesia is important because many of them originate from such *adat* communities, from ethnic communities on the "outer islands," and from regions that experienced ethnic unrest in the tumultuous years following the end of Suharto's rule.[33] Examples of such GIs include Gayo coffee and patchouli oil from Aceh, Kalosi and Toraja coffee from Sulawesi, and Adan Krayan rice from Kalimatan. The long struggle of Aceh against incorporation into the Netherlands East Indies and the string of rebellions since then have been well documented, with Anthony Reid noting that there were only "relatively short periods of the twentieth century during which Aceh was not disturbed by rebellion against Jakarta."[34] Coffee plantations were established by the Dutch after they had incorporated Aceh into their colonial empire. Coffee is a relatively recent addition to the livelihood of some of the Gayo people in the highlands of Aceh, which live in communities that have seen a strong influx of transmigrants from Java. Around 2000, there was interethnic violence in the Aceh region involving the *Gerakan Merdeka Aceh* (Free Aceh Movement) and what John Bowen describes as militias of unclear origins and composition, with some of them being allegedly linked to the Indonesian army.[35] In Kalimantan, there was widespread violence between local Dayak groups and transmigrants from the island of Madura off the north shore of Java between 1996 and 2001.[36] As for the Toraja region of Sulawesi, Kathleen Adams reports disputes between locals and the central authorities about the

---

[32] Noer Fauzi Rachman & Mia Siscawati, *Forestry Law, Masyarakat Adat, and Struggles for Inclusive Citizenship in Indonesia*, in THE ROUTLEDGE HANDBOOK OF ASIAN LAW 224–249 (Christoph Antons ed., 2017).
[33] *See* the GI Registration List, DIRECTORATE GENERAL OF INTELLECTUAL PROPERTY RIGHTS, laman.dgip.go.id/layanan-kekayaan-intelektual/indikasi-geografis/berita-resmi-ig (last visited February 7, 2017) (showing twenty-one of the thirty-nine registered GIs in Indonesia (including three from foreign countries) are from the islands outside of Java).
[34] Anthony Reid, *Indonesia, Aceh and the Modern Nation State*, in THE POLITICS OF THE PERIPHERY IN INDONESIA: SOCIAL AND GEOGRAPHICAL PERSPECTIVES 84, 94 (Minako Sakai, Glenn Banks & J.H. Walker eds., 2009).
[35] JOHN R. BOWEN, ISLAM, LAW AND EQUALITY IN INDONESIA: AN ANTHROPOLOGY OF PUBLIC REASONING 24 (2003); Edward Aspinall, *Modernity, History and Ethnicity: Indonesian and Acehnese Nationalism in Conflict*, in AUTONOMY AND DISINTEGRATION IN INDONESIA 128, 141 (Damien Kingsbury & Harry Aveling eds., 2003).
[36] Mary Hawkins, *Violence and the Construction of Identity: Conflict between the Dayak and Madurese in Kalimantan, Indonesia*, in THE POLITICS OF THE PERIPHERY IN INDONESIA: SOCIAL AND GEOGRAPHICAL PERSPECTIVES 153–172 (Minako Sakai, Glenn Banks & J.H. Walker eds., 2009).

diversion of income from tourism and the question on whether jobs as tour guides should go to locals or to people from elsewhere in Indonesia.[37] The last mentioned example of a national development initiative using local culture shows that disputes can arise if locals take a more exclusive view of who should benefit from their culture than the government and development planners in Jakarta. GIs, as another national initiative for the marketing of local culture, could raise similar concerns.

Legal academics and social scientists have long been showing the increasing role of governments in discourses about heritage and tradition that are linked to IP rights.[38] It was only a matter of time before claims to centralized and national control of such rights and the benefits flowing from licensing and royalty collections would encounter counterclaims from local communities, indigenous communities, and regional governments. In Indonesia, this is now becoming visible with the emergence of regional IP laws, which put local governments rather than the central government in charge of granting licenses and collecting royalties. Unsurprisingly, the first set of such local regulations was proclaimed in 2008 in the province of Papua to protect the IP rights of indigenous Papuans.[39] Papua had remained under Dutch administration until 1962 and was incorporated into Indonesia after a controversial referendum in 1969, a move resisted by the *Organisasi Papua Merdeka* (Free Papua Organisation) ever since.[40] Apart from Aceh, it was the only province granted "special autonomy" in 2001.[41] Richard Chauvel, in his analysis of the

---

[37] Kathleen M. Adams, *Touting Touristic "Primadonas": Tourism, Ethnicity, and National Integration in Sulawesi, Indonesia*, in TOURISM, ETHNICITY AND THE STATE IN ASIAN AND PACIFIC SOCIETIES 160–72 (Michel Picard & Robert E. Wood eds., 1997).

[38] See, e.g., Christoph Antons, *Traditional Knowledge and Intellectual Property Rights in Australia and Southeast Asia*, in NEW FRONTIERS OF INTELLECTUAL PROPERTY LAW: IP AND CULTURAL HERITAGE, GEOGRAPHICAL INDICATIONS, ENFORCEMENT AND OVERPROTECTION 37–51 (Christopher Heath & Anselm Kamperman Sanders eds., 2005); Christoph Antons, *What Is "Traditional Cultural Expression"? International Definitions and Their Application in Developing Asia*, 1 WIPO J. 103 (2009); Rosemary Coombe, *The Expanding Purview of Cultural Properties and Their Politics*, 5 ANN. REV. L. & SOC. SCI. 393 (2009); Lorraine V. Aragon & James Leach, *Arts and Owners: Intellectual Property Law and the Politics of Scale in Indonesian Arts*, 35 AM. ETHNOLOGIST 607 (2008); Jinn Winn Chong, *"Mine, Yours or Ours?": The Indonesia-Malaysia Disputes over Shared Cultural Heritage*, 27 SOJOURN: J. SOC. ISSUES SE. ASIA 1–53 (2012).

[39] Peraturan Daerah Khusus Provinsi Papua Nomor 19 Tahun 2008 Tentang Perlindungan Hak Kekayaan Intelektual Orang Asli Papua.

[40] M.C. RICKLEFS, A HISTORY OF MODERN INDONESIA SINCE C. 1200 328, 358–59 (3rd edn. 2001).

[41] Richard Chauvel, *Papua and Indonesia: Where Contending Nationalisms Meet*, in AUTONOMY AND DISINTEGRATION IN INDONESIA 115, 122 (Damien Kingsbury & Harry Aveling eds., 2003) (quoting Decrees of the People's Advisory Assembly (MPR) No. IV/MPR/1999, No. VIII/MPR/2000, Appendix 1.1.a).

negotiations for the special autonomy law, describes the negotiations as a bargaining process between the provincial government and a committee from the central parliament in Jakarta.[42] The autonomy law makes a distinction between indigenous Papuans and other residents of the province. It defines "indigenous Papuans" as *"rumpun ras Melanesia"* (i.e., "descending from Melanesian racial stock"), who are members of indigenous tribes or people recognized as indigenous by the Papuan *adat* communities.[43] The same definition is also used in the Special Regional Regulation of the Province Papua No. 19 of 2008 on the Protection of Intellectual Property Rights of Indigenous Papuans.[44] The Regulation extends to "indigenous Papuan GIs" focusing on the "specific indigenous Papuan circumstances" and the specific Papuan character and quality of such GIs.[45] What this Regulation means in practice for the administration and registration of Papuan GIs is not clear at this stage as none have been successfully registered so far.

Although Papua is a rather special case, other provinces are beginning to draft their own rules and regulations on IP rights. In 2012, West Java issued a Regional Regulation of the Province of West Java No. 5 of 2012 on the Protection of Intellectual Property.[46] The province of Bangka Belitung is currently drafting a regional regulation on intellectual property. A spokesperson for the regional law and human rights office there has made it clear that the regulation is meant to raise income and to channel royalties, which are currently going to the central government, to the regional government.[47] Discussions about a regional regulation have also started in East Java, where the Governor has identified 253 potential GIs and 154 indications of origin as "communal intellectual property" owned by the "East Java community."[48] Needless to say, the proliferation of local IP regulations could well create inconsistencies among local and national IP laws. In the West Java IP protection regulation, GIs are included, rather confusingly, in a category called *hak*

---

[42] *Id.*, 122–27.
[43] Art. 1 t. of Law No. 21 of 2001 on Special Autonomy for the Papua Province.
[44] Art. 1 No. 8 of the Special Regional Regulation of the Province Papua No. 19 of 2008 on the Protection of Intellectual Property Rights of Indigenous Papuans.
[45] Art. 1 No. 16 of Special Regulation No. 19/2008.
[46] Peraturan Daerah Provinsi Jawa Barat Nomor 5 Tahun 2012 Tentang Perlindungan Kekayaan Intelektual.
[47] BE, *Kanwilkumham Babel Ajukan Perda HAKI*, Belitong Ekspres (December 13, 2014), http://belitongekspres.co.id/2014/12/13/kanwilkumham-babel-ajukan-perda-haki/.
[48] *Pemprov Diminta Terbitkan Perda HKI*, Ubaya (June 11, 2015), www.ubaya.ac.id/2014/content/news_detail/1548/Pemprov-Diminta-Terbitkan-Perda-HKI.html.

terkait (neighboring rights),[49] a term otherwise and elsewhere in this regulation used for neighboring rights in copyright.[50] Also, the object of GI protection as defined in Article 16 of Regional Regulation No. 5 of 2012 (i.e., the "specification of a production method, the specification of the quality of a product, the name, reputation or other characteristic, which distinguishes [it] from a product of the same kind") differs from the definition of a GI in the new Trade Marks Act.[51]

Whether local governments are authorized to enact such wide-ranging regulations may be found in Article 70 of the new Trade Marks and Geographical Indications Act and in Law No. 23 of 2014 on Regional Government Administration, which implements the general framework outlined in the Constitution. Article 70 leaves the matter undecided and states merely that guidance, including legal protection, with regards to GIs is the responsibility of the central and/or regional government, depending on their respective authority. Law No. 23 of 2014 reserves a few areas to the national government and includes an Annex stating fields in which both national and regional governments have powers to act. Here, the central government is put in charge of community IP rights in the field of culture[52] and of the development of the national creative industries sector using IP rights.[53] All government levels are responsible, depending on their locations, for the empowerment of *adat* communities.[54] The recognition of *adat* communities, their traditional knowledge, and their related rights are discussed in the section on the environment and is the responsibility of local authorities unless the communities inhabit several provinces, in which case the central government would be responsible.[55] As will be explained in the following, the associations representing GI users are not normally identical with *adat* communities, so that the authority of the central government will probably prevail in most cases. In any case, Law No. 10 of 2004 on the Forming of Legislative Provisions envisages a hierarchy of laws in which regional regulations stand at a lower level than national laws and are not valid in so far as they contradict national laws.[56]

---

[49] Art. 7(2) Regional Regulation of the Province of West Java on the Protection of Intellectual Property.
[50] In art. 8(3), (4), the term is used to cover performances, recordings, and broadcasting rights.
[51] Art. 1 No. 6 Trade Marks and Geographical Indications Act (defining a GI as "a sign, which indicates the geographical origin of a good and/or product, with this origin giving a certain reputation, quality and characteristic to the good because of the geographical environment, the human factor or a combination of the two.").
[52] Annex to Law No. 23 of 2014 under V.   [53] Annex to Law No. 23 of 2014 under Z.
[54] Annex to Law No. 23 of 2014 under M.   [55] Annex to Law No. 23 of 2014 under K.
[56] Simon Butt, *Regional Autonomy and Legal Disorder: The Proliferation of Local Laws in Indonesia*, 32 SYDNEY L. REV. 177–97 (2010); Simon Butt, *National Control Over Local*

How much of the regional regulation of IP will survive such scrutiny remains, therefore, to be seen. What the regulations enacted thus far indicate, however, is that the various levels of government may not always have the same interests when it comes to IP relating to heritage and tradition. Clearly, some regional governments see local culture as a source of income that should benefit their provinces rather than the central government. Also, it is equally clear that some provinces would like to ensure that benefits go first and foremost to locals rather than to, for example, transmigrants. While the central government may be interested in initiating regional development projects, it may also encourage controlled migration into an area and, consistent with the concept of a unitary state, cannot allow for distinctions among different sections of the population. Conversely, regional governments may not share such goals and concerns.

Finally, there are the customary law or *adat* communities. In spite of the aforementioned landmark decision in their favor, their position in the Indonesian political structure remains weak. Following the reinterpretation of the relevant provision of the Forestry Act by the Constitutional Court, these communities and their rights are recognized "as long as they are still in existence and in accordance with the development of society and the principles of the unitary Republic of Indonesia regulated by law."[57] However, these communities are not part of the regional government as defined in Law No. 23 on Regional Government Administration. Instead, they depend on the regional government's recognition of their rights, which are only mentioned in the context of the protection and management of the environment. If this implies a role of custodians only, communities dissatisfied with this role can take the matter to the courts, as some have done recently in the Constitutional Court Case mentioned above regarding recognition of their traditional rights under the Forestry Act.[58] However, the large discretionary powers that laws grant the authorities and courts in relation to *adat* communities provide a strong incentive to work with regional authorities in getting local culture and traditions recognized and promoted.

In the end, much will depend in every single case on the relationship between *adat* communities and the government and how far locals regard their interests as well represented, their traditions as respected, and benefits from commercialization as fairly distributed. As for GIs, appropriate

---

Lawmaking in Indonesia, in THE ROUTLEDGE HANDBOOK OF ASIAN LAW, 203–223 (Christoph Antons ed., 2017).

[57] See the Constitutional Court's re-interpretation of Article 4(3) of Law No. 41 of 1999 on Forestry, Decision of the Constitutional Court No. 35/PUU-X/2012 of May 16, 2013, 185–86.

[58] *Id.* at 1–188.

representation of the various stakeholder interests in the associations managing them will be decisive. Madhavi Sunder fears that within such associations, "traditional leaders may impose their will on members, reifying traditional hierarchies."[59] At least in the case of Indonesia, however, associations formed for the protection of GIs are not "traditional." They are government constructs with varying degrees of involvement of "traditional leaders." If one examines the registrations of GIs so far, the majority of registering associations simply call themselves "Association for" (*Asosiasi*) or "Community for the Protection of" (*Masyarakat Perlindungan*) a particular GI. There is only a single registration referring to an *adat* community and this is the GI for Adan Krayan rice registered by the Adat Community Association for the Protection of Adan Krayan Rice. This example will be discussed further below. Prior to examining individual case studies, however, it is necessary to look at the structure of the legal framework for GI protection in Indonesia.

3 THE LEGAL FRAMEWORK FOR GEOGRAPHICAL INDICATIONS

So, who is in charge of GIs in Indonesia and what is the legal framework for them? GIs and indications of origin are regulated in Chapters VIII, IX, X, and XI of the Indonesian Trade Marks and Geographical Indications Act of 2016, with further details stated in an implementing Government Regulation No. 51 of 2007 Regarding Geographical Indications. A GI is defined as "a sign, which indicates the geographical origin of a good and/or a product with this origin giving a certain reputation, quality, and characteristic to the good and/or product because of the geographical environment, the human factor or a combination of the two" under Article 1 No. 6 of the Trade Marks and Geographical Indications Act, which overrides a differently worded definition in Article 1 No. 1 of Government Regulation No. 51/2007. The "sign" can be the name of the place or the region or any other sign that indicates the origins of the goods.[60] The government's explanation accompanying Article 2(1) of Government Regulation No. 51/2007 gives the following examples: (a) the word "Minang" indicates that a good's origin is West Sumatra; and (b) the picture of a Toraja adat house indicates that a good comes from the Toraja region in South Sulawesi.

---

[59] Madhavi Sunder, *The Invention of Traditional Knowledge*, 70 L. & CONTEMP. PROBS. 97–124 (2007).
[60] Art. 2(1) Government Regulation No. 51/2007.

GIs can be used for goods obtained from nature, agricultural goods, manufactured products, crafts, or other goods.[61] The 2007 Government Regulation foresees that, once registered, GIs can no longer become generic[62] and that this protection does not extend to indications that have become generic in the past and prior to registration.[63] This reason for not registering a GI has now been left out in Article 56 of the new Trade Marks and Geographical Indications Act and Article 56, therefore, overrides Article 3(d) Government Regulation No. 51/2007.

The frequent use of Indonesian place names abroad could be one of the reasons for this change. The government's explanation to the relevant Article 3(d) of Government Regulation No. 51/2007 gives examples of the names of fruits that have been linked to certain islands and have now become commonly known in Indonesia (e.g., *pisang Ambon* (Ambon banana) and *jeruk Bali* (Bali grapefruit)). Incidentally, *pisang Ambon* is also known outside of Indonesia as a liqueur manufactured in the Netherlands.[64] However, it is not the only Indonesian place name registered in the Netherlands. Gayo coffee producers from Aceh found to their dismay that the term "Gayo" was trademark-registered by a coffee-trading company in the Netherlands.[65] If such place names are in the future no longer regarded as generic, bona fide users or owners of trademarks using the name may in the future have to rely on Article 68(1), (2) Trade Marks and Geographical Indications Act, which grants them a 2-year grace period to phase out the infringing use.

Other reasons that prevent registration are listed in Article 56 of the Trade Marks and Geographical Indications Act. Accordingly, GI registration will be refused if it conflicts with the state ideology, legal provisions, morality, religion, ethics, and the public order.[66] The state ideology of Indonesia is *Pancasila*. It consists of five broad principles, initially pronounced by Indonesia's first President Sukarno, and enshrined in the preamble of the Indonesian Constitution of 1945. The five principles are belief in a supreme

---

[61] Art. 2(2) Government Regulation No. 51/2007.
[62] Art. 2(4) Government Regulation No. 51/2007.
[63] Art. 3(d) Government Regulation No. 51/2007.
[64] Wikipedia, Pisang Ambon, https://en.wikipedia.org/wiki/Pisang_Ambon (last visited June 10, 2016).
[65] *Dutch Company Claims Int'l Trade Rights Over Gayo Coffee*, JAKARTA POST (February 11, 2008), http://imo.thejakartapost.com/news/2008/02/11/dutch-company-claims-into39l-trade-rights-over-gayo-coffee.html; Mark Forbes, *Aceh Heads for New Conflict – Over the Name of a Coffee*, SYDNEY MORNING HERALD (February 16, 2008), www.smh.com.au/news/world/aceh-heads-for-new-conflict--over-the-name-of-a-coffee/2008/02/15/1202760599951.html.
[66] Art. 56(1)a. Trade Marks and Geographical Indications Act.

god; just and civilized humanity; Indonesian unity; democracy guided by the wisdom of consultation and representation; and social justice for the whole of the Indonesian people.[67] *Pancasila* also informs the interpretation of "religion" in this context. It prescribes religious tolerance as far as the major religions are concerned, while animist belief systems are not officially recognized.[68] In accordance with a similar provision in the previous Trade Marks Act and the relevant Government Explanation, "religious morality" would only become of concern in exceptional cases where religious symbolism is used in an insulting and insensitive manner.[69] The question of disturbance of the "public order" has, in the past, occasionally been used in cases of consumer confusion about trademarks, especially in relation to the geographical origin of a product.[70] This interpretation is no longer relevant after the introduction of GIs and the prohibition in the Trade Marks Act to register GI-protected signs as trademarks.[71] Consumer confusion relating to the reputation, quality, characteristics, origin, production process, and/or use of the goods also prevents registration of a GI according to Article 56(1)b. Trade Marks and Geographical Indications Act.[72] A further obstacle to GI registration is if the geographical name is already used as the name for a plant variety as indicated in Article 56(1) c. Trade Marks and Geographical Indications Act, unless there is an addition of comparable words which indicates that there exists a geographical indication of the same kind. Further reasons that lead to an application being declined are when the content of a document describing the GI cannot be verified (Article 56(2)a.) and when the indication to be registered is substantially identical with the registered one (Article 56(2)b.).

The Act and Regulation also mention the applicants and principal right holders under the legislation. According to the Preamble to the Government Explanation on Government Regulation No. 51 of 2007, these parties are the local community groups where the goods originate and who are competent to maintain, defend, and use a GI in connection with their businesses and/or enterprises.[73] Article 53(3) of the Trade Marks and Geographical Indications Act narrows this wide scope down to two types of organizations: organizations

---

[67] CHRISTOPH ANTONS, INTELLECTUAL PROPERTY LAW IN INDONESIA 19–20 (2000).
[68] Persoon, *supra* note 30.
[69] See the Government Explanation to Article 5 a. of the former Trade Marks Act of 2001: "Included in the understanding of conflicting with religious morality, ethics or the public order is where the use of the aforementioned sign may hurt the feeling, politeness, calm or religiousness of the general public or of a certain group in society."
[70] ANTONS, *supra* note 67, 221.
[71] Article 56(2)b. Trade Marks and Geographical Indications Act.
[72] Art. 56 (4) Trade Marks Act; Article 3 b. of Government Regulation No. 51/2007.
[73] Preamble, Government Regulation No. 51/2007.

representing the communities in production areas; and the local government at provincial, district, or city level. According to the government explanation accompanying Article 53(3)a. typical representative organisations are producer associations, cooperations, and "communities for the protection of geographical indications." Of the thirty-nine GIs registered in the GI registry so far,[74] three (Champagne, Pisco, and Parmigiano Reggiano) were registered by foreign organizations and one (Muntok White Pepper) directly by a government agency.[75]

The remaining GIs were registered by various organizations representing the communities in production areas referred to as "communities," "associations," "community forums," or "networks" for GI protection with widely varying membership.[76] According to Article 5(3) of Government Regulation No. 51/2007, and the accompanying government explanation, membership should include local cultivators of natural resources, producers of agricultural goods, crafts or industrial goods, or traders selling such goods.[77] Article 53(3) of the Trade Marks and Geographical Indications Act speaks of communities that work with goods and/or products in the form of natural resources, handicrafts or industrial products. According to the government explanation, the latter term includes any raw material transformed into goods and mentions as examples typical textiles from the provinces of Bali (*Tenun Gringsing*) and East Nusa Tenggara (*Tenun Sikka*). "Natural resouces" is given a very wide interpretation in the government explanation and includes not just animals, plants, and microorganisms, but also oil, natural gas, certain types of metal, water, and soil.

In practice, it seems that in many cases the initiative to set up such an association comes from the local government, with government leaders at the provincial and regency levels being involved in the leadership of the association or in the roles of *pembina* (senior members), *penasehat* (advisers), or *pengawas* (supervisors). Other members not immediately involved in the production or trading can be lawyers, university experts, or members of institutions for skills training.[78]

---

[74] GI Registration List, *supra* note 33.   [75] Id.
[76] Directorate General of Intellectual Property Rights, http://119.252.174.21/indikasi-geografis/ (last visited March 9, 2016) (providing links to the various *buku persyaratan* (books of rules and regulations), from which details about the membership can be collected).
[77] Art. 5(3) Government Regulation No. 51/2007.
[78] For example, the executive committee of the association administering the GI for Jepara furniture, discussed in the following section, includes representatives from artisan centers and craft schools. *See* Directorate General of Intellectual Property Rights, http://119.252.174.21/indikasi-geografis/ (last visited March 9, 2016).

The executive committee of such associations is usually formed by decree of the local government.[79] It is usually authorized to draft the *buku persyaratan* (Book of rules and regulations), which accompanies the application for registration.[80] In the new Trade Marks and Geographical Indications Act it is referred to as a document describing the GI (*Dokumen Deskripsi Indikasi Geografis*).[81] This book specifies all the details about the good, what is special about it, as well as the logo that will be used for it.[82] It also contains an explanation about the territory that the GI relates to and the territorial borders. This explanation, however, must be endorsed by a government agency in the relevant field of production in a recommendation letter. Other important tasks of committees of the associations at the local level include the standardization of products, supervision of training and education, certification that producers using the GI have the necessary skills, and certification and control of the materials involved in the production process.[83]

The ultimate decision about the appropriateness of the local regulations rests with a powerful *Tim Ahli Indikasi Geografis* (Expert Team for Geographical Indications) in Jakarta, which is appointed by the Minister of Justice.[84] When the first Expert Team was appointed in 2008, it included central government officials from various departments, from the Directorate General of Intellectual Property Rights (DGIP), and members of relevant research institutes.[85] In the future, it will comprise a representative of the Minister, respresentatives of the Ministries of agriculture, industry, trade and/or other related Ministries, respresentatives of the supervisory and quality assurance bodies, and other experts.[86] An Expert Team like this is supported by a Technical Evaluation Team.[87] What was particularly surprising about the previous regulation was the lengthy period that the Expert Team was allowed to take of up to two years

---

[79] *See, e.g.*, Decision of the Regent of Jepara No. 78 of 2010 Regarding the Formation of the Operational Organization of Geographical Indications Products, 55–59, http://119.252.174.21/indikasi-geografis/filemedia/Buku-Persyaratan-Mebel-Ukir-Jepara-Perubahan1/mobile/index.html (last visited March 9, 2016) [hereinafter Decision of the Regent of Jepara].

[80] Art. 6(3) Government Regulation No. 51/ 2007.

[81] See Arts. 56(2)a., 66a. Trade Marks and Geographical Indications Act.

[82] Art. 6 (3) Government Regulation No. 51/2007.

[83] *See, e.g.*, Decision of the Regent of Jepara, *supra* note 79.

[84] Arts. 8, 14 58, 59 Trade Marks and Geographical Indications Act.

[85] *Pemerintah angkat tim ahli indikasi geografis*, KOPI GAYO COFFEE (July 21, 2008), http://kopigayo.blogspot.com.au/2008/07/pemerintah-angkat-tim-ahli-indikasi.html (last visited June 3, 2016). For the regulation of membership of the team see Art. 14 (2) Government Regulation No. 51/2007.

[86] See Art. 59(2) of the Trade Marks and Geographical Indications Act.

[87] Article 59(5) Trade Marks and Geographical Indications Act.

for a decision on a GI application.[88] The new Trade Marks and Geographical Indications Act now brings the time table for the substantive examination into accordance with the much tighter framework of 150 days of the trademarks examination process by referring to Arts. 23 to 26 Trade Marks and Geographical Indications Act.[89] The new law also foresees a new Ministerial Regulation regarding the details of the registration process of GIs and the various expert teams,[90] which may finally replace Government Regulation No. 51/2007.

The central and regional levels of government also become involved in monitoring the use of the GI,[91] but the wider society, including communities and other interested parties, can also become involved.[92] Producers and producer organisations can also oppose registrations,[93] sue violators in the Commercial Court for damages, ceasing of the infringing activities as well as destruction of relevant labels and apply for an injunction to stop the infringing activities.[94] Article 18 of Government Regulation No. 51/2007 further offers a claim for deletion of an infringing registration.

4 THE CASE STUDIES OF *ADAN KRAYAN* RICE AND *JEPARA* FURNITURE

The significance of *adat* communities was discussed earlier. There are currently thirty-nine registered GIs in Indonesia, with most of them registered for agricultural products. One of these has been registered by the *Asosiasi Masyarakat Adat Perlindungan Beras Krayan* (Customary Community Association for the Protection of Adan Krayan Rice). This rice comes from the Krayan region of the province of North Kalimantan. The customary community in question is one of the many sub-groups of people that outsiders collectively refer to as the Dayak tribes,[95] who live on the island of Borneo, and are often the majority population in the island's interior. Those living in the Krayan region refer to themselves as Lundayeh, which means "people of the

---

[88] Art. 8(2) Government Regulation No. 51/2007.
[89] See Art. 58(2) Trade Marks and Geogreaphical Indications Act and Article 23(5) for the length of the substantive examination process..
[90] Art. 60 Trade Marks and Geographical Indications Act.
[91] Art. 71(1) Trade Marks and Geographical Indications Act.
[92] Article 71(2) Trade Marks and Geographical Indications Act.
[93] Articles 53(4), 16 Trade Marks and Geographical Indications Act.
[94] Article 69 Trade Marks and Geographical Indications Act.
[95] Robert L. Winzeler, Introduction to INDIGENOUS PEOPLES AND THE STATE: POLITICS, LAND, AND ETHNICITY IN THE MALAYAN PENINSULA AND BORNEO 1, 3 n. 2 (Robert L. Winzeler ed., 1997).

interior."[96] Like many other tribal population groups, they are spread over a fairly large territory and related groups are to be found in the Indonesian provinces of East and North Kalimantan as well as across the border in the states of Sabah and Sarawak in the Malaysian part of Borneo, where they are called Lun Bawang (people of the place).[97] The Kelabit people are another related group in the north-east of Sarawak who grow the same type of rice.[98] According to Cristina Eghenter, it is a two-hour motorcycle ride from the village of Long Bawan in Indonesia to the Kelalan Valley in Malaysia and "[f]or centuries this border has done little to divide communities and families on its two sides."[99] Ardhana et al. point out that "[t]hese people, while living in two different countries, share a common border and are bound to one another by ties of ethnicity, language, kinship, religion and economics" and are "linguistically and culturally the same."[100]

The people in this region practice a system of wet rice cultivation, which the Lundayeh call Lati'ba. It involves a combination of irrigation techniques, buffalos to soften the land and fertilize the soil with their waste, and bamboo to bind the soil and use as construction material for water pipes and fences.[101] The resulting organic rice comes in white, red, and black varieties and is famous for its quality and taste.[102] It is known as "Bario rice" in Malaysia and as "Adan Krayan rice" in Indonesia. However, while communities in Malaysia have road connections to major markets to sell their surplus rice, the Lundayeh on the Indonesian side of the border are well connected to the nearest village in Malaysia but need expensive air transport to reach the nearest provincial capitals in Indonesia.[103] As a result, surplus Adan Krayan rice is sold mainly in Ba Kelalan, the nearest border town in Malaysia.[104]

---

[96] I Ketut Ardhana, Jayl Langub & Daniel Chew, *Borders of Kinship and Ethnicity: Cross-Border Relations Between the Kelalan Valley, Sarawak, and the Bawan Valley, East Kalimantan*, 35 BORNEO RESEARCH BULLETIN 144–45 (2004).

[97] *Id.*

[98] Dora Jok, *Adan Rice*, in THE HUMAN HEART OF BORNEO 45 (Nancy Ariaini et al., (eds.), not dated), www.wwf.org.au/our_work/saving_the_natural_world/forests/forests_work/heart_of_borneo/the_human_heart/ (last visited June 6, 2016).

[99] Cristina Eghenter, *Borneo: One Island One Sustainable Future*, in THE HUMAN HEART OF BORNEO, *supra* note 98, at 57.

[100] Ardhana et al., *supra* note 96, at 144–145.

[101] Jayl Langub, *Lati'ba: The Process of Wet-Rice Cultivation*, in THE HUMAN HEART OF BORNEO, *supra* note 98, at 44.

[102] Jok, *supra* note 98, at 45; Ardhana et al., *supra* note 96, at 144–145.

[103] *Beras Adan Resmi Dipatenkan*, KOMPAS: REGIONAL (January 15, 2012), http://regional.kompas.com/read/2012/01/15/18453496/Beras.Adan (last visited February 15, 2016)

[104] Ardhana et al., *supra* note 96, at 144–145.

The Malaysian side allows border trade to be free of customs duties only in this border area so that it would not be economically feasible for the Indonesians to circumvent the traders in the town by selling further inland.[105]

When a GI for Adan Krayan rice was registered in Indonesia in 2012, the Indonesian press was quick in celebrating the registration as a victory over what they regarded as copycats on the Malaysian side of the border, following several disputes about cultural and IP rights to cultural material in recent years.[106] What was "temporarily claimed by Malaysia," as stated in one article, "was now the property of Indonesia."[107] The "claiming by Malaysia" referred to a GI registration for Bario rice in Malaysia in 2008 by the Sarawak Information Technology and Resources Council, a state agency of the government of Sarawak. The same newspaper article also explained that because of their geographical isolation, Adan Krayan people were forced to sell their rice on the Malaysian side of the border. Some local government officials subsequently went as far as to claim in the media that all rice sold on the Malaysian side as "Bario rice" in fact originated in the Krayan region of Indonesia and that the rice could not be grown elsewhere.[108] Studies of the border trade indeed confirm the economic grip of the Malaysian side over the Indonesian communities but also explain that the rice is grown on both sides of the border, on the Malaysian side not only in Sarawak but also in Sabah. The climate and altitude on both sides of the border are similar, as is the "human factor" of irrigation techniques and the other elements described above as part of the Lati'ba system.[109] Quite clearly, these techniques are practiced on both sides of the border by these related communities and, consequently, both GIs continue to be used.

In what commentators regard as a further attempt by the government to stop Malaysian claims, the local government of the regency has also registered Adan Krayan as plant variety.[110] According to Article 7(1) of the Plant Varieties Protection Act,[111] local varieties are "owned by the community, but controlled by the state." In the implementing

---

[105] Id. at 169, 172. [106] Antons, supra note 18.
[107] Andi Saputra, Sempat Diklaim Malaysia, Beras Adan Krayan Kini Milik Indonesia, DETIKNEWS (January 13, 2012), http://news.detik.com/berita/1815286/sempat-diklaim-malaysia-beras-adan-krayan-kini-milik-indonesia (last visited February 15, 2016)
[108] Beras Adan Resmi Dipatenkan, supra note 97; Agus Candra, Malaysia Klaim Padi Adan Indonesia, KOMPASIANA (March 14, 2011), www.kompasiana.com/aguscandra/malaysia-klaim-padi-adan-indonesia_5500959da333113e0950fe67 (last visited February 15, 2016)
[109] Ardhana et al., supra note 96, at 144–145. [110] Candra, supra note 108.
[111] Undang-Undang Republik Indonesia Nomor 29 Tahun 2000 Tentang Perlindungan Varietas Tanaman.

Government Regulation,[112] local government officers are put in charge of registering them and, accordingly, all local varieties registered since 2005 have been registered by governors of provinces, mayors of towns, and regency officers.[113] For instance, the Krayan rice varieties were registered in 2006 by the Head of the local Regency of Nunukan.[114] The Trade Marks and Geographical Indications Act seeks to avoid overlaps between plant variety protection and GIs by stipulating in Article 56(1)c. that a local geographical name registered for a plant variety can no longer be used to register a GI for the same plant, unless further words are used that indicate that it concerns a geographical indication. In the case of Krayan rice, only the white variety is registered in the Plant Variety Register using the term *Adan*, but with the additional term *putih* (white).[115] Also, the Indonesian language has different words for rice in the field (*padi*) and harvested rice (*beras*). Thus, the GI is registered for harvested rice and not for the plant and this could be an additional reason why the subsequent GI registration has been allowed in this case.

Although the word "*adat*" used here is the same as that recognized in Article 18B(2) of the Constitution, the GI Protection Association formed here for the purposes of administering the GI is an organization in the context of the IP legislation and not necessarily identical with the constitutionally recognized "*adat* law community." The Heads of the various local *adat* communities are involved as *penasehat* (advisers), while the whole association stands under the *pelindung* (patronage) of the highest local government officials, including the *Bupati* (government officer in charge of the regency).[116] In sum, government officials and the population have high hopes for the legal protection of this rice via the registered GI. However, they may be disappointed because the registration in Indonesia does not seem to help much as long as the lack of transportation and market access problems persist. The geographical isolation of the Krayan communities means that these communities have to continue to

---

[112] Peraturan Pemerintah Republik Indonesia Nomor 13 Tahun 2004 Tentang Penamaan Pendaftaran dan Penggunaan Varietas Asal untuk Varietas Turunan Esensial.
[113] Rajeswari Kanniah & Christoph Antons, *Plant Variety Protection and Traditional Agricultural Knowledge in Southeast Asia*, 13 AUSTL. J. ASIAN L. 16 (2012).
[114] Plant Variety Register, PUSAT PERLINDUNGAN VARIETAS TANAMAN (CENTRE FOR PLANT VARIETY PROTECTION) OF THE MINISTRY OF AGRICULTURE, http://ppvt.setjen.pertanian.go.id/ppvtpp//tinymcpuk/gambar/File/VL-2014(1).pdf (last visited March 10, 2016).
[115] *Id.*
[116] For the composition of the management of the association see the "Book of rules and regulations" *Buku Persyaratan Indikasi Geografis – Asosiasi Masyarakat Adat Perlindungan Beras Adan Krayan*, http://119.252.174.21/indikasi-geografis/?paged=2 (last visited February 15, 2016).

sell their rice to their main competitors in Malaysia,[117] and the GI protection cannot allow them to raise prices under such circumstances. With regard to the division of income and responsibilities in the context of decentralization policies, the Krayan region was not affected by the violent clashes between local Dayak groups and transmigrants elsewhere in Kalimantan. Reports indicate in fact that there is outmigration from the area and the relatively small population of non-Lundayeh people is welcome to join the workforce, in particular on the Malaysian side of the border.[118] Nevertheless, a discourse regarding indigenous IP rights is forming in the central parts of Borneo. This is visible from the main points that a newly formed "Alliance of Indigenous Peoples of the Highlands of Borneo" regards as its mission, which includes the protection of cultural sites, historical sites, and "the collective intellectual property rights of the Indigenous Peoples of the Highlands."[119]

Of the thirty-nine GIs registered so far, all but one relate to agricultural goods. The only registration for traditional crafts on the list is Jepara furniture, a highly valued and popular traditional type of Javanese furniture produced in the Jepara Regency on the north coast of Java.[120] This GI is registered by an Association called *Jepara Indikasi Geografis Mebel Ukir Jepara* (Jepara Geographical Indication for Carved Jepara Furniture). The Executive Committee of this association consists of many government officers at the regency level and representatives from producer associations, artisan centers, and craft schools.[121] The regency government also forms a committee that evaluates relevant products and recommends producers and artisans that may register as users of the GI. This committee also maintains the quality control of the materials used and checks the qualification of the artisans involved in the production process.[122]

The low number of registrations of craft-related GIs in comparison to those relating to agriculture is surprising in a culturally rich country like Indonesia.

---

[117] Ardhana et al., *supra* note 96, at 147, 169, 172. [118] *Id.* at 174.
[119] THE HUMAN HEART OF BORNEO, *supra* note 98, at 59.
[120] See the relevant "Book of rules and regulations" *Buku Persyaratan Indikasi Geografis – Indikasi Geografis Mebel Ukir Jepara* 1–2, http://119.252.174.21/indikasi-geografis/?book=mebel-ukir-jepara (last visited March 10, 2016).
[121] *Id.* at 57–59.
[122] *Id.* at 60–62; *see also* Farisa Adilan, *Hak Indikasi Geografis Mebel Ukir Jepara (IG MUJ) dalam Peningkatan Ekonomi Daerah Kabupaten Jepara*, www.academia.edu/10110570/Hak_Indikasi_Geografis_Mebel_Ukir_Jepara_IG_MUJ_dalam_Peningkatan_Ekonomi_Daerah_Kabupaten_Jepara (last visited February 15, 2016); *HaKI IG Melindungi Mebel Ukir*, KOMPAS (December 27, 2010), http://edukasi.kompas.com/read/2010/12/27/03545334/HaKI.IG.Melindungi.Mebel.Ukir (last visited February 15, 2016).

One reason for this relatively low interest in GIs in the craft sector could be that the products of the larger producers of Batik and similar craft products are already protected by trademarks that are well known in Indonesia. Hence, while GIs could provide an additional marketing tool for such producers, they are already well served by other parts of the IP system. Another reason could be that the borders of the region of protection are more difficult to establish for cultural products that rely strongly on the skills of people involved in the production rather than on climatic or soil conditions as in agriculture. In the case of Jepara furniture, the GI is supposed to help in competition with not just international furniture producers from countries like China and Vietnam but also other local producers that have been inspired by the success of Jepara furniture but are producing at lower costs.[123]

Again, however, the GI offers only a marketing tool in the competition with low-cost producers elsewhere in Indonesia but does not prevent these producers from producing furniture in Jepara style. Ensuring greater exclusivity by relying on copyright or design registration is not possible with regard to traditional motifs in Indonesia. This is because Indonesian design law requires a "new design,"[124] while the new Indonesian Copyright Act of 2014 establishes the state as the fictional copyright holder over traditional cultural expressions.[125]

5 CONCLUSION

GIs have often been discussed in the context of local and rural development and the safeguarding of cultural heritage. This link to rural and regional developments means that an assessment of the impact of GIs in such fields needs to take into account Indonesia's efforts at decentralizing the political and administrative power structure since 1999. Discussions in this field could become enmeshed in complicated bargaining processes between central and regional authorities, and between different levels of government and local communities about the scope and direction of development projects and the usefulness of GIs in this context. Differences about such directions have occasionally come to the fore on the fringes of the vast Indonesian archipelago in provinces such as Aceh and Papua and on the island of Sulawesi, for example. The decentralization process is now leading to the emergence of regional IP laws, which, in the example of Papua, create different IP rights for

---

[123] *HaKI IG Melindungi Mebel Ukir*, supra note 116; Adilan, supra note 116.
[124] Art. 2(1) of Law No. 31 of 2000 on Industrial Designs.
[125] Art. 38 of Law No. 28 of 2014 on Copyright.

Papuans. There is also an emerging indigenous peoples' movement in other parts of Indonesia, which in some cases wants to see the indigenous peoples' collective IP rights being protected.

Indonesia's current GI legislation makes the community organizations representing the GI users the principal right holders. Such community organizations are not to be confused with traditional *adat* communities. They are usually set up with substantial involvement of local government agencies to administer the GIs and to maintain the quality of the goods for which they are used. Although they have strong supervisory roles at the local level, the ultimate decision about the registration of the GIs and the appropriateness of rules and regulations relating to them is made by an expert team in Jakarta.

The case studies presented in this chapter show widespread hope with regard to GIs at both the community and government levels. They show, however, that the expectations are often exaggerated. GIs are marketing tools and not instruments to exclude competitors at the national or international level. Their effects on heritage and the environment will only become visible in the longer term. In neighboring Malaysia, for example, the success of highland rice has occasionally led to attempts to raise the output by introducing double cropping and inorganic chemical inputs.[126] In remote and isolated settings, as in the Krayan in Kalimantan, GIs can be of little help if it is too costly to actually reach the target markets and products have to be sold in the markets of competitors. Nevertheless, there are positive assessments of the effect of GIs established elsewhere, such as in Bali. It is further surprising to see that the registration for Jepara furniture is so far the only GI relating to traditional crafts in a country as rich in traditional culture as Indonesia. Perhaps the reason is that the larger commercial players in industries such as Batik are already well served by other parts of the IP system. Nevertheless, the GI for Jepara furniture could prove advantageous for Jepara producers in differentiating their products from their numerous competitors.

---

[126] Ardhana et al., *supra* note 96, at 175.

21

When Geographical Indications Meet Intangible Cultural Heritage: The New Japanese Act on Geographical Indications

Steven Van Uytsel[*]

1 INTRODUCTION

'Some scholars have begun to acknowledge the symmetries between formal recognition as GI [geographical indications] and as ICH [intangible cultural heritage]',[1] Dev Gangjee reports in his paper *Geographical Indications and Cultural Rights: The Intangible Cultural Heritage Connection?*[2] Gangjee then tells us that 'Brazilian researchers have identified the strategic potential for GI protection for the clay pots of Goiabeiras, from the Brazilian state of Espirito Santo'.[3] Subsequently, not only did Brazil formally recognize these pots under their intangible cultural heritage (ICH) laws, but also registered it as a geographical indication (GI). The idea behind this double recognition was to boost the marketing of this ICH and, if necessary, provide 'protection in the international markets'.[4]

The Brazilian example shows that GIs are not necessarily restricted to agricultural products. The extension of the scope of GIs beyond strictly agricultural products is the subject of intensive research.[5] In fact, several

---

[*] Associate Professor, Graduate School of Law, Kyushu University (Japan). The author would like to thank the International Research Centre for Intangible Cultural Heritage in the Asia-Pacific Region (IRCI) for their financial contribution to facilitate this research. The views and opinions expressed in this chapter are those of the author and do not necessarily reflect the official policy or position of IRCI.

[1] Dev S. Gangjee, *Geographical Indications and Cultural Rights: The Intangible Cultural Heritage Connection?*, in RESEARCH HANDBOOK ON HUMAN RIGHTS AND INTELLECTUAL PROPERTY 544, 555–556 (Christophe Geiger ed., 2015) [hereinafter Gangjee, *GIs and Cultural Rights*].

[2] *Id.* at 556.   [3] *Id.*   [4] *Id.*

[5] *See, e.g.,* Michael Blakeney, *Geographical Indications, Traditional Knowledge, Expressions of Culture and the Protection of Cultural Products in Africa*, in EXTENDING THE PROTECTION OF GEOGRAPHICAL INDICATIONS: CASE STUDIES OF AGRICULTURAL PRODUCTS IN AFRICA 120

countries, such as Japan, have already taken the step to adopt legislation with a broad protective scope for GIs.[6] The Japanese Parliament – the Diet – has amended what is regarded as 'the' Geographical Indications Act (GI Act) of Japan,[7] the *Tokutei Norin Suisan Butsu to no Meisho no Hogo ni Kansuru Horitsu* (Act for the Protection of the Names of Designated Agricultural, Forestry and Fishery Products and Foodstuffs) (GI Act),[8] to include derivatives of agricultural products[9] (e.g., Japanese lacquer, an organic substance made from the sap of the urushi tree).

The extended scope of protection for 'non-edible agricultural, fishery or forestry products and products manufactured or processed using agricultural, forestry and fishery products'[10] opens the discussion of applying the GI Act to ICH, as Brazil already has. Because this is already a reality, the idea cannot simply be dismissed with arguments that GIs are not suitable for protecting ICH. It does not matter that the reasoning behind such arguments is valuable; there has to be some guidance for communities – the holders of ICH – about the possible hidden dangers of applying for a GI in relation to products based on ICH.

This chapter is structured as follows. Section 2 will introduce that the debate on GIs and ICH has mainly two opposing views on the role GIs can play for ICH. By unveiling the scope of the new Japanese GI Act, the section

---

(Michael Blakeney, Thiery Coulet, Getachew Mengistie, & Marcelin Tonye Mahop eds., 2012); Michael Blakeney, *Protection of Traditional Knowledge by Geographical Indications*, 3 INT'L J. INTELL. PROP. MGMT 357 (2009); INSIGHT CONSULTING, REDD AND ORIGIN, STUDY ON GEOGRAPHICAL INDICATIONS PROTECTIONS FOR NON-AGRICULTURAL PRODUCTS IN THE INTERNAL MARKET: FINAL REPORT (2013) available at http://ec.europa.eu/internal_market/in dprop/docs/geo-indications/130322_geo-indications-non-agri-study_en.pdf.

[6] In several countries, protection for GIs extends beyond agricultural products. Among these countries are Brazil, Chile, China, Colombia, Russia, and Switzerland. *See, e.g.*, INSIGHT CONSULTING, REDD & ORIGIN, *supra* note 5, at 19–20.

[7] *See, e.g.*, MINISTRY OF AGRICULTURE, FORESTRY AND FISHERIES, *Geographical Indication (GI) Protection System in Japan*, MAFF, www.maff.go.jp/e/japan_food/gi_act/pdf/gi_pamph. pdf (last visited March 10, 2016); Junko Kimura, *Dawn of Geographical Indications in Japan: Strategic Marketing Management of GI Candidates* (2015), available at http://ageconsearch .umn.edu/bitstream/200232/2/J.%20Kimura%20(2015)%20Dawn%20of%20Geographical%20 Indications%20in%20Japan%20Strategic%20Marketing%20Management%20of%20GI%20 Products%20Candidates.pdf (last visited 15 September 2015).

[8] *Tokutei Norin Suisan Butsu to no Meisho no Hogo ni Kansuru Horitsu* [Act for the Protection of the Names of Designated Agricultural, Forestry and Fishery Products and Foodstuffs], 25 June 2014, available at www.maff.go.jp/j/shokusan/gi_act/outline/pdf/doc4.pdf [hereinafter GI Act]. *See* Juichi Hayashi, *Japan to Implement GI System on June 1, 2015*, GAIN Report Number JA5008 (2015), available at http://gain.fas.usda.gov/Recent%20GAIN%20Publication s/Japan%20to%20Implement%20GI%20system%20on%20June%201_2015_Tokyo_Japan_3-10- 2015.pdf.

[9] GI Act, *supra* note 8, art. 2.   [10] *Id.*.

will show that part of the debate has become obsolete because, in reality, GIs could sometimes overlap with ICH. Section 3 will describe in detail the conceptualization of the new Japanese GI Act. This will pave the way for further analysis in Section 4 of the perils and promises that the extension of the GI Act has on ICH. In conclusion, Section 5 will hold that although the GI Act extends to ICH, holders of ICH should still be careful when they seek to register products that incorporate their ICH as part of the GI.

2 GEOGRAPHICAL INDICATIONS AND INTANGIBLE CULTURAL HERITAGE: THE JAPANESE GEOGRAPHICAL INDICATIONS ACT

Without denying the existence of sophisticated studies,[11] the academic debate on the use of GIs in relation to ICH is divided.[12] On the one hand, scholars have defended the vision that GIs and ICH are two worlds apart.[13] On the other hand, scholars have opined that GIs could have a positive contribution to ICH.[14] These two visions probably emerged from the fact that GIs and ICH

---

[11] See, e.g., Justin Hughes, *Coffee and Chocolate – Can We Help Developing Country Farmers through Geographical Indications?* (Washington, DC: International Intellectual Property Institute, 2010), available at http://papers.ssrn.com/sol3/papers.cfm?abstract_id=1684370.

[12] The debate is mainly conducted within the framework of traditional knowledge (TK) or traditional cultural expressions (TCE). The current chapter adopts the preposition that what has been said for TK and TCE can be transferred to intangible cultural heritage (ICH) as well. This is based on the parallels between the definitions that have been adopted or are being elaborated at the international level. See respectively Convention for the Safeguarding of the Intangible Cultural Heritage, U.N. Doc. MISC/2003/CLT/CH/14 (17 October 2003) [hereinafter ICH Convention]; The Protection of Traditional Knowledge: Draft Articles, WIPO Document No. WIPO/GRTKF/IC/28/5, June 2, 2014 www.wipo.int/meetings/en/doc_details.jsp?doc_id=276361; The Protection of Traditional cultural expressions: WIPO Document No. WIPO/GRTKF/IC/28/6, June 2, 2014 www.wipo.int/meetings/en/doc_details.jsp?doc_id=276220.

[13] See, e.g., Tomer Broude, *A Diet Too Far? Intangible Cultural Heritage, Cultural Diversity, and Culinary Practices*, in DIVERSITY IN INTELLECTUAL PROPERTY: IDENTITIES, INTERESTS, AND INTERSECTIONS 472 (Irene Calboli & Srividhya Ragavan eds., 2015); Susy Frankel, *The Mismatch of Geographical Indications and Innovative Traditional Knowledge* 29(3) PROMETHEUS 253–267 (2011), available at http://papers.ssrn.com/sol3/papers.cfm?abstract_id=1953033; Toshiyuki Kono, *Geographical Indication and Intangible Cultural Heritage*, in LE INDICAZIONI DI QUALITÀ DEGLI ALIMENTI: DIRITTO INTERNAZIONALE ED EUROPEO 289 (Benedetta Ubertazzi & Esther Muñiz Espada eds., 2009); Tomer Broude, *Taking 'Trade and Culture' Seriously: Geographical Indications and Cultural Protection in WTO Law*, 26 U. PA. J. INT'L L. 623 (2005) [hereinafter Broude, *Trade and Culture*].

[14] See, e.g., Gangjee, *GIs and Cultural Rights*, supra note 1, at 544; Irene Calboli, *Of Markets, Culture, and Terroir: The Unique Economic and Culture-Related Benefits of Geographical Indications of Origin*, in RESEARCH HANDBOOK ON INTERNATIONAL INTELLECTUAL PROPERTY 433 (Daniel Gervais ed., 2014); Delphine Marie-Vivien, *The Protection of Geographical Indications for Handicrafts: How to Apply the Concepts of Natural and Human Factors to All Products*, 4 WIPO J. 191 (2013); Daniel Gervais, *Traditional Innovation and the*

have 'their focus on old creativity and community ownership, rather than new knowledge and individual ownership'.[15]

Among these debating scholars, it is not only possible to distinguish two different views – one stating that GIs and ICH are two worlds apart, and one arguing in favour of using GIs to safeguard ICH – but it is also possible to discern the two distinct approaches to support each view. One approach focuses on the definition of GIs and ICH to argument either for or against a supportive role.[16] The other approach places emphasis on whether a GI could, in practice, mean something for ICH in order to conclude in favour, or disfavour, of a supportive role.[17]

Reaching different outcomes for a similar question may lead to the conclusion that there is confusion on the substantive matter. But one could attempt to disentangle the different understandings and bring clarity in the confusion: it could be argued that GIs have a different understanding of the collectivity concept.[18] However, that does not mean that the holders of ICH are excluded from using the ICH just because a GI has been attached to a product produced by this heritage. In the same way, ICH may not have a monopoly right,[19] but that does not necessarily mean that GIs are attributing a monopoly right to it. In fact, it is possible that a GI may not permanently preserve ICH, but that would equally deny the very nature of ICH. Theoretical statements made on the indirect support of GIs for ICH risk falling down a slippery slope if they are not supported by empirical evidence.[20]

However, any attempt to achieve uniformity in the discussion on GIs and ICH may be obsolete. The reality is that legislators have created GI regimes that allow the registration of non-edible products. Japan, be it in a limited way, is one such example. The Japanese Diet passed the GI Act in 2014[21] and has been operating under the supervision of the Ministry of Agriculture, Forestry and Fishery (MAFF) since 1 June 2015.[22]

Ongoing Debate on the Protection of Geographical Indications, in INDIGENOUS PEOPLES' INNOVATION: INTELLECTUAL PROPERTY PATHWAYS TO DEVELOPMENT 121, 132–143 (Peter Drahos & Susy Frankel eds., 2012) (admitting that the support is limited to non-secret traditional knowledge); Cerkia Bramley, *A Review of the Socio-Economic Impact of Geographical Indications: Considerations for the Developing World* (24 June 2011), available at www.wipo.int/e docs/mdocs/geoind/en/wipo_geo_lim_11/wipo_geo_lim_11_9.pdf.

[15] Marsha A. Echols, *Geographical Indications for Foods, TRIPS and the Doha Development Agenda*, 47 J. AFR. L. 199 (2003).
[16] See references *supra* note 13 and 14.   [17] *Id.*   [18] See Frankel, *supra* note 13, at 8.
[19] See Kono, *supra* note 13, at 298.   [20] See Calboli, *supra* note 14, at 452.
[21] GI Act, *supra* note 8.
[22] The focus of the Abe Cabinet on raising the profile of the agricultural sector as one of the pillars of the Japanese economy has facilitated the promulgation of a GI Act that solely focuses

MAFF being in charge of operating the GI Act (which may be explained by the fact that the agricultural sector wanted an extra layer of protection in place given the ongoing negotiations for the Trans-Pacific Partnership Agreement (TPPA))[23] has an impact on the definition of products eligible for a GI. Only products and foodstuffs that relate to agriculture, forestry, and fishery are within the protective scope of the GI Act.[24] However, the legislator did not limit the scope to only edible or drinkable agricultural, forestry, or fishery products and foodstuffs. Instead, it was decided that protection would also extend to non-edible manufactured or processed agricultural, forestry, and fishery products.

Article 2 of the GI Act enables the designation of the following products with a GI:

(1) Edible agricultural, forestry, and fishery products
(2) Food and beverages
(3) Non-edible agricultural, forestry, and fishery products
(4) Products manufactured or processed using agricultural, forestry, and fishery products.[25]

---

on agricultural, forestry, and fishery products and foodstuffs. *See* Ministry of Agriculture, Forestry and Fisheries, *Abe Cabinet Agricultural Reform*, MAFF, http://fpcj.jp/wp/wp-content/uploads/2014/07/a89885aa705c72d976dd953518d82140.pdf (last visited 8 October 2015).

[23] *See* Nami Togawa, *Report on the New Japanese Law on Protection of Geographical Indications*, INTERNATIONAL ASSOCIATION FOR THE PROTECTION OF INTELLECTUAL PROPERTY (2014) available at http://aippi.org/wp-content/uploads/committees/220/GR220japan.pdf. MAFF had been trying to set up a *sui generis* system for the protection of GIs in 2003. However, in a power struggle with the Ministry of Economy, Trade and Industry of Japan (METI), MAFF had to recognize its superior in METI, which developed the regionally based collective trademark system. *See* Louis Augustin-Jean & Kae Sekine, *From Products of Origin to Geographical Indications in Japan: Perspectives on the Construction of Quality for the Emblematic Productions of Kobe & Matsusaka Beef*, in GEOGRAPHICAL INDICATIONS AND INTERNATIONAL AGRICULTURAL TRADE: THE CHALLENGE FOR ASIA 139, 148 (Louis Augustin-Jean, Hélène Ilbert, & Neantro Saavedra-Rivano eds., 2012); Daisuke Kojo, *Comment: The Importance of the Geographic Origin of Agricultural Products: A Comparison of Japanese and American Approaches*, 14 MO. ENVTL. L. & POL'Y REV. 275, 294 (2007). On the regionally based collective trademarks, *see* Kenneth Port, *Regionally Based Collective Trademark System in Japan: Geographical Indicators by a Different Name or a Political Misdirection?* 6 CYBARIS, AN INTEL. PROP. L. REV. 2 (2015).

[24] This definition is narrower than the internationally accepted minimal standard for GIs formulated in Article 22(1) of TRIPS. Geographical indications, as defined in TRIPS, can include all kind of products, as long as there is a 'quality, reputation or other characteristic' linked to these products that can be attributed to a specific geographical region. *See* Calboli, *supra* note 14, at 457–59; Marie-Vivien, *supra* note 14, at 194–95.

[25] GI Act, *supra* note 8, art. 2.

In the same Article, we see that alcohol, pharmaceuticals, quasi-pharmaceutical products, cosmetics, and regenerative medicine are excluded from the list of products that could be categorized as agricultural, forestry, and fishery products. Alcoholic drinks, such as *sake, shochu*, wine, or spirits, can obtain a GI under the *Act Concerning Liquor Business Associations and Measures for Securing Revenue from Liquor Tax*.[26]

However, eggs, vegetables, fruits, seafood, milk, or eggs can be categorized under the first section of Article 2 of the GI Act,[27] and bread, tofu, olive oil, soft drinks, or prepared food[28] under the second section. A Cabinet Order further explains sections 3 and 4 of Article 2 of the GI Act. MAFF categorizes ornamental plants, industrial crops, ornamental fish, and pearls under non-edible agricultural, forestry, and fishery products.[29] Products manufactured or processed using agricultural, forestry, and fishery products include feed (limited to things manufactured or processed from agricultural, forestry, or fishery products as raw produce or as ingredients), lacquer, bamboo material, essential oil, charcoal, timber, tatami facing, and raw silk.[30]

By including manufactured or processed products, the GI Act is embracing know-how, skills, and practices necessary for transforming agricultural, forestry, and fishery products into other products. These know-how, skills, and practices could have developed in response to the external environment and have since been passed down from generation to generation. Thus, they have been recognized as part of the identity of the beholders. Moreover, such know-how, skills, and practices constitute craftsmanship, which is also recognized as a category of ICH internationally[31] and in

---

[26] *See* Concerning Liquor Business Associations and Measures for Securing Revenue from Liquor Tax, No. 7 of 1953, art. 86.6 (Japan). The powers attributed to the Minister of Finance in this article have been used to create a GI system for liquors, *see* Standard for Indication in Relation to Geographical Indications, (Notification No. 4 of National Tax Agency, Revised Edition Notification No. 9, 2006) 28 December 1994, WIPO Lex No. JP068, available at www.wipo.int/edocs/lexdocs/laws/ja/jp/jp068ja.pdf (for an unofficial translation: www.wipo.int/edocs/lexdocs/laws/en/jp/jp068en.pdf). There are currently six geographical indications recognized for wine (Yamanashi), sake (Hakusan), and *sochu* (Iki, Kuma, Satsuma, and Ryukyu).

[27] *See* MINISTRY OF AGRICULTURE, FORESTRY AND FISHERIES, *Establishment of Japan's Geographical Indication*, (GI) Protection System, MAFF, www.eu-japan.eu/sites/eu-japan.eu/files/SAKA_EN_0.pdf (last visited 8 October 2015) (stipulating that there is no need for a Cabinet Order to further specify the products that are included).

[28] *See id.* (stipulating that there is no need for a Cabinet Order to further specify the products that are included).

[29] *See* Implementation of Act for the Protection of the Names of Designated Agricultural, Forestry and Fishery Products and Foodstuffs, Law No. 227 of 2015, art. 1 (Japan) available at www.maff.go.jp/j/shokusan/gi_act/outline/pdf/doc7.pdf.

[30] *See* Cabinet Order No. 227, *supra* note 29, art 2.

[31] *See* ICH Convention, *supra* note 12, arts. 2(1)–(2). *See also* JANET BLAKE, COMMENTARY ON THE UNESCO 2003 CONVENTION ON THE SAFEGUARDING OF THE INTANGIBLE CULTURAL HERITAGE 31, 39 (2006).

Japan.[32] Holders of such an ICH, whether or not recognized under any of the ICH regimes, should therefore carefully consider the regime that each jurisdiction has for GIs before filing an application. The next section explains how the GI regime is implemented in Japan.

3 THE PROCESS TOWARDS OBTAINING A GEOGRAPHICAL INDICATION IN JAPAN

3.1 Registering a Geographical Indication

In order for agricultural, forestry, and fishery products, and foodstuffs to be eligible for a GI, they first need to be identifiable based on location,[33] quality, or reputation linked to that location.[34] If producers or processors of agricultural, forestry, and fishery products think that their products fulfil these criteria, they can form an association of producers.[35]

An association of producers is in principle composed of members who can be, but are not limited to,[36] the direct producers of the agricultural, forestry, and fishery produce. If the association is organized as a legal person, a representative or a manager has to be appointed. The association has multiple tasks: first, it has the responsibility of applying for the GI to MAFF and therefore has to prepare all the necessary documents. Second, once a GI registration has been granted, the association is responsible for the management and control of the production processes described in the product specification (as filed in the application).

Once the association of producers has been formed, it can proceed to file an application with MAFF for a GI.[37] The application needs to contain the following information:[38]

(1) Name and address of the association of producers and its representative
(2) Classification of the agricultural, forestry, or fishery product

---

[32] See Law for the Protection of Cultural Property, Law No. 2014 of 1950, art. 2(2) (Revised Edition 2007), available at www.unesco.org/culture/natlaws/media/pdf/japan/japan_lawprotectionculturalproperty_engtof.pdf (hereinafter Law No. 2014) (intangible cultural heritage is referred to in this law as intangible cultural properties and folk-cultural properties. Know-how, techniques, and traditional craftsmanship are categorized under intangible cultural properties). See also CULTURAL PROPERTIES DEPARTMENT (AGENCY FOR CULTURAL AFFAIRS), CULTURAL PROPERTIES FOR FUTURE GENERATIONS – OUTLINE OF THE CULTURAL ADMINISTRATION OF JAPAN (March 2015), www.bunka.go.jp/tokei_hakusho_shuppan/shuppanbutsu/bunkazai_pamphlet/pdf/pamphlet_en_03_vero4.pdf.
[33] See GI Act, supra note 8, arts. 2(1), 3.   [34] See id. at arts. 2(2), 3.   [35] See id. at art. 2(5).
[36] See Hayashi, supra note 8, at 4 (mentioning that producers, processors, and local branding associations can form an association of producers).
[37] See GI Act, supra note 8, art. 7.   [38] See id. at art. 7(1) 1–8.

(3) Name of the agricultural, forestry, or fishery product
(4) Region of the agricultural, forestry, or fishery product
(5) Distinct characteristic of the agricultural, forestry, or fishery product (shape, taste, etc.)
(6) Method of production of the agricultural, forestry, or fishery product.

This list of requirements can be expanded by MAFF to include other necessary information.[39] The producer association must also submit detailed product specifications and quality-control guidelines together with the application form.[40] These guidelines should specify how the group will manage the production process. Since the specification of the product is supposed to be done within the specified community, the local producers or processors who want the recognition of their products as GIs will be consulted.

Once the GI application is submitted, MAFF will publish the application on a dedicated website.[41] Subsequently, for a period of three months thereafter, any person may submit an opinion regarding the application to MAFF.[42] The opinions are then forwarded to the applying association.[43]

After the three months, MAFF must consult experts (persons with specialized knowledge and experience) to see whether the application should be rejected under one of the categories listed in the GI Act.[44] The experts will also be given the opinions expressed during the three-month public notice period.[45] If the experts deem it necessary, they can also directly consult the stakeholders.[46] In the process of formulating their opinion, the experts have a duty of confidentiality regarding the information they have obtained. Furthermore, they should not use this information fraudulently.[47] If the experts' screening process does not reveal any reason to reject the application, MAFF will proceed to register the GI,[48] inform the applicant of its successful registration,[49] and notify the public by posting it on a designated MAFF website.[50]

3.2 Refusal of an Application for a Geographical Indication

There are several reasons why a GI application may be denied. The main reasons can be divided into the following categories: the nature or behaviour of

---

[39] See id. at art. 7(1) 9. [40] See id. at art. 7(2). [41] See id. at art. 8.
[42] See id. at art. 9(1). [43] See GI Act, supra note 8, art. 9(2). [44] See id. at art. 11.
[45] See id. at art. 11(2). [46] See id. at art. 11(3). [47] See id. at art. 11(4).
[48] See id. at art. 12(1). [49] See GI Act, supra note 8, art. 12(3). [50] See id.

the applicant,[51] the quality-control guidelines,[52] the nature of the product,[53] and the name of the product.[54]

A prospective applicant may have to wait two years before applying again if his organization's (association of producers) GI had previously been cancelled for any of the following reasons:[55]

(1) the association of producers no longer meet the requirements of being an association of producers;
(2) the association of producers has disobeyed an order of MAFF; or
(3) the association of producers has submitted an application by unlawful means.

Next, quality-control guidelines are an important part of the application. They should stipulate how the organization plans to ensure that the association's members comply with the methods of production described in the application.[56] Registration may be refused if the guidelines are insufficient to fairly ensure compliance with the stipulated methods of production.[57] Equally, if the organization does not prove to have enough financial or technical ability to maintain quality control, MAFF will refuse the application.[58]

MAFF will also refuse a GI application if the products do not meet the definition of the designated agricultural, forestry, and fishery products, and foodstuffs.[59] This has two aspects. Items that fall outside the definition of agricultural, forestry, and fishery products, and foodstuffs in Article 2(1) may be refused application.[60] Another basis for refusal is the lack of a geographic link, specific quality, reputation, or other characteristic that is attributable to the location in question.[61]

Finally, the MAFF may refuse an application if the name of the product is a generic term,[62] or if it is identical or similar to a registered trademark.[63] However, it is possible that the owner of a registered trademark, or an authorized user, could have applied for GI recognition.[64] In such a case, the name will be protected under both the trademark law and the GI Act.

3.3 Amendments to a Geographical Indication Registration

In Japan, the terms of registration of a GI are not necessarily permanently fixed. Even though it is compulsory to submit a description of the production

---

[51] See id. at art. 13(1). [52] See id. at art. 13(2). [53] See id. at art. 13(3).
[54] See id. at art. 13(4). [55] See GI Act, supra note 8, arts. 13(1), 22. [56] See id. at art. 13(2).
[57] See id. [58] See id. [59] See id. at art. 13(3). [60] See id. at art. 2(1).
[61] See GI Act, supra note 8, art. 2(2). [62] See id. at art. 13(4)(a). [63] See id. at art. 13(4)(b).
[64] See id.

process and to implement quality-control guidelines to ensure compliance, the GI Act gives the association of producers the opportunity to revise their registration.[65] The process of amending a GI's registration is, just like the registration process itself, a time-consuming one under the supervision of MAFF. The amendments may be related to either the eligibility of the association of producers[66] or the application documents.[67]

The association of producers in charge of checking for compliance with the quality-control guidelines can apply to add another association of producers.[68] This application requires the name and address of the added association of producers and its representative.[69]

Amendments to application documents have to be supported by all the associations of producers that have applied for the registration of a GI.[70] In other words, all associations of producers need to submit a joint application for an amendment. The request for an amendment can relate to the name, the region, the characteristic of the product, the production process, or if MAFF requires extra information.[71] The application for an amendment needs to mention the registration number and a description of the part that requires amendment.[72]

The procedure for these amendments is *mutatis mutandis* the same as that for registration. This means that there is a publication of the amendments, an opposition period, and consultation with experts.[73] The duration for each of these steps is the same as in the original registration.[74] Once the amendments are approved, MAFF will publish it on its website.[75]

3.4 Cancellation of a Geographical Indication Registration

Besides the cases in which a registration as a GI loses its effects, which is when an association of producers has been dissolved or the quality-control guidelines have been abolished, MAFF may also, *ex officio*, cancel a registration.[76] A cancellation can be done for reasons pertaining to the association of producers,[77] the information in the application for registration,[78] or the product name.[79]

First, an association of producers is meant to be an organization that groups producers, processors, or brand organizations.[80] Moreover, the organization is required to accept members on fair conditions comparable with that

---

[65] See id. at arts. 15–19. [66] See id. at art. 15. [67] See GI Act, supra note 8, art. 16
[68] See id. at art. 15(1). [69] See id. at art. 15(2). [70] See id. at art. 16(2).
[71] See id. at art. 16(3). [72] See id. [73] See GI Act, supra note 8, arts. 15(2), 16(3).
[74] See id. [75] See id. at art. 17(3). [76] See id. at art. 22. [77] See id. at arts. 22(1)–(3).
[78] See id. at art. 22(4). [79] See GI Act, supra note 8, art. 22(5). [80] See id. at art. 2(4).

applicable to current members.[81] Thus, no legitimate candidate should be refused participation. A violation of any of these conditions means that an 'association of producers' is not in compliance with the definition of an association of producers.[82] Because of this, MAFF could cancel the registered GI.[83]

Second, an association of producers has several obligations. Members of an association of producers have the right to use the GI for the registered products. But the flipside of the coin is the obligation not to use the GI for products that are similar to the registered product.[84] The use of designated symbol for a GI is allowed, but the use of a similar symbol is forbidden.[85] Any other use not described in the previous two examples is caught by a general obligation to refrain from any unlawful use of the GI.[86] If any of these obligations are violated, MAFF is entitled to cancel the registration.[87]

Quality control is an essential element for obtaining a GI registration and maintaining the registration. Therefore, the association of producers are obligated to implement the best guidelines to ensure that the quality of GI products is upheld up to the expectations of the consumers and as indicated in the product specification. This requires guidelines that ensure compliance with the method of production, that there is sufficient financial capacity to implement the guidelines, and competent technical ability to carry out the required measures.[88] If any of these are not present, MAFF has the right to cancel the registration because the 'authenticity' of the product may be compromised.[89]

Lastly, MAFF can also cancel a GI registration if the description in the application regarding the origin and characteristics of the product are inaccurate or false.[90] MAFF has a similar right if the product no longer originates from a specific region, or if the quality, reputation, or other characteristics essentially attributable to its geographical origin cease to exist.[91] The registration will also be cancelled if the registered name of a designated product has become a generic term.[92]

4 THE GEOGRAPHICAL INDICATIONS ACT AND INTANGIBLE CULTURAL HERITAGE

4.1 Positioning Intangible Cultural Heritage within the Geographical Indications Act

Since he came to power in 2012, Prime Minister Abe has emphasized achieving economic growth – by a system often referred to as

---

[81] See id. [82] See id. [83] See id. at art. 22(1). [84] See id. at art. 3(2).
[85] See GI Act, *supra* note 8, art. 4. [86] See id. at art. 5. [87] See id. at art. 22(2).
[88] See id. at art. 13(2). [89] See id. at art. 22(3).
[90] See GI Act, *supra* note 8, arts 2(2), 22(4). [91] See id. [92] See id. at art. 22(5).

'Abenomics'.[93] Since the revitalization of the agricultural sector fits within this economic strategy,[94] a system of GIs for agricultural, forestry, and fishery products was implemented to facilitate this revitalization.[95]

In particular, MAFF has supported that GIs can contribute to this revitalization in two different ways. First, GIs will enable product differentiation based upon the GI name and the branding can be associated with the GI name. This, together with quality assurance that is embodied in GI-denominated products, should lead to higher prices for GI products. In turn, rural villages will reap the benefits of these higher prices, and thus these villages will be economically revitalized.[96] Second, by highlighting the truly Japanese origin of local produce, GIs will make the products more attractive for foreign consumers and the interest of these consumers for Japanese products will increase, therefore spurring the export of Japanese agricultural, forestry, and fishery products, and foodstuffs.[97]

In this context, however, consumer protection only enters the picture as an indirect consequence of the quality-control requirement that GI producers have to fulfil as part of the GI specification. Due to quality control, only products that abide with the predetermined quality standards reach the market. Still, the requirement that GI producers have to guarantee a certain product quality and exert quality control is, according to MAFF, beneficial to consumers.[98]

Moreover, ICH is not mentioned by MAFF as one of the goals of the GI Act, except for the assistance to inheriting traditional food culture.[99] Likewise, MAFF does not indicate the importance and the implication for GIs of traditional food, and traditional food culture. Hence, traditional food culture could be relevant in two aspects in the context of GI protection. On the one hand, traditional food culture may relate to

---

[93] See Naoyuki Yoshino & Farhad Taghizadeh Hesary, *Three Arrows of 'Abenomics' and the Structural Reform of Japan: Inflation Targeting Policy of the Central Bank, Fiscal Consolidation, and Growth Strategy* 3 (Asian Development Bank Institute, Working Paper No. 492, 2014), available at http://papers.ssrn.com/sol3/papers.cfm?abstract_id=2475730.

[94] See Ministry of Agriculture, Forestry, and Fisheries, *Abe Cabinet Agricultural Reform*, MAFF http://fpcj.jp/wp/wp-content/uploads/2014/07/a89885aa705c72d976dd953518d82140.pdf (last visited 9 March 2016).

[95] See id. at 5.

[96] See Ministry of Agriculture, Forestry, and Fisheries, *Establishment of Japan's Geographical Indication (GI) Protection System*, MAFF www.eu-japan.eu/sites/eu-japan.eu/files/SAKA_EN_0.pdf (last visited 9 March 2016); Ministry of Agriculture, Forestry, and Fisheries, *Geographical Indication (GI) Protection System in Japan*, MAFF www.maff.go.jp/e/japan_food/gi_act/pdf/gi_pamph.pdf (last visited 9 March 2016).

[97] See id.   [98] See id.   [99] See id.

traditional techniques of preparing agricultural products into food,[100] which could be relevant as part of the GI specification and in turn the quality control to which GI products should be subjected as part of the GI Act. On the other hand, traditional food culture could contribute to the success of GI products as it incentivizes maintaining a culture of consuming local produce.[101]

Because of its limited scope, this chapter does not need to assess whether the GI Act will be able to attain the goals identified by MAFF. Also, this chapter cannot address the question of whether the GI Act has underlying unstated goals and whether they could be realized. For the purposes of this chapter, it suffices to point out that economic goals are the most prominent in MAFF's discourse. Therefore, it is likely that MAFF will gear the operation of the GI Act towards attaining the economic goals without necessarily paying attention to other stakes, such as safeguarding ICH. Furthermore, MAFF is not a ministry that deals with culture and thus has no expertise in this respect. But this lack of expertise could be compensated for by relying on experts who are well versed not only in GIs but also in ICH issues.[102]

Notwithstanding MAFF's lack of interest or expertise in safeguarding ICH, the broad scope of the GI Act, combined with the necessity to describe the production process, means that ICH can be part of a GI. But when holders of ICH register for a GI, they should consider the problems relating to the association of producers, the authenticity of the production process, and the product specification.

4.2 Association of Producers and Communities

A GI regime is an attractive legal instrument for ICH holders because it is 'based upon collective traditions and a collective decision-making process'.[103] The GI Act stipulates that the collective decision-making must occur within the context of an association of producers.[104] The GI Act leaves open the question of whether or not the association takes the form of a legal person. If the association takes the form of a legal person, it needs to appoint a representative. In the context of ICH, one could argue that the holders of ICH, as a community, could be considered an association, and thus they may be eligible to apply for a GI.

---

[100] See Broude, *Trade and Culture*, supra note 13, at 651.   [101] See id. at 656.
[102] See GI Act, *supra* note 8, art.11.
[103] See Shivani Singhal, *Geographical Indication and Traditional Knowledge*, 3 J. INTELL. PROP. L. & PRAC. 732, 733 (2008).
[104] See *supra* Section 3.1.

In the context of indigenous communities, Rosemary Coombe, Sarah Ives, and Daniel Huizenga have identified that it will most likely not be difficult for the communities to assume the role of an association of producers.[105] These communities would usually have already been 'subjectified'[106] to this role in their interaction with norms of other discourses, maybe human rights or environmental issues.[107] These experiences would help them recognize the 'economic and political opportunities that GI protections afford'.[108]

However, ICH in Japan is not necessarily linked to indigenous communities seeking protection.[109] Nonetheless, Japan has a relatively old law dealing with ICH. The Law for the Protection of Cultural Property was adopted in 1950.[110] Under this law, ICH, including traditional craftsmanship, can be designated as important intangible cultural property. Where there has been a designation of important intangible cultural property under this law, the population group[111] holding the ICH will have identified itself as a community,[112] which then can subsume the role of an association of producers.

Even though the population group is considered a community for the purposes of ICH, this community may not necessarily be sufficiently homogenous to agree that a GI registration is mutually beneficial for all.[113] Coombe, Ives, and Huizenga reflect on the minoritarian bias,[114] in which a small group

---

[105] See Rosemary J. Coombe, Sarah Ives, & Daniel Huizenga, *Geographical Indications: The Promise, Perils and Politics of Protecting Place-Based Products*, in THE SAGE HANDBOOK OF INTELLECTUAL PROPERTY 207, 215 (Matthew David & Debora Halbert eds., 2015).

[106] See Rosemary J. Coombe, *Cultural Agencies, The Legal Construction of Community Subjects and Their Properties*, in MAKING AND UNMAKING INTELLECTUAL PROPERTY: CREATIVE PRODUCTION IN LEGAL AND CULTURAL PERSPECTIVE 79, 83 (Mario Biagioli, Peter Jaszi & Martha Woodmansee eds., 2011).

[107] See Coombe, Ives, & Huizenga, *supra* note 105, at 215.   [108] *Id.*

[109] See, e.g., NATSUKO AKAGAWA, HERITAGE CONSERVATION IN JAPAN'S CULTURAL DIPLOMACY: HERITAGE, NATIONAL IDENTITY AND NATIONAL INTEREST 134 (2015) (stating that communities have a lesser role to play in the Japanese intangible cultural heritage regime).

[110] See Law No. 2014, *supra* note 32.

[111] See CULTURAL PROPERTIES DEPARTMENT, *supra* note 32, at 2. (Note that under the Law for the Protection of Cultural Property the application process for important cultural property does not necessarily have to be done by a group. It can also be done by an individual.).

[112] See Law for the Protection of Cultural Property, *supra* note 110, arts. 71–77.

[113] See Coombe, Ives, & Huizenga, *supra* note 105, at 214.

[114] Neil Komesar has pointed out that the more agencies participate and the more complex the issue at stake, there is an 'enhanced possibility of minoritarian bias and the prospect of "rent-seeking"'. The ideas or interest of the majority risk being underrepresented. See NEIL KOMESAR, LAW'S LIMITS: THE RULE OF LAW AND THE SUPPLY AND DEMAND OF RIGHTS 153 (2001).

of producers, often the wealthy ones, steer the rest towards the registration for a GI.[115] Thus, this small group may be able to construct the collective organization to suit their demands. Their demands may impact the description of the GI in several ways. For example, the production process could favour the practices of this group. Moreover, the criteria for participation in the collective organization may also be determined during application, possibly creating a burden for future entry.

The risk of a minoritarian bias may be problematic in light of the often-heard critique that a GI creates a monopoly right.[116] Accordingly, one could argue that the creation of a monopoly right would further strengthen the grip this small group has on the ICH. However, it should be noted that a monopoly right is an indirect consequence of a GI. The 'monopoly right' created by a GI is one that mainly delineates who may have an individual 'entitlement to the collective'.[117] In other words, the regime is set up to determine the 'group of qualified individuals who can use the GI for their independent business purposes'.[118] Therefore, the 'monopoly right' does not deprive anyone from using techniques or knowledge that underlie the GI. ICH holders who refuse to join the collective association in applying for a GI will still be able to produce their products, but will be limited in their marketing efforts. Their marketing must not resemble the GI's marketing, something the GI Act confirms in Article 3(2).

Even if the ICH is not yet designated, a collective association must still be formed. However, the risk associated with this situation is the artificial creation of a community[119] or an industry, or by the state driving the formation of the association.[120] It has been described by Coombe, Ives, and Huizenga that this may have an industrialization effect. They describe this effect in relation to Chucucanas ceramics and Mexican tequila. In the case of ceramics, government interference led to 'promoting economies of scale and forms of industrialized manufacture that [...] seriously damaged the social relations of production which historically sustained egalitarian communities of

---

[115] See Coombe, Ives, & Huizenga, *supra* note 105, at 214; *See also* Singhal, *supra* note 103, at 737 (expanding on the problem of disagreements between small groups, even families).
[116] For a discussion on geographical indications, monopoly rights, and intangible cultural heritage, *see* Kono, *supra* note 13, at 298.
[117] Frankel, *supra* note 13, at 8.
[118] *Id.*; *see also* Singhal, *supra* note 103, at 733 (noting that, even though there is a creation of a monopoly right, this right 'simply limits the class of people who can use a certain symbol').
[119] See Broude, *Trade and Culture*, *supra* note 13, at 674.
[120] See Coombe, Ives, & Huizenga, *supra* note 105, at 217–218; *see also* Delphine Vitrolles, *When Geographical Indication Conflict with Food Heritage Protection*, 8 ANTHROPOLOGY OF FOOD §§ 28–31 (2011).

producers'.[121] Industry elites working together with the government to nominate tequila as ICH resulted in the 'introduction of highly industrialized standards and volumes of production which marginalized smaller producers'.[122]

It is difficult to be sure that these problems will not occur in Japan. However, the fact that associations have a long history in Japan[123] means that many holders of ICH are most likely linked to associations that date back to the late nineteenth or early twentieth centuries (often changing names in the post-war period)[124] and that were often formed under state guidance to, for example, improve the flow of information and quality control.[125] A unifying or industrializing effect on the production process – if any – might have happened at the time these associations were formed. But this does not take us away from the fact that the above-described minoritarian biases can be removed in associations that have been operating for decades, especially if the local associations are under the control of a nationwide association.

Moreover, it could be argued that the likelihood of a minoritarian bias or the effect of the industrial elite's influence will be minor in an environment that allows producers with a pending GI application to participate widely.[126] The GI Act has only two broad guarantees for having such a participatory role. First, the GI Act requires the formation of an association of producers in order to apply for a GI.[127] The formation of an association might lead to communication between the various stakeholders, but will not necessarily exclude a minoritarian bias or an industrial elite's influence. Second, the GI Act provides the possibility of filing complaints against a GI application.[128] These complaints may express concern over the loss of diversity of ICH. However, MAFF and its experts may not take complaints seriously because the safeguarding of ICH is not its main aim. But ultimately, the loss of diversity

---

[121] Coombe, Ives, & Huizenga, *supra* note 105, at 217.   [122] *Id.* at 218.
[123] *See* Sheldon Garon, *From Meiji to Heisei: The State and Civil Society in Japan*, in THE STATE OF CIVIL SOCIETY IN JAPAN 42, 49 (Frank J. Schwartz & Susan J. Pharr eds., 2003). To name a few, the Japan Lacquer Association (Nihon Shikkoukai) was established in 1891. The Greater Japan Ceramic Industry Association (Dai Nippon Yougyou Kyoukai) was set up in 1892. *See* DOUSHIN SATOU, MODERN JAPANESE ART AND THE MEIJI STATE: THE POLITICS OF BEAUTY 119 (Hiroshi Nara trans., 2011) (1999).
[124] The Wajima Lacquerware Craftsman Association was founded in 1899, but changed its name to Wajima Urushi Ware Commerce and Industry in 1947. *See* Digital Archives of Ishikawa Japan, *History of Wajima Lacquerware*, WAJIMA LACQUERWARE http://shofu.pref.ishikawa.jp /shofu/wajima_e/h_nenpyou.html (last visited 8 March 2015).
[125] *See* Coombe, Ives, & Huizenga, *supra* note 105, at 218.   [126] *See id.* at 214–215.
[127] *See supra* Section 3.1   [128] *See id.*

is not a reason to refuse the registration of a GI. Nevertheless, it could encourage internal discussion among the producers.[129]

In order to somehow prevent the above-described problems from occurring, producers could turn to the flexibility offered in substantive law provisions.[130] The GI Act requires a product specification that describes the production process. There is no indication in the law that such a production process should be homogenous among the members of the association of producers.[131] The application guidelines offer some further insight into this.

First of all, the guidelines indicate that, when dealing with the relevant characteristics for an application, plural criteria can be included.[132] The application form itself refers to several elements, such as the technical basis, special ingredients, special raw materials, delivery basis or standard, feedstuff, or cultivated breed, that could make up the production process.[133] The application form indicates that this list of examples is neither exhaustive nor compulsory.[134] However, neither the guidelines nor the application form indicate whether the plurality points to more than one element or whether that one element could have different varieties. In the latter case, the applicant could explicitly stipulate the differences in the production process.[135] A more indirect approach would be to not directly mention the differences, but instead stipulate the 'normally-followed' production process.[136] Nevertheless, whether the former or the latter approach is followed, both enable holders of ICH to participate actively in the registration process.

Second, more than one association of producers can be registered to use the GI.[137] The guidelines stipulate that only one single application form can be submitted, but the product specification needs to be submitted by each

---

[129] See supra Section 3.2.
[130] See Dwijen Rangnekar, *Geographical Indications and Localisation: A Case Study of Feni* 20–32 (24 September 2009), available at www2.warwick.ac.uk/fac/soc/pais/research/research centres/csgr/research/projects/2007/protecting_feni/proj_pbl/esrc_report_english.pdf.
[131] See GI Act, supra note 8, art. 6.
[132] See MAFF, *Chiritekihyouji Hogo Seido Moushikomisha Gaidorain* [The System for the Protection of Geographical Indications – Guidelines for Applicants] 38 (27 October 2015), available at www.maff.go.jp/j/shokusan/gi_act/process/pdf/doc11.pdf.
[133] See id. at 89.   [134] See id.
[135] See, e.g., Rangnekar, supra note 130, at 31 (indicating that a revision of the application for Feni could include both apples and coconut as raw materials for the product carrying the GI).
[136] See, e.g., id. at 30 (indicating that the GI Feni has been defined as 'fallen and ripe apples are "normally" used', indicating that sometimes different approaches could be followed).
[137] See GI Act, supra note 8, art. 6. See also MAFF, *Chiritekihyouji Touroku no Moushikomi Houhou ni Tsuite* [About the Way how to Apply for Geographical Indications] 6 (27 October 2015), available at www.maff.go.jp/j/shokusan/gi_act/process/pdf/doc11.pdf.

respective association.[138] It is explicitly acknowledged in the guidelines that the respective product specifications can differ from each other.[139] Since the product specification also has a section on the production process, the differences could be identified there as well. To accommodate these interpretations of the law, MAFF should use application forms that allow for enough flexibility.

Even though the substantive law seems to enable flexibility and thus a broader participation by different holders of ICH, the remaining question is how the controlling institutions – the experts and MAFF – will judge the acceptability of the inclusion of difference in the production process, or of a vague formulation of the production process. Quality control will most likely be the main criterion by which this decision will be made. Vague formulations will make such quality-control assessments difficult and give the producers much leeway to breach the appropriate standards. A detailed formulation will allow for better quality assessment, but it requires a more sophisticated and expensive quality-control mechanism.

While the GI Act may be able to accommodate diversity, we need to reflect on whether the unifying force of a minoritarian bias or industrial elite should be automatically considered as problematic. ICH is a living heritage, prone to change in response to the outside environment.[140] Thus, it could be questioned whether the application for a GI should necessarily mean the fixation on preserving the diversity of ICH. This issue links to authenticity, a concept often heard within the context of GIs.

4.3 Authenticity of the Production Process and Intangible Cultural Heritage

GIs are often linked to the concept of authenticity. This link stems from the fact that the production process must adhere to what has been described in the application for a GI. In other words, a product is no longer authentic if a different production process, other than the one put forward during the application, is deployed. Non-compliance with the production process, which is most likely 'inseparably linked to geography',[141] could eventually affect the quality of the product that the GI is supposed to represent. This interpretation excludes any form of divergence from the stipulated production process.

---

[138] See MAFF, *supra* note 132, at 56.   [139] See id.
[140] Steven Van Uytsel, *Philosophies behind the Intangible Cultural Heritage Convention: Equality in Heritage Protection, Community Re cognition and Cultural Diversity* 9–10 (9 February 2012), available at http://papers.ssrn.com/sol3/papers.cfm?abstract_id=2001835.
[141] Kono, *supra* note 13, at 298.

Therefore, GIs are described as stabilizing a 'historically validated production process',[142] and this runs counter to the characteristic of the living nature of ICH.[143]

After pointing out that other scholars have already indicated that the timeliness of the production process should not be too strongly overstated,[144] Dev Gangjee provides a way out of the authenticity issue. He posits that as long as the understanding of authenticity refers to a state of antiquity, the concepts of GIs and ICH will not be reconcilable with each other. By shifting the understanding of authenticity to the designation of a 'strong link with a specific community',[145] goods will be authentic if they are produced by what the community considers the appropriate method of production. This allows for a specific community to actively (re-)interpret the intergenerational transmissions of production processes.

Gangjee's vision on the interpretation of authenticity is not foreign to the recent ICH debate. In his article *Intangible Cultural Heritage: The Living Culture of Peoples*, Federico Lenzerini argues that authenticity, even though not included in the ICH Convention, could be valuable to ICH.[146] More specifically, authenticity could guarantee the connection between ICH and the cultural identity of the creators and bearers. Authenticity would be the concept preventing ICH from being used for purposes that the community does not ascribe to. ICH would be authentic if 'such heritage is constantly tailored to the cultural identity of the communities, groups, and or persons concerned'.[147]

However, suggesting that authenticity should be devoid of the meaning of originality still requires the GI Act and its enforcement structure to suit such an interpretation. As mentioned above, the GI Act provides the possibility for amending the GI registration. One area that could be amended is the description of the production process to give the impression that, in theory at least, a community could apply to amend the registration whenever it deems desirable. If MAFF accepts some flexibility in the formulation of the production

---

[142] Gangjee, *supra* note 1, at n. 60–63.   [143] See Kono, *supra* note 13, at 298.
[144] Gangjee, *GIs and Cultural Rights*, *supra* note 1, at 557. See also Broude, *Trade and Culture*, *supra* note 13, at 623.
[145] Fransesca Cominelli, *Governing Cultural Commons: The Case of Traditional Craftsmanship in France*, http://dlc.dlib.indiana.edu/dlc/bitstream/handle/10535/7212/726.pdf?sequenc e=1&isAllowed=y (last visited 8 March 2016); *see also* Gangjee, *GIs and Cultural Rights*, *supra* note 1, at 558.
[146] See Federico Lenzerini, *Intangible Cultural Heritage: The Living Culture of Peoples*, 22 EUR. J. INT. L. 101 (2011).
[147] *Id.* at 113–114.

process, the change in the production process could be printed just next to the original description of the production process.

In the absence of flexibility, and presuming that a process of change will most likely be gradually initiated by some members of the community, two scenarios could develop. The first is that the more vocal members of the community could change their production process, thereby forcing the others to follow suit. Thus, when less outspoken or minority community members change the production process of the ICH, the more outspoken or the majority members may keep that group in line via the quality-control mechanisms enforced by the association of producers. Whatever the case may be, a strict application of the GI Act could either cause the standardization of ICH or stifle its development.

The second scenario could be that changes to the ICH mentioned in a GI registration may only be recorded with the consent of the association of producers. Therefore, individual members cannot apply for a change in the registration because all the members must be in agreement. There is no role for MAFF to play if there is any disagreement between the members. The best way for MAFF to accommodate the blurry boundaries of ICH is to do away with an overly legalistic application of the GI Act and allow flexibility in the application documents.

4.4 Openness of the Product Specification and Intangible Cultural Heritage

Generally speaking, the product specification must be drawn up before a product may be registered as a GI. In principle, the product specification should concentrate on the 'product's unique connection to its particular place of origin'.[148] Ultimately, the connection to a place is 'definitional to a GI'.[149] This means that the legitimacy of a GI can be sustained if 'weather and topology'[150] make out the 'claimed nexus between place and product qualities'.[151] The GI Act also requires a description of the production process.[152] The production process – especially when we talk about products made from agricultural, fishery, or forestry products – may well be based on knowledge that the community has gathered in order to make valuable products with what they had on hand.[153] ICH is formed through years of

---

[148] Hughes, *supra* note 11, at 72. [149] *Id.* [150] *Id.* at 76. [151] *Id.*
[152] See GI Act, *supra* note 8, arts. 6–7.
[153] See, e.g., N.S. Gopalakrishnan, Prabha S. Nair & Aravind K. Babu, *Exploring the Relationship between Geographical Indications and Traditional Knowledge: An Analysis of*

passing down this knowledge and then transforming it into an identifier for that community.[154] Thus, it is likely that this ICH also characterizes the unique qualities of the product.

The process of describing ICH is also found in the ICH discourse. The ICH Convention, for example, imposes an obligation on its member states to create one or more inventories of their ICH.[155] But there is one difference between the ICH Convention and the GI Act: the ICH Convention is quite flexible as to what these inventories could mean.[156] For example, it could be a listing of ICH identified in the member state's sovereign territory. Within the listing, separate categories can be made depending on their local, regional, or national importance. Another listing could be categorized depending on its need for extra safeguards. The inventory could also be a detailed description of what the ICH is. In other words, the ICH Convention leaves enough freedom to the member states to create inventories that cater to the specific needs of the communities.[157]

In the previous sections, speculation was made about the flexibility of the GI Act to accommodate diversity and change. The registration guidelines are much more direct about the inclusion of elements that could be considered as trade secrets or know-how of the community. The guidelines mention that the applicant should think carefully about including such secrets or know-how in the application documents, as these documents are generally made public.[158] The only limitation that the guidelines put to this flexibility is that the trade secret or the know-how should not be directly related to the product's characteristics.[159] MAFF and its experts have a margin of appreciation as to what aspects of the production process should be revealed. But, as Hughes

---

the Legal Tools for the Protection of Geographical Indications in Asia (Geneva: International Centre For Trade and Sustainable Development, Working Paper, 2007).

[154] See Steven Van Uytsel, *Philosophies behind the Intangible Cultural Heritage Convention: Equality*, in Heritage Protection, Community Recognition and Cultural Diversity 8–9 (9 February 2012), available at http://papers.ssrn.com/sol3/papers.cfm?abstract_id=2001835.

[155] See ICH Convention, supra note 12, art. 12; see also Steven Van Uytsel & Toshiyuki Kono, *Intangible Cultural Heritage Identified: Inventories as an Essential Part of the Safeguarding Process*, in INTANGIBLE CULTURAL HERITAGE AND INTELLECTUAL PROPERTY: COMMUNITIES, CULTURAL DIVERSITY AND SUSTAINABLE DEVELOPMENT 113 (Toshiyuki Kono ed., 2009).

[156] See Steven Van Uytsel, *Inventory Making and Fairy Tales: Safeguarding of Intangible Cultural Heritage in Historical Perspective*, in INTANGIBLE CULTURAL HERITAGE AND INTELLECTUAL PROPERTY: COMMUNITIES, CULTURAL DIVERSITY AND SUSTAINABLE DEVELOPMENT 143 (Toshiyuki Kono ed., 2009).

[157] See id. at 143.   [158] See MAFF, supra note 132, at 38.

[159] See id.; but see Gopalakrishnan, Nair & Babu, supra note 153, at 48–49 (arguing for a strong exception for secrets).

mentions in one of his studies, what is the point of a GI when something essentially relevant to characterize the product is not part of the description made to obtain the registration?[160]

5 CONCLUSION

With the adoption of the GI Act, Japan has left the negative protection system for GIs. The GI Act applies not only to edible agricultural, forestry, and fishery products but also to manufactured and processed agricultural, forestry, and fishery products. Therefore, in an application for a GI, the production process must be adequately described, and a control mechanism checking for compliance with the production process must be established. The combination of these two elements means that know-how, skills, and practices will also be protected. Such know-how, skills, and practices can also fulfil the definition of ICH such that GIs and ICH could coexist under the GI Act.

Bringing GIs and intangible heritage together in one legal framework is controversial. However, it is unavoidable and must be dealt with. Through a flexible interpretation of the substantive law relating to the production process; allowing amendments to the original application process; and a choice for applicants to decide what to include in the product specification, the GI Act could potentially accommodate difficult issues such as minoritarian biases, industrial elites, authenticity, or openness of product specification. The only question to be answered in practice is the extent to which MAFF will comply with these suggestions in order to contribute to the safeguarding of ICH.

[160] Hughes, *supra* note 11, at 76–77.

Index

Abenomics, 518–19
Act for the Protection of the Names of Designated Agricultural, Forestry and Fishery Products and Foodstuffs (GI Act) (Japan), 508–9, 510–14
   ICH and, 518–29
   scope of protections, 512
Adan Kayan rice, 501–6
adat communities, in Indonesia, 495–96
Administration of Quality Supervision, Inspection, and Quarantine (AQSIQ) system, 387–90
Agreement of Trade-Related Aspects to Intellectual Property Rights (TRIPS)
   appellations of origin in, 442–45
   Bangladesh and, 439–40, 450
   GI Act of 2013 and, compatibility with, 448–54
   EU violations of, 171–72
   GATT and, 39
   geographical origins protections under, 30–33
   GIs and, 6, 7, 12–14, 40–41, 87–88, 441–44
   definitions of, 52–54, 126
   in EU, 190, 195
   minimum requirements for, 151
   reputation-based, 24–25
   India and, 341
   Inter-American Convention and, 216
   ISDS and, 180
   levels of protections in, 128–29
   Malaysia and, 281, 288
   Singapore under, 240
   Sri Lanka under, 411–12, 413
   sui generis systems and, 449
   Taiwan and, 359–61, 364–65, 370–71
   terroir under, 64–65
   trademarks under, 141
      conflicts between, 134–35
      definitions of, 453
   under WTO law, 180
Agreement on Technical Barriers to Trade (TBT), 171–72
Agricultural and Processed Food Products Export Development Authority (APEDA), 355–56
agricultural products. *See also* coffee production; non-agricultural products and handicrafts; wine labeling
   in India, 337, 340–41
   APEDA certification, 355–56
   MOA practice for, 393
   in Southeast Asia, from plantations, 97–102
AGWA Act. *See* Australian Grape and Wine Authority Act
AICs. *See* authorities for industry and commerce
AIPP. *See* Asian Indigenous Peoples' Pact
Algeria, 196
Alphonso mango, 354–57
alternative food networks, 118
Ambalangoda masks, 428–30
American Viticultural Areas (AVAs), 64
Anti-Unfair Competition Law (China), 395
AO. *See* Appellation d'Origine
AOC. *See* Appellation d'Origine Contrôlée
APEDA. *See* Agricultural and Processed Food Products Export Development Authority
Appellation d'Origine (AO), 44–45, 62
Appellation d'Origine Contrôlée (AOC), 44–45

530

Index

appellations of origin
　in Geneva Act, 441–42
　in Lisbon Agreement, 23–27, 441–42
　in TRIPS, 442–45
　in Vietnam, 314, 320
AQSIQ system. *See* Administration of Quality Supervision, Inspection, and Quarantine system
Argumedo, Alejandro, 120
Arunachal Pradesh state, biocultural diversity in, 107–9
ASEAN. *See* Association of South-East Asian Nations
ASEAN-Australia-New Zealand Free Trade Agreement, 285–86
Asia, GIs in. *See also* Southeast Asia; tea production
　marketing of, 91
　MICOs in, 88–89, 90–92, 113–20
　　alternative food networks and, 118
　　gender equity in, 116, 117–18
　protections frameworks for, 211, 230–33
　　in bilateral agreements, 192–94
　　under EU trademark law, 198–208
　　in international multilateral agreements, 194–97
　　non-proprietary, 208–10
　　scope of, 191–92
　purpose of, 186
　registration of, 190–91
　TCEs in, 88
　TEK in, 88
Asian Indigenous Peoples' Pact (AIPP), 100–1
association of producers and communities, 520–25
Association of South-East Asian Nations (ASEAN)
　ASEAN-Australia-New Zealand Free Trade Agreement, 285–86
　Geneva Act and, 142–43
　GI protections among, 17
　multilateral aspects of, 151
Australia. *See also* wine GIs, in Australia
　AGWA Act in, 262–63, 271–72
　　enforcement procedures under, 264–67
　ASEAN-Australia-New Zealand Free Trade Agreement, 285–86
　EU and, trade agreements with, 166
　GIs in, 149, 164
　　boundary setting for, 263
　　costs of, 267–68

　　enforcement of, 266–67
　　perceptions of, 268–72
　　regional benefits of, 272–74, 279
　　PDOs in, 269–70
　　PGIs in, 269–70
　　terroir in, 63, 164
　　under TPP Agreement, 156
　　wine making in, 260–66
　　terroir and, 63, 164
Australian Grape and Wine Authority (AGWA) Act, 262–63, 271–72
　enforcement procedures under, 264–67
Australia-United States Free Trade Agreement, 279
authenticity, in ICH, 483, 525–27
authorities for industry and commerce (AICs), 387
AVAs. *See* American Viticultural Areas
ayllu (holistic territorial approach to life and development), 120

Banarasi sarees, 333–35, 347–50
Bangladesh, GIs in
　definition of, 448–49
　Fazli mango, 447
　under GI Act of 2013, 440–41, 459–60
　　development history for, 446–48
　　infringement actions, 451–52
　　protections under, 449–52
　　registration strategies under, 451
　　TRIPS and, compatibility of, 448–54
　IPRs and, 453–54
　Jamdani, 440–41, 447
　　historical value of, 456–57
　　as traditional knowledge, 455–59
　NakshiKantha, 447
　protections for, 449–52
　　Jamdani as traditional knowledge, 455–59
　　rationale for, 444–48
　terroir and, 455
　trademarks and, 452–54
　TRIPS and, 439–40, 450
　　GI Act of 2013 and, compatibility of, 448–54
Basmati rice, 230–32
Basole, Amit, 487–88
Beeralu lace, 430–31
Besky, Sarah, 92
bilateral trade agreements
　Asia GIs and, 192–94
　EU GIs and, protection frameworks for, 192–94

bilateral trade agreements (cont.)
    for wine making, 192–93
    ISDS clauses and, 181–82
bilateral trade and investment agreements (BTIAs)
    with EU, 169–70
        under TFEU, 169
    ISDS and, 178
    WTO law and, 178
biocultural diversity
    in India, 107–9
        in Arunachal Pradesh state, 107–9
    MICOs and, 119
    in Southeast Asia, 96–113. *See also* swidden agriculture
        on agricultural lands, 100
        under CBD, 103–4
        ecosystem services and, 102–5
        on forest lands, 100
        livelihood security and, 102–5
biocultural rights, 119
    through community protocols, 119–20
    of indigenous farmers, 119–20
        collective marks and, 120
    of indigenous peoples, 119–20
biomass, in swidden agriculture, 98, 103
border enforcement, under GI Act 2014, 246
Bosnia, 196
Brazil, ICH in, 508
BTIAs. *See* bilateral trade and investment agreements
Bulgaria, 196
Burkina Faso, 196
business practice laws, in Sri Lanka, 412–13, 415–17

CAA Act of 2003. *See* Consumer Affairs Authority Act of 2003
Calboli, Irene, 38, 65, 163–64, 188
Cambodia, swidden agriculture in, 99–100
Canada-EU Trade Agreement (CETA), 157–58, 169
carbon stocks, in swidden agriculture, 98, 102
case studies
    in India, 344–57
        Alphonso mango, 354–57
        Banarasi sarees, 333–35, 347–50
        Darjeeling Tea, 351–54
        Kashmir Pashminas, 350–51

    in Vietnam, 320–27
        Hạ Long fried calamari, 321–24, 330
        Lạng Sơn star anise, 324–27
CBD. *See* Convention on Biodiversity
certification marks, 137–38
    for Cognac, 138–41
    defined, 252
CETA. *See* Canada-EU Trade Agreement
Ceylon Cinnamon, 423–24
Ceylon Sapphires, 425–26
Ceylon Tea, 409–10, 421–23
    SLTB and, 422–23
champagne, under *sui generis* regime, 122–23
Chauvel, Richard, 492–93
Chew, Daniel, 502
Chile, Malaysia-Chile Free Trade Agreement, 285–86
China, GIs in
    AICs and, 387
    under Anti-Unfair Competition Law, 395
    approval of, 389
    collective marks, 385–87
    control and supervision of, 390
    examination of, 389
    historical development of, 380–81
    international protections for, 405–6
        for domestic right holders, 405–6
        for foreign right holders, 406
    Lạng Sơn star anise, 326–27
    under Law on Protection of Consumer Rights and Interests, 395
    legal considerations for, 404–8
        administrative appeals in, 406–8
        international protections, 405–6
        through judicial review, 406–8
        trademark law and, hierarchy for, 404–5
    under Lisbon Agreement, 405
    under Madrid Agreement, 405–6
    under Paris Convention, 380–81
    producer applications for, 390
    under Product Quality Law, 395
    protections of, 230–33, 381, 390–91, 396–402
        through enforcement procedures, 390–91
        for foreign products, 391
        legislative history for, 382–84
    under SAIC, 380–81
    under trademark system, 381–87
    registration procedures for, 389, 403–4

under *sui generis* regimes, 387–91, 392–94, 402–4. *See also* Ministry of Agricultural Practice
  AQSIQ system, 387–90
  costs of, 403
  exclusive rights, 403–4
  PPGIP system, 388–89, 390–91
  trademarks in conflict with, 400–2
  under TM Law 1993, 382–83
  under TM Law 2013, 387, 397, 399, 400–1
  trademark system in, protections through, 381–87, 402–4
  conflicts between, 396–400
  costs of, 403
  enforcement of, 387
  exclusive rights, 403–4
  legislative history for, 382–84
  registration for, 385–87
Chromy, Josef, 277–78
Civil Code of Vietnam, 320
CJEU. *See* Court of Justice of the European Union
Cleary, Jen, 149, 261
coffee production
  in Ethiopia, 75–80
    as export, 80
    geographic certification and, 77–79
    history of, 79–80
  in Indonesia, 491
  labeling in, 75–80
  in PNG, 84–86
    infrastructure for, 84
    labeling schemes for, 84–85
    non-traditional sources of, 85
  Starbucks and, 75–80
    single-origin coffees and, 77–80
  trademark registrations and, 75–80
Cognac, certification marks for, 138–41
collective action
  with India GIs, 345
  with Vietnam GIs, 310, 331
collective goodwill, trademarks and, 137–38
collective marks, 62, 120, 139
  Darjeeling Tea as, 203–4
  defined, 252
  EU GIs and, 202–4
  in Vietnam, 328–29
collective trademarks, in Taiwan, 372–73
common law, trademarks under, 137–41
  collective goodwill under, 137–38
  "first-in-time, first-in-right" approach to, 137

  in United States, 138
Community Trade Mark Regulation (CTMR), 201–2, 204
conflict palm oil, 113
Consortium for Common Food Names, 248–49
Consumer Affairs Authority Act of 2003 (CAA Act of 2003) (Sri Lanka), 416
Consumer Protection Act 1999 (CPA 1999) (Malaysia), 287, 301
consumer protections, in Sri Lanka, 415–17
contemporary reputation-based GIs, 55–56
Convention for the Safeguarding of the Intangible Cultural Heritage (CSICH) (2003), 21, 461–62
  property rights under, 462
  purpose of, 467–68
  Representative List in, 468–69
Convention on Biodiversity (CBD), 103–4
Convention on the Protection and Promotion of the Diversity of Cultural Expressions (2005), 21
Coombe, Rosemary, 487–88, 521
Costa Rica, 196
Court of Justice of the European Union (CJEU)
  EU-Singapore Free Trade Agreement ratification by, 255
  Greek Yoghurt case, 42, 43, 209
  IP protections and, 176–77
  reputation-based GIs and, 42–43
  trademark law cases, 198–201
Cowen, Tyler, 74
CPA 1999. *See* Consumer Protection Act 1999
CSICH. *See* Convention for the Safeguarding of the Intangible Cultural Heritage
CTMR. *See* Community Trade Mark Regulation
Cuba, 196
culinary diplomacy, 477
culinary practices, definitions of, 475
cultural diversity
  criteria for, 471–72
  culinary practices and, 474–83
    Kimjang, Making and Sharing Kimchi in the Republic of Korea, 478–83
    Mediterranean Diet, 474–77
  GIs and, 469–74
  ICH and, 469–74
  law's impact on, 469–74

cultural diversity (cont.)
  safeguarding of, 484
  UNESCO and, 470–71
customary law communities, 490–91
Czech Republic, 196
Czechoslovakia, 196

Darjeeling Tea, 92–96, 232–33, 351–54
  as collective mark, 203–4
  cultural impact of, 93
  fair trade and, 93–94
    political marginalization and, 95–96
  female workers and, 94–95
  production techniques for, 92–93
Database of Origin and Registration
    (DOOR), 41
  PDOs in, 171
  PGIs in, 171
  TSGs in, 171
deceptive trademarks, 200
deforestation, in Southeast Asia, 97–102
  through palm oil production, 97–99
Democratic Republic of the Congo, 196
denomination of origin, 441–42
dereism, defined, 362
dereistic policies, in Taiwan, 362–67
  as IP-centred, 363
  negative protections in, 365–67
  positive protections in, 365–77
  trademarks in, 363–65
design registration, in India, 61
Desseauve, Thierry, 63
developing countries. *See also* geographical
    indications
  farmers in
    economic rents for, 74
    in Ethiopia, 75–80. *See also* coffee
        production
    in India, 80–83. *See also* Feni liquor
    labeling practices for, 73–86
    in PNG, 84–86. *See also* coffee
        production
    under *sui generis* systems, 74
development. *See* economic development;
    social development
Directorate General of Intellectual Property
    Rights (DGIP), 500–1
dispute settlement understanding (DSU), 178
DOOR. *See* Database of Origin and
    Registration
Drahos, Peter, 149

DSU. *See* dispute settlement understanding
Dumbara mats, 427–28
Dusong, Jean-Luc, 205–6, 207
Dutfield, Graham, 487

EC. *See* European community
ECHR. *See* European Convention on Human
    Rights
economic development
  GIs for, 15–22
  in Indonesia, through GIs, 485–88
  in Taiwan, through GIs, 377–79
ecosystem services, swidden agriculture and,
    102–5
ECtHR. *See* European Court of Human Rights
Eghenter, Cristina, 502
Equal Exchange, 95–96
Ethiopia
  coffee production in, 75–80
    as export, 80
    geographic certification and, 77–79
    history of, 79–80
  farmers in, 75–80
  Starbucks in, 75–80
  trademark registrations in, 75–80
EU. *See* European Union
EU-Canada Comprehensive Trade
    Agreement, 14
European Commission
  on GI protections claims, 65–66
  on PDOs, 68
  on PGIs, 68
European community (EC)
  GATT and, 39
  reputation-based GIs recognized by, 51–54
European Convention on Human Rights
    (ECHR), GIs under, 175
European Court of Human Rights (ECtHR),
    GIs protections and, 175–76
European Union (EU). *See also* geographical
    indications, in EU
  Australia and, trade agreements with, 166
  BTIAs and, 169–70
  GATT and, violations of, 171–72
  IP in
    under BTIAs, 169–70
    ISDS and, 169–70
    under TFEU, 169
    under NAFTA, 170
  New Zealand and, trade agreements
      with, 166

PDOs in, 168, 189
  in DOOR, 171
PGIs in, 168, 189
  in DOOR, 171
reputation-based GIs in, as multilateral compromise, 51–54
under TPP, 170
trademark regulations in, 133
TRIPS and
  GIs and, 190, 195
  violations of, 171–72
TSGs in, 168, 189
  in DOOR, 171
under TTIP, 169, 212
European Union-Singapore Free Trade Agreement (EUSFTA), 286
EU-Singapore Free Trade Agreement, 166–67, 169, 247–49
  CJEU ratification of, 255
  establishment of, 235
  purpose of, 235
EU-South Korea Free Trade Agreement, 169, 192, 193–94
EU-Vietnam Free Trade Agreement, 169, 305
"evocation" imitation and, 191
Examination Guidelines of 2007 (Taiwan), 371–75

Fair and Equitable Treatment (FET), 181
Fair Trade Act (Taiwan), 360–61
fair trade label, 72
  for Darjeeling Tea, 93–94
    political marginalization in production of, 95–96
Fair Trade Labelling Organizations International (FLO), 95
Fair Trade USA, 95–96, 117–18
fallow periods, in swidden agriculture, 103, 104
farmers. *See also* coffee production
  in developing countries
    economic rents in, 74
    in Ethiopia, 75–80. *See also* coffee production
    in India, 80–83. *See also* Feni liquor
    labeling practices for, 73–86
    in PNG, 84–86. *See also* coffee production
    under *sui generis* systems, 74
  indigenous, in Southeast Asia, 101–2
  subsistence, women as, 109
Fazli mango, 447

female genital mutilation, 467
Feni liquor, 80–83
  GI application for, 81–83
  production of, 81
  types of, 81, 82
FET. *See* Fair and Equitable Treatment
"first-in-time, first-in-right" approach, 137
FLO. *See* Fair Trade Labelling Organizations International
foodstuffs, in India, 337
forest lands, in Southeast Asia, 100
FPIC principles. *See* Free, Prior and Informed Consent principles
France
  GIs in, 10–12
    INAO regulation of, 219
    wine labeling laws, 10–11
  Lisbon Agreement and, 196
  terroir and, 62–63, 122–23
  wine making in, 62–63
Free, Prior and Informed Consent (FPIC) principles, 108–9
  of indigenous peoples, 119–20
free market economies, *terroir* in, 136
free trade agreements (FTAs). *See also* mega-regional trade agreements; Trans-Pacific Partnership
  bilateral, 152
  expansion of, 151
  GIs and, 4–5, 14–15, 17–18
    status of play, 14
  Guatemala and, 178–79
  international, 14
  ISDS and, 185
  Malaysia in, 285–86
  multilateral, 151
  Peru and, 178–79
  policy approaches to, incompatibilities between, 158–65
    local law as factor in, 160
  terroir and, 159
  with US, 222
  under WTO law, 178–79
From Modern Production to Imagined Primitive: The Social World of Coffee from Papua New Guinea (West), 84
FTAs. *See* free trade agreements

Gabon, 196
Gangjee, Dev, 24, 137, 508, 526
gastrodiplomacy, 477

GATT. *See* General Agreement on Tariffs and Trade
gender equity, in MICOs, 116, 117–18. *See also* women
gendered labour. *See also* women
  in Southeast Asia, 109–13
General Agreement on Tariffs and Trade (GATT)
  EU violations of, 171–72
  TRIPS and, 39
General Inter-American Convention for Trademark and Commercial Protection (Inter-American Convention), 212–24
  geographical terms in, 216, 219
  GI protections under, 229–30
  in Latin America, 221–22
  long-term influence of, 221–24
  objective of, 220–21
  purpose of, 214–15
  as self-executing treaty, 223
  signatory countries, 214
  standard-setting by, 218–19
  TRIPS and, 216
  unfair competition protections in, 216–17, 218
  US Trademark Act and, 213, 220
generic names. *See* names
genericide
  defined, 131
  Geneva Act prohibitions against, 132, 135
  IP and, 131–32
  Lisbon Agreement and, 131–32
  sui generis systems and, 132
Geneva Act of the Lisbon Agreement for the Protection of Appellations of Origin and their International Registration (Geneva Act), 4–5, 26–27. *See also* trademarks
  appellations of origin in, 441–42
  ASEAN countries and, 142–43
  development of, 122–26
  future of, 141–43
  genericide prohibition in, 132, 135
  GIs under
    definitions of, 40–41
    in EU, 197
  levels of protections under, 128–29
  maintenance fees under, 129
  OAPI and, 141
  registration-related issues, 129–31
  reputation-based GIs under, 40–41

sui generis systems under, 142
terminological issues, 126–27
terroir and, 64–65, 123
TPP and, 143
WIPO and, 122
geographical collective trademarks, 375–76
Geographical Indication (Registration and Protection) Act 2013 (GI Act 2013) (Bangladesh), 440–41, 459–60
  development history for, 446–48
  infringement actions, 451–52
  protections under, 449–52
  registration strategies under, 451
  TRIPS and, compatibility with, 448–54
Geographical Indication of Goods (Registration & Protection) Act of 1999 (GI Act) (India), 344–45, 346
Geographical Indication of Goods (Registration & Protection) Rules of 2002 (GI Rules) (India), 344
geographical indications (GIs). *See also* Geneva Act of the Lisbon Agreement for the Protection of Appellations of Origin and their International Registration; Lisbon Agreement; reputation-based GIs
  ASEAN and, 17
  in Australia, 149, 164
  as badge of accountability, 18–19
  benefits of, 15–22
  under common law, 135–43
    in free market economies, 135–37
    trademarks and, 137–41
  consumer information through, 19–21
  culinary cultural practices and, 462–63
  cultural diversity and, 469–74
  defined, 25–26, 36–37
  delocalized model of production and, 23
  denomination of origin, 441–42
  diverse stakeholders and, 89–90
  under ECHR, 175
  for economic development, 15–22
  for Feni liquor, application for, 81–83
  under French laws, 10–12
    wine labeling laws, 10–11
  FTAs and, 4–5, 14–15, 17–18
    status of play, 14
  generic names and, 13
  global debates on, 3–4, 8–15
    expansion of, 9–10, 34
    geographical origins protections, 11–12

global reputations of, 159
green, 118–19
indication of source, 441–42
IP regimes and, 37
ISDS and, 180–84
limitations of, 90–91
Lisbon Agreement and, 6, 23–24
localized reputations of, 159
as marketing tool, 28–29
   in Asia, 91
PDOs, 25–26, 37
PGIs, 25–26, 37, 62
as policy tool, 86
poorly designed, 89
prices influenced by, 124
problems of, 15–22
production focus of, 124–25
promises of, 15–22
as property, 175–78
purpose of, 123–24
registries for, 5, 18
   in Asia, 190–91
   in EU, 38
terroir and, 24–25
rural development and, 259
scope of, 62
for social development, 15–22
sui generis systems and, 5, 9–10
terroir and, 62–65
   in France, 62–63
third-party use of, 29
traditional knowledge compared to, 165
TRIPS and, 6, 7, 12–14, 24–25, 40–41, 87–88, 441–44
   definitions of GIs under, 52–54, 126
   minimum requirements for GIs, 151
under UNESCO framework, 21
Western interests and, 9
WIPO and, 37
WTO and, 4, 36–37
   EU violations of, 168, 171–72
   member requirements for, 12
   protections for GIs, 12
geographical indications (GIs), in EU, 165–67
Asia and, protection frameworks for, 211
   in bilateral agreements, 192–94
   under EU trademark law, 198–208
   in international multilateral agreements, 194–97
   non-proprietary, 208–10
   scope of, 191–92

cultural factors in, 187–89
economic factors in, 187–89
   increased costs of GI products, 188
under EU trademark law, 198–208
   collective marks, 202–4
   geographical term use, 198–201
   protection as trademark, 198–201
   registration of, 198–201
   scope of protections, 201–2
"evocation" and, 191
under Geneva Act, 197
incompatibilities in, 167
legal factors in, 187–89
under Lisbon Agreement, 196–97
under Madrid Agreement, 195–96
under Paris Convention, 194
PDOs, 168, 189
PGIs, 168, 189
product specifications for, 171–75, 185
as property, 175–78
protection frameworks for, 189–97, 226, 227–28
   in bilateral agreements, 192–94
   comparisons to US, 224–28
   in international multilateral agreements, 194–97
   non-proprietary, 208–10
   scope of, 191–92
registered names and, protections of, 210
registries for, 38
under Regulation 1151/2012, 189–91
under Regulation 2081/92, 189–91
TRIPS and, 190, 195
TSGs, 168, 189
WTO and, 168, 171–72, 190
geographical indications (GIs), protections of, 65–70. *See also* protected geographical indications
in Asia, 211, 230–33
   in bilateral agreements, 192–94
   under EU trademark law, 198–208
   in international multilateral agreements, 194–97
   non-proprietary, 208–10
   scope of, 191–92
in Bangladesh, 449–52
   for Jamdani, as traditional knowledge, 455–59
   rationale for, 444–48
in China, 230–33, 381, 390–91, 396–402
   through enforcement procedures, 390–91

geographical indications (GIs) (cont.)
  for foreign products, 391
  international, 405–6
  legislative history for, 382–84
  under SAIC, 380–81
  under trademark system, 381–87
 EC claims on, 65–66
 in ECtHR cases, 175–76
 in EU
  alternate approaches to, 228–30
  compared to US, 224–28
  generic terms and, 226
  legal approaches to, 227–28
 GI prices correlated to, 66
 under Inter-American Convention, 229–30
 in Japan
  non-proprietary, 209
  scope of, 509
 in Kenya, 67
 through legal means, 67–69
 PDOs and, 68
 as policy tool, 86
 public beliefs in, 69–70
 in Singapore, 237–40, 247–54
  after GI Act (1999), 238–40
  before GI Act (1999), 237–38
  through registration systems, 247–49
  relationships between owners and rights holders, 249–54
 in Sri Lanka, 412–21
  through business practice laws, 412–13, 415–17
  through consumer protections, 415–17
  through *sui generis* regimes, 414–15, 419–20, 434–35
  through trademark law, 413–14, 417–19
 in US
  alternate approaches to, 228–30
  compared to EU, 224–28
  history of, 212–14
  legal approaches to, 227–28
  under trademark law, 227–28
  weakness of, 420–21
Geographical Indications Act (GI Act) (1999) (Singapore), 235, 237–40
Geographical Indications Act (GI Act) (2014) (Singapore), 235–36, 240–46
  border enforcement measures, 246
  enhanced protections through, 245–46
  existing holders under, 250–51

 GIs under
  cancellations of, 245
  definitions of, 242
  PGI owners under, 250–54
  registry establishment under, 241–45
  trademarks under, 242
  owners of, 251–53
  users of signs, 253–54
Geographical Indications Act 2000 (GIA Act 2000) (Malaysia), 281–83, 287–96
 amendment of, 287
 institution of proceedings under, 293–96
 PGIs under, 289
 registration system under, 289–91
 rights and exceptions under, 291–93
geographical origins
 marketing of, 70–73
  appeal of, 70–72
  in developed countries, 71–72
  in developing countries, 71–72
  labeling and, 72–73
 protections for, 11–12, 28–34
  interpretations of, 30–31
  under Lisbon Agreement, 11–12
  under Madrid Agreement for the Repression of False and Deceptive Indications of Source on Goods (Madrid Agreement), 11
  under Paris Convention for the Protection of Industrial Property, 11
  under TRIPS, 30–33
geographical terms
 under EU trademark law, 198–201
 in Inter-American Convention, 216, 219
 in Madrid Agreement, 219
Georgia, 196
Germany
 Ethiopian coffee imported into, 80
 non-proprietary protections of GIs, 210
 reputation-based GIs in, 47–48
 terroir paradigm in, 47–48
GI Act. *See* Act for the Protection of the Names of Designated Agricultural, Forestry and Fishery Products and Foodstuffs; Geographical Indication of Goods Act of 1999
GI Act (1999). *See* Geographical Indications Act
GI Act (2014). *See* Geographical Indications Act

GI Act 2013. *See* Geographical Indication
    (Registration and Protection) Act 2013
GI Rules. *See* Geographical Indication of
    Goods Rules of 2002
GIA Act 2000. *See* Geographical Indications
    Act 2000
GIs. *See* geographical indications
gluten-free labels, 72
Government Regulation No. 51/2007
    (Indonesia), 498–99
Greek Yoghurt case, 42, 43, 209
green GIs, 118–19
Guatemala, FTAs and, 178–79

Hạ Long fried calamari, 321–24, 330
Haiti, 196
handicrafts. *See* non-agricultural products and
    handicrafts
historic reputation-based GIs, 55–56, 58–59, 60
holistic territorial approach to life and
    development. *See ayllu*
Howard, Sir Albert, 63
Hughes, Justin, 22
Huizenga, Daniel, 521
human rights, in ICH, 467
Hungary, 196

ICH. *See* intangible cultural heritage
ICSID. *See* International Center for
    Settlement of Investment Disputes
INAO. *See* Institut National de l'Origine et de
    la Qualité
India, GIs in
    for agricultural products, 337, 340–41
    APEDA certification, 355–56
    Banarasi sarees, 333–35, 347–50
    Basmati rice, 230–32
    biocultural diversity in, 107–9
        in Arunachal Pradesh state, 107–9
    case studies for, 344–57
        Alphonso mango, 354–57
        Banarasi sarees, 333–35, 347–50
        Darjeeling Tea, 351–54
        Kashmir Pashminas, 350–51
    collective action problems, 345
    Darjeeling Tea, 92–96, 232–33, 351–54
        as collective mark, 203–4
        cultural impact of, 93
        fair trade and, 93–94, 95–96
        female workers and, 94–95
        production techniques for, 92–93

    design registration applications in, 61
    farmers in, 80–83
    for foodstuffs, 337
    under GI Act, 344–45, 346
    under GI Rules, 344
    information asymmetry regarding, 336–37
    Lạng Sơn star anise in, 326–27
    liquor production in, 84–86
        for Feni, 80–83
    patent applications in, 61
    PDOs, 341–42
    PGIs, 338, 341–42
    quality for, relevance of, 336–39
    under Regulation 510/2006, 340
    under Regulation 1151/2012, 189–91, 340
    regulations of, 339–43
        EU influences on, 339–42
        for geographical names, 342–43
        under *sui generis* systems, 339–42
        trademark-style protections in, 342–43
        US influences on, 342–43
    reputation-based GIs in, 59–60
    SMOI and, 349–50
    Sri Lankan policy influenced by, 432–33
    sui generis systems in, 339–42, 445
    Tea Act in, 352, 353
    Tea Board and, 352–54
    trademark registration applications in, 61
    traditional knowledge libraries for, 432
    under TRIPS, 341
    vanity GIs, 335
    women's TEK in, 107–9
indication of source, 441–42
indigenous farmers
    biocultural rights of, 119–20
    collective marks and, 120
    FPIC of, 119–20
    in Southeast Asia, 101–2
    swidden agriculture and, 101–2
Indonesia, GIs in
    Adan Kayan rice, 501–6
    adat communities and, 495–96
    for coffee production, 491
    cultural heritage and, 485–88
    customary law communities and, 490–91
    decentralization policies for, 488–96, 506–7
    economic development and, 485–88
    Government Regulation No. 51/2007 in,
        498–99
    IPR and, 492–95
        DGIP and, 500–1

Indonesia, GIs in (cont.)
  Jepara furniture, 501–6
  legal framework for, 496–501
  palm oil production and
    monocropping and, 112
    RSPO certification, 112
    smallholder schemes, 111
    women's role in, 109–13
  under Plant Varieties Protection Act, 503–4
  under Protection of Intellectual Property
    Rights of Indigenous Papuans, 493
  Trade Marks Act of 2001 in, 496, 498–99
Institut National de l'Origine et de la Qualité
    (INAO), 37
  establishment of, 219
intangible cultural heritage (ICH)
  authenticity in, 483
  in Brazil, 508
  CSICH and, 21, 461–62, 464–69
    property rights under, 462
    purpose of, 467–68
    Representative List in, 468–69
  culinary practices and, 462–63, 474–83
    *Kimjang, Making and Sharing Kimchi in
      the Republic of Korea*, 478–83
    Mediterranean Diet, 474–77
  cultural diversity and, 469–74
  culture and, definitions of, 467
  definition of, 466
  domains of, 465
  human rights context for, 467
  Indonesia and, 485–88
  intergenerational nature of, 465
  in Japan, 510–14
    association of producers and
      communities and, 520–25
    authenticity of production process and,
      525–27
    GI Act and, 518–29
    openness of product specification and,
      527–29
  law's impact on, 469–74
  for traditional culture, 465–66
  UNESCO and, 461–62
intellectual property (IP)
  in CJEU cases, 176–77
  disincentivizing of, 161–62
  in EU
    under BTIAs, 169–70
    ISDS and, 169–70
    under TFEU, 169
  GIs and, 37
  global trade rules for, 150, 160–62
  incentivizing of, 161–62
  ISDS and, 169–70, 182–83
  in Malaysia, GIs as distinct from, 281–82
  national treatment principle for, 453
  property-style rules for, 162–63
  in Taiwan
    under dereistic policies, 363
    laws for, 359–60
  under WTO rules, 162–63
Intellectual Property Act of 2003 (IP Act of
    2003) (Sri Lanka), 415–16, 418, 419–20,
    426, 428
Intellectual Property Law (IP Law) (Vietnam),
    313–14
intellectual property rights (IPR) systems
  in Bangladesh, 453–54
  in Indonesia, 492–95
    DGIP and, 500–1
  MICOs and, 120
  in Taiwan, 359–60
Inter-American Convention. *See* General
    Inter-American Convention for
    Trademark and Commercial
    Protection
International Center for Settlement of
    Investment Disputes (ICSID), 182
investor–state dispute settlement (ISDS)
  in bilateral trade agreements, 181–82
  FET and, 181
  GIs and, 180–84
    BTIAs and, 178
    FTAs under, 178–79
    TRIPS and, 180
  ICSID and, 182
  IP and, 169–70, 182–83
  NAFTA and, 181–83
  plain packaging and, 178
  UNCITRAL and, 180–81, 182
  WTO and, 178–80, 185
    BTIAs and, 178
    FTAs under, 178–79
    TRIPS and, 180
IP. *See* intellectual property
IP Act of 2003. *See* Intellectual Property Act of
    2003
IP Law. *See* Intellectual Property Law
IPR systems. *See* intellectual property rights
    systems
Iran, 196

ISDS. *See* investor–state dispute settlement
Israel, 196
Italy
  geographical origins protections in, 32
  Lisbon Agreement and, 196
    invalidation of, 197–98
  non-proprietary protections of GIs, 209
  PDOs in, 174–75
  reputation-based GIs in, 60
Ives, Sarah, 521

Jamdani, 440–41, 447
  historical value of, 456–57
  as traditional knowledge, 455–59
Japan, GIs in
  Abenomics and, 518–19
  application process for, 514–18
    amendments to, 516–17
    cancellations in, 517–18
    quality control in, 518
    refusal of, 515–16
    registration as part of, 514–15
  GI Act in, 508–9, 510–14
  ICH and, 518–29
  scope of protections of, 512
  ICH and, 510–14
    association of producers and communities and, 520–25
    authenticity of production process and, 525–27
    GI Act and, 518–29
    openness of product specification and, 527–29
    under Law for the Protection of Cultural Property, 521
  monopoly rights and, 522
  protections for
    non-proprietary, 209
    scope of, 509
  TCE and, 510
  TPP and, 512
  traditional knowledge and, 510
Jepara furniture, 501–6

Kashmir Pashminas, 350–51
Kenya, GI protections in, 67
Keys, Ancel, 475
Kimjang, Making and Sharing Kimchi in the Republic of Korea, 478–83
  Codex standard for, 481–82
knowledge, traditional, 165
  in India, libraries for, 432
  Jamdani as, 455–59
  in Japan, 510
Kobe beef, 208–9
Kolia, Marina, 50–51
Komesar, Neil, 521

labels, labeling and
  in coffee production, 75–80
  in PNG, 84–85
  farmers and, in developing countries, 73–86
  geographical origin marketing and, 72–73
  types of, 72
  for wine, in France, 10–11
Ladas, Stephen, 213, 215, 220. *See also* General Inter-American Convention for Trademark and Commercial Protection
landholders, women as, 109
Lạng Sơn star anise
  in China, 326–27
  in India, 326–27
  as Vietnam GI, 324–27
Lanham Act (US), 140, 342–43
Latin America, Inter-American Convention in, 221–22
Latvia, reputation-based GIs in, 58
Law for the Protection of Cultural Property (Japan), 521
Law of Passing Off (Malaysia), 296–99
Law on Protection of Consumer Rights and Interests (China), 395
Layton, Ron, 78
Lenzerini, Federico, 526
Li, Tania, 109–10
Limburg, Germany, 183
Limburg Grotto Cheese, 183–84
liquor production
  for Cognac, 138–41
  Feni, 80–83
    GI application for, 81–83
    production of, 81
    types of, 81, 82
  in India, 80–83
Lisbon Agreement (1958). *See also* Geneva Act of the Lisbon Agreement for the Protection of Appellations of Origin and their International Registration; trademarks
  appellations of origin in, 23–27, 441–42
  future of, 141–43

Lisbon Agreement (1958) (cont.)
    generic terms under, 133–35
    genericide, 131–32
    geographical origins protections under, 11–12
    GIs and, 6
        in China, 405
        in EU, 196–97
        Geneva Act definitions of, 40–41
        invalidation of, 197–98
        level of protections under, 127–29
        maintenance fees under, 130–31
        national parties to, 125
        original member states of, 196
        registration-related issues, 129–31
        reputation-based GIs under, 23–24, 45
            Geneva Act, 40–41
        scope of protections under, 196–97
        Sri Lanka under, 410–11
        terminological issues, 126–27
        terroir under, 64–65
        travaux in, 127
        usurpation in, 127
        Vietnam GIs under, 313
livelihood security, 102–5
Loong, Lee Hsien, 255–56

Macedonia, 196
Madrid Agreement for the Repression of False and Deceptive Indications of Source on Goods (Madrid Agreement), 11, 195
    China and, 405–6
    geographical terms in, 219
    Sri Lanka under, 410–11
maintenance fees, for trademarks
    under Geneva Act, 129, 130–31
    under Lisbon Agreement, 130–31
    under PCT, 130
Malaysia, GIs in
    applications for, 282–83
    ASEAN-Australia-New Zealand Free Trade Agreement and, 285–86
    CPA 1999 in, 287, 301
    for cultural heritage, 285
    establishment of, 281–84
    EUSFTA and, 286
    in FTAs, 285–86
    GIA 2000 in, 281–83, 287–96
        amendment of, 287
        institution of proceedings under, 293–96

    PGIs under, 289
    registration system under, 289–91
    rights and exceptions under, 291–93
    IP as distinct from, 281–82
    Law of Passing Off in, 296–99
    legal protections of, 286–303
        scope of, 301–3
    Malaysia-Chile Free Trade Agreement and, 285–86
    MEUFTA, 286
    sui generis systems and, 445
    TDA 2011 in, 300–1
    TMA 1976 in, 287, 299–300
    Trade Marks (Amendment) Act 2000 in, 299–300
    as trade tool, 284–86
    TRIPS and, 281, 288
Malaysia-Chile Free Trade Agreement, 285–86
Malaysia-European Union Free Trade Agreement (MEUFTA), 286
Malmström, Cecilia, 152
Marie-Vivien, Delphine, 38–39
marketing
    of Asian GIs, 91
    in Vietnam, 330
    of geographical origins, 70–73
        appeal of, 70–72
        in developed countries, 71–72
        in developing countries, 71–72
        labeling and, 72–73
    GIs as tool in, 28–29
marks. *See also* certification marks; geographical indications; names; trademarks
    collective, 62, 120, 139
    under Lanham Act, 140
marks indicating conditions of origin (MICOs)
    Argumedo on, 120
    in Asia, 88–89, 90–92, 113–20
        alternative food networks and, 118
        gender equity in, 116, 117–18
        biocultural diversity and, 119
        biocultural rights and, 119
            through community protocols, 119–20
        of indigenous peoples, 119–20
    collective marks, 62, 120
    IPR systems and, 120
    WIPO and, 91
Mediterranean Diet, 474–77
    mutations in, 477

mega-regional trade agreements, 153–58. *See also* Trans-Pacific Partnership Agreement
  CETA, 157–58
  RCEP, 151, 156–57
    negotiating members of, 156–57
MEUFTA. *See* Malaysia-European Union Free Trade Agreement
Mexico, 196
MICOs. *See* marks indicating conditions of origin
Ministry of Agricultural (MOA) practice, 392–94
  for agricultural products, 393
  approval in, 392–93
  control and supervision in, 393
  examination in, 392–93
  protection terms in, 393
    enforcement and, 394
    for foreign GIs, 394
  registration procedures, 392
Moldova, 196
monocropping
  palm oil production and, 112
  in swidden agriculture, 106
  women and, 106
monopoly rights, 522
Montenegro, 196
Moratuwa furniture, 430–31
multilateral trade agreements, Asia GIs and, 194–97

NAFTA. *See* North American Free Trade Agreement
NakshiKantha, 447
names, generic
  GIs and, 13
  under Lisbon Agreement, 133–35
national identity, *terroir* and, 122–23
National Office of Intellectual Property (NOIP), 311–12
national treatment principle, 453
Naylor, Lindsay, 117
New Zealand
  ASEAN-Australia-New Zealand Free Trade Agreement, 285–86
  EU and, trade agreements with, 166
  exports from, 166
Nicaragua, 196
NOIP. *See* National Office of Intellectual Property

non-agricultural products and handicrafts, reputation-based GIs for, 43–44
non-GMO labels, 72
North American Free Trade Agreement (NAFTA)
  EU under, 170
  ISDS and, 181–83
North Korea, 193–94
  Lisbon Agreement and, 196

OAPI. *See* Organisation Africaine de la Propriété Intellectuelle
OLPs. *See* Origin Labelled Products
organic labels, 72
Organisation Africaine de la Propriété Intellectuelle (OAPI), 141
Origin Labelled Products (OLPs), 310
Oxfam, 76, 77, 80

palm oil production
  conflict palm oil, 113
  deforestation through, 97–99
  Fair Trade USA and, 117–18
  in Indonesia
    monocropping and, 112
    RSPO certification, 112
    smallholder schemes, 111
    women's role in, 109–13
  industry reform for, 113–15
    through certification regimes, 114–15
    by corporations, 113–14
    regulatory standards for, 115–16
    through sustainability, 115
  Snack Food 20 and, 113
Papua New Guinea (PNG)
  coffee production in, 84–86
  infrastructure for, 84
  labeling schemes for, 84–85
  non-traditional sources of, 85
  farmers in, 84–86
Paris Convention for the Protection of Industrial Property, 11
  China GIs under, 380–81
  EU GIs under, 194
  patents under, 131–32
  Sri Lanka under, 410–11
  trademarks under, 131–32
  unfair competition and, 218

Patent Cooperation Treaty (PCT), 130
patents
　applications for, in India, 61
　under Paris Convention, 131–32
PCT. *See* Patent Cooperation Treaty
PDOs. *See* protected designation of origins
Peru
　FTAs and, 178–79
　Lisbon Agreement and, 196
　PRS in, 178–79
PGIs. *See* protected geographical indications
the Philippines, swidden agriculture in, 100–1
Phu Quoc products, 22
Plant Varieties Protection Act (Indonesia), 503–4
plantation agriculture, in Southeast Asia, 97–102
　female landholders and, 109
　gendered labour and, 109–13
　for palm oil production, 109–13
　subsistence farming and, 109
PNG. *See* Papua New Guinea
Portugal, 196
PPGIP system. *See* Provisions on the Protection of Geographical Indication Products system
price range system (PRS), 178–79
prices, GIs as influence on, 124
Product Quality Law (China), 395
property rights, under CSICH, 462
protected designation of origins (PDOs), 25–26, 37, 62
　in Australia, 269–70
　in EU, 168, 189
　GI protections and, 68
　in India, 341–42
　in Italy, 174–75
　TPP and, 153–54
protected geographical indications (PGIs), 25–26, 37, 62
　in Australia, 269–70
　in EU, 168, 189
　European Commission on, 68
　under GI Act 2014, 250–54
　under GIA Act 2000, 289
　in India, 338, 341–42
　reputation-based GIs and, 44–47
　in Taiwan, 362
　TPP and, 153–54
　in Vietnam, 315

Protection of Intellectual Property Rights of Indigenous Papuans (Indonesia), 493
Provisions on the Protection of Geographical Indication Products (PPGIP) system, 388–89, 390–91
PRS. *See* price range system

qualitative methodology, 311–12
quality control
　for Japan GIs, 518
　for wine GIs, 277–78

Raja, Indranee, 249
Rangnekar, Dwijen, 69, 74, 80–81. *See also* Feni liquor
Regional Comprehensive Economic Partnership (RCEP), 151, 156–57
　negotiating members of, 156–57
registered names, 210
registration protection principle, 366
registries and registrations, of GIs
　in China, 385–87
　　MOA practice for, 392
　DOOR, 41
　　PDOs in, 171
　　PGIs in, 171
　　TSGs in, 171
　under EU trademark law, 198–201
　under GI Act 2013, 451
　under GI Act 2014, 241–45
　under GIA Act 2000, 289–91
　for GIs, 5, 18
　　in Asia, 190–91
　　in EU, 38
　　terroir and, 24–25
　　in Japan, 514–15
　　in Singapore, 247–49
　　in Sri Lanka, 410, 435
　　in Taiwan, 370–71
　　TRIPS and, 370–71
　　in Vietnam, 312–20
　　　criteria requirements for, 312–14
　　　product types and, 314–15
　　　public policies for, 318–20
　　　as state-driven top-down process, 316–18, 329
Regulation 510/2006 (India), 340
Regulation 1151/2012 (India), 189–91, 340
Regulation 2081/92 (European Union), 189–91

reputation-based GIs, 23–28, 40–54
  attributability of, 54–59
    in India, 59–60
    in Italy, 60
    in Latvia, 58
    relevance of, 54–55
    in Spain, 57–58
  in CJEU cases, 42–43
    Greek Yoghurt case, 42, 43, 209
  as compromise, 44–54
    as multilateral template, within EU, 51–54
    for PGIs, 44–47
  contemporary aspects of, 55–56
  defined, 40–41
  DOOR and, 41
  EC recognition of, 51–54
  historic aspects of, 55–56, 58–59, 60
  under Lisbon Agreement, 23–24, 45
    Geneva Act, 40–41
  for non-agricultural products and handicrafts, 43–44
  product history and, 55–56, 57
  production techniques in, 56
  terroir paradigm and, 24–25, 47–51
    in Germany, 47–48
    under TFEU, 48
  trademarks and, 137
  under TRIPS, 24–25
  under unfair competition laws, 45–47
  WTO legislation and, 40
Rogers, Edward, 213, 220. *See also* General Inter-American Convention for Trademark and Commercial Protection
Roundtable on Sustainable Palm Oil (RSPO), 112
Ruhunu Curd, 426–27
rules of origin, WTO criteria for, 150
rural development, GIs and, 259
Ryan, Paul, 152

SAIC. *See* State Administration for Industry and Commerce
Saudi Arabia, Ethiopian coffee imported into, 80
Sen, Debarati, 94
Serbia, 196
shade-grown labels, 72
shifting cultivation. *See* swidden agriculture
Silk Mark Organization of India (SMOI), 349–50

Singapore. *See also* Geographical Indications Act
  EU-Singapore Free Trade Agreement, 166–67, 169
    CJEU ratification of, 255
    establishment of, 235
    purpose of, 235
  under GI Act (1999), 235, 237–40
  GI protections in, 237–40, 247–54
    after GI Act (1999), 238–40
    before GI Act (1999), 237–38
    through registration systems, 247–49
    relationships between owners and rights holders, 249–54
  Trade Marks Act 1938 in, 237
  Trade Marks Act 1998 in, 237–38
  Trade Marks (Amendment) Act 2004 in, 254
  under TRIPS, 240
  US-Singapore Free-Trade Agreement, 166–67, 254
Singh, Ranjay K., 107
single-origin coffees
  from Ethiopia, 77–79
  Starbucks and, 77–80
Slovakia, 196
SLTB. *See* Sri Lanka Tea Board
smallholder schemes, 111
SMOI. *See* Silk Mark Organization of India
Snack Food 20, 113
social development
  GIs for, 15–22
  in Vietnam, through GIs, 308–9, 320–27
social movements, swidden agriculture and, 100–1
The Soil and Health (Howard), 63
soil fertility, swidden agriculture and, 103
South Korea
  EU-South Korea Free Trade Agreement, 169, 192, 193–94
  Kimjang, Making and Sharing Kimchi in the Republic of Korea, 478–83
  Codex standard for, 481–82
  under TPP Agreement, 156
Southeast Asia. *See also* Bangladesh; China; India; South Korea; Sri Lanka; Taiwan
  biocultural diversity in, 96–113. *See also* swidden agriculture
  on agricultural lands, 100
  under CBD, 103–4
  ecosystem services and, 102–5

Southeast Asia (cont.)
  on forest lands, 100
    livelihood security and, 102–5
  deforestation in, 97–102
    through palm oil production, 97–99
  indigenous farmers in, 101–2
  plantation agriculture in, 97–102
    female landholders and, 109
    gendered labour and, 109–13
    for palm oil production, 109–13
    subsistence farming and, 109
Spain, reputation-based GIs in, 57–58
species richness, swidden agriculture and, 103
Sri Lanka, GIs in
  Ambalangoda masks, 428–30
  Beeralu lace, 430–31
  CAA Act of 2003 in, 416
  Ceylon Cinnamon, 423–24
  Ceylon Sapphires, 425–26
  Ceylon Tea, 409–10, 421–23
    SLTB and, 422–23
  definitions of, 410–12
  Dumbara mats, 427–28
  Indian influences on, 432–33
  IP Act of 2003 in, 415–16, 418, 419–20, 426, 428
  under Lisbon Agreement, 410–11
  under Madrid Agreement, 410–11
  Moratuwa furniture, 430–31
  under Paris Convention, 410–11
  protections for, 412–21
    through business practice laws, 412–13, 415–17
    through consumer protections, 415–17
    through *sui generis* regimes, 414–15, 419–20, 434–35
    through trademark law, 413–14, 417–19
    weakness of, 420–21
  registration-based system for, 410, 435
  Ruhunu Curd, 426–27
  sui generis regimes in, 414–15, 419–20, 434–35, 445
  under TRIPS, 411–12, 413
Sri Lanka Tea Board (SLTB), 422–23
stakeholders, diverse, 89–90
Starbucks, 75–80
  single-origin coffees and, 77–80
State Administration for Industry and Commerce (SAIC), 380–81
status of play, 14
subsistence farming, women and, 109

sui generis systems. *See also* Ministry of Agricultural practice
  in Asian countries, 445
  champagne under, 122–23
  in China, 387–91, 392–94, 402–4. *See also* Ministry of Agricultural practice
    AQSIQ system, 387–90
    costs of, 403
    exclusive rights, 403–4
    PPGIP system, 388–89, 390–91
    trademarks in conflict with, 400–2
  farmers under, in developing countries, 74
  genericide and, 132
  under Geneva Act, 142
  GIs and, 5, 9–10
  in India, 339–42, 445
  in Sri Lanka, 414–15, 419–20, 434–35
  in Taiwan, 378
  TPP and, 142
  TRIPS and, 449
  in Vietnam, 308, 312
sustainable, as label, 72
swidden agriculture, 97–102
  biomass in, 98, 103
  carbon stocks in, 98, 102
  under CBD, 103–4
  criminalization of, 99–100
  ecosystem services and, 102–5
  fallow periods in, 103, 104
  in global social movements, 100–1
  indigenous farmers and, 101–2
  livelihood security and, 102–5
  political and strategic advantages of, 100
  soil fertility and, 103
  species richness and, 103
  women's TEK in, 105–9
Sykes, Friend, 63

Taiwan, GIs in
  dereistic policies for, 362–67
    as IP-centred, 363
    negative protections in, 365–67
    positive protections in, 365–77
    trademarks in, 363–65
  economic development through, 377–79
  under Examination Guidelines of 2007, 371–75
  under Fair Trade Act, 360–61
  IP and
    under dereistic policies, 363
    laws for, 359–60

IPRs and, 359–60
PGIs, 362
registration of, 370–71
  TRIPS and, 370–71
registration protection principle and, 366
sui generis systems, 378
under TMA 2003, 360–61, 366, 367, 368–70, 373–74
under TMA 2012, 368, 375–77
under Tobacco and Alcohol Administration Act, 360–61
trademarks and
  collective, 372–73
  under dereistic policies, 363–65
  geographical collective, 375–76
TRIPS and, 359–61, 364–65, 370–71
for wine and spirits, 362
in WTO, 359, 360–61
Taiwan Intellectual Property Office (TIPO), 360–61, 364–65, 372, 373–74
TBT. *See* Agreement on Technical Barriers to Trade
TCEs. *See* traditional cultural expressions
TDA 2011. *See* Trade Descriptions Act 2011
Tea Act (India), 352, 353
Tea Board, in India, 352–54
tea production, Darjeeling Tea, 92–96
  cultural impact of, 93
  fair trade and, 93–94, 95–96
  female workers and, 94–95
  production techniques for, 92–93
TEK. *See* traditional environmental knowledge
terroir. *See also* geographical origins
  in Bangladesh, 455
  cultural context for, 63
  defined, 36, 63
  in France, 62–63, 122–23
  in free market economies, 136
  FTA policy and, 159
  GATT and, 39
  Geneva Act and, 64–65, 123
  under Lisbon Agreement, 64–65
  microclimactic elements of, 63
  national identity and, 122–23
  reputation-based GIs and, 24–25, 47–51
    in Germany, 47–48
    under TFEU, 48
  soil composition and, 63
  TPP Agreement and, 123
  under TRIPS, 64–65

wine making and, 62–65
  in Australia, 63, 164
  in France, 62–63
  in United States, 64
TFEU. *See* Treaty on the Functioning of the European Union
Thailand, *sui generis* systems and, 445
TIPO. *See* Taiwan Intellectual Property Office
TM Law 1993. *See* Trade Mark Law of 1993
TM Law 2001. *See* Trade Mark Law of 2001
TM Law 2013. *See* Trade Mark Law of 2013
TMA 1976. *See* Trade Marks Act 1976
TMA 2003. *See* Trade Mark Act 2003
TMA 2012. *See* Trade Mark Act 2012
Tobacco and Alcohol Administration Act (Taiwan), 360–61
Togo, 196
TPP Agreement. *See* Trans-Pacific Partnership Agreement
Trade Descriptions Act 2011 (TDA 2011) (Malaysia), 300–1
Trade Mark Act 2003 (TMA 2003) (Taiwan), 360–61, 366, 367, 368–70, 373–74
Trade Mark Act 2012 (TMA 2012) (Taiwan), 368, 375–77
Trade Mark Law of 1993 (TM Law 1993) (China), 382–83
Trade Mark Law of 2001 (TM Law 2001) (China), 383
Trade Mark Law of 2013 (TM Law 2013) (China), 387, 397, 399, 400–1
trade marks. *See* trademarks
Trade Marks Act 1938 (Singapore), 237
Trade Marks Act 1976 (TMA 1976) (Malaysia), 287, 299–300
Trade Marks Act 1998 (Singapore), 237–38
Trade Marks (Amendment) Act 2000 (Malaysia), 299–300
Trade Marks (Amendment) Act 2004 (Singapore), 254
Trade Marks Act of 2001 (Indonesia), 496, 498–99
Trademark Act (US), 213, 220
trademark law
  in China, 404–5
  in Sri Lanka, 413–14, 417–19
trademarks. *See also* General Inter-American Convention for Trademark and Commercial Protection
  in Bangladesh, 452–54

trademarks (cont.)
　certification marks and, 137–38
　　for Cognac, 138–41
　in China, 381–87, 402–4
　　conflicts between GIs and, 396–400
　　costs of, 403
　　enforcement of, 387
　　as exclusive rights, 403–4
　　legislative history for, 382–84
　　registration for, 385–87
　in CJEU cases, 198–201
　collective
　　geographical, 375–76
　　in Taiwan, 372–73
　under common law, 137–41
　　collective goodwill under, 137–38
　　"first-in-time, first-in-right" approach to, 137
　　in United States, 138
　conflicts over
　　EU Council regulations for, 133
　　under Geneva Act, 135
　　under Lisbon Agreement, 133–35
　　under TRIPS, 134–35
　CTMR and, 204
　deceptive, 200
　EU GIs under, 198–208
　　collective marks, 202–4
　　geographical term use, 198–201
　　protection as trademark for, 198–201
　　registrability of, 198–201
　　scope of protections for, 201–2
　under GI Act 2014, 242
　owners of trademarks, 251–53
　under Lanham Act, 140, 342–43
　maintenance fees for
　　under Geneva Act, 129, 130–31
　　under Lisbon Agreement, 130–31
　　under PCT, 130
　under Paris Convention, 131–32
　registrations for
　　in Ethiopia, 75–80
　　in India, 61
　　Starbucks and, 75–80
　reputation-based GIs and, 137
　in Taiwan
　　collective, 372–73
　　under dereistic policies, 363–65
　　geographical collective, 375–76
　under TRIPS, 134–35, 141
　　definitions of, 453

　in Vietnam, 328–29
traditional cultural expressions (TCEs)
　in Asia, 88
　in Japan, 510
traditional environmental knowledge (TEK)
　in Asia, 88
　for women, 105–9
　　FPIC principles and, 108–9
　　in India, 107–9
traditional knowledge. *See* knowledge
traditional specialties guaranteed (TSGs), 153–54
　in EU, 168, 189
Trans-Atlantic Trade and Investment Partnership (TTIP)
　EU under, 169, 212
　multilateral aspects of, 151
　US under, 212
Trans-Pacific Partnership (TPP) Agreement, 14–15, 153–56, 225
　Australia under, 156
　EU under, 170
　Geneva Act and, 143
　Japan and, 512
　member nations in, 15
　multilateral aspects of, 151
　PDOs and, 153–54
　PGIs and, 153–54
　South Korea under, 156
　sui generis systems and, 142
　terroir and, 123
　TSG and, 153–54
travaux, 127
Treaty of Athens, 193–94
Treaty on the Functioning of the European Union (TFEU)
　IP under, 169
　reputation-based GIs and, 48
　terroir paradigm and, 48
TRIPS. *See* Agreement of Trade-Related Aspects to Intellectual Property Rights
TSGs. *See* traditional specialties guaranteed
TTIP. *See* Trans-Atlantic Trade and Investment Partnership
Tunisia, 196

UNCITRAL. *See* United Nations Commission on International Trade Law
UNCTAD. *See* United Nations Conference on Trade and Development

UNESCO. *See* United Nations Educational, Scientific and Cultural Organization
unfair competition
  under Anti-Unfair Competition Law, 395
  Inter-American Convention and, 216–17, 218
  Paris Convention and, 218
  reputation-based GIs and, 45–47
United Nations Commission on International Trade Law (UNCITRAL), 180–81, 182
United Nations Conference on Trade and Development (UNCTAD), 337
United Nations Educational, Scientific and Cultural Organization (UNESCO), 21, 440–41
  cultural diversity and, 470–71
  ICH and, 461–62
United States (US). *See also* General Inter-American Convention for Trademark and Commercial Protection
  Australia-United States Free Trade Agreement, 279
  AVAs in, 64
  FTAs with, 222
  GIs in, 165–67
    incompatibilities in, 167
  Lanham Act in, 140, 342–43
  protection of GIs in
    comparisons with EU, 224–28
    history of, 212–14
    legal approaches to, 227–28
    under trademark law, 227–28
  terroir and, for wine making, 64
  Trademark Act in, 213, 220
  trademarks in, 138
  under TTIP, 212
  wine making in, 64
US-Singapore Free-Trade Agreement, 166–67, 254
usurpation, 127

van Caenegem, William, 149, 261
Vietnam, GIs in
  appellations of origin and, 314, 320
  case studies for, 320–27
    Hạ Long fried calamari, 321–24, 330
    Lạng Sơn star anise, 324–27
  Civil Code of Vietnam, 320
  collective action dynamics in, 310, 331
  collective marks in, 328–29
  commercial channels for, 330

development and establishment of, 305–10
EU-Vietnam Free Trade Agreement, 169, 305
institutional frameworks for, 309–10, 328–29
IP Law in, 313–14
legal frameworks for, 309–10, 328–29
under Lisbon Agreement, 313
marketing channels for, 330
NOIP and, 311–12
OLPs and, 310
PGIs in, 315
qualitative methodology approach to, 311–12
registration of, 312–20
  criteria requirements, 312–14
  product types and, 314–15
  public policies for, 318–20
  as state-driven top-down process, 316–18, 329
socio-economic development through, 308–9, 320–27
sui generis systems and, 308, 312
trademarks in, 328–29
Vietnam Intellectual Property Law, 311–12

West, Paige, 84–85
wine GIs, in Australia, 260–66
  communities and, 277–78
  costs of, 267–68
  enforcement procedures for, 266–67
  in Granite Belt, 274–76, 280
  quality standards for, 277–78
  reciprocal spillovers for, 280
  size of region for, 263–65, 274–76
  in Tasmania, 271–72
wine labeling, laws on
  in France, 10–11
  in Taiwan, 362
wine making
  in Australia, 260–66
    terroir and, 63, 164
  AVAs and, 64
  bilateral trade agreements for, 192–93
  terroir and, 62–65
    in Australia, 63, 164
    in France, 62–63
    in United States, 64
WIPO. *See* World Intellectual Property Organisation
women
  in alternative food networks, 118

women (cont.)
    in Darjeeling Tea production, 94–95
    as landholders, 109
    in plantation economies, 109–13
        in palm oil production, 109–13
    in subsistence farming, 109
    in swidden agriculture, 105–9
        monocropping and, 106
        rice cultivation, 106
    TEK for, 105–9
        FPIC principles and, 108–9
        in India, 107–9
World Intellectual Property Organisation (WIPO)
    Geneva Act and, 122
    GIs and, 37
    MICOs and, 91

World Trade Organization (WTO)
    discrimination between trading partners, 453
    DSU, 178
    GIs and, 4, 36–37
        in EU, 168, 171–72, 190
        member requirements for, 12
        protections for, 12
    IP and, 162–63
    ISDS and, 178–80, 185
        BTIAs and, 178
        FTAs under, 178–79
        TRIPS and, 180
    reputation-based GIs and, 40
    rules of origin criteria, 150
    Taiwan accession to, 359, 360–61

Yugoslavia, 196